Money Laundering Compliance

Dedication

For three special people
Ploypailin, Petchnapa
and Lucy

Money Laundering Compliance

Third edition

Tim Bennett

LLB, LLM, TEP, Solicitor

FOR REFERENCE

ONLY

Bloomsbury Professional

BLOOMSBURY PROFESSIONAL LTD, MAXWELTON HOUSE, 41–43 BOLTRO ROAD, HAYWARDS HEATH, WEST SUSSEX, RH16 1BJ

© Bloomsbury Professional 2014

Bloomsbury Professional is an imprint of Bloomsbury Publishing plc

A CIP Catalogue record for this book is available from the British Library.

ISBN 978 1 78043 496 4

Typeset by Phoenix Photosetting, Chatham, Kent
Printed and bound in Great Britain by CPI Group (UK) Ltd, Croydon, CR0 4YY

Preface

Since completing the Second Edition in 2007, an increasing a number of books and websites have appeared on the subject of Money Laundering Compliance. This book does not pretend to be a comprehensive AML-CFT textbook of the black-and-white letter laws on the topic, but rather to serve as a practical reference to technical compliance and procedural aspects, and how to deal with the difficulties of the contemporary AML-CFT environment.

AML rules are not new: they have been around for 30 years or more, but every year, AML-CFT procedures are having an increasing impact on business and private life issues for most people. AML-CFT compliance is no longer a minor inconvenience for 99.9% of the law-abiding population: it has become almost a full-time preoccupation, with armies of people spending all of their day-time on gathering, submitting, checking and updating compliance materials.

The Book is structured as follows:

- Chapter 1 introduces the Core Principles, and notes the trend towards a 'cashless society'.

- Chapters 2 – 6 describe the UK AML-CFT framework, the principal UK ML offences, the offences of 'failure to disclose' and 'tipping-off', the mechanisms of tracing, asset recovery and forfeiture, and the Money Laundering Regulations 2007 (and JMLSG Guidance).

- Chapter 7 examines technical issues, including the concept of 'suspicion'.

- Chapter 8 considers of dual criminality in relation to fiscal offences, foreign tax enforcement, 'legacy' issues, FATCA and Amnesty Programmes.

- Chapter 9 is on Tax Transparency, TIEAs and the workings of the new OECD Multilateral Automatic Exchange of Tax Information program and the Common Reporting Standard.

- Chapter 10 looks at EU Initiatives and the Money Laundering Directives, especially matters arising from new '4MLD'.

- Chapter 11 examines Customer Due Diligence, Compliance & Risk Management.

- Chapter 12 considers STR Reporting procedures and dealings with the Client.

- Chapters 13–16 are sector-specific, focussing on issues facing legal professionals and practitioners (Chapter 13), Trustees, Executors and TSPs (Chapter 14), CSPs (Chapter 15), and Banks and Investment Managers (Chapter 16).

- Chapter 17 and Appendix 9 look in detail at the AML-CFT regimes in ten selected non-UK jurisdictions.

- Chapter 18 covers Bribery and Corruption in relation to AML and the proceeds of crime,

And finally, Chapter 19 summarises concerns and offers conclusions on where all this is leading.

The new OECD Multilateral Automatic Exchange of Tax Information program and the Common Reporting Standard comprise an entirely new area of enforcement since the previous edition, and Chapter 9 merits particularly careful study.

Those who will find this book most useful will be directly or indirectly involved in the financial services industry, be that as a professional; advisor, administrator of wealth-planning structures, private banker, trust or company service provider, regulator, or legislator.

Whilst every care has been taken to ensure the accuracy of the contents of this work, no responsibility for loss occasioned to any person acting or refraining from action as a result of any statement in it can be accepted by either the Author or the publisher.

Finally, the Author invites reader's feedback and (positive or negative) comments by email to tim@belgrave.ch are most welcome, as is feedback on errors/omissions, points of clarification, and ideas or suggestions for development in future editions. Your support is appreciated!

Tim Bennett
7 November 2014

Contents

Contents

Contents

Contents

Appendices

Contents

Table of Cases

References at the right-hand side of the column are to Division and paragraph numbers.

Table of Statutes

References at the right-hand side of the column are to Division and paragraph numbers.

Table of Statutory Instruments

References at the right-hand side of the column are to Division and paragraph numbers.

Table of Foreign Legislation

References at the right-hand side of the column are to Division and paragraph numbers.

Table of European Legislation

References at the right-hand side of the column are to Division and paragraph numbers.

Abbreviations and References

ABA	American Bar Association; American Bankers Association
ABCO	Association of Bermuda Compliance Officers
ACAMS	Association of Certified Anti-Money Laundering Specialists
ACPO	Association of Chief Police Officers (UK)
AIBT	Association of International Banks and Trustees (Bahamas)
AML	Anti-Money Laundering
AMLO	Asian Money Laundering Office
AnCorR	Anti-Corruption Ring Online (OECD)
APT	Asset Protection Trust
ARA	Assets Recovery Agency
ATF	Anti Terrorist Financing
AUM	'Assets under Management'
BALT	Bermuda Association of Licensed Trustees
BBA	British Bankers' Association
BEE	Bahamas Executive Entity
BFSB	Bahamas Financial Services Board
BIBA	Bermuda International Business Association
BIAC	Business and Industry Advisory Committee (OECD)
BMA	Bermuda Monetary Authority
BOI	British Offshore Islands (Jersey, Guernsey, Alderney, Isle of Man)
BOT	British Overseas Territories (Anguilla, Ascension St Helena and Tristan da Cunha, Bermuda, British Antarctic Territory, BVI, Cayman Islands, Chagos Archipelago (British Indian Ocean Territory), Falkland Islands and South Georgia, Gibraltar, Montserrat, Pitcairn Islands, South Sandwich Islands, Turks and Caicos, plus the Sovereign base area in Cyprus)
BPI	Bribe Payers Index (Transparency International)
BSA	Bank Secrecy Act (US)
BVI	The British Virgin Islands
CAA	Competent Authority Agreement (OECD)
CARA	Criminal Assets Recovery Agency (UK)
CATA	Commonwealth Association of Tax Administrators
CARICOM	The Caribbean Community
CBI	Confederation of British Industry
CCAB	Consultative Committee of Accountancy Bodies (UK)
CCBE	Council of Bars and Law Societies of Europe
CDCFFI	Certified Deemed Compliant FFI
CDs	Crown Dependencies (Jersey, Guernsey & Alderney, and Isle of Man)
CDD	Customer Due Diligence
CED	Customs & Excise Department (Hong Kong)
CFA	Committee on Fiscal Affairs (OECD Directorate)
CFA	Court of Final Appeal (Hong Kong)

CFATF	Caribbean Financial Action Task Force
CFC	Controlled Foreign Corporation (US); Controlled Foreign Company (UK)
CFT	Countering Terrorist Finances (sometimes also shown as "CTF")
CIAT	Inter-American Centre of Tax Administrators
CICAD	Inter-American Drug Abuse Control Commission (OAS)
CICFA	Concerted Inter-Agency Criminal Finances Action Group (UK)
CIMA	Cayman Islands Monetary Authority
CIS	Commonwealth of Independent States
CJA	Criminal Justice Act (UK)
CLASS	Consular Lookout and Support System
CMIR	[International Transportation of] Currency or Monetary Instruments Report (US)
CoE	Council of Europe
CoI	Certificate of Incorporation
CoI	Certificate of Incumbency
COTA	Cariant Organisation of Tax Administrators
CPI	Corruption Perceptions Index (Transparency International)
CRE-DAF	Centre des Rencontres et d'Etudes des Dirigeants des Administrations Fiscales
CRS	Common Reporting Standard (OECD)
CSE	Child Sexual Exploitation
CSSF	Commission de Surveillance du Secteur Financier
CSPs	Corporate Service Providers
CTC	Certified True Copy
CTF	variant of Countering Terrorist Finances
CTR	Cash Transaction Report
DEA	Drug Enforcement Agency
DFNBP	Designated Non-Financial Businesses and Professions (FATF)
DFS	Department of Financial Services (New York)
DFSA	Dubai Financial Services Authority
DoJ	Department of Justice (US)
DTA	Double Taxation Agreement
DTI	Department of Trade and Industry (UK)
DLR	Dominion Law Reports
DNFBP	Designated Non-Financial Business or Profession
DPP	Director of Public Prosecutions
EoI	Exchange of Information
EBRD	European Bank for Reconstruction and Development (est 1991)
EC	European Commission
ECOFIN	Economic and Finance Ministers (EU Council)
ECHR	European Convention for the Protection of Human Rights and Fundamental Freedoms (Council of Europe, 4 November 1950)
ECJ	European Court of Justice (EU)
ECtHR	European Court of Human Rights
EESAAMLG	Eastern and Southern Africa Anti-Money Laundering Group
EFF	European Financial Forum

EIN	Employee Identification Number (US)
EoI	Exchange of Information
EU	European Union
EUROPOL	European Police Office
EUDTOSI	EU Directive on Taxation of Savings Income
F&PP	Fit and Proper Person
FATCA	Foreign Account Tax Compliance Act
FATF	Financial Action Task Force
FBC	'No Longer Business as Usual – Fighting Bribery and Corruption' (The FBC Report), OECD, June 2000
FCA	Financial Conduct Authority (UK)
FCO	Foreign and Commonwealth Office (UK)
FCPA	Foreign Corrupt Practices Act (US)
FDAP	Fixed, Determinable, Annual, Periodical (US)
FFI	Foreign Financial Institution (US)
FIAMLA	Financial Intelligence and Anti Money Laundering Act 2002 (Mauritius)
FIC	Foreign Investment Corporation (US)
FinCEN	Financial Crimes Enforcement Network (US Department of the Treasury)
FINTRAC	Financial Transactions and Reports Analysis Centre (Canada)
FIS	Financial Intelligence Service (Guernsey)
FIU	Financial Intelligence Unit
FOPAC	Bureau des Fonds Provenant d'Activités Criminelles (Interpol)
FPHC	Foreign Personal Holding Corporation (US)
FR	Fully Reportable (UK)
FSA	former Financial Services Authority (UK)
FSAP	Financial Sector Assessment Program (IMF, WB)
FSB	Financial Service Business
FSB	Federal Security Bureau (Russia) (previously the KGB)
FCS	Financial Services Commission
FSE	Foreign Sanctions Evaders (OFAC) (US)
FSMA	Financial Services and Markets Act 2000 (UK)
FSI	Financial Secrecy Index
FT	Financial Times
G7	'Group of Seven' most industrialised nations (Britain, Canada, France, Germany, Italy, Japan and the United States)
G8	'Group of Eight' (the 'G7' countries plus Russia)
G15	'Group of 15 developing countries' (Algeria, Argentina, Brazil, Chile, Egypt, Indonesia, Jamaica, Kenya, Malaysia, Mexico, Nigeria, Peru, Senegal, Venezuela and Zimbabwe)
G20	'Group of Twenty' (Argentina, Australia, Brazil, Britain, Canada, China, France, Germany, India, Indonesia, Italy, Japan, Mexico, Russia, Saudi Arabia, South Africa, South Korea, Turkey, the United States, the EU)
GAFI	Groupement d'Action Financière (FATF's French initials)
GAFISUD	FATF regional grouping for South America
GAO	General Accounting Office
GATS	General Agreement on Trade in Services (part of GATT)

GATT	General Agreement on Tariffs and Trade (now the WTO)
GCC	Gulf Cooperation Council (Bahrain, Kuwait, Oman, Qatar, Saudi Arabia and the UAE)
GFSC	Guernsey Financial Services Commission
GIFSA	Grenada International Financial Services Authority
GIIN	Global Intermediary Identification Number (US)
GPML	Global Program against Money Laundering (UN)
GRID	Global Regulatory Information Database
GRO	General Register Office
HAM	"Hold All Mail"
HKICS	Hong Kong Institute of Chartered Secretaries
HKMA	Hong Kong Monetary Authority
HKTA	Hong Kong Association of Licensed Trustees
HMRC	Her Majesty's Revenue & Customs (UK)
HNWI	High-Net-Worth Individual
HMSO	Her Majesty's Stationery Office (UK) (old term)
HRA	Human Rights Act 1998 (UK)
IACC	International Anti-Corruption Conference (TI)
IAM	Independent Asset Manager
IBA	International Bar Association
IBC	International Business Corporation
ICA	International Compliance Association
ICC	International Chamber of Commerce
ICIJ	International Consortium of Investigative Journalists
IFA	International Fiscal Association
IFC	International Financial Centre
IFLR	International Financial Law Review
IFS	Institute of Fiscal Studies (London)
IGA	Inter-Governmental Agreement
IJGDF	Isle of Man Guernsey Jersey Disclosure Facility (UK)
IMF	International Monetary Fund
IMLPO	Institute of Money Laundering Prevention Officers
IOFC	International Offshore Financial Centre
IOTA	Intra-European Organisation of Tax Administrators
IPB	International Private Banking
IRS	Internal Revenue Service (US)
ISP	Internet Service Provider
ITLR	International Tax Law Reports
ITELR	International Trust & Estate Law Reports
ITCA	International Trust Companies Association
ITIO	International Tax and Investment Organisation
ITO	International Tax Organisation
ITPA	International Tax Planning Association
JCESA	Joint Committee of European Supervisory Authorities (EU)
JCFU	Joint Police and Customs Financial Crime Unit
JFCU	Joint Financial Crime Unit (Jersey)
JFSC	Jersey Financial Services Commission
JFIU	Joint Police and Customs Financial Investigation Unit (Guernsey)
JFIU	Joint Financial Intelligence Unit (Hong Kong)
JIBFL	Journal of International Banking & Finance Law
JITCP	Journal of International Trust and Corporate Planning
JLR	Jersey Law Reports

JMLSG	Joint Money Laundering Steering Group (UK)
JP	Justice of the Peace
KYC	'Know Your Customer' (former acronym for what is now known as 'CDD')
LDF	Liechtenstein Disclosure Facility (UK)
LLC	Limited Liability Company; Limited Life Company
LLP	Limited Liability Partnership
LLU	London Liaison Unit (UK HMR&C)
LPP	Legal Professional Privilege
M&AA	Memorandum and Articles of Association
MAS	Monetary Authority of Singapore
MCAA	Model Competent Authority Agreement (FATCA)
MCV	The Misuse of Corporate Vehicles, including TSPs and CSPs' (FATF, 13.10.2006)
MFSC	Mauritius Financial Services Commission
MiFID	The Markets in Financial Instruments Directive (UK)
ML	Money Laundering
MLAT	Mutual Legal Assistance Treaty
MLCO	Money Laundering Compliance Officer
MLRO	Money Laundering Reporting Officer
MS	Member State (EU)
NCA	National Crime Agency
NCCTs	Non-Cooperative Countries or Territories (OECD)
NCIS	[former] National Criminal Intelligence Service (UK)
NFFE	Non Financial Foreign Entity (FATCA)
NFR	Non Fully Reportable (UK)
NGO	Non-Governmental Organisation
NRA	Non-Resident Alien (US)
OAS	Organisation of American States
OBS	Offshore Banking Supervisors
ODCCP	Office for Drug Control and Crime Prevention (UN)
OECD	Organisation for Economic Co-operation and Development (French Initials = OECE)
ODT	Overseas Dependant Territory/ies (UK)
OFAC	Office of Foreign Asset Control (US)
OFC	Offshore Financial Centre
OFLR	Offshore Financial Law Reports
OGBS	Offshore Group of Banking Supervisors
OJCE	Official Journal (EU)
OLAF	European Anti-Fraud Office (French acronym)
OSCE	Organisation for Security and Cooperation in Europe
OSCO	Organised and Serious Crimes Ordinance (Hong Kong)
OTRCIS	The Overseas Territories Regional Criminal Intelligence System
OT	The Overseas Territories (the British Overseas Territories)
OUP	Oxford University Press
PAC	Programme of Action Against Corruption
PBIG	Private Banking Industry Group (Singapore)
PCB	Private Client Business
PC-R-EV	Select Committee of Experts on Evaluating AML Measures (CoE)
PEP	Politically Exposed Person (& see PSP)
PFIC	Personal Foreign Investment Corporation (US)

PfSB	Program for Swiss Banks (US)
PIC	Private Investment Company
PIF	Pacific Islands Forum (Cook Islands, Nauru, Niue, Marshall Islands, Samoa, Tonga, and Vanuatu)
PRA	Prudential Regulation Authority
PSC	People with Significant Control (EU 4MLD)
PSP	Politically Sensitive Person (& see PEP)
PTC	Private Trading Company
PTN	Portcullis TrustNet
RICO	Racketeer Influenced Corrupt Organisations (US)
ROSC	Report on the Observance of Standards and Codes (IMF, WB)
SAICSA	Singapore Association of the Institute of Chartered Secretaries and Administrators
SAR	Suspicious Activity Report (new terminology)
SAR	Special Administrative Region (Hong Kong)
SARG	Scottish Asset Recovery Group
SARS	Specific Acquired Respiratory Syndrome
SCO	Special Compliance Office (UK HMRC)
SCO	Shanghai Cooperation Organisation (China, Russia, Kazakhstan, Kyrgyzstan. Tajikistan and Uzbekistan)
SDE	Small and Developing Economies
SDN	Specially Designated National (US)
SFC	Securities and Futures Commission
SFO	Serious Fraud Office (UK)
SPC	Standards and Practices Committee (Bahamas)
SOCA	[former] Serious Organised Crime Agency (UK)
SOCPA	Serious Organised Crime and Police Act (UK)
SPSCI	Senate Permanent Sub-committee on Investigations (US)
SRA	Solicitors Regulatory Authority (England & Wales)
STEP	Society of Trust and Estate Practitioners (UK)
STR	Suspicious Transaction Report
SYSC	Senior Management Arrangements System and Controls module (FCA Handbook) (UK)
TA	Technical Assistance
TCI	The Turks and Caicos Islands
TI	Transparency International
TIEA	Tax Information Exchange Agreement
TIN	Taxpayer Identification Number (US)
TLI	Tax Law International
TRACFIN	Office for the Repression of Large-scale Financial Crime (France)
UBO	Ultimate Beneficial Owner
UHNWI	Ultra-High-Net-Worth Individual
UKFIU	United Kingdom Financial Intelligence Unit
UN	United Nations
UNOF	Offshore Forum (UN)
USBTCA	USA Bermuda Tax Convention Act 1986 (as amended)
USVI	The US Virgin Islands
WB	World Bank
WCCIT	White Collar Criminal Investigation Team
WGOFC	Working Group on Offshore Financial Centres (FSF)
WTO	World Trade Organisation (successor to the GATT)

Glossary of Terms

The following basic definitional contrasts should be noted.

'Tax haven' versus 'financial centre'

These terms are largely synonymous, although the expression 'financial centre' is preferred, being less pejorative and thus more politically correct. Note that there is no single clear objective test which permits the identification of a country as a tax haven[1].

'Offshore' versus 'onshore'

These are relative terms, depending on one's position and point of view. In a geographical sense, 'offshore' simply denotes a place far from the shore. In a fiscal sense, 'offshore' is generally used to refer to a no-tax or low-tax financial centre.

'Offshore' versus 'international'

Again, these terms are largely synonymous, and are generally used together with the expression 'financial centre'. There is possibly some connotation of size, and it might be argued that an 'international financial centre' is larger and better-established than a mere 'offshore financial centre': it all depends on the context. Thus, whilst New York and Singapore are 'money centres', Cayman and Bermuda might be IFCs, and Malta and Seychelles 'offshore centres' or OFCs.

'Industry' versus 'business'

Again, largely synonymous, and used in the context of the 'international offshore trust business' ('trust industry'). The word 'industry' does not connote 'smokestacks', but it may have a manufacturing or production connotation in the sense of many thousands of people being employed in it[2].

'Country' versus 'jurisdiction'

These terms may be used interchangeably, but 'jurisdiction' is the correct term to describe a somewhere with a largely autonomous legal system but which may fall short of being a full-blown 'country'. Issues of independence (nationhood, statehood) and federalism (having more than one legal system within a nation or country) are key elements in differentiating a country from a jurisdiction. As many of the OFCs are not countries in a strict constitutional sense, they must be referred to as jurisdictions.

---

1 Per 'Tax Havens and their Use by United States Taxpayers – An Overview' by Richard Gordon of the US Department of the Treasury (1981).

2 But hopefully does not connote 'those dark satanic mills' referred to by William Blake.

ADDITIONAL DEFINITIONS

Tax avoidance

A transaction or operation whereby a taxpayer engages in a lawful act or omission whereby a tax burden is avoided or reduced.

Anti-avoidance

Measures whereby the tax authorities (or the tax courts) counteract attempted tax avoidance so as to reduce or eliminate the effectiveness of the desired transaction or operation and/or to penalise the taxpayer.

Tax haven or international offshore financial centre (IOFC)

"There is no internationally agreed definition of a tax haven" per Lord McIntosh, HL Debates 02 Feb 1998; and "Tax haven is not a concept defined in European Law" per EU Taxation Commissioner Monti, 02 Feb 1998

Nevertheless, the expression is generally used to refer to a jurisdiction:

(a)   where there are no relevant taxes;

(b)   where taxes are levied only on internal taxable events, but not at all (or at low rates) on profits from foreign sources; or

(c)   where special tax privileges are granted to certain types of taxable persons or events.

Such special tax privileges may be accorded by the domestic internal tax system or may derive from a combination or domestic tax and treaty provisions.

As Giles Clarke states in his introduction to *Spitz and Clarke: Offshore Service*:

> 'For many years, the normal term for offshore jurisdictions was 'tax haven': this reflected their importance in tax planning, and the fact that some were favoured destinations of those seeking to emigrate to avoid tax. The term "offshore jurisdiction" has recently become more appropriate, as it better reflects the wide range of commercial and financial activities carried on in the jurisdictions concerned.'

International (Offshore) Financial Centre (IOFC or IFC)

A politically correct term for what used to be called a tax haven. The use of this term makes the important point that a jurisdiction may provide specific financial services without necessarily being a tax haven in any general sense. An important requirement of a successful IFC is that international financial business transacted there should not be subject to inconvenient controls or withholding taxes.

Offshore

Originally used to refer to the tax havens off the shores of the United Kingdom and the United States, and by extension to any company or trust located in a tax haven or a country where tax can be kept low. Nowadays it is used more and more in connection with financial transactions. The offshore scene is currently undergoing important changes; the main development is the amount of money offshore (estimated at 60% of the world's money).

Trust[1]

Refers to the aggregate duties and obligations that rest upon persons described as 'trustees' having responsibilities in relation to property held by them or under their control. A trustee is obliged to administer the trust property in the manner lawfully prescribed by the trust instrument (trust deed or settlement), or in the absence of specific provision, in accordance with equitable principles or statute law. Administration will be undertaken in such a manner that the consequential benefits and advantages accrue to the beneficiaries, not to the trustees. An Anglo-Saxon trust is not a legal entity, but is merely a bundle of rights and obligations in equity and law. Though the law of trusts varies from legal system to system, those based on the English law of trusts resemble one another closely. In civil law systems where trusts occur, for example in Liechtenstein and Panama, it is usually a statute-based system. In recent years large numbers of offshore trusts have been set up: these usually contain provisions allowing the situs and proper law of the trust to be transferred from one jurisdiction to another.

Trust Services

Most international banks and all trust companies located in tax havens offer trust services. Such services normally include a wide range of trusteeship, management and related administration services relating both to trusts and to investment companies (often called 'PICs') and trading companies (often called 'PTCs').

---

1 The *Words and Phrases Legally Defined* Third Edition, Butterworths (2001) contains an alternative definition of the term 'Trust'.

Introduction: the core principles, and towards a 'cashless society'

1.1 A simple definition of money laundering (ML) is to describe it as the concealment of the identity of illegally obtained money, so that it appears to have come from a legitimate source. This definition requires anti-money laundering (AML) attention to be paid to the *Source of Funds* (see **11.10.2**). Since '9-11' the definition has been extended to 'countering the financing of terrorism' (CFT), which requires attention to be paid to the *Destination of Funds* (see **11.10.3**). These are coupled with enforcement by suspicious transactions reports (**Chapter 12**) and the related dislike of cash transactions above a certain minimum value (**Chapter 10**).

These then are the basic AML-CFT principles. But the challenges they bring for financial and professional services and related businesses as regards both *source* and *destination* of funds need to be clearly understood: AML-CFT has added hugely to the operational burdens, whilst perhaps not proved, striking the desired targets.

1.2 In this book, the study of AML-CFT compliance commences with a close look at the United Kingdom. Since the Proceeds of Crime Act 2002 ('PoCA 2002') (see **Chapters 2–6),** professionals in the United Kingdom have become the soft target for legislative policy enforcement, and the European Union continues to widen the scope further through the Third Money Laundering Directive ('3MLD') and now the Fourth Money Laundering Directive ('4MLD').

It is appropriate for this book to have its primary focus on the United Kingdom, since the United Kingdom is the second biggest money centre after the United States and thus arguably the second biggest ML centre in the world. Another key reason for this UK focus derives from the UK's historical position as one of the biggest centres of expertise in the planning of international structures using the laws of present and many former colonies, near and far (the Financial Secrecy Index in **Appendix 11** contains a preponderance of such present or past British possessions and territories). These jurisdictions are nowadays referred to as Offshore Financial Centres ('OFCs'), as the term 'tax haven' has become pejorative. Many of these structures involve the use of Offshore Trusts and Offshore Companies, as these provide the architecture for wealth preservation, confidentiality and good governance.

It is inevitable that some of the Trust and Company structures established internationally may indeed conceal ML as currently broadly defined. Execution/administration of these structures is undertaken by Trust Service Providers ('TSPs' – **Chapter 14**) and Corporate Service Providers

('CSPs' – **Chapter 15**) away from the United Kingdom, but often the strings lead back to the United Kingdom in terms of professional and financial service providers. Thus, the UK 'string-pullers' also need an informative guide as to what they can (and cannot) do, and what they must (and must not) do to prevent themselves from becoming inadvertent money launderers, tippers-off, etc. And of course those in the OFCs also need reliable reference and support materials.

1.3   The addition of the proceeds of tax evasion (see **3.4** ('**predicate offences**') and **Chapter 8**) to anti-money laundering law (AML-CFT) and regulation makes it all-embracing, and of constant concern to professionals and practitioners both onshore and offshore of the United Kingdom.

1.4   The book goes on to consider AML-CFT in an international context (both onshore and offshore), as many overseas jurisdictions (especially most the offshore jurisdictions) derive their AML-CFT framework from the United Kingdom. The author's extensive experience in dealing with international business derives from his lengthy spells living and working in a number of offshore jurisdictions, and enables the book to refer authoritatively to the AML-CFT laws and practices of many other jurisdictions.

1.5   Individual Chapters deal with specific Issues facing different groups of professional or financial players, namely:

- Legal Professionals and Practitioners (**Chapter 13**);
- Trustees, Executors and TSPs (**Chapter 14**);
- CSPs (**Chapter 15**); and
- Banks and Investment Managers (**Chapter 16**).

Please be reassured that this Book is not just another *Compliance Manual*, or *Operations and Procedures Manual*, although the Author has included certain passages of his own from such Manuals that he has previously drafted.

TOWARDS A 'CASHLESS SOCIETY'

1.6   Cash is anonymous! But as *The Economist* of 17 February 2007 famously remarked 'the suspicion clings that where you find anonymity you find drugs, fraud, money-laundering, terrorist financing, and a huge amount of humdrum tax evasion.'

As a result of AML-CFT initiatives, large denomination bank-notes are rapidly disappearing! As a Swiss Citizen, my favourite is the purple CHF1,000 note: The total value of all CHF1,000 notes in circulation was more than CHF35 billion in 2012. Their share in the CHF55 billion total of all Swiss banknotes rose to a record 60 per cent in 2012 (from 50 per cent in 2012). However, in April 2014 the Swiss Federal Council considered requests to abolish the note, to reduce the risk of money laundering.

The World's highest value note in circulation is still Singapore's Sing$10,000 note. However following the MAS decision of 2 June 2014, this ceased to be printed as of 1 October 2014, and will gradually be retired 'to reduce the risk of money laundering'. The notes will remain legal tender until all the notes slowly get returned 'as they get damaged'. New note issues (and retirement or 'demonetizing' old ones by requiring exchange at a bank) is an effective way of controlling the underground cash economy.

3MLD adopted a threshold approach of €15,000 for payments in cash for goods (see **10.4**) and 4MLD will lower this to €7,500. Despite this, there are currently €295 billion of €500 notes in circulation!

The Economist of 20 September 2014 cited Professor Rogoff of Harvard University's view that scrapping physical currency entirely would help governments to collect more tax, fight crime and develop better monetary policy.

ELECTRONIC MONEY

1.7   Wikipedia tells us that:

> 'In theory, electronic money should provide as easy a method of transferring value (without revealing identity) as untracked banknotes, especially wire transfers involving anonymity-protecting numbered bank accounts. In practice, however, record-keeping capabilities of ISPs tend to frustrate that intuition. While some cryptocurrencies … have aimed to provide for more possibility of transaction anonymity for various reasons, the degree to which they succeed—and, in consequence, the degree to which they offer benefits for money laundering efforts—is controversial.'

Of even greater interest is the EU's 4MLD (see **10.9**), which is also causing concern from experts within the financial services sector due to its failure to co-ordinate cross-border issues for electronic businesses, the risk that it will be disproportionately burdensome and costly for European businesses, it will damage innovation in new business areas such as the regulated e-money and payment services sectors (eg prepaid cards, e-wallets and money remittances) and will perversely increase the use of cash where there are less controls and there is less monitoring information available to the relevant authorities and law enforcement agencies.

Note that where references to statutes, etc appear, these refer to the United Kingdom unless otherwise stated.

Chapter 2

The UK AML-CFT framework – background

LEGISLATIVE HISTORY

2.1   There is nothing new about the notion of criminal offences similar to anti-money laundering ('AML') offences! Section 22(1) of the Theft Act 1968 (also see the Theft Act 1978 and the Theft (Amendment) Act 1996) was the first 'money laundering' ('ML') style offence created under English law, involving the receipt of goods derived from an underlying crime of theft, prior to a dishonest involvement in their retention, removal, disposal or realisation on behalf of another person.

Although the provision is confined to 'goods' and the underlying offences of theft and robbery, it has a wide-ranging effect covering a multitude of 'laundering' activities (that is, retention, removal, disposal or realisation) and it is significant that, by virtue of s 34 of the Theft Act 1968, 'goods' includes money.

The offence has consistently been applied to those laundering money and facilitating the realisation of unlawfully obtained property. In addition, the inchoate offences of aiding and abetting, counselling or procuring have long been part of the English legal system, thereby rendering those who somehow participate in the crime of another as criminal.

MEASURES AGAINST DRUG TRAFFICKING

2.2   With the enactment of the Misuse of Drugs Act 1971 it became possible under s 27(1) for the courts to order the forfeiture of property -whether it be money, drugs, weapons or vehicles - of a person convicted of a drugs-related offence classified as an 'offence under this Act'. However, the House of Lords severely curtailed the application of s 27(1) in *R v Cuthbertson* [1981] AC 470, [1980] 2 All ER 401: as a result of *Cuthbertson*, the Hodgson Committee Report of 1984 recommended the introduction of specific offences to deal with persons laundering the proceeds of drug trafficking. This in turn prompted a 1985 report by the Home Affairs Committee, resulting in the enactment of the Drug Trafficking Offences Act 1986 ('DTOA 1986') which created the forerunner to s 50 of the Drug Trafficking Act 1994 (DTA 1994) by establishing the offence of 'assisting another to retain the benefits of drug trafficking'.

The enactment of specific AML legislation in relation to drug trafficking prompted Parliament in 1989 to introduce an offence modelled on s 24 of the DTOA 1986 in relation to terrorism. Given the increasing concern that terrorist organisations were involved in organised crime and were effectively laundering the resulting proceeds, s 11 of the Prevention of

Terrorism (Temporary Provisions) Act 1989 (PT(TP)A1989) created *inter alia* the offence of 'assisting in the retention or control of terrorist funds'.

On 5 April 1990, the Criminal Justice (International Co-operation) Act 1990 received Royal Assent, thereby enabling the UK Government to ratify both the *European Convention on Mutual Assistance 1957* and the AML legislative obligations imposed by the *Vienna Convention against Illicit Traffic in Narcotic Drugs and Psychotropic Substances 1988* which created a new offence in s 14 of concealing or transferring proceeds of drug trafficking. This offence has since been consolidated into s 51 of the DTA 1994.

The enactment of the 1990 Act took place within the background of a review of drug trafficking and AML laws by the House of Commons Home Affairs Committee, whose November 1989 report resulted in the extension of AML laws in s 14.

CJA 1988; AND CJA 1993: EXTENSION TO 'OTHER SERIOUS CRIMES'

2.3   The Criminal Justice Act 1993 ('CJA 1993') extended the scope of the AML offences in the 1988 Act from specific defined crimes (drugs, terrorism, etc) to the non-specific category of 'other serious crimes', pursuant to The First EC Money Laundering Directive 91/308/EEC (1MLD) and the Second EU AML Laundering Directive (2MLD) – see **10.2** and **10.3**.

The principal AML offences created by the CJA 1993 were as follows:

(a)   Assisting the retention or control of the proceeds of criminal conduct by another, knowing or suspecting that other to be involved in ML (s 93A of the CJA 1988);

(b)   Acquisition, possession or use of proceeds of criminal conduct, *knowing* the property concerned to be tainted (s 93B of the CJA 1988); and

(c)   Concealing or transferring property, *knowing or having reasonable grounds to suspect* that the property is the proceeds of criminal conduct (s 93C of the CJA 1988). This includes transferring or removing property from the jurisdiction.

THE PROCEEDS OF CRIME ACT 2002

2.4   In 2002, the PoCA 2002 replaced the CJA 1988 and CJA 1993 provisions noted at **2.3** above: the impact of this important piece of legislation is reviewed in detail in **Chapters 3, 4** and **5**.

THE SERIOUS ORGANISED CRIME AND POLICE ACT 2005

2.5   The Serious Organised Crime and Police Act 2005 ('SOCPA 2005') amended the PoCA 2002 with effect from 1 January 2006 in the following ways:

- providing a territorial defence to charges under ss 327–329 of the PoCA 2002 where the conduct took place outside the United Kingdom (and see **7.2**);

- creating a new offence – 'Failure to Report on the required Form' (and see **Chapter 4**);

- establishing 'internal' STR procedures (and see **Chapter 12**);

- establishing a defence to 'failure to report', where there is insufficient information either of the alleged perpetrator or of the 'property' in question (see **Chapter 4**); and

- establishing SOCA as a new law enforcement agency (the UK's FIU) (although since 7 October 2013, the NCA replaced SOCA and has taken over running the UK FIU).

SOCA assumed its responsibilities on 1 April 2006, and assumed all functions previously held by NCIS; and in 2007 (as noted in **2.6** immediately below) SOCA assumed the role and functions of the (former) ARA: however in October 2013 SOCA was replaced by the NCA, which came into being under the Crime and Courts Act 2013 (Royal Assent 25 April 2013).

It is a bit of a complicated genealogy! Let's hope things have settled down now!

THE SERIOUS CRIME ACT 2007

2.6   The Serious Crime Act 2007 (SOCA 2007) introduced the concept of a *'Serious Crime Prevention Order'* to be effected by means of a civil injunction. This remedy is available to the applicant where the Court is satisfied that the person enjoined has been involved in a 'serious crime' in the jurisdiction, and that grant of such an Order would protect the public by preventing, restricting or disrupting involvement by that person in a serious crime in the jurisdiction. Applications may only be brought by the DPP; the Director of HMRC Prosecutions; or the Director of the SFO (and see **4.4**).

The Serious Crime Act also introduced a range of inchoate offences, including 'intentionally encouraging or assisting an offence', 'encouraging or assisting an offence believing it will be committed' and 'encouraging or assisting offences believing one or more will be committed'.

As noted at **2.5** above, the SOCA 2007abolished the ARA and transferred its role and functions to SOCA; but in 2013 SOCA was in turn replaced by the NCA (see **5.1–5.2**).

Schedule 4 to the SOCA 2007 contains detailed complex provisions relating to 'extraterritoriality' of the Defendant's behaviour relating to a serious crime, and whether such behaviour (if committed wholly or partly *outside* the jurisdiction) would nonetheless be triable within the jurisdiction. The key condition is that 'D knows or believes that what he anticipates might take place wholly or partly in a place outside England and Wales' (see **7.2** and **8.11**).

THE EU INITIATIVES ('3MLD' AND '4MLD')

2.7   Directive 2005/60 (known as The Third Money Laundering Directive or 3MLD) (see **10.4**) was implemented by the National Parliaments of all 28 EU Member States by 15 December 2007. In the United Kingdom, the current Money Laundering Regulations were published on 27 July 2007 (see **6.1** and **Appendix 1.3**).

3MLD introduced a number of important changes, including:

- applying to a broader range of persons;
- overlaying a 'risk-based' approach to all CDD requirements;
- defining *Politically Exposed Persons* ('PEPs');
- codifying how institutions should deal with 'third parties'; and
- requiring the licensing/registration of all TSPs (see **Chapter 14**) and CSPs – see **Chapter 15**).

2.8   The draft Directive 2014/ (known as The Fourth Money Laundering Directive or '4MLD') (see **10.9**) was up for approval by the European Parliament during October 2014, and to come into force by December 2014: thereafter it falls to be implemented by the National Parliaments of the 28 EU Member States, which in the case of the UK will lead to a new set of Money Laundering Regulations some time in early 2015

The broader impact of the brand-new 4MLD is discussed in greater detail in **Chapter 10.**

Chapter 3

The UK AML-CFT framework - the principal UK ML offences

INTRODUCTION AND BACKGROUND

3.1　　The principal statute is the Proceeds of Crime Act 2002 ('PoCA 2002') which received Royal Assent on 24 July 2003 (see **Appendix 1.1** for its key sections 327–330). PoCA 2002 replaced the anti-money laundering provisions of the Criminal Justice Act 1988, the Criminal Justice Act 1993 and the Drug Trafficking Act 1994.

PoCA introduced a requirement for mandatory reporting on an 'all crimes' basis. PoCA 2002 restates the money laundering offences, and has replaced the parallel drug- and nondrug-crime money laundering (ML) offences with single offences that do not distinguish between the proceeds of drug trafficking and other crime.

As noted in **2.5**, the Serious Organised Crime and Police Act 2005 (SOCPA 2005) amended PoCA with effect from 1 January 2006 and created and added a further offence of 'Failure to Report on the Required Form' (and see **Chapter 12**).

As noted at **6.1**, the Money Laundering Regulations 2007 implement 3MLD (see **10.4**), with further amendments under the Money Laundering (Amendment) Regulations 2012.

THE PRINCIPAL OFFENCES

3.2　　There are three principal offences, as follows:

(1)　concealing, etc (PoCA 2002, s 327);

(2)　assisting with arrangements, etc (PoCA 2002, s 328); and

(3)　acquisition, use or possession, etc (PoCA 2002, s 329).

- *Concealing, etc*: the offence is committed where a person conceals, disguises, converts, transfers or removes 'criminal property' from the jurisdiction (PoCA 2002, s 327).

- *Assisting with arrangements, etc*: the offence is committed where a person enters into or becomes concerned in an arrangement which facilitates another person to acquire, retain, use or control 'criminal property' and the person concerned also 'knows' or 'suspects' that the property constitutes or represents benefit from 'criminal conduct (PoCA 2002, s 328).

- *Acquisition, use or possession, etc*: the offence is committed where a person 'knows' or 'suspects' that the property which he

8

acquires, uses or has possession of constitutes or represents his own or another's benefit from 'criminal conduct' (PoCA 2002, s 329).

THE FOUR ELEMENTS

3.3   There are four elements of the main ML offences:

- criminal (unlawful) conduct; leading to
- criminal property; with
- some act in relation to the 'criminal property'; and coupled with
- knowledge or suspicion.

There must be criminal conduct (known as the 'predicate offence', and see **3.4**) which results in 'criminal property' (defined as property which the alleged offender 'knows' or 'suspects' constitutes or represents benefit from such 'criminal conduct') (see **7.5** on the technical issues relating to the concept of 'knowledge' or 'suspicion'). And note that there will often be cases where an AML-CFT offence will automatically arise in consequence of conviction of a predicate offence - even though (as noted in **7.2**) a conviction for the predicate offence is not required to support an AML-CFT prosecution. Examples include the famous 'Society Madam' Heidi Fleiss (who spent 21 months in prison for conspiracy and tax evasion); or Benazir Bhutto who received a six-month suspended prison sentence in Switzerland for laundering USD 11 million through Swiss accounts: it is noteworthy that neither led to an AML-CFT prosecution.

There must also be some act in relation to the 'criminal property' (the *actus reus)* such as concealing, assisting with arrangements, or acquisition/use/possession (see **3.2**). Knowledge or suspicion is also required (the *mens rea)* (see **7.5**). Also refer to the principles stated by Lord Scarman in *Gammon (Hong Kong) Ltd v A-G of Hong Kong* [1984] 2 All ER 503 on the presumption of *mens rea* and strict liability.

PREDICATE OFFENCES

3.4   The range of predicate offences is extremely wide. It includes (but without limitation) the following:

- robbery;
- theft;
- illicit trafficking in stolen and other goods;
- piracy;
- forgery;
- counterfeiting and piracy of products;
- smuggling;
- extortion;
- kidnapping;

- illegal restraint and hostage taking;
- sexual exploitation, including CSE;
- trafficking in human beings and migrant smuggling;
- murder, grievous bodily injury;
- corruption and bribery;
- fraud and tax evasion;
- environmental crime;
- insider trading and market manipulation;
- illicit trafficking in narcotic drugs and psychotropic substances;
- participation in an organised criminal group and racketeering;
- illicit arms trafficking;
- terrorism, including terrorist financing; and
- no doubt others!

PENALTIES

3.5   The maximum penalty for each of the above offences is 14 years' imprisonment and an unlimited fine for conviction on indictment. Summary conviction carries the lesser penalties of six months' imprisonment and a fine not exceeding the statutory maximum.

DEFENCES

3.6   It is a defence to each of these PoCA 2002 offences for the person in question to have reported his/her knowledge or suspicion to a constable, or if the law enforcement agency has given permission (a consent) for the transaction to proceed (see **12.5**). The Author refers to this as the statutory 'Get-Out-Of-Jail Free' Card, rather like the one in 'Monopoly')

In fact, internal suspicious activity reports ('SAR') (previously known as suspicious transaction reports or 'STRs') are made to the money laundering reporting officer ('MLRO') of the firm or business in which the person works. The SAR must, of course, have been made at the person's own volition, and either before any criminal conduct occurred, or as soon as it was reasonable for him/her to make it.

Since October 2013, external SARs within the UK are now made to the NCA www.nationalcrimeagency.gov.uk: the NCA website has a number of useful joint NCA & UKFIU publications, including:

- Submitting a SAR within the Regulated Sector (July 2014);
- SAR Guidance Notes (July 2014);
- SAR Glossary Codes Revision Explained (July 2014);
- Home Office Circular 53 2005 Confidentiality and Sensitivity of SARs (July 2014).

The NCA also has an 'SAR Online' reporting service (see **12.4**) and also a July 2014 publication on its website to assist with online filings. See also **Chapter 17** and **Appendix 9** for the procedures in the other selected jurisdictions.

Filing an external SAR does not, however, provide a defence to the person filing it in respect of common law offences such as fraud, false accounting or cheating the revenue, or inchoate offences such as conspiring or inciting, or the related offences of aiding and abetting, counselling or procuring. There is a conundrum here, in that filing an SAR may appear to be an act of exoneration or expiation, rather like making confession for Catholics; however, it may be an evidence of guilt in some circumstances, but (unlike a church confession), an SAR could even be used as an evidence against the reporter (see **Chapter 12**).

SOCPA 2005 added a defence to 'failure to report', where there is insufficient information either of the alleged perpetrator or of the 'property' in question.

Chapter 4

The UK AML-CFT framework – failure to disclose and tipping-off

FAILURE TO DISCLOSE/FAILURE TO REPORT

4.1   Proceeds of Crime Act 2002 ('PoCA 2002'), s 330 widened the scope of the former 'drug money' reporting offence to the proceeds of any *criminal conduct*.

There is a negligence test for liability under the offence of 'failure to disclose' or negligently failing to report a money laundering (ML) offence. The provisions apply to those working in the UK 'regulated financial sector', thus including accountants, lawyers, trustees, tax advisers and many other categories (see **6.2**). The new negligence threshold replaces the requirement for *'suspicion'* of an offence with an *objective* standard, namely whether it was reasonable for a professional in that position to have had a suspicion. The maximum penalty for the offence is five years' imprisonment and/or an unlimited fine.

The offence is committed if the following three conditions are satisfied:

- a person knew or suspected, *or has reasonable (ie objective) grounds for knowing or suspecting*, that another person is engaged in ML, even if they did not actually know or suspect [Author's emphasis, and see **7.5.1** and **7.5.2**];

- the information or other matter on which the knowledge or suspicion is based, or which gives reasonable grounds for such knowledge or suspicion, came to the person in the course of a business in the 'regulated sector'; and

- the person failed to report the information or suspicion of ML by means of a suspicious activity report (SAR) to the authorities as soon as was practicable after it came to that person.

The duty to report/ disclose (by filing an SAR) is restricted to persons receiving information in the course of a business in the regulated sector (as defined in PoCA 2002, Sch 9). This reflects the fact that persons who are carrying out activities in the regulated sector should be expected to exercise a higher level of diligence in handling transactions than those employed in other businesses.

An article by Ryan Myint, *Solicitors Beware: Money Laundering after R v Duff* ((2003) 10(2) JICTCP), noted the difficulties inherent in the concept of *suspicion* in the statutory offence (and see **7.5**).

There is a defence for a person who has a reasonable excuse for not disclosing the information; and also for lawyers where the information came to them in privileged circumstances (see **13.3-13.6**). Once a disclosure is made, the NCA has seven days to respond.

There is also a defence for staff who have not had adequate training (see **6.7** concerning the identification of transactions which may be indicative of ML). However, in order to use this defence successfully, the defendant would have to show that he did not actually know or suspect that another person was engaged in ML, and that, in his case, his employer had not complied with requirements to provide employees with the training specified by relevant Ministerial Order (such an Order referring to the training which all employers are required to provide to employees under The Money Laundering Regulations 2007 (SI 2007/2157) (and see **6.7** on Training).

TIPPING-OFF

4.2   One of the keystones of the Anti-Money Laundering (AML) legislation is the concept of gaining immunity from future prosecution for an offence under the PoCA 2002 by filing a SAR with the proper authorities (see **3.6** and **Chapter 12**).

In order to address the possible temptation a professional or practitioner may have to warn their client (perhaps out of loyalty, or for some other reason), the legislation also includes the offence of 'tipping-off' in relation to criminal conduct (PoCA 2002, s 333). This applies when a suspicion of ML has been disclosed to the authorities by means of a SAR, and when a ML investigation is being, or is about to be, conducted. The 'tipping-off' offence is in making a disclosure likely to prejudice the ML investigation.

Section 330(8) of the PoCA 2002 elevated the Joint Money Laundering Steering Group (UK) (JMLSG) *Guidance Notes* (see **6.6**) to a formal status as the Court is required to consider such *Guidance Notes* in deciding whether a person has committed this AML-CFT offence.

The penalties for 'tipping-off' are five years' imprisonment and an unlimited fine for conviction on indictment. Summary conviction carries the lesser penalty of six months' imprisonment, and a fine not exceeding the statutory maximum.

Conflicting issues, involving tipping-off and constructive trust arguments (and see **14.8**), arose in *Bank of Scotland v A Ltd* [2001] EWCA Civ 52. This case illustrates the tensions between the criminal law provisions relating to tipping-off and the potential civil liability that may arise if an institution deals with the proceeds of a serious crime. In this case, the Bank applied to the Court for directions as to what it should do, and the Court subsequently made an Order freezing the accounts. The customer whose account had been frozen (and who had not been notified of the reason) brought proceedings for the release of the funds. At first instance, Laddie J laid down guidelines as to what an institution should do in the future, either if it wants to make payments from the account, or if it does not. The Court of Appeal did not endorse the guidelines, but confirmed the likelihood of a constructive trust arising in circumstances of suspicion of its customer's dishonesty: but the Court suggested that the Serious Fraud Office should have been made a party to the directions application.

The bankers' concern in this case was that their failure to implement their customer's instructions would in and of itself serve to tip him off.

In a subsequent English case (*Amalgamated Metal Trading Ltd v City of London Police Financial Investigation Unit* [2003] EWHC 703 (Comm) the Judge distinguished the Bank of Scotland decision. He found that 'tipping-off' was not an issue in the case, and ruled that in such circumstances a bank or other financial institution which suspects that it holds funds that are the proceeds of crime should not seek declaratory relief from the Court but must make a commercial decision whether or not to contest proceedings if they are brought by the account holder. The judge alluded to some other tipping-off cases heard in private, where a refusal to comply with a customer's instruction might tip off a customer that there was an investigation: in those cases, Commercial Court Judges in the United Kingdom had made 'show cause' s against the police, and this no doubt influenced the way this case was resolved.

There are few if any reported cases on tipping off, which is surprising, as the consequences of an FSB making an SAR may lead to the rapid 'freezing' of the bank account in question, which in turn puts pressure on the FSB to explain to its customer what is going on (which of course they cannot do, without technically 'tipping off' the customer). See also the *Shah* case in **Appendix 7** and **12.6**.

REPORTING

4.3   The procedure relating to both 'internal' reporting to an MLRO and the 'external' filing of a SAR is covered in detail in **Chapter 12**. Since October 2013 the NCA is the UK national agency to which external SARs are made (previously SOCA and before that NCIS).

Note also that the NCA's SARs Annual Report 2013 is the latest in the series of reports that started with Sir Stephen Lander's detailed review of the UK SAR regime in April 2006: the 2013 Report (see **Appendix 6**) is also available on the NCA website at http://www.nationalcrimeagency.gov.uk/contact-us

CIVIL INJUNCTIONS

4.4   As noted at **2.6**, The Serious Crime Act 2007 introduced the concept of a 'Serious Crime Prevention Order', to be effected by means of a civil injunction. This remedy is available to the applicant where the Court is satisfied that the person enjoined has been involved in a 'serious crime' in the jurisdiction, and that grant of such an Order would protect the public by preventing, restricting or disrupting involvement by that person in a serious crime in the jurisdiction.

Applications may only be brought by the DPP; the Director of HMR&C Prosecutions; or the Director of the SFO.

Chapter 5

The UK AML-CFT framework – tracing, asset recovery and forfeiture

ASSETS RECOVERY AGENCY

5.1   Part 1 of the Proceeds of Crime Act 2002 ('PoCA 2002') established the Assets Recovery Agency (ARA); while Parts 2–5 of the Act provide for confiscation, civil recovery and recovery of cash. These Parts of the Act had two purposes:

- to enable the ARA to bring civil proceedings in the High Court to recover property that is or represents property obtained through *unlawful conduct* (civil recovery) (this right of action is reserved to the enforcement authority); and

- to enable cash which is (or represents) property obtained through *unlawful conduct*, or is intended to be used in such conduct, to be forfeited in civil proceedings before a magistrates' court.

THE NCA

5.2   As noted at **2.6**, the Serious Crime Act 2007 abolished the ARA and transferred its responsibilities and powers to the SOCA, which in October 2013 was replaced by the NCA.

The Concerted Inter-Agency Criminal Finances Action ('CICFA') Group (launched in 2002, with the aim of improving the UK's response to the financial aspects of crime, particularly criminal asset recovery) was linked to the ARA. CICFA members consisted of senior representatives of the main government agencies involved in asset recovery (thus the Police, ACPO, the National Crime Squad and the ARA).

And in January 2008, The Scottish Asset Recovery Group ('SARG') came into effect, with the dissolution of the former CICFA Scotland Group ('CICFAS')

CONFISCATION

5.3   Parts 2-4 of PoCA 2002 provide for Confiscation Orders following a conviction in the criminal Courts. The leading case in this area is the House of Lords' decision in *R v May* [2008] UKHL 28 (the Case Note is set out in **Appendix 7.12**) where the Committee set out the three preliminary questions a Court must address before making a confiscation order:

- The first question is: has the defendant (D) benefited from the relevant criminal conduct?

If the answer to that question is negative, the inquiry ends. If the answer is positive, the second question is:

- what is the value of the benefit D has so obtained?

- The third question is: what sum is recoverable from D?

In some cases (such as *R v Chrastny* (No 2) [1991] 1 WLR 1385, *R v Walls* [2003] 1 WLR 731 and *R v Ahmed* [2005] 1 WLR 122) there may be no dispute how one or more of these questions should be answered, but the questions are distinct and the answer given to one does not determine the answer to be given to another.

CIVIL RECOVERY AND 'RECOVERY ORDER'

5.4   Part 5 of the PoCA 2002 provides for the civil recovery of the proceeds, etc of 'unlawful conduct' and allows for forfeiture of assets even following a criminal acquittal if a civil Court determines that the accused had a 'criminal lifestyle' (see **5.6**), ie has demonstrably benefited from criminal activity with reference to a specified number of convictions within a specified, time period.

'Unlawful conduct' is broadly defined in s 241 of the PoCA 2002 so as to cover conduct that is, or would be, unlawful under the criminal law, wherever it occurred. Note the 'territorial' issue of 'wherever it [the conduct] occurred' (and see **7.2**).

RECOVERY OF CASH

5.5   Part 5 of the PoCA 2002 also provides for the recovery of cash in summary proceedings.

CRIMINAL LIFESTYLE

5.6   'Criminal lifestyle' is defined in s 75 of the PoCA 2002 in particular connection with whether the defendant has committed any one of the 'lifestyle offences' set out in Sch 2 to the PoCA 2002: these are set out in **Appendix 1.1**, and include drug trafficking, directing terrorism, people trafficking, arms trafficking, counterfeiting, intellectual property offences, sexual offences relating to pimps and brothels, and blackmail.

In addition, the 'lifestyle offences' include not only the anti-money laundering (AML) offences under s 327 or 328 of the PoCA 2002, but also the *inchoate* offences of attempting, conspiring or inciting the commission of a 'lifestyle offence', and of aiding, abetting, counselling or procuring the commission of any such offence.

There must also be a 'course of criminal activity', which is defined as three or more convictions in the instant proceedings, or two convictions in the last six years. The defendant must also be shown to have benefited for the conduct.

There is no general examination into whether an accused may be living beyond his/her means with respect to his/her declared sources of income and gains, although this may be taken into account, judged on a balance of probabilities (ie to the civil Court standard of proof) *and not* beyond all reasonable doubt (the criminal Court standard of proof).

And the Court of Appeal confirmed in 2008 in *R v NW, SW, RC & CC* [2008] EWCA Crim 2, 23/1/08 that the prosecution could not simply point to 'unexplained wealth' and assert that as there was no legitimate explanation, *it must therefore emanate from the proceeds of crime* [Author's emphasis]. The Court made it clear that the prosecution had to identify specifically the criminal conduct (or category of criminal conduct) that allegedly generated the money.

FREEZING AND CONFISCATION OF THE PROCEEDS OF CRIME

5.7   On 29 April 2014 the text of EU Directive 2014/42/EU of the European Parliament and of the Council of 3 April 2014 [on the freezing and confiscation of instrumentalities and proceeds of crime in the EU] was published in the OJ. This Directive introduces measures intended to make it easier for national authorities to confiscate and recover the profits made by criminals from cross-border and organised crime: it entered into force on 19 May 2014 (the 20th day following its OJ publication) (the Text is set out in **Appendix 1.9**).

However, the UK has decided, for the time being, not to opt in to the Directive.

COMMENTS

5.8   Note that the recovery provisions of PoCA 2002 do not extend to seizing the financial receipts from, for example, writing a book or newspaper article, or giving an interview about a crime that has taken place and for which a conviction was obtained. For example, Tony Martin was jailed for killing a burglar on his property: in October 2003, on his release from prison he gave an exclusive interview to *The Daily Mirror* who paid him £125,000: after investigation, the Press Complaints Commission ruled that the payment was justified and in the public interest because Martin 'had a unique insight into an issue of great public concern'.

And not all crimes lead to AML-CFT charges. For example, no AML-CFT charges were brought against the Scotland Yard detectives who laundered over £15 Million in drug money as part of a ten-year undercover sting operation in Gibraltar known as 'Operation Cotton' and who may have undoubtedly enjoyed elements of a 'criminal lifestyle' funded by laundered public money, albeit as undercover agents.

TRACING

5.9   'Tracing' is a remedy available to a defrauded party in conjunction with constructive trust arguments: it literally concerns following the money, or its proceeds or fruits, as it is moved around and invested and transformed. The remedy exists in parallel with a finding that a constructive trust exists – see **14.6** and the cases referred to therein.

Tracing is quite different from asset forfeiture, which is a right or remedy available to the State; relevant English cases include *Foskett v McKeown* [2001] 1 AC 102; *Shalson v Russo* [2003] WTLR1169

Nevertheless, s 305 of the PoCA 2002 (see **Appendix 1.1**) contains provisions on tracing, which provide for virtually unlimited tracing in respect of the 'recoverable property' (defined as property obtained through unlawful conduct): such tracing is limited by s 308(1) of the PoCA 2002 if the property is disposed of to a person who 'obtains it in good faith, for value and without notice that it was recoverable property' (the 'equitable superhero' and possibly now also 'the money launderer's darling').

Note that there is no requirement for the disposal to be for money or money's worth, but in practice it is unlikely that a gift could fall within this exception, as 'without notice' must be taken to include constructive notice: in any event, it might be caught by the 'tainted gifts' provisions of s 77 of the PoCA 2002.

PIERCING THE CORPORATE VEIL

5.10   There are interesting issues about 'piercing the corporate veil' in relation to assets belonging to a convicted defendant that are held in a company owned or controlled by that defendant. *R v Gokal* [2001] EWCA Civ 368 sets out general principles. But once the corporate veil is pierced, the assets of the company become available by way of recovery from its controller: see the House of Lords' Decision in *R v May* [2008] UKHL 28 (**Appendix 7.9**). See also *Prest v Petrodel Resources Ltd* [2013] UKSC 34, a decision of the UK Supreme Court on the doctrine of 'piercing the corporate veil'.

The UK AML-CFT framework – the Money Laundering Regulations 2007 and JMLSG Guidance

THE MONEY LAUNDERING REGULATIONS

6.1   The first Money Laundering Regulations were published by the UK Treasury in 1993 (SI 1993/1933). Since then they have formed an essential part of the United Kingdom's anti-money laundering (AML) defences. The Regulations require financial institutions to put in place systems to deter money laundering (ML) and to assist the authorities to detect ML activities.

The current Money Laundering Regulations 2007 (SI 2007/2157) (set out at **Appendix 1.3**) replaced the 1993, 2001 and 2003 Regulations and came into force on 15 December 2007 pursuant to Directive 2005/60 (known as The Third Money Laundering Directive or '3MLD') (see **10.4**). 3MLD was subsequently amended by the Money Laundering (Amendment) Regulations 2012 (SI 2012/2298).

SCOPE AND DEFINITIONS

6.2   The 2007 Regulations apply to the following relevant persons or relevant businesses (as defined):

- credit and financial institutions (see **Chapter 16**);
- auditors, insolvency practitioners, external accountants and tax advisers;
- independent legal professionals (see **Chapter 13**);
- trust or company service providers (see **Chapters 14** and **15**); and
- estate agents, high value dealers and casinos [beyond the scope of this Book].

'Independent legal professional' means a firm or sole practitioner who by way of business provides legal or notarial services to other persons, when participating in financial or real property transactions concerning:

(a)   the buying and selling of real property or business entities;

(b)   the managing of client money, securities or other assets;

(c)   the opening or management of bank, savings or securities accounts;

(d)   the organisation of contributions necessary for the creation, operation or management of companies; or

(e)   the creation, operation or management of trusts, companies or similar structures,

and, for this purpose, a person participates in a transaction by assisting in the planning or execution of the transaction or otherwise acting for or on behalf of a client in the transaction'.

And 'Trust or company service provider' means a firm or sole practitioner who by way of business provides any of the following services to other persons—

(a)   forming companies or other legal persons;

(b)   acting, or arranging for another person to act:-

(i)   as a director or secretary of a company;

(ii)   as a partner of a partnership; or

(iii)   in a similar position in relation to other legal persons;

(c)   providing a registered office, business address, correspondence or administrative address or other related services for a company, partnership or any other legal person or arrangement;

(d)   acting, or arranging for another person to act, as:-

(i)   a trustee of an express trust or similar legal arrangement; or

(ii)   a nominee shareholder for a person other than a company whose securities are listed on a regulated market,

when providing such services.

The 2007 Regulations continue to define ML broadly, as 'an act which falls within s 340(11) of the Proceeds of Crime Act 2002 ('PoCA 2002') or an offence under s 18 of the Terrorism Act 2000'.

The 2007 Regulations tie in with the criminal provisions in PoCA 2002 and Serious Organised Crime and Police Act 2005 (UK) ('SOCPA 2005'), and further define standards in key areas, including:

- identification procedures (customer due diligence) (regs 4, 5 and 6) (**Chapter 11**);

- record-keeping procedures relating to customer due diligence, the business relationships and occasional transactions (reg 13);

- systems and training for employees who are involved in the recognition and handling of transactions which may relate to AML-CFT (regs 14 and 16) (see **6.7** and **6.8**);

- internal reporting procedures (reg 13) (see **Chapter 12**).

Part 1 of the 2007 Regulations (regs 1–3) constitute the general provisions, and include detailed definitions in reg 2, mostly drawn from 3MLD. Regulation 6 defines 'beneficial owner', and has specific provisions (in reg 6(1) for a body corporate, in reg 6(3) for a trust, and in reg 6(6) for 'any legal entity or legal arrangement' which does not fall within regs 6(1), 6(2) or 6(3)).

BENEFICIAL OWNER

6.3   It is worth setting out *in extenso* the definition for a trust, which states that:

'6(3) In the case of a trust, "beneficial owner" means—

(a)   any individual who is entitled to a specified interest in at least 25% of the capital of the trust property;

(b)   as respects any trust other than one which is set up or operates entirely for the benefit of individuals falling within sub-paragraph (a), the class of persons in whose main interest the trust is set up or operates;

(c)   any individual who has control over the trust.

6(4) In paragraph (3)—

"specified interest" means a vested interest which is—

(a)   in possession or in remainder or reversion (or, in Scotland, in fee); and

(b)   defeasible or indefeasible;

"control" means a power (whether exercisable alone, jointly with another person or with the consent of another person) under the trust instrument or by law to—

(a)   dispose of, advance, lend, invest, pay or apply trust property;

(b)   vary the trust;

(c)   add or remove a person as a beneficiary or to or from a class of beneficiaries;

(d)   appoint or remove trustees;

(e)   direct, withhold consent to or veto the exercise of a power such as is mentioned in sub-paragraph (a), (b), (c) or (d).'

As noted in **9.6** (FATCA), **9.8** and **9.9** (OECD), **10.5** and **14.2.1** and **Appendix 1.3** this definition is of great significance in relation to discretionary trusts, as it moves the focus away from the 'discretionary beneficiaries', towards those *'who have legal control over a trust'*. The newest definition is 'people with significant control' ('PSCs') (see **10.5, 14.5** and **15.7**).

Part 2 of the 2007 Regulations (regs 4–12) relates to customer due diligence. Regulation 5 provides that every relevant person must apply customer due diligence measures when establishing a business relationship or where there are doubts about the veracity or adequacy of documents, data or information previously obtained for the purpose of customer identification (and of course if there is any suspicion of ML or terrorist financing). Regulation 4 defines 'Customer due diligence measures'.

Regulation 9 deals with simplified due diligence; and reg 10 with enhanced customer due diligence.

The detailed definition of 'politically exposed persons' is set out in para 4 of Sch 2 to the Regulations (and see **10.10** and **11.15**).

Regulation 12 deals with reliance on third parties. Regulation 12(2) defines 'third party' in a detailed waterfall, first with reference to persons in the United Kingdom, then with reference to persons who carry on business in another 'EEA State', and finally with reference to persons who carry on business in a non-EEA State.

'EQUIVALENT COUNTRIES'

6.4   In the international context, these definitions require careful study, whilst the accompanying narrative to the 2007 Regulations discusses the concept of 'third country equivalence' (meaning third countries that are considered to have equivalent AML and CFT systems to those in the EU): the European Commission list of 'equivalent third countries' as at 26 June 2012 (see **Appendix 1.8** and see also **10.6**) comprises the 28 EU MSs plus:

- Australia
- Brazil
- Canada
- Hong Kong
- India
- Japan
- South Korea
- Mexico
- Singapore
- Switzerland
- South Africa
- The United States of America

(this also being the 'white list' drawn up under 3MLD to reflect *FATF Recommendations*).

Part 3 of the Regulations (regs 13–16) deals with record keeping, systems, training, etc. The provisions relating to 'internal reporting procedures' and the MLRO (a person nominated to receive disclosures) are contained in s 15. Regulation 16 deals with training, requiring that all relevant employees are made aware of the law relating to AML-CFT, and are regularly given training in how to recognise and deal with transactions which may be related thereto.

Part 4 of the Regulations (regs 22–35) deals with supervision and registration. Regulations 25–30 relate in particular to the registration of TSPs or CSPs, and within this group of regulations, the 'fit and proper test' is contained in reg 28, as a negative clearance approach (whereby an applicant will not be registered as a F&PP if they possess any of the negative indicia (convictions etc).

Regulation 23 designates the 'supervisory authorities'. For TSPs and CSPs 'The Authority' is defined in reg 2 as the FSA (now changed to the FCA – see **6.5**). In relation to accountants, barristers, solicitors, etc, Sch 3 Part 1 to the Regulations lists the professional bodies that are the 'supervisory authority' in relation to their own members (lawyers, accountant etc).

Part 5 of the Regulations (regs 30–43) deals with enforcement, including, within regs 41–43, the definition of the criminal offences created and the accompanying tariffs for fine or imprisonment on conviction.

FSMA, FSA AND FCA

6.5   The Financial Services and Markets Act 2000 ('FSMA 2000') came into force in the United Kingdom in November 2001, when the Financial Services Authority ('FSA') became the sole regulator of all financial services in the United Kingdom, with power to make and enforce regulatory rules on ML, prosecute criminal breaches of AML-CFT regulations and publicise the outcome of disciplinary proceedings. The FSA also had the responsibility of reducing financial crime, by a combination of supervision and training.

The Financial Services Act 2012 came into force on 1 April 2013 (having received royal assent on 19 December 2012). The Act created a new regulatory framework for financial services, abolishing the Financial Services Authority, giving the Bank of England responsibility for financial stability, and creating a new regulatory structure consisting of the Bank of England's Financial Policy Committee, the Prudential Regulation Authority and the Financial Conduct Authority ('FCA')

The FCA Money Laundering Sourcebook, coupled with the JMLSG Guidance Notes, used to be the AML-CFT standard reference point for the UK financial services sector. However in August 2006 the *Sourcebook* was revoked and replaced by the provisions of the *Senior Management Arrangements System and Controls Handbook* ('SYSC'), effectively binding senior management of FCA-regulated bodies to ensure appropriate AML-CFT risk sensitive controls and systems are in place. These Rules were further reviewed and updated as a result of the implementation of MiFID in late 2007.

THE JOINT MONEY LAUNDERING STEERING GROUP GUIDANCE FOR THE UK FINANCIAL SECTOR (2013 REVISED VERSION)

6.6   The JMLSG of the British Bankers Association has for a number of years published AML-CFT guidance notes for the UK financial sector (available at http://www.jmlsg.org.uk/industry-guidance/article/further-amendments-to-2007-guidance1), in association with the Building Societies Association and the law enforcement authorities. Similar guidance notes have also been produced for the insurance and investment business sectors.

The original JMLSG *Guidance Notes* were first published in June 1997, and have since been periodically reviewed and updated as required. An important revision took place in 2003 to reflect the implementation of PoCA 2002. And a major revision was published in January 2006 (based on a number of fundamental principles - including that of senior management accountability and the adoption of a risk-based approach, the latter allowing firms to focus their AML/CFT resources on areas where the risk of money laundering/terrorist financing is higher, and therefore embodying proportionate and cost-effective approach to managing these risks.)

JMLSG subsequently amended its *Guidance* to reflect the provisions of Money Laundering Regulations 2007, which in turn implemented 3MLD.

The current version is JMLSG Guidance for the UK Financial Sector (2013 Revised version, published on 20 November 2013). The revised Guidance is 359 pages long: certain sections are extracted at **Appendix 1.4**. The Guidance has the following seven 'key pillars':

1   Senior management responsibility;

2   Internal controls;

3   The nominated officer or MLRO;

4   Risk-based approach;

5   Customer identification/due diligence;

6   Suspicious activities, reporting and data protection;

7   Staff awareness, training and alertness; and

8   Record keeping; and

with two further massive 'Parts' (each approximately 100 pages long) on 'sectoral guidance'.

The actual Guidance has eight chapters, each of which begins with a definition of the relevant law/regulation, and also the core obligations of each. Thus:

Chapter 1	Senior Management Responsibility core obligations are to identify and manage effectively the risks in their businesses, and (if in the regulated sector) to appoint a nominated officer to process disclosures. Adequate resources must be devoted to AML-CFT. Also, the senior management may be subject to potential personal liability if the legal obligations are not met.
Chapter 2	Internal Controls core obligations are to establish and maintain appropriate procedures to forestall and prevent ML, whilst appropriate controls should take account of the risks faced by the business.

Chapter 3	Nominated Officer or MLRO core obligations are to receive and review internal disclosures, and make external reports. Threshold competence is required, and the MLRO should be able to act on his/her own authority. The business itself must devote adequate resources to AML-CFT. And the MLRO is responsible for oversight of compliance with requirements in respect of staff training.
	In addition to their JMLSG Guidance, the British Bankers' Association (BBA) has an AML-CFT Reporting Officer's Reference Guide (see **10.6**).
Chapter 4	Risk-based Approach core obligations are for appropriate systems and controls to reflect the degree of risk associated with the business and its customers, and to take into account the greater potential for ML and terrorist financing which arises when the customer is not physically present. The detailed provisions on 'Risk-based Approach' (see **10.4** and **11.16**) are extremely helpful (see **Appendix 1.4**.)
Chapter 5	Customer Due Diligence core obligations are to have processes for identifying different types of customers; to have systems to deal with identification issues in relation to those who cannot produce this standard evidence; to ensure the processes take account of the greater potential for ML which arises when the customer is not physically present when being identified; to ensure that certain types of person/entities must not be dealt with; to halt the business relationship if satisfactory evidence of identity is not obtained; and to have a system for updating customer information.
Chapter 6	Suspicious Activities, Reporting and Data Protection core obligations (these are highly detailed, and are set out in **Appendix 1.4**.
Chapter 7	Staff Awareness, Training and Alertness (and see **6.7**) core obligations are again highly detailed and are set out in **Appendix 1.4**.
Chapter 8	Record keeping core obligations are to retain copies of the evidence of customer identity for five years after the end of the customer relationship, and details of customer transactions for five years from the date of each transaction. Also, to retain details of actions taken in respect of both internal and external suspicious activity reports (SAR), as well as details of information considered by the nominated officer (MLRO) in respect of an 'internal report' where no 'external report' is made.

The JMLSG *Guidance Notes* have been approved by HM Treasury and carry a degree of 'force of law', in that, in considering a charge under s 330 of the PoCA 2002 (see **4.1**), a UK Court is required to consider whether an individual has complied with them. The Money Laundering Regulations 2007 also provide in reg 41(2) that 'in deciding whether a person has committed an offence under these Regulations, the Court must consider whether he followed the relevant guidance' which was issued by a supervisory body or other appropriate authority, approved by the Treasury and published.

In October 2013, the Law Society issued its updated **AML Practice Note** (see **Appendix 7**) to help Solicitors comply with the PoCA 2002, the Terrorism Act 2000 and the Money Laundering Regulations 2007 (and all amending legislation up to October 2013). It also details good practice. The Practice Note has also been updated following the replacement of SOCA by the National Crime Agency - see http://www.lawsociety.org. uk/advice/practice-notes/aml/#sthash.3wl5ADxM.dpuf (and see **7.5.3** and **13.2**).

And the ICAEW (in conjunction with the other members of the CCAB) has issued The CCAB AML-CFT Guidance (see www.icaew.com/ en/technical/legal-and-regulatory/money-laundering/uk-law-and-guidance to assist its members in fulfilling AML-CFT requirements. The guidance was issued in August 2008, to assist those providing audit, accountancy, tax advisory, insolvency or related services in the United Kingdom (including such firms providing trust or company services) in fulfilling their AML-CFT requirements under PoCA 2002 and the Money Laundering Regulations 2007, it replaces the previous Handbook section 7.2 and technical releases issued in October 2007 (Tech 05/07) and December 2007 (Tech 07/07). The Guidance was been approved by Treasury (approval granted in July 2008).

TRAINING

6.7   Effective staff training is essential for an effective AML-CFT machine in the private sector. This requirement is also reflected in Art 35 of The Third Money Laundering Directive or 3MLD (see **10.4** and **Appendix 1.6**). It is covered by the 2007 Regulations in reg 14. Importance of training is one of the seven key pillars of the revised Guidance Notes.

Chapter 4 notes that s 330 of the PoCA 2002 created the offence of negligently failing to report a ML offence, which is applicable only to those working in the 'regulated financial sector', thus including UK accountants, lawyers and trustees.

Note also the defence for staff who have not had adequate training concerning the identification of transactions which may be indicative of ML. However, in order to use this defence successfully, the defendant would have to show that he/she did not actually know or suspect that another person was engaged in ML, and that, in his case, his/her the employer had not complied with requirements to provide employees with such training specified by the Secretary of State by Order (such an Order will reference to training which all employers are required to provide to employees under the Money Laundering Regulations).

TRAINING INITIATIVES AND RESOURCES

6.8   There are now a host of training initiatives, both in the United Kingdom and internationally, and both from government agencies and private sector, for example:

- British Bankers Association online training initiative at www. bbae-learning.com/_corpsite/ default. asp

- The FCA courses and workshops: see www.fca.gov.uk/industry-training/ml_workshop. html.

- The International Compliance Association and the University of Manchester Business School, with the approval of STEP and the International Trust Companies Association offer international diplomas: *'International Diploma in Anti-Money Laundering'* and *'International Diploma in Compliance'* see www.step.org.

- The International Compliance Association (ICA) see *www.int-comp. com* offers In-house Anti-Money Laundering Awareness Training – available world wide

Other AML-CFT training resources and publications include:

- Compliance Training http://www.mlro.net/

- Money Laundering Reporting Officer's Practical Handbook 2015 www.mlro.net/products/display/mloph-general

- *International Enforcement Law Reporter* edited by Bruce Zagaris, Washington DC;

- Money Laundering Bulletin, by *Informa;*

- SWAT's Money Laundering *The New Law and Your Obligations* training CD;

- AML-CFT multimedia and e-learning by www. Moneylaunder. co.uk;

- ACAMS (the Association of Certified Anti-Money Laundering Specialists), a US-based organisation www.acams.org.

Chapter 7

The UK AML-CFT framework – technical issues

'ALL CRIMES' OFFENCES

7.1 The Proceeds of Crime Act 2002 ('PoCA 2002') definition of 'criminal conduct' refers to conduct comprising a criminal offence. There is no limitation of the type of predicate offence covered, and there is no requirement for the predicate offender to be convicted in order to support an anti-money laundering (AML-CFT) prosecution against the AML defendant (see **7.2**).

FATF Recommendation 3 (issued on 15 February 2012, see **Appendix 2**) states that countries should apply the crime of money laundering to 'all serious offences' with a view to including the widest range of predicate offences.

Although the 'all crimes' approach is logical (and clears up overlapping legislation), it tends to cause difficulty in relation to fiscal and tax-related offences, where learned commentators take the view that 'there is a fundamental separation between tax evaders and corrupt money launders'[1] and 'the widening of AML-CFT legislation to include tax offences, specifically tax avoidance, creates an impossible situation for banks and demands vast resources'[2] (see **8.12**).

And even if the position is relatively clear in relation to domestic offences, there are analytical difficulties where the offence occurs overseas (see **2.6**, **5.4** and **7.2** below on 'extraterritoriality').

TERRITORIAL LIMITS AND 'DUAL CRIMINALITY'

7.2 Complex and technical issues abound! In terms of territoriality, criminal law traditionally confines itself to offences where some element of the activities of the underlying crime occur within the territorial borders of the jurisdiction (although long arm' statutes are increasingly common). In other words, the basic principle is that there can be no extra-territorial application to AML-CFT laws.

The PoCA 2002 is for the most part consistent with this, in that it does not apply unless some element of the *actus reus* is connected with the United Kingdom, in the sense of either occurring in the United Kingdom, or (if it

---

1 *Per* Bruce Zagaris writing in (2005) 21 (9) International Enforcement Law Reporter.
2 *Per* Alon Kaplan writing in (2005) (March) Globes.

occurred elsewhere) then at least having the criminal proceeds enter the United Kingdom.

As noted at **3.3** and **8.11**, s 340(2) of the PoCA 2002 contains a dual definition of 'criminal conduct', namely:

- conduct which constitutes an offence in any part of the United Kingdom; or

- in relation to conduct which occurs *outside* the United Kingdom, conduct which *would* constitute an offence *if it had* occurred in any part of the United Kingdom.

The concept of 'criminal property', as defined in s 340(3), links directly to the requirement of 'criminal conduct'.

In terms of 'dual criminality', the position is more obscure. The three principal anti-money laundering (AML-CFT) offences (see **3.2**) clearly do not have 'dual criminality' requirements, so the conduct does not also need to be unlawful under the criminal law of the foreign country in which it occurred. In contrast, the drafting of the *Civil Recovery* definition of 'unlawful conduct' in s 241 curiously does require dual criminality.

The notes to FATF Recommendation 3 (February 2012) (see **Appendix 2**) provides that predicate offences for money laundering *should* extend to conduct that occurred in another country, which constitutes an offence in that country, and which would have constituted a predicate offence had it occurred domestically.

Despite the territorial limitation of the criminal law (see above), these provisions establish a high degree of extraterritoriality (and a Home Office Circular in March 2003 failed to clarify the position). The provisions enable property obtained through conduct abroad to be recovered, or cash so obtained to be forfeited, even if the conduct was lawful where it took place but provided only that it would have been unlawful in any part of the United Kingdom had it occurred there, which rather obviously, it did not (see *HKSAR v Look Kar Win* [1999] 4 HKC 783 4 in **Chapter 17**, involving Hong Kong residents gambling in Thailand).

Fortunately, s 102 of the SOCPA 2005 (see **Appendix 1.2**) added a territorial defence to charges under ss 327–329 of the PoCA 2002, where the conduct took place outside the United Kingdom and in a country where such conduct is lawful.

And as noted at **2.6** and **8.11**, Sch 4 to the SOCPA 2005 contains detailed complex provisions relating to 'extraterritoriality' of the Defendant's behaviour relating to a serious crime, and whether such behaviour (if committed wholly or partly *outside* the jurisdiction) would nonetheless be triable within the jurisdiction. The key condition is that 'D knows or believes that what he anticipates might take place wholly or partly in a place outside England and Wales'.

There is also bizarrely no requirement for the predicate offender to be convicted in order to support an AML prosecution against a linked

AML defendant, although human rights issues of legal 'certainty' and 'proportionality' would inevitably arise if no conviction at all was obtained in any country in relation to the underlying predicate offence/offender. To that extent therefore, AMM-CFT offences have inchoate features.

Thus, in the context of securing an AML-CFT conviction for a foreign fiscal offence (see **Chapter 17** relating to other jurisdictions) s 340(2) of the PoCA 2002 seems to necessitate a 'double deeming', not only that the offence was committed in the United Kingdom, but also that the 'deemed victim' was (presumably) HMRC (the actual 'victim' of course being a foreign revenue administration). Thus, the extra-territorial effect is enlarged along with the difficulties in applying the section to the offence.

PROCEEDS

7.3   There is also a technical debate about the concept of the 'proceeds' of a foreign tax crime.

Some have argued that money laundering (ML) is a type of crime that does not directly result in any 'proceeds'. Clearly, if an individual has an undisclosed fortune held on deposit offshore and also has substantial funds in a bank at home, there is an argument that the funds at home might primarily contain the 'proceeds' of the domestic tax offence committed through non-reporting of (and non-payment of tax on) the offshore fortune.

An alternative view is that the offshore fortune is also the proceeds of crime, at least partially and possibly pro rata the sum onshore, on the basis that the offshore fortune may 'directly or indirectly' represent them. Certainly the point is not free from doubt.

In the 2003 English criminal case *R v Foggon* [2003] EWCA Crim 270 the Court of Appeal confirmed that tax avoided or attempted to be avoided could also be a pecuniary advantage (see *R v Moran* [2002] 1 WLR 253; and *R v Dimsey* [2000] QB 744 (CA) and 2001 UKML 46; [2001] 3 WLR 843) obtained by an accused (in the context of a confiscation order).

And in *R v IK* [2007] EWCA Crim 491 the Court examined the question of whether the proceeds of cheating the revenue could be 'criminal property'. The prosecution alleged that not all of the takings of a retail business had been declared for tax purposes, and that the shopkeeper was therefore cheating the revenue. The Crown Court Judge threw out the money laundering prosecution, ruling that as the cash did not emanate from an actual crime there could not be any 'criminal property'. However, the Court of Appeal held that the undeclared income could in part 'represent' the proceeds of crime, and that the undeclared amount represented the 'benefit' of tax evasion.

Wikipedia notes that 'Different countries may or may not treat tax evasion as money laundering. Some jurisdictions differentiate these for definition purposes, and others do not. Some jurisdictions define money laundering as obfuscating sources of money, either intentionally or by merely using financial systems or services that do not identify or track sources or destinations. Other jurisdictions define money laundering to include money from activity that *would have been a crime in that jurisdiction, even if it were legal where the actual conduct occurred.* This broad brush of applying the term "money laundering" to merely incidental, extraterritorial, or simply privacy-seeking behavior has led to the label "financial thoughtcrime".[1]

TIME LIMITS AND RETROSPECTIVITY

7.4   Although PoCA 2002 expressly provides that it is immaterial when the criminal conduct occurred, there is no apparent intention to create wholesale retrospectivity (in any event prohibited under European Convention on Human Rights, Art 7, and see *Welch v United Kingdom (Application 17440/90)* (1995) 20 EHHR 247), and it is just the difference in time between the underlying predicate offence and the subsequent AML-CFT offence that is intended.

It is, however, clear that *due diligence* (CDD) obligations, and the principal money laundering offences themselves, do extend backward in time *without time limit* in respect of all businesses whenever taken on. This position may be mitigated by local statute or regulation.

'KNOWLEDGE', 'SUSPICION' AND 'REASONABLE GROUNDS'

7.5   The requisite mental elements (*mens rea*) of the PoCA 2002 AML-CFT offences are 'knowledge' or 'suspicion' that the property in question constitutes or represents the benefit of criminal conduct. An understanding of the concepts of 'knowledge' or 'suspicion' is crucial, as lawyers can attest that plain words do not always mean what they seem to mean. A more detailed consideration of the differing 'mental' elements of the offences follows; this becomes particularly relevant in relation to foreign (ie non-UK) fiscal offences (see **8.7**). And as discussed in the JMLSG Guidance, these states of mind (along with the test of 'reasonable ground') all have differing thresholds.

7.5.1   'Knowledge' is an absolute – one either knows or one does not – hence the legislation includes the lesser requirement of mere 'suspicion' to cover the case where someone does not actually know but still has suspicions or doubts. The key to keeping a UK professional or financial institution from falling within the principal AML-CFT offences is, therefore, the requirement for there to be neither 'knowledge' nor 'suspicion' that the property in question emanates from criminal conduct.

Case law in the area of constructive trusts (see **14.8**) shows there are various types of knowledge:

(a)   actual knowledge;

(b)   'Nelsonian' knowledge – this would also suffice for the offence; and

---

1 Coined by Jon Matonis (May 7, 2013). 'Money Laundering Is Financial Thoughtcrime'. AmericanBanker.com

(c)   imputed or constructive knowledge – this introduces an objective standard of knowledge, whereby one might be deemed to 'know' something if it could have been ascertained from enquiries which 'the reasonable person' would have made in the same circumstances (see *Baden Delvaux v Société Générale* 1992; *Royal Brunei Airlines Ltd v Tan* [1995] 2 AC 378 and *BCCI (Overseas) v Akindele* [2000] 4 All ER 221).

Directive 2005/60 (known as the Third Money Laundering Directive or 3MLD) (see **10.4**) has reconfirmed verbatim in its Art 1(5) the expansive test of knowledge originally in (now superseded) EU Directive 91/308, stating:

'5. Knowledge, intent or purpose required as an element of the activities mentioned in para 2 and 4 [of Article 1] may be inferred from objective factual circumstances.'

The standard of knowledge under PoCA 2002 is subjective. It is usually quite difficult to prove a person's actual knowledge, but if there is less than actual subjective knowledge, then there may still be a residual suspicion. The requisite 'suspicion' does not need to relate to the particular underlying crime that gave rise to the criminal proceeds, and it is sufficient simply to show that there was suspicion as to the tainted nature of the source of funds that gave rise to the 'property'. A 'suspicious activity' report or 'SAR' is what is then filed.

7.5.2   'Suspicion' is different and has a lower threshold. 'Suspicion' is a very unusual connecting factor for attributing criminal liability, let alone for something as important as an AML-CFT offence with a lengthy prison term attached. Suspicion is not an easy state of mind to define, and the difficulties for those working with the Act are exacerbated by the fact that there is no definition in the primary legislation.

The JMLSG *Guidance* 2013 (see **6.6**) states at its Para 6.10 that suspicion is more subjective and falls short of proof based on firm evidence. Suspicion has been defined by the Courts as being beyond mere speculation and based on some foundation, for example:

'A degree of satisfaction and not necessarily amounting to belief but at least extending beyond speculation as to whether an event has occurred or not'; and

'Although the creation of suspicion requires a lesser factual basis than the creation of a belief, it must nonetheless be built upon some foundation.'

This almost echoes exactly Lord Scott of Foscote's remarks in the House of Lords case in 2001 that: 'suspicion is a word that can be used to describe a state of mind that may, at one extreme, be no more than a vague feeling of unease, and at the other extreme reflect a firm belief in the existence of the relevant facts' (*Manifest Shipping Co v Uni-Polaris Shipping Co* [2001] UKHL 1) at [116]).

Other attempts have, however, been made to define *suspicion* in case law:

- In his learned article in 2003 ('Solicitors Beware: Money Laundering after R v Duff', [2003] 10 (2) JICTCP) Ryan Myint noted the difficulties inherent in such a broad definition in the context of the statutory offence of failing to report a *suspicion* of money laundering (and see Cases in **Appendix 5**).

- In *Hussein v Chong Fook Kam* [1969] 3 All ER 1626, PC, it was held that the word suspicion in its ordinary meaning is a state of conjecture or surmise where proof is lacking: 'I suspect, but I cannot prove'.

- Similarly, in the case of *Corporate Affairs Comr v Guardian Investments* [1984] VR 1019 it was stated that the word 'suspect' requires a degree of satisfaction, not necessarily amounting to belief, but at least extending beyond speculation as to whether an event has occurred or not.

- In contrast, mere speculation was excluded in the case of *Walsh v Loughman* [1992] 2 VR 351 where it was held that 'although the creation of suspicion requires a lesser factual basis than the creation of a belief it must nonetheless be built upon some foundation'.

- See also *Abou-Rahmah v Abacha* [2006] EWCA 1492, where the appeal was dismissed against a finding that the Nigerian bank was not liable for knowing/dishonest assistance in breach of trust. The manager had suspected in a general way that the parties may have been involved in money laundering, but did not have suspicions about two concessions that gave rise to the claim.

- Other recent cases include *R v Liaquat Ali, Akhtar Hussain and Mohsan Khan* [2005] EWCA Crim 87.

- In *R v Da Silva* [2006] EWCA Crim 1654 the Court of Appeal held that 'the essential element in the word "suspect" is that the Defendant must think there is a possibility, which is more than merely fanciful, that the relevant facts exist'.

- In *K Ltd v National Westminster Bank* [2006] ECWA Civ 1039 the Court adopted the definition in *Da Silva* and found that the existence of a suspicion *is a subjective fact* and that *there is no legal requirement that there should be reasonable grounds for a suspicion*.

- In *R v Saik* [2006] UKHL 18 the defendant suspected but did not actually 'know' that the money he was laundering was the proceeds of crime, and was therefore acquitted. Lord Nicholl's speech in this leading case explains and clarifies the law of conspiracy in relation to the ML offences.

- The question 'whatever happened to the concept of a 'duty of care' and the 'neighbour principle'?' was answered in *Shah v HSBC Private Bank (UK) Limited* [2009] EWHC 79 (QB) and [2010] EWHC 31, an important decision on the apparent lack of a bank's duty of care (and see **Chapter 12** and **Appendix 7**). Mr Shah's subsequent claim for alleged negligence/breach of contract in reporting of money laundering suspicions failed in the High Court of Justice QBD on 16 May 2012 [2012] EWHC 1283 (QB).

- See the Jersey position on the *subjective* standard, referred to in **Appendix 9** para 28.74

As regards 'suspicion' in relation to foreign tax offences, the JMLSG *Guidance Notes* 2003 conceded that there is no requirement for institutions to have knowledge of the tax (or other) laws in the countries in which criminal conduct may have occurred (see **8.9**) but the revised JMLSG Guidance omits this comment (see in contrast the position in Singapore at **17.10**).

Also note that *FATF Recommendation* 3 (February 2012) provides that the intent and knowledge required to prove an AML offence should be consistent with the standards set out in the Vienna Convention (*Vienna Convention against Illicit Traffic in Narcotic Drugs and Psychotropic Substances 1988*) and the Palermo Convention (the 2000 UN Convention on *Transnational Organised Crime*): this includes that such a subjective mental state can be inferred from objective factual circumstances (if so, a person could be convicted of any AML-CFT offence for being 'wilfully blind').

7.5.3   The balance: there should be a degressive scale, beginning with 'knowledge', then moving to 'belief', then 'strong suspicion' (or gut feel), then to 'speculation', and finally to 'doubt' or 'uncertainty'. It is submitted that the latter two categories ('speculation' and 'doubt'/'uncertainty') cannot be constitutive of the required mental element. In any event, a 'speculation' or a doubt/uncertainty should be resolved either way by some further action on the part of the professional, such as directing specific questions to the client as to what is going on, and if the responses are unsatisfactory it automatically converts into an actual suspicion.

The current GFSC *Handbook for Financial Service Businesses on Countering Financial Crime and Terrorist Financing* (15 December 2007, updated March & April 2013) (and see **Appendix 5**) summarises the position admirably as follows:

'297. What may constitute reasonable grounds for knowledge or suspicion will be determined from facts or circumstances from which an honest and reasonable person engaged in a financial services business would have inferred knowledge or formed the suspicion that another was engaged in money laundering or terrorist financing.

'298. A transaction or activity which appears unusual, is not necessarily suspicious. An unusual transaction or activity is, in the first instance, likely to be a basis for further enquiry, which may in turn require judgement as to whether it is suspicious. For example, an out of the ordinary transaction or activity within a business relationship should prompt the financial services business to conduct enquiries about the transaction or activity.

'299. There may be a number of reasons why the financial services business is not entirely happy with CDD information or where the financial services business otherwise needs to ask questions. Enquiries of their customer should be made where the financial services business has queries, regardless of their level of suspicion, to either assist them in formulating a suspicion, or conversely to negate it, having due regard to the tipping off provisions.

'300. Although a financial services business is not expected to conduct the kind of investigation carried out by law enforcement agencies, it must act responsibly and ask questions to satisfy any gaps in the CDD or its understanding of a particular transaction or activity or proposed transaction or activity.'

It is also interesting to note that the previous version of the GFSC Handbook also requires persons submitting SARs to provide 'full evidence to demonstrate why the suspicion has been raised'. Whilst it is clear what is intended, there may be difficulties in providing 'full evidence' of the type admissible in Court proceedings. Given the fundamental distinction between 'knowledge' and 'suspicion', if the person only has a 'suspicion' then there is unlikely to be any 'full evidence', as if there was, the suspicion becomes 'knowledge' by corroboration.

The clear and present danger for professionals lies in allowing knowledge or suspicion to be judged with hindsight or objectively. If this is indeed the test (outside of the regulated sector offence of 'negligently failing to report'), then it is no longer merely a question of what you actually knew (or did not know) or suspected (or did not suspect); what may matter is what the 'reasonable lawyer', 'reasonable private banker', 'reasonable accountant' or 'reasonable TSP or CSP' would have concluded if faced with the same circumstances. On the face of it, the PoCA 2002 at present only introduces an objective test of suspicion for the offence of failure to disclose (see **Chapter 4**). And see Lord Reid's speech in *Healthcare at Home Ltd v The Common Services Agency (Scotland)* [2014] UKSC 49 for the analysis of what happened to 'the man on the Clapham omnibus' (now more politically correctly called the 'ORPP' (or 'Ordinary Reasonable Prudent Person').

In October 2013 the Law Society issued its updated AML Practice Note (see **Appendix 7**) to help Solicitors comply with the Proceeds of Crime Act 2002, the Terrorism Act 2000 and the Money Laundering Regulations 2007 (and all amending legislation up to October 2013), and updated following the replacement of SOCA by the National Crime Agency: see http://www. lawsociety.org.uk/advice/practice-notes/aml/#sthash.3wl5ADxM.dpuf (and see **8.8** and **13.4**).

Most of the offshore centres (and the UK in particular) also have a purely subjective test, whilst Hong Kong, Liechtenstein, and Singapore have a 'mixed' test, that is both objective and subjective. It is not yet clear if the subjective standard will stand alone, or if an objective element will be grafted on as well. Some time ago the Association of Bermuda Compliance Officers in Bermuda lobbied the Bermuda Monetary Authority to keep the test objective, arguing that a clear definition of *mens rea* should be adopted since what a jury may regard as 'reasonable grounds to suspect', after the fact and in the light of evidence that may not have been obvious when the transaction took place, may not at the time have triggered suspicion from the employee concerned.

So it seems that the legal position is mixed, that the subjectivity of a decision cannot be challenged if it was an over-reaction, but can be challenged if it is an under-reaction (in either case, that no reasonable banker would have reached that conclusion). So a subjective mental state can be inferred from objective factual circumstances. 'You should have suspected' becomes the cry, rather than 'you over-reacted'. The 2000 decision of the UK Court of Appeal in interlocutory proceedings in *Walker v Stones* [2000] 4 All ER 412 backs up this approach in relation to the definition of' dishonesty' within the context of a trustee exemption clause shows the Courts' willingness to substitute a 'hindsight' test for a subjective belief genuinely held in good faith. On the other hand, a later House of Lords decision (*Twinsectra*

Ltd v Yardley [2002] UKHL 12) found a Surrey solicitor to have possibly been naive or misguided, but not dishonest. But the tests for establishing 'dishonesty' in a criminal trial, as laid down in *R v Ghosh* [1982] 1 QB 1053, are whether the accused's act was 'dishonest' by the standards of reasonable and honest men, and did the accused realise his act would be so regarded: thus a clear objective standard applies.

By way of contrast, in 1990 (some three years before the Criminal Justice Act 1993 amendments), the Judge at first instance in *Agip (Africa) Ltd v Jackson* [1990] Ch 265 (Millett J as he then was, now Lord Millett); affd [1991] Ch 547 (CA) considered the merits of an argument put forward on behalf of the accountants that they did not act dishonestly because what they suspected was 'only' a breach of exchange control or 'only' a case of tax evasion. This approach received a dusty answer from the Judge, who said this at 294H:

> 'What did Mr. Jackson and Mr. Griffin think was going on? There is some evidence of this in the minutes of the first meeting of the Directors of Keclward Limited of 22 March 1984 and it will be wrong of me to ignore it. This suggests that they thought that their clerk was engaged in evading Tunisian Exchange Control, possibly with the connivance of the Plaintiffs and on their behalf – though the minutes do not say so. In my judgment, however, it is no answer for a man charged with having knowingly assisted in a fraudulent and dishonest scheme to say that he thought that it was "only" a breach of exchange control or "only" a case of tax evasion. It is not necessary that he should have been aware of the precise nature of the fraud or even of the identity of its victim. A man who consciously assists others by making arrangements which he knows are calculated to conceal what is happening from the third party, takes the risk that they are part of a fraud practised on that party.'

This is salutary advice. Once a professional sinks to a position of knowing that his client is involved in fraudulent activity, he will find it very difficult to argue that he was not sufficiently on notice of a fraud on a particular party.

In a civil case against an alleged money launderer for dishonest assistance in breach of trust, the Privy Council held in *Barlow Clowes International Ltd v Eurotrust International Ltd* [2005] UKPC 37 that a person could know and could certainly suspect that he was assisting in misappropriation of money, without knowing that the money was held in trust or what a trust meant.

While the Courts are traditionally very reluctant to enforce, directly or indirectly, a foreign revenue law, they will not look kindly on professionals who get involved in what they know to be dishonest activity, even if the professional believes that it is 'only' a fraud on a foreign tax authority or exchange control authority. Commission of a money laundering offence is an automatic consequence, and an SAR should also be filed.

Overall, therefore, this area remains fraught with danger. But these may become a 'future thing of the past' once the new OECD Multilateral tax assistance convention providing for Automatic Exchange of Tax Information, coupled with the Common Reporting Standard, comes into effect (see **9.8** and **9.9**), as these will substantially stamp out simple tax evasion by concealment.

Chapter 8

Fiscal offences, foreign tax enforcement, 'legacy' issues, FATCA and Amnesty programmes

HISTORICAL BACKGROUND

8.1 Historically the stance of the English Courts has been to subscribe to the generally accepted principle of international law that, in the absence of specific treaty provisions to the contrary, no government will enforce the revenue claims of another.

The House of Lords comprehensively reviewed English case law in the 1955 case of *Government of India v Taylor* [1955] AC 491, HL, a case where the Indian Government was attempting to recover through the English Courts an Indian tax liability from the liquidator of an Indian company because he was resident in the UK. Viscount Simonds gave the leading judgment in the House of Lords, in which he relied on four main points:

1   Case law going back over 200 years, including a series of 18th Century cases in which Lord Mansfield had clearly repeated the dictum 'for no country ever takes notice of the revenue laws of another';

2   The fact that the Foreign Judgments (Reciprocal Enforcement) Act 1933 excluded 'a sum payable in respect of taxes or other charges of a like nature or in respect of a fine or other penalty';

3   Evidence produced that other countries (such as Eire, France and the United States) would not allow the collection of foreign taxes through their Courts; and

4   The rule as stated in *Dicey's* authoritative treatise *The Conflict of Laws* that 'the English Courts have no jurisdiction to entertain an action for the enforcement, either directly or indirectly, of a penal, revenue, or other public law of a foreign state'.

The philosophical basis of the rule was debated in the case. Lord Keith concluded that enforcement of such claims is an extension of the sovereign power which imposed the taxes and that 'an assertion of sovereign authority by one state within the territory of another... is (treaty or convention apart) contrary to all concepts of independent sovereignties'.

Also, it was just generally thought inappropriate for one country to become involved in what might turn out to be the penal or confiscatory actions of another.

It was argued that the English Courts might consider collecting taxes which they could classify as non-penal, in other words "the sort of tax which is recognised in this country", but Viscount Simonds stated that he was not 'disposed to introduce so nice a refinement into a rule which has hitherto been stated in terms that are so easy to understand and apply'.

In taking this line the English Courts in effect left it to the Government to determine which tax regimes, if any, should be assisted by introducing specific enforcement provisions in tax treaties.

8.2 In 1997 the English Court of Appeal reaffirmed this traditional position in *Camdex International Ltd v Bank of Zambia (No 2)* [1997] 1 WLR 632, [1997] 1 All ER 728, which held that the English Courts had no power to entertain an action for enforcement in the United Kingdom of a public law of a foreign state (in the event, a garnishee Order, sought by the Bank of Zambia, to remit funds to Zambia pursuant to their exchange control legislation). Interestingly, the same divergence of approach is reflected in two Jersey Cases, *Le Marquand and Backhurst v Chiltmead Ltd (by its Liquidator)* 1987–88 JLR 86, and *In the Matter of Tucker* 1987–88 JLR 473.

The collection of foreign taxes is not the only factor to be considered, as demonstrated by the different approach taken some ten years earlier by the Court of Appeal in the *Nuland* case (*R v Chief Metropolitan Stipendiary Magistrate, ex p Secretary of State for the Home Department* [1988] 1 WLR 1204). That case concerned an extradition application by the Norwegian Government against a Norwegian tax offender who had been convicted in Norway of eleven offences (including five offences relating to evasion of Norwegian tax) and had fled to London. The Court of Appeal (Divisional Court) confirmed that, even though the offences related to foreign tax evasion, extradition could still be ordered. Stuart Smith LJ suggested that the principle enunciated in *Government of India v Taylor* 'plainly relates to civil proceedings'. In other words, recovery of tax would not be enforced, but return of a criminal fugitive would.

FISCAL OFFENCES

8.3 Given this background, even by the time of 2MLD in 2000, few professionals would have considered that the UK's AML-CFT laws extended to tax offences. Or if they did, then surely *non-UK* tax offences, committed *outside the UK* by *non-UK citizens* could not possibly be caught (see **7.2**). And so, two schools of thought emerged:

- Constitutional purists argued for the narrower, more restrictive interpretation based on the historical position and the principle of construing criminal statutes narrowly (see *DPP v Ottewell* [1970] AC 642, HL at 649), and concluded that the new AML-CFT legislation could not criminalise UK practitioners or financial institutions who were simply involved with the proceeds of a foreign client's tax evasion in an overseas country, while recognising that active assistance in evasionary acts (fraud, conspiring to cheat, false accounting, etc) would render the UK person liable. The debate also focused on whether there can be such a thing as a 'proceeds' of a tax crime (see **7.3**), although this question was resolved in relation to tracing and identifying such 'proceeds' following the House of

Lords decision in *Foskett v McKeown* [2000] 3 All ER 97, [2000] 2 WLR 1299, HL (see **5.9** and **14.8**).

- Other practitioners advanced a more extensive purposive interpretation, echoing the JMLSG Guidelines at the time (see **6.1**), namely that 'tax-related offences are not in a special category', concluding that the broader application was not only appropriate and inevitable, but was also fully in accordance with the UK's international obligations.

8.4 So despite the initial ambiguity in its legislative history, it is now beyond doubt that the UK Government has extended the concept of 'other serious crime' to include tax evasion (domestic or foreign). First the Criminal Justice Acts and then the PoCA 2002, have brought within the scope of the UK AML-CFT offences any dealings by UK professionals or financial institutions with the proceeds of tax evasion. So the prudent course must be to assume that tax evasion is a predicate offence, as it is likely to be accompanied by other tax-related offences such as fraud, cheating the public revenue or false accounting, and inchoate offences such as conspiracy to cheat, etc (offences which would in any event give rise to criminal liability in most jurisdictions).

Cases where the common law concept of cheating the public revenue are considered include *R v Mulligan* [1990] Crim LR 427: also *R v Hudson* [1956] 2 QB 252, [1956] 2 WLR 914, [1956] 1 All ER 814, 40 Cr App R 55, [1956] Crim LR 814; *R v Mavji* [1987] 2 All ER 758, 84 Cr App R 34, [1987] Crim LR 39, CA; and *R v Redford*, 89 Cr App R 1, [1989] Crim LR 152, CA; and *R v Hunt* [1994] Crim LR 747, CA.

THE ALL-CRIMES APPROACH

8.5 Despite the above, the 'all crimes' approach still causes difficulty in relation to fiscal and tax-related offences, as a number of learned commentators have noted the fundamental separation between tax evaders and corrupt money launderers,[1] and how the widening of AML legislation to include tax offences (specifically tax avoidance), creates an impossible situation for banks and demands vast resources.[2]

We will see at **8.13** and **14.14** below how banks, TSPs and CSPs have had to address these (euphemistically called) 'legacy' issues.

FRAUDULENT EVASION OF INCOME TAX

8.6 Prior to the Finance Act 2000 ('FA 2000'), the United Kingdom Taxes Acts did not contain any criminal offence of 'tax evasion'. FA 2000 introduced new provisions that were debated and passed by Parliament within two days of their first publication, s 144 of which introduced the statutory offence of fraudulent evasion of income tax:

---

1 *Per* Bruce Zagaris writing in (2005) 21 (9) International Enforcement Law Reporter.
2 *Per* Alon Kaplan writing in (2005) (March) Globes.

A person commits such an offence if he is 'knowingly concerned in the fraudulent evasion of income tax by him or any other person'. In the UK HMRC has clarified that s 144 does not criminalise conduct which is already an offence under current law, and that its ambit should be regarded as similar to the common law offence of 'cheating the public revenue' (see **8.4** and **8.7**).

So the s 144 offence will only be committed if the taxpayer (or his adviser):

- has actual knowledge of the income tax fraud, or at least wilful blindness to it (so *constructive knowledge* – that is, what the defendant ought to have known – is not enough); and

- has acted in some way dishonestly.

FOREIGN TAX EVASION

8.7 As is explained in more detail at **7.2**, the AML-CFT panoply of the proceeds of tax offences does not differentiate where the offence took place. A foreign act of tax evasion, provided it results from conduct the equivalent of which in the United Kingdom is an offence, can by itself amount to criminal conduct under the PoCA 2002. This view (see *Money Laundering Law*) relies on the fact that tax evasion in the United Kingdom can be an offence by virtue of ss 17 and 32 of the former Theft Act 1968 and under the Fraud Act 2006. HMRC brings criminal prosecutions against tax evaders under these sections, albeit infrequently, for:

- false accounting (s 17 of the Theft Act 1968);

- the old common law offence of cheating the public revenue (s 32 of the Theft Act 1968); and

- evading liability by deception (s 2 of the Theft Act 1978 – since repealed by the Fraud Act 2006 (see below)).

Since an act (as opposed to an omission) of foreign tax evasion usually results from a deception of some kind, it is the deception which, if committed in the United Kingdom, would constitute the criminal conduct required under the PoCA 2002. In this regard, the *dictum* in *Hawkins Pleas of the Crown* that 'all frauds affecting the Crown and public at large are indictable as cheats at common law', cited favourably in *R v Mulligan* [1990] Crim LR 427 (a case on the offence of cheating), would nowadays probably not be taken to exclude 'cheating a foreign revenue'.

In other words, an offence under the PoCA 2002 can occur where the serious crime is tax evasion, and the UK Courts should not differentiate whether the taxes that were evaded were domestic or foreign. All that is required is that some element of the activities of the underlying crime occur within the territorial borders of the jurisdiction, such as either the evasionary act itself occurring in the United Kingdom, or (if it occurred elsewhere) then at least having the criminal proceeds of the tax evasion enter the United Kingdom.

Note that the Fraud Act 2006 has abolished the deception offences in the Theft Acts of 1968 and 1978 and its s 1(1) created one new offence of 'fraud', which could be committed in three different ways. However, the Fraud Act did not repeal any of the 'offences against the revenue' (such as s 72 of the Value Added Tax Act 1974 on VAT frauds (and see **Appendix 1.2.2**).

SUSPICION

8.8   As regards *suspicion* (see **7.5.2** for a more detailed analysis) in relation to foreign tax offences, the earlier JMLSG *Guidance Notes* in 2003 conceded that there is no requirement for institutions to have knowledge of the tax (or other) laws in the countries in which criminal conduct may have occurred. The current JMLSG Guidance seems to be silent on this topic. While this may be of considerable assistance to an 'average' practitioner, it surely aggravates the position for large international businesses and professional organisations with offices in different countries around the world, as these may well have the 'in house' capability of checking the position on overseas taxes and the likelihood of evasion with their sister offices in such overseas jurisdictions. Against this background, one wonders how the Senior Management of UBS turned a blind eye to soliciting US taxpayers as their Clients. An article in *Magazine* of 26 September 2014 entitled 'UBS, Histoire d'un Scandale' provides an interesting insight into the methods and procedures adopted by UBS Private Bankers, and the timeline of UBS's alleged assistance with French Clients' tax evasionary activities.

On the other hand, they do need to be absolutely clear on whether the conduct abroad would constitute an offence if committed in the United Kingdom. In the United Kingdom there is no policy ambiguity on this point: the UK Courts only need to answer one question, namely would the facts have constituted criminal activity had they occurred in the United Kingdom?

In other jurisdictions, the position on this crucial point is less clear, and **Chapters 17** and **Appendix 9** review the approach in eleven selected jurisdictions.

PRACTICAL DIFFICULTIES

8.9   Writing in the *Chase Journal* some years ago John Rhodes summed up the difficulties in the UK position thus:

> 'I am not condoning or encouraging tax evasion: to do so is quite simply untenable. Life is less complicated when people pay their taxes. If everyone willingly did so, no doubt tax rates everywhere could fall. I therefore agree in principle with the overall objective of stamping out tax evasion, but I still question the route the UK government has taken. Anecdotal evidence suggests that there is far more tax evasion (as opposed to tax planning/avoidance) outside the US and the United Kingdom; yet the UK government has gone out on a limb on this issue. In doing so it has apparently:
>
> - made no attempt to distinguish between OECD-type taxes and those imposed by regimes it abhors (Iraq, Libya, Serbia, etc);

- paid no attention to the fact that a large proportion of funds in question were originally "hidden" in time of war, or by families who had suffered religious or political persecution;

- not offered the present generation of such families any sensible way in which to reintroduce funds into the open without threat of criminal prosecution;

- ignored the fact that almost all the funds were invested one way or another back in the Western economies via New York, London, or Zurich;

- ignored the proportion they may represent of such markets;

- ignored the difficulty this rapid change of agenda causes some of the world's largest financial institutions, most of which are major players and employers in the City of London and elsewhere.'

In the same article, John Rhodes referred to the dilemma of two 'awful alternatives':

'If situations involving suspicion of foreign tax evasion alone are within the CJA, UK bankers, accountants and lawyers are already faced with two awful alternatives, particularly in relation to families for whom they were acting prior to 15 February 1995, when these new provisions took effect:

[either:] They report the clients (without telling them) to [the NCA], knowing this may now result in the immediate transfer of information to the clients' home revenue authority.

[or:] They don't report and risk prosecution.'

per John Rhodes 'The United Kingdom's Pursuit of Fiscal Crime' (1998) 2(3) Chase Journal at p 58.

The UK approach to foreign fiscal offences also ignores the politics of foreign countries and administrations. For example, some countries have a procedure in their fiscal code whereby a minister or tax official can deliver a 'certificate' that a certain transaction is approved: the law also allows for such certifications to be obtained after the event. An arbitrary refusal of such a certificate to a political 'enemy' or member of a former regime would thus trigger UK AML-CFT sanctions.

COUNTRIES THAT INCLUDE FISCAL CRIME IN MONEY LAUNDERING

8.10   Along with the United Kingdom, a number of countries now include fiscal crime in money laundering, provided the same type of taxation exists in both jurisdictions. Therefore the rule is asymmetric: for example as Hong Kong and Singapore both abolished Estate Duty some seven years ago, the receipt of funds that have not paid foreign Estate or Death Duties does not fall within AML reporting. For more specific information, see **Chapter 17** and **Appendix 9**.

OTHER LEGAL AND TECHNICAL ISSUES RELATING TO FISCAL OFFENCES BEING AML-CFT OFFENCES

8.11   If an offshore trust is found to have been established in its entirety with the proceeds of a domestic fraud or a foreign tax crime (including a VAT offence), then there is a possibility that the purported settlor did not have title to any assets purportedly 'settled'. In circumstances where a trust has no trust fund to 'bite' on, the trust is improperly constituted as a matter of law (there being no certainty of subject matter). So, the trust is simply non-existent (neither 'void' nor even 'voidable') and the trustee would be no more than a custodian of the property for whomever could establish proper title, for example via *tracing* (see **14.8** on constructive trust issues). Further difficulties will ensue for the 'trustee' in respect of any distributions made to 'beneficiaries' in the interim.

In the context of a foreign fiscal offence, s 340(2) of the PoCA 2002 provides as follows:

'(2)   Criminal conduct is conduct which:-

(a)   constitutes an offence in any part of the United Kingdom, or

(b)   would constitute an offence in any part of the United Kingdom if it occurred there'.

Thus it is necessary to deem that the offence was committed in the United Kingdom and (in the case of a fiscal offence) that the 'deemed victim' was (presumably) HMRC (see **7.2**). Thus, there is a high element of extraterritoriality. The JMLSG *Guidance Notes 2003* suggested that a SAR should still be made (this may be prudent, albeit technically incorrect), even though the concerned UK professional need not (or could not possibly) have an encyclopaedic knowledge of world tax systems. The current JMLSG Guidance seems to be silent on this topic.

The territorial limits of AML offences are further reflected the PoCA 2002, the SOCPA 2005 and the Serious Crimes Act 2007 (see **Chapters 2–5** and **7.2**). And the JMLSG Guidance 2013 states in its Para 6.25 that:

'The offence of money laundering, and the duty to report under POCA, apply in relation to the proceeds of any criminal activity, *wherever conducted* (including abroad), that would constitute an offence if it took place in the UK. This broad scope excludes offences (other than those referred to in paragraph 6.26) which [you] know or believe on reasonable grounds, to have been committed in a country or territory outside the UK *and not to be unlawful under the criminal law then applying in the country or territory concerned.*' [Author's emphasis]

As noted at **2.6**, Sch 4 to of The Serious Crime Act contains detailed complex provisions relating to 'extraterritoriality' of the Defendant's behaviour relating to a serious crime, and whether such behaviour (if committed wholly or partly *outside* the jurisdiction) would nonetheless be triable within the jurisdiction. The key condition is that 'D knows or believes that what he anticipates might take place wholly or partly in a place outside England and Wales': and the words 'what he anticipates' refers to the planned and intended criminal conduct.

Para 6.26 of the JMLSG Guidance goes on to add that:

> 'Offences committed overseas which the Secretary of State has prescribed by Order as remaining within the scope of the duty to report under POCA are those which are punishable by imprisonment for a maximum term in excess of 12 months in any part of the United Kingdom if they occurred there' [other than certain gambling offences].

So is it sufficient simply to judge the acts giving rise to the 'proceeds' against UK legislation, with which a UK professional is deemed to be entirely familiar? If that were the correct approach, the underlying acts may well be a 'crime' in the United Kingdom, whilst in reality only being subject to civil or administrative penalties in the 'home' country. A perverse result would ensue, as a UK AML-CFT offence could arise on the basis of the deeming that the acts would have been a crime in the United Kingdom albeit that the acts were *not* committed in the United Kingdom and the 'victim' *was not* based in the United Kingdom.

WIDER ISSUES AFFECTING INTERNATIONAL PRIVATE BANKING

8.12   The inclusion within the AML-CFT panoply of the proceeds of tax offences (domestic or foreign) inevitability means that a significant amount of tax evasionary assets will be jettisoned by the international private banking industry. However, world prosperity and economic growth over the last five years will have more than adequately reinstated those jettisoned AUM (Assets Under Management).

Nevertheless, international private banking (IPB) has an Achilles heel in its general inability to deal with the customer or client's specific taxation profile in their 'home' country. In AUM terms this is a very significant issue for customers or clients from parts of South East Asia, the Indian subcontinent, Africa, Central America and South America and is still also an issue in the European context. And do not overlook the fact that the proceeds of bribery and corruption are also within the AML-CFT definition of the proceeds of serious crime (see **Chapter 18**).

In terms of tax avoidance, some individuals may be fortunate enough to live in countries without taxation such as Bermuda or Saudi Arabia. A smaller number of individuals may manage to construct their lives so they are not officially resident anywhere (which is achievable by spending time in a number of different countries without triggering the specific 'days spent' residence criteria of any one of them).

Some individuals may be fortunate enough to live in countries where taxation is only imposed on a territorial or 'source' basis, so that income or gains earned 'offshore' that country may not be subject to home country taxation either at all (as in Hong Kong) or if it is 'captured' in an offshore

44

company, such as was the case in the United States prior to the 1967 tax reform, and/or is not 'remitted' to the home country, as in Singapore.

In response to this, many developing countries have recently introduced, or are in the process of introducing, controlled foreign corporation (US)/ controlled foreign company (UK)-type legislation or anti-tax haven legislation. Anti-tax haven legislation may involve a given country publishing a prescribed 'blacklist' of jurisdictions, and introducing rules that penalise transactions with such 'blacklisted' countries (for example, the 'blacklists' promulgated by Mexico, Venezuela, Argentina, Peru, Brazil, Portugal and Spain).

The Mexico 'black list' of low tax jurisdictions was recently abandoned (although the list is still in existence) when Mexico adopted CFC rules.

However, the vast majority of individual private banking clients (both in numerical terms and in asset value terms) do officially reside somewhere, generally in countries with systems of taxation and a functioning tax administration. Typically, such an individual has accumulated funds in a bank in a country other than his/her home country, and those funds and/ or the income and gains arising on them, may not have been declared to the home country tax authorities. Indeed, one of the reasons most frequently advanced for *not* using the domestic banking sector in the home country is the lack of confidentiality, coupled with the risk of possible kidnap and financial blackmail.

Thus, the international private banker from (say) Hong Kong, London, Luxembourg or New York is aware that the funds are 'undeclared' to the home country tax authorities. It is unlikely that there is a detailed discussion of how to (or whether to) get back into compliance with the home country tax laws (private bankers usually make it clear to their clients that they do not give specific tax advice), unless some sort of tax amnesty is available (see **8.16** below and **Appendix 3**).

Such funds therefore, on the UK analysis, constitute or include the 'proceeds of crime'.

In the European context, the Luxembourg private banker is in the same position vis-a-vis clients from (say) Germany or France.

Chief Justice Smellie of the Cayman Islands noted in an article in December 2000:

> 'Nowadays, in the more advanced financial centres, it is my understanding that the more sophisticated practitioners routinely seek to clarify the true nature of the client's transactions and will inform the client that he or she must comply with domestic tax laws and that he or she is not prepared to assist in the evasion of such laws. Moreover, in appropriate cases practitioners will require tax opinions vouchsafing compliance with the tax laws of the clients' domicile. I believe that we can now all agree that there can be little, if any, objection to the imposition of a code of practice which discourages the breach of foreign tax laws as a concomitant to the principles and obligations of international comity.'

As 'onshore' governments (led initially by the UK and more recently by the US through FATCA) have now refocused their AML-CFT legislation so as to bring within its ambit anyone who assists with the concealment or retention of the proceeds of foreign tax evasion, it follows that the proceeds of tax evasion (whether domestic or foreign) are now comprised in the definition of the 'proceeds of... serious crime' and are thus immediately reportable.

LEGACY ISSUES

8.13 It follows that the international private banker is, by the UK definition, participating in foreign tax evasion and is in his/her own right committing a criminal money laundering offence, punishable with a prison term. And at industry level, the employer company (namely the private banking institution itself) would likewise appear to be indulging in wholesale institutional money laundering, since the gathering in of cross-border assets would have been central to its strategy over the last 15 to 20 years.

Clearly some protection can be gained by filing SARs. And practitioners can also review with clients whether they may wish to (or be able to) avail of tax amnesty legislation in their home country.

However, a key question is how financial institutions themselves should deal with any partially or even wholly tainted portfolio of IPB clients (see **14.14**).

THE FOREIGN ACCOUNT TAX COMPLIANCE ACT (FATCA) AND US ISSUES

8.14 FATCA seems to have been a 'sledgehammer to crack a walnut' response to international financial institutions seemingly targeting US Citizens and assisting them to hide wealth and evade US Taxation. One key difference between the US and the rest of the world is that 'US Persons' are subject to global reporting and taxation, whereas the other Western countries all allow for their citizens to become 'non-resident for tax purposes' subject to fulfilling the necessary preconditions.

The Swiss banking industry came more directly into the sights with the Swiss DoJ 'Program for Swiss Banks' ('PfSB') which was announced on 29 August 2013, and followed their direct prosecution of UBS for allegedly hiding USD17 billion on behalf of 52,000 Clients), Wegelin (founded in 1741 but closed down in January 2012 as a result), Bank Frey (which announced its closure on 17 October 2013) and 11 other Swiss banks, all for assisting US citizens evade their US tax liabilities. The PfSB voluntary disclosure program requires all Swiss Banks to determine which 'category' they fall into, and then make disclosures accordingly: the level of fines for non-compliance will be up to 50% of the highest bank balance of such US clients back to 1 August 2008. And on 03 September 2013 the Swiss Banks issued a formal apology for helping US Clients evade taxes, and confirmed that they will reach final settlements with the US over tax disputes by 2015.

FATCA was to have been fully applied as of 1 July 2014, although that date was subject to some slippage as banks worldwide insisted on a single set of software changes and procedures to accommodate not only the US FATCA, but also the various other 'mini-FATCAs' and Model 1 and Model 2 IGAs currently being promulgated mainly between the Western European countries (and based on the FATCA principle of flushing out a given country's citizens who use international/ offshore financial centres).

To date, some 88,000 financial institutions have agreed to pass information to the IRS. But it is worth noting the criticism of FATCA voiced in *The Economist* of 28 June 2014 and subsequently frequently repeated. It is also noteworthy how FATCA has been a bonanza for US Attorneys: 'the Americans are over here' in Europe again (especially in Switzerland), just as they were 70 years ago in 1944.

The Model 1 IGA route excludes FFIs from making direct bilateral reports to a foreign Tax Department (in contrast to the TIEA mechanisms which do), and provide for reporting instead to their own national body (typically the tax department or the regulator, and known as the 'competent authority'): offshore jurisdictions going the Model 1 IGA route include: BVI, Cayman, Guernsey, Isle of Man, Jersey, Malta and Mauritius. Model 2 IGAs are currently in place (or contemplated) by Bermuda, Switzerland (and in due course by Hong Kong), thus providing for direct bilateral reports to a foreign Tax Department. It is worth referring to the STEP webpages on FATCA and the IGAs at www.step.org/fatca.

RISKS

8.15   The 21 October 2013 arrest of Raoul Weill (former head of UBS private clients) in Bologna and his subsequent extradition to the US underscores how seriously the US are taking their enforcement efforts.

One leading commentator has asked rhetorically whether the Swiss experience could foreshadow an attack on the entire global private wealth industry, using FATCA and the OECD Multilateral Convention on Administrative Assistance in Tax Matters Standard (see **9.8**). The Author's reply is an unqualified 'Yes'.

AMNESTIES/DISCLOSURE FACILITIES, 'WHISTLEBLOWING' AND DISENGAGEMENT

8.16   Over the last five years, a number of countries have launched Amnesty programmes. Details of these are set out in **Appendix 3**. There is no doubt that these have been successful. A *Financial Times* report on 24 July 2014 confirmed that Governments across the world have collected more than €37 billion of tax from secret offshore accounts, via disclosure schemes offered in countries including the US, France and the UK.

Also included in **Appendix 3** is a useful flowchart that enables interested parties to determine if they are eligible to use the UK's *Disclosure Facilities* relating to hidden assets located in the Isle of Man, Guernsey, Jersey and Liechtenstein. One of the most chilling aspects of such arrangements in general (taken to the extreme in the Swiss DoJ Program or 'PfSB – see **8.14**) is the 'reach back' aspect, whereby accounts that may have been closed several years ago still have to be disclosed.

It is also worth noting that under the US IRS's Whistleblower programme (established in 2006), the IRS Whistleblower Office pays money to people who 'shop' the tax evasionary activities of US Persons, where the information provided leads to the recovery of tax. If the IRS uses the information provided by the whistleblower, it can award the whistleblower up to 30 percent of the additional tax, penalty and other amounts it collects (essentially reward payments for the provision of information).There is a detailed formula for determining the size of the reward, depending on how egregious the case is, or if the tipster has sat on the information.

As noted at **8.12** and **8.13**, the inclusion within the AML-CFT panoply of the proceeds of tax offences (domestic or foreign) inevitability means that a significant amount of tax evasionary assets will be jettisoned by the international private banking industry. One learned commentator has recently remarked that 'whilst it may be darkest before the dawn, those institutions that do in fact go ahead and reject their 'legacy portfolios' will have a great future ahead of them'. Meaning that those that don't, won't!

Chapter 9

Tax transparency, TIEAs, OECD automatic exchange of tax information and the Common Reporting Standard

9.1 Since the 2nd Edition of this Book was published (in 2007), seismic shifts have occurred as regards government-to-government Exchange of Information. The tectonic plates have been well and truly on the move. The background to this is the long-standing campaign within OECD and by the OECD countries to stamp out tax havens: this dates from their 1999 publication *Towards a Level Playing Field* (see **14.12**).

FATF reinforced this around the same time by persuading Governments to add 'tax evasion' to the list of predicate crimes for money-laundering purposes. Thenceforth, undeclared money (often called 'black money') became the 'proceeds of a tax crime', and any financial institution (including trustees and CSPs) 'assisting with its retention' became a principal offender under AML-CFT statutes, and liable to up to 14 years in prison.

9.2 The 2001 assault on mainland USA by Al-Qaeda operatives (including destroying the iconic Twin Towers, with over 2,500 lives lost) resulted in 'terrorism' being added to the scope of AML-CFT legislation, while at the same time forcing people to take AML-CFT prevention far more seriously than ever before.

DATA LEAKS, THEFT AND PENETRATION

9.3 Then the mid-2000s saw a series of data leaks from big banks (first LGT in Liechtenstein; then UBS in Zürich; then HSBC in Geneva), with insiders or IT consultants literally selling their banks' client lists to neighbouring tax departments in return for a cash reward. Bradley Birkenfeld (formerly of UBS) was awarded USD104 million under the US Whistleblower programme (see **8.16**) for shopping UBS to the US authorities, despite having been sentenced to 40 months in a Federal Prison (thus earning USD4,600 per hour for each hour he spends behind bars).

More recently in early 2013, two BVI service providers (Commonwealth and Portcullis TrustNet Group) had massive data leaks/thefts, and the information on over 40,000 BVI companies was passed to the International Consortium of Investigative Journalists who processed it and put a great deal of the information on the Internet (on the ICIJ website). In many cases, the information on the ICIJ site includes the name of the UBO and the name(s) of their related BVI companies.

The motivation for these types of data leaks/thefts fall into four categories: internal (by staff); semi-authorized access (eg by trusted third parties such as IT specialists); unauthorised access (eg by office cleaners via USB drives); and external (eg by hackers). In almost all cases (other than a disgruntled staff member with a score to settle) the motive is purely financial, although it is sometimes cloaked in morality and a desire to do good. Clearly 'end-to-end encryption' would permit this.

For further reading the Author recommends the Article 'Roll Up' $ Millions available in the name and shame game' by Howard Fisher and others, published in Offshore Investment December 2012/January 2013. This phenomenon is considered in further detail in **Appendix 11**.

THE 2008 ECONOMIC CRISIS

9.4   The financial recession than began in 2008 (triggered by the sub-Prime Lending scandal in the US, for which the US banks and in particular *Bank of America* (where the Author used to work) have been heavily fined in recent months) went on to hit the world economies extremely hard, and is still being felt even now (six years later).

The OECD countries' public finances are in disarray, with unprecedented levels of deficits, and interest rates close to zero. Against this dire background, politicians in those countries have had no difficulty in targeting tax evasion and tax schemes as a 'public enemy'. And likewise continuing the campaign to stamp out OFCs.

9.5   The US Government became so outraged against the egregious conduct of particularly the Swiss Banks, that they launched prosecutions against UBS and 13 other Swiss Banks, and also persuaded the Swiss Government to sign a treaty forcing all Swiss Banks to give up their US clients and customers (see **8.14**). Credit Suisse was fined USD 2.6 billion in May 2014 (see **Appendix 10**) and pleaded guilty to helping US citizens evade tax. Its CEO Brady Dougan (himself a US Citizen) remarkably stated in February 2014 that 'Swiss-based private bankers went to great lengths to disguise their bad conduct from Credit Suisse executive management,' which constantly pushed the bank to enhance its compliance policies.

TIEAs

9.6   The OECD's 'blacklist' and 'whitelist' approach to the OFCs led over the last decade to large numbers of bilateral Tax Information Exchange Agreements being put in place. The critical number per OFC was initially set at 12 TIEAS so as to ensure 'whitelist' status.

Chapter 17 and **Appendix 9** track the way that 'onshore' government applications for information pursuant to TIEAs is being challenged. Recent case law includes:

- *MH Investments and JA Investments v The Cayman Islands Tax Information Authority* [2013] Cayman Islands Grand Court.

- *Minister of Finance v Bunge Ltd* [2013] Bermuda Law Reports 83.

- *Volaw Trust & Corporate Services and Larsen v Comptroller of Taxes* [2013] JRC 095; and CA 239 Jersey Court of Appeal.

- *APEF Management Company 5 Limited v Comptroller of Taxes* [2013] JRC 262, Jersey Royal Court.

Of course, TIEA-based information exchange is shortly to be replaced by automatic EoI (see **9.8–9.10**).

FATCA

9.7   The US 'FATCA' legislation (see **8.14**) is a further step in forcing the financial sectors in all serious countries to identify their US customers and clients. FATCA is a kinder, gentler approach than was adopted against Switzerland, but will lead to the same result on a global scale.

Other EU and OECD governments studied FATCA and liked what they saw, so decided to copy it in an attempt to force the financial sectors in the EU and OECD countries to identify, reciprocally, their own nationals (customers and clients) to their fellow government members. The 'Type 1 IGAs' and 'Type 2 IGAs' (see **8.14**) are the solution adopted where the EU or OECD member country has overseas possessions (for which read 'tax havens')

THE OECD MULTILATERAL CONVENTION ON ADMINISTRATIVE ASSISTANCE IN TAX MATTERS (AUTOMATIC EXCHANGE OF INFORMATION IN TAX MATTERS)

9.8   According to the OECD Website:

> "Co-operation between tax administrations is critical in the fight against tax evasion and protecting the integrity of tax systems. A key aspect of that co-operation is exchange of information. Starting in 2012, political interest has increasingly focussed on the opportunities provided by automatic exchange of information [which] involves the systematic and periodic transmission of "bulk" taxpayer information by the source country to the residence country concerning various categories of income (e.g. dividends, interest, etc.). It can provide timely information on non-compliance where tax has been evaded either on an investment return or the underlying capital sum, even where tax administrations have had no previous indications of non-compliance.

> "On 19 April 2013, the G20 Finance Ministers endorsed automatic exchange as the expected new standard. On 6 September 2013, the G20 Leaders committed to automatic exchange of information as the new global standard and fully supported the OECD work, with G20 countries, aimed at presenting such a single standard in 2014. And on 23 February 2014, the G20 Finance Ministers endorsed the Common Reporting Standard for automatic exchange of tax

information, now contained in Part II of the full version of the Standard [see **9.9** below].

On 6 May 2014, the OECD Declaration on Automatic Exchange of Information in Tax Matters was endorsed by all 34 member countries along with several non-member countries. More than 65 jurisdictions have publicly committed to implementation,

On 21 July 2014, the OECD released the full version of the Standard for Automatic Exchange of Financial Account Information in Tax Matters. The Standard calls on governments to obtain detailed account information from their financial institutions and exchange that information automatically with other jurisdictions on an annual basis.

On 30 October 2014 the Standard was endorsed by 58 'Early Adopter' jurisdictions and 35 other jurisdictions at the annual OECD Global Forum meetings and is up for formal approval by the G-20 (now the "G-19") at their meeting in Brisbane in November 2014.

THE MODEL CAA AND THE CRS

9.9   As noted above, the OECD scored another triumph in its campaign to stamp out tax evasion, by persuading 44 countries to commit to early adoption ('the Early Adopters' – see **9.10** below) of the new standard for automatic exchange of information ('AEoI') between the tax departments of those countries, and thus commit themselves to a specific and ambitious timetable leading to the first automatic information exchanges in 2017 (see timetable below).

The Standard (comprising the Model Competent Authority Agreement ('Model CAA') and the Common Reporting Standard ('CRS') was published on 21 July 2014 on the OECD website http://www.oecd.org/ctp/exchange-of-tax-information/standard-for-automatic-exchange-of-financial-information-in-tax-matters.htm

The CRS contains the reporting and due diligence requirements that are the foundation of automatic information exchange. Participating jurisdictions will have to enact rules in domestic laws that are consistent with the provisions of the CRS. FIs covered by the scope of the CRS will be required to report financial account information on account holders that are tax resident in other participating jurisdictions (see the 'Early Adopters' list at **9.10** below). The CRS definition of an Reportable Account holder's 'residence address' is currently based on a bank statement or utility bill etc (see **Appendix 4**), thus effectively self-certification: inevitably this will change.

The timetable for implementing the CRS and its variables are as follows:

- 'new accounts' [accounts that are opened after 1 January 2016] have to record tax residence at the time of opening

- 'Pre-existing accounts' from 31 December 2015 identify 'high value' accounts, and for pre-existing accounts have the due diligence completed by 31 December 2016 by 30 September 2017

- The first exchange of information for new accounts and for 'high value' pre-existing accounts

- complete the due diligence on 'low value' pre-existing accounts by 31 December 2017

Thereafter each signatory jurisdiction will automatically exchange information on an annual basis with every other signatory ('recipient') jurisdiction in respect of the financial affairs of the nationals/taxpayers of each recipient jurisdiction.

And 'reportable accounts' include accounts held by individuals and entities such as trusts and foundations. Companies likewise must be 'looked through' to their UBOs if they are passive (ie have no real business). The new 'PSC' definition of 'Beneficial Ownership' (based on the 'control concept') is already appearing in Bank Account opening forms, so the information gathering exercise has begun (see **6.3**, **10.5**, **19.5** and **15.7**).

The EY Global Tax Alert dated 13 August 2014 notes one positive aspect for FIs, namely that:

> 'the OECD has modelled the CRS on the intergovernmental approach to the Foreign Tax Account Compliance Act (FATCA), which means that in part it should be possible to leverage existing and planned FATCA processes and systems. It should be noted, however, that the data required under the CRS is different, and the volumes of customers and clients affected are likely to be significantly greater'.

As noted at **19.4**, the OECD recognised these same issues in their 2012 Report *'Keeping It Safe: The OECD Guide on the Protection of Confidentiality of Information Exchanged for Tax Purposes'* published on 23 July 2012

THE EARLY ADOPTERS AND OTHER COMMITTED PARTIES

9.10   The 45 'Early Adopters' include all EU member states, some OECD countries, and (*inter alia*) Jersey, Guernsey, Mexico, South Africa and the BVI. A full list of Early Adopters and Other Committed Parties is in **Appendix 4**. Bahamas is a significant omission.

Panama, Switzerland and the UAE are currently among the list of 14 countries that haven't yet met the OECD Global Forum peer review tests of having adequate legal and regulatory frameworks in place for EoI.

The only crumbs of comfort are that (similar to 'dual criminality'), a requesting jurisdiction cannot seek tax information (hence exchange thereof) if there is no equivalent type of tax in the requested jurisdiction; and also that to participate in the AEoI and CRS process, the receiving country must have adequate safeguards to ensure the confidentiality of the information received.

Whilst of course o the political and procedural level, each such adhering country has to go through their internal Parliamentary ratification processes to bring the provisions into effect in their domestic law.

COMMENTS ON THE OECD CRS

9.11   The Author speculates on the deliberate misnomer of the OECD initiative, in referring to itself as an exchange of 'tax information'. It is not. It is nothing more than a mechanism for exchanging 'wealth information'. The fact that FIs are required to disclose assets held in structures for PSCs entirely fails to take into account that properly tax-planned structures are entitled to be left alone.

SEIZURE OF INFORMATION

9.12   In contrast to Exchange of Information (which is a bilateral process, government to government) and in further contrast to 'hacking' (which is an involuntary data leak – see **Appendix 11**) there have been some recent instances of unilateral data seizure. In June 2014 the Hamburg port authorities apparently seized 14,000 documents that were being shipped from Grand Cayman to Geneva, and which were suspected of containing information about Coutts/RBSI bank accounts used for tax evasion.

> 'The Cayman Compass reported that 'The German finance ministry confirmed to the newspaper that the seizure was in relation to a criminal investigation carried out by tax investigators in the German state of North Rhine-Westphalia under the order of the public prosecutor's office in Duesseldorf. It is believed that the investigation is related to a CD containing the records of German taxpayers suspected of tax evasion, which investigators in Duesseldorf acquired in 2013.'

A subsequent *Huffington Post* article by Asa Bennett (the Author's younger son) reported a slightly different version of the saga.

Chapter 10

EU initiatives and the Money Laundering Directives

INTRODUCTION

10.1   The main elements of EU anti-money laundering (AML) policy (the four AML Directives) come under internal market and comprise the 'first pillar' initiatives. Since the Amsterdam Treaty entered into force (1 May 1999) several key policy areas in the area of justice and home affairs, including organised crime, were moved from the national level to the EU level, and now comprise the 'third pillar' initiatives. The 'second pillar' deals with EU common foreign and security policy, so that EU legislation on terrorist financing, although strictly a 'first pillar' initiative, derives from 'second pillar' initiatives. EU efforts to combat money laundering (ML) rest on the original five-year action programme adopted in 2004 in The Hague.

It is beyond the scope of this Book to provide a detailed explanation of the functions and powers of the institutions of the European Union (EU) or in particular the different types of EU legislation and legal instruments. Suffice it to say that in the area of AML-CFT, the EU legislates through the instrument of 'Directives, which are not 'EU legislation' as such (unlike EU 'Regulations' which are directly applicable and have immediate binding effect). 'Directives' require each Member State to enact further domestic implementing legislation in order to give effect to their terms. Nevertheless, some provisions of EU Directives are capable of having a 'direct effect' and creating rights or obligations between the state and individuals (see eg *Van Gend & Loos* Case 26/62, [1970] CMLR 1, ECJ; and *Grad v Finanzamt Traunstein* Case 9/70, [1970] ECR 825, ECJ) but not horizontally between individuals (see eg *Defrenne v SABENA* Case 2/74, [1974] ECR 631, ECJ; *Doughty v Rolls-Royce plc* [1992] ICR 538, CA).

Suffice it to say that EU-wide cooperation on AML-CFT operates at a number of levels:

- An *Expert Group on Money Laundering and Terrorist Financing* meets regularly to share views and help the EU Commission define policy and draft new legislation;

- A *Committee on the Prevention of Money Laundering and Terrorist Financing* may also be convened to give its opinion on implementing measures put forward by the Commission;

- The *European Commission* also takes part in the informal network of *Financial Intelligence Units* (the EU FIUs Platform); and

- The *Joint Committee of European Supervisory Authorities* also works on measures to combat ML.

✎ THE FIRST MONEY LAUNDERING DIRECTIVE OF 1991 ('1MLD')

10.2   The first EC ML Directive 91/308/EEC ('1MLD) was adopted on 16 June 1991, and required Member States to prevent the use of their financial systems for ML by:

- criminalising ML;

- taking measures to identify laundered proceeds with a view to confiscation;

- passing laws and establish systems to prevent the proceeds of crime being laundered in the first place.

1MLD also set out requirements to be placed on financial businesses in the Member States: this included customer identification (then known as KYC and now CDD), and retention of records relating to identification and transactions for a period of five years. 1MLD also required member states to require financial institutions to inform the authorities about suspected ML activity.

In the United Kingdom, 1MLD spawned the Criminal Justice Act 1993 (see **2.3**).

But 1MLD itself was repealed in its entirety by 3MLD, whose Annex contains a useful 'Correlation Table', showing into which Articles of 3MLD the key provisions of 1MLD were transferred.

EXTENSION OF 1MLD: THE SECOND MONEY ✎ LAUNDERING DIRECTIVE 2000 ('2MLD')

10.3   In September 2000, the EU Council of Ministers voted to extend the AML rules in 1MLD (approved by the European Parliament in April 2001) so as to cover *all* serious crimes, and 'to include notaries and other independent legal professionals (ie lawyers) as well as accountants, auditors and other professionals along with financial intermediaries'.

This also tied into FATF-XII Typologies initiatives, which had in tandem recommended including lawyers, notaries, accountants and other legal professionals; 2MLD extended the CDD regime to a broader range of businesses and professional or service activities (no longer just 'financial businesses' as before).

The definition of 'serious crimes' was left to a subsequent instrument, and has now been elaborated on in 3MLD Art 3(5) see **10.4** below and **Appendix 1.8**).

'Tax evasion' was not specifically included within the scope of the Directive, although the definition of 'criminal activity' was widely drafted, covering 'fraud, corruption or any other illegal activity'.

As noted at **2.4**, 2MLD was enacted into UK law as the PoCA 2002.

THE THIRD MONEY LAUNDERING DIRECTIVE (EU DIRECTIVE 2005/60) ('3MLD')

10.4   On 26 October 2005, the EU Council of Ministers voted to extend further the AML-CFT rules in 1MLD and 2MLD, and brought into force Directive 2005/60 (known as 3MLD) see **Appendix 1.8**.

The implementation date for the National Parliaments of all 28 EU Member States was 15 December 2007. Implementation in the United Kingdom followed the publication of The 2007 Money Laundering Regulations 2007 (on 27 July 2007) (see **Appendix 1.5**).

The main changes were:

- under Art 2, it applies to a wide range of institutions and persons, including lawyers, accountants, tax advisors, TSPs, CSPs, and estate agents (see **6.2** and The Money Laundering Regulations 2007 (SI 2007/2157) (**Appendix 1.5**);

- a detailed codification of CDD requirements in Arts 6–19;

- in Art 3(6)(b) a clear definition of Beneficial Owner in relation to Trusts (see **6.3**, **10.5** and **14.2.1**);

- a definition of 'serious crime' (with reference to the penalties);

- overlaying a 'risk-based' approach to all CDD requirements (see Art 8(1)(b) and (2), wherein institutions can 'use intelligence and judgment rather than a tick-box approach to mitigate AML-CFT risks effectively' (and see **Chapter 11**);

STEP Journal, September 2006, p 11.

- clarification of when either 'simplified CDD' (Arts 11–12) or 'enhanced CDD' (Art 13) is required;

- explicitly, coverage of CFT (reflecting changes introduced *via* FATF's original (Special Recommendations);

- definition of *Politically Exposed Person* (PEP) (see **10.10** and **11.15**);

- definition of *Business Relationship* in Art 3(9);

- codification of how institutions should deal with 'third parties' (see Arts 14–19); and

- a requirement for licensing/registration requirements of all TSPs and CSPs and a 'fit and proper' test (Art 36).

10.5   Problems of interpretation always emerge from new legislation. UK Professionals have responded to some of 3MLD's vague drafting with a mixture of indignation and frustration! The President of the Law Society of England and Wales stated in February 2007 that:

> 'It is unacceptable for the government to pass the responsibility of interpreting the incomprehensible language of this directive to solicitors, who face possible imprisonment if they get it wrong.' (see **Chapter 13**)

From a professional practitioner's standpoint, the important areas (the first three of which are looked at in more detail below) are:

(1)   the definition of *Beneficial Owner* in relation to Trusts (see below and in **6.3**, **11.4**, **14.2.1** and **Appendix 1.5**);

(2)   the issue of reliance on third parties' CDD;

(3)   the requirement for all TSPs and CSPs to be licensed/registered under a 'fit and proper' test; and

(4)   'Gold Plating' (dealt with in detail in Art 5 and in **11.13**).

BENEFICIAL OWNER

(1)   3MLD Art 3(6)(b) contains a two-stage definition of 'beneficial owner' in relation to Trusts.

- For trusts where the 'future beneficiaries have already been determined', 3MLD Art 3(6)(b)(i) requires identification of every natural person who is the beneficiary of '25% or more of the property'.

- For trusts where the 'individuals that benefit have yet to be determined', 3MLD Art 3(6)(b)(ii) requires identification of 'the class of persons in whose main interest the arrangement is set up or operates'.

Clearly, where one is dealing with a trust with a named and closed class (i.e. where the 'future beneficiaries have already been determined') it may still be impossible if it is a discretionary trust for the trustees to know from the outset who is to be the beneficiary of '25% or more of the property'.

The 2007 Regulations provide further clarification on the definition of 'beneficial owner' in its Appendix 2 (and see **Appendix 1.5**). The definition operates broadly:

- in relation to a body corporate,

- in relation to a trust, and also

- in relation to 'any other legal entity (other than a body corporate) or legal arrangement (other than a trust)'

and is of great significance in relation to discretionary trusts, as it has moved the focus away from the 'discretionary beneficiaries' and towards those 'who have legal control over a trust' (see also **14.2**).

In terms of risk, one industry expert recently stated that in his view the risk of ML in trust structures is highest at the time the trust is set up and the assets placed into trust On this basis, verification of the Settlor and of the source of funds is the 'sensible priority'. 3MLD's emphasis on beneficiaries is misplaced. The EU's requirements to effect this are impractical, and reveal a misunderstanding of the modern use of trusts. This misunderstanding, which is causing much of the difficulty with the definitional concepts, emanates from reports and publications of the OECD and FATF, where trusts have been lumped together with companies and described (obviously incorrectly) as having 'beneficial owners': for example the FATF 2006 Report on the Misuse of Corporate Vehicles.

(2) Articles 14–16 deal with the issue of reliance on 'third parties' CDD where such 'third parties' may be either in the same Member State or in another EU Member State. The wording is imprecise, as it states that Member States 'may' allow third-party verification, but the 'ultimate responsibility' remains with the party relying on the third party. So it will be left to individual Member States how they implement this.

Institutions will therefore be unlikely to rely on information from regulated third parties, and will probably elect to conduct their own original checks themselves.

Where such a 'third party' is not in an EU Member State, then Arts 16(1) and (2) facilitate CDD to be received from third countries that impose 'equivalent requirements' to those laid down in 3MLD, and enable the Member States to inform each other and the Commission of cases where they consider the condition is met.

(3) The more recent definition of 'Persons of Significant Control' (or 'PSCs') will become more relevant (see **6.3**, **14.5** and **15.7**).

EQUIVALENT JURISDICTIONS

10.6   In June 2013, JMLSG published its amended *Guidance for the UK Financial Sector – Part III: Specialist Guidance* – see www.bba.org.uk and www.jmlsg.co.uk. The extracted text is set out in **Appendix 1.6** (and see also **6.6**). This divides the world into two broad categories:

- 'Countries for which equivalence may be presumed'; and

- 'Countries for which equivalence should not be presumed'.

The former category are what the UK regards as a 'comparable jurisdiction' (also sometimes called 'equivalent countries and territories') from an AML-CFT standpoint, and comprise these groups:

- EU Member States and EEA Countries;

- Gibraltar;

- The EU Agreed List; and

- The UK Crown Dependencies

The latter category (where 'equivalence should not be presumed') includes other FATF Members, the GCC Countries, and 'other jurisdictions'.

Thus a number of important jurisdictions have not yet been accorded 'comparable jurisdiction' status, including the GCC countries; also Mauritius which has its own FSC, and panoply of AML-CFT legislation.

The GFSC Handbook 2013 also sets out in its *Appendix C* a list of 'Countries or Territories whose regulated financial services businesses may be treated as if they were local FSBs: this is reproduced at **Appendix 1.8.**

FATF are not *per se* involved in defining 'black lists' or 'white lists'; that is left to its sister organisation, the OECD. Nevertheless FATF does, through its assessments and peer reviews end up with lists that are almost as compelling from a risk avoidance standpoint. As noted in **Appendix 2**, the November 2013 FATF List identified 15 countries as jurisdictions that have strategic deficiencies posing a risk to the international financial system.

Chapter 6 notes that in the international context, the 2007 Regulations sets out 'the list of countries that cannot be treated as 'equivalent'.

TSPs & CSPs

10.7   (3)TSPs and CSPs are defined broadly in 3MLD Art 3(7). And 3MLD Art 36(1) requires all TSPs and CSPs to be licensed/ registered, and for Member States' 'competent authorities' to refuse licencing/registration of TSPs and CSPs if they are not satisfied that the controllers are 'fit and proper' persons (and see **14.1** for TSPs and **16.1** for CSPs).

As 3MLD is a Directive, it does not establish the licensing/registration body, but leaves it to each Member State to define. In the United Kingdom, the Law Society continues to monitor/regulate Solicitors who offer TSP and CSP services; while those other previously unregulated TSP and CSP practitioners have the FCA as their monitoring body.

FEEDBACK

10.8   3MLD established a number of feedback channels:

- publication of STR statistics (Recital 38 and Arts 30-33: now done per Member State, and for the UK by FCA see **12.8** and **Appendix 5**);

- under Art 42, a legislative impact assessment, which led to the adoption of draft 4MLD; and

- under Art 43, a Commission Report to the European Parliament in December 2010 which recommended retaining the 25% percentage (see **10.7**)

THE FOURTH MONEY LAUNDERING DIRECTIVE (EU DIRECTIVE) ('4MLD')

EU Directive 2014 (known as '4MLD')

10.9   The Fourth Anti-Money Laundering Directive ('4MLD') (published in draft on 5 February 2013 and scheduled for adoption in November 2014) changes the nature of AML compliance across the EU, moving to a risk-based and evidence-based approach to identifying and managing ML and CFT risks (rather than a tick-box approach to compliance). It supersedes 3MLD that has been effective since 2005 (and see **Appendix 1.8**).

The Fourth Directive defines 'beneficial owner' as 'any natural person(s) who ultimately owns or controls the customer and/or the natural person on whose behalf a transaction or activity is being conducted.' This approximates to the PSC test!

For corporate entities the beneficial owner 'shall at least' include the natural person who 'owns or controls the legal entity through direct or indirect ownership or control over a sufficient percentage of the shares or voting rights.' The 25% threshold in 3MLD is retained, plus one share, to constitute sufficient evidence of ownership or control.

For other legal entities, such as foundations and trusts, the beneficial owner would be:

● the natural person(s) who (1) control 25% or more of the property or entity or

● who is the beneficiary of 25% or more of the property or entity.

4MLD brings TSPs and CSPs into the 'regulated sector', and will require every company, legal entity and trust to hold adequate, accurate and up-to-date information about their UBOs.

4MLD brings 'domestic PEPs' within the scope of the enhanced due diligence aspects of 3MLD and the Regulations.

3MLD: Directive 2006/70 on PEPs

10.10   3MLD Arts 3(8) and 13(4) (and Recital 25) refer to 'Politically Exposed Persons' ('PEPs') and Directive 2006/70 of 1 August 2006 contains more detailed measures to implement EU Directive 2005/60 on the definition of 'Politically Exposed Person'.

The issue of PEPs (or PSPs) relates to clients and beneficial owners who hold public offices, who have (or have had) positions of public trust, such as government officials, senior executives of government corporations, politicians, important political party officials, etc. and their families and close associates (and see also **11.15**), where the driver is the risk of corruption, by abuse of public funds and/or by corrupt payments and kickbacks on contract awards.

There is an automatic presumption of 'suspicion' in any transaction involving a PEP, and therefore enhanced CDD is required in order to dispel this presumption. This may be a more difficult issue to check, although recourse can now be to database services (see **11.16**). Major public figures may be a household name (especially in their home countries), but monitoring all possibilities of relationship is difficult, as the PEP concept extends widely – not only to government officials, but also to relatives and even business associates of government officials.

There is a practical one-year cooling off period for retired PEPs whereby after a one-year break from any official position they resume their former non-PEP status. (Art of the 3(4) of EU Directive 2005/60).

The most important aspect of dealing with a PEP lies in the requirement for enhanced due diligence (see **11.15**).

As noted above, 4MLD will also bring 'domestic PEPs' within the scope of the Regulations.

ADDITIONAL EU INITIATIVES

10.11.1 The European Union Savings Directive ('EUSTD') (Council Directive 2003/48/EC) ('the Directive') aims to counter cross-border tax evasion by collecting and exchanging information about EU Citizens living in any one MS who receive savings income from Banks etc located in any other MS (or related third country such as Guernsey, Jersey and Isle of Man). The EUSTD also contains a withholding tax mechanism, which in the transitional phase was accepted as an alternative for Luxembourg and Austria refusing to divulge customer information.

On 21 March 2014 Austria and Luxembourg capitulated against EU pressure, and agreed to abolish bank secrecy for EU citizens resident in an EU member state by 31 January 2017: the latest EUSTD amendments now encapsulate this.

As a result of the ECOFW Agreement of 14 October 2014, the EU Commission has decided to repeal the EUSTD (see **10.11.14**).

Directive 2014/42 on the Freezing and Confiscation of the Proceeds of Crime

10.11.2 On 29 April 2014 EU Directive 2014/42 was published in the EU Official Journal and entered into force on 19 May 2014. This Directive introduces measures intended to make it easier for national authorities to confiscate and recover the profits made by criminals from cross-border and organised crime. However, the UK decided not to opt in to the Directive.

10.11.3 The European Commission is currently working on other EU initiatives in the AML-CFT area. The Europol Convention of 1995 has been extended to ML in general. Member States have signed the protocol to the convention on mutual assistance in criminal matters between the member states and with third countries (such as the United States), with a view to exchange of information, suspension of banking secrecy, information on beneficial ownership and freezing of assets. Once the model agreement is adopted, the EU Council will authorise the opening of negotiations with third countries.

10.11.4 On 14 October 2014, ECOFW decided to implement the OECD CRS (**9.8–9.10**) through amendments to EU Directive 2011/16 on administrative cooperation in direct taxation (also called 'DAC 2').

BRIBERY AND CORRUPTION

10.12   The EU has also launched a number of initiatives in the area of bribery and corruption (and see **18.8**):

- EU Convention on Combating Corruption, 26 May 1997;

- EU Common Positions (EC OJ L 279 13 October 1997) and (EC OJ L 320 21 November 1997); and

- The EU Convention on the Fight against Corruption involving Officials of the European Communities or Officials of Member States (EC OJ C 195, 25 June 1997): this is of narrow scope, being limited to EU officials: www.europa.eu.int.

Chapter 11

Customer due diligence, compliance and risk management

CUSTOMER DUE DILIGENCE – INTRODUCTION

11.1   Since 9-11, lawmakers and regulators have significantly tightened up on their general AML–CFT policies and procedures as part of the exercise of eliminating the financial supports for terrorism. In the United Kingdom (and in the overseas dependencies and territories) it is now an absolute requirement for financial services and related businesses to be entirely clear that neither the *Source of Funds* (see **11.10.2**) nor the *Destination of Funds* (see **11.10.3**) involves money laundering (ML) activity. This is not an easy task – a bit like looking for the proverbial needle in a haystack. A large bank might typically handle between 100,000 and 150,000 wire transfers per day. The enlargement of the scope of AML–CFT laws simply makes the haystack bigger. And the key to all of this is Customer Due Diligence ('CDD') (previously known as know-your-customer or 'KYC').

It is a trite fact that it is often extremely difficult to make distinctions between good and bad customers or clients, and between acceptable or illicit transactions. Unfortunately the AML-CFT panoply has reversed the long-standing 'presumption of innocence', and now requires the normal innocent participant in the modern economic system to 'prove' his/her innocence over and over again, often at great cost, delay and inconvenience. This scattergun approach doesn't really hit many guilty players. The truly villainous carry on unimpeded. The banks (our principal modern-day 'financial gatekeepers') are terrified and demoralized: they continue to be hit by vast and ever-increasing fines, not for actually 'assisting in AML-CFT' but now just for seemingly not having adequate systems in place. The expression 'gatekeepers' is used to describe not only banks, but also accountants, lawyers, notaries and other professionals: all of these now act unpaid as amateur detectives and plain-clothes agents of the State, and are expected actively to participate in the detection and prevention of crime.

We all have stories about delays to payments and transfers, missed deal deadlines etc. We are all now reduced to being supplicants to banks, to allow us to get on with our day-to-day lives and businesses. And meanwhile the drug-dealers and pornographers and terrorists continue to thrive. We seem to be stuck with this nightmare system, and nobody (with the exception of Professor Jason Sharman – see **15.9** and a few others) dare to criticise the fact that the 'Emperor's new clothes' are invisible!

64

CDD REQUIREMENTS

11.2   The general requirements for CDD are the most important element in this process. As a result, financial institutions both onshore and offshore, have to strive to obtain initial CDD and to maintain their CDD information on an updated basis whenever necessary.

As noted at **10.4**, 3MLD established a detailed codification of CDD requirements in its Arts 6–19, and, *via* the Money Laundering Regulations 2007, this became the reference point for institutions.

Article 8 of 3MLD states that CDD measures shall comprise the following:

- identifying the customer and verifying the customer's identity on the basis of documents, data or information obtained from a reliable and independent source;

- identifying, where applicable, the beneficial owner, and taking risk–based and adequate measures to verify his identity so that the institution is satisfied that it knows who the beneficial owner is, including as regards legal persons [=companies], trusts or 'other legal arrangements' taking risk–based and adequate measures to understand 'the ownership and control structure' of the customer;

- obtaining information on the purpose and intended nature of the business relationship; and

- conducting ongoing monitoring of the business relationship including scrutiny of transactions undertaken throughout the course of that relationship to ensure that the transactions being conducted are consistent with the institution's knowledge of the customer, the business and the risk profile, including where necessary the source of funds and ensuring that the documents, data or information held are kept up-to-date.

(See also **Chapters 13, 14, 15** and **16**)

IDENTIFYING THE CUSTOMER, VERIFYING CUSTOMER IDENTITY AND WHAT IT ENTAILS

11.3   In the FSA discussion paper 'Reducing money laundering risk' (August 2003), the term 'identification' meant the basic information (name and address) collected to meet the legal and regulatory identification requirements. And CDD referred to the additional information (for example, occupation) that an institution may obtain for AML risk management purposes.

Now, as noted above, the requirements are codified, and Art 8 of 3MLD requires:

i.   identifying the customer and verifying the customer's identity and residence;

ii.   identifying the beneficial owner;

iii. understanding for companies and trusts 'the ownership and control structure' of the customer; and

iv. obtaining information on 'the purpose and intended nature of the business relationship';

each of which element can be accompanied by different degrees of difficulty depending on the complexity of the arrangement. If the CDD information on file is not up-to-date, then remediation will be required.

COMPANIES

11.4 When dealing with companies there is an important and immediately applicable distinction between public listed companies, and private unlisted companies:

- For public listed companies, no further evidence of identity is required if the company is listed on a recognised stock exchange, or is a subsidiary of such a listed company.

- For private unlisted companies, more detailed information is sought, requiring the identification of (and proof of residence items for) the principal shareholders (in practice holding 10% or more). In some countries, this information may be obtainable through a government search (at the Company's Registry, Companies House, or Register of Commerce), where these are open to public inspection. There can be no indication in such registers if any shares are registered in nominee names, so this method is imperfect.

In countries and jurisdictions where the registry is essentially private, the requirement to identify the influential shareholders or those who ultimately own and control the company may be less easy to satisfy to a level capable of extrinsic proof.

If two or more companies are involved in the chain of ownership, CDD requires 'piercing the veil' (see **5.10**) of all intermediate layers, so as to identify the individual(s) owner(s). The requirement essentially boils down to identifying one or more 'warm bodies' and obtaining the same identification and proof of residence items.

TRUSTS

11.5 CDD for Trusts is different: these requirements are considered in more detail in **Chapter 14**. If a trust is included in the ownership structure, then it becomes necessary to identify the 'control' elements (or 'PSCs') (in terms of both the settlor, the Trustees and any Protector); plus the principal beneficiary/ies. So for 'trusts, foundations and similar entities', it is necessary to identify first what type of trust is involved, and then to determine what detailed information on the 'beneficial owners' should be obtained corresponding to the type of trust in question (see the JMLSG revised Guidance 2013 at **6.6** and in **Appendix 1.6**).

PROOF OF IDENTITY

11.6   The common standard for proof of identity is a certified true copy of the identity page of an in-date passport. Alternatively, a CTC of the official identity card is also acceptable: however, that may not be acceptable to a FSB in a third country, as it may not be in a readily recognised format or in a language th read or transliterated.

Passport styles can be easily verified in Keesing Technologies at www. documentchecker.com which gives users access to thousands of passports, ID cards, residence permits, visas and driving licenses from more than 200 countries.

Interpol's 'I-Checkit' is an innovative tool, still in its pilot phase, which will assist in detecting and preventing illicit transactions www.interpol. com/en. I-Checkit is being developed to Identify the fraudulent use of stolen travel documents to cross borders, often in connection with AML-CFT activities.

Some banks will try to 'gold plate' a CTC Passport by phoning the individual and seeking to do a 'Video Log' of the individual, holding up their Passport. Many banks also require the CTC signature of the certifier (see **11.9**) to be a 'wet ink' signature. (see **11.13**).

The spelling of Middle Eastern or Asian names can be a cause of problem as unfortunately there is no 'correct' equivalent spelling in English. Full names in Arabic, Thai, Chinese etc are often complex, and as there is no standard way of 'romanising' such scripts, one name can be (and often is) rendered in English in many different ways.

'Mistaken identity' is a matter of potentially great concern, where a crucial payment may be mistakenly blocked, or a bank or investment account mistakenly frozen by a similarity between the name of the account owner with a name on a 'banned' list (such as the OFAC list – see **11.19**). There are many examples not just in the financial sector, but in aviation, immigration, indeed across the board. Great harm can be done, and there may be little or no recourse.

PROOF OF RESIDENCE (VERIFICATION OF ADDRESS)

11.7   There should be, but is not any common standard for 'proof of residence'. The UK and other jurisdictions each have lists of types of proof of address that they recommend their FSBs consider as acceptable. These include

- an account statement from a recognised bank or a recognised bank credit card. The statement should be the most recent available, and an original, not a copy. Statements featuring a 'care of' or an office building address are not acceptable. Non-bank cards, such as store cards, are not acceptable;
- a recent rates, property tax or utility bill. Care must be taken that the document is an original and not a copy;

- the most recent original mortgage statement from a recognised lender;

- checking a register of electors;

- a credit reference agency search;

- Recent correspondence from a Government department or agency;

- making a record of a personal visit to the home of an applicant for business; or

- using one of the address validation/verification services on offer.

In practice, for international clients, only the first two 'proofs' above will be acceptable. Usually, clients are advised to produce an original bank statement or utility bill (within the last three months). As there is no central registry of different countries' utility bills, this could be abused: also, as sophisticated copying (forging) techniques are readily available in many non-OECD countries, a number of FSB groups do not accept utility bills as an adequate 'proof'. As noted, a Home Visit Form completed by a senior staff member can also suffice: but not all FSBs are willing or able to make personal visits to the homes of applicants for business.

So, the best 'proof becomes a recent original utility bill; or a recent original bank account statement (or credit card statement) from a recognised bank.

The 'gold-plating' here arises in relation to the word 'recognised' bank, where some major international banks have stated that they will only accept a recent original bank account statement from 'a bank incorporated or licensed in EU/FATF Countries'.

And see the Report dated 'Bank Accounts: problems of identification' issued by the UK House of Commons Library (see **Appendix 5**).

Even more bizarrely, some banks will not use their own bank statement (mailed to the home address) as 'Proof of Residence' for a customer who wishes to open a new account (such as a 'No 2 Account' or a Rent Account).

And remember: a utility bill may be no more than proof of the place to where the bill is sent, and not of residency itself (and see **9.9**).

See further on 'Verification Issues' at **11.11** below

'RESIDENCE'

11.8   What is meant by 'residence'?

Proving 'residence' will be difficult for some individuals if they have utility bills in the name of a company, or if they live in a country where the use of PO boxes or Mailboxes is prevalent. For example, the Bermuda Post Office http://www.bpo.bm/default.aspx lists 5 of the main benefits of renting a PO box:

'1. Privacy – When you use our post box service, you do not have to publish your home, business and charitable address and location.

2. Security – When you have a post box rental, your packages and mail are kept safe for you to pick up. You continue to receive your mail when you are away on business or vacation. That means no more putting a hold on mail or having it pile up in your mailbox while you are away for that unwelcomed attention.

3. Reliability – Even in bad weather, you can receive important letters or packages quicker and with 24 hour access.

4. Affordable – We do not apply hidden costs, additional fees and provide a value added service.

5. Mobility – You can change your residence, but your mail always goes to the same permanent location.'

The UK HMRC's 'Savings Income reporting Guidance Notes' dated September 2013 provide guidance on various aspects of the 'EU Savings Directive' (the Directive on the Taxation of Savings Income or EUSD) www.hmrc.gov.uk. Paragraphs 132–158 contain detailed rules for establishing the identity and residence' of individuals for EUSD purposes. Note especially para 138 in which HMRC stated that 'The country of residence for tax purposes is **not** affected by these rules'. The basic rule in para 136 is that the country of residence is where the individual has his 'permanent address': individuals with more than one address are dealt with in paras 154–155; and PO Boxes and 'c/o' addresses in paras 156–158. See www.hmrc.gov.uk/esd-guidance/sir-guidance.pdf. The EUSTD itself is recently up for repeal (see **10.11.1**).

WHO CAN 'CERTIFY'?

11.9 Currently a suitable certifier is defined as:

● Bank Staff from a banks that is headquartered in (or is a branch of a bank that has its HQ in an Equivalent Jurisdiction (see **6.4**)

● Lawyers, Accountants, Notaries Public, Commissioners of Oaths or Diplomatic Missions based in an Equivalent Jurisdiction (see **6.4** and **Appendix 5**).

One well-known global bank nowadays 'gold-plates' by insisting that CTCs it receives must be certified by a CPA, lawyer, banker or notary public 'in a European Union or a FATF member jurisdiction': this immediately disqualifies over 100 other countries and the named professionals who live/work there from participating in the verification process.

And as noted in **Chapter 15** and **Appendix 5**, one well-known Asia-based CSP has its own 'Certification of Due Diligence' Form (relating to CDD Proof of Identity and Proof of Residence), to be executed by the 'Approved Certifier', who must be one of the following:

- Notary Public;
- Certified Public Accountant;
- Registrar/Deputy-Registrar of a Court;
- Justice of the Peace ('JP');
- Legal practitioner/solicitor;
- An officer or employee of a licenced bank, trust company or insurance company in a 'recognised jurisdiction';
- An associate member of the Hong Kong Institute of Chartered Secretaries ('HKICS');
- An associate member of the Singapore Association of the Institute of Chartered Secretaries and Administrators ('SAICSA').

SOURCE OF WEALTH AND SOURCE OF FUNDS AND DESTINATION OF FUNDS

11.10 Three critically important concepts in the CDD matrix are:

- Source of Wealth (see **11.10.1**);
- Source of Funds (see **11.10.2**); and
- Destination of Funds source of funds (see **11.10.3**).

SOURCE OF WEALTH

11.10.1 Verify the Source of Wealth: at the outset of a business relationship, the extent and source of the client's wealth should be established. This is to address the 'proceeds of crime' aspect of AML-CFT in terms of the general relationship being formed. It is entirely to do with 'looking up the pipe'.

So the FSB needs to consider his/her:

- Employment or former employment
- Business interests;
- Family history;
- Existing investments, savings and other assets.

This information should be established and recorded. Such factors as the age of the client and his/her nationality must also be borne in mind. The service provider must be satisfied that the level of wealth displayed by the client is consistent with the client's background. Particular care must be taken where clients have connections with 'sensitive jurisdictions' (see **Appendices 2** and **4**) or where they can be regarded as PEPs (see **10.10** and **11.15**).

In co-operation with the client, obtain sufficient information to establish his/her source of wealth, and that it is legitimate in nature. Explain to the client that the purpose is both to satisfy AML-CFT regulations and also to ensure that appropriate services are being offered.

The client is not obliged to disclose *all* their assets and income, but should be made aware that business may be declined if information received is inadequate: as a minimum, the Source of Wealth must be established for the portion of the client's assets that are to be placed with the service provider. Documentary evidence should be obtained in relation to this portion. This should be independently verified wherever possible.

Typical check-list options for Source of Wealth include:

- Proceeds from a trade, profession or business;
- Inheritance;
- Trust Fund;
- Financial Investments or Insurance Policy;
- Asset sale(s);
- Loan Repayment;

and the like.

If the source of wealth cannot be verified and supported by documentary evidence, the business of a prospective client must not be accepted. Furthermore, if evidence is seen to create a suspicion that wealth has been derived from criminal conduct or the client shows a reluctance to provide information which could reasonably be expected to be provided, a suspicious transaction report could still be made to the MLRO (albeit that no legal/ contractual relations have been entered into yet, and so no 'client relationship' or 'customer relationship' or 'debtor-creditor relationship' has yet been brought into existence).

SOURCE OF FUNDS

General

11.10.2 This is different from 'Source of Wealth' and is also to address the 'proceeds of crime' aspect of AML-CFT *on specific transactions*. It is also entirely to do with 'looking *up* the pipe'

During the ongoing business relationship, the source of funds employed for each transaction should be verified. This should be the original source, not simply the last bank account in which the assets rested and must be consistent with the client profile. If the funds do not form part of wealth that has already been verified, additional checks should be undertaken.

Record should be made of the bank account from which funds have been received, including the name and address of the bank. Special attention should be paid where the source account is not in the name of the client.

Where funds appear from a source inconsistent with the client profile or one that cannot be fully verified, consider whether the transaction should be regarded as 'suspicious'.

11.10.3 *Customer due diligence, compliance and risk management*

If it is not possible to verify the source of funds for a particular transaction, *that transaction must not proceed*, and in particular:

- Cash may not be accepted.

- A cheque or bankers order should be returned uncashed. If already paid into an account at the company, repayment must be made by cheque crossed and payable to the same account name as on the original cheque.

- A wire transfer payment must be returned to source, ensuring that account number and name and the destination bank are the same as on the original payment.

If evidence is seen to create a suspicion that the funds were derived from criminal conduct or the client shows a reluctance to provide information that could reasonably be expected, a suspicious transaction report must be made to the MLRO. In such cases funds should not be returned until the MLRO has said that they can be. A request by the client for repayment to a different name or different destination might also be sufficient to trigger an STR.

Interestingly, in November 2005 'senior figures in Ardent Productions (the Earl of Wessex's film production company) said that they did not know the identity of the benefactor behind the £350,000 investment that came from a company based in the BVI' *The Times* 14 November 2005.

DESTINATION OF FUNDS

11.10.3 This is purely a CDD aspect of specific transactions, and is designed to address whether the money that has been held in or generated from the account or transaction, does not, when remitted or transferred, go to assist terrorist financing. It is thus more to do with 'looking down the pipe' at the 'CFT' aspect of AML-CFT. Of course, there is a residual concern that it is not being used to pay for drugs or weapons etc as well.

Of course, difficult questions arise. How should a gift or transfer to a Middle Eastern Charity be regarded? Could it possibly 'assist terrorism'? What if it is a hospital charity in the Gaza Strip?

11.11   Verification issues on Source of Wealth and Source of Funds

Clients may be naturally reticent about their affairs, and may make general statements about their wealth which lack sufficient detail to satisfy requirements: it is important to look beneath such statements and obtain sufficient documentary evidence to verify source of funds.

- **Bank Account**: This is simply a location, not a true source of wealth. The original source of the money should be established and should be consistent with the client profile.

- **Savings**: It must be satisfied that it has been possible for the client to save or amass this money via the known 'Source of Wealth' in addition to maintaining his/her lifestyle.

- **Earnings:** Current and past employment may explain savings, account for the ownership of assets or provide for ongoing investment on a regular basis. Where appropriate, the client's employment should be verified, for example by a letter from the employer or a pay slip. A senior professional's name may feature in corporate literature, company accounts, on professional registers or appear in the public domain (ie in the phonebook or in press cuttings). The wealth displayed by the client should be reasonable for the type of employment followed.

- **Commissions, Dividends and Royalties:** A client with business interests can be expected to receive due payment. The source and size of payments must be in line with known business interests. Particular care should be exercised when payments are received from 'sensitive jurisdictions' (see **Appendices 2** and **4**) or in connection with government contracts, the oil industry or defence suppliers. In the case of substantial or one- off payments, copy contracts, commission or royalty statements could be requested.

- **Property:** Property might include not only real estate, but also portable wealth such as cars, boats, antiques or jewellery. Ownership should be consistent with the client's profile. If funds are due to the sale of property, the manner by which the property was acquired in the first instance may require to be established. Documentary proof of the sale might consist of a copy of a solicitor's letter or bill of sale.

- **Inheritance:** The size and the timing of the inheritance must be consistent with the client's family background. Documentary evidence could include a solicitor's letter, extract of the will, copy death certificate, or a copy of press announcement for local clients.

- **Investments:** Ownership of investments such as securities, bonds or fund holdings should be consistent with the client profile. Where funds arise from the sale of investments, the source can be verified by copy contract notes or by settlement being made directly by a broker or investment manager. It will be necessary to establish the source of funds used to purchase the investments where the amounts are inconsistent with other factors known about the client or where the investments have only been held for a short time.

- **Pensions:** A copy of a statement from the former employer or the pension provider, whether yielding a lump sum or regular payment can verify the existence of a pension

- **Private Income, Trust Funds and Settlements:** The client may be the beneficiary of a trust fund, divorce settlement or may receive an allowance from a spouse, parent or other relation. This must be consistent with the client's background, and may be verified by taking a copy of a relevant letter from a solicitor, banker or accountant. It may in some instances be necessary to verify the source of funds used to create the wealth from which the benefit is drawn.

- **Gifts:** Where the sudden appearance of funds is attributable to a gift, this should be consistent with the client's profile, particularly family history. The circumstances of the gift should be fully documented and it should be clear that the ownership properly rests with the client and does not remain under the control of a third party. It will be necessary to establish the source of funds used to purchase the gift where the value or relationship is inconsistent with other factors known about the client.

- **Prizes:** Documentary proof will be required where money is said to originate as the proceeds of gambling (i.e. lottery ticket prize, casino or horse racing winnings). Special care must be taken where the prize was won abroad or if winnings are presented on more than one occasion.

- **Loans and Debt:** Where funds arise as the result of a loan, the creditor should be established by sight of the loan agreement. This should be checked to ensure that its terms are not unusual. It should be ascertained what assets have been pledged as collateral and the origin of those assets also confirmed. Special care should be taken where the collateral is cash held in another jurisdiction (a 'back to back' loan). Where a payment arises from repayment of a debt the source of the original money credited should be verified.

A WORKED EXAMPLE

11.12   For the purposes of this analysis, let us take as an example a situation where a BVI Company 'B Ltd' wishes to open a bank account with 'Bank K', and the shares of the B Ltd are held in a Bermuda Trust established by Mr. X for his family (comprising Mr. X, Mrs. X and the two children X1 and X2): and the trustees are a licensed and regulated Bermuda trust company TrustCo'. In relation to such a structure:

(i)   'identifying the customer and verifying the customer's identity' will primarily relate to obtaining current documentation on B Ltd (namely its CoI, M&AA and Certificate of Incumbency). Bank K should have its own standard list of requirements for offshore companies, with differences according to the different jurisdictions. Also, some banks will inevitably 'gold plate' their list of requirements, and ask for items that do not clearly define 'the customer' or address AML-CFT risk, but go more to mere 'box ticking';

(ii)   'identifying the beneficial owner' will relate to the X Trust, and will require production to Bank K of CTCs of the Passport of the Settlor Mr. X, the Protector (if any), and also probably the adult Trust beneficiaries (being Mr. X and his family members, Mrs X and their children X1 and X2); plus of course their proofs of residence. Technical questions arise depending on the type of trust ('fixed interest' or 'discretionary'). In this regard, in relation to discretionary trusts, the definition of 'beneficial owner' and PSC (see **6.3**, **10.5**, **14.2.1**, **14.5**, **15.7** and **Appendix 1.3**) focusses on those 'who have legal control over a trust'. Practical issues will also arise if the children are very young and/or do not have passports. As noted, if there is a 'Protector', that person will also have to be identified and verified.

(iii)   'understanding for companies and trusts the ownership and control structure of the customer', meaning obtaining for Bank K a detailed diagram showing every entity in the structure plus the details of each such entity.

(iv)   In addition, K Bank will also want CDD on the directors of B Ltd, and those who it proposed will be authorised signatories (comprising their certified passport copies and their proofs of residence);

(v)   K Bank will want the same items of corporate identification and verification on the trust company TrustCo' as are noted at (i) above for B Ltd.;

(vi)   K Bank will also want the same items of personal identification and verification on the directors of TrustCo (comprising their certified passport copies and their proofs of residence); and

(vii)   K Bank will want the same items of personal identification and verification on the shareholders/beneficial owners of TrustCo (comprising their certified passport copies and their proofs of residence): although K Bank could in theory waive the requirement in respect of TrustCo's shareholders/beneficial owners and *in lieu* accept a copy of TrustCo's current trust licence issued by its regulator (in this example, the Bermuda Monetary Authority) they will in practice prefer to 'Gold Plate' (see **11.13**).

In addition, there will be all of the Bank's account opening forms, resolutions/mandates, etc. and a system for the Bank to capture the necessary information on 'the purpose and intended nature of the business relationship'.

So you can see how, for a relatively commonplace and simple structure, a huge amount of paperwork is required. Small wonder there is climate change!

GOLD PLATING

11.13   'Gold Plating' refers to the conversion of defined CDD requirements into overly-elaborate procedures. But 'gold plating' is driven by nothing more complicated than institutions that react to the threat of fines or criminal convictions for those found negligent in making the checks, and therefore encouraging excessive paperwork requirements. Most institutions for some years now have their own internal CDD checklists both for individual and for corporate clients and customers: a sample checklist is attached at **Appendix 5**: 'gold plating' is also mentioned in **10.5**, **13.9** and **15.5**.

A balance needs to be struck between requests for specific CDD information, and wider 'gold–plated' trawls for competitive or marketing information. For example, one UK bank that caters to some 16,000 racehorse owning customers (large numbers of whom are not based in the United Kingdom, at least from a domicile standpoint) sent a detailed questionnaire to its customers asking for details of marital status, residential status, other main bank accounts and credit cards held, employment details, income details, and details of their fixed monthly household expenditure. Although the questions were asked in good faith in an effort to be ahead of the evolution of CDD requirements, many of their customers simply disregarded them or returned the form incomplete, on grounds of intrusiveness.

ENSURING COMPLIANCE

11.14 AML-CFT compliance is fundamental to the ongoing viability of a professional practice or a fiduciary business: it is mandatory, non–negotiable, and an integral part of any system of regulation or licensing supervision. Any institution connected with a ML scandal may lose its good reputation in the market-place: more seriously, its licence may be suspended or revoked or may not be renewed in the face of blatant noncompliance.

To help companies and professionals comply, a range of compliance products are available, for example the International Compliance Association's *International Diploma in Compliance www.int-comp.com*. Training obligations are also closely linked – see **6.7** and **6.8**.

In the UK regulated sector, across-the-board compliance is essential in order to avoid conviction of the criminal offence (punishable by a maximum of two years' imprisonment and/or a fine) of not maintaining the administrative procedures and staff training required under reg 16 of the Money Laundering Regulations 2007 (SI 2007/2157) (see **Chapter 6**). An offence is capable of being committed irrespective of whether or not any substantive money laundering has taken place (**7.2** notes that an AML-CFT conviction under ss 327–334 of the PoCA 2002 astonishingly can occur even if there has been no conviction for the ultimate 'serious crime' from which the alleged 'proceeds' flowed). And the case of *R v Burke* [2006] EWCA Crim 3122 the Court of Appeal decided that an ML conviction against one defendant could be upheld even when the other defendant was acquitted for the substantive predicate offence which was alleged to have generated the 'proceeds of crime'.

As regards the Regulations, the situation is similar, in that non-compliance with the Regulations is a stand-alone offence, eg failure to organise training is an offence under reg 41 of the Money Laundering Regulations 2007, punishable by a fine and/or up to two years' imprisonment.

The substantial level of fines for getting it wrong are noted in **Appendix 10**.

POLITICALLY EXPOSED PERSONS

11.15 As noted in **10.4**, 3MLD (EU Directive 2005/60) refers in its Art 3(8) to 'Politically Exposed Persons', and Directive 2006/70 contains measures to implement EU Directive 2005/60 on the definition of PEPs (see **10.10**, **Appendices 1.8** and **1.9**).

The EU policy on dealing with politically exposed persons ('PEPs') does not say that a business may *not* have PEPs as Clients, merely that far more scrutiny ('enhanced due diligence') should be applied to Clients who *are* PEPs.

CDD requires identification of the individual client or ultimate beneficial owner, and PEPs are defined as clients/ beneficial owners who hold public offices, who have (or have had) positions of public trust (such as government officials, senior executives of government corporations, politicians, important political party officials etc) and their families and close associates. The following are covered:

- **Senior political figure** is a senior figure in the executive, legislative, administrative, military or judicial branches of a government (elected or non- elected), a senior figure of a major political party, or a senior executive of a government owned corporation. It includes any corporate entity, partnership or trust relationship that has been established by, or for the benefit or, a senior political figure.

- **Immediate family** typically includes the person's parents, siblings, spouse, children, in laws, grandparents and grandchildren.

- **Close associate** typically includes a person who is widely and publicly known to maintain an unusually close relationship with the PEP and includes a person who is in a position to conduct substantial domestic and international financial transactions on the PEP's behalf.

It is difficult but essential to be sure one is not dealing with a PSP/PEP. There is no central database of such persons, let alone of relationships such as their family members and close associates. Such a matrix list would be a key resource, provided it was accessible. At present, approaches to government agencies and regulators are generally met only with copies of published terrorism sanctions lists.

Also as noted at **10.10**, 4MLD also brings 'domestic PEPs' within the scope of AML-CFT regulation.

DATABASES

11.16   As far as concerns PEPs, Colin Powell (the then Director General of the Jersey Financial Services Commission) proposed as long ago as July 2001 that banks and other institutions should have access to databases detailing at least the identity of ministers and senior public officials, and listing friends and associates of politicians in corrupt regimes.

Regulatory DataCorp Int'l LLC (see www.rdc.com) was established in 2002 by a consortium of 17 leading banks. Their GRID ('Global Regulatory Information Database') system sources government lists, PEPs, etc. This initiative is extremely useful. Iit also raises other concerns:

- To be truly useful, the information needs to be available to those in the industry as a whole. It is unclear who will be able to gain access and at what price. The private sector would benefit enormously from the information in avoiding being tainted by a genuine AML-CFT or corruption case.

● The information must be of pinpoint accuracy. It is not difficult to imagine a payment being held up and a commercial opportunity or contractual obligation missed simply through a name being (wrongly as it might turn out) linked on such a database to being a business associate or even a relative of a government official.

The issue of remedies for error become important. It is unclear whether individuals should have the right to inspect their entries and correct errors. In this context, be mindful of the harsh decision in *Shah v HSBC* (see **Appendix 7**)

There is an obvious issue of data protection and access to overcome. Data protection legislation has already been in place for several years, whilst human rights legislation is a more recent phenomenon. Data protection principles must be observed just as strictly, and should prevent any form of unauthorised access.

Private database services are also available: however their user subscriptions tend to be set at levels that make them attractive only to the larger institution. These include:

● BEST-AML-CFT software

● Worldcheck (see www.isys.ch/products/prods/amlf.html)

● Complinet (see info@complinet.com

● Regulatory DataCorp GRID – see above

● C6

And note FATF Recommendation 1 (February 2012) setting out a 'risk-based' approach to combatting ML and terrorist financing in relation to banks and securities institutions: Recommendations 24 and 25 apply respectively to CSPs and TSPs. The 'risk-based' approach is very welcome in order to maintain the AML-CFT regime in a workable manner, reducing customer disruption while raising intelligence value. STRs should be kept just as a vital enforcement tool and not be turned into CYA defensive bureaucracy.

PROLIFERATION OF GOVERNMENT DATABASES

11.17   Given the pressures on the financial sector (and including lawyers, TSPs, CSPs etc.) to 'get it right', governments, EUROPOL, INTERPOL, the CIA, etc. need to share their blacklists, since they are in effect recruiting the financial sector as their (unpaid) policemen and subjecting them to huge fines or even prison sentences in an effort to force them to 'comply'. However, such an 'open source' data sharing is unlikely ever to happen, for obvious political reasons.

In the United States, the financial database is administered by the Financial Crimes Enforcement Network (FinCEN), located in Vienna, Virginia (in effect, the US's Financial Intelligence Unit (FIU)). FinCEN reports are made available to US criminal investigators, as well as other FIU's around the globe, and FinCEN conducts computer-assisted analyses of these reports to determine trends and refer investigations

Some readers will remember back in December 2003, when so-called hard 'intelligence' led to the cancellation of BA 223 and several Air France flights just before Christmas: the 'extremely detailed and explicit intelligence' was provided by the US, but the passenger suspected of being a Tunisian radical turned out to be a child who coincidentally shared the same name (a case of 'mistaken identity' – see **11.6**).

Conversely, in 2013 a US District Court Judge held that the US 'No Fly' list violated the Constitutional Right to Travel in so far as it offered no adequate method for people to challenge their placement on the list.

The United States, and no doubt other countries, regulatory agencies have so far been reluctant to co-ordinate their efforts. But the US *Homelands Security* initiative (which involves all foreign visitors to the US being photographed and fingerprinted) is leading to a 'searchable and integrated' master list of suspected foreign terrorists, known as 'TIPOFF'. This feeds into other databases such as CLASS (Consular Lookout and Support System) and other US Government watchlists maintained by the FBI, the CIA, several Pentagon departments and other US Government bureaus.

The United Nations Office on Drugs and Crime maintains a website (the International Money Laundering Information Network, www.imolin.org) that provides information and software for anti-money laundering data collection and analysis.

And the World Bank website, www.worldbank.org, provides policy advice and best practices to governments and the private sector on anti-money laundering issues.

BLACKLISTS

11.18   In this context, blacklists should also be of great assistance in providing some sort of negative clearance on customers and clients. However, security concerns at government level and data protection concerns at the private level mean that practitioners and professionals are all but on their own when it comes to identifying potential AML-CFT offenders.

In terms of international transactions, FATF has no 'black lists' or 'white lists' as such; that is left to its sister organisation, the OECD: nevertheless FATF monitors and identifies , and as noted in **Appendix 5**, the November 2013 FATF List identified 15 countries as jurisdictions that have strategic deficiencies posing a risk to the international financial system.

And the OECD NCCT list now includes only five countries/jurisdictions (Liechtenstein, Monaco, Liberia, the Marshall Islands and Andorra).

Monaco's signature in mid-October 2014 of the OECD Mutual Administrative Assistance in Tax Convention (not the automatic EOI) will help remove it from this 'blacklist'.

A rebuttable presumption can be operated that a transaction or payment involving any of the countries/jurisdictions on the FATF or OECD lists will automatically trigger a response. But in reality, it is also transactions with some 85 or so other jurisdictions (non-EU, non-EEA, non-OECD and non-FATF) that will also raise queries according to lists maintained by some of the leading banks.

And dealings with countries at the bad end or the Transparency International Corruption Perceptions Index (CPI) or Bribe Payers Index (BPI) will also raise a presumption that enhanced due diligence is called for (see **11.15**).

As far as concerns, CDD and transactions of individuals and companies, at present most of the relevant databases are owned and maintained by governments, and thus not available to or accessible by the private sector. It is thus particularly galling for the private sector to be made legally responsible on the one hand for monitoring and controlling AML-CFT prevention, while on the other hand being denied access to the very databases of information that would enable professionals, etc. to enquire about a given individual or company's background. Governments and regulators have such tools at their own disposal. This is not a very level information or enforcement playing field, and results in the practitioner or professional being squeezed as the 'piggy in the middle'.

OFAC LISTS, KINGPIN DESIGNATIONS ETC

11.19   The Office of Foreign Assets Control ('OFAC'): OFAC is an agency of the United States Department of the Treasury under the auspices of the Under Secretary of the Treasury for Terrorism and Financial Intelligence.

OFAC administers and enforces US economic and trade sanctions (based on US foreign policy and national security goals) against targeted foreign states, organizations, and individuals. 'Blocked persons', Foreign Sanctions Evaders ('FSE'), and Specially Designated Nationals ('SDN') are listed online.

OFAC also has powers under the US Foreign Narcotics Kingpin Designation Act 1999 (also known as the 'Kingpin Act').

For further information see www.ustreas.gov/offices/enforcement/ofac and www.treasury.gov/resource-center/sanctions/OFAC-Enforcement/Pages/OFAC-Recent-Actions.aspx

SANCTIONS LISTS

11.20   The OFAC List is the most comprehensive sanction list available as a public source: it includes the UN sanction list and also specific economic sanctions specifically imposed by the US: www.treasury.gov/about/organizational-structure/offices/Pages/Office-of-Foreign-Assets-Control.aspx

The following searchable sources are also of use:

- The EU List: www.eeas.europa.eu/cfsp/sanctions/consol-list/index_en.htm;

- The United Nations Sanction list (on the UN website) www.un.org/sc/committees/list_compend.shtml.

CONCLUSIONS

11.21 Overall, the slavish demand for passports and utility bills has produced a high level of consumer irritation – but at the same time has probably failed to flush out a single Al-Qaeda supporter.

FI face adverse publicity and fines (see **Appendix 10**) if they turn out to have had AML-CFT perpetrators within their client and customer lists, or even merely to have had procedures deemed inadequate.

Chapter 12

STR reporting procedures and dealing with the client

INTRODUCTION: THE MLRO

12.1　　The Money Laundering Reporting Officer ('MLRO') is the official interface the professional firm or business has with the NCA (the Financial Intelligence Unit ('FIU')): he or she receives and screens internal suspicious activity reports ('SARs') and passes those of concern on to the FIU.

Since October 2013 the NCA is the United Kingdom's FIU (having previously been named NCIS and SOCA).

A financial services business must also nominate another person to receive disclosures in the absence of the MLRO, and must communicate the name of the Nominated Officer to all staff. The Nominated Person must be of at least management level, and must be 'appropriately qualified' [not defined].

SUSPICIOUS TRANSACTIONS AND CLIENT REPORTING

12.2　　We have already explored what is meant by 'suspicion' – see **7.5.2**.

Unfortunately it is not possible to provide an exhaustive list of what constitutes a 'suspicious transaction'. It is also not acceptable training simply to say that 'you will know it is suspicious when you come across it'.

In this regard, the various Regulations, Guidance Notes and Handbooks have moved from a list of things to look out for (as *indicia*) to a risk-based viewpoint. As an example, the GFSC Handbook 2013 now enumerates two categories of High Risk Indicators:

(a)　relating to Customers and Clients:

- complex ownership structures, which can make it easier to conceal underlying beneficial owners and beneficiaries;

- structures where there is no apparent legitimate economic or other rationale;

- customers or structures which are associated with a specific industry activity which carries a higher exposure to the possibility of bribery and corruption (such as in natural resource extraction, infrastructure construction or the defence industry); an individual who may be regarded as a commercially exposed person because of his or her position as a senior executive of a well-known commercial enterprise;

- customers based in, or conducting business in or through, a country or territory with known higher levels of bribery and corruption, or organised crime, or involved in illegal drug production/processing/distribution, or associated with terrorism; involvement of an introducer from a country or territory which does not have an adequate AML/CFT infrastructure;

- where a customer wants a product or service in one country or territory when there are very similar products or services in his home country or territory, and where there is no legitimate economic or other rationale for buying the product or service abroad;

- requests to adopt undue levels of secrecy with a transaction; and

- business relationships or occasional transactions where the source of wealth and source of funds cannot be easily verified or where the audit trail has been deliberately broken and/or unnecessarily layered.

(b) relating to Products and Services:

- complex structures of legal persons and/or legal arrangements;

- hold mail or retained mail arrangements;

- safe custody arrangements;

- significant and/or frequent cash transactions;

- high value balances or investments, which are disproportionately large to that particular customer, product or service set;

- bearer shares and other bearer instruments; and

- inappropriate delegation of authority.

By way of contrast, previous Guidance Notes did give more practical examples of what, in the absence of a satisfactory explanation, should be regarded as suspicious transactions. Some of these are set out below, despite their being 'blindingly obvious':

- the establishment of an administered entity with no obvious purpose;

- sales invoice values exceeding the known or expected value of goods or services;

- sales or purchases at inflated or undervalued prices;

- payments or settlements to or from an administered entity, of a size or source, that had not been expected; an administered entity, entering into transactions which have little or no obvious purpose or which are unrelated to the anticipated objects;

  – a request for, or the discovery of, and unnecessarily complicated trust or corporate structure involving several different jurisdictions;

  – excessive use of wide ranging powers of attorney;

- – unnecessarily complex group structure; and
- arrangements established with the apparent objective of fiscal evasion.

The Author personally finds FINTRAC more helpful: their examples are comprehensive and detailed: their website www.fintrac.com provides the following examples of common indicators that may point to a suspicious transaction, whether completed or attempted.

General

- Client admits or makes statements about involvement in criminal activities.
- Client does not want correspondence sent to home address.
- Client appears to have accounts with several financial institutions in one area for no apparent reason.
- Client conducts transactions at different physical locations in an apparent attempt to avoid detection.
- Client repeatedly uses an address but frequently changes the names involved.
- Client is accompanied and watched.
- Client shows uncommon curiosity about internal systems, controls and policies.
- Client has only vague knowledge of the amount of a deposit.
- Client presents confusing details about the transaction or knows few details about its purpose.
- Client appears to informally record large volume transactions, using unconventional bookkeeping methods or 'off-the-record' books.
- Client over justifies or explains the transaction.
- Client is secretive and reluctant to meet in person.
- Client is nervous, not in keeping with the transaction.
- Client is involved in transactions that are suspicious but seems blind to being involved in money laundering activities.
- Client's home or business telephone number has been disconnected or there is no such number when an attempt is made to contact client shortly after opening account.
- Normal attempts to verify the background of a new or prospective client are difficult.
- Client appears to be acting on behalf of a third party, but does not tell you.
- Client is involved in activity out-of-keeping for that individual or business.
- Client insists that a transaction be done quickly.

- Inconsistencies appear in the client's presentation of the transaction.
- The transaction does not appear to make sense or is out of keeping with usual or expected activity for the client.
- Client appears to have recently established a series of new relationships with different financial entities.
- Client attempts to develop close rapport with staff.
- Client uses aliases and a variety of similar but different addresses.
- Client spells his or her name differently from one transaction to another.
- Client uses a post office box or General Delivery address, or other type of mail drop address, instead of a street address when this is not the norm for that area.
- Client provides false information or information that you believe is unreliable.
- Client offers you money, gratuities or unusual favours for the provision of services that may appear unusual or suspicious.
- Client pays for services or products using financial instruments, such as money orders or traveller's cheques, without relevant entries on the face of the instrument or with unusual symbols, stamps or notes.
- You are aware that a client is the subject of a money laundering or terrorist financing investigation.
- You are aware or you become aware, from a reliable source (that can include media or other open sources), that a client is suspected of being involved in illegal activity.
- A new or prospective client is known to you as having a questionable legal reputation or criminal background.
- Transaction involves a suspected shell entity (that is, a corporation that has no assets, operations or other reason to exist).

Knowledge of reporting or record keeping requirements

- Client attempts to convince employee not to complete any documentation required for the transaction.
- Client makes inquiries that would indicate a desire to avoid reporting.
- Client has unusual knowledge of the law in relation to suspicious transaction reporting.
- Client seems very conversant with money laundering or terrorist activity financing issues.
- Client is quick to volunteer that funds are 'clean' or 'not being laundered.'
- Client appears to be structuring amounts to avoid record keeping, client identification or reporting thresholds.

- Client appears to be collaborating with others to avoid record keeping, client identification or reporting thresholds.
- Client performs two or more cash transactions of less than $10,000 each just outside of 24 hours apart, seemingly to avoid the 24-hour rule.

Identity documents

- Client provides doubtful or vague information.
- Client produces seemingly false identification or identification that appears to be counterfeited, altered or inaccurate.
- Client refuses to produce personal identification documents.
- Client only submits copies of personal identification documents.
- Client wants to establish identity using something other than his or her personal identification documents.
- Client's supporting documentation lacks important details such as a phone number.
- Client inordinately delays presenting corporate documents.
- All identification presented is foreign or cannot be checked for some reason.
- All identification documents presented appear new or have recent issue dates.
- Client presents different identification documents at different times.
- Client alters the transaction after being asked for identity documents.
- Client presents different identification documents each time a transaction is conducted.

Cash transactions

- Client starts conducting frequent cash transactions in large amounts when this has not been a normal activity for the client in the past.
- Client frequently exchanges small bills for large ones.
- Client uses notes in denominations that are unusual for the client, when the norm in that business is different.
- Client presents notes that are packed or wrapped in a way that is uncommon for the client.
- Client deposits musty or extremely dirty bills.
- Client makes cash transactions of consistently rounded-off large amounts (eg, $9,900, $8,500, etc).
- Client consistently makes cash transactions that are just under the reporting threshold amount in an apparent attempt to avoid the reporting threshold.

- Client consistently makes cash transactions that are significantly below the reporting threshold amount in an apparent attempt to avoid triggering the identification and reporting requirements.

- Client presents uncounted funds for a transaction. Upon counting, the client reduces the transaction to an amount just below that which could trigger reporting requirements.

- Client conducts a transaction for an amount that is unusual compared to amounts of past transactions.

- Client frequently purchases traveller's cheques, foreign currency drafts or other negotiable instruments with cash when this appears to be outside of normal activity for the client.

- Client asks you to hold or transmit large sums of money or other assets when this type of activity is unusual for the client.

- Shared address for individuals involved in cash transactions, particularly when the address is also for a business location, or does not seem to correspond to the stated occupation (ie, student, unemployed, self-employed, etc).

- Stated occupation of the client is not in keeping with the level or type of activity (for example a student or an unemployed individual makes daily maximum cash withdrawals at multiple locations over a wide geographic area).

- Cash is transported by a cash courier.

- Large transactions using a variety of denominations.

Economic purpose

- Transaction seems to be inconsistent with the client's apparent financial standing or usual pattern of activities.

- Transaction appears to be out of the normal course for industry practice or does not appear to be economically viable for the client.

- Transaction is unnecessarily complex for its stated purpose.

- Activity is inconsistent with what would be expected from declared business.

- A business client refuses to provide information to qualify for a business discount.

- No business explanation for size of transactions or cash volumes.

- Transactions of financial connections between businesses that are not usually connected (for example, a food importer dealing with an automobile parts exporter).

- Transaction involves non-profit or charitable organisation for which there appears to be no logical economic purpose or where there appears to be no link between the stated activity of the organisation and the other parties in the transaction.

Transactions involving accounts

- Opening accounts when the client's address is outside the local service area.

- Opening accounts in other people's names.

- Opening accounts with names very close to other established business entities.

- Attempting to open or operating accounts under a false name.

- Account with a large number of small cash deposits and a small number of large cash withdrawals.

- Funds are being deposited into several accounts, consolidated into one and transferred outside the country.

- Client frequently uses many deposit locations outside of the home branch location.

- Multiple transactions are carried out on the same day at the same branch but with an apparent attempt to use different tellers.

- Activity far exceeds activity projected at the time of opening of the account.

- Establishment of multiple accounts, some of which appear to remain dormant for extended periods.

- Account that was reactivated from inactive or dormant status suddenly sees significant activity.

- Reactivated dormant account containing a minimal sum suddenly receives a deposit or series of deposits followed by frequent cash withdrawals until the transferred sum has been removed.

- Unexplained transfers between the client's products and accounts.

- Large transfers from one account to other accounts that appear to be pooling money from different sources.

- Multiple deposits are made to a client's account by third parties.

- Deposits or withdrawals of multiple monetary instruments, particularly if the instruments are sequentially numbered.

- Frequent deposits of bearer instruments (for example, cheques, money orders or bearer bonds) in amounts just below $10,000.

- Unusually large cash deposits by a client with personal or business links to an area associated with drug trafficking.

- Regular return of cheques for insufficient funds.

- Correspondent accounts being used as 'pass-through' points from foreign jurisdictions with subsequent outgoing funds to another foreign jurisdiction.

- Multiple personal and business accounts are used to collect and then funnel funds to a small number of foreign beneficiaries, particularly when they are in locations of concern, such as countries known or suspected to facilitate money laundering activities.

Whilst the CDD process does requires a proactive investigative role, it does not as such turn a professional into an informer – this may only arise if an SAR is required.

Conversely, in an SAR the professional's role is reactive, as an informant, and is (probably) subjective (see **7.5.1** and **7.5.2**). The client is uninformed and is non-participative, and must be kept unaware because of the tipping-off rules. There is an inherent conflict between a professional acting with professional confidentiality (such as a solicitor) and him/her filing an SAR: this conflict is explored more fully in **Chapter 13**. One solution to this is to make the prospective client aware at the 'prospect' stage of the possibility of a report being filed in the future, based on any future concerns, suspicions, etc although **11.10.1** makes it clear that Reporting *before* he/she becomes a 'Client' is not logically possible. It is prudent to warn prospective Clients, but perhaps it is daydreaming to expect everyone to do so. Some prospective Clients will accept the discussion and move along with their planning. A small number of prospective Clients will (hopefully) get up and leave.

THE REPORTING PROCESS AND PROCEDURES – INTERNAL

12.3 Every professional firm, financial institution and fiduciary business is required to have a MLRO. This person should be sufficiently senior to command authority and have considerable practical experience in the business. The MLRO must also ensure that each relevant employee (meaning those employees who are in the areas of business relating to customers and their activities) knows:

- who the MLRO is;

- to whom he/she should report suspicions; and

- that there is a clear reporting chain under which those suspicions will be passed without delay to the MLRO.

The internal reporting form should encourage employees to be as detailed as possible, even if their comments are wholly subjective.

If an employee makes a report to the MLRO, he/she is discharged from further individual responsibility under the PoCA 2002, ss 337–339 [the 'Statutory Get-out-of-Jail Free' Card]. As noted in **3.6**, it is a complete defence to the principal PoCA 2002 offences for the employee in question to have reported his/her knowledge or suspicion.

The MLRO or institution then has to determine whether or not to make a formal SAR. If after completing a review of the activity/ies reported (including discussions with the individual employee (s) concerned) the MLRO decides that the initial report *does indeed* give rise to a knowledge or suspicion of money laundering (ML) (see **7.5**), then the MLRO must disclose this information to the appropriate law enforcement agency.

It is presumably open to an employee to 'go direct' if he/she is aware that the MLRO has not followed up, although such a course could be career altering (see **12.7**). Such a course would not be necessary in relation to the PoCA 2002 offences, but could still provide valuable protection in the case of common law anti-money laundering (AML-CFT) crimes (see **12.4** below).

However, filing an SAR does *not* provide a defence, either to employee or the institution, in relation to AML-CFT offences arising as a result of common law offences such as fraud, false accounting or cheating the revenue, or the inchoate offences of conspiring or inciting, or aiding and abetting, counselling or procuring. Herein lies a dilemma: it is unlikely that a Court would be very sympathetic with an employer institution that failed to report externally, even if the employee who reported internally would have evidence justifying his/her exoneration.

In addition, as regards any suspicious transaction report (STR), the issue is not the size of the transaction: it is the 'quality' of the STR in terms of materiality that matters.

The term 'AML-CFT Prevention Officer' is generic, referring both to MLROs and Nominated Person/Nominated Officer. There is also an Institute of Money Laundering Prevention Officers contactable at www.imlpo.com/

THE REPORTING PROCESS AND PROCEDURES – EXTERNAL

12.4 Once an employee makes a report to the MLRO, the MLRO or institution then has to determine whether or not to make a formal SAR.

If after completing a review of the activity/ies reported (including discussions with the individual employee(s) concerned) the MLRO decides that the internal report does indeed give rise to a knowledge or suspicion of ML, then the MLRO must disclose this information to the appropriate external law enforcement agency.

Since October 2013, external SARs within the United Kingdom should be made in the first instance to the NCA (the new national agency which replaced SOCA which in turn replaced NCIS). The NCA is staffed by police and by HMRC officers. The NCA website is www.nationalcrimeagency.gov.uk. The NCA website has a number of useful joint NCA & UKFIU publications, including:

- Submitting a SAR within the Regulated Sector (July 2014);
- SAR Guidance Notes (July 2014);
- SAR Glossary Codes Revision Explained (July 2014);
- SARs Explained (July 2014); and
- Home Office Circular 53 2005 Confidentiality and Sensitivity of SARs (July 2014).

The NCA also has an 'SAR Online' reporting service (see **3.6**) and also a July 2014 publication on its website to assist with Online filings. Disclosures can be made online, using the NCA's *'SAR Online'* system on www.ukciu. gov.uk/saronline.aspx

For information or assistance with submitting SARs to NCA or UKFIU, *SAR Online* enquiries and consent, visit www.nationalcrimeagency.gov.uk or contact the UKFIU as follows:

UKFIU: Tel: +44 20 7238 8282
Press '2' – SAR Management
Press '3' – SAR Online
Press '4' – Consent

General UKFIU matters may be emailed to www.ukfiusars@nca.x.gsi.gov.uk

SARs can be sent by post to:

UKFIU, PO Box 8000,
London, SE11 5EN
or by fax on +44 20 7238 8286.

The web-based reporting system allows SARs to be constructed and submitted in a secure and efficient manner, and there is no need to complete, post or fax a SAR. There are no certification processes. SAR Online standardises reports and accelerate procedures. It is well worth visiting the NCA website and the SAR Online site to view their template formats!

NCA also provides technical support to FSBs relating to SARs, and advice and assistance on reporting suspicions of money laundering: interested persons can contact the NCA on their 24/7 phone number +44 370 496 7622 (either for general enquiries, or to verify a person as an NCA officer) or by mail to NCA at:

Units 1 – 6 Citadel Place,
Tinworth Street,
London SE11 5EF

or by email to communication@nca.x.gsi.gov.uk

There can be no objection to the MLRO consulting outside professional legal advisors in reaching his/her conclusion as to whether to report. However, the advice of prudence will invariably be 'when in doubt, report'. Unfortunately the CYA approach is the default option.

Note also the SOCPA 2005, s 105 offence of 'Failure to Report on the required Form' (see **2.5** and **4.1**).

See also **Chapter 17** and **Appendix 9** for the procedures in the other selected jurisdictions).

CONSENT OR OTHERWISE

12.5   Obtaining consent to proceed with the transaction is in many circumstances the essential next step. The NCA will acknowledge to the reporting business their receipt of the SAR disclosure.

PoCA 2002, s 335 (as amended) requires the NCA to give or refuse consent within seven days. In most cases, the NCA will give the reporting business their written consent to continue, or if the NCA have not responded within seven days, such consent is deemed to have been given.

In the case of the reporting business being a professional firm, the *consent* relates to continuing to process the particular transaction or activity. In the case of the reporting business being a bank, a fiduciary business, or other financial institution, the *consent* relates to continuing to operate the account or relationship.

In exceptional cases the reporting business will not receive such *consent*. In such a case, the information disclosed in the SAR will be allocated to trained professionals in HMRC or in the relevant Regional Crime Squad. Either of the latter will then follow up with the MLRO of the reporting business, and probably also with the individual employee(s) concerned. However, if the NCA does refuse to give *consent*, then for the 31-day period from the date of the refusal the transaction or arrangement *may not* be proceeded without the reporting business being at risk of committing an AML-CFT offence. Only at the end of this 'moratorium period' may the reporting business continue freely.

In other jurisdictions, in particular offshore financial centres, the position in terms of obtaining consent may be by no means as clear cut. Time frames and time limits are central to the UK system. If a different jurisdiction does not have corresponding time frames and time limits, then practical difficulties will ensue.

This was indeed the case in the offshore trust case in Jersey involving the State of Qatar (see **14.4.2**). And see also *Squirrel v NatWest Bank plc* [2005] EWHC 664 (Ch); and *K Ltd v NatWest Bank plc* [2006] EWCA Civ 1039

INDEMNITY

12.6   An institution may wish for an indemnity from its customer/ client against claims for breach of confidentiality in respect of an SAR that is made: an indemnity may be obtained if the institution requests the NCA investigating team for a Production Order. Or an indemnity relating to AML-CFT disclosures may be contained within the terms of business.

This issue is, of course, of great importance to legal professionals and practitioners, and is considered in greater detail in **Chapter 13**.

In the event an SAR leads to a criminal prosecution of the client/customer of the reporting institution, the source of the SAR (ie the identity of the reporting institution) is supposed to be protected. But it remains to be seen how much weight can in practice be attached to this promise, in the light of recent cases on SARs (where the identity of the institutional party is revealed when the matter turns complex). See eg *Shah v HSBC Private Bank (UK) Limited* [2009] EWHC 79 (QB) and [2010] EWHC 31 (see **4.2**, **7.5.2** and **Appendix 7**).

FALSE REPORTING

12.7   This is a comparatively recent phenomenon. The issue is simple: a *de facto* 'External STR' is signed by a junior staff member, but is otherwise entirely unknown to the institution let alone its MLRO. So is that an 'official STR'? Possibly yes if the 'going direct' option in **12.3** is pursued.

But if not, does it have the status nonetheless as an unofficial STR? What if the employee is disaffected (a 'renegade', possibly having already resigned, and determined to cause damage to his/her future ex-colleagues and ex-boss)? In such circumstances, should the institution later (when it discovers what has transpired) insist that the employee signs a letter withdrawing any and all STRs as not having been made officially by the institution?

There is a fine balance here. What the employee has done in these circumstances is serious and potentially damaging to the 'accused' institution:

- like a schoolteacher wrongly being accused of molesting a pupil; or
- like a person subjected to a false accusation of rape.

In the pure criminal law, a so-called victim can eventually (when the allegation is shown to have been false) be prosecuted for 'wasting police time'. But in anti-money laundering (AML-CFT) law, the 'whistle-blower' is not the victim, merely a bystander. And the AML-CFT codes generally seek to encourage suspicion transaction reporting.

The AML-CFT structure has in effect handed a loaded gun to every employee, however junior and however poorly educated, in effect to make an anonymous tip-off against their employer. Small wonder if occasionally one of these loaded guns goes off!

FIUs have now started to look at systems for testing the possibility of an STR being 'renegade' if it does not look official. At least one jurisdiction has convened an industry round table to address this issue.

INTERNATIONAL REPORTING STATISTICS

12.8   There are profound potential criminal, reputational and public relations risks ('media risk') for employees, professionals and financial institutions themselves in committing an AML-CFT offence. The statutory procedure for obtaining exoneration from the principal AML-CFT offences appears straightforward, involving nothing more than the filing of an SAR. On this basis it would be no surprise to find that that the authorities have been inundated with SARs.

From an initial 18,400 SARs in 2000, the numbers have increased steadily, with a significant jump in 2003 following the coming into force of the PoCA 2002 in February 2003.

Since 1 March 2004, when UK Solicitors, Accountants and other 'relevant businesses' (see **10.3**) became subject to the Money Laundering Regulations, the rate of SAR reporting should also have experienced a quantum leap: but despite that, overall numbers of SARs remain small in relation to the number of financial professionals and activities/transactions in any 12-month period. SOCA (the predecessor of the NCA) used repeatedly to criticise UK legal professionals for their alleged failure to ensure that their clients are honest people dealing with legitimate funds.

There is no doubt that many banks have been panicked into making large numbers of unnecessary 'defensive' SARs. But only a very small percentage of the total SARs filed are from solicitors; and a similarly low percentage of the total are from accountants. The Law Society has in the past questioned publicly whether some city firms of solicitors are being used by money launderers: property/conveyancing departments of law firms are now within the AML-CFT net, and it is not unlikely that valuation levels in the UK property market remain high in part as a result of foreign ML activity through this sector (see 'The UK threat of serious and organised crime', NCIS Report 2003).

3MLD (see **10.4**) established a feedback channel by requiring publication of STR statistics (Recital 38 and arts 30–33) after its implementation in December 2007. And as noted in **4.3**, the annual SAR Annual Report 2013 is the latest in the series of reports that started with Sir Stephen Lander's detailed review of the UK SAR regime in April 2006: the 2013 Report (see **Appendix 6**) is also available on the NCA website at www. nationalcrimeagency.gov.uk/contact-us

It would be useful and fascinating to have a detailed impact assessment study of the effect of the last ten years of the AML-CFT STR reporting regime. As not all FIUs publish STR reporting statistics, and those that do publish, generally limit the information to the 'raw' number of STRs and do not disclose in any detail the types/categories of alleged underlying suspicion (hence suspected offence(s)), the 'quality' of the STRs (as opposed to their 'quantity') is hard to probe.

In this regard it is appropriate to echo Professor Jason Sharman's Article entitled *'Look at 20 Years of Anti-Money Laundering: Does the System Work?'* published in December 2013 in the IFC Review. Selected extracts make the following points:

'It is now just over 20 years since the first international anti-money agreements were concluded. Notable amongst these are the 40 Recommendations compiled by FATF), which have come to define the international state-of-the-art in AML standards.

'At the time they were first created, AML rules were seen as another front in the 'War on Drugs'. Since then, the monitoring and implementation of AML standards have morphed into a global industry. Rather than just the rich countries that originally comprised the FATF membership, over 180 states have now signed up to the 40 Recommendations, which have since been augmented by the 9 Special Recommendations on the financing of terrorism. A vast array of financial institutions, from banks to brokers, insurance firms to casinos, money remitters to hedge funds, have now been conscripted into monitoring their clients for signs of suspicious financial activity. All this has imposed substantial costs on governments, private financial firms, and, indirectly, consumers, with the burden being especially significant for International Financial Centres.

'While this broadening and deepening of the global AML regime can be taken as evidencing the extraordinary strides made since the early 1990s, it is disconcerting how seldom the most obvious questions about this system are asked. **First amongst these is whether AML standards actually work**. That is to say, is there any less money laundered now than there was 20 years ago? Is there any less predicate crime that gives rise to these dirty funds in the first place? Despite all the evaluations performed by the FATF, other international organisations, national governments and the army of private AML experts that has grown up, it is striking that these sort of first-order questions are almost never asked, let alone answered. Although definite answers are elusive, I argue these hard questions should be asked. For all the time, effort and money devoted to combating money laundering over the last few decades, there is very little evidence that the standards have done much good in achieving their original aims.

'The appropriate starting point for this enquiry is to re-examine what AML standards were supposed to do…while the proximate goal of AML systems is, rather obviously, to reduce money laundering, the ultimate aim is to reduce profit-driven crime in general. So in judging the success or failure of AML standards these two concerns (the scale of money laundering, and the incidence of profit-driven crime) provide the logical benchmarks to be applied.

'Surprisingly, however, one can read through thousands of pages of FATF reports, covering everything from football to free-trade zones, without finding much, if any, attention devoted to these measures. Instead, the international surveillance and monitoring system that judges almost every country to see whether they have 'the right stuff' in AML terms has tended to foster **a bureaucratic game of goal displacement: means to an end have become ends in themselves**. For example, rather than a suspicious transaction reporting system being assessed on the grounds of its contribution to reducing money laundering and predicate crime, having a reporting system becomes an end in itself. This tendency towards goal displacement, of means becoming ends, has also filtered through to private firms, thanks to pressure exerted by national regulators, themselves keen to obtain a good FATF scorecard.

'While there is a rhetorical commitment to measuring effectiveness, the extent of this seems to be counting the number of convictions and totals of assets seized. In most countries these numbers are very low, which would tend to indicate that the AML system is not very effective. But even putting this to one side, there is the fact that the number of convictions is a very ambiguous measure of success. Is a high number of convictions good news (because lots of launderers are being caught) or bad news (because lots of laundering is going on)? Clearly having a few or no convictions is similarly ambiguous. There is also the point that giving the world's many dictatorial governments (for whom the rule of law is a foreign concept) an incentive to 'find' money launderers will probably result in the conviction of innocent individuals.

'The most careful studies of effectiveness note the mismatch whereby we have an incredibly extensive and intrusive policy apparatus, but **very little knowledge about the results produced**. On the basis of the fragmentary evidence that is available, however, it is hard to see any impact that AML rules have made on the incidence of crime. The general conclusion is that **the expansion of the AML regime owes more to a political imperative to 'do something' in response to hot-button issues like crime or terrorism, rather than any track record of success.**

'As we enter the third decade of anti-money laundering, it is thus time to ask simple, direct questions concerning the effectiveness of the system. Rather than caricaturing those questioning the effectiveness of AML systems as somehow 'soft on crime', the onus should be on those defending the status quo to show how the results justify the costs, direct and indirect, that have been incurred so far. It is a fundamental expectation that government policy should create more benefits for society than it does costs. So far there is little evidence that AML systems pass this test.'

From the statistics that are available, there is only one observable pattern, namely huge growth in the number of STRs – see **Appendix 6**. The statistics seem to confirm that UK-based STRs are all too often just be defensive bureaucracy. They should be a vital enforcement tool if a workable AML-CFT regime is to be maintained. The Author shares Professor Sharman's concern, that 'mission creep' has moved the AML-CFT imperatives to not much more than a tedious set of form filling, coupled with increasing statistics of STRs filed. But not a word about the success of the overall mission.

Chapter 13

Legal professionals and practitioners – specific issues

INTRODUCTION

13.1   As noted at **6.2**, the Money Laundering Regulations 2007 (SI 2007/2157) apply to every 'relevant business', which includes lawyers, accountants and tax advisers (reg 2(2)(i)).

By being thrust to the forefront of AML-CFT's 'privatised' law enforcement initiatives aimed at stamping out Money Laundering ('ML') by third parties, professionals and practitioners now for the first time ever, face an array of potential criminal offences, including both offences of commission and offences of omission, for the ultimate acts of other people, whether or not clients. So the AML-CFT rules and procedures have entirely changed the position of professionals and practitioners in terms of their traditional duty of confidentiality towards their clients.

The CDD process is central to this, coupled with the requirement to file a SAR where knowledge or suspicion of an AML-CFT offence arises.

As noted in **12.2**, the CDD process requires a proactive investigative role. The professional or practitioner becomes an informer where an SAR is required, while the client must be kept unaware because of the tipping-off rules.

FATF Recommendation 23 (February 2012) ('transparency of legal persons and arrangements') is specifically aimed at lawyers and makes it clear that lawyers are within the AML-CFT regime:

> '**23. DNFBPs: Other Measures:** The requirements set out in Recommendations 18–21 apply to all designated non-financial businesses and professions, subject to the following qualifications:
>
> a)   Lawyers, notaries, other independent legal professionals and accountants should be required to report suspicious transactions when, on behalf of or for a client, they engage in a financial transaction in relation to the activities described in Recommendation 22. Countries are strongly encouraged to extend the reporting requirement to the rest of the professional activities of accountants, including auditing.'

The FATF Notes do go on to add however, that 'lawyers, notaries, other independent legal professionals and accountants acting as independent legal professionals are not required to report their suspicions if the relevant information was obtained in circumstances where they are subject to professional secrecy or LPP.'

LAW SOCIETY AML-CFT PRACTICE NOTE

13.2   The Law Society updated **AML Practice Note** (October 2013, see **Appendix 7**) helps Solicitors comply with the Proceeds of Crime Act 2002, the Terrorism Act 2000 and the Money Laundering Regulations 2007 (and all amending legislation up to October 2013), and also details good practice. The **Practice Note** was updated following the replacement of SOCA by the –NCA – see www.lawsociety.org.uk/advice/practice-notes/aml/#sthash.3wl5ADxM.dpuf.

The **Practice Note** Chapter 8 on STRs does not discuss the issues of 'suspicion' and 'cause for concern' (and see **7.5**), merely requiring a disclosure after you 'have formed a reportable suspicion'.

Note that the Law Society SRA Handbook provides a Professional Ethics Helpline on +44 (876) 02577 and email address report@sra.org.uk where Solicitors or law firm MLROs may wish to seek help on some of these delicate issues. The latest SRA Handbook (version 10) was published on 1 July 2014 and contains a Code of Conduct. It is worth noting Principle 4, which states:

'Principle 4: You must act in the best interests of each client.

You should always act in good faith and do your best for each of your clients. Most importantly, you should observe:

(a)   your duty of confidentiality to the client – see Chapter 4 (Confidentiality and disclosure) of the Code of Conduct; and

(b)   your obligations with regard to conflicts of interests – see Chapter 3 (Conflicts of interests) of the Code of Conduct.'

LEGAL PROFESSIONAL PRIVILEGE AND CONFIDENTIALITY – GENERAL POSITION

13.3   Chapter 6 of the Law Society **Practice Note** on Legal Professional Privilege ('LPP') is delightfully clear and straightforward! So it is helpful to review the evolution of Solicitors' LPP and confidentiality, and then highlight how the AML-CFT laws (especially the PoCA 2002 and *P v P*) have altered this.

There is an absolute privilege as to communications between a lawyer and a client in relation to legal proceedings, whereby information is inadmissible as evidence in a Court of law, and the Judge will not allow it to be elicited. As regards LPP, the key feature is that a communication passing between lawyer and client conveying legal advice or relating to the conduct of on-going litigation need not be given in evidence or disclosed by the client and, without the client's consent, may not be given in evidence or disclosed by the legal adviser. This especially covers anything disclosed to a lawyer in the context of a retainer to defend the client of a particular criminal offence.

The scope of LPP is broad (see P O'Hagan's article on the English Court of Appeal case *Barclays Bank v Eustice* [1995] 4 All ER 511 in Private Client Business ([1997] PCB 131). Also see *Canada Trust Co v Century Holdings BVI* July 1998, 1 ITELR 056), in that it can also extend as between lawyer and client to legal advice outside the context of on-going litigation.

In the United Kingdom, there is a statutory formulation of the privilege in the Police and Criminal Evidence Act 1984, s 10(1), which provides that:

'(1) Subject to subsection (2) below in this Act "items subject to legal privilege" means:

(a) Communications between a professional legal adviser and his client or any person representing his client made in connection with the giving of legal advice to the client;

(b) Communications between a professional legal adviser and his client or any person representing his client or between such an adviser or his client or any such representative and any other person made in connection with or in contemplation of legal proceedings and for the purpose of such proceedings; and

(c) Items enclosed with or referred to in such communications and made:

(i) In connection with the giving of legal advice; or

(ii) In connection with or in contemplation of legal proceedings and for the purpose of such proceedings; when they are in the possession of a person who is entitled to possession of them'.

This section has been authoritatively stated to reproduce the common law of the United Kingdom (see Lord Goff in *R v Central Criminal Court, ex p Francis and Francis* [1989] AC 346 and *Cross and Tapper on Evidence* (12th Edition, OUP, 2010).

The professional duty of confidentiality is (or was) the essence of a lawyer's function. The Law Society SRA Handbook (version 10, published on 1 July 2014) declares confidentiality to be a fundamental right and duty of the lawyer (Principle 4 and Chapter 4 of the Code of Conduct) thus:

'Protection of confidential information is a fundamental feature of your relationship with clients. It exists as a concept both as a matter of law and as a matter of conduct. This duty continues despite the end of the retainer and even after the death of the client.'

In the House of Lords case *Bolkiah v KPMG* [1999] 2 AC 222, the professional duty of confidentiality was considered in detail. Lord Hope stated that it

'...extends well beyond that of refraining from deliberate disclosure...'
And Lord Millett said (at p 236):

> 'It is of overriding importance to the proper administration of
> justice that a client should be able to have complete confidence
> that what he tells his solicitor will remain secret. This is a matter
> of perception as well as substance.'

See also *Koch Shipping Inc v Richards Butler* [2002] 2 All ER (Comm) 957;
[2002] EWCA Civ 1280.

In the House of Lords Case *R v Special Commrs, ex p Morgan Grenfell* [2002]
UKHL 21, Lord Hoffmann restated that 'the policy of LPP requires that the
client should be secure in the knowledge that protected documents and
information will not be disclosed at all'.

It should be noted that a common law 'crime/fraud exception' has existed
for some decades. This is referred to in the *2013 Practice Note* and also in
the post-*Bowman v Fels* Guidance (**13.6**).

As is demonstrated in **13.4** below, the PoCA 2002 and its aftermath very
much changed the rules.

LEGAL PROFESSIONAL PRIVILEGE AND CONFIDENTIALITY ISSUES POST-POCA 2002

13.4   Although the 'crime/fraud exception has existed for some decades,
the concept of a 'statutory exception' to the common law professional duty
of confidentiality is entirely the result of AML-CFT legislation. It started
with the Drug Trafficking Act 1994, and was expanded, first of all by the
Terrorism Act 2000 (as amended), and then by ss 337 and 338 of the PoCA
2002.

Sections 331 and 332 of the PoCA 2002 create offences of failure of a Money
Laundering Reporting Officer (MLRO) (whether or not in the regulated
sector) to disclose to the authorities any knowledge or reasonable suspicion
of the client's receipt or dealing in the proceeds of any of the scheduled
offences – see **4.1** and also **12.3** in relation to 'authorised disclosure' under
s 338 and 'protected disclosure' under s 337 of the PoCA 2002.

As noted in **6.2**, the 2MLD, 3MLD and The Money Laundering Regulations
2007 (see **6.4**) have extended the definition of 'relevant financial business'
so that solicitors and accountants are now subject to these provisions.

The types of legal work included in the scope of the Directive are:

- assisting in the planning or execution of transactions for a client
  concerning the:
- buying and selling of real property or business entities;
- managing of clients' money, securities or other assets;
- opening or management of bank, savings or securities accounts;

- organisation of contributions necessary for the creation, operation or management of companies;

- creation, operation or management of trusts, companies or similar structures.

- acting on behalf of and for a client in any financial or real estate transaction.

They also apply to those engaged in investment business, to tax advisers (persons providing tax advice), and to trustees (see Chapter 14). Thus, the professional duty of confidentiality is no longer an absolute, but is outweighed by an overriding positive duty to the State, to protect the public interest.

Section 330(10) of the PoCA 2002 contains an exception for the need to report privileged information, when the knowledge or suspicion is based on information or some other matter which came to him/her in privileged circumstances. However, s 330(11) excludes from the 'privilege defence', information or other matters which are communicated or given with the intention of furthering a criminal purpose, thus restricting the operation of privilege.

Privilege has always been vitiated by a criminal purpose, and it is the purpose of the person who communicates the information (which need not be shared by the person receiving it) which is important – see *R v Central Criminal Court, ex p Francis and Francis* [1989] 1 AC 346. This means that before a lawyer can decide not to report knowledge or suspicion, on the grounds of privilege, he will have to first satisfy himself as to the reason he was given the information.

This overriding duty to the State is reflected in The Law Society's/SRA Handbook (version 10, published on 1 July 2014) which allows a solicitor to report his/her client to the authorities rather than be dragged into providing assistance in the perpetration of a crime (see Principle 4 and Chapter 4 (Confidentiality and Disclosure) in the SRA Code of Conduct).

Thus, while these may be more of a concern to solicitors than accountants, there is a general concern within both professions in the apparent conflict created by the AML-CFT legislation in requiring disclosure by an SAR of details about client's affairs, where the professional has concerns as to AML-CFT issues.

Non-Disclosure is not a practical option, as there are severe penalties for such a course of action or inaction.

Section 106 of the SOCPA 2005 (see **Appendix 1.2**) ameliorated s 330 of the PoCA 2002 (regulated sector: failure to disclose), so that a professional legal adviser making a disclosure need not be regarded as making a STR if the disclosure is made for the purpose of obtaining advice about making a disclosure, and he/she does not intend it to be a disclosure.

It is, perhaps, a result of the United Kingdom not having a written constitution that has allowed such a long-standing common law principle to be diluted. In contrast, in two Canadian cases the statutory AML-CFT provisions requiring disclosure were themselves held to be unconstitutional; also Canadian Supreme Court in *Lavalee Rackel and Heintz v Canada (A-G)* [2002] SCC 61, 12 September 2002; also *British Columbia Supreme Court in Law Society of British Columbia v A-G of Canada* [2000] BC Supreme Court 1593.

And see *Michaud v France* (ECHR, 6 December 2012) on the clash between reporting obligations and LPP/right to privacy (and **Appendix 7**) where the ECHR held unanimously that the obligation on lawyers to report suspicions in the context of the fight against money laundering does not interfere disproportionately with professional privilege.

See www.lawsociety.org.uk/advice/articles/case-summaries/michaud-v-france/#sthash.EyvMsbgr.dpuf

Robert Pang v Commr of Police (2 December 2002, unreported) was an important Hong Kong case in relation to issues of LPP. The applicant, a well-known barrister, sought four Declarations, and obtained two, in the context of his arrest under s 5A(1) of the Organised and Serious Crimes Ordinance (Hong Kong) ('OSCO'). The declarations sought were in the following terms:

- that on the true construction of s 25A OSCO, it does not cover information and communications communicated to counsel which are covered by LPP when taking instructions and rendering legal advice (Declaration granted);

- further or alternatively, that s 25A OSCO, insofar as it relates to information and communications communicated to counsel which are covered by LPP contravenes Arts 35, 39 and 87 of the Basic Law and Art 14 of the International Covenant on Civil and Political Rights 1996 (Declaration not granted);

- further or in the further alternative, that s.25A OSCO, insofar as it requires a barrister of Hong Kong to disclose any matters which are covered by LPP contravenes Arts 35, 39 and 87 of the Basic Law and Art 14 of the International Covenant on Civil and Political Rights 1996 (Declaration not granted); and

- that the arrest and detention of the applicant on 14 March 2002 was arbitrary and unlawful (Declaration granted).

P v P

13.5   The case of *P v P* [2003] EWHC 2260 (Fam); [2003] 4 All ER 843 (decided in October 2003 in the UK High Court (Family Division)) concerned matrimonial proceedings where in the course of the negotiations on financial relief for the wife, her solicitors became aware by the husband's disclosures that part of his substantial assets were derived from untaxed income. As such, the wife's solicitors became concerned that they might be committing an offence under s 328 of the PoCA 2002

The two main AML-CFT issues arose in the proceedings:

(i) whether and in what circumstances it is permitted to continue to act in relation to a potential AML-CFT 'arrangement'; and

(ii) whether and in what circumstances a legal adviser, having made an authorised disclosure, is permitted to tell others of the fact that he/ she has done so.

The judgment of the President of the Family Division, Dame Elizabeth Butler-Sloss, gave guidance on a number of vexed issues, including:

- the extent to which a solicitor handling a divorce case for a client might come within the ambit of s 328 of the PoCA 2002 (arrangements, etc) in relation to a proposed financial settlement, where part of the funds had not been declared for tax; and

- that the facts should be disclosed to ARA in the form of a SAR;

- and also that there is no professional privilege exemption under s 327, 328 or 329 of the PoCA 2002 (although there is under s 330(6) (b)).

Because the issues raised were important, a number of third parties to the matrimonial proceedings intervened in the case by way of written submissions, namely NCIS (at that time), both The Law Society and The Bar Council, and (also at that time) the Inland Revenue (now HMRC).

Interestingly, the Judge held (para 56) that there is no distinction between degrees of criminal property, whether the illegally obtained sum is ten pounds or a million pounds. Whatever may be the resource implications, the legal profession would appear to be bound by the provisions of the Act in all cases, however big or small.'

The case of *P v P* confirmed that practitioners' concerns in relation to the scope of s 328 of the PoCA 2002 were justified, and as a result of *P v P*, The Law Society (which had intervened in the case by way of written submissions) provided detailed clarification on the case in their *Money Laundering: Guidance for Solicitors* (Pilot, January 2004). And a critical article in October 2003 by *The Times'* legal correspondent commented that, PoCA 2002 '… now appears to reach far beyond its original purpose, and needs to have its scope restricted'. So, the overall position was acute until eased less than 18 months later by *Bowman v Fels* (see **13.6**).

CONFIDENTIALITY ISSUES, CONFLICT OF INTEREST, AND REPORTING – POST *BOWMAN V FELS*

13.6 *Bowman v Fels* (2005) ECWA Civ 226: The Court of Appeal judgment in *Bowman v Fels* arose as a result of county court litigation involving a property dispute between ex-cohabitees, during the course of which one party's legal adviser reported the other side for ML to NCIS (as it then was). The Court of Appeal considered s 328 of the PoCA 2002, and in particular whether the meaning of the phrase *'enters into all becomes concerned in an arrangement'* could encompass, the ordinary conduct of legal proceedings.

The Court concluded that neither the EU legislation nor the UK Government had intended that 1MLD/2MLD and the PoCA 2002 should interfere with the 'ordinary conduct of litigation'. Specifically, the Court concluded:

> '... as a matter of ordinary language, our impression on reading s 328 was and remains that, whatever Parliament may have had in mind by the phrase "entering into all becomes concerned in an arrangement which ... facilitates ...", it is most unlikely that it was thinking of legal proceedings' [para 64]; and

> ' to our mind, it is improbable that Parliament, being the UK legislature, had the ordinary conduct of legal proceedings to judgment in mind under s 328 (or indeed ss 327 and 329...' [para 63]

The Court went on to consider whether, if it was wrong about the scope of s 328 of the PoCA 2002, LPP could in any event be overridden, and concluded that it could not. Parliament would have had to use express words to allow lawyers to breach their professional confidence with clients. The Court stated:

> ' Much stronger language would have been required if s.328 could be interpreted as having a necessary implication that LPP was to be overridden'.

As Lord Hoffmann said in *R v Secretary of State for the Home Department, ex p Simms:*

> 'fundamental rights cannot be overridden by general words.' [para 87]

Similarly, the Court decided that Parliament could not have intended SARs to have been made in breach of the 'implied undertaking' not to disclose documents to a third party, referring to Lord Hoffmann in *Taylor v Serious Fraud Office*, and concluding that:

> 'We are of the firm opinion that it would require much clearer language than is contained in s 328 and its ancillary sections before a Parliamentary intention could be gleaned to the effect that a party's solicitor is obliged, in breach of this implied duty to the Court, and in breach of the duty of confidence he owes to his own Client as his litigation solicitor, to disclose to NCIS a suspicion he may have that documents disclosed under compulsion by the other party evidence, one of the matters referred to in s 328.' [para 89]

The *Bowman v Fels* judgment excluded certain activities from the scope of the s 328 'arrangements' offence in the PoCA 2002. Thus, importantly, the judgment in *Bowman v Fels* effectively overturned the decision in *PvP*.

Whilst the *Bowman v Fels* judgment was on litigation and similar work, the judgment also makes references to how Parliament could not have intended the authorised disclosure defence to the principal POCA 2002 offences (ss 327–329) to override LPP. Therefore, whenever solicitors have to consider whether to make a report in relation to the ss 327–329 offences, they need to consider whether the information on which their knowledge or suspicion is based is itself subject to common law LPP.

Whereas the range of those whose communications fall within the s 330(6) exemption may be broader than within common law LPP, under both heads the communications must relate to legal advice' A definition on the scope of common law advice privilege (approved by the House of Lords) can be found in *Three Rivers District Council v Governor and Company of the Bank of England* [2004] UKHL 48 at 111 as covering:

> 'all communications between a solicitor and his client relating to a transaction in which the solicitor has been instructed for the purpose of obtaining legal advice … notwithstanding that they do not contain advice on matters of law and construction provided that they are directly related to the performance by the solicitor of his professional duty as legal adviser of his client';

and see [2005] 1 AC 610 at para 34.

There is also clear guidance on the 'crime/fraud exception', where neither LPP nor the s 330(6) exemption apply to communications made with the intention of furthering a criminal purpose.

Finally, the judgment contains important clarification as to how solicitors conducting transactions should approach the exemption for professional legal advisers to the tipping-off offences under ss 333 and 342 of the PoCA 2002. Solicitors who are acting in transactions in circumstances where they have knowledge or suspicion of ML, and so are going to risk 'being concerned in an arrangement' at some future date, have a legal duty to give legal advice to clients for whom they act, including on the possibility of their client committing ML offences if the transaction proceeds without 'appropriate consent' having been obtained. It should, however, be noted that this exemption does not apply if in discussing the issues with the client, the solicitor has a criminal intention.

CLIENT CARE LETTERS, LPP AND REPORTING

13.7   Given the requirements of LPP and the Solicitor's statutory AML-CFT Reporting obligations, prospective clients must be made clearly aware at the 'prospect' stage that public duties now outweigh the duty of confidentiality. Existing clients should be similarly advised by circular letter or notice attached to the next fee note (if not so already advised). Thus, they need to be made aware of the possibility of an SAR being filed in the future, based on any future suspicions, etc. relating either to the prospective client or indeed to third parties with whom the prospective client is (or was) engaged in a transaction. Such a procedure is prudent. Most prospective clients (and existing clients) will accept the discussion as not applicable to them, and will proceed to the advice stage. If the occasional prospect or client just ups and leaves, then the legal professional or practitioner may have succeeded in avoiding a problem further down the road.

Specific wording must be included in the client care letter (or Standard Terms & Conditions of Business), stating clearly the position of the professional or practitioner in this regard.

Senior English solicitor John Rhodes' October 2002 conference paper on *'Reporting Suspicious Transactions'* for the Offshore Trust and Tax Planning Summit in Miami included a letter to clients setting out the position in relation to LPP, foreign tax evasion and the effect of the (then anticipated) PoCA 2002: his concluding paragraph wisely counselled, 'I suggest that we arrange to speak later on this week if you have any further questions arising from this analysis'.

And at the same time, Barrister David Dabbs' New Law Journal article included the following sample paragraphs for a client care letter:

> 'Under this retainer we shall abide by our professional duty to keep secret and in strict confidence information received from you concerning your personal, financial or other circumstances. We shall not disclose such information to any person without your consent; save where we have reached the conclusion (whether justified or not) that this information ("incriminating information") implies that you are, or were once, engaged in criminal activity of a kind proscribed by law. In such circumstances, we shall be entitled to conclude that our duty to the public outweighs our duty of confidence to you; and we reserve the right to disclose incriminating information to the proper authorities for the sake of our duty to comply with the law.

> 'In such circumstances, either such disclosure will not amount to a breach of our duty of confidence; alternatively, in so far as such disclosure might otherwise amount to a breach, save where malice is proved, we will accept no liability whatsoever for any loss or damage, direct or indirect, and howsoever occasioned (death or serious injury aside) as a result of such disclosure.'

The Law Society (England and Wales) Practice Notes (26 March 2013) provide its Solicitor Members with approved paragraphs for Client Care Letters or Terms & Conditions of engagement. The Client Care information Section 5 includes the following:'

> '5.2.8 Money laundering and terrorist financing

>> Your anti-money laundering obligations depend on whether you are providing services to this client within the regulated sector. If you are providing a client with regulated services, you must conduct client due diligence and monitor your client's retainer for warning signs of money laundering or terrorist financing. If you are not providing a client with regulated services, you must still monitor your client's retainer for warning signs of money laundering or terrorist financing.'

- for advice on AML requirements, see the Law Society's anti-money laundering practice note.

- for further advice on your CFT obligations, see the Law Society's anti-terrorism practice note.

5.2.8.1 Client Due Diligence (CDD): For more information on how to conduct CDD, see Chapter 4 of the Law Society's anti-money laundering practice note. While you may have already obtained CDD material before sending out the client care letter, you should still include information in the terms and conditions about your CDD obligations. You should cover all of the following points in your terms and conditions:

The Money Laundering Regulations 2007 require you to:

- obtain information about a client's identity and to verify that information

- obtain identity information about people related to the client (beneficial owners), where relevant, and at times verify that information

- continue to monitor the transaction and keep identity information up to date

You may verify a client's identity in a number of ways. You should state your practice's preferred method of verification, eg passport. If the client has difficulty providing the information you requested, you should ask them to contact you to discuss other ways to verify their identity. For example:

'The law requires solicitors to get satisfactory evidence of the identity of their clients and sometimes people related to them. This is because solicitors who deal with money and property on behalf of their client can be used by criminals wanting to launder money. To comply with the law, we need to get evidence of your identity as soon as possible. Our practice is to [insert your standard practice]. If you cannot provide us with the specific identification requested, please contact us as soon as possible to discuss other ways to verify your identity'

'5.2.8.2 Making a disclosure. If you suspect a client is engaged in money laundering or terrorist financing, you may risk committing a principal money laundering or terrorism offence, or an offence of failing to disclose your suspicions to relevant authorities. For further information on your legal options in these circumstances, see Chapter 5 of the Law Society's AML practice note. Making a disclosure may require you to either temporarily cease work on the client's retainer or to withdraw completely. It is not tipping-off to include a paragraph about your obligations under the money laundering legislation in your terms of business. For example:

'We are professionally and legally obliged to keep your affairs confidential. However, solicitors may be required by statute to make a disclosure to [NCA] where they know or suspect that a transaction may involve money laundering or terrorist financing. If we make a disclosure in relation to your matter, we may not be able to tell you that a disclosure has been made. We may have to stop working on your matter for a period of time and may not be able to tell you why.'

See more at: www.lawsociety.org.uk/advice/practice-notes/client-care-letters/#sthash.FRbwtXs0.dpuf.

CONSTRUCTIVE TRUST ISSUES

13.8 Of great importance is the issue of a professional/practitioner or fiduciary being found liable as a constructive trustee, and having to return (or reimburse) funds after the event to their 'proper' owner (see also **14.8**).

In an ideal world, adequate KYC and CDD procedures would highlight the most blatant cases of a so-called client in fact dealing with property belonging to another. But it would be naive to think that all such cases can be prevented from the outset.

And the AML-CFT reporting regime does not assist in exonerating a professional/practitioner or fiduciary against this risk area, as constructive trusteeship arises through application of trust law and principles of equity, and has nothing to do with ML as such. The two issues only overlap where funds that are found to be subject to a constructive trust are at the same time identified as having passed under the possession or control of the 'client' through some fraud or deception practiced on the true owner. At that stage ML issues arise, and an STR is appropriate.

Note that the former ARA disclosure template (now the NCA) had at its data box at top left an item entitled 'constructive trust'.

3MLD, THE MONEY LAUNDERING REGULATIONS 2007 AND 4MLD

13.9 The useful Report issued by the UK House of Commons Library on 14 November 2012 deals in its Section 2.4 with the impact of 3MLD on the legal profession (see extract at **Appendix 7**).

Back in 2007 when the Money Laundering Regulations 2007 were first published in draft, the Law Society response concluded that there were grave problems of interpretation, with the Law Society President stating that:

'It is unacceptable for the government to pass the responsibility of interpreting the incomprehensible language of this directive to solicitors, who face possible imprisonment if they get it wrong.'

and expressing concerns: that the draft Regulations could impose significant extra costs on solicitors for compliance; could reduce the competitiveness of UK firms due to 'gold plating' of the EU directive; and put even conscientious solicitors at risk of conviction and imprisonment. The Law Society campaigned vigorously to ensure that the final version of the Money Laundering Regulations 2007 were (and are) proportionate and workable, and as backup obtained an Opinion from leading counsel Rabinder Singh QC, which clearly stated that the (then) current definition of beneficial interest was unlawful, and that the Regulations as then currently formulated were open to challenge on grounds of 'lack of legal certainty'. Fortunately the UK Government heeded these concerns and (despite concerns over LPP) the Money Laundering Regulations 2007 (SI 2007/2157) were well received.

4MLD AND CLIENT ACCOUNTS

13.10   In his Law Society Gazette Article on 5 September 2014 (see **Appendix 7**), CCBE Secretary General Jonathan Goldsmith notes the impact of the proposed 4MLD provisions on Solicitor Client Accounts, thus:

> 'The current draft 4th Directive was some way through its legislative process when it was noticed there was a difference in the treatment of what are called pooled accounts (which we know as client accounts) between this version and 3MLD. According to 3MLD Article 11.2(b), Member States may allow CDD not to be applied in respect of beneficial owners of pooled accounts run by independent legal professionals. This is good, because it eliminates a burden which would otherwise be considerable. [However] 4MLD aims to abolish this explicit exception [as] the authorities feel that the simplified due diligence provisions in 3MLD are overly permissive, because certain categories of client or transaction are given outright exemption: 4MLD proposes to tighten the rules. Under the new system, it would be left to the member states to determine which areas they believe present a lower risk, so resulting in simplified customer due diligence measures (4MLD, Article 13). My organisation, the CCBE, believes that the current system of pooled accounts works smoothly, and meets the requirements of preventing money laundering. The Law Society agrees. If pooled accounts for lawyers are abolished, lawyers would have to open a separate account for each individual case, then make a separate transfer from that account and close the account afterwards, which would be extremely burdensome.'

There will be much lobbying on this point.

STRs, FRAUD ALLEGATIONS AND 'FREEZE ORDERS'

13.11   A prima facie suspicion that the client or prospective client is involved in a 'fraud', is generally enough to justify filing an STR against one's client.

On the other hand, a third party allegation of 'fraud' or 'ML' *against* one's client is a different story. Nowadays, all too frequently, litigation has become a tool in commercial negotiations particularly, in high-value contracts and divorce.

The point is: 'expect the unexpected' (unless it is The Spanish Inquisition!), and be aware that complicated corporate structures may get unravelled and/or frozen in the event that there is a serious dispute where fraud/AML is alleged. It may take months or years to reinstate or unfreeze bank accounts that have been caught in the crossfire. And the AML-CFT regime in many jurisdictions may lack clear procedures on how to appeal (or seek to quash) a freeze order imposed or improved by (eg) the Attorney-General's office.

THE IBA INTERNATIONAL ANTI-MONEY LAUNDERING FORUM

13.12 The IBA has established an International AML Forum www. anti-moneylaundering.org. Their Lawyer's Guide to Legislation and Compliance is a well-designed internet-based network which can be used to assist lawyers in dealing with their current responsibilities in connection with AML-CFT matters. In addition, the IBA website announces that they are:

> 'continuing the examination and follow-up of the implementations and developments which have taken place all over the world on this topic. Following the success and quality of the European country templates, the IBA website has started to focus on other regions that are rapidly developing their internal AML laws and regulations, such as Latin America, Africa, Asia Pacific and the Caribbean. As many countries adjust their protective measures against ML, the FATF Recommendations have continued their permeation into multiple jurisdictions. A number of these new laws and regulations have started to include lawyers as one of the non-designated businesses and professions, although the extent of the obligations varies from country to country'.

OTHER SUPRANATIONAL ISSUES

13.13 Case C-305/05 in the European Court of Justice (ECJ), involved a challenge to 2MLD brought by four European bar associations. On 14 December 2006, the advocate general ruled that the Directive does apply to lawyers, but that they should be exempted from SAR filing requirements involving conduct 'before, during, or after a judicial proceeding, or during the provision of legal advice'. The ECJ's decision of 2 July 2007 (Times Law Reports) upheld the advocate general in relation to the exemption from SAR filing in the context of advising, defending and appraising their client.

On the other hand, in relation to involvement of Canadian lawyers in certain transactions (essentially ones of a financial nature or concerning real estate), the Provincial Bars have resisted encroachment. Japanese lawyers are trying to do likewise. More recently the December 2012 ECHR decision of *Michaud v France* reviewed whether the AML reporting requirements applicable to lawyers are consistent with the right to privacy – see www.hudoc.echr.coe.int/sites/eng/pages/search.aspx?i=001-115377#{"itemid":["001-115377"]}. And see **Appendix 7** for other recent cases.

Chapter 14

Trustees, executors and TSPs – specific issues

INTRODUCTION

14.1 FATF Recommendation 25 (February 2012) (aiming at 'transparency of legal persons and arrangements') is specifically aimed at Trusts and Trustees/TSPs:

> '25 Countries should take measures to prevent the misuse of legal persons for money laundering or terrorist financing. Countries should ensure that there is adequate, accurate and timely information on express trusts, *including information on the Settlor, trustee and beneficiaries*, that can be obtained or accessed in a timely fashion by competent authorities. Countries could consider measures to facilitate access to beneficial ownership and control information to financial institutions and DNFBPs undertaking the requirements set out in Recommendations 10 and 12' [Author's emphasis]

UK-based TSPs have been within the regulated sector since 2007: and reg 2(8) of the Money Laundering Regulations 2007 (SI 2007/2157) apply to every 'relevant business', which includes UK TSPs (based on the requirements of 3MLD) (see **6.4**). Part 4 of the Regulations (regs 22–35) deals with supervision and registration. Regulations 25–30 relate in particular to the registration of TSPs, and within this group of regulations reg 28 contains the 'fit and proper test', as a negative clearance approach, whereby an applicant will not be registered as a F&PP if they possess any negative indicia (previous convictions etc).

In most offshore jurisdictions, TSPs have been subject to licencing and regulation for many years, either by being 'trustees'/TSPs or by being within the broader definition of 'fiduciaries' (eg the 'regulation of fiduciaries' in Guernsey and Jersey).

It is clear from many of OECD and FATF's international initiatives over the last few years that offshore trusts are regarded as having a high degree of risk from an ML standpoint. This may in part result from the fact that structures involving trusts and companies are often complex and difficult to understand. We have already seen how they require greater initial CDD work by institutions to identify controllers and beneficiaries (see **10.5**, **14.2.1** and **14.2.2**).

So this chapter will address the following issues relating to Trusts, Trustees and Executors:

- CDD on Trusts, the 'control elements' of a Trust, verification etc;

- Regulation of TSPs by virtue of Money Laundering Regulations 2007 and AML-CFT issues;

- Regulation of Trustees outside the UK and AML-CFT issues;

- Reporting by Trustees;

- Registration of Trustees;

- Issues facing Executors; and

- Constructive Trust issues

'CORE CDD' ON TRUSTS: PROOF OF IDENTITY/PROOF OF RESIDENCE

14.2   As noted in **11.10**, if a trust is somewhere included in an ownership structure, then it is necessary to identify the controlling elements – see **14.2.1** and **Appendix 1.3**. Plus it is necessary to identify both the *Source of Funds* and the *Destination of Funds*, in terms of both the settlor and the beneficiaries. And also

WHO IS THE 'BENEFICIAL OWNER' OF A TRUST?

14.2.1   The key (but misleading) question that Civil Law jurisdictions have been raising for years is 'who is the 'owner' or 'economic owner' of a trust?'. The Swiss have long required a name or names for the mandatory *Form A* disclosure on opening a bank account for a trust, and since 2008 have used their newer 'Form T'; and in Luxembourg, a similar question has been put to trustees for the last 15 or more years under (former IML, now CSSF) rules.

From a regulatory and CDD standpoint, this question, among others, has now answered by 3MLD and in the Money Laundering Regulations 2007 (see **Appendix 1.3**).

These issues of 'beneficiary' identification have been brought more sharply into focus by 3MLD (see **10.4**). 3MLD Article 8(1)(a) sets out the requirement to 'identify' the customer and then 'verify' that identification. 'Identification' involves getting details of full name, date of birth, nationality and address, whereas 'verification' involves *proving* 'identification' by, for example, a copy of the passport (and see **Chapter 11** generally).

But note also the following:

- *Identification*. Trust law has long required 'certainty of objects' (see *McPhail v Doulton* [1971] AC 424 and more recently *Re Rosewood* [2003] UKPC 26) so it is not going far beyond pre-existing law to require the full name and date of birth of discretionary beneficiaries. This can be easily proved by a passport; or by a birth certificate copy (coupled as the case may be with a subsequent marriage certificate or change of name deed).

- *Nationality* is only provable by means of an official document such as a passport or national identity card.

- *Addresses* can and do change, although in the case of adult beneficiaries there are a number of acceptable ways of establishing proof of residence ('verifying' it) (see **Appendix 5**).

As a pragmatic assistance for practitioners, in the case of a family trust (established typically by a parent) and including minor children in the beneficiary group, the trustees should do whatever they feel is sensible to define with certainty the identities of the minor beneficiaries. If the settlor is a parent there can be no difficulty in getting a copy of the birth certificate, as it is their legal obligation to register the birth.

The UK definition of 'beneficial owner' emanating from the Money Laundering Regulations 2007 set out in **Appendix 1.4** applies in relation to a body corporate, to a trust, and to 'any legal entity (other than a body corporate) or legal arrangement (other than a trust)' (such as a Foundation). This definition is most important in relation to discretionary trusts, as it moves the focus away from 'discretionary beneficiaries' and towards those 'who have legal control over a trust'. In this regard, the new definition states that, in the case of a discretionary trust, 'beneficial owner' means 'any individual who has control over the trust', and it goes on to define the word 'control' in detail, as follows:

'control' means a power (whether exercisable alone, jointly with another person or with the consent of another person) under the trust instrument or by law to:

(a) dispose of, advance, lend, invest, pay or apply trust property;

(b) vary the trusts;

(c) add or remove a person as a beneficiary or to a class of beneficiaries;

(d) appoint all remove trustees; or

(e) direct, withhold consent to all detail the exercise of a power such as is mentioned in subparagraph (a), (b), (c) or (d).

Since this definition refers to 'any individual', it must quite sensibly be taken not to include corporate trustees within its scope: after all, they are not the beneficial owners, but are merely the legal owners. On the other hand, the 'control'; test automatically includes typical 'protector' functions (such as the power to appoint/remove trustees), and may also include any person exercising some of what in certain jurisdictions are known as 'reserved powers', and may typically be reserved by or to the settlor.

14.2.2   CDD on Beneficiaries: Also, given the focus on the 'CFT' side of AML-CFT, it becomes essential to apply a broader CDD to a beneficiary recipient at the time of (and in advance of) receipt of a trust distribution: after all, who is to know if the fresh-faced three-year-old cherub smiling out of a baby passport page might not grow up at 22 years into a manic sociopath. So, in terms of risk, the process of 'verification' is a much more profound exercise than just getting a 'current valid passport' and having it certified correctly!

There is no real difficulty nowadays in getting passports for minor beneficiaries over (say) four or five years old – possibly just inconvenience – but there may be no passport for a new-born for a number of years, or at least until that child starts to travel by air. It may be more difficult for a relative or god-parent (as settlor) to get a copy of the birth certificate, but is still good practice to seek such an official confirmation of identity. A birth announcement from a reputable newspaper would also suffice.

As noted in **11.6** and **11.7**, nationality and country of residence may anyway serve as further 'alerts' to the possibility of money laundering (ML). Although only five countries/jurisdictions remain on the OECD NCCT list, and FATF has identified only 15 remaining countries with deficiencies, many FIs maintain their own internal lists of yet other countries that they wish to monitor closely or even prefer not to do business with at all.

These problems are certainly not insuperable, and primarily involve an increased administrative burden imposed on TSPs: hence the higher fees.

Note also that for' trusts, foundations and similar entities', the 2013 JMLSG Guidance (see **6.1**) sets out in its Paras 5.3.243–5.3.269 an explanation of the different types of trust and what detailed information should be obtained for each.

APPROVED CERTIFIERS

14.2.3 This is becoming standardised, subject always to 'Gold-Plating' requirements. See **11.13** and **15.3**.

REGULATION OF TSPs

14.3 Within the United Kingdom, TSPs are now within the regulated sector. As noted in **Chapter 6**, the Money Laundering Regulations 2007 apply to every 'relevant business', which includes UK fiduciaries (TSPs) as broadly defined by 3MLD and reg 2(8) of the 2007 Regulations. And as noted above, Regulations 25–30 relate in particular to the registration of TSPs, and within this group of regulations, reg 28 contains the 'fit and proper test' as a negative clearance approach, whereby an applicant will not be registered as a F&PP if they possess any negative indicia (previous convictions etc.) along with a broader set of criteria based on risk of AML-CFT.

In July 2013, HMR&C published their updated *Notice MLR9C Registration Guide for Trust or Company Service Providers*.

The detailed issues pertaining to Trusts and Trustees that arose as a result of 3MLD, and as further developed in 4MLD, are referred to in greater detail in **10.4** and **10.9**.

14.3.1 *Trustees, executors and TSPs – specific issues*

In most of the offshore jurisdictions, TSPs have been subject to licencing and regulation for many years, either by falling within the definition of 'Fiduciary' for fiduciary regulation (eg Guernsey and Jersey), or specifically as 'TSPs'. Some jurisdictions (eg Hong Kong) still do not licence or regulate TSPs other than by virtue of the general law, including AML-CFT provisions.

It is beyond the scope of this book to list or analyse the statutory provisions whereby TSPs themselves are regulated in the jurisdictions cited: reference on this can be made to 'The Regulation of Trust and Company Service Providers' (STEP, June 2006), to STEP's Jurisdiction Guides www.step. org and to the relevant FSC or Monetary Authority websites in each jurisdiction.

ONSITE INSPECTION VISITS

14.3.1 Trust (or 'fiduciary') businesses are now regulated in nearly all reputable offshore jurisdictions. As part of the licensing process, their regulator has the right to make annual or occasional onsite inspection visits. Onsite inspections are generally regarded as a necessary fact of life. An element of such visits involves checking the extent to which the fiduciary business is complying with the applicable *Regulations* and *Guidance Notes* and *Codes of Practice* (see **Chapter 17** and **Appendix 9**). The inspection visit generally involves substantive checking on a random sample of trust files (and related or corporate files) drawn from an anonymised master list, to ensure CDD is in place, and that Mandates and documentation are correctly drawn up, dated etc. Staff are also to be asked about their AML-CFT training, and AML-CFT training records are checked (see **6.7**).

It is interesting to note (**14.4.3** and **Appendix 9, para 28.12**) that JFSC apparently identified the *Caversham* AML-CFT offences during their onsite inspection visit. However, there may first have been unofficial tip-offs.

Note also that even regulators are not perfect: the former executive director of the Grenada International Financial Services Authority (Michael Creft) was famously described as 'the village idiot of offshore regulators'.

THE EFFECT OF REGULATION

14.3.2 Being regulated obviously raises standards, service quality and professionalism, and can only therefore be positive for the 'customer'. However there is one evident side-effect, namely that the rising high tide of regulation in some of the more mature Trust Jurisdictions has made trustees in those jurisdictions increasingly risk-conscious and defensive, and with one eye always looking in *'the rear view mirror'* in case their regulator might spring a surprise inspection and find something (however trivial) that could lead to criticism. This can ultimately be a drag on service quality. And it triggers a debate as to whether 'too much regulation' is a 'good thing'.

The Economist of 16 February 2013 reported in relation to Jersey that the Island had tried to turn regulation to its advantage, marketing itself as being at the high value respectable end of the tax haven industry. But 'its time consuming rules for everything from corporate registration to verifying the provenance of bank deposits are scaring off clean as well as dirty business.'

The trick, therefore, is to find the right balance.

OPENING ACCOUNTS FOR TRUSTS

14.3.3   As we all know, this is becoming more and more difficult! The STEP Journal commented in January 2011 that:

> 'Every Trust Officer's least favourite job is dealing with the administration of opening a new bank account. The costs to service providers (and consequently to their clients) in terms of staff time and effort required to deal with what used to be a simple operation, have escalated beyond all expectation in recent years'.

TSPs: REPORTING BY TRUSTEES AND MANDATE PROVISIONS TO DEAL WITH AML-CFT AND REPORTING

14.4.1   In the *Nearco* case in Jersey (Royal Court, August 2002) the Deputy Bailiff had to consider the consequences of a fiduciary business filing a SAR in response to a client instruction for them to resign all positions and transfer the company to another jurisdiction. Paragraph 17 of the judgment found as follows:' [w]e fully accept that Quorum acted in good faith, but in our judgment it was wholly mistaken in the attitude that it adopted'. In other words, they could not (with judicial hindsight) have had a suspicion, and should not have filed a SAR. In consequence, the fiduciary business was ordered to bear the costs of the hearing. And see on 'Suspicion' (the standard) at **7.5**.

14.4.2   The State of Qatar litigation in Jersey is an offshore trust case involving a SAR. It began in July 2000, when the trustees filed an SAR, and continued until the day the Iraq war broke out in March 2003. There were two main sets of concerns: first as to corruption arising by way of commissions paid to three Jersey trusts by arms companies; and secondly that the trust fund might properly be held on constructive trust for the State of Qatar, rather than for the individual beneficiaries of the trusts in question.

In response to an application brought by Sheikh Hamad (the then Foreign Minister of Qatar), as beneficiary of the trusts, the Jersey Royal Court apparently declared on 17 May 2001 that there was no breach of fiduciary duty owed to the State of Qatar, and there was no constructive trust in favour of the State of Qatar or any other person.

However, as the trustees had made an SAR, but had not received any form of consent from the Jersey police, they were caught on the horns of a dilemma. The Jersey police were unwilling (ie had refused) to grant consent to any distribution from the trusts at what was said to be an early stage of a complex enquiry. The effect of the police refusal to grant *consent* was in effect to paralyse the administration of the trusts, and to expose the trustees to liability for breach of trust.

In the summer of 2001, Sheikh Hamad made a second application, seeking directions from the Court:

> '… that will enable the trustees to resume the administration of [the trusts] in accordance with their terms within such a time and to such an extent as may be reasonable in all the circumstances of the case.'

The Jersey Attorney-General objected to this application, contending that it would be contrary to public policy to grant the Order sought, because the Sheikh's clear collateral purpose was to use any declaration granted to hinder any criminal investigation and any subsequent criminal proceedings (presumably by asking the trustees to transfer the trust assets out of Jersey).

An article entitled 'The State of Qatar and Jersey – the litigation and the lessons for trustees' by Simon Gould and David Hopwood of Mourant du Feu & Jeune, Jersey ((2003) 2(3) STEP Journal Quarterly Review 17) notes how the trustee found itself on the horns of a dilemma between the risk of prosecution for a ML offence, and liability for a breach of trust:

> 'On the assumption that a trustee will normally risk civil liability for a breach of trust rather than a criminal prosecution, this also means that the police have, in effect, acquired the ability to freeze assets which are suspected to be the proceeds of criminal conduct, for an indefinite period, simply by refusing a trustee's request for consent to distribute those assets.'

Given the formal procedures and safeguards that exist in Jersey for the Attorney-General to apply for a *saisie judiciaire,* this shortcut method is unusually oppressive, and provides a vivid example of where the offshore jurisdictions need to emulate the strict time frames that are already laid down in the United Kingdom (see **12.5**).

The article also notes how unsatisfactory it is that the law 'should place professional trustees in such a dilemma when they are endeavouring to assist the criminal justice system'.

The article ends with a review of possible countermeasures that a trustee can adopt to resolve being caught in such a dilemma. One interesting suggestion is that fiduciaries should arrange for a release from liability for breaches of trust in the event an SAR is made on reasonable grounds. As noted at **15.6**, whilst it would certainly be wise for CSPs to amend their terms of business accordingly, it is less easy for trustees to do so, as to be most effective the provision would have to be included within the trust itself, which may not be capable of being amended without consent of the Court.

CAVERSHAM TRUSTEES CASE, JERSEY

14.4.3 The *Caversham Trustees* case in Jersey was a criminal prosecution brought against a trust company and one of its directors for AML-CFT offences dating back to 2002. The facts emerged as a result of an onsite inspection visit by the Jersey Financial Services Commission (JFSC). Following their AML-CFT convictions, the Royal Court passed sentence on 25 November 2005, fining the Caversham companies a total of £65,000 and Mr. Bell £35,000: in addition the defendants were ordered to pay the prosecution costs. A full case note is located in **Appendix 8** courtesy of *Mourants* and see also **Appendix 9** at para 28.125.

PUBLIC REGISTER OF PSCs OF TRUSTS

14.5 This initiative is in its early days. It is a spin-off from the EU AML-CFT policies, as reflected in the March 2014 amendments to 4MLD. The proposal involves identifying and disclosing 'people with significant control' (or 'PSCs') in relation to the 'beneficial ownership' of trusts (and see **6.3**, **10.5** and **Appendix 1.3**).

The proposal is highly political, since the UK is one of very few EU MS that uses trusts, and it smacks of 'Trust Bashing' by the Civil Law non-trust jurisdictions (see **14.13**). The UK Government is less in favour of transparency for trusts than transparency of beneficial ownership of companies, but the other MS do not generally support the UK's position.

The proposal is highly controversial within the trust industry, and is also being studied within the OFCs (see for example the May 2014 review entitled 'A Public Register of Beneficial Ownership' prepared by Jersey Finance as a briefing document for interested parties).

Actual implementation of a public register of Trust PSCs is fraught with difficulties, and raises complex issues that are beyond the scope of this Edition of this book. And as the driving force behind Public Registers is the countering of tax evasion, it must be questioned whether this additional layer of complexity is actually needed, given the global trend towards AEOI as reflected in FATCA (**8.14** and **9.6**), the OECD Multilateral Convention on Administrative Assistance in Tax Matters (**9.8** and **Appendix 4**) and the CRS (**9.9**).

AML-CFT ENFORCEMENT ACTIONS AGAINST TRUSTS AND UNDERLYING COMPANIES

14.6 See **Appendix 9** in relation to this. In addition, the Mauritius Court of Appeal in 2005 confirmed the freeze order over the Bank account of a company owned by a trust, on the grounds that the company was engaged in a criminal activity and the money in the account represented 'the proceeds of crime': *Mauritius, ex p ICAC* [2005] SCJ 72.

EXECUTORS AND PROBATE

14.7   For completeness, it is appropriate to look briefly at executorships and will trusts.

In the United Kingdom, probate business is not a 'regulated sector' unless the executor is, or is advised by, a legal professional. In any event a Court approved Grant of Probate or Letters of Administration is first required.

The likelihood of ML occurring in connection with a deceased's estate is extremely low, as death is generally not a premeditated 'transaction'. Nevertheless, AML-CFT rules will still generally apply, so that those involved should still consider filing an SAR if they have relevant suspicions.

Perhaps, persons named as executors in a will, who discover the appointment only after the death of the testator, will have to conduct retroactive due diligence on the business and affairs of the deceased prior to accepting the appointment, however, it is always open to them to renounce.

There should also be a general *caveat* in respect of legacies or donations to minor or obscure charities established in jurisdictions where there is little or no charitable regulation. In this regard FATF Recommendation Notes on charities are of interest (see **Appendix 2.1**).

Consider also the issues that an Executor is faced with on discovering a secret or undisclosed bank or investment account as part of the deceased's Estate. In such circumstances, entering a Disclosure/Amnesty program is likely to be the only course of action.

CONSTRUCTIVE TRUST ISSUES

14.8   The risk of being found liable as a constructive trustee is of great importance. The funding of a trust with property not belonging to the 'Settlor' raises complex tracing rights and remedies, and in such circumstances, the trustees could find themselves holding a trust fund on constructive trust for the defrauded party (for cases on constructive trusts see *Paragon Financier Plc v D B Thakerar & Co* [1999] 1 All ER 400, CA and *Foskett v McKeown* [2000] 3 All ER 97; [2000] 2 WLR1299 HL). As the funds themselves are the proceeds of the fraud, they constitute laundered money, and a suspicious activity report (SAR) is appropriate. If they have, in the meantime, paid the funds away, they may be liable to reinstate the true owner in the full amount, thus being exposed to a financial double jeopardy.

Even partial funding with property not belonging to the settlor raises the same issues of constructive trust for the defrauded party, or the foreign revenue authority that is due the unpaid tax. This position will always arise in the event of proven criminality, in contrast, a settlor's pre-existing civil indebtedness, or civil judgment debt, will only give rise to a constructive trusteeship in narrowly-defined circumstances.

As noted at **4.2**, constructive trust issues arose in *Bank of Scotland v A Ltd* [2001] EWCA Civ 52 which illustrates the tensions between criminal law provisions relating to tipping-off and the potential civil liability that may arise if an institution deals with the proceeds of a serious crime. In this case, the bank applied to the Courts for directions as to what it should do, and the Court made an Order freezing the accounts. The customer whose account had been frozen (and who had not been notified of the reason) brought proceedings for the release of the funds.

At first instance, Laddie J laid down guidelines as to what an institution should do in the future, either if it wants to make payments from the account, or if it does not. The Court of Appeal did not endorse the guidelines, but did confirm the likelihood of a constructive trust arising in circumstances of suspicion of its customer's dishonesty. However, the Court suggested that the Serious Fraud Office should have been made a party to the directions application.

The standard of 'knowledge' is central to the 'constructive trustee' issue (as noted in **7.5**): and the case law on constructive trusts identifies different degrees of knowledge:

- actual knowledge;

- 'Nelsonian' knowledge; and

- imputed or constructive knowledge (see *Baden Delvaux v Société Générale 1992; Royal Brunei Airlines v Tan* [1995] 2 AC 378 and *BCCI (Overseas) v Akindele* [2000] 4 All ER 221).

In the *State of Qatar* case (see **14.4.2**) a trust beneficiary brought an application and obtained confirmation of the Jersey Royal Court that there was no constructive trust in favour of the State of Qatar or any other person. This was a highly unusual form of application, but showed what could be done if the circumstances require unusual action.

The *Esteem (Abacus (CI)) Ltd, Trustee of the Esteem Settlement v Grupo Torras SA* [2003] JCR 092) case in Jersey is a graphic example of claims against a trust alleging assets tainted by fraud, infringement of public policy, and seeking a remedial constructive trust to be grafted on so as to provide restitution to the victim of the fraud. Wherever a constructive trust is found, a SAR should not be far behind (see the discussion on *Tracing* in **5.9**).

Most recently the UK Supreme Court in *FHR European Ventures LLP & Ors v Cedar Capital Partners LLC* [2014] UKSC 45 analysed the treatment of bribes and secret commissions, holding that these are held on constructive trust for the principal. Lord Neuberger's single short judgement is worthy of study, not least as the decision overruled the 1890 decision in the *Lister* case [1890] 45 ChD 1, and substantially overruled the decision in the *Sinclair* case [2012] Ch 453 (and see **Chapter 19** on Bribery & Corruption).

COMMON FAILINGS

14.9   The first rule of ML prevention is to recognise and deal with one's own weaknesses (and see **15.6**). Once you understand why you or your business is attractive to the wrong type of client, you are well placed to erect meaningful AML-CFT defences.

Conversely, the more control powers over a trust that are reserved by or delegated back to a client, the more vulnerable you become to ML risk. Therefore, fiduciaries should monitor common forms of delegated control such as powers of attorney, bank signatory rights and direct access to funds via, for example, credit cards.

At a macro level, there may be a rebuttable presumption of 'suspicion' in any transaction involving any of the three FATF 'monitoring status' countries (Myanmar, Nigeria and Indonesia) or any of the five countries/ jurisdictions on the OECD 'NCCT' list (Liechtenstein, Monaco, Liberia, the Marshall Islands and Andorra). Plus of course the 'Sanctioned' countries (Cuba, Iran, DPR Korea, Sudan/South Sudan and Syria). But in reality, it is also transactions with some 119 or so other 'Higher Risk Jurisdictions' (non-EU, non-EEA, non-OECD and non-FATF) that will also raise queries according to lists maintained by some of the leading banks (see **11.7, 11.18, 16.5** and **Appendix 5**).

And dealings with countries at the bad end or the Transparency International Corruption Perceptions Index (CPI) or Bribe Payers Index (BPI) will also raise a presumption that enhanced due diligence is called for (see **11.15**).

And there should also be a strong presumption of 'suspicion' in any transaction involving a politically exposed person (PEP). This may be a more difficult issue to check, although recourse can now be to the database services referred to in **14.9**. Although major public figures are a household name (especially in their home countries), monitoring all possibilities of relationship is difficult, as the PEP concept extends not only a government official, but also to relatives of a government official, or even to their business associates.

As noted in **Chapter 7** and **18.12**, the slippery slope for the offshore industry lies in where the definition and concept of the AML-CFT 'proceeds of crime' test will extend, as it would appear to bring within its scope any of the following types of payment either arising out of false or sham documentation, or where the recipient of the funds is not clearly reporting them for tax:

- commissions;
- fees;
- brokers' fees and other similar remuneration;
- subcontract payments; or
- consulting agreements;

all of which 'proceeds' can be the 'proceeds of crime' for AML-CFT purposes. So, professionals and practitioners involved with offshore trusts and offshore companies (and the bankers to offshore trusts and offshore companies) must exercise the utmost vigilance.

BLACKLISTED JURISDICTIONS

14.10   Dealings with any jurisdiction on the FATF 'blacklist' or any OECD 'NCCT will raise a presumption of risk. A transaction or payment involving any of these countries/jurisdictions requires considerably more CDD, and may be blocked.

In reality, there is a wider 'blacklist' of some 85 or so other countries (that are non-EU, non-EEA, non-OECD non-FATF) with whom transactions or payments in or out are likely to be regarded initially with concern, and then at risk of being elevated to suspicions! See **15.9** and **Appendix 2**.

REFERENCE RESOURCES

14.11

STEP AML Commentary (in relation to Trusts)

14.11.1
The current STEP AML commentary is available on the STEP website at www.step.org. The original STEP AML Commentary (2004) is a helpful reference: the following passages from section 3 should be noted:

> 'Often, for drafting reasons a trust deed will include a wide class of beneficiaries, many of whom are not entitled to benefit from the trust fund other than in remoter circumstances. Instructions to verify every future contingent beneficiary might be unduly onerous and in certain circumstances impossible. FATF Recommendation 10 (February 2012) allows financial institutions to determine the extent of the customer due diligence measures on a risk sensitive basis depending on the type of customer, business relationship or transaction.

> 'In low risk cases and in order not to interrupt the normal conduct of business, practitioners should be permitted to undertake the verification of beneficiaries after having established the business relationship. However, in all such cases, verification of beneficiaries should occur prior to a distribution of assets.

> 'For example in the case of a beneficiary in a discretionary trust who is entitled to a distribution when he or she reaches the age of twenty-one and who is presently a minor, there would be no verification process required until distribution was expected. Since the aim is to prevent criminals from having access to the trust assets, this effectively manages the money laundering risks.

> 'However verification should be initiated at the outset where the money laundering risk is considered high even if a distribution is not in immediate prospect.'

Case studies – 'trustees as money launderers'

14.11.2   Over ten years ago, the Law Society of Hong Kong hosted a presentation by James Wadham and Shane Kelly entitled *Trustees as money launderers*. This title was chosen deliberately to get the attention of solicitors in Hong Kong, many of whom may not have hitherto realised the scope of the AML-CFT legislation. Whilst OSCO in Hong Kong derives from different sources than the UK PoCA, its effect is broadly similar.

Appendix 8 contains some of the case studies used in the presentation. Although these are now over three years old, they were taken very much from day-to-day fiduciary life in Hong Kong. They still merit careful study, as some of the types of client, the planning structures adopted, and the behaviour of the fiduciaries involved (trustees or CSPs) can be found in just about any jurisdiction, both onshore and offshore.

In addition, consider the complex AML-CFT aspects of a fiduciary business becoming involved with superficial documentation, whether a sham trust, or bogus sham or false commercial agreements (so-called consultancy agreements, agency commission agreements, loan agreements, etc.).

In relation to international trading activities, private trading companies (PTCs) may be used in customs fraud, by under- (or over-) invoicing, or by relying on forged documents such as false certificates of origin or bills of lading. Re-invoicing operations by a PTC also raises AML-CFT and reporting issues.

Lord Millett's reasoning in the *Agip (Africa) Ltd* case (see quote at **7.5.3** is equally applicable in current AML-CFT era to any sort of arrangement that facilitates 'just' foreign tax evasion. Lord Millett's speech in the important stamp duty case in the Hong Kong Court of Final Appeal – *Comr of Stamp Revenue v Arrowtown Assets Ltd*, 4 December 2003 – is also illustrative. With a nod to *Ozymandias*, 'Offshore fiduciaries should tremble and beware'!

'TRUST BASHING': THE SUPRA-NATIONAL INITIATIVES AND PERCEPTION ISSUES

14.12   The offshore world first came into the headlights of the supranational bodies back in 1998 (when the OECD published '*Harmful Tax Competition: An Emerging Global Issue*') and what this Author describes as "Offshore Bashing" and "Trust Bashing" has continued more or less continuously since then.

To illustrate, 2006 saw the publication of three 'Offshore Bashing' and 'Trust Bashing' reports:

- 'Tax Cooperation – Towards a Level Playing Field' (OECD, 29 May 2006);
- 'Tax Haven Abuses: The enablers, the Tools and Secrecy', US Senate Permanent Committee on Investigations, (1 August 2006); and

- 'The Misuse of Corporate Vehicles, including TSPs and CSPs' (FATF, 13 October 2006).

The abortive US 'Stop Tax Haven Abuse' Bill (HR1554 sponsored in 2007 by Senator Carl Levin, then Senator Barack Obama and Senator Norm Coleman) listed 34 'offshore secrecy jurisdictions' to which the US Treasury estimated it was losing $100 billion in revenue annually. The response of the Cayman Islands in March 2007 was that they 'deeply resent and seek to dispel the idea that because we are not located onshore, we are illegitimate': this neatly summarised the problem.

Interestingly, in *The Regulation of Trust and Company Service Providers* (published by STEP in June 2006) the authors say that as their research progressed, they realised that suggestions from law enforcement agencies that trusts are popular vehicles for criminals to hide and launder money are 'an oversimplification and do not reflect the current state of regulation, or the efforts of many jurisdictions to counter ML'. In this Author's view, the real drivers of the continued growth in the international private client fiduciary sector are primarily estate and succession planning, and also legitimate tax planning structures both for individuals and commercial businesses.

Some reports had favourable aspects (in particular, the Edwards Report on the Crown Dependencies (commissioned by the UK Government), which described the Channel Islands and the Isle of Man as being in 'the top division' from a regulatory standpoint).

However, the perception remains that 'offshore is bad', and that both offshore trusts and offshore companies are also automatically bad. This, of course, is certainly not the case.

Publications of both OECD and FATF have consistently demonstrated a shockingly high level of technical confusion between companies and trusts (for example, referring to trusts as having 'beneficial owners', analogous to shareholders). The negative perception of both offshore trusts and offshore companies seems to have originated in the FATF 'Report on Money Laundering Typologies 2000–2001' (published (1 February 2001), wherein it states at para 29:

> '29. This exercise was the first to focus on trusts as another legal mechanism that could be misused for money laundering purposes. In many ways, this use is similar to and associated with the role of corporate entities and company formation agents discussed in earlier typologies studies. Consequently, the actions proposed by the experts this year for dealing with trusts should also be viewed in the larger context of confronting the misuse of all legal mechanisms for money laundering purposes, increasing transparency with regard to such formations, more closely ensuring the integrity of the professionals involved in the creation of these mechanisms, and working toward some universal standards that could preclude the establishment of systems in certain jurisdictions that facilitate and protect such misuse.'

Offshore structures certainly can be used to enable (or assist) people to hide income and assets, just as motor vehicles can be used to kill –although that is not the primary purpose of either. Private offshore companies such as an international business corporation (IBC) can provide highly effective vehicles for criminals to hide the proceeds of crime of all sorts, and for others to hide assets from family members, future creditors and others with legitimate expectations. Yet this is by no means exclusively an offshore problem, as shown by the burgeoning number of LLC incorporations in Delaware and other states of the United States.

To take the BCV Report as an example, trusts were also included in the remit, and the *Report* noted at para 25 that a trust is an important, useful, and legitimate vehicle for the transfer and management of assets. However, the BCV report also noted the 'dark side', whereby these entities are, under certain conditions, misused for illicit purposes, including ML, bribery/corruption, hiding and shielding assets from creditors, illicit tax practices, self-dealing/defrauding assets/diversion of assets, market fraud, circumvention of disclosure requirements, and other forms of illicit behaviour:

The BCV Report noted that part of the attractiveness of misusing trusts lies in the fact that trusts enjoy a greater degree of privacy and anonymity than other corporate vehicles. 'Given the private nature of trusts and the fact that a trust is essentially a contractual agreement between two private persons, virtually all jurisdictions recognising trusts have purposely chosen not to regulate trusts like other corporate vehicles such as corporations. This also means that, unlike corporations, there are no registration requirements or central registries and there are no authorities charged with overseeing trusts' (p 25). Although current moves may change this, the fallacy in these reports and studies is that just because something is *capable* of being abused does not automatically mean that the vast majority of people will or do abuse it. The vast majority of trusts are perfectly legitimate in the same way as the vast majority of people are law-abiding citizens

Other reports (including those mentioned in **14.14**) have continued the general (and specific) offshore trust/offshore company bashing tendencies. And most recently, The Economist in its 9th November 2013 issue put the extreme position thus:

> 'So-called discretionary trusts are particularly open to abuse. Their assets sit in a kind of ownerless limbo; given away, legally speaking, but without a recipient, so long as beneficiaries are not defined. They may even be children or grand-children as yet unborn. Trustees can be guided by a 'letter of wishes' which may allow the settlor to control assets even though legally they do not belong to him. Such trusts are an 'important and tricky' issue for tax authorities, says Konstantin Lozev, a European Commission official.'

And in its leader in the same edition stated that:

> '...trust law has become a murky world' and a concept '...that was set up to protect the wives of medieval crusaders has ended

up being used by the sort of businesspeople who greet the Russian leader as 'Vladimir'.

Charming!

THE PROBLEM OF INSTITUTIONAL TAX EVASION

14.13   **Chapter 13** looked at the wider issues that affect international private banking. The same wider issues affect offshore fiduciaries and CSPs.

A December 2003 paper to the STEP winter conference by John Nugent (entitled *Practical implications of Money Laundering Regulations – Tax Evasion*, extracts of which are set out in **Appendix 9**) was of pinpoint accuracy in its examination of the potential implications of advanced AML-CFT for organisations that have, perhaps unconsciously, assisted in the evasion of taxes. Mr. Nugent notes that tax evasion involves some blameworthy act or omission *and is in reality equivalent to* fraud: in essence tax evasion involves the concealment of the true facts of an arrangement, in contrast to tax avoidance.

Mr. Nugent noted that regulation of trustees, CDD/KYC, and EoI is undermining offshore tax evasion, but that PoCA legislation will work to greater effect as it has fatally wounded 'institutionalised tax evasion', namely mass tax evasion facilitated by organisations who honestly do not know; or turn a blind eye to; or do not care about; or actively encourage the fact that their clients and customers are evading taxes. These organisations are normally based in offshore centres, although they may be owned by or have related entities in the onshore jurisdictions, those most immediately affected will be medium to large size organisations who have wide-ranging business interests beyond the entity containing the tax evasion arrangements, and whose executives sitting at the group headquarters may be blissfully unaware of what is being done in their name in some of their more remote outposts.

The recommendation is that offshore organisations providing offshore arrangements should review their services, to ensure that they are not running the risk of attracting new tax evasion arrangements; and should analyse their existing clients and customers to identify any existing tax evasion arrangements. Such organisations could be considered as 'critically ill' depending on the extent of their infection with tax evasion: if they are critically ill (ie a very substantial proportion of their business could be classed as tax evasion) they face serious and urgent problems. Prosecution could follow if tax evasion monies have been actively sought or the organisations welcomed such business when it arrived.

Perhaps, the most chilling comment is that:

> 'although incomprehensible to most onshore professionals, the fact is that such organisations do exist. And the fact is though that some onshore parents may not be fully aware of the deep seated problem that their seemingly successful offshore children have stored up'.

Mr. Nugent concludes that sale of such a business is unlikely to be viable as there may not be much worth selling, and the market for certain sorts of businesses has already evaporated, so there may therefore be no choice but to break up the business.

These are harsh views indeed, but they simply describe the observed reality in most if not all of the offshore financial centres, and the issue of the 'legacy book' described in **8.13**.

Chapter 15

CSPs: specific issues

INTRODUCTION

15.1 FATF Recommendation 24 (aiming at 'transparency and beneficial ownership of legal persons) make it clear that CSPs are within the FATF remit:

> '24. Countries should take measures to prevent the misuse of legal persons for money laundering or terrorist financing. Countries should ensure that there is adequate, accurate and timely information on the beneficial ownership and control of legal persons that can be obtained or accessed in a timely fashion by competent authorities. In particular, countries that have legal persons that are able to issue bearer shares or bearer share warrants, or *which allow nominee shareholders or nominee directors*, should take effective measures to ensure that they are not misused for money laundering or terrorist financing. Countries should consider measures to facilitate access to beneficial ownership and control information by financial institutions and DNFBPs undertaking the requirements set out in Recommendations 10 and 22.' [Author's emphasis]

Within the United Kingdom, CSPs have been within the regulated sector since 2007: and reg 2 (8) of the Money Laundering Regulations 2007 (SI 2007/2157) applies to every 'relevant business', which includes UK CSPs (based on the requirements of 3MLD) (see **6.4**).

Part 4 of the Regulations (regs 22–35) deals with supervision and registration. Regulations 25–30 relate in particular to the registration of CSPs, and within this group of regulations, the 'fit and proper test' is contained in reg 28, as a negative clearance approach (whereby an applicant will not be registered as a F&PP if they possess any of the negative indicia (convictions etc).

In July 2013, HMR&C published their updated *'Notice MLR9C Registration Guide for Trust or Company Service Providers*. This is the new OECD-driven transparency regime in the UK.

In most of the offshore jurisdictions, CSPs have been subject to licencing and regulation for many years, either by falling within the definition of 'Fiduciary' for fiduciary regulation (eg Guernsey and Jersey), or specifically as 'CSPs' (as distinct from 'TSPs'). Some jurisdictions (eg Singapore and Hong Kong) still do not licence or regulate CSPs other than by virtue of the general law, including AML-CFT provisions.

It is beyond the scope of this book to list or analyse the statutory provisions whereby CSPs themselves are regulated in the jurisdictions cited: reference on this can be made to 'The Regulation of Trust and Company Service Providers' (STEP, June 2006), to STEP's Jurisdiction Guides www.step.org and to the relevant FSC or Monetary Authority websites in each jurisdiction.

15.2 'Core CDD': Proof of identity/Proof of residence (and verification)

These items are non-negotiable, and must be provided by the Client/UBO(s). If there are intermediate entities in the shareholder chain, these must also all 'undress' until the individual(s) is/are identified. So this is normal, logical and consistent.

Additional CDD

15.3   Many CSPs demand additional CDD, including details of the following:

- any bank accounts in the name of the PIC/PTC;
- any assets in the name of the PIC/PTC;
- any company 'connected with' the PIC/PTC;
- specific activities carried out by the PIC/PTC; and
- the countries where those activities are conducted.

If the CSP were providing directors or bank account signatories (what the Author calls 'fully in') then some of these items would be justifiable. But it is hard to understand the need for this level of information if all that the CSP is doing is acting as registered office and registered agent/company secretary (what the Author calls 'fully out'). And the legal basis for demanding this even is less clear.

APPROVED CERTIFIERS

15.4   As noted at **11.9**, one well-known Asia-based CSP has its own 'Certification of Due Diligence' Form (relating to CDD Proof of Identity and Proof of Residence), to be executed by the 'Approved Certifier', who must be one of the following:

- Notary Public;
- Certified Public Accountant;
- Registrar/Deputy-Registrar of a Court;
- Justice of the Peace '(JP');
- Legal practitioner/solicitor;
- An officer or employee of a licensed bank, trust company or insurance company in a 'recognised jurisdiction';
- An associate member of the Hong Kong Institute of Chartered Secretaries ('HKICS');

- An associate member of the Singapore Association of the Institute of Chartered Secretaries and Administrators ('SAICSA').

CSPs: APPOINTMENT OF FIRST DIRECTORS

15.5   As noted in **11.13**, some FSBs used to 'gold plate' by asking for certified copies of the 'appointment of first directors' of offshore companies, along with the other standard documentation normally required. Happily this 'gold plating' exercise has now ceased. Itw as pointless anyway, as most 'first director' appointments are provided by the incorporating CSP themselves, prior to handing the company over to the 'end user'. Very few ultimate clients take on 'first director' appointments.

CSPs: MANDATE PROVISIONS TO DEAL WITH AML-CFT AND REPORTING

15.6   Given the observations in **15.3**, it is appropriate to ask whether CSPs need to respond to the AML-CFT challenges in any specific way over and beyond the legal and regulatory requirements?

CSPs should of course amend their mandates or terms of business so as to allow (or restrict) certain types of activity: sample wording might comprise:

- **'Source of Funds and Prevention of Money Laundering and Countering the Financing of Terrorism**: The client acknowledges that the funds entrusted to CSP derive solely from the activities described herein, that he/she is not and will not be engaged in any illegal activities and that the origin of the funds entrusted or to be entrusted are not and will not be connected in any way to the proceeds of serious crime (AML-CFT) as defined by law. In addition, the client acknowledges that CSP may be required to disclose any suspicions it may have to the relevant AML-CFT authorities in its jurisdiction, and is hereby exonerated for not advising the client in the event of any such disclosure

- **Confidentiality**: CSP undertakes to treat all information contained herein as strictly personal and confidential and to make use of it solely for the purpose of performing its duties hereunder and/or for the purpose of complying with current applicable requirements, such as but not restricted to maintaining adequate records in accordance with applicable procedures for the prevention of money laundering (AML-CFT) and/or for opening and maintaining banking relations with Banks on behalf of the Client.'

Of course, confidentiality has been an issue of late, and the famous 'data leaks' at Commonwealth and at PTN in early 2013 sent shock-waves through the industry (see **9.3** and **Appendix 11**), and upset many of the UBOs of such PICs.

PUBLIC REGISTER OF PSCs OF COMPANIES

15.7   As noted at 14.5 this initiative is in its early days, and is a spin off from the EU AML-CFT policies, as reflected in the March 2014 amendments to 4MLD. The proposal involves identifying 'people with significant control' (or 'PSCs') in relation to the beneficial ownership of companies, and for that information to be filed with the local Registrar of Companies, where it will be open for public inspection. 'Significant control' currently means individuals with an interest in more than 25% of the voting rights, or who otherwise control the management of a company. This type of information is not currently available or publicly searchable in most financial centres (whether onshore or offshore) or there is a limited disclosure requirement in the accounts of companies from an EU MS in respect of who such a company regards as its 'controller' or 'ultimate controlling party'.

The UK Government is in favour of transparency of beneficial ownership of companies, and wants to impose it within the British OFCs (the overseas territories and possessions), where it is currently being studied [see for example the May 2014 review entitled 'A Public Register of Beneficial Ownership' prepared by Jersey Finance as a briefing document for interested parties].

The driving force behind such Public Registers is the countering of tax evasion. However it must be questioned whether this additional layer will serves any practical purpose, given the global trend towards AEOI as reflected in FATCA (**8.14** and **9.6**), the OECD Multilateral Convention on Administrative Assistance in Tax Matters (**9.8** and **Appendix 4**) and by the CRS (**9.9**).

CSP INDUSTRY ISSUES

15.8   As noted in **14.13**, the first rule of ML prevention is to recognise and deal with one's own potential weaknesses and vulnerabilities. Once you understand why you or your CSP business may be attractive to the wrong type of client, you are well placed to erect meaningful AML-CFT defences.

Where the CSP is 'fully out', it's hard to see what they should do to 'monitor', or what legal basis they might cite for so doing. The more direct 'control' a client has over the PIC/PTC then the less oversight abilities the CSP has, or arguably needs to have.

Conversely, where the CSP is 'fully in', but the CSP has also delegated control back to the Client (such as by a power of attorney, or direct access to the company's funds by, for example being bank signatory or having a credit card), then that is the point where the CSP becomes highly vulnerable and at risk of being connected to ML risk.

THE JASON SHARMAN CASE STUDY

15.9   During 2012, Professor Jason Sharman designed and carried out an experiment to test the willingness of CSPs around the world to accept business introductions by email or fax from his research team, posing as wealthy individuals from different backgrounds, and with three customer profiles:

- Baseline: respectable retired family man from a small EU/OECD country;

- West African or Central Asian government officer with procurement responsibilities;

- Citizen of one of four Islamic countries perceived as having a high terrorism risk, working for an Islamic Charity in Saudi Arabia.

The results are fascinating, and demonstrate that the OFCs were the most rigorous in turning away the 'Dodgy Shoppers', whilst the onshore countries were fairly indifferent to the degree of dodginess. The full result of the study is available from j.sharman@griffith.edu.au along with a 'Table of Dodginess' of 54 countries, showing as the most compliant the UAE, Seychelles, Jordan, Jersey, Israel, Denmark, Cayman and Bahamas; and among the least compliant, possibly surprisingly Canada and the US.

BLACKLISTED JURISDICTIONS

15.10   Dealings with any jurisdiction on the FATF 'blacklist' or any OECD 'NCCT will raise a presumption of risk. A transaction or payment involving any of these countries/jurisdictions requires considerably more CDD, and may be blocked.

In reality, there is a wider 'blacklist' of some 85 or so other countries (that are non-EU, non-EEA, non-OECD non-FATF) with whom transactions or payments in or out are likely to be regarded initially with concern, and then at risk of being elevated to suspicions!

Dealings with countries at the 'bad end' of TI's CPI or BPI will also raise a presumption that enhanced due diligence is called for (see **11.15**).

Bribery and corruption is also an ML issue – see **18.1**. As these 'proceeds' can be the 'proceeds of crime' for AML-CFT purposes, then CSPs to offshore PICs/ PTCs must exercise the utmost vigilance.

Chapter 16

Banks (internal policies) and investment managers – specific issues

INTRODUCTION: BANKS ARE ONE OF THE 'KEY GATEKEEPERS' IN THE AML-CFT WAR

16.1 Customer Due Diligence (CDD) has taken on paramount importance for banks, since it is their raw material (money) that inevitably forms the subject matter of AML-CFT investigations. In addition, as banks tend to be, by their nature, both risk-averse and large and publicly identifiable institutions, they have a far greater sensitivity to being connected with AML-CFT scandals on the front pages of business newspapers such as the Financial Times, International New York Times/Herald Tribune or the Wall Street Journal.

For these reasons, banks tend to 'gold plate' the basis of AML-CFT requirements, by which is meant taking the published legal and regulatory standards as a starting point, then adapting them by additional requirements so as to be on the safe side.

CUSTOMER DUE DILIGENCE FOR BANKS

16.2 **Proof of identity; Proof of residence (verification of address)**

This is a standard requirement and is dealt with comprehensively in **11.2–11.11** above)

However two further aspects arise:

- Different banks applying differing requirements or standards of what they will accept as Proof of Identity or Proof of Residence (and see the September 2013 Report *'Bank Accounts: problems of identification'* issued by the UK House of Commons Library and included in **Appendix 5**); and

- The similar but broader issue of 'Gold-Plating', whereby Banks go beyond the basic CDD requirements (see in detail at **11.13** and elsewhere).

RISK PROFILING

16.3 As each FSB is best placed to decide the risk profile of its own customer base, the following risk criteria (which are not in order of importance and should not be considered exhaustive) must be considered in isolation or in combination:

- turnover;
- geographical origin of customer;
- geographical sphere of customer's activities;
- nature of activity (eg whether trading or identified as 'sensitive' by an Island regulator);
- frequency of activity;
- type and complexity of account/business relationship;
- value of account/business relationship;
- customer type, eg potentates/politically exposed persons;
- whether Hold All Mail ('HAM') arrangements are in place;
- whether an account/business relationship is dormant;
- whether there is any form of delegated authority in place (e.g. power of attorney, 'mixed' boards and representative offices);
- cash withdrawals/placement activity in or outside the jurisdiction; and
- suspicion or knowledge of money laundering or other crime.

TRIGGER EVENTS

16.4   The following are regarded as 'trigger events', and justify (in isolation or in combination) a CDD update review:

- a significant transaction (relative to a relationship);
- a material change in the operation of a business relationship;
- a transaction which is out of keeping with previous activity;
- a new product or account being established within an existing relationship;
- a change in an existing relationship which increases a risk profile;
- the early redemption of a fixed-term investment or insurance product;
- the assignment or transfer of ownership of any product;
- a non-regular 'top-up' of an existing insurance product;
- the addition of or a change to a principal in any relationship;
- the roll-over of any fixed-term product (taking into account the length of the roll-over period); and
- an insurance claim.

and the above is not to be considered an exhaustive list.

The reference to 'an initial CDD review' arises through FSBs having been set the gargantuan task of reviewing CDD on all account relationships, and their practical need to phase these reviews over time.

There is discretion on FSBs to update CDD on any account at any time. But there is perhaps excessive leeway in the broadly formulated 'material change in the operation of a business relationship'. The Author recalls one case where the FSB ordered a full updated CDD on the stated basis that one of the signatories on a corporate account has done nothing more sinister than request a cheque-book for the company.

BANKING INITIATIVES

The 'Wolfsberg AML Principles'

16.5   The Wolfsberg Group comprises 11 of the world's leading private banks (so-called because important working sessions were held in the Wolfsberg Centre of UBS in north-east Switzerland).

> Banco Santander, Bank of Tokyo-Mitsubishi, Barclays, Citigroup, Credit Suisse, Deutsche Bank, Goldman Sachs, HSBC, JP Morgan Chase, Société Générale and UBS.

The 'Wolfsberg AML Principles' (see www.wolfsberg-prinicples.com) were first published on 30 October 2000, by way of a formal AML-CFT policy statement. These global AML-CFT guidelines are aimed primarily at international private bankers, including both relationship managers and those involved with fiduciary activities in the offshore havens. The principles were drawn up in conjunction with Transparency International (the global anticorruption organisation, see **18.11**). The initial Principles were a response to scandals and events over the then preceding two years, and at the time were the latest word on appropriate KYC (CDD) policies, guidelines for dealing with international HNWI and UHNWI clients, and identification and follow-up of unusual or suspicious transactions.

The current Wolfsberg AML Principles 2012 remain an important document: they are reproduced in **Appendix 5** together with a very useful set of FAQs with *'Regard to Beneficial Ownership in the Context of Private Banking'*. Topically it is worth citing the joint study 'Performance of Swiss Private Banks' published in September 2014 by KPMG and the University of St Gallen.

To those with experience in IPB and the offshore field, the principles will seem pretty much like an exercise in common sense, and as such contain no surprises; the key points and procedural requirements are as follows:

(a)   Accept only those clients whose source of wealth and funds can be reasonably established to be legitimate. Primary responsibility for this lies with the private banker who sponsors the client for acceptance, and mere fulfilment of internal review procedure does not relieve the private banker of this basic responsibility. In other words, slavishly following a checklist is insufficient.

(b) The identity of natural persons will be established by reference to official identity papers (note that identification documents must be current at the time).

(c) Beneficial ownership must be established for all accounts. Due diligence must be done on all principal beneficial owners identified in accordance with the following principles:

- *individuals* – establish whether the client is acting on his/her own behalf. If doubt exists, establish the capacity in which and on whose behalf the account holder is acting;

- *offshore companies* – understand the structure of the company sufficiently to determine the provider of funds, principal owner(s) of the shares and those who have control over the funds (eg the directors) and those with the power to give direction to the directors of the company;

- *trusts* – understand the structure of the trust sufficiently to determine the provider of funds (eg the Settlor), those who have control over the funds (eg the trustees), and any persons or entities who have the power to remove the trustees (eg a protector).

(d) Due diligence information must be collected and recorded covering the following categories:

- purpose and reasons for opening the account;

- anticipated account activity;

- source of wealth (description of the economic activity which has generated the net worth);

- estimated net worth;

- source of funds (description of the origin and the means of transfer for monies that are accepted for the account opening); and

- references or other sources to corroborate reputation information where available.

(e) Unless other measures reasonably suffice to conduct the due diligence on a client (eg favourable and reliable references), a client will be met prior to account opening.

(f) Additional diligence/heightened scrutiny is required on clients and beneficial owners resident in and funds sourced from 'high-risk countries' (ie countries having inadequate anti-money laundering standards, or representing a high risk for crime and corruption).

(g) Additional diligence/heightened scrutiny is also required on clients and beneficial owners who hold public offices, who have (or have had) positions of public trust (such as government officials, senior executives of government corporations, politicians, important political party officials, etc) and their families and close associates. These can be referred to as a politically exposed person (PEP) or a politically sensitive person (PSP).

(h) Legitimate aids to identifying unusual or suspicious activities may include:

– monitoring of transactions;

– contacts (meetings, discussions, in–country visits, etc);

– third–party information (eg newspapers, Reuters, the Internet); and

– knowledge of the client's environment (eg the political situation in his/her country).

Record retention requirements for all anti-money laundering related documents are that these must be retained for a minimum of six years. An interesting question arises in relation to this concept, as most institutions will err on the side of caution and retain more paperwork rather than less, thus raising a similar issue to that discussed in relation to audits of qualified intermediaries (see **Chapter 5**).

The two areas ('f' and 'g' above) where additional diligence/heightened scrutiny is required merit further comment:

● High-risk countries is not a concept defined in a single list. The FATF has its blacklist of jurisdictions (see **Appendix 5**). The OECD has its 'NCCT list (see **Appendix 4**). There are many countries that have never either been on or off the FATF blacklist, through never having been part of the FATF process in the first place (two extreme examples being Libya and Cuba). The Transparency International's (TI) Corruption Perceptions Index (CPI) and Bribe Payers Index (BPI) (see **11.18, 14.9, 15.10, 18.2** and **18.11**) provide a clear ranking of countries in terms of the risk for crime and corruption. However, there is no 'bright line' or cut-off point on the scale, above which it is fine to deal, and below which it is not. Customer Due Diligence requires professionals to be sure whether clients and beneficial owners are resident in, or funds are sourced from, such countries. Given that financial institutions dislike imprecision, many have taken to developing their own internal blacklists. Such lists will vary from institution to institution. And as it is always prudent to err on the side of safety, many of such lists will go wider than may have been strictly necessary.

● The issue of PEPs/PSPs, namely clients and beneficial owners who hold public offices, who have (or have had) positions of public trust, such as government officials, senior executives of government corporations, politicians, important political party officials, etc *and* their families *and* close associates (and see **10.10** and **11.15**). The driver here is the risk of corruption, by abuse of public funds and/or by corrupt payments and kickbacks on contract awards.

As noted, 3MLD refers in its Arts 3(8) and 13(4) to 'Politically Exposed Person's; and Directive 2006/70 (issued on 1 August 2006) contains measures to implement EU Directive 2005/60 on the definition of 'Politically Exposed Person'.

There is an automatic presumption of 'suspicion' in any transaction involving a PEP, and therefore enhanced CDD is required in order to dispel this presumption. This may be a more difficult issue to check, although recourse can now be to database services (see **11.6**). Major public figures may be a household name (especially in their home countries), but monitoring all possibilities of relationship is difficult, as the PEP concept extends widely – not only to government officials, but also to relatives and even business associates of government officials.

There is a practical one-year cooling off period for retired PEPs whereby after a one-year break from any official position they resume their former non-PEP status (see **7.6** and Art.3.4 of EU Directive 2005/60).

OTHER WOLFSBERG GROUP INITIATIVES

16.6　The Group also identified areas for further discussion with governments. Three areas merit particular note:

- Governments should be more precise in publishing name lists, as Arabic names published in the Roman alphabet are capable of being spelled in numerous different ways.

- Governments should include better details on official lists, such as (for individuals) date of birth, place of birth and passport number, and (for companies) place of incorporation and details of principals, and in all cases stating the reason for inclusion on the list.

- Governments should permit financial institutions to report unusual or suspicious transactions that may relate to terrorism without breaching any duty of customer confidentiality.

In the AML-CFT field, the Wolfsberg Group has also published:

- a Statement on the Suppression of the Financing of Terrorism (January 2002);

- the Wolfsberg Anti-Money Laundering Principles for Correspondent Banking (November 2002);

- the Wolfsberg Statement on Monitoring Screening and Searching (September 2003);

- Development of a due diligence model for financial institutions, in co-operation with *Banker's Almanac*, thereby fulfilling one of the recommendations made in the Correspondent Banking Principles.

- Guidance on a Risk-Based Approach for Managing Money Laundering Risks (June 2006);

- FAQs on Beneficial Ownership (referred to above);

- FAQs on Politically Exposed Persons; and

- FAQs on Intermediaries.

These various papers make a valuable contribution to the fight against money laundering. As well as providing general assistance to industry participants and regulatory bodies when shaping their own policies and guidance.

ISSUES FOR THE BANKS

16.7   Although AML-CFT has supposedly moved away from 'Box Ticking' towards a risk weighted approach, the benefits of this have not yet filtered through to the consuming public. 'War stories' abound of banks imposing effective unilateral freezes on accounts that have been in operation for some time, just on the basis of some minor change within the setup (four example, the customer, merely requesting a cheque-book) (see 'trigger events' at **16.4**). Pending wire transfer instructions are secretly and unilaterally placed on hold, and apparently without any regard to the commercial consequences to the customer. All of this presupposes that there is no actual 'suspicion', and that no SAR has been made either internally or externally.

So what is the analysis for the bank? It would seem that, unless the bank has provisions within its banking mandate allowing it effectively to disregard any and all instructions at any and all times in its entire discretion and without giving a reason(!), then the bank would appear to be in breach of contract vis-a-vis the client. If so, then the bank would be engaging potential liability for any consequential and foreseeable loss flowing from that breach. See also the case of *Shah v HSBC Private Bank (UK) Limited* [2009] EWHC 79 (QB) and [2010] EWHC 31 where the bank was held not to be under a duty of care (**12.6** and **Appendix 7.1**).

On the other hand, the level of fines handed out to banks can be extremely high and disproportionate to the actual danger or risk in issue: recent examples are set out in **Appendix 10**: in a sense, banks, as the licenced financial 'gatekeepers' are 'piggy in the middle', and face an understandably difficult series of judgment calls.

INITIATIVES AFFECTING FUNDS AND INVESTMENT MANAGERS

16.8   It is self-evident that hedge funds, mutual funds and investment management businesses are required (as FIs) to comply with all aspects of modern AML-CFT, and there are specific CFT Regulations for this important sector. It is less clear whether 'independent asset managers' ('IAMs') are similarly subject to AML-CFT regulation if they do not have actual custody of the underlying assets, and where the assets and funds under management are held by external banks and securities custodians: some jurisdictions (eg Switzerland) err on the safe side, requiring IAMs also to be aware of the underlying reasons for payments and transfer instructions into and out of the accounts.

Chapter 17

AML in selected non-UK Jurisdictions

17.1 For understandable constitutional reasons, the UK Anti-Money Laundering (AML-CFT) rules, as originally defined in the Criminal Justice Acts 1988 and 1993 (and as now set out in PoCA 2002 and SOCPA 2005) form the basis of the statutory AML-CFT regimes in the Crown Dependencies and the 14 British Overseas Territories.

AML-CFT rules have evolved differently in other jurisdictions such as the United States and Canada, being less connected with the United Kingdom,

There are subtle differences in the approaches that some of the offshore jurisdictions have adopted in implementing their AML-CFT legislation. Whilst it is beyond the scope of this Book to provide a comprehensive comparative analysis, we nevertheless note the salient features and differences of a number of key jurisdictions in this **Chapter 17** and in **Appendix 9**: the Appendix also contains a more detailed overview of the AML-CFT treatment of fiscal offences in those key jurisdictions, and comments on two key legal issues, namely: (a) 'extra-territoriality'; and (b) the 'subjective/objective' standard for 'suspicion'.

The following key jurisdictions are reviewed in this Chapter:

- Bahamas;
- Bermuda;
- Canada;
- Cayman Islands;
- Gibraltar;
- Guernsey;
- Hong Kong;
- Isle of Man;
- Jersey;
- Singapore;
- Switzerland; and
- United States;

with a list of their principal statutes and regulations etc being set out in the *Table of Foreign Legislation* set out at the beginning of the book.

It remains beyond the scope of this Chapter to list or analyse the statutory provisions whereby TSPs and CSPs themselves are regulated in the jurisdictions cited: reference on this can be made to 'The Regulation of Trust and Company Service Providers' (STEP, June 2006), to STEP's Jurisdiction Guides www.step.org and to the relevant FSC or Monetary Authority websites in each jurisdiction.

Appendix 9 contains detailed extracts from the corresponding country/ jurisdiction chapters of *International Guide to Money Laundering Law and Practice* (Bloomsbury professional, 3rd Edition, 2012). The Author wishes to express his appreciation to the Publishers for organising and agreeing to this. However, please note that, finally, in the interests of brevity, these detailed 'country' extracts do not include materials relating to terrorist – or drug/narcotic – AML-CFT, as the Author wishes this book to maintain a consistent focus.

THE BAHAMAS

17.2 The Bahamas' AML-CFT code is contained in the Financial Transactions Reporting Act 2000 and the Proceeds of Crime Act 2000 (PoCA 2000). The Commonwealth of the Bahamas, which is an independent sovereign nation, has modelled its substantive AML-CFT offences on the UK Criminal Justice Act (CJA) offences. The scope of the offences covered includes any other offence triable in the Bahamas Supreme Court.

As regards fiscal offences, there is no direct taxation in the Bahamas – foreign tax evasion is not regarded as a predicate offence, but as foreign tax evasion is frequently accompanied by a charge of fraud or a related offence, this would fall into PoCA 2000, Schedule, para 'd'. Note that the Bahamas' Tax Information Exchange Agreement (ITEA) with the United States (signed on 25 January 2002) defines 'criminal matter' as 'an examination, investigation or proceeding concerning conduct that constitutes a criminal tax offence' under US law.

BERMUDA

17.3 Bermuda's principal AML-CFT statute is the Proceeds of Crime Act 1997 (as amended). The Taxes Management Amendment Act 2000 and the Proceeds of Crime (Amendment) Act 2000 broadened the scope by redefining 'relevant offence' to cover all serious crime, including fraudulent tax evasion which occurs outside Bermuda if such evasion is actively facilitated within Bermuda. The US-Bermuda Tax Information Exchange Agreement (TIEA) of July 1986 provides for disclosure in cases of tax fraud and the evasion of taxes.

Thus, the overseas commission of a tax offence can fall within the definition of 'suspicious transaction' reporting (it should be noted that there is a three-year cut-off date). Under the Taxes Management Amendment Act 2000 the definition of criminal tax evasion was revised, and 'tax fraud' is defined as 'any deliberate or wilful act by a person with intent to defraud where that person knows that a substantial amount of tax would otherwise be due, and the conduct involved constitutes a *systematic effort or pattern of activity* (a definition which is similar to that of 'tax offence' contained in other US TIEAs, for example, with the Cayman Islands – see **16.5)** designed to falsify material records to the relevant authorities'.

CANADA

17.4   The Canadian AML-CFT framework is contained in the Proceeds of Crime (Money Laundering) and Terrorist Financing Act 2000 (as amended), and related regulations. The provisions follow loosely the UK CJA provisions, and encompass the proceeds of a 'designated offence' committed in Canada, or an offence committed elsewhere which would constitute a 'designated offence' had it been committed in Canada. A 'designated offence' is essentially an indictable offence. There is thus a high element of extraterritoriality. However, offences under the Canadian Income Tax Act are excluded from the definition of 'designated offence' as the statutes already provide for specific rules and penalties for dealing with tax evasion and recovering any unpaid tax. For this reason, practitioners do not see that the Canadian AML-CFT regime can be extended to cover tax evasion against non-Canadian tax authorities committed outside Canada.

THE CAYMAN ISLANDS

17.5   The Cayman Islands' AML-CFT provisions are contained in the Proceeds of Criminal Conduct Law (as amended) and follow the UK model. There is no need for dual criminality in the substantive law, but the Regulations contain a dual criminality approach.

The current version of the *Guidance Notes on the Prevention and Detection of Money Laundering and Terrorist Financing in the Cayman Islands* was published in March 2010.

The Cayman Islands' TIEA with the United States (signed on 27 November 2001) defines 'criminal tax evasion' in Art 4 as:

> 'wilfully, with dishonest intent to defraud the public revenue, evading or attempting to evade any tax liability… [which] must be of a significant or substantial amount… and the conduct involved must constitute a systematic effort or pattern of activity designed or tending to conceal pertinent facts from the tax authorities'.

GUERNSEY

17.6   The Guernsey AML-CFT provisions are contained in The Criminal Justice (Proceeds of Crime) (Bailiwick of Guernsey) Law 1999 as amended, which is closely based on the UK model. The Guernsey position on fiscal offences (domestic or foreign) is broadly the same as in Jersey (see **17.9**), it is a common law offence in Guernsey to cheat the Guernsey Revenue, and the GFSC Handbook 2007 (updated) states expressly that proceeds of a tax-related offence may fall within the AML-CFT offences.

The position on foreign fiscal offences is less clear. It should be noted that Guernsey signed a TIEA with the United States in September 2002 which (following the OECD commitment) requires exchange of information in criminal tax matters as of 1 January 2004, and in civil/administrative tax matters as of 1 January 2006.

HONG KONG

17.7   The Hong Kong AML-CFT framework, contained in the Organized and Serious Crimes Ordinance (OSCO) (as amended), is not based on the UK model, and is reflective of Hong Kong's autonomous status since 1 July 1997 as a Special Administrative Region of the People's Republic of China. The AML-CFT offences are linked to the proceeds of indictable offences, irrespective of where the offence was committed: the maximum penalty is 14 years. The position on fiscal offences is unclear, but is likely to follow the common law position.

The AML & CFT (Financial Institutions) Ordinance ('AMLO') (effective1 April2012), sets up various criminal offences, and also codifies requirements relating to PEPs (including domestic PEPs), CDD and record-keeping for specified FIs. AMLO, s 1, Schedule 2 also defines 'Equivalent Jurisdiction' as one that is a FATF member or that imposes requirements similar to those under Schedule 2.

The HKMA introduced new AML Guidelines in 2012, and on 29 April 2014 published an important Circular dealing with Data Security within External Service Providers to Authorized Institutions. Hong Kong's Joint Financial Intelligence Unit ('JFIU') was set up by the Police and the Customs & Excise Departments. AML-CFT is jointly administered by the Narcotics Bureau, the Organised Crime & Triad Bureau of the Hong Kong Police Force or the Customs Drug Investigation Bureau of the Customs & Excise Department ('CED').

Hong Kong has had some interesting money laundering (ML) cases. In *HKSAR v Li Ching* [1997] 4 HKC108 the Court of Appeal held in December 1997 that it was sufficient to constitute an AML-CFT offence if the defendant believed he was dealing with property representing the proceeds of an indictable offence (which would include tax evasion), even if as it turned out, he was not. The case also confirmed that under OSCO it is not necessary that there has to be a successful prosecution of the underlying serious crime, Justice Mayo holding that'… it is obviously the case that tax evasion must be a crime in China'.

In *HKSAR v Look Kar Win* [1999] 4 HKC 783 4 the Court held that a football match-fixing that occurred in Thailand (where it may not have been illegal) could be prosecuted under corruption laws in Hong Kong, as the offence could be deemed to have taken place in Hong Kong (where it would have been illegal). The *Lam Yiu Chung* case was an ML case brought following an ICAC investigation, where the prosecution argued that 'it was reasonable for anyone involved in the operation to assume the cash was either illegitimate or evading the tax man'. And the *Robert Pang v Cmr of Police* [2002] case is also important in relation to issues of LPP – see **Chapter 13.**

Recent high profile convictions for ML include Luo Juncheng (January 2013) convicted of laundering HKD13.1 billion and imprisoned for ten and a half years. And Yet Lam Mei-Ling (March 2013) convicted of laundering HKD6.7 billion and imprisoned for ten years. It is clear that there is an aggressive prosecution strategy (to satisfy FATF) and that the Judiciary want convictions.

ISLE OF MAN

17.8   The principal AML-CFT statute in the Isle of Man is the Criminal Justice (Money Laundering Offences) Act, which is directly modelled on the UK CJA. The Isle of Man position on whether a fiscal offence can constitute an AML-CFT offence is similar to that in the Channel Islands (see **17.6** and **17.9**). Any conduct, wherever transacted, that is sufficiently serious to be triable 'on information' is caught by the Act. As offences under the Isle of Man Income Tax Acts are triable only summarily, at present they fall outside the scope of the AML-CFT offences. It is also unclear whether there are Manx equivalents to the UK common law offences of defrauding and/or cheating the revenue which are triable either summarily or on information. On the other hand, false accounting which may be part of a tax evasion scheme is an offence under the Manx Theft Act 1981, thus falling within the scope of the Manx AML-CFT code. It seems likely that the Isle of Man Courts would extend the statutory AML-CFT provisions to cover fiscal offences.

JERSEY

17.9   Jersey's Proceeds of Crime (Jersey) Law also follows the UK model. It defines 'criminal conduct' as a conduct which, if committed in Jersey, might lead to a sentence of imprisonment of one year or more. The case of *Re Kaplan* (Jersey Royal Court 29 April 2009) left undecided per curiam whether the words 'beneficially entitled' under PC(J)L should have a broader meaning than the conventional trusts law meaning

As regards fiscal offences, since tax evasion in Jersey (in the sense of negligently or fraudulently making incorrect statements in connection with a tax return) is punishable under the Income Tax (Jersey) Law by a fine rather than imprisonment, it appears that fiscal offences do not fall within the scope of the AML-CFT offences. However, if a tax-related offence is accompanied by a common law offence (see **17.3** and **17.5**) such as forgery, fraud or false accounting – see *Foster v A-G* [1992] JLR 6 (Jersey Court of Appeal) 1992 JLR 6 – the position may differ. The Jersey Handbook for AML-CFT prevention and detection (effective 4 February 2008 and updated to 14 August 2014) no longer contains clarification of whether a tax-related offence committed outside of the Island may be within the definition of "criminal conduct" it is likely that the purposes of the Law, not all overseas tax offences will necessarily amount to such conduct. Advocate Alan Binnington writing in the Jersey Law Review concludes his 12 March 2014 Article entitled '*Money Laundering and Tax Evasion – The Banker's Dilemma*' as follows:

> 'Reporting one's customer to the police on the basis that one suspects him of having engaged in criminal conduct is a drastic

step. On the other hand, failing to report a suspicious transaction and, as a result, being convicted of a money laundering offence, which carries with it a potential sentence of imprisonment of up to 14 years, is an extremely serious matter. For understandable reasons neither government nor prosecutors wish to give greater guidance as to the application of all crimes money laundering legislation to fiscal offences. *This is an unsatisfactory state of affairs but it would seem that we shall have to wait for the first test case before the matter is clarified'.*

(the full article attached in **Appendix 9**).

During the year to 31 December 2013, 3,036 SARs were made in Jersey.

Note Jersey's 2002 TIEA with the United States. The TIEA Regulations were substantially amended in November 2013 so as to limit the role of the Jersey Courts in relation to foreign requests for the provision of tax information: key provisions of the amended TIEA Regulations include:

* limiting the scope for Judicial Review;

* the removal of the requirement on the Comptroller of Taxes *'to act reasonably'* in deciding whether to respond to a request;

* requiring (even where a Judicial Review has been commenced) the recipient of the Notice to provide the information requested to the Comptroller, even without a Court Order, for onward disclosure to the foreign tax authority until the Judicial Review has been determined; and

* limiting the right to appeal unless the Privy Council has given permission.

SINGAPORE

17.10   Since 1 July 2013, Singapore Law now regards the proceeds of foreign tax evasion ('serious tax crimes', eg wilful or fraudulent tax evasion) as coming within their AML-CFT offences. Private Banking divisions that accept such funds will be severely penalised. A 'Private Banking Industry Group' ('PBIG') has been set up to develop a framework and guidelines to ensure such funds do not enter the Singapore financial system. The Industry Sound Practices can be accessed on the website of the Association of Banks in Singapore (ABS), as an addendum to the Private Banking Code of Conduct: www.abs.org.sg/industry_private.php

The MAS confirmed in a response to feedback on its Consultation paper that FIs are not required to determine whether their Clients are compliant with all relevant tax obligations globally. The scope is further limited in that a foreign 'serious tax crime' is an ML predicate offence if the foreign tax evaded is of a kind which is also imposed (so the principle of 'dual criminality' applies in Singapore): this means that if the foreign tax evaded has no equivalent in Singapore (eg inheritance, gift or wealth taxes), then the FI *does not need* to file an STR.

The new 2014 Income Tax amendments bring EoI requests under the Income Tax Act up to the OECD Standard.

SWITZERLAND

17.11 The Federal Act on the Swiss Financial Market Supervisory Authority (FINMASA) established

FINMA on the 22 June 2007, merging the previous Federal Office of Private Insurance (FOPI), the Swiss Federal Banking Commission and the Anti-Money Laundering Control Authority. FINMA is now responsible for all financial regulation in Switzerland, and the Swiss Federal Banking Commission (in existence since at least 1934) is no more. FINMA's financial services regulations follow international standards, while keeping the overall regulatory burden and related costs at a reasonable level.

Disclosure Requirements under Know Your Customer ('KYC') Rules

Swiss financial services providers are subject to the KYC principles contained in the FATF 2012 Recommendations, requiring Swiss banks, investment managers and lawyers rendering financial services to establish the identity of their clients and keep records on the identity of beneficial ownership of assets under management. In this respect, banking secrecy and professional secrecy laws will also apply. In this regard, the disclosure 'Form A' has existed for over 30 years, and in 2008 'Form T' for Trusts was added.

International Cooperation in Criminal and Tax Matters

In tax matters, Switzerland for decades limited legal assistance to cases of demonstrated tax fraud (ie tax matters of criminal nature involving fraudulent activity such as the forgery of documents). However since 2009, Switzerland revised this long standing policy while maintaining the principle of protecting bank clients' privacy. The first limb of this new strategic approach is called the 'White Money' policy ('Weissgeld' in German) and commits Switzerland to being a tax compliant financial centre, acquiring and managing only taxed assets The second limb involved negotiating amendments to existing double taxation agreements (DTAs) granting administrative assistance in tax matters according to worldwide accepted OECD standards. Agreements are being reached with EU countries, the US and many offshore jurisdictions, while negotiations with other countries are still pending.

This newly adopted policy aims to give Switzerland's advantageous tax system better international recognition, both in the field of corporate and individual taxation. At the same time, Switzerland grants partner nations of high importance and its direct neighbouring countries a favourable position with regard to the lifting of Swiss banking secrecy in cases of tax evasion on a case-by-case basis when an alleged infraction of tax laws can sufficiently substantiated. Legal assistance in case of mere tax evasion (ie cases 'simple' incomplete declaration of income and, if applicable, assets for tax purposes) will not be granted outside the framework of double taxation treaties and *vis-à-vis* countries with restrictions on currency export and on foreign investments.

The newly adopted policy ensures that Swiss banking secrecy continues to exist in a framework compatible with the FATF Forty Recommendations and OECD standards while still being focused on the protection of individual privacy. A recent Referendum Vote in 2013 rejected the outright removal of bank secrecy.

Criminalisation of Money Laundering

Switzerland has implemented all of the requisite international norms (including the 2012 FATF Recommendations) to prevent money laundering and terrorist finance (AML-CFT), and has been praised internationally for its achievements. KYC requirements are set out in the Money Laundering Act, which requires suspicious transaction reporting to the Money Laundering Reporting Office. Swiss law distinguishes between tax evasion (non-reporting of income) and tax fraud (active deception). In March 2009 the distinction was abolished in dealings with foreign clients (interestingly, the distinction remains in place for Swiss taxpayers), and since then Switzerland has granted international legal assistance under OECD standards with regard to administrative assistance in tax matters (OECD Model Tax Convention, in particular Article 26). Switzerland does not yet operate a full 'dual criminality' approach to predicate AML-CFT offences in the field of taxation.

Exchange of Information (EOI)

EUSTD: The EU has for several years complained about EU nationals using the Swiss banks to avoid taxation in their home countries, and has long sought a harmonised tax regime among its member states. As Switzerland did not want to be seen as an obstacle to closer tax cooperation among EU-member states it has supported the EU efforts to tax cross-border investment income, and the 'retention tax' agreed with the EU as part of the overall Savings Tax Directive (EUSTD) was a suitable and efficient means of doing so

The 'Rubik' Agreements

These bilateral agreements were intended to reinforce the approach to EUSTD retention tax for nationals of the UK and Germany with bank accounts in Switzerland. The Swiss-UK Tax Cooperation Agreement required Swiss banks to identify those 'in scope' and notify the affected individuals no later than 28 February 2013 ('in scope' referring to customers with significant UK connections, but excluding UK-Resident Non-Domiciliaries), and on 31 May 2013 to subject their Swiss bank accounts to a one-off levy of between 21% and 41% which resulted in payment of a total of £340 Million to the UK HMRC. Annual deductions will thereafter be made and paid over, albeit on an anonymous basis. Conversely, the Swiss-Germany Tax Cooperation Agreement did not go ahead having been blocked in December 2012 by the upper house of the German Parliament. Since then, the German state of Rhineland-Palatinate announced in April 2013 that it has bought a CD containing data on secret

Swiss bank accounts in order to track down more than 10,000 suspected German tax evaders with accounts in Switzerland, and hopes to recover half a billion euros (CHF608 million) in unpaid tax.

FATCA and US issues

FATCA (see **9.6**) was to have been applied in Switzerland as of 1 July 2014 and Switzerland has opted for the Model-2 IGA.

Mutual Administrative Assistance in Tax Matters

On 15th October 2013 Switzerland became the 58th country to sign the OECD's *Multilateral Convention on Mutual Administrative Assistance in Tax Matters.* Switzerland's adherence to the Convention sends a clear and strong signal that Switzerland is part of the community of states which consider international tax co-operation as a necessity. This signature is also an important step for Switzerland to resolve the issues identified in its Peer Review by the Global Forum on Transparency and Exchange of Information on June 2011.

THE UNITED STATES

17.12   The AML-CFT framework in the United States has also been updated, and the United States has moved in the same direction as the United Kingdom in its interpretation of AML-CFT laws as covering the proceeds of all crimes, including fiscal offences, but with discussion of the same academic issues that were encountered in the United Kingdom over a decade ago. The American College of Trust and Estate Counsel take the view that tax offences are not and should not be understood to be the type of criminal acts that can be held to produce 'proceeds of crime' for AML-CFT purposes, and that international transactions that led to underpayment or non-payment of tax should not be criminalised or made part of the AML-CFT STR structure.

IRS Code ss 1956 and 1957 prohibited engaging in a financial transaction knowing or being wilfully blind to the fact that the property involved represents the proceeds of 'some form of unlawful activity', where the person inter alia intends to engage in tax fraud or tax evasion of either US or non-US taxes. Recent cases in the United States have held that evasion of non-US taxes and exchange control violations is an AML-CFT offence.

The USA PATRIOT Act of Congress was signed into law by President George W Bush on 26 October 2001 (only six weeks after the '9-11' attacks). It is an acronym of 'Uniting and Strengthening America by Providing the Appropriate Tools Required to Intercept and Obstruct Terrorism'. The law inter alia requires US financial institutions to identify the foreign beneficial owners of accounts with them. These measures have been applied strictly, with some institutions requiring compulsory redemption or closure of an existing relationship if the name(s) is/are not provided. The Patriot Act measures run counter to the current position under US Qualified Jurisdictions and Qualified Intermediaries programme, where the 'beneficial owner' concept stops at a 'real' company (ie one that is not a nominee or pass through entity) (current QI Rules do not seek to pierce through to the ultimate individual beneficial owners). QI has been followed by FATCA with its far-reaching effects (see **8.4** and **9.6**).

The 2003 *Pasquantino* case (*United States of America v David Pasquantino* US App LEXIS 14453 (2003)); 336F. 3d 321 (4th Cir. 2003) confirmed that the US Courts have expanded the territorial limitation to enforcing foreign revenue laws (similar to the UK – see **7.2**). The decision in *US v Hebroni* 2002 US Dist. LEXIS 8836 is also noteworthy, as the US Courts secured a conviction of ML and conspiracy to launder drugs money: the case was exceptional as all of the trading activities had taken place in Panama. The accused mainly seems to have sold jewellery to drug barons, knowing that it was being paid for with the proceeds of drug trafficking.

Conversely, the United States is currently self-examining its own domestic CSP sector in relation to the hundreds of thousands of Limited Liability Corporations ('LLCs') that have been spawned at state level, in particular in Delaware, Wyoming and Nevada, where no prior disclosure of beneficial ownership is required by state law, while the Federal Government has said it is purely a state-level issue: the US needs to get its own house in order rapidly!

Chapter 18

Bribery and corruption

INTRODUCTION

18.1   This chapter will look at the concepts of bribery and corruption in the Anti-Money Laundering-Countering Terrorist Finances (AML-CFT) context. At first sight it may not be entirely clear why this book should contain a chapter about bribery and corruption: the simple answer is that the subject is currently receiving a high level of focus from the main supranational bodies, including the EU, the Council of Europe, the EBRD, the IMF, the World Bank, the WTO, and the United Nations; and also from numerous private sector bodies including the ICC and BIAC. It is worth reflecting that the United States FCPA has been on the statute books for nearly 40 years, since 1977.

Recurring scandals in Europe (*Clearstream*; Siemens; VW) indicate that corporate governance still has a long way to go. The UNICORN organisation (founded by three leading international trade union bodies) maintains a comprehensive list of recent bribery cases – see www. againstcorruption.org/BriberyCases.asp. This is well worth a look!

So another level of reply is that the main thrust of the AML-CFT panoply is hitherto against the private sector: so why not start to try to subject politicians and civil servants to the same standards/levels of financial cleanliness that the private sector has been subjected to for some time!

Being a predicate crimes, both bribery and corruption are, of course, also ML issues. Back in 2002 this was confirmed by the Grand Court of Cayman in *Corporacion Nacional del Cobra de Chile v Interglobal Inc* [2002] CILR 298. And even before that, the Levin Report entitled 'Private banking and money laundering – a case study of opportunities and vulnerabilities' (published in November 1999) had examined the vulnerability of private banking operations to such ML and described four illustrative case histories at Citibank Private Bank.

One of the case histories concerned Asif Ali Zardari, the husband of Benazir Bhutto the former Prime Minister of Pakistan. Ms Bhutto was elected Prime Minister in 1988 and dismissed for alleged corruption in 1990. She was re-elected Prime Minister in October 1993 and dismissed again in November 1996. At various times Mr Zardari held political office and in the period between the two Bhutto administrations he was imprisoned for corruption.

DEFINITIONS

18.2   First, it is necessary to define terms:

> *Corruption,* as legally defined, involves the use of public power for private gain (as such it does not apply to the private sector, although it may apply to 'parastatal' bodies); and

> *Bribery,* which involves an unlawful payment or other inducement for private gain; it can and does feature in corruption as the means by which 'corrupters' corrupt officials.

Although corruption can also be defined more broadly (to include all forms of dishonesty, such as fraud, embezzlement, tax evasion and bribery), this chapter will use the narrower definition noted above. It also seems that there is a quantitative test, and that genuine corruption needs to be distinguished from 'grease payments', gratuities and other forms of petty corruption (a sort of *de minimis* standard).

The Bribe Payers Index (BPI) and Corruption Perceptions Index (CPI) published by Transparency International ('TI') (see **11.18**, **14.9**, **15.10**, **16.5** and **18.11**) show that corruption is a phenomenon occurring mainly in developing and transitional countries, whilst in democratic countries, where the rule of law is deeply rooted and state institutions are well developed, it occurs less or not at all.

THE BRIBERY ACT 2010

18.3   Wikipedia summarises The Bribery Act 2010 (c 23) as being UK Act of that covers the criminal law relating to bribery. Introduced to Parliament in the Queen's Speech in 2009 after several decades of reports and draft bills, the Act received the Royal Assent on 8 April 2010 following cross-party support. Initially scheduled to enter into force in April 2010, this was changed to 1 July 2011. The Act repeals all previous statutory and common law provisions in relation to bribery, instead replacing them with the crimes of bribery, being bribed, the bribery of foreign public officials, and the failure of a commercial organisation to prevent bribery on its behalf.

The penalties for committing a crime under the Act are a maximum of 10 years' imprisonment, along with an unlimited fine, and the potential for the confiscation of property under POCA2002, as well as the disqualification of directors under the Company Directors Disqualification Act 1986. The Act has a near-universal jurisdiction, allowing for the prosecution of an individual or company with links to the United Kingdom, regardless of where the crime occurred. Described as 'the toughest anti-corruption legislation in the world', concerns have been raised that the Act's provisions criminalise behaviour that is acceptable in the global market, and puts British business at a competitive disadvantage.

See **Appendix 4** for extracted sections.

The SFO is the principal enforcer of the Bribery Act 2010, which has been designed to encourage good corporate governance and enhance the reputation of the City of London and the UK as a safe place to do business. Guidance is available on www.gov.uk/government/publications/ bribery-act-2010-guidance.

SUPRANATIONAL: CONVENTION ON COMBATING BRIBERY OF FOREIGN PUBLIC OFFICIALS IN INTERNATIONAL BUSINESS TRANSACTIONS (OECD 1997)

18.4   Article 1(1) of the **OECD's 1997 Anti-Bribery Convention** states that it is an offence for any person intentionally to:

'... offer, promise or give any undue pecuniary or other advantage, whether directly or through intermediaries, to a foreign public official, for that official or for a third party, in order that the official act or refrain from acting in relation to the performance of official duties, in order to obtain or retain business or other improper advantage in the conduct of international business.'

It is irrelevant whether the bribe goes to a third party, such as a relative, or to the corrupt official in person.

On the basis of Art 1(2), complicity (participation) and incitement to corruption also constitute criminal offences. They include 'authorisation'. Thus, if a company in an OECD country authorises a foreign subsidiary to pay a bribe, the parent company and those directors and managers involved will commit the offence.

Article 1(3) defines 'foreign public official' as any person in a foreign country who holds a legislative, administrative or judicial office, or who exercises a public function, including a public agency or enterprise, and any official of an international organisation. As regards extension of the offence to the behaviour of managers of private companies controlled by the state, the commentary on the 1997 Convention specifies that a company is deemed 'public' if the state can exercise a dominant influence on it.

Article 7 of the Convention states that each party that has made bribery of its own public official a predicate offence for the purposes of the application of its AML-CFT legislation shall do so on the same terms for the bribery of a foreign public official, without regard to the place where the bribery occurred.

This is an enormously significant provision which raises some of the same territorial arguments that arose in the United Kingdom in relation to the extension of the UK AML-CFT offences to include the proceeds of 'foreign fiscal offences' (see **8.11**). The rule essentially requires 'national treatment'.

As a result of the 1997 Convention, corruption is a crime, so the 'proceeds' of corruption are now the 'proceeds of crime'. They thus fall within the definition of the AML-CFT regime (see **2.3** and **7.3**). And since the general adherence to the OECD 1997 Bribery Convention, local AML regulations (including their reporting and disclosure obligations, and seizure and confiscation of the funds) will apply when an offence of corrupting a foreign public official is at issue.

Participating in such dubious financial transactions will incur the risk of criminal responsibility.'

The 1997 Convention binds the parties to criminalise in their national law the 'active' corruption (ie bribery) of officials of other countries, whether or not those countries are signatories to the 1997 Convention, and whether or not the country in which the official receiving the bribe is based has itself applied and enforced criminal laws on 'passive corruption' (ie the taking of bribes) of its officials.

The parties thus intended not to accept either corruption of foreign officials, nor tolerance thereof by such officials' governments. This 'level playing field' approach was sought to ensure that there were common rules for companies of different origins operating in international markets.

Each signatory is required to punish the offence by 'effective, proportionate and dissuasive criminal penalties', including imprisonment. Other punitive measures are to be applied, such as seizure and confiscation of the bribe, and of the proceeds of the bribery.

The UK adopted legislation to comply with the 1997 Convention fairly rapidly, as part of the UK's 'package' approach to financial crime, and came into force in the United Kingdom early in 2002.

Thereafter, the legislation was extended to the Crown dependencies and the British overseas territories, by virtue of AML-CFT legislation and requirements.

REPORTS: NO LONGER BUSINESS AS USUAL – FIGHTING BRIBERY AND CORRUPTION (THE FBC REPORT), OECD, JUNE 2000

18.5   In its time, this was a seminal document on the subject of bribery and corruption. The FBC Report states:

> 'It is well known that bribes of high-ranking foreign officials are paid "from abroad to abroad", through banking channels and financial intermediaries in third countries, usually offshore financial centres protected by bank secrecy and hostile to international co-operation.' Such payments hitherto did not entail money laundering, because transnational corruption was not a crime.

The FBC Report is also a fascinating study of the OECD's own internal processes, and the development of structures for 'global governance'. It notes that as OECD decisions must be unanimous to be binding on its members, the OECD possesses only a limited power.

> 'Unanimity also means that arguments have a chance for consideration on their merits, rather than merely on the political and economic clout of the speaker. Power play does occur, of course, and sometimes things can get rough, especially when countries use the media to support their points in a crucial phase of the negotiation.'

Thus, it can be a long and formidable negotiating task to get such a 'consensus' (OECD parlance). The OECD's technique is, therefore, to draft a 'soft law' instrument (typically a recommendation) and seek agreement on it. In this particular case, member countries were invited to confront bribery with dissuasive actions outside of criminal law, and to remove provisions (such as tax deductibility) that might facilitate bribery.

Thereafter, the OECD will move from the 'soft law' instrument to a 'hard law' instrument (such as a convention) within a relatively short space of time, supervising and monitoring implementation in national legislatures. 'The process could serve as a template for building dams against the wild streams of economic globalisation when it generates noxious effects.'

On this basis it is easy to see how the OECD process was able to move towards the Multilateral Convention on Administrative Assistance in Tax Matters Standard described at **9.8** and **9.9**, even if (through their own admission) officials at the OECD were taken aback by the speed at which this was adopted in the early part of 2014.

REPORTS: BEHIND THE CORPORATE VEIL – USING CORPORATE ENTITIES FOR ILLICIT PURPOSES (OECD, NOVEMBER 2001)

18.6   It is also worth mentioning the OECD report *'Behind the Corporate Veil – Using Corporate Entities for Illicit Purposes'* (previously known as the Report on 'Misuse of Corporate Vehicles for Illicit Purposes') ('the BCV Report'), which was published in 2001.

SUPRANATIONAL: THE UN CONVENTION AGAINST CORRUPTION (2003)

18.7   Note that the UN convention against corruption came into force on 14 December 2005. www.unodc.org/unodc/crimeconventioncorruption

EU INITIATIVES AGAINST CORRUPTION

18.8   Also for completeness, The EU also has some initiatives on bribery and corruption:

- EU Convention on Combating Corruption, 26 May 1997 Official Journal C 195, 25/06/1997; and

- EU Common Positions (EC OJ L 279 13 October 1997) and (EC OJ L 320 21 November 1997).

- The EU Convention on the Fight against Corruption involving Officials of the European Communities or Officials of Member States (EC OJ C 195, 25 June 1997): this is of narrow scope, being limited to EU officials.

www.europa.eu.int.

But the EU itself is none too clean: The Economist of 26 April 2014 reported at length about waste and fraud at EU level, noting in particular that:

> 'the European Anti-Fraud Office ('OLAF') opens hundreds of cases every year… [and] …The Court of Auditors worries about the 'error rate' in the EU's accounts, which stood at an enormous 4.8% of total spending in 2012.'

In February 2014 the EU Commission published a its first detailed Report on Corruption within the 28 Member States (COM(2014) 38 final), providing a clear picture of the situation in each Member State, measures in place, outstanding issues, policies that are working and areas that could be improved. The Report shows that the nature and scope of corruption varies from one Member State to another and that the effectiveness of anti-corruption policies is quite different. It also shows that corruption deserves greater attention in all EU Member States. It was a bit of a whitewash, 'couching criticism in terms of recommendations for improvement'. The Economist Article at the time noted that the so-called '29th Chapter' (on the EU institutions themselves) had been mysteriously shelved!

THE COUNCIL OF EUROPE ANTI-CORRUPTION CONVENTION

18.9

- The Council of Europe has two binding policies against corruption:

- The Criminal Law Convention on Corruption was adopted in 1998 and represents a regional consensus on what states should do in the areas of criminalisation and international cooperation with respect to corruption. The convention covers the public sector and private sector corruption and a broad range of offences including bribery (domestic and foreign), trading in influence, ML and accounting offences. This Convention is complemented by an additional Protocol covering bribery offences committed by and against arbitrators and jurors. These two groups of persons do not legally qualify as public officials and are therefore not covered by the Criminal Law Convention.

- The Civil Law Convention on Corruption was adopted in 1998 and came into force in 2003. It provides for compensation for damages resulting from corruption, invalidity of corrupt contracts and whistle-blower protection.

APEC CORRUPTION INFORMATION-SHARING AGREEMENT 2014

18.9A The 21 APEC Member Countries agreed on 8 November(2014) to set up a network to share information on corruption, essentially so as to deny safe haven to anyone engaged in corruption and to formalise the Agreement at their 9-11 November summit in Beijing.

THE WOLFSBERG GROUP'S STATEMENT AGAINST CORRUPTION

18.10   Also for completeness, note that in early 2007 the Wolfsberg Group published a 'Statement against corruption' – see **16.5**), in close association with TI (see **19.11**) and the Basel *Institute on Governance*, to describe the role of the Wolfsberg Group and financial institutions more generally in support of international efforts to combat corruption.

The Statement against Corruption identified some of the measures financial institutions may consider in order to prevent corruption in their own operations, and protect themselves against the misuse of their operations in relation to corruption. The Statement distinguished between the internal measures a financial institution may take with respect to its own staff to prevent involvement in corruption, and the misuse of a financial institution's products and services by their customers in connection with corruption.

The Wolfsberg Statement recognised that the fight against corruption requires a comprehensive, multi-stakeholder approach which has to be led by supranational and national government agencies and law enforcement, assisted by civil society and the wider business community. The members of the Wolfsberg Group are committed to participating in this fight and are of course, opposed to all forms of corruption and commit to abide by laws designed to fight corruption. The Wolfsberg Group members support a publicly led multi-stakeholder approach to addressing a number of important areas where further dialogue and cooperation may lead to improvements in preventing and deterring bribery and other corrupt activity as it affects the financial sector.

MEASURING CORRUPTION

Transparency International

18.11   Transparency International (TI) is a Berlin-based NGO, dedicated to increasing governmental accountability and curbing both international and national corruption. TI is active in more than 70 countries. See www.transparency.org.

Since 1995, TI has published each year, in the autumn, its CPI. This ranks how people perceive countries in terms of the likelihood of being asked to pay bribes when doing business there. A clean score is 10, and the lower the score the higher the corruption. The CPI thus ranks the 'demand side'.

Since 1999, TI has also published its BPI. This ranks the leading exporting countries in terms of the degree to which they are perceived as the homes of bribe-paying companies. The BPI thus ranks the 'supply side'.

How precisely the tables can be of use in the offshore fiduciary field is not exactly clear. Clearly there is a tie-in, in that the *'Wolfsberg Anti-Money Laundering Principles'* (see **16.5**) recommend 'Additional Diligence/ Heightened Scrutiny' in relation to transactions with Clients from 'High-risk Countries'. But there is no 'brightline' or cut-off point on the scale, above which it is acceptable to deal, and below which it is not.

ISSUES FOR THE FUTURE – DANGERS FOR TSPs, CSPs, BANKS AND LEGAL PRACTITIONERS

18.12 The hidden dangers for the offshore trust and company sector need to be highlighted, and the Wolfsberg Anti-Money Laundering Principles' (see **16.5**) contains the following principle relating to public officials in its para 2.5:

> 'Individuals who have or have had positions of public trust (such as government officials, senior executives of government corporations, politicians, important political party officials etc.) and their families and close associates require heightened scrutiny.'

Clearly, there are possibilities that offshore trusts and offshore companies can be used in connection with receiving or paying bribes or corrupt payments. Enhanced vigilance is called for, depending on the profile of the client or customer involved. The slippery slope for the offshore industry lies in where the definition and concept of corruption will extend. Taken as a whole, the Initiatives noted above could collectively bring within its scope any of the following types of payment:

- commissions;

- fees;

- brokers' fees; other remuneration; subcontract payments; and consulting agreements (see the FINTRAC examples of suspicious transactions listed at **12.2**).

Monitoring all of these possibilities is an extremely difficult task, as the initiatives also include, not only situations where the payment is made to a government official, but also where the payment is to a relative of a government official, or even to a business associate of a government official. Once the anticorruption regime is extended to the private sector, then there are greater risks of corruption becoming an issue in offshore financial services. Furthermore, it will be confusing to monitor, as many newly appointed government officials have been (and still may be) active in business, so their commercial activities may be perfectly legitimate as regards such types of payment. The wider issue of PEPs/PSPs is looked at in **10.10** and **11.15**.

Note that the joint FATF/Asia-Pacific Group is working on corruption issues.

In terms of its impact on the financial havens, the problem of corruption is that the individuals or groups who engage in corruption need to find ways to use and benefit from the profits thereof without drawing attention to the underlying criminal activity. They are thus naturally drawn to jurisdictions offering secrecy or enhanced confidentiality, and to non-transparent entities such as International Business Corporation (IBCs).

And corruption clearly has 'proceeds'. A 'wake-up call' on this specific point is necessary, to alert professionals and practitioners in the offshore jurisdictions of the extent of this risk to their businesses, and ultimately their individual liberty. So as the 'proceeds' of a corrupt payment are the 'proceeds of crime' for AML-CFT purposes, then the professionals and practitioners involved with offshore trusts and offshore companies (and the bankers to offshore trusts and offshore companies) will have to exercise the utmost vigilance to avoid the risk of a '14-year holiday'.

As noted at **14.8**, the UK Supreme Court in *FHR European Ventures LLP & Ors v Cedar Capital Partners LLC* [2014] UKSC 45 analysed the treatment of bribes and secret commissions, holding that these are held on constructive trust for the principal. Lord Neuberger's single short judgement is worthy of study, not least as FHR has overruled the *Lister* case [1890] 45 ChD 1, and substantially overruled the *Sinclair* case [2012] Ch 453. Jeremy Gordon and Jolyon Connell note in their Article in the STEP Journal (August/September 2014) that it is possible the FHR decision might extend to other breaches of duty by any fiduciary: they also note that there may not be any Limitation Act restriction in respect of claims to recover trust property.

Whether or not anti-corruption legislation will work in all countries round the world is a moot point: but if Governments remain committed to the crusade to purify public life, they may succeed in the end.

Chapter 19

Concerns and conclusions

CHANGES SINCE '9-11'

19.1   Since 9-11, the offshore sector has undergone a radical change. Many offshore financial centres have elected to remain part of the global financial system, and have changed their laws to remain in business. Others have withered away. The current wave of regulatory and compliance initiatives is likened to a Tsunami or tidal-wave: the rate of change has never been higher

Internationally, Anti-Money Laundering-Countering Terrorist Finances (AML-CFT) legislation coupled with increased exchange of information (EoI) and the associated huge fines and criminal prosecutions have reined in the worst excesses of the 'offshore industry' that had (by the late 1990s) gotten completely out of control. Those who assisted in barefaced tax evasion have learned the perils, and the issues involved (criminalisation, extradition, prison) are now well-publicised. Existing tax evasionary clients and customers ('the legacy book') are at high risk; future such prospective clients should not be taken on (see **8.13**).

THE AML-CFT MISSION: ACCOMPLISHED OR NOT?

19.2   It is less clear whether all the AML-CFT legislation has been at all successful in preventing or curtailing serious crime or terrorism. It has certainly succeeded in slowing down and disrupting commerce and the private financial affairs of hundreds of millions of people around the world. And it has succeeded in generating loads of Reports and statistics, let alone a whole industry of compliance specialists (advisors, trainers, analysts etc).

There is clear political hypocrisy in any purported linkage of 'AML' to 'CFT': the two are unconnected! The effectiveness of the former has been diluted by being 'tied' it to the latter. Cash notes still circulate in huge quantities, the worst example being the USD465 million cash windfall that ISIS acquired in June 2014 (along with six Blackhawk Helicopter fighters) on capturing Mosul. And electronic 'virtual cash' alternatives are developing fast.

THE COSTS OF AML-CFT ENFORCEMENT?

19.3   The financial services industry has become more vocal about the rising costs of AML-CFT regulation and the benefits that governments claim it brings. Douglas Flint (HSBC's Chairman) complained in early August 2014 that regulators were making unprecedented demands on banks that had increased red tape and deterred managers from pursuing necessary risks, and that around 10% of the HSC's staff now work in risk and compliance. Compliance is no longer just a 'minor inconvenience'.

And earlier, Dr. Jackie Harvey of Newcastle Business School had noted that:

> '[w]ithout facts, [anti-money laundering] legislation has been driven on rhetoric, and by ill-guided activism responding to the need to be "seen to be doing something" rather than by an objective understanding of its effects on predicate crime. The social panic approach is justified by the language used—we talk of the battle against terrorism or the war on drugs'.

The Economist magazine (20 October 2005) started to criticize AML-CFT regulation nearly a decade ago, particularly with reference to CFT, referring to it simply as a 'costly failure'.

Professor Sharman picks up this theme, quoting the lack of any precise measurement of the costs of regulation balanced against the harms associated with ML. Given the evaluation problems involved in assessing such an issue, it is unlikely that the effectiveness of AML-CFT laws *can* be determined with any degree of accuracy. Ten years ago, *The Economist* (14 October 2004) estimated the annual costs of the then European and US/ Canadian AML-CFT efforts at US$5 billion in 2003, citing an increase from US$700 million in 2000. The costs will have risen exponentially since then.

Inevitably, the increased FATCA and OECD-CRS-driven levels of information gathering for compliance purposes will only serve to increase banking and professional fees and costs.

PRIVACY CONCERNS

19.4 Besides the economic costs of implementing AML-CFT laws, improper attention to data-protection practices also entails disproportionate costs to individuals' privacy rights. In June 2011, the EU's Data Protection Working Party issued 'Opinion 14/2011 on data protection issues related to the prevention of money laundering and terrorist financing': this identified numerous transgressions against the established legal framework on privacy and data protection, and made recommendations how to address AML-CFT in ways that safeguard personal privacy rights and data-protection laws.

And the OECD has recognised these same issues in their 2012 Report *Keeping It Safe: The OECD Guide on the Protection of Confidentiality of Information Exchanged for Tax Purposes* published on 23 July 2012 (see **9.7**). The mantra should be *Don't Collect what you can't Protect*, as data leaks and penetration occur also at the levels of government departments.

In parallel, in the United States, the American Civil Liberties Union has expressed its concerns that the AML-CFT regime (requiring banks to report on their own customers) has essentially conscripted private businesses 'into agents of the surveillance state'. I fully endorse those concerns, as the issue of reporting a Client (see **Chapter 12**) has long been one of the two principal dilemmas of AML-CFT.

US Supreme Court Justice Louis D. Brandeis famously said in his dissenting speech in *Olmstead v US*, 277 US 438 (1928):

> 'Experience should teach us to be most on our guard to protect liberty when the government's purposes are beneficent. Men born to freedom are naturally alert to repel invasion of their liberty by evil-minded rulers. The greatest dangers to liberty lurk in insidious encroachment by men of zeal, well-meaning but without understanding'.

HUMAN RIGHTS

19.5 The FATF Recommendations (February 2012) www.fatf-gafi.org requires in their Notes that 'strict safeguards be established to ensure that EoI is consistent with national and international provisions on privacy and data protection'. Human rights law is relatively new in the UK legal arena, but the human rights that are worthy of protection in relation to AML-CFT legislation are fundamental, and include the Human Right to privacy, the right of property, the right to a fair trial, and of course the presumption of innocence! In purely AML terms, there is no automatic presumption that persons seeking privacy over their financial affairs are necessarily suspicious! Governments who use flawed logic to argue 'if you have nothing to hide then you shouldn't object to disclosure' are deliberately missing the point. It is a false premise to argue that 'privacy is used to hide bad things'.

Application of post 9-11 anti-terrorist laws also requires a careful balancing of traditional democratic freedoms with security requirements – for a more in-depth discussion than this book allows, see Baroness Helena Kennedy QC *Just Law* (2004). New laws and regulations always need a settling-in period, but as the AML-CFT regime roughly coincides with both the introduction of codified human rights legislation, and their curtailment as a result of 9-11, practitioners and their clients are left with uncertainties on the scope of the AML-CFT regime and the strength of the human rights protections and remedies.

FOREIGN TAX EVASION

19.6 The other principal dilemma is the issue of foreign tax evasion (see **Chapter 7**). We all know and accept that overly aggressive tax planning ('avoidance') may shade into 'evasion', may trigger registration as a 'scheme', and in any event will requires extreme caution, as harsh cases that fall on the wrong side of the line will be subject to heavy penalties. For the time being, the Private Banking/Private Client/Wealth Management/Family Office sector continues to thrive, and tax avoidance/tax mitigation planning continues to be used. Human nature continues to drive individuals and families to diversify their assets and investments across more than one country or jurisdiction, so as to provide a hedge against political or economic risks. Tax optimisation and confidentiality issues are an intrinsic part of this process. But maybe the IFCs will start to lose business as the CRS first exchange deadline (September 2017) looms closer. 'Tax Evasion 101', being the simple hiding of funds offshore, will become a thing of the past.

The simple answer is that 'tax' is the 'low-hanging fruit'. The OECD lacks the mandate to go after organised crime, narco-business or terrorism. The US government spent USD 7.6 billion in battling the opium trade in Afghanistan, and lost. So, to adapt a phrase, 'we are all now unpaid policemen'.

ASSET FORFEITURE

19.7   The continuing evolution of AML-CFT legislation has placed greater powers of asset forfeiture and asset recovery in the hands of prosecutors and revenue gatherers – see the NCA's powers in **Chapter 5**. Issues on human rights are being increasingly invoked in AML-CFT proceedings, both in connection with forfeiture, and on the wider issue of EoI generally.

Note also that the ability of US Government Departments to earn and retain a percentage of fines successfully imposed on Banks etc. (by way of departmental 'rewards' or bonuses) must surely skew the objectivity of their enforcement approach.

THE FUTURE

19.8   The pendulum has clearly swung too far, and will never swing back, unless/until the banks combine to point out to Governments that it is the job of Governments to stamp out crime and eliminate terrorism and not the job of private practice professionals or the financial sector. Although the idea behind AML-CFT policy is sound, the AML-CFT panoply will never lead to a terrorism-free world (through striking at terrorist finances) and it is naive to believe that it will achieve its mission (see **12.8** on 'mission creep' and **Appendix 6** on statistics). Sadly, we can never be safe from terrorism. Recent unofficial reports suggest that the finances Al-Qaeda (and other terrorist organisations') are still in good shape despite over five years of focused application of AML-CFT laws. This should come as no surprise, as it is likely that only a tiny percentage of money destined for, or owned by, terror organisations actually flows through 'co-operative countries or territories' (in FATF-speak), with the bulk flowing through underground networks or unregulated jurisdictions.

Some ten years ago, Richard Pease's closing remarks to the annual STEP Conference predicted a future world of total financial transparency, bank account information publicly available, and registers of trust beneficiaries and company beneficial owners. At the time, we found the idea amusing, not believing for one moment that it would or could come to pass. We now inhabit that Brave New 'post-FATCA' World with its total transparency requirements and global onslaught on Undeclared Money and its related tax evasion (see **19.6**). This and The AML-CFT regime will continue to raise issues of concern over privacy and human rights (see **19.4** and **19.5**). The era of 'Big Brother', that has been stealthily slouching our way since 1984, has now well and truly arrived!

Appendix 1

Statutory and EU Provisions

Contents

Appendix 1.1   Proceeds of Crime Act 2002

2002 Chapter 29

Proceeds of Crime Act 2002

Part 2
Confiscation: England and Wales

Interpretation

75   Criminal lifestyle

(1)   A defendant has a criminal lifestyle if (and only if) the following condition is satisfied.

(2)   The condition is that the offence (or any of the offences) concerned satisfies any of these tests—

(a)   it is specified in Schedule 2;

(b)   it constitutes conduct forming part of a course of criminal activity;

(c)   it is an offence committed over a period of at least six months and the defendant has benefited from the conduct which constitutes the offence.

(3)   Conduct forms part of a course of criminal activity if the defendant has benefited from the conduct and—

(a)   in the proceedings in which he was convicted he was convicted of three or more other offences, each of three or more of them constituting conduct from which he has benefited, or

(b)   in the period of six years ending with the day when those proceedings were started (or, if there is more than one such day, the earliest day) he was convicted on at least two separate occasions of an offence constituting conduct from which he has benefited.

(4)   But an offence does not satisfy the test in subsection (2)(b) or (c) unless the defendant obtains relevant benefit of not less than £5000.

(5)   Relevant benefit for the purposes of subsection (2)(b) is—

(a)   benefit from conduct which constitutes the offence;

(b)   benefit from any other conduct which forms part of the course of criminal activity and which constitutes an offence of which the defendant has been convicted;

(c)   benefit from conduct which constitutes an offence which has been or will be taken into consideration by the court in sentencing the defendant for an offence mentioned in paragraph (a) or (b).

(6)   Relevant benefit for the purposes of subsection (2)(c) is—

(a)   benefit from conduct which constitutes the offence;

(b)   benefit from conduct which constitutes an offence which has been or will be taken into consideration by the court in sentencing the defendant for the offence mentioned in paragraph (a).

(7)   The Secretary of State may by order amend Schedule 2.

(8)   The Secretary of State may by order vary the amount for the time being specified in subsection (4).

Notes

Extent

This Part does not extend to Scotland: see s 461(1).

---

76   Conduct and benefit

(1)   Criminal conduct is conduct which—

(a)   constitutes an offence in England and Wales, or

(b)   would constitute such an offence if it occurred in England and Wales.

(2)   General criminal conduct of the defendant is all his criminal conduct, and it is immaterial—

(a)   whether conduct occurred before or after the passing of this Act;

(b)   whether property constituting a benefit from conduct was obtained before or after the passing of this Act.

(3)   Particular criminal conduct of the defendant is all his criminal conduct which falls within the following paragraphs—

(a)   conduct which constitutes the offence or offences concerned;

(b)   conduct which constitutes offences of which he was convicted in the same proceedings as those in which he was convicted of the offence or offences concerned;

(c)   conduct which constitutes offences which the court will be taking into consideration in deciding his sentence for the offence or offences concerned.

(4)   A person benefits from conduct if he obtains property as a result of or in connection with the conduct.

(5)   If a person obtains a pecuniary advantage as a result of or in connection with conduct, he is to be taken to obtain as a result of or in connection with the conduct a sum of money equal to the value of the pecuniary advantage.

(6)   References to property or a pecuniary advantage obtained in connection with conduct include references to property or a pecuniary advantage obtained both in that connection and some other.

(7)   If a person benefits from conduct his benefit is the value of the property obtained.

Notes

Extent

This Part does not extend to Scotland: see s 461(1).

Part 5
Civil recovery of the proceeds etc. of unlawful conduct

Chapter 1
Introductory

240   General purpose of this Part

(1)   This Part has effect for the purposes of—

(a)   enabling the enforcement authority to recover, in civil proceedings before the High Court or Court of Session, property which is, or represents, property obtained through unlawful conduct,

(b)   enabling cash which is, or represents, property obtained through unlawful conduct, or which is intended to be used in unlawful conduct, to be forfeited in civil proceedings before a magistrates' court or (in Scotland) the sheriff.

(2)   The powers conferred by this Part are exercisable in relation to any property (including cash) whether or not any proceedings have been brought for an offence in connection with the property.

241   'Unlawful conduct'

(1)   Conduct occurring in any part of the United Kingdom is unlawful conduct if it is unlawful under the criminal law of that part.

(2)   Conduct which—

(a)   occurs in a country [or territory]¹ outside the United Kingdom and is unlawful under the criminal law [applying in that country or territory]², and

(b)   if it occurred in a part of the United Kingdom, would be unlawful under the criminal law of that part,

is also unlawful conduct.

(3)   The court or sheriff must decide on a balance of probabilities whether it is proved—

(a)   that any matters alleged to constitute unlawful conduct have occurred, or

(b)   that any person intended to use any cash in unlawful conduct.

Notes

Amendments

1   Inserted by the Serious Organised Crime and Police Act 2005, s 109, Sch 6, paras 4, 8(a). Date in force: 1 January 2006: see the Serious Organised Crime and Police Act 2005 (Commencement No.3) Order 2005, SI 2005/3136, art 3(b), (c).
2   Substituted by the Serious Organised Crime and Police Act 2005, s 109, Sch 6, paras 4, 8(b). Date in force: 1 January 2006: see the Serious Organised Crime and Police Act 2005 (Commencement No.3) Order 2005, SI 2005/3136, art 3(b), (c).

---

242 'Property obtained through unlawful conduct'

(1) A person obtains property through unlawful conduct (whether his own conduct or another's) if he obtains property by or in return for the conduct.

(2) In deciding whether any property was obtained through unlawful conduct—

(a) it is immaterial whether or not any money, goods or services were provided in order to put the person in question in a position to carry out the conduct,

(b) it is not necessary to show that the conduct was of a particular kind if it is shown that the property was obtained through conduct of one of a number of kinds, each of which would have been unlawful conduct.

Chapter 2
Civil recovery in the High Court or Court of Session

Proceedings for recovery orders

243 Proceedings for recovery orders in England and Wales or Northern Ireland

(1) Proceedings for a recovery order may be taken by the enforcement authority in the High Court against any person who the authority thinks holds recoverable property.

(2) The enforcement authority must serve the claim form—

(a) on the respondent, and

(b) unless the court dispenses with service, on any other person who the authority thinks holds any associated property which the authority wishes to be subject to a recovery order,

wherever domiciled, resident or present.

(3) If any property which the enforcement authority wishes to be subject to a recovery order is not specified in the claim form it must be described in the form in general terms; and the form must state whether it is alleged to be recoverable property or associated property.

(4) The references above to the claim form include the particulars of claim, where they are served subsequently.

[(5) Nothing in sections 245A to 255 limits any power of the court apart from those sections to grant interim relief in connection with proceedings (including prospective proceedings) under this Chapter.][1]

Notes

Amendment

1   Inserted by the Serious Organised Crime and Police Act 2005, s 109, Sch 6, paras 4, 9. Date in force: 1 January 2006: see the Serious Organised Crime and Police Act 2005 (Commencement No.3) Order 2005, SI 2005/3136, art 3(b), (c).

Property freezing orders (England and Wales and Northern Ireland)

[245A   Application for property freezing order

(1)   Where the enforcement authority may take proceedings for a recovery order in the High Court, the authority may apply to the court for a property freezing order (whether before or after starting the proceedings).

(2)   A property freezing order is an order that—

(a)   specifies or describes the property to which it applies, and

(b)   subject to any exclusions (see section 245C(1)(b) and (2)), prohibits any person to whose property the order applies from in any way dealing with the property.

(3)   An application for a property freezing order may be made without notice if the circumstances are such that notice of the application would prejudice any right of the enforcement authority to obtain a recovery order in respect of any property.

(4)   The court may make a property freezing order on an application if it is satisfied that the condition in subsection (5) is met and, where applicable, that the condition in subsection (6) is met.

(5)   The first condition is that there is a good arguable case—

(a)   that the property to which the application for the order relates is or includes recoverable property, and

(b)   that, if any of it is not recoverable property, it is associated property.

(6)   The second condition is that, if—

(a)   the property to which the application for the order relates includes property alleged to be associated property, and

(b)   the enforcement authority has not established the identity of the person who holds it,

the authority has taken all reasonable steps to do so.][1]

Notes

Amendment

1   Inserted by the Serious Organised Crime and Police Act 2005, s 98(1). Date in force: 1 January 2006: see the Serious Organised Crime and Police Act 2005 (Commencement No.3) Order 2005, SI 2005/3136, art 3(a).

[245B   Variation and setting aside of order

(1)   The court may at any time vary or set aside a property freezing order.

(2)   If the court makes an interim receiving order that applies to all of the property to which a property freezing order applies, it must set aside the property freezing order.

(3)   If the court makes an interim receiving order that applies to some but not all of the property to which a property freezing order applies, it must vary the property freezing order so as to exclude any property to which the interim receiving order applies.

(4)   If the court decides that any property to which a property freezing order applies is neither recoverable property nor associated property, it must vary the order so as to exclude the property.

(5)   Before exercising power under this Chapter to vary or set aside a property freezing order, the court must (as well as giving the parties to the proceedings an opportunity to be heard) give such an opportunity to any person who may be affected by its decision.

(6)   Subsection (5) does not apply where the court is acting as required by subsection (2) or (3).]¹

Notes

Amendment

1   Inserted by the Serious Organised Crime and Police Act 2005, s 98(1). Date in force: 1 January 2006: see the Serious Organised Crime and Police Act 2005 (Commencement No.3) Order 2005, SI 2005/3136, art 3(a).

[245C   Exclusions

(1)   The power to vary a property freezing order includes (in particular) power to make exclusions as follows—

(a)   power to exclude property from the order, and

(b)   power, otherwise than by excluding property from the order, to make exclusions from the prohibition on dealing with the property to which the order applies.

(2)   Exclusions from the prohibition on dealing with the property to which the order applies (other than exclusions of property from the order) may also be made when the order is made.

(3)   An exclusion may, in particular, make provision for the purpose of enabling any person—

(a)   to meet his reasonable living expenses, or

(b)   to carry on any trade, business, profession or occupation.

(4)   An exclusion may be made subject to conditions.

(5)   Where the court exercises the power to make an exclusion for the purpose of enabling a person to meet legal expenses that he has incurred, or may incur, in respect of proceedings under this Part, it must ensure that the exclusion—

(a)   is limited to reasonable legal expenses that the person has reasonably incurred or that he reasonably incurs,

(b)   specifies the total amount that may be released for legal expenses in pursuance of the exclusion, and

(c)   is made subject to the required conditions (see section 286A) in addition to any conditions imposed under subsection (4).

(6)   The court, in deciding whether to make an exclusion for the purpose of enabling a person to meet legal expenses of his in respect of proceedings under this Part—

(a) must have regard (in particular) to the desirability of the person being represented in any proceedings under this Part in which he is a participant, and

(b) must, where the person is the respondent, disregard the possibility that legal representation of the person in any such proceedings might, were an exclusion not made, be [made available under arrangements made for the purposes of Part 1 of the Legal Aid, Sentencing and Punishment of Offenders Act 2012 or funded by][1] or the Northern Ireland Legal Services Commission.

(7) If excluded property is not specified in the order it must be described in the order in general terms.

(8) The power to make exclusions must, subject to subsection (6), be exercised with a view to ensuring, so far as practicable, that the satisfaction of any right of the enforcement authority to recover the property obtained through unlawful conduct is not unduly prejudiced.

(9) Subsection (8) does not apply where the court is acting as required by section 245B(3) or (4).][2]

Notes

Amendments

1   Substituted by the Legal Aid, Sentencing and Punishment of Offenders Act 2012, s 39(1), Sch 5, paras 58, 59. Date in force: 1 April 2013; see the Legal Aid, Sentencing and Punishment of Offenders Act 2012 (Commencement No. 6) Order 2013, SI 2013/453, art 3(a), (h), subject to saving and transitional provisions as specified in the Legal Aid, Sentencing and Punishment of Offenders Act 2012 (Consequential, Transitional and Saving Provisions) Regulations 2013, SI 2013/534, regs 6–13.
2   Inserted by the Serious Organised Crime and Police Act 2005, s 98(1). Date in force: 1 January 2006: see the Serious Organised Crime and Police Act 2005 (Commencement No.3) Order 2005, SI 2005/3136, art 3(a).

[245D   Restriction on proceedings and remedies

(1)   While a property freezing order has effect—

(a)   the court may stay any action, execution or other legal process in respect of the property to which the order applies, and

(b)   no distress may be levied against the property to which the order applies except with the leave of the court and subject to any terms the court may impose.

(2)   If a court (whether the High Court or any other court) in which proceedings are pending in respect of any property is satisfied that a property freezing order has been applied for or made in respect of the property, it may either stay the proceedings or allow them to continue on any terms it thinks fit.

(3)   If a property freezing order applies to a tenancy of any premises, no landlord or other person to whom rent is payable may exercise the right of forfeiture by peaceable re-entry in relation to the premises in respect of any failure by the tenant to comply with any term or condition of the tenancy, except with the leave of the court and subject to any terms the court may impose.

(4)   Before exercising any power conferred by this section, the court must (as well as giving the parties to any of the proceedings concerned an opportunity to be

heard) give such an opportunity to any person who may be affected by the court's decision.]¹

Notes

Amendment

1   Inserted by the Serious Organised Crime and Police Act 2005, s 98(1). Date in force: 1 January 2006: see the Serious Organised Crime and Police Act 2005 (Commencement No.3) Order 2005, SI 2005/3136, art 3(a).

---

280   Applying realised proceeds

(1)   [Subsection (2) applies to sums which are in the hands of the trustee for civil recovery if they are]¹—

(a)   sums which represent the realised proceeds of property which was vested in the trustee for civil recovery by a recovery order or which he obtained in pursuance of a recovery order,

(b)   sums vested in the trustee by a recovery order or obtained by him in pursuance of a recovery order.

(2)   The trustee is to make out of the sums—

(a)   first, any payment required to be made by him by virtue of section 272,

[(aa)   next, any payment of legal expenses which, after giving effect to section 266(8B), are payable under this subsection in pursuance of provision under section 266(8A) contained in the recovery order,]²

(b)   [then]³, any payment of expenses incurred by a person acting as an insolvency practitioner which are payable under this subsection by virtue of section 432(10),

and any sum which remains is to be paid to the enforcement authority.

[(3)   The [enforcement authority (unless it is the Scottish Ministers)]⁴ may apply a sum received by [it]⁴ under subsection (2) in making payment of the remuneration and expenses of—

(a)   the trustee, or

(b)   any interim receiver appointed in, or in anticipation of, the proceedings for the recovery order.

(4)   Subsection (3)(a) does not apply in relation to the remuneration of the trustee if the trustee is a member of the staff of the [enforcement authority concerned]⁴ [(but it does apply in relation to such remuneration if the trustee is a person providing services under arrangements made by that enforcement authority)]⁵.]⁶

Notes

Amendments

1   Substituted by the Crime and Courts Act 2013, s 48(6)(b), Sch 18, paras 4, 5. Date in force: 24 February 2003: see the substitution deemed always to have had effect subject to transitional provisions and savings specified in 2013 c.22 s.15, s.48(8) and Sch.8)
2   Inserted by the Serious Organised Crime and Police Act 2005, s 109, Sch 6, paras 4, 18(a). Date in force: 1 January 2006: see the Serious Organised Crime and Police Act 2005 (Commencement No.3) Order 2005, SI 2005/3136, art 3(b), (c).
3   Substituted by the Serious Organised Crime and Police Act 2005, s 109, Sch 6, paras 4, 18(b). Date in force: 1 January 2006: see the Serious Organised Crime and Police Act 2005 (Commencement No.3) Order 2005, SI 2005/3136, art 3(b), (c)

4   Substituted by the Serious Crime Act 2007, s 74(2), Sch 8, paras 85, 88. Date in force: 1 April 2008: see the Serious Crime Act 2007 (Commencement No. 2 and Transitional and Transitory Provisions and Savings) Order 2008, SI 2008/755, art 2(1)(a), subject to transitional and transitory provisions and savings as specified in the Serious Crime Act 2007 (Commencement No. 2 and Transitional and Transitory Provisions and Savings) Order 2008, arts 3–14.

5   Inserted by the Serious Crime Act 2007 (Amendment of the Proceeds of Crime Act 2002) Order 2008, SI 2008/949, art 2. Date in force: 1 April 2008: see the Serious Crime Act 2007 (Amendment of the Proceeds of Crime Act 2002) Order 2008, art 1.

6   Inserted by the Serious Organised Crime and Police Act 2005, s 99(1), (2). Date in force: 1 July 2005: see the Serious Organised Crime and Police Act 2005 (Commencement No. 1, Transitional and Transitory Provisions) Order 2005, SI 2005/1521, art 2(1)(b).

Extent

This version of this section does not extend to Northern Ireland.

Chapter 3
Recovery of cash in summary proceedings

Searches

290   Prior approval

(1)   The powers conferred by section 289 may be exercised only with the appropriate approval unless, in the circumstances, it is not practicable to obtain that approval before exercising the power.

(2)   The appropriate approval means the approval of a judicial officer or (if that is not practicable in any case) the approval of a senior officer.

(3)   A judicial officer means—

(a)   in relation to England and Wales and Northern Ireland, a justice of the peace,

(b)   in relation to Scotland, the sheriff.

(4)   A senior officer means—

(a)   in relation to the exercise of the power by [an officer of Revenue and Customs, such an officer][1] of a rank designated by the Commissioners of Customs and Excise as equivalent to that of a senior police officer,

(b)   in relation to the exercise of the power by a constable, a senior police officer,

[(c)   in relation to the exercise of the power by an accredited financial investigator, an accredited financial investigator who falls within a description specified in an order made for this purpose by the Secretary of State under section 453.][2]

(5)   A senior police officer means a police officer of at least the rank of inspector.

(6)   If the powers are exercised without the approval of a judicial officer in a case where—

(a)   no cash is seized by virtue of section 294, or

(b)   any cash so seized is not detained for more than 48 hours [(calculated in accordance with section 295(1B))][3],

the [officer of Revenue and Customs][1][, constable or accredited financial investigator][4] who exercised the powers must give a written report to the appointed person.

(7)   The report must give particulars of the circumstances which led him to believe that—

(a)   the powers were exercisable, and

(b)   it was not practicable to obtain the approval of a judicial officer.

(8)   In this section and section 291, the appointed person means—

(a)   in relation to England and Wales ...[5], a person appointed by the Secretary of State,

(b)   in relation to Scotland, a person appointed by the Scottish Ministers,

[(c)   in relation to Northern Ireland, a person appointed by the Department of Justice.][6]

(9)   The appointed person must not be a person employed under or for the purposes of a government department or of the Scottish Administration; and the terms and conditions of his appointment, including any remuneration or expenses to be paid to him, are to be determined by the person appointing him.

Notes

Amendments

1   Substituted by the Finance Act 2013, s 224, Sch 48, paras 1, 3(a). Date in force: 17 July 2013.
2   Inserted by the Serious Crime Act 2007, s 79, Sch 11, paras 1, 3(1), (2). Date in force: 6 April 2008: see the Serious Crime Act 2007 (Commencement No. 2 and Transitional and Transitory Provisions and Savings) Order 2008, SI 2008/755, art 17(1)(f).
3   Inserted by the Serious Organised Crime and Police Act 2005, s 100(1), (3). Date in force: 1 July 2005: see the Serious Organised Crime and Police Act 2005 (Commencement No. 1, Transitional and Transitory Provisions) Order 2005, SI 2005/1521, art 2(1)(c).
4   Substituted by the Serious Crime Act 2007, s 79, Sch 11, paras 1, 3(3). Date in force: 6 April 2008: see the Serious Crime Act 2007 (Commencement No. 2 and Transitional and Transitory Provisions and Savings) Order 2008, SI 2008/755, art 17(1)(f).
5   Repealed by the Northern Ireland Act 1998 (Devolution of Policing and Justice Functions) Order 2010, SI 2010/976, art 12, Sch 14, paras 47, 58(a). Date in force: 12 April 2010: see the Northern Ireland Act 1998 (Devolution of Policing and Justice Functions) Order 2010, art 1(2), subject to transitional provision specified in the Northern Ireland Act 1998 (Devolution of Policing and Justice Functions) Order 2010, art 28.
6   Inserted by the Northern Ireland Act 1998 (Devolution of Policing and Justice Functions) Order 2010, SI 2010/976, art 12, Sch 14, paras 47, 58(b). Date in force: 12 April 2010: see the Northern Ireland Act 1998 (Devolution of Policing and Justice Functions) Order 2010, art 1(2), subject to transitional provision specified in the Northern Ireland Act 1998 (Devolution of Policing and Justice Functions) Order 2010, art 28.

Seizure and detention

295   Detention of seized cash

(1)   While the [officer of Revenue and Customs][1][, constable or accredited financial investigator][2] continues to have reasonable grounds for his suspicion, cash seized under section 294 may be detained initially for a period of 48 hours.

[(1A)   The period of 48 hours mentioned in subsection (1) is to be calculated in accordance with subsection (1B).

(1B)   In calculating a period of 48 hours in accordance with this subsection, no account shall be taken of—

(a)   any Saturday or Sunday,

(b)   Christmas Day,

(c)   Good Friday,

(d)   any day that is a bank holiday under the Banking and Financial Dealings Act 1971 in the part of the United Kingdom within which the cash is seized, or

(e)   any day prescribed under section 8(2) of the Criminal Procedure (Scotland) Act 1995 as a court holiday in a sheriff court in the sheriff court district within which the cash is seized.][3]

(2)   The period for which the cash or any part of it may be detained may be extended by an order made by a magistrates' court or (in Scotland) the sheriff; but the order may not authorise the detention of any of the cash—

(a)   beyond the end of the period of [six months][4] beginning with the date of the order,

(b)   in the case of any further order under this section, beyond the end of the period of two years beginning with the date of the first order.

(3)   A justice of the peace may also exercise the power of a magistrates' court to make the first order under subsection (2) extending the period.

(4)   An application for an order under subsection (2)—

(a)   in relation to England and Wales and Northern Ireland, may be made by the Commissioners of Customs and Excise[, a constable or an accredited financial investigator][2],

(b)   in relation to Scotland, may be made by the Scottish Ministers in connection with their functions under section 298 or by a procurator fiscal,

and the court, sheriff or justice may make the order if satisfied, in relation to any cash to be further detained, that either of the following conditions is met.

(5)   The first condition is that there are reasonable grounds for suspecting that the cash is recoverable property and that either—

(a)   its continued detention is justified while its derivation is further investigated or consideration is given to bringing (in the United Kingdom or elsewhere) proceedings against any person for an offence with which the cash is connected, or

(b)   proceedings against any person for an offence with which the cash is connected have been started and have not been concluded.

(6)   The second condition is that there are reasonable grounds for suspecting that the cash is intended to be used in unlawful conduct and that either—

(a)   its continued detention is justified while its intended use is further investigated or consideration is given to bringing (in the United Kingdom or elsewhere) proceedings against any person for an offence with which the cash is connected, or

(b)   proceedings against any person for an offence with which the cash is connected have been started and have not been concluded.

(7)   An application for an order under subsection (2) may also be made in respect of any cash seized under section 294(2), and the court, sheriff or justice may make the order if satisfied that—

(a)   the condition in subsection (5) or (6) is met in respect of part of the cash, and

(b)   it is not reasonably practicable to detain only that part.

(8)   An order under subsection (2) must provide for notice to be given to persons affected by it.

Notes

Amendments

1   Substituted by the Finance Act 2013, s 224, Sch 48, paras 1, 7. Date in force: 17 July 2013.
2   Substituted by the Serious Crime Act 2007, s 79, Sch 11, paras 1, 7. Date in force: 6 April 2008: see the Serious Crime Act 2007 (Commencement No. 2 and Transitional and Transitory Provisions and Savings) Order 2008, SI 2008/755, art 17(1)(f).
3   Inserted by the Serious Organised Crime and Police Act 2005, s 100(1), (2). Date in force: 1 July 2005: see the Serious Organised Crime and Police Act 2005 (Commencement No. 1, Transitional and Transitory Provisions) Order 2005, SI 2005/1521, art 2(1)(c).
4   Substituted by the Policing and Crime Act 2009, s 64(1). Date in force: 25 January 2010: see the Policing and Crime Act 2009 (Commencement No. 1 and Transitional and Saving Provisions) Order 2009/3096, art 3(i).

---

296   Interest

(1)   If cash is detained under section 295 for more than 48 hours [(calculated in accordance with section 295(1B))][1], it is at the first opportunity to be paid into an interest-bearing account and held there; and the interest accruing on it is to be added to it on its forfeiture or release.

(2)   In the case of cash detained under section 295 which was seized under section 294(2), the [officer of Revenue and Customs][2][, constable or accredited financial investigator][3] must, on paying it into the account, release the part of the cash to which the suspicion does not relate.

(3)   Subsection (1) does not apply if the cash or, as the case may be, the part to which the suspicion relates is required as evidence of an offence or evidence in proceedings under this Chapter.

Notes

Amendments

1   Inserted by the Serious Organised Crime and Police Act 2005, s 100(1), (3). Date in force: 1 July 2005: see the Serious Organised Crime and Police Act 2005 (Commencement No. 1, Transitional and Transitory Provisions) Order 2005, SI 2005/1521, art 2(1)(c).
2   Substituted by the Finance Act 2013, s 224, Sch 48, paras 1, 8. Date in force: 17 July 2013.
3   Substituted by the Serious Crime Act 2007, s 79, Sch 11, paras 1, 8. Date in force: 6 April 2008: see the Serious Crime Act 2007 (Commencement No. 2 and Transitional and Transitory Provisions and Savings) Order 2008, SI 2008/755, art 17(1)(f).

Supplementary

302   Compensation

(1)   If no forfeiture order is made in respect of any cash detained under this Chapter, the person to whom the cash belongs or from whom it was seized may make an application to the magistrates' court or (in Scotland) the sheriff for compensation.

(2)   If, for any period beginning with the first opportunity to place the cash in an interest-bearing account after the initial detention of the cash for 48 hours

[(calculated in accordance with section 295(1B))][1], the cash was not held in an interest-bearing account while detained, the court or sheriff may order an amount of compensation to be paid to the applicant.

(3)   The amount of compensation to be paid under subsection (2) is the amount the court or sheriff thinks would have been earned in interest in the period in question if the cash had been held in an interest-bearing account.

(4)   If the court or sheriff is satisfied that, taking account of any interest to be paid under section 296 or any amount to be paid under subsection (2), the applicant has suffered loss as a result of the detention of the cash and that the circumstances are exceptional, the court or sheriff may order compensation (or additional compensation) to be paid to him.

(5)   The amount of compensation to be paid under subsection (4) is the amount the court or sheriff thinks reasonable, having regard to the loss suffered and any other relevant circumstances.

(6)   If the cash was seized by [an officer of Revenue and Customs][2], the compensation is to be paid by the Commissioners of Customs and Excise.

(7)   If the cash was seized by a constable, the compensation is to be paid as follows—

(a)   in the case of a constable of a police force in England and Wales, it is to be paid out of the police fund from which the expenses of the police force are met,

(b)   in the case of a constable of a police force in Scotland, it is to be paid by the [Scottish Police Authority][3],

[(ba)   in the case of a constable of the Police Service of Scotland, it is to be paid by the Scottish Police Authority,][4]

(c)   in the case of a police officer within the meaning of the Police (Northern Ireland) Act 2000 (c. 32), it is to be paid out of money provided by the Chief Constable.

[(7A)   If the cash was seized by an accredited financial investigator who was not an officer of Revenue and Customs or a constable, the compensation is to be paid as follows–

(a)   in the case of an investigator–

   [(i)   who was a member of the civilian staff of a police force, including the metropolitan police force, (within the meaning of that Part of that Act), or][5]

   (ii)   who was a member of staff of the City of London police force,

   it is to be paid out of the police fund from which the expenses of the police force are met,

(b)   in the case of an investigator who was a member of staff of the Police Service of Northern Ireland, it is to be paid out of money provided by the Chief Constable,

(c)   in the case of an investigator who was a member of staff of a department of the Government of the United Kingdom, it is to be paid by the Minister of the Crown in charge of the department or by the department,

(d)   in the case of an investigator who was a member of staff of a Northern Ireland department, it is to be paid by the department,

(e)   in any other case, it is to be paid by the employer of the investigator.

(7B)   The Secretary of State may by order amend subsection (7A).][6]

(8)   If a forfeiture order is made in respect only of a part of any cash detained under this Chapter, this section has effect in relation to the other part.

[(9)   The power in subsection (7B) is exercisable by the Department of Justice (and not by the Secretary of State) so far as it may be used to make provision which could be made by an Act of the Northern Ireland Assembly without the consent of the Secretary of State (see sections 6 to 8 of the Northern Ireland Act 1998).][7]

Notes

Amendments

1   Inserted by the Serious Organised Crime and Police Act 2005, s 100(1), (3). Date in force: 1 July 2005: see the Serious Organised Crime and Police Act 2005 (Commencement No. 1, Transitional and Transitory Provisions) Order 2005, SI 2005/1521, art 2(1)(c).
2   Substituted by the Finance Act 2013, s 224, Sch 48, paras 1, 10. Date in force: 17 July 2013.
3   Substituted by the Police and Fire Reform (Scotland) Act 2012 (Consequential Modifications and Savings) Order 2013, SSI 2013/119, art 4, Sch 1, para 19(1), (3)(a). Date in force: 1 April 2013: see the Police and Fire Reform (Scotland) Act 2012 (Consequential Modifications and Savings) Order 2013, art 1.
4   Inserted by the Police and Fire Reform (Scotland) Act 2012 (Consequential Modifications and Savings) Order 2013, SSI 2013/119, art 4, Sch 1, para 19(1), (3)(b). Date in force: 1 April 2013: see the Police and Fire Reform (Scotland) Act 2012 (Consequential Modifications and Savings) Order 2013, art 1.
5   Substituted by the Police Reform and Social Responsibility Act 2011, s 99, Sch 16, paras 304, 306. Date in force: 16 January 2012: see the Police Reform and Social Responsibility Act 2011 (Commencement No. 3 and Transitional Provisions) Order 2011, SI 2011/3019, art 3, Sch 1.
6   Inserted by the Serious Crime Act 2007, s 79, Sch 11, paras 1, 11. Date in force: 6 April 2008: see the Serious Crime Act 2007 (Commencement No. 2 and Transitional and Transitory Provisions and Savings) Order 2008, SI 2008/755, art 17(1)(f).
7   Inserted by the Northern Ireland Act 1998 (Devolution of Policing and Justice Functions) Order 2010, SI 2010/976, art 12, Sch 14, paras 47, 62. Date in force: 12 April 2010: see the Northern Ireland Act 1998 (Devolution of Policing and Justice Functions) Order 2010, art 1(2), subject to transitional provision specified in the Northern Ireland Act 1998 (Devolution of Policing and Justice Functions) Order 2010, art 28.

337, 338, 339, 340, 364, 415, 444, 447

Chapter 4
General

Recoverable property

305   Tracing property, etc.

(1)   Where property obtained through unlawful conduct ('the original property') is or has been recoverable, property which represents the original property is also recoverable property.

(2)   If a person enters into a transaction by which—

(a)   he disposes of recoverable property, whether the original property or property which (by virtue of this Chapter) represents the original property, and

(b)   he obtains other property in place of it,

the other property represents the original property.

(3)   If a person disposes of recoverable property which represents the original property, the property may be followed into the hands of the person who obtains it (and it continues to represent the original property).

308   General exceptions

(1)   If—

(a)   a person disposes of recoverable property, and

(b)   the person who obtains it on the disposal does so in good faith, for value and without notice that it was recoverable property,

the property may not be followed into that person's hands and, accordingly, it ceases to be recoverable.

(2)   If recoverable property is vested, forfeited or otherwise disposed of in pursuance of powers conferred by virtue of this Part, it ceases to be recoverable.

(3)   If—

(a)   in pursuance of a judgment in civil proceedings (whether in the United Kingdom or elsewhere), the defendant makes a payment to the claimant or the claimant otherwise obtains property from the defendant,

(b)   the claimant's claim is based on the defendant's unlawful conduct, and

(c)   apart from this subsection, the sum received, or the property obtained, by the claimant would be recoverable property,

the property ceases to be recoverable.

In relation to Scotland, 'claimant' and 'defendant' are to be read as 'pursuer' and 'defender'.

(4)   If—

(a)   a payment is made to a person in pursuance of a compensation order under Article 14 of the Criminal Justice (Northern Ireland) Order 1994 (S.I. 1994/2795 (N.I. 15)), section 249 of the Criminal Procedure (Scotland) Act 1995 (c. 46) or section 130 of the Powers of Criminal Courts (Sentencing) Act 2000 (c. 6) or in pursuance of a service compensation order under the Armed Forces Act 2006, and

(b)   apart from this subsection, the sum received would be recoverable property,

the property ceases to be recoverable.

(5)   If—

(a)   a payment is made to a person in pursuance of a restitution order under section 27 of the Theft Act (Northern Ireland) 1969 (c. 16 (N.I.)) or section 148(2) of the Powers of Criminal Courts (Sentencing) Act 2000 or a person otherwise obtains any property in pursuance of such an order, and

(b)   apart from this subsection, the sum received, or the property obtained, would be recoverable property,

the property ceases to be recoverable.

(6)   If—

(a)   in pursuance of an order made by the court under section 382(3) or 383(5) of the Financial Services and Markets Act 2000 (c. 8) (restitution orders), an amount is paid to or distributed among any persons in accordance with the court's directions, and

(b) apart from this subsection, the sum received by them would be recoverable property,

the property ceases to be recoverable.

(7) If—

(a) in pursuance of a requirement of the Financial Conduct Authority, the Prudential Regulation Authority or the Bank of England under or by virtue of section 384(5) of the Financial Services and Markets Act 2000 (power to require restitution), an amount is paid to or distributed among any persons, and

(b) apart from this subsection, the sum received by them would be recoverable property,

the property ceases to be recoverable.

[(7A) If—

(a) a payment is made to a person in pursuance of an unlawful profit order under section 4 of the Prevention of Social Housing Fraud Act 2013, and

(b) apart from this subsection, the sum received would be recoverable property,

the property ceases to be recoverable.]¹

(8) Property is not recoverable while a restraint order applies to it, that is—

(a) an order under section 41, 120 or 190, or

(b) an order under any corresponding provision of an enactment mentioned in section 8(7)(a) to (g).

(9) Property is not recoverable if it has been taken into account in deciding the amount of a person's benefit from criminal conduct for the purpose of making a confiscation order, that is—

(a) an order under section 6, 92 or 156, or

(b) an order under a corresponding provision of an enactment mentioned in section 8(7)(a) to (g),

and, in relation to an order mentioned in paragraph (b), the reference to the amount of a person's benefit from criminal conduct is to be read as a reference to the corresponding amount under the enactment in question.

(10) Where—

(a) a person enters into a transaction to which section 305(2) applies, and

(b) the disposal is one to which subsection (1) or (2) applies,

this section does not affect the recoverability (by virtue of section 305(2)) of any property obtained on the transaction in place of the property disposed of.

Notes

Amendment

1   Inserted by the Prevention of Social Housing Fraud Act 2013, s 10, Schedule, paras 11, 23. Date in force (England): 15 October 2013: see the Prevention of Social Housing Fraud Act 2013 (Commencement) (England) Order 2013, SI 2013/2622, art 2. Date in force (Wales): 5 November 2013: see the Prevention of Social Housing Fraud Act 2013 (Commencement) (Wales) Order 2013, SI 2013/2861, art 2.

Extent

This version of this section does not extend to Northern Ireland and Scotland.

_____

Part 7
Money laundering

Offences

327   Concealing etc

(1)   A person commits an offence if he—

(a)   conceals criminal property;

(b)   disguises criminal property;

(c)   converts criminal property;

(d)   transfers criminal property;

(e)   removes criminal property from England and Wales or from Scotland or from Northern Ireland.

(2)   But a person does not commit such an offence if—

(a)   he makes an authorised disclosure under section 338 and (if the disclosure is made before he does the act mentioned in subsection (1)) he has the appropriate consent;

(b)   he intended to make such a disclosure but had a reasonable excuse for not doing so;

(c)   the act he does is done in carrying out a function he has relating to the enforcement of any provision of this Act or of any other enactment relating to criminal conduct or benefit from criminal conduct.

[(2A)   Nor does a person commit an offence under subsection (1) if—

(a)   he knows, or believes on reasonable grounds, that the relevant criminal conduct occurred in a particular country or territory outside the United Kingdom, and

(b)   the relevant criminal conduct—

(i)   was not, at the time it occurred, unlawful under the criminal law then applying in that country or territory, and

(ii)   is not of a description prescribed by an order made by the Secretary of State.

(2B)   In subsection (2A) 'the relevant criminal conduct' is the criminal conduct by reference to which the property concerned is criminal property.]¹

[(2C)   A deposit-taking body that does an act mentioned in paragraph (c) or (d) of subsection (1) does not commit an offence under that subsection if—

(a)   it does the act in operating an account maintained with it, and

(b)   the value of the criminal property concerned is less than the threshold amount determined under section 339A for the act.]²

(3)   Concealing or disguising criminal property includes concealing or disguising its nature, source, location, disposition, movement or ownership or any rights with respect to it.

Notes

Amendments

1   Inserted by the Serious Organised Crime and Police Act 2005, s 102(1), (2). Date in force:
     15 May 2006: see the Serious Organised Crime and Police Act 2005 (Commencement
     No. 6 and Appointed Day) Order 2006, SI 2006/1085, art 3.
2   Inserted by the Serious Organised Crime and Police Act 2005, s 103(1), (2). Date in force:
     1 July 2005: see the Serious Organised Crime and Police Act 2005 (Commencement No.
     1, Transitional and Transitory Provisions) Order 2005, SI 2005/1521, art 3(1)(c).

328   Arrangements

(1)   A person commits an offence if he enters into or becomes concerned in an arrangement which he knows or suspects facilitates (by whatever means) the acquisition, retention, use or control of criminal property by or on behalf of another person.

(2)   But a person does not commit such an offence if—

(a)   he makes an authorised disclosure under section 338 and (if the disclosure is made before he does the act mentioned in subsection (1)) he has the appropriate consent;

(b)   he intended to make such a disclosure but had a reasonable excuse for not doing so;

(c)   the act he does is done in carrying out a function he has relating to the enforcement of any provision of this Act or of any other enactment relating to criminal conduct or benefit from criminal conduct.

[(3)   Nor does a person commit an offence under subsection (1) if—

(a)   he knows, or believes on reasonable grounds, that the relevant criminal conduct occurred in a particular country or territory outside the United Kingdom, and

(b)   the relevant criminal conduct—

  (i)   was not, at the time it occurred, unlawful under the criminal law then applying in that country or territory, and

  (ii)   is not of a description prescribed by an order made by the Secretary of State.

(4)   In subsection (3) 'the relevant criminal conduct' is the criminal conduct by reference to which the property concerned is criminal property.]¹

[(5)   A deposit-taking body that does an act mentioned in subsection (1) does not commit an offence under that subsection if—

(a)   it does the act in operating an account maintained with it, and

(b)   the arrangement facilitates the acquisition, retention, use or control of criminal property of a value that is less than the threshold amount determined under section 339A for the act.]²

Notes

Amendments

1   Inserted by the Serious Organised Crime and Police Act 2005, s 102(1), (3). Date in force:
     15 May 2006: see the Serious Organised Crime and Police Act 2005 (Commencement
     No. 6 and Appointed Day) Order 2006, SI 2006/1085, art 3.

2   Inserted by the Serious Organised Crime and Police Act 2005, s 103(1), (3). Date in force: 1 July 2005: see the Serious Organised Crime and Police Act 2005 (Commencement No. 1, Transitional and Transitory Provisions) Order 2005, SI 2005/1521, art 3(1)(c).

---

329   Acquisition, use and possession

(1)   A person commits an offence if he—

(a)   acquires criminal property;

(b)   uses criminal property;

(c)   has possession of criminal property.

(2)   But a person does not commit such an offence if—

(a)   he makes an authorised disclosure under section 338 and (if the disclosure is made before he does the act mentioned in subsection (1)) he has the appropriate consent;

(b)   he intended to make such a disclosure but had a reasonable excuse for not doing so;

(c)   he acquired or used or had possession of the property for adequate consideration;

(d)   the act he does is done in carrying out a function he has relating to the enforcement of any provision of this Act or of any other enactment relating to criminal conduct or benefit from criminal conduct.

[(2A)   Nor does a person commit an offence under subsection (1) if—

(a)   he knows, or believes on reasonable grounds, that the relevant criminal conduct occurred in a particular country or territory outside the United Kingdom, and

(b)   the relevant criminal conduct—

(i)   was not, at the time it occurred, unlawful under the criminal law then applying in that country or territory, and

(ii)   is not of a description prescribed by an order made by the Secretary of State.

(2B)   In subsection (2A) 'the relevant criminal conduct' is the criminal conduct by reference to which the property concerned is criminal property.][1]

[(2C)   A deposit-taking body that does an act mentioned in subsection (1) does not commit an offence under that subsection if—

(a)   it does the act in operating an account maintained with it, and

(b)   the value of the criminal property concerned is less than the threshold amount determined under section 339A for the act.][2]

(3)   For the purposes of this section—

(a)   a person acquires property for inadequate consideration if the value of the consideration is significantly less than the value of the property;

(b)   a person uses or has possession of property for inadequate consideration if the value of the consideration is significantly less than the value of the use or possession;

(c)   the provision by a person of goods or services which he knows or suspects may help another to carry out criminal conduct is not consideration.

Notes

Amendments

1   Inserted by the Serious Organised Crime and Police Act 2005, s 102(1), (4). Date in force: 15 May 2006: see the Serious Organised Crime and Police Act 2005 (Commencement No. 6 and Appointed Day) Order 2006, SI 2006/1085, art 3.
2   Inserted by the Serious Organised Crime and Police Act 2005, s 103(1), (4). Date in force: 1 July 2005: see the Serious Organised Crime and Police Act 2005 (Commencement No. 1, Transitional and Transitory Provisions) Order 2005, SI 2005/1521, art 3(1)(c).

330   Failure to disclose: regulated sector

(1)   A person commits an offence if [the conditions in subsections (2) to (4) are satisfied][1].

(2)   The first condition is that he—

(a)   knows or suspects, or

(b)   has reasonable grounds for knowing or suspecting,

that another person is engaged in money laundering.

(3)   The second condition is that the information or other matter—

(a)   on which his knowledge or suspicion is based, or

(b)   which gives reasonable grounds for such knowledge or suspicion,

came to him in the course of a business in the regulated sector.

[(3A)   The third condition is—

(a)   that he can identify the other person mentioned in subsection (2) or the whereabouts of any of the laundered property, or

(b)   that he believes, or it is reasonable to expect him to believe, that the information or other matter mentioned in subsection (3) will or may assist in identifying that other person or the whereabouts of any of the laundered property.

(4)   The fourth condition is that he does not make the required disclosure to—

(a)   a nominated officer, or

(b)   a person authorised for the purposes of this Part by [the Director General of the National Crime Agency][2],

as soon as is practicable after the information or other matter mentioned in subsection (3) comes to him.

(5)   The required disclosure is a disclosure of—

(a)   the identity of the other person mentioned in subsection (2), if he knows it,

(b)   the whereabouts of the laundered property, so far as he knows it, and

(c)   the information or other matter mentioned in subsection (3).

(5A)   The laundered property is the property forming the subject-matter of the money laundering that he knows or suspects, or has reasonable grounds for knowing or suspecting, that other person to be engaged in.

(6)   But he does not commit an offence under this section if—

(a)   he has a reasonable excuse for not making the required disclosure,

(b)   he is a professional legal adviser [or ...³ relevant professional adviser]⁴ and—

    (i)   if he knows either of the things mentioned in subsection (5)(a) and (b), he knows the thing because of information or other matter that came to him in privileged circumstances, or

    (ii)   the information or other matter mentioned in subsection (3) came to him in privileged circumstances, or

(c)   subsection (7) [or (7B)]⁴ applies to him.]⁵

(7)   This subsection applies to a person if—

(a)   he does not know or suspect that another person is engaged in money laundering, and

(b)   he has not been provided by his employer with such training as is specified by the Secretary of State by order for the purposes of this section.

[(7A)   Nor does a person commit an offence under this section if—

(a)   he knows, or believes on reasonable grounds, that the money laundering is occurring in a particular country or territory outside the United Kingdom, and

(b)   the money laundering—

    (i)   is not unlawful under the criminal law applying in that country or territory, and

    (ii)   is not of a description prescribed in an order made by the Secretary of State.]⁶

[(7B)   This subsection applies to a person if—

(a)   he is employed by, or is in partnership with, a professional legal adviser or a relevant professional adviser to provide the adviser with assistance or support,

(b)   the information or other matter mentioned in subsection (3) comes to the person in connection with the provision of such assistance or support, and

(c)   the information or other matter came to the adviser in privileged circumstances.]⁴

(8)   In deciding whether a person committed an offence under this section the court must consider whether he followed any relevant guidance which was at the time concerned—

(a)   issued by a supervisory authority or any other appropriate body,

(b)   approved by the Treasury, and

(c)   published in a manner it approved as appropriate in its opinion to bring the guidance to the attention of persons likely to be affected by it.

(9)   A disclosure to a nominated officer is a disclosure which—

(a)   is made to a person nominated by the alleged offender's employer to receive disclosures under this section, and

(b)   is made in the course of the alleged offender's employment ...⁷.

[(9A) But a disclosure which satisfies paragraphs (a) and (b) of subsection (9) is not to be taken as a disclosure to a nominated officer if the person making the disclosure—

(a) is a professional legal adviser [or ...³ relevant professional adviser]⁴,

(b) makes it for the purpose of obtaining advice about making a disclosure under this section, and

(c) does not intend it to be a disclosure under this section.]⁸

(10) Information or other matter comes to a professional legal adviser [or ...³ relevant professional adviser]⁴ in privileged circumstances if it is communicated or given to him—

(a) by (or by a representative of) a client of his in connection with the giving by the adviser of legal advice to the client,

(b) by (or by a representative of) a person seeking legal advice from the adviser, or

(c) by a person in connection with legal proceedings or contemplated legal proceedings.

(11) But subsection (10) does not apply to information or other matter which is communicated or given with the intention of furthering a criminal purpose.

(12) Schedule 9 has effect for the purpose of determining what is—

(a) a business in the regulated sector;

(b) a supervisory authority.

(13) An appropriate body is any body which regulates or is representative of any trade, profession, business or employment carried on by the alleged offender.

[(14) A relevant professional adviser is an accountant, auditor or tax adviser who is a member of a professional body which is established for accountants, auditors or tax advisers (as the case may be) and which makes provision for—

(a) testing the competence of those seeking admission to membership of such a body as a condition for such admission; and

(b) imposing and maintaining professional and ethical standards for its members, as well as imposing sanctions for non-compliance with those standards.]⁴

Notes

Amendments

1   Substituted by the Serious Organised Crime and Police Act 2005, s 104(1), (2). Date in force: 1 July 2005: see the Serious Organised Crime and Police Act 2005 (Commencement No. 1, Transitional and Transitory Provisions) Order 2005, SI 2005/1521, art 3(1)(c).
2   Substituted by the Crime and Courts Act 2013, s 15(3), Sch 8, paras 108, 129. Date in force: 7 October 2013: see the Crime and Courts Act 2013 (Commencement No. 2 and Saving Provision) Order 2013, SI 2013/1682, art 3(u), (v), subject to savings and transitional provisions specified in the Crime and Courts Act 2013, s 15, Sch 8.
3   Repealed by the Terrorism Act 2000 and Proceeds of Crime Act 2002 (Amendment) Regulations 2007, SI 2007/3398, reg 3, Sch 2, paras 1, 2. Date in force: 26 December 2007: see the Terrorism Act 2000 and Proceeds of Crime Act 2002 (Amendment) Regulations 2007, reg 1(2).
4   Inserted by the Proceeds of Crime Act 2002 and Money Laundering Regulations 2003 (Amendment) Order 2006, SI 2006/308, art 2. Date in force: 21 February 2006: see the Proceeds of Crime Act 2002 and Money Laundering Regulations 2003 (Amendment) Order 2006, art 1.

5   Subsections (3A)-(6) substituted for sub-ss (4)-(6) by the Serious Organised Crime and Police Act 2005, s 104(1), (3). Date in force: 1 July 2005: see the Serious Organised Crime and Police Act 2005 (Commencement No. 1, Transitional and Transitory Provisions) Order 2005, SI 2005/1521, art 3(1)(c), subject to transitional provisions specified in SI 2005/1521, art 3(4).
6   Inserted by the Serious Organised Crime and Police Act 2005, s 102(1), (5). Date in force: 15 May 2006: see the Serious Organised Crime and Police Act 2005 (Commencement No. 6 and Appointed Day) Order 2006, SI 2006/1085, art 3.
7   Repealed by the Serious Organised Crime and Police Act 2005, ss 105(1), (2), 174(2), Sch 17, Pt 2. Date in force: 1 July 2005: see the Serious Organised Crime and Police Act 2005 (Commencement No. 1, Transitional and Transitory Provisions) Order 2005, SI 2005/1521, art 3(1)(c), (ee)(vi).
8   Inserted by the Serious Organised Crime and Police Act 2005, s 106(1), (2). Date in force: 1 July 2005: see the Serious Organised Crime and Police Act 2005 (Commencement No. 1, Transitional and Transitory Provisions) Order 2005, SI 2005/1521, art 3(1)(c).

---

331   Failure to disclose: nominated officers in the regulated sector

(1)   A person nominated to receive disclosures under section 330 commits an offence if the conditions in subsections (2) to (4) are satisfied.

(2)   The first condition is that he—

(a)   knows or suspects, or

(b)   has reasonable grounds for knowing or suspecting,

that another person is engaged in money laundering.

(3)   The second condition is that the information or other matter—

(a)   on which his knowledge or suspicion is based, or

(b)   which gives reasonable grounds for such knowledge or suspicion,

came to him in consequence of a disclosure made under section 330.

[(3A)   The third condition is—

(a)   that he knows the identity of the other person mentioned in subsection (2), or the whereabouts of any of the laundered property, in consequence of a disclosure made under section 330,

(b)   that that other person, or the whereabouts of any of the laundered property, can be identified from the information or other matter mentioned in subsection (3), or

(c)   that he believes, or it is reasonable to expect him to believe, that the information or other matter will or may assist in identifying that other person or the whereabouts of any of the laundered property.

(4)   The fourth condition is that he does not make the required disclosure to a person authorised for the purposes of this Part by [the Director General of the National Crime Agency][1] as soon as is practicable after the information or other matter mentioned in subsection (3) comes to him.

(5)   The required disclosure is a disclosure of—

(a)   the identity of the other person mentioned in subsection (2), if disclosed to him under section 330,

(b)   the whereabouts of the laundered property, so far as disclosed to him under section 330, and

(c)   the information or other matter mentioned in subsection (3).

(5A)   The laundered property is the property forming the subject-matter of the money laundering that he knows or suspects, or has reasonable grounds for knowing or suspecting, that other person to be engaged in.

(6)   But he does not commit an offence under this section if he has a reasonable excuse for not making the required disclosure.][2]

[(6A)   Nor does a person commit an offence under this section if—

(a)   he knows, or believes on reasonable grounds, that the money laundering is occurring in a particular country or territory outside the United Kingdom, and

(b)   the money laundering—

  (i)   is not unlawful under the criminal law applying in that country or territory, and

  (ii)   is not of a description prescribed in an order made by the Secretary of State.][3]

(7)   In deciding whether a person committed an offence under this section the court must consider whether he followed any relevant guidance which was at the time concerned—

(a)   issued by a supervisory authority or any other appropriate body,

(b)   approved by the Treasury, and

(c)   published in a manner it approved as appropriate in its opinion to bring the guidance to the attention of persons likely to be affected by it.

(8)   Schedule 9 has effect for the purpose of determining what is a supervisory authority.

(9)   An appropriate body is a body which regulates or is representative of a trade, profession, business or employment.

Notes

Amendments

1   Substituted by the Crime and Courts Act 2013, s 15(3), Sch 8, paras 108, 130. Date in force: 7 October 2013: see the Crime and Courts Act 2013 (Commencement No. 2 and Saving Provision) Order 2013, SI 2013/1682, art 3(u), (v), subject to savings and transitional provisions specified in the Crime and Courts Act 2013, s 15, Sch 8.
2   Subsections (3A)-(6) substituted for sub-ss (4)-(6) by the Serious Organised Crime and Police Act 2005, s 104(1), (4). Date in force: 1 July 2005: see the Serious Organised Crime and Police Act 2005 (Commencement No. 1, Transitional and Transitory Provisions) Order 2005, SI 2005/1521, art 3(1)(c), subject to transitional provisions specified in SI 2005/1521, art 3(4).
3   Inserted by the Serious Organised Crime and Police Act 2005, s 102(1), (6). Date in force: 15 May 2006: see the Serious Organised Crime and Police Act 2005 (Commencement No. 6 and Appointed Day) Order 2006, SI 2006/1085, art 3.

---

332   Failure to disclose: other nominated officers

(1)   A person nominated to receive disclosures under section 337 or 338 commits an offence if the conditions in subsections (2) to (4) are satisfied.

(2)   The first condition is that he knows or suspects that another person is engaged in money laundering.

(3)   The second condition is that the information or other matter on which his knowledge or suspicion is based came to him in consequence of a disclosure made under [the applicable section][1].

[(3A)   The third condition is—

(a)   that he knows the identity of the other person mentioned in subsection (2), or the whereabouts of any of the laundered property, in consequence of a disclosure made under the applicable section,

(b)   that that other person, or the whereabouts of any of the laundered property, can be identified from the information or other matter mentioned in subsection (3), or

(c)   that he believes, or it is reasonable to expect him to believe, that the information or other matter will or may assist in identifying that other person or the whereabouts of any of the laundered property.

(4)   The fourth condition is that he does not make the required disclosure to a person authorised for the purposes of this Part by [the Director General of the National Crime Agency][2] as soon as is practicable after the information or other matter mentioned in subsection (3) comes to him.

(5)   The required disclosure is a disclosure of—

(a)   the identity of the other person mentioned in subsection (2), if disclosed to him under the applicable section,

(b)   the whereabouts of the laundered property, so far as disclosed to him under the applicable section, and

(c)   the information or other matter mentioned in subsection (3).

(5A)   The laundered property is the property forming the subject-matter of the money laundering that he knows or suspects that other person to be engaged in.

(5B)   The applicable section is section 337 or, as the case may be, section 338.

(6)   But he does not commit an offence under this section if he has a reasonable excuse for not making the required disclosure.][3]

[(7)   Nor does a person commit an offence under this section if—

(a)   he knows, or believes on reasonable grounds, that the money laundering is occurring in a particular country or territory outside the United Kingdom, and

(b)   the money laundering—

(i)   is not unlawful under the criminal law applying in that country or territory, and

(ii)   is not of a description prescribed in an order made by the Secretary of State.][4]

Notes

Amendments

1   Substituted by the Serious Organised Crime and Police Act 2005, s 104(1), (5). Date in force: 1 July 2005: see the Serious Organised Crime and Police Act 2005 (Commencement No. 1, Transitional and Transitory Provisions) Order 2005, SI 2005/1521, art 3(1)(c).

2   Substituted by the Crime and Courts Act 2013, s 15(3), Sch 8, paras 108, 131. Date in force: 7 October 2013: see the Crime and Courts Act 2013 (Commencement No. 2 and Saving Provision) Order 2013, SI 2013/1682, art 3(u), (v), subject to savings and transitional provisions specified in the Crime and Courts Act 2013, s 15, Sch 8.

3   Subsections (3A)-(6) substituted for sub-ss (4)-(6) by the Serious Organised Crime and Police Act 2005, s 104(1), (6). Date in force: 1 July 2005: see the Serious Organised Crime and Police Act 2005 (Commencement No. 1, Transitional and Transitory Provisions) Order 2005, SI 2005/1521, art 3(1)(c), subject to transitional provisions specified in SI 2005/1521, art 3(4).

4   Inserted by the Serious Organised Crime and Police Act 2005, s 102(1), (7). Date in force: 15 May 2006: see the Serious Organised Crime and Police Act 2005 (Commencement No. 6 and Appointed Day) Order 2006, SI 2006/1085, art 3.

---

333   ...[1]

...[1]

Notes

Amendment

1   Repealed by the Terrorism Act 2000 and Proceeds of Crime Act 2002 (Amendment) Regulations 2007, SI 2007/3398, reg 3, Sch 2, paras 1, 3. Date in force: 26 December 2007: see the Terrorism Act 2000 and Proceeds of Crime Act 2002 (Amendment) Regulations 2007, reg 1(2).

[333A   Tipping off: regulated sector

(1)   A person commits an offence if—

(a)   the person discloses any matter within subsection (2);

(b)   the disclosure is likely to prejudice any investigation that might be conducted following the disclosure referred to in that subsection; and

(c)   the information on which the disclosure is based came to the person in the course of a business in the regulated sector.

(2)   The matters are that the person or another person has made a disclosure under this Part—

(a)   to a constable,

(b)   to an officer of Revenue and Customs,

(c)   to a nominated officer, or

(d)   to a [National Crime Agency officer][1] authorised for the purposes of this Part by the Director General of that Agency,

of information that came to that person in the course of a business in the regulated sector.

(3)   A person commits an offence if—

(a)   the person discloses that an investigation into allegations that an offence under this Part has been committed is being contemplated or is being carried out;

(b)   the disclosure is likely to prejudice that investigation; and

(c)   the information on which the disclosure is based came to the person in the course of a business in the regulated sector.

(4)   A person guilty of an offence under this section is liable—

(a)   on summary conviction to imprisonment for a term not exceeding three months, or to a fine not exceeding level 5 on the standard scale, or to both;

(b)   on conviction on indictment to imprisonment for a term not exceeding two years, or to a fine, or to both.

(5)   This section is subject to—

(a)   section 333B (disclosures within an undertaking or group etc),

(b)   section 333C (other permitted disclosures between institutions etc), and

(c)   section 333D (other permitted disclosures etc).][2]

Notes

Amendments

1   Substituted by the Crime and Courts Act 2013, s 15(3), Sch 8, paras 108, 132. Date in force: 7 October 2013: see the Crime and Courts Act 2013 (Commencement No. 2 and Saving Provision) Order 2013, SI 2013/1682, art 3(u), (v), subject to savings and transitional provisions specified in the Crime and Courts Act 2013, s 15, Sch 8.
2   Inserted by the Terrorism Act 2000 and Proceeds of Crime Act 2002 (Amendment) Regulations 2007, SI 2007/3398, reg 3, Sch 2, paras 1, 4. Date in force: 26 December 2007: see the Terrorism Act 2000 and Proceeds of Crime Act 2002 (Amendment) Regulations 2007, reg 1(2).

[333B   Disclosures within an undertaking or group etc

(1)   An employee, officer or partner of an undertaking does not commit an offence under section 333A if the disclosure is to an employee, officer or partner of the same undertaking.

(2)   A person does not commit an offence under section 333A in respect of a disclosure by a credit institution or a financial institution if—

(a)   the disclosure is to a credit institution or a financial institution,

(b)   the institution to whom the disclosure is made is situated in an EEA State or in a country or territory imposing equivalent money laundering requirements, and

(c)   both the institution making the disclosure and the institution to whom it is made belong to the same group.

(3)   In subsection (2) 'group' has the same meaning as in Directive 2002/87/EC of the European Parliament and of the Council of 16th December 2002 on the supplementary supervision of credit institutions, insurance undertakings and investment firms in a financial conglomerate.

(4)   A professional legal adviser or a relevant professional adviser does not commit an offence under section 333A if—

(a)   the disclosure is to professional legal adviser or a relevant professional adviser,

(b)   both the person making the disclosure and the person to whom it is made carry on business in an EEA State or in a country or territory imposing equivalent money laundering requirements, and

(c)   those persons perform their professional activities within different undertakings that share common ownership, management or control.][1]

[333C   Other permitted disclosures between institutions etc

(1)   This section applies to a disclosure—

(a)   by a credit institution to another credit institution,

(b)   by a financial institution to another financial institution,

(c)   by a professional legal adviser to another professional legal adviser, or

(d)   by a relevant professional adviser of a particular kind to another relevant professional adviser of the same kind.

(2)   A person does not commit an offence under section 333A in respect of a disclosure to which this section applies if—

(a)   the disclosure relates to—

(i)   a client or former client of the institution or adviser making the disclosure and the institution or adviser to whom it is made,

(ii)   a transaction involving them both, or

(iii) the provision of a service involving them both;

(b)   the disclosure is for the purpose only of preventing an offence under this Part of this Act;

(c)   the institution or adviser to whom the disclosure is made is situated in an EEA State or in a country or territory imposing equivalent money laundering requirements; and

(d)   the institution or adviser making the disclosure and the institution or adviser to whom it is made are subject to equivalent duties of professional confidentiality and the protection of personal data (within the meaning of section 1 of the Data Protection Act 1998).][1]

[333D   Other permitted disclosures etc

(1)   A person does not commit an offence under section 333A if the disclosure is—

(a)   to the authority that is the supervisory authority for that person by virtue of the Money Laundering Regulations 2007 (S.I. 2007/2157); or

(b)   for the purpose of—

(i)   the detection, investigation or prosecution of a criminal offence (whether in the United Kingdom or elsewhere),

(ii)   an investigation under this Act, or

(iii)   the enforcement of any order of a court under this Act.

(2)   A professional legal adviser or a relevant professional adviser does not commit an offence under section 333A if the disclosure—

(a)   is to the adviser's client, and

(b)   is made for the purpose of dissuading the client from engaging in conduct amounting to an offence.

(3)   A person does not commit an offence under section 333A(1) if the person does not know or suspect that the disclosure is likely to have the effect mentioned in section 333A(1)(b).

(4)   A person does not commit an offence under section 333A(3) if the person does not know or suspect that the disclosure is likely to have the effect mentioned in section 333A(3)(b).][1]

Notes

Amendment

1   Inserted by the Terrorism Act 2000 and Proceeds of Crime Act 2002 (Amendment) Regulations 2007, SI 2007/3398, reg 3, Sch 2, paras 1, 4. Date in force: 26 December 2007: see the Terrorism Act 2000 and Proceeds of Crime Act 2002 (Amendment) Regulations 2007, reg 1(2).

[333E   Interpretation of sections 333A to 333D

(1)   For the purposes of sections 333A to 333D, Schedule 9 has effect for determining—

(a)   what is a business in the regulated sector, and

(b)   what is a supervisory authority.

(2)   In those sections—

'credit institution' has the same meaning as in Schedule 9;

'financial institution' means an undertaking that carries on a business in the regulated sector by virtue of any of paragraphs (b) to (i) of paragraph 1(1) of that Schedule.

(3)   References in those sections to a disclosure by or to a credit institution or a financial institution include disclosure by or to an employee, officer or partner of the institution acting on its behalf.

(4)   For the purposes of those sections a country or territory imposes 'equivalent money laundering requirements' if it imposes requirements equivalent to those laid down in Directive 2005/60/EC of the European Parliament and of the Council of 26th October 2005 on the prevention of the use of the financial system for the purpose of money laundering and terrorist financing.

(5)   In those sections 'relevant professional adviser' means an accountant, auditor or tax adviser who is a member of a professional body which is established for

accountants, auditors or tax advisers (as the case may be) and which makes provision for—

(a) testing the competence of those seeking admission to membership of such a body as a condition for such admission; and

(b) imposing and maintaining professional and ethical standards for its members, as well as imposing sanctions for non-compliance with those standards.][1]

Notes

Amendment

1   Inserted by the Terrorism Act 2000 and Proceeds of Crime Act 2002 (Amendment) Regulations 2007, SI 2007/3398, reg 3, Sch 2, paras 1, 4. Date in force: 26 December 2007: see the Terrorism Act 2000 and Proceeds of Crime Act 2002 (Amendment) Regulations 2007, reg 1(2).

334   Penalties

(1)   A person guilty of an offence under section 327, 328 or 329 is liable—

(a) on summary conviction, to imprisonment for a term not exceeding six months or to a fine not exceeding the statutory maximum or to both, or

(b) on conviction on indictment, to imprisonment for a term not exceeding 14 years or to a fine or to both.

(2)   A person guilty of an offence under [section 330, 331 or 332][1] is liable—

(a) on summary conviction, to imprisonment for a term not exceeding six months or to a fine not exceeding the statutory maximum or to both, or

(b) on conviction on indictment, to imprisonment for a term not exceeding five years or to a fine or to both.

[(3)   A person guilty of an offence under section 339(1A) is liable on summary conviction to a fine not exceeding level 5 on the standard scale.][2]

Notes

Amendments

1   Substituted by the Terrorism Act 2000 and Proceeds of Crime Act 2002 (Amendment) Regulations 2007, SI 2007/3398, reg 3, Sch 2, paras 1, 5. Date in force: 26 December 2007: see the Terrorism Act 2000 and Proceeds of Crime Act 2002 (Amendment) Regulations 2007, reg 1(2).
2   Inserted by the Serious Organised Crime and Police Act 2005, s 105(1), (3). Date in force: 1 July 2005: see the Serious Organised Crime and Police Act 2005 (Commencement No. 1, Transitional and Transitory Provisions) Order 2005, SI 2005/1521, art 3(1)(c).

Part 7
Money laundering

Consent

335   Appropriate consent

(1)   The apropriate consent is—

(a) the consent of a nominated officer to do a prohibited act if an authorised disclosure is made to the nominated officer;

(b) the consent of a constable to do a prohibited act if an authorised disclosure is made to a constable;

(c) the consent of a customs officer to do a prohibited act if an authorised disclosure is made to a customs officer.

(2)   A person must be treated as having the appropriate consent if—

(a) he makes an authorised disclosure to a constable or a customs officer, and

(b) the condition in subsection (3) or the condition in subsection (4) is satisfied.

(3)   The condition is that before the end of the notice period he does not receive notice from a constable or customs officer that consent to the doing of the act is refused.

(4)   The condition is that—

(a) before the end of the notice period he receives notice from a constable or customs officer that consent to the doing of the act is refused, and

(b) the moratorium period has expired.

(5)   The notice period is the period of seven working days starting with the first working day after the person makes the disclosure.

(6)   The moratorium period is the period of 31 days starting with the day on which the person receives notice that consent to the doing of the act is refused.

(7)   A working day is a day other than a Saturday, a Sunday, Christmas Day, Good Friday or a day which is a bank holiday under the Banking and Financial Dealings Act 1971 (c. 80) in the part of the United Kingdom in which the person is when he makes the disclosure.

(8)   References to a prohibited act are to an act mentioned in section 327(1), 328(1) or 329(1) (as the case may be).

(9)   A nominated officer is a person nominated to receive disclosures under section 338.

(10)   Subsections (1) to (4) apply for the purposes of this Part.

336   Nominated officer: consent

(1)   A nominated officer must not give the appropriate consent to the doing of a prohibited act unless the condition in subsection (2), the condition in subsection (3) or the condition in subsection (4) is satisfied.

(2)   The condition is that—

(a) he makes a disclosure that property is criminal property to a person authorised for the purposes of this Part by [the [Director General of the National Crime Agency]¹]², and

(b) such a person gives consent to the doing of the act.

(3)   The condition is that—

(a) he makes a disclosure that property is criminal property to a person authorised for the purposes of this Part by [the [Director General of the National Crime Agency]¹]², and

(b) before the end of the notice period he does not receive notice from such a person that consent to the doing of the act is refused.

(4) The condition is that—

(a) he makes a disclosure that property is criminal property to a person authorised for the purposes of this Part by [the [Director General of the National Crime Agency]¹]²,

(b) before the end of the notice period he receives notice from such a person that consent to the doing of the act is refused, and

(c) the moratorium period has expired.

(5) A person who is a nominated officer commits an offence if—

(a) he gives consent to a prohibited act in circumstances where none of the conditions in subsections (2), (3) and (4) is satisfied, and

(b) he knows or suspects that the act is a prohibited act.

(6) A person guilty of such an offence is liable—

(a) on summary conviction, to imprisonment for a term not exceeding six months or to a fine not exceeding the statutory maximum or to both, or

(b) on conviction on indictment, to imprisonment for a term not exceeding five years or to a fine or to both.

(7) The notice period is the period of seven working days starting with the first working day after the nominated officer makes the disclosure.

(8) The moratorium period is the period of 31 days starting with the day on which the nominated officer is given notice that consent to the doing of the act is refused.

(9) A working day is a day other than a Saturday, a Sunday, Christmas Day, Good Friday or a day which is a bank holiday under the Banking and Financial Dealings Act 1971 (c. 80) in the part of the United Kingdom in which the nominated officer is when he gives the appropriate consent.

(10) References to a prohibited act are to an act mentioned in section 327(1), 328(1) or 329(1) (as the case may be).

(11) A nominated officer is a person nominated to receive disclosures under section 338.

Notes

Amendments

1   Substituted by the Crime and Courts Act 2013, s 15(3), Sch 8, paras 108, 133. Date in force: 7 October 2013: see the Crime and Courts Act 2013 (Commencement No. 2 and Saving Provision) Order 2013, SI 2013/1682, art 3(u), (v), subject to savings and transitional provisions specified in the Crime and Courts Act 2013, s 15, Sch 8.

2   Substituted by the Serious Organised Crime and Police Act 2005, s 59, Sch 4, paras 168, 173. Date in force: 1 April 2006: see the Serious Organised Crime and Police Act 2005 (Commencement No. 5 and Transitional and Transitory Provisions and Savings) Order 2006, SI 2006/378, art 4(1), Schedule, para 10.

Disclosures

337   Protected disclosures

(1)   A disclosure which satisfies the following three conditions is not to be taken to breach any restriction on the disclosure of information (however imposed).

(2)   The first condition is that the information or other matter disclosed came to the person making the disclosure (the discloser) in the course of his trade, profession, business or employment.

(3)   The second condition is that the information or other matter—

(a)   causes the discloser to know or suspect, or

(b)   gives him reasonable grounds for knowing or suspecting,

that another person is engaged in money laundering.

(4)   The third condition is that the disclosure is made to a constable, a customs officer or a nominated officer as soon as is practicable after the information or other matter comes to the discloser.

[(4A)   Where a disclosure consists of a disclosure protected under subsection (1) and a disclosure of either or both of—

(a)   the identity of the other person mentioned in subsection (3), and

(b)   the whereabouts of property forming the subject-matter of the money laundering that the discloser knows or suspects, or has reasonable grounds for knowing or suspecting, that other person to be engaged in,

the disclosure of the thing mentioned in paragraph (a) or (b) (as well as the disclosure protected under subsection (1)) is not to be taken to breach any restriction on the disclosure of information (however imposed).][1]

(5)   A disclosure to a nominated officer is a disclosure which—

(a)   is made to a person nominated by the discloser's employer to receive disclosures under [section 330 or][2] this section, and

(b)   is made in the course of the discloser's employment …[3].

Notes

Amendments

1   Inserted by the Serious Organised Crime and Police Act 2005, s 104(1), (7). Date in force: 1 July 2005: see the Serious Organised Crime and Police Act 2005 (Commencement No. 1, Transitional and Transitory Provisions) Order 2005, SI 2005/1521, art 3(1)(c), subject to transitional provisions specified in SI 2005/1521, art 3(4).
2   Inserted by the Serious Organised Crime and Police Act 2005, s 106(1), (3). Date in force: 1 July 2005: see the Serious Organised Crime and Police Act 2005 (Commencement No. 1, Transitional and Transitory Provisions) Order 2005, SI 2005/1521, art 3(1)(c).
3   Repealed by the Serious Organised Crime and Police Act 2005, ss 105(1), (2), 174(2), Sch 17, Pt 2. Date in force: 1 July 2005: see the Serious Organised Crime and Police Act 2005 (Commencement No. 1, Transitional and Transitory Provisions) Order 2005, SI 2005/1521, art 3(1)(c), (ee)(vi).

---

338   Authorised disclosures

(1)   For the purposes of this Part a disclosure is authorised if—

(a)   it is a disclosure to a constable, a customs officer or a nominated officer by the alleged offender that property is criminal property,

(b)   ...[1] and

(c)   the first[, second or third][2] condition set out below is satisfied.

(2)   The first condition is that the disclosure is made before the alleged offender does the prohibited act.

[(2A)   The second condition is that—

(a)   the disclosure is made while the alleged offender is doing the prohibited act,

(b)   he began to do the act at a time when, because he did not then know or suspect that the property constituted or represented a person's benefit from criminal conduct, the act was not a prohibited act, and

(c)   the disclosure is made on his own initiative and as soon as is practicable after he first knows or suspects that the property constitutes or represents a person's benefit from criminal conduct.][3]

(3)   The [third][2] condition is that—

(a)   the disclosure is made after the alleged offender does the prohibited act,

(b)   [he has a reasonable excuse][4] for his failure to make the disclosure before he did the act, and

(c)   the disclosure is made on his own initiative and as soon as it is practicable for him to make it.

(4)   An authorised disclosure is not to be taken to breach any restriction on the disclosure of information (however imposed).

(5)   A disclosure to a nominated officer is a disclosure which—

(a)   is made to a person nominated by the alleged offender's employer to receive authorised disclosures, and

(b)   is made in the course of the alleged offender's employment ...[1].

(6)   References to the prohibited act are to an act mentioned in section 327(1), 328(1) or 329(1) (as the case may be).

Notes

Amendments

1   Repealed by the Serious Organised Crime and Police Act 2005, ss 105(1), (2), (4), 174(2), Sch 17, Pt 2. Date in force: 1 July 2005: see the Serious Organised Crime and Police Act 2005 (Commencement No. 1, Transitional and Transitory Provisions) Order 2005, SI 2005/1521, art 3(1)(c), (ee)(vi).
2   Substituted by the Serious Organised Crime and Police Act 2005, s 106(1), (4), (6). Date in force: 1 July 2005: see the Serious Organised Crime and Police Act 2005 (Commencement No. 1, Transitional and Transitory Provisions) Order 2005, SI 2005/1521, art 3(1)(c).
3   Inserted by the Serious Organised Crime and Police Act 2005, s 106(1), (5). Date in force: 1 July 2005: see the Serious Organised Crime and Police Act 2005 (Commencement No. 1, Transitional and Transitory Provisions) Order 2005, SI 2005/1521, art 3(1)(c).
4   Substituted by the Terrorism Act 2000 and Proceeds of Crime Act 2002 (Amendment) Regulations 2007, SI 2007/3398, reg 3, Sch 2, paras 1, 6. Date in force: 26 December 2007: see the Terrorism Act 2000 and Proceeds of Crime Act 2002 (Amendment) Regulations 2007, reg 1(2).

---

339   Form and manner of disclosures

(1)   The Secretary of State may by order prescribe the form and manner in which a disclosure under section 330, 331, 332 or 338 must be made.

[(1A)   A person commits an offence if he makes a disclosure under section 330, 331, 332 or 338 otherwise than in the form prescribed under subsection (1) or otherwise than in the manner so prescribed.

(1B)   But a person does not commit an offence under subsection (1A) if he has a reasonable excuse for making the disclosure otherwise than in the form prescribed under subsection (1) or (as the case may be) otherwise than in the manner so prescribed.

(2)   The power under subsection (1) to prescribe the form in which a disclosure must be made includes power to provide for the form to include a request to a person making a disclosure that the person provide information specified or described in the form if he has not provided it in making the disclosure.

(3)   Where under subsection (2) a request is included in a form prescribed under subsection (1), the form must—

(a)   state that there is no obligation to comply with the request, and

(b)   explain the protection conferred by subsection (4) on a person who complies with the request.]¹

(4)   A disclosure made in pursuance of a request under subsection (2) is not to be taken to breach any restriction on the disclosure of information (however imposed).

(5)   ...²

(6)   ...²

(7)   Subsection (2) does not apply to a disclosure made to a nominated officer.

Notes

Amendments

1   Subsections (1A)-(3) substituted for sub-ss (2)-(3) by the Serious Organised Crime and Police Act 2005, s 105(1), (5). Date in force: 1 July 2005: see the Serious Organised Crime and Police Act 2005 (Commencement No. 1, Transitional and Transitory Provisions) Order 2005, SI 2005/1521, art 3(1)(c).
2   Repealed by the Serious Organised Crime and Police Act 2005, s 174(2), Sch 17, Pt 2. Date in force: 1 July 2005: see the Serious Organised Crime and Police Act 2005 (Commencement No. 1, Transitional and Transitory Provisions) Order 2005, SI 2005/1521, art 3(1)(c), (ee)(vi).

[339ZA   Disclosures to [the NCA]¹

Where a disclosure is made under this Part to a constable or an officer of Revenue and Customs, the constable or officer of Revenue and Customs must disclose it in full to a person authorised for the purposes of this Part by the [Director General of the National Crime Agency]¹ as soon as practicable after it has been made.]²

Notes

Amendments

1   Substituted by the Crime and Courts Act 2013, s 15(3), Sch 8, paras 108, 134. Date in force: 7 October 2013: see the Crime and Courts Act 2013 (Commencement No. 2 and Saving Provision) Order 2013, SI 2013/1682, art 3(u), (v), subject to savings and transitional provisions specified in the Crime and Courts Act 2013, s 15, Sch 8.
2   Inserted by the Terrorism Act 2000 and Proceeds of Crime Act 2002 (Amendment) Regulations 2007, SI 2007/3398, reg 3, Sch 2, paras 1, 7. Date in force: 26 December 2007: see the Terrorism Act 2000 and Proceeds of Crime Act 2002 (Amendment) Regulations 2007, reg 1(2).

[Threshold amounts

339A   Threshold amounts

(1)   This section applies for the purposes of sections 327(2C), 328(5) and 329(2C).

(2)   The threshold amount for acts done by a deposit-taking body in operating an account is £250 unless a higher amount is specified under the following provisions of this section (in which event it is that higher amount).

(3)   An officer of Revenue and Customs, or a constable, may specify the threshold amount for acts done by a deposit-taking body in operating an account—

(a)   when he gives consent, or gives notice refusing consent, to the deposit-taking body's doing of an act mentioned in section 327(1), 328(1) or 329(1) in opening, or operating, the account or a related account, or

(b)   on a request from the deposit-taking body.

(4)   Where the threshold amount for acts done in operating an account is specified under subsection (3) or this subsection, an officer of Revenue and Customs, or a constable, may vary the amount (whether on a request from the deposit-taking body or otherwise) by specifying a different amount.

(5)   Different threshold amounts may be specified under subsections (3) and (4) for different acts done in operating the same account.

(6)   The amount specified under subsection (3) or (4) as the threshold amount for acts done in operating an account must, when specified, not be less than the amount specified in subsection (2).

(7)   The Secretary of State may by order vary the amount for the time being specified in subsection (2).

(8)   For the purposes of this section, an account is related to another if each is maintained with the same deposit-taking body and there is a person who, in relation to each account, is the person or one of the persons entitled to instruct the body as respects the operation of the account.]¹

Notes

Amendment

1   Inserted by the Serious Organised Crime and Police Act 2005, s 103(1), (5). Date in force: 1 July 2005: see the Serious Organised Crime and Police Act 2005 (Commencement No. 1, Transitional and Transitory Provisions) Order 2005, SI 2005/1521, art 3(1)(c).

Interpretation

340   Interpretation

(1)   This section applies for the purposes of this Part.

(2)   Criminal conduct is conduct which—

(a)   constitutes an offence in any part of the United Kingdom, or

(b)   would constitute an offence in any part of the United Kingdom if it occurred there.

(3)   Property is criminal property if—

(a)   it constitutes a person's benefit from criminal conduct or it represents such a benefit (in whole or part and whether directly or indirectly), and

(b)   the alleged offender knows or suspects that it constitutes or represents such a benefit.

(4)   It is immaterial—

(a)   who carried out the conduct;

(b)   who benefited from it;

(c)   whether the conduct occurred before or after the passing of this Act.

(5)   A person benefits from conduct if he obtains property as a result of or in connection with the conduct.

(6)   If a person obtains a pecuniary advantage as a result of or in connection with conduct, he is to be taken to obtain as a result of or in connection with the conduct a sum of money equal to the value of the pecuniary advantage.

(7)   References to property or a pecuniary advantage obtained in connection with conduct include references to property or a pecuniary advantage obtained in both that connection and some other.

(8)   If a person benefits from conduct his benefit is the property obtained as a result of or in connection with the conduct.

(9)   Property is all property wherever situated and includes—

(a)   money;

(b)   all forms of property, real or personal, heritable or moveable;

(c)   things in action and other intangible or incorporeal property.

(10)   The following rules apply in relation to property—

(a)   property is obtained by a person if he obtains an interest in it;

(b)   references to an interest, in relation to land in England and Wales or Northern Ireland, are to any legal estate or equitable interest or power;

(c)   references to an interest, in relation to land in Scotland, are to any estate, interest, servitude or other heritable right in or over land, including a heritable security;

(d)   references to an interest, in relation to property other than land, include references to a right (including a right to possession).

(11)   Money laundering is an act which—

(a)   constitutes an offence under section 327, 328 or 329,

(b)   constitutes an attempt, conspiracy or incitement to commit an offence specified in paragraph (a),

(c)   constitutes aiding, abetting, counselling or procuring the commission of an offence specified in paragraph (a), or

(d)   would constitute an offence specified in paragraph (a), (b) or (c) if done in the United Kingdom.

(12)   For the purposes of a disclosure to a nominated officer—

(a)   references to a person's employer include any body, association or organisation (including a voluntary organisation) in connection with whose activities the person exercises a function (whether or not for gain or reward), and

(b)   references to employment must be construed accordingly.

(13)   References to a constable include references to a person authorised for the purposes of this Part by [the [Director General of the National Crime Agency][1]][2].

[(14)   'Deposit-taking body' means—

(a)   a business which engages in the activity of accepting deposits, or

(b)   the National Savings Bank.][3]

Notes

Amendments

1   Substituted by the Crime and Courts Act 2013, s 15(3), Sch 8, paras 108, 135. Date in force: 7 October 2013: see the Crime and Courts Act 2013 (Commencement No. 2 and Saving Provision) Order 2013, SI 2013/1682, art 3(u), (v), subject to savings and transitional provisions specified in the Crime and Courts Act 2013, s 15, Sch 8.
2   Substituted by the Serious Organised Crime and Police Act 2005, s 59, Sch 4, paras 168, 174. Date in force: 1 April 2006: see the Serious Organised Crime and Police Act 2005 (Commencement No. 5 and Transitional and Transitory Provisions and Savings) Order 2006, SI 2006/378, art 4(1), Schedule, para 10.
3   Inserted by the Serious Organised Crime and Police Act 2005, s 103(1), (6). Date in force: 1 July 2005: see the Serious Organised Crime and Police Act 2005 (Commencement No. 1, Transitional and Transitory Provisions) Order 2005, SI 2005/1521, art 3(1)(c).

Part 8
Investigations

Chapter 4
Interpretation

415   Money laundering offences

(1)   An offence under section 327, 328 or 329 is a money laundering offence.

[(1A)   Each of the following is a money laundering offence—

(a)   an offence under section 93A, 93B or 93C of the Criminal Justice Act 1988;

(b)   an offence under section 49, 50 or 51 of the Drug Trafficking Act 1994;

(c) an offence under section 37 or 38 of the Criminal Law (Consolidation) (Scotland) Act 1995;

(d) an offence under article 45, 46 or 47 of the Proceeds of Crime (Northern Ireland) Order 1996.]¹

(2) Each of the following is a money laundering offence—

(a) an attempt, conspiracy or incitement to commit an offence specified in subsection (1);

(b) aiding, abetting, counselling or procuring the commission of an offence specified in subsection (1).

Notes

Amendment

1 Inserted by the Serious Organised Crime and Police Act 2005, s 107(1), (4). Date in force: 1 July 2005: see the Serious Organised Crime and Police Act 2005 (Commencement No. 1, Transitional and Transitory Provisions) Order 2005, SI 2005/1521, art 3(1)(c).

Schedule 2
Lifestyle offences: England and Wales

1 Drug trafficking

(1) An offence under any of the following provisions of the Misuse of Drugs Act 1971 (c. 38)—

(a) section 4(2) or (3) (unlawful production or supply of controlled drugs);

(b) section 5(3) (possession of controlled drug with intent to supply);

(c) section 8 (permitting certain activities relating to controlled drugs);

(d) section 20 (assisting in or inducing the commission outside the UK of an offence punishable under a corresponding law).

(2) An offence under any of the following provisions of the Customs and Excise Management Act 1979 (c. 2) if it is committed in connection with a prohibition or restriction on importation or exportation which has effect by virtue of section 3 of the Misuse of Drugs Act 1971—

(a) section 50(2) or (3) (improper importation of goods);

(b) section 68(2) (exploration of prohibited or restricted goods);

(c) section 170 (fraudulent evasion).

(3) An offence under either of the following provisions of the Criminal Justice (International Co-operation) Act 1990 (c. 5)—

(a) section 12 (manufacture or supply of a substance for the time being specified in Schedule 2 to that Act);

(b) section 19 (using a ship for illicit traffic in controlled drugs).

Notes

Extent

This Part does not extend to Scotland: see s 461(1).

2   Money laundering

An offence under either of the following provisions of this Act—

(a)   section 327 (concealing etc criminal property);

(b)   section 328 (assisting another to retain criminal property).

Notes

Extent

This Part does not extend to Scotland: see s 461(1).

3   Directing terrorism

An offence under section 56 of the Terrorism Act 2000 (c. 11) (directing the activities of a terrorist organisation).

Notes

Extent

This Part does not extend to Scotland: see s 461(1).

[4   People trafficking

(1)   An offence under section 25, 25A or 25B of the Immigration Act 1971 (c. 77) (assisting unlawful immigration etc.).

[(2)   An offence under [section 59A of the Sexual Offences Act 2003][3] (trafficking for sexual exploitation).][2]

[(3)   An offence under section 4 of the Asylum and Immigration (Treatment of Claimants, etc.) Act 2004 (exploitation).][4]][1]

Notes

Amendments

1   Substituted by the Nationality, Immigration and Asylum Act 2002, s 114(3), Sch 7, para 31. Date in force: 10 February 2003: see the Nationality, Immigration and Asylum Act 2002 (Commencement No. 2) Order 2003, SI 2003/1, art 2, Schedule.
2   Substituted by the Sexual Offences Act 2003, s 139, Sch 6, para 46(1), (2). Date in force: 1 May 2004: see the Sexual Offences Act 2003 (Commencement) Order 2004, SI 2004/874, art 2.
3   Substituted by the Protection of Freedoms Act 2012, s 115, Sch 9, para 138. Date in force: 6 April 2013: see the Protection of Freedoms Act 2012 (Commencement No. 5 and Saving and Transitional Provision) Order 2013, SI 2013/470, art 2(c), (d), subject to savings and transitional provisions as specified in the Protection of Freedoms Act 2012 (Commencement No. 5 and Saving and Transitional Provision) Order 2013, arts 3(b), 8.
4   Inserted by the Asylum and Immigration (Treatment of Claimants, etc.) Act 2004, s 5(7). Date in force: 1 December 2004: see the Asylum and Immigration (Treatment of Claimants, etc.) Act 2004 (Commencement No. 2) Order 2004, SI 2004/2999, art 2.

Extent

This Part does not extend to Scotland: see s 461(1).

5   Arms trafficking

(1)   An offence under either of the following provisions of the Customs and Excise Management Act 1979 if it is committed in connection with a firearm or ammunition—

(a)   section 68(2) (exportation of prohibited goods);

(b)   section 170 (fraudulent evasion).

(2)   An offence under section 3(1) of the Firearms Act 1968 (c. 27) (dealing in firearms or ammunition by way of trade or business).

(3)   In this paragraph 'firearm' and 'ammunition' have the same meanings as in section 57 of the Firearms Act 1968 (c. 27).

Notes

Extent

This Part does not extend to Scotland: see s 461(1).

---

6   Counterfeiting

An offence under any of the following provisions of the Forgery and Counterfeiting Act 1981 (c. 45)—

(a)   section 14 (making counterfeit notes or coins);

(b)   section 15 (passing etc counterfeit notes or coins);

(c)   section 16 (having counterfeit notes or coins);

(d)   section 17 (making or possessing materials or equipment for counterfeiting).

Notes

Extent

This Part does not extend to Scotland: see s 461(1).

---

7   Intellectual property

(1)   An offence under any of the following provisions of the Copyright, Designs and Patents Act 1988 (c. 48)—

(a)   section 107(1) (making or dealing in an article which infringes copyright);

(b)   section 107(2) (making or possessing an article designed or adapted for making a copy of a copyright work);

(c)   section 198(1) (making or dealing in an illicit recording);

(d)   section 297A (making or dealing in unauthorised decoders).

(2)   An offence under section 92(1), (2) or (3) of the Trade Marks Act 1994 (c. 26) (unauthorised use etc of trade mark).

Notes

Extent

This Part does not extend to Scotland: see s 461(1).

[8   Prostitution and child sex

(1)   An offence under section 33 or 34 of the Sexual Offences Act 1956 (keeping or letting premises for use as a brothel).

(2)   An offence under any of the following provisions of the Sexual Offences Act 2003–

(a)   section 14 (arranging or facilitating commission of a child sex offence);

(b)   section 48 (causing or inciting child prostitution or pornography);

(c)   section 49 (controlling a child prostitute or a child involved in pornography);

(d)   section 50 (arranging or facilitating child prostitution or pornography);

(e)   section 52 (causing or inciting prostitution for gain);

(f)   section 53 (controlling prostitution for gain).]¹

Notes

Amendment

1   Substituted by the Sexual Offences Act 2003, s 139, Sch 6, para 46(1), (3). Date in force: 1 May 2004: see the Sexual Offences Act 2003 (Commencement) Order 2004, SI 2004/874, art 2.

Extent

This Part does not extend to Scotland: see s 461(1).

---

9   Blackmail

An offence under section 21 of the Theft Act 1968 (c. 60) (blackmail).

Notes

Extent

This Part does not extend to Scotland: see s 461(1).

[9A

An offence under section 12(1) or (2) of the Gangmasters (Licensing) Act 2004 (acting as a gangmaster other than under the authority of a licence, possession of false documents etc).]¹

Notes

Amendment

1   Inserted by the Gangmasters (Licensing) Act 2004, s 14(4). Date in force: 1 October 2006: see the Gangmasters (Licensing) Act 2004 (Commencement No.3) Order 2006, SI 2006/2406, art 2(e).

Extent

This Part does not extend to Scotland: see s 461(1).

---

10   Inchoate offences

(1)   An offence of attempting, conspiring or inciting the commission of an offence specified in this Schedule.

[(1A)   An offence under section 44 of the Serious Crime Act 2007 of doing an act capable of encouraging or assisting the commission of an offence specified in this Schedule.][1]

(2)   An offence of aiding, abetting, counselling or procuring the commission of such an offence.

Notes

Amendment

1   Inserted by the Serious Crime Act 2007, s 63(2), Sch 6, para 62. Date in force: 1 October 2008: see the Serious Crime Act 2007 (Commencement No. 3) Order 2008, SI 2008/2504, art 2(a).

Extent

This Part does not extend to Scotland: see s 461(1).

Appendix 1.2   Serious Organised Crime and Police Act 2005

2005 Chapter 15

Serious Organised Crime and Police Act 2005

Part 2
Investigations, prosecutions, proceedings and proceeds of crime

Chapter 6
Proceeds of crime

97   Confiscation orders by magistrates' courts

(1)   The Secretary of State may by order make such provision as he considers appropriate for or in connection with enabling confiscation orders under—

(a)   Part 2 of the Proceeds of Crime Act 2002 (c. 29) (confiscation: England and Wales), ...[1]

(b)   ...[1]

to be made by magistrates' courts in England and Wales ...[1].

[(1A)   The Department of Justice in Northern Ireland may by order make such provision as the Department considers appropriate for or in connection with enabling confiscation orders under Part 4 of the 2002 Act (confiscation: Northern Ireland) to be made by magistrates' courts in Northern Ireland.][2]

(2)   But an order under subsection (1) [or (1A)][2] may not enable such a confiscation order to be made by any magistrates' court in respect of an amount exceeding £10,000.

(3)   An order under subsection (1) [or (1A)][2] may amend, repeal, revoke or otherwise modify any provision of Part 2 or 4 of the 2002 Act [(as the case may be)][2] or any other enactment relating to, or to things done under or for the purposes of, [that Part (or any provision of that Part)][3].

Notes

Amendments

1   Repealed by the Northern Ireland Act 1998 (Devolution of Policing and Justice Functions) Order 2010, SI 2010/976, art 13, Sch 15, paras 1, 23(1), (2). Date in force: 12 April 2010: see the Northern Ireland Act 1998 (Devolution of Policing and Justice Functions) Order 2010, art 1(2), subject to transitional provision specified in the Northern Ireland Act 1998 (Devolution of Policing and Justice Functions) Order 2010, art 28.
2   Inserted by the Northern Ireland Act 1998 (Devolution of Policing and Justice Functions) Order 2010, SI 2010/976, art 13, Sch 15, paras 1, 23(1), (3), (4), (5)(a). Date in force: 12 April 2010: see the Northern Ireland Act 1998 (Devolution of Policing and

Justice Functions) Order 2010, art 1(2), subject to transitional provision specified in the Northern Ireland Act 1998 (Devolution of Policing and Justice Functions) Order 2010, art 28.

3   Substituted by the Northern Ireland Act 1998 (Devolution of Policing and Justice Functions) Order 2010, SI 2010/976, art 13, Sch 15, paras 1, 23(1), (5)(b). Date in force: 12 April 2010: see the Northern Ireland Act 1998 (Devolution of Policing and Justice Functions) Order 2010, art 1(2), subject to transitional provision specified in the Northern Ireland Act 1998 (Devolution of Policing and Justice Functions) Order 2010, art 28.

Appendix 1.3   Fraud Act 2006

2006 Chapter 35

Fraud Act 2006

Fraud

1   Fraud

(1)   A person is guilty of fraud if he is in breach of any of the sections listed in subsection (2) (which provide for different ways of committing the offence).

(2)   The sections are–

(a)   section 2 (fraud by false representation),

(b)   section 3 (fraud by failing to disclose information), and

(c)   section 4 (fraud by abuse of position).

(3)   A person who is guilty of fraud is liable–

(a)   on summary conviction, to imprisonment for a term not exceeding 12 months or to a fine not exceeding the statutory maximum (or to both);

(b)   on conviction on indictment, to imprisonment for a term not exceeding 10 years or to a fine (or to both).

(4)   Subsection (3)(a) applies in relation to Northern Ireland as if the reference to 12 months were a reference to 6 months.

2   Fraud by false representation

(1)   A person is in breach of this section if he–

(a)   dishonestly makes a false representation, and

(b)   intends, by making the representation–

    (i)   to make a gain for himself or another, or

    (ii)   to cause loss to another or to expose another to a risk of loss.

(2)   A representation is false if–

(a)   it is untrue or misleading, and

(b)   the person making it knows that it is, or might be, untrue or misleading.

(3)   'Representation' means any representation as to fact or law, including a representation as to the state of mind of–

(a)   the person making the representation, or

(b)   any other person.

(4)   A representation may be express or implied.

(5)   For the purposes of this section a representation may be regarded as made if it (or anything implying it) is submitted in any form to any system or device designed to receive, convey or respond to communications (with or without human intervention).

3   Fraud by failing to disclose information

A person is in breach of this section if he–

(a)   dishonestly fails to disclose to another person information which he is under a legal duty to disclose, and

(b)   intends, by failing to disclose the information–

  (i)   to make a gain for himself or another, or

  (ii)   to cause loss to another or to expose another to a risk of loss.

4   Fraud by abuse of position

(1)   A person is in breach of this section if he–

(a)   occupies a position in which he is expected to safeguard, or not to act against, the financial interests of another person,

(b)   dishonestly abuses that position, and

(c)   intends, by means of the abuse of that position–

  (i)   to make a gain for himself or another, or

  (ii)   to cause loss to another or to expose another to a risk of loss.

(2)   A person may be regarded as having abused his position even though his conduct consisted of an omission rather than an act.

5   'Gain' and 'loss'

(1)   The references to gain and loss in sections 2 to 4 are to be read in accordance with this section.

(2)   'Gain' and 'loss'–

(a)   extend only to gain or loss in money or other property;

(b)   include any such gain or loss whether temporary or permanent;

and 'property' means any property whether real or personal (including things in action and other intangible property).

(3)   'Gain' includes a gain by keeping what one has, as well as a gain by getting what one does not have.

(4)   'Loss' includes a loss by not getting what one might get, as well as a loss by parting with what one has.

6   Possession etc. of articles for use in frauds

(1)   A person is guilty of an offence if he has in his possession or under his control any article for use in the course of or in connection with any fraud.

(2)   A person guilty of an offence under this section is liable–

(a)   on summary conviction, to imprisonment for a term not exceeding 12 months or to a fine not exceeding the statutory maximum (or to both);

(b)   on conviction on indictment, to imprisonment for a term not exceeding 5 years or to a fine (or to both).

(3)   Subsection (2)(a) applies in relation to Northern Ireland as if the reference to 12 months were a reference to 6 months.

7   Making or supplying articles for use in frauds

(1)   A person is guilty of an offence if he makes, adapts, supplies or offers to supply any article–

(a)   knowing that it is designed or adapted for use in the course of or in connection with fraud, or

(b)   intending it to be used to commit, or assist in the commission of, fraud.

(2)   A person guilty of an offence under this section is liable–

(a)   on summary conviction, to imprisonment for a term not exceeding 12 months or to a fine not exceeding the statutory maximum (or to both);

(b)   on conviction on indictment, to imprisonment for a term not exceeding 10 years or to a fine (or to both).

(3)   Subsection (2)(a) applies in relation to Northern Ireland as if the reference to 12 months were a reference to 6 months.

8   'Article'

(1)   For the purposes of–

(a)   sections 6 and 7, and

(b)   the provisions listed in subsection (2), so far as they relate to articles for use in the course of or in connection with fraud,

'article' includes any program or data held in electronic form.

(2)   The provisions are–

(a)   section 1(7)(b) of the Police and Criminal Evidence Act 1984 (c. 60),

(b)   section 2(8)(b) of the Armed Forces Act 2001 (c. 19), and

(c)   Article 3(7)(b) of the Police and Criminal Evidence (Northern Ireland) Order 1989 (S.I. 1989/1341 (N.I. 12));

(meaning of 'prohibited articles' for the purposes of stop and search powers).

9   Participating in fraudulent business carried on by sole trader etc.

(1)   A person is guilty of an offence if he is knowingly a party to the carrying on of a business to which this section applies.

(2)   This section applies to a business which is carried on–

(a)   by a person who is outside the reach of [section 993 of the Companies Act 2006][1] (offence of fraudulent trading), and

(b)   with intent to defraud creditors of any person or for any other fraudulent purpose.

(3)   The following are within the reach of [that section][1]–

(a)   a company [(as defined in section 1(1) of the Companies Act 2006)][2];

(b)   a person to whom that section applies (with or without adaptations or modifications) as if the person were a company;

(c)   a person exempted from the application of that section.

(4)   …[3]

(5)   'Fraudulent purpose' has the same meaning as in [that section][1].

(6)   A person guilty of an offence under this section is liable–

(a)   on summary conviction, to imprisonment for a term not exceeding 12 months or to a fine not exceeding the statutory maximum (or to both);

(b)   on conviction on indictment, to imprisonment for a term not exceeding 10 years or to a fine (or to both).

(7)   Subsection (6)(a) applies in relation to Northern Ireland as if the reference to 12 months were a reference to 6 months.

Notes

Amendments

1   Substituted by the Companies Act 2006 (Commencement No. 3, Consequential Amendments, Transitional Provisions and Savings) Order 2007, SI 2007/2194, art 10(1), Sch 4, para 111(1), (2), (3)(a), (5). Date in force: 1 October 2007: see the Companies Act 2006 (Commencement No. 3, Consequential Amendments, Transitional Provisions and Savings) Order 2007, art 1(3)(a).
2   Substituted by the Companies Act 2006 (Consequential Amendments, Transitional Provisions and Savings) Order 2009, SI 2009/1941, art 2(1), Sch 1, para 257. Date in force: 1 October 2009: see the Companies Act 2006 (Consequential Amendments, Transitional Provisions and Savings) Order 2009, art 1(2).
3   Repealed by the Companies Act 2006 (Commencement No. 3, Consequential Amendments, Transitional Provisions and Savings) Order 2007, SI 2007/2194, art 10(1), (3), Sch 4, para 111(1), (4), Sch 5. Date in force: 1 October 2007: see the Companies Act 2006 (Commencement No. 3, Consequential Amendments, Transitional Provisions and Savings) Order 2007, art 1(3)(a).

---

10   …[1]

…[1]

Notes

Amendments

1   Repealed by the Companies Act 2006 (Consequential Amendments, Transitional Provisions and Savings) Order 2009, SI 2009/1941, art 2(2), Sch 2. Date in force: 1 October 2009: see the Companies Act 2006 (Consequential Amendments, Transitional Provisions and Savings) Order 2009, art 1(2).

Obtaining services dishonestly

11 Obtaining services dishonestly

(1) A person is guilty of an offence under this section if he obtains services for himself or another–

(a) by a dishonest act, and

(b) in breach of subsection (2).

(2) A person obtains services in breach of this subsection if–

(a) they are made available on the basis that payment has been, is being or will be made for or in respect of them,

(b) he obtains them without any payment having been made for or in respect of them or without payment having been made in full, and

(c) when he obtains them, he knows–

    (i) that they are being made available on the basis described in paragraph (a), or

    (ii) that they might be,

but intends that payment will not be made, or will not be made in full.

(3) A person guilty of an offence under this section is liable–

(a) on summary conviction, to imprisonment for a term not exceeding 12 months or to a fine not exceeding the statutory maximum (or to both);

(b) on conviction on indictment, to imprisonment for a term not exceeding 5 years or to a fine (or to both).

(4) Subsection (3)(a) applies in relation to Northern Ireland as if the reference to 12 months were a reference to 6 months.

Supplementary

12 Liability of company officers for offences by company

(1) Subsection (2) applies if an offence under this Act is committed by a body corporate.

(2) If the offence is proved to have been committed with the consent or connivance of–

(a) a director, manager, secretary or other similar officer of the body corporate, or

(b) a person who was purporting to act in any such capacity,

he (as well as the body corporate) is guilty of the offence and liable to be proceeded against and punished accordingly.

(3) If the affairs of a body corporate are managed by its members, subsection (2) applies in relation to the acts and defaults of a member in connection with his functions of management as if he were a director of the body corporate.

13 Evidence

(1) A person is not to be excused from–

(a) answering any question put to him in proceedings relating to property, or

(b) complying with any order made in proceedings relating to property, on the ground that doing so may incriminate him or his spouse or civil partner of an offence under this Act or a related offence.

(2)   But, in proceedings for an offence under this Act or a related offence, a statement or admission made by the person in–

(a)   answering such a question, or

(b)   complying with such an order,

is not admissible in evidence against him or (unless they married or became civil partners after the making of the statement or admission) his spouse or civil partner.

(3)   'Proceedings relating to property' means any proceedings for–

(a)   the recovery or administration of any property,

(b)   the execution of a trust, or

(c)   an account of any property or dealings with property,

and 'property' means money or other property whether real or personal (including things in action and other intangible property).

(4)   'Related offence' means–

(a)   conspiracy to defraud;

(b)   any other offence involving any form of fraudulent conduct or purpose.

14   Minor and consequential amendments etc.

(1)   Schedule 1 contains minor and consequential amendments.

(2)   Schedule 2 contains transitional provisions and savings.

(3)   Schedule 3 contains repeals and revocations.

15   Commencement and extent

(1)   This Act (except this section and section 16) comes into force on such day as the Secretary of State may appoint by an order made by statutory instrument; and different days may be appointed for different purposes.

(2)   Subject to subsection (3), sections 1 to 9 and 11 to 13 extend to England and Wales and Northern Ireland only.

(3)   Section 8, so far as it relates to the Armed Forces Act 2001 (c. 19), extends to any place to which that Act extends.

(4)   Any amendment in section 10 or Schedule 1, and any related provision in section 14 or Schedule 2 or 3, extends to any place to which the provision which is the subject of the amendment extends.

16   Short title

This Act may be cited as the Fraud Act 2006.

Schedule 2
Transitional provisions and savings

1   Maximum term of imprisonment for offences under this Act

In relation to an offence committed before the commencement of section 154(1) of the Criminal Justice Act 2003 (c. 44), the references to 12 months in sections 1(3)(a), 6(2)(a), 7(2)(a), 9(6)(a) and 11(3)(a) are to be read as references to 6 months.

2   Increase in penalty for fraudulent trading

Section 10 does not affect the penalty for any offence committed before that section comes into force.

3   Abolition of deception offences

(1)   Paragraph 1 of Schedule 1 does not affect any liability, investigation, legal proceeding or penalty for or in respect of any offence partly committed before the commencement of that paragraph.

(2)   An offence is partly committed before the commencement of paragraph 1 of Schedule 1 if–

(a)   a relevant event occurs before its commencement, and

(b)   another relevant event occurs on or after its commencement.

(3)   'Relevant event', in relation to an offence, means any act, omission or other event (including any result of one or more acts or omissions) proof of which is required for conviction of the offence.

4   Scope of offences relating to stolen goods under the Theft Act 1968 (c. 60)

Nothing in paragraph 6 of Schedule 1 affects the operation of section 24 of the Theft Act 1968 in relation to goods obtained in the circumstances described in section 15(1) of that Act where the obtaining is the result of a deception made before the commencement of that paragraph.

5   Dishonestly retaining a wrongful credit under the Theft Act 1968

Nothing in paragraph 7 of Schedule 1 affects the operation of section 24A(7) and (8) of the Theft Act 1968 in relation to credits falling within section 24A(3) or (4) of that Act and made before the commencement of that paragraph.

6   Scope of offences relating to stolen goods under the Theft Act (Northern Ireland) 1969 (c. 16 (N.I.))

Nothing in paragraph 11 of Schedule 1 affects the operation of section 23 of the Theft Act (Northern Ireland) 1969 in relation to goods obtained in the circumstances described in section 15(1) of that Act where the obtaining is the result of a deception made before the commencement of that paragraph.

7   Dishonestly retaining a wrongful credit under the Theft Act (Northern Ireland) 1969

Nothing in paragraph 12 of Schedule 1 affects the operation of section 23A(7) and (8) of the Theft Act (Northern Ireland) 1969 in relation to credits falling within section 23A(3) or (4) of that Act and made before the commencement of that paragraph.

8   Limitation periods under the Limitation Act 1980 (c. 58)

Nothing in paragraph 18 of Schedule 1 affects the operation of section 4 of the Limitation Act 1980 in relation to chattels obtained in the circumstances described in section 15(1) of the Theft Act 1968 where the obtaining is a result of a deception made before the commencement of that paragraph.

9   Limitation periods under the Limitation (Northern Ireland) Order 1989 (S.I. 1989/1339 (N.I. 11))

Nothing in paragraph 22 of Schedule 1 affects the operation of Article 18 of the Limitation (Northern Ireland) Order 1989 in relation to chattels obtained in the circumstances described in section 15(1) of the Theft Act (Northern Ireland) 1969 where the obtaining is a result of a deception made before the commencement of that paragraph.

10   Scheduled offences under the Terrorism Act 2000 (c. 11)

Nothing in paragraph 30 of Schedule 1 affects the operation of Part 7 of the Terrorism Act 2000 in relation to an offence under section 15(1) of the Theft Act (Northern Ireland) 1969 where the obtaining is a result of a deception made before the commencement of that paragraph.

11   Powers of arrest under Asylum and Immigration (Treatment of Claimants, etc.) Act 2004 (c. 19)

(1)   Nothing in paragraph 35 of Schedule 1 affects the power of arrest conferred by section 14 of the Asylum and Immigration (Treatment of Claimants, etc.) Act 2004 in relation to an offence partly committed before the commencement of that paragraph.

(2)   An offence is partly committed before the commencement of paragraph 35 of Schedule 1 if–

(a)   a relevant event occurs before its commencement, and

(b)   another relevant event occurs on or after its commencement.

(3)   'Relevant event', in relation to an offence, means any act, omission or other event (including any result of one or more acts or omissions) proof of which is required for conviction of the offence.

Appendix 1.4   Bribery Act 2010

2010 Chapter 23

Bribery Act 2010

General bribery offences

1   Offences of bribing another person

(1)   A person ('P') is guilty of an offence if either of the following cases applies.

(2)   Case 1 is where—

(a)   P offers, promises or gives a financial or other advantage to another person, and

(b)   P intends the advantage—

    (i)   to induce a person to perform improperly a relevant function or activity, or

    (ii)   to reward a person for the improper performance of such a function or activity.

(3)   Case 2 is where—

(a)   P offers, promises or gives a financial or other advantage to another person, and

(b)   P knows or believes that the acceptance of the advantage would itself constitute the improper performance of a relevant function or activity.

(4)   In case 1 it does not matter whether the person to whom the advantage is offered, promised or given is the same person as the person who is to perform, or has performed, the function or activity concerned.

(5)   In cases 1 and 2 it does not matter whether the advantage is offered, promised or given by P directly or through a third party.

2   Offences relating to being bribed

(1)   A person ('R') is guilty of an offence if any of the following cases applies.

(2)   Case 3 is where R requests, agrees to receive or accepts a financial or other advantage intending that, in consequence, a relevant function or activity should be performed improperly (whether by R or another person).

(3)   Case 4 is where—

(a)   R requests, agrees to receive or accepts a financial or other advantage, and

(b)   the request, agreement or acceptance itself constitutes the improper performance by R of a relevant function or activity.

(4)   Case 5 is where R requests, agrees to receive or accepts a financial or other advantage as a reward for the improper performance (whether by R or another person) of a relevant function or activity.

(5)   Case 6 is where, in anticipation of or in consequence of R requesting, agreeing to receive or accepting a financial or other advantage, a relevant function or activity is performed improperly—

(a) by R, or

(b) by another person at R's request or with R's assent or acquiescence.

(6)   In cases 3 to 6 it does not matter—

(a)   whether R requests, agrees to receive or accepts (or is to request, agree to receive or accept) the advantage directly or through a third party,

(b)   whether the advantage is (or is to be) for the benefit of R or another person.

(7)   In cases 4 to 6 it does not matter whether R knows or believes that the performance of the function or activity is improper.

(8)   In case 6, where a person other than R is performing the function or activity, it also does not matter whether that person knows or believes that the performance of the function or activity is improper.

3   Function or activity to which bribe relates

(1)   For the purposes of this Act a function or activity is a relevant function or activity if—

(a) it falls within subsection (2), and

(b) meets one or more of conditions A to C.

(2)   The following functions and activities fall within this subsection—

(a) any function of a public nature,

(b) any activity connected with a business,

(c) any activity performed in the course of a person's employment,

(d) any activity performed by or on behalf of a body of persons (whether corporate or unincorporate).

(3)   Condition A is that a person performing the function or activity is expected to perform it in good faith.

(4)   Condition B is that a person performing the function or activity is expected to perform it impartially.

(5)   Condition C is that a person performing the function or activity is in a position of trust by virtue of performing it.

(6)   A function or activity is a relevant function or activity even if it—

(a) has no connection with the United Kingdom, and

(b) is performed in a country or territory outside the United Kingdom.

(7)   In this section 'business' includes trade or profession.

4 Improper performance to which bribe relates

(1) For the purposes of this Act a relevant function or activity—

(a) is performed improperly if it is performed in breach of a relevant expectation, and

(b) is to be treated as being performed improperly if there is a failure to perform the function or activity and that failure is itself a breach of a relevant expectation.

(2) In subsection (1) 'relevant expectation'—

(a) in relation to a function or activity which meets condition A or B, means the expectation mentioned in the condition concerned, and

(b) in relation to a function or activity which meets condition C, means any expectation as to the manner in which, or the reasons for which, the function or activity will be performed that arises from the position of trust mentioned in that condition.

(3) Anything that a person does (or omits to do) arising from or in connection with that person's past performance of a relevant function or activity is to be treated for the purposes of this Act as being done (or omitted) by that person in the performance of that function or activity.

5 Expectation test

(1) For the purposes of sections 3 and 4, the test of what is expected is a test of what a reasonable person in the United Kingdom would expect in relation to the performance of the type of function or activity concerned.

(2) In deciding what such a person would expect in relation to the performance of a function or activity where the performance is not subject to the law of any part of the United Kingdom, any local custom or practice is to be disregarded unless it is permitted or required by the written law applicable to the country or territory concerned.

(3) In subsection (2) 'written law' means law contained in—

(a) any written constitution, or provision made by or under legislation, applicable to the country or territory concerned, or

(b) any judicial decision which is so applicable and is evidenced in published written sources.

Bribery of foreign public officials

6 Bribery of foreign public officials

(1) A person ('P') who bribes a foreign public official ('F') is guilty of an offence if P's intention is to influence F in F's capacity as a foreign public official.

(2) P must also intend to obtain or retain—

(a) business, or

(b) an advantage in the conduct of business.

(3) P bribes F if, and only if—

(a) directly or through a third party, P offers, promises or gives any financial or other advantage—

    (i)   to F, or

    (ii) to another person at F's request or with F's assent or acquiescence, and

(b) F is neither permitted nor required by the written law applicable to F to be influenced in F's capacity as a foreign public official by the offer, promise or gift.

(4)   References in this section to influencing F in F's capacity as a foreign public official mean influencing F in the performance of F's functions as such an official, which includes—

(a) any omission to exercise those functions, and

(b) any use of F's position as such an official, even if not within F's authority.

(5)   'Foreign public official' means an individual who—

(a) holds a legislative, administrative or judicial position of any kind, whether appointed or elected, of a country or territory outside the United Kingdom (or any subdivision of such a country or territory),

(b) exercises a public function—

    (i)   for or on behalf of a country or territory outside the United Kingdom (or any subdivision of such a country or territory), or

    (ii) for any public agency or public enterprise of that country or territory (or subdivision), or

(c) is an official or agent of a public international organisation.

(6)   'Public international organisation' means an organisation whose members are any of the following—

(a) countries or territories,

(b) governments of countries or territories,

(c) other public international organisations,

(d) a mixture of any of the above.

(7)   For the purposes of subsection (3)(b), the written law applicable to F is—

(a) where the performance of the functions of F which P intends to influence would be subject to the law of any part of the United Kingdom, the law of that part of the United Kingdom,

(b) where paragraph (a) does not apply and F is an official or agent of a public international organisation, the applicable written rules of that organisation,

(c) where paragraphs (a) and (b) do not apply, the law of the country or territory in relation to which F is a foreign public official so far as that law is contained in—

    (i)   any written constitution, or provision made by or under legislation, applicable to the country or territory concerned, or

    (ii) any judicial decision which is so applicable and is evidenced in published written sources.

(8)   For the purposes of this section, a trade or profession is a business.

7   Failure of commercial organisations to prevent bribery

(1)   A relevant commercial organisation ('C') is guilty of an offence under this section if a person ('A') associated with C bribes another person intending—

(a)   to obtain or retain business for C, or

(b)   to obtain or retain an advantage in the conduct of business for C.

(2)   But it is a defence for C to prove that C had in place adequate procedures designed to prevent persons associated with C from undertaking such conduct.

(3)   For the purposes of this section, A bribes another person if, and only if, A—

(a)   is, or would be, guilty of an offence under section 1 or 6 (whether or not A has been prosecuted for such an offence), or

(b)   would be guilty of such an offence if section 12(2)(c) and (4) were omitted.

(4)   See section 8 for the meaning of a person associated with C and see section 9 for a duty on the Secretary of State to publish guidance.

(5)   In this section—

'partnership' means—

  (a)   a partnership within the Partnership Act 1890, or

  (b)   a limited partnership registered under the Limited Partnerships Act 1907,

  or a firm or entity of a similar character formed under the law of a country or territory outside the United Kingdom,

'relevant commercial organisation' means—

  (a)   a body which is incorporated under the law of any part of the United Kingdom and which carries on a business (whether there or elsewhere),

  (b)   any other body corporate (wherever incorporated) which carries on a business, or part of a business, in any part of the United Kingdom,

  (c)   a partnership which is formed under the law of any part of the United Kingdom and which carries on a business (whether there or elsewhere), or

  (d)   any other partnership (wherever formed) which carries on a business, or part of a business, in any part of the United Kingdom,

and, for the purposes of this section, a trade or profession is a business.

8   Meaning of associated person

(1)   For the purposes of section 7, a person ('A') is associated with C if (disregarding any bribe under consideration) A is a person who performs services for or on behalf of C.

(2)   The capacity in which A performs services for or on behalf of C does not matter.

(3)   Accordingly A may (for example) be C's employee, agent or subsidiary.

(4)   Whether or not A is a person who performs services for or on behalf of C is to be determined by reference to all the relevant circumstances and not merely by reference to the nature of the relationship between A and C.

(5)   But if A is an employee of C, it is to be presumed unless the contrary is shown that A is a person who performs services for or on behalf of C.

9   Guidance about commercial organisations preventing bribery

(1)   The Secretary of State must publish guidance about procedures that relevant commercial organisations can put in place to prevent persons associated with them from bribing as mentioned in section 7(1).

(2)   The Secretary of State may, from time to time, publish revisions to guidance under this section or revised guidance.

(3)   The Secretary of State must consult the Scottish Ministers [and the Department of Justice in Northern Ireland][1] before publishing anything under this section.

(4)   Publication under this section is to be in such manner as the Secretary of State considers appropriate.

(5)   Expressions used in this section have the same meaning as in section 7.

1   Words inserted by Northern Ireland Act 1998 (Devolution of Policing and Justice Functions) Order 2012/2595 art.19(2) (October 18, 2012: insertion has effect subject to transitional provisions specified in SI 2012/2595 art. 24 to 27).

Appendix 1.5   Money Laundering Regulations 2007 SI 2007/2157

Money Laundering Regulations 2007

SI 2007/2157

Part 1
General

1   Citation, commencement etc.

(1)   These Regulations may be cited as the Money Laundering Regulations 2007 and come into force on 15th December 2007.

(2)   These Regulations are prescribed for the purposes of sections 168(4)(b) (appointment of persons to carry out investigations in particular cases) and 402(1) (b) (power of the Authority to institute proceedings for certain other offences) of the 2000 Act.

(3)   The Money Laundering Regulations 2003 are revoked.

2   Interpretation

(1)   In these Regulations—

'the 2000 Act' means the Financial Services and Markets Act 2000;

'Annex I financial institution' has the meaning given by regulation 22(1);

['auction platform' has the meaning given by regulation 3(13A);]¹

'auditor', except in regulation 17(2)(c) and (d), has the meaning given by regulation 3(4) and (5);

'authorised person' means a person who is authorised for the purposes of the 2000 Act;

'the Authority' means the [Financial Conduct Authority]²;

…³

'beneficial owner' has the meaning given by regulation 6;

['bill payment service provider' means an undertaking which provides a payment service enabling the payment of utility and other household bills;]⁴

'business relationship' means a business, professional or commercial relationship between a relevant person and a customer, which is expected by the relevant person, at the time when contact is established, to have an element of duration;

['the capital requirements directive' means Directive 2013/36/EU of the European Parliament and of the Council of 26 June 2013 relating to the activity of credit institutions and the prudential supervision of credit institutions and

225

investment firms, amending Directive 2002/87/EC and repealing Directives 2006/48/EC and 2006/49/EC;

'the capital requirements regulation' means Regulation (EU) 575/2013 of the European Parliament and of the Council of 26 June 2013 on prudential requirements for credit institutions and investment firms and amending Regulation (EU) No 648/2012;][5]

'cash' means notes, coins or travellers' cheques in any currency;

'casino' has the meaning given by regulation 3(13);

'the Commissioners' means the Commissioners for Her Majesty's Revenue and Customs;

...[6]

'credit institution' has the meaning given by regulation 3(2);

'customer due diligence measures' has the meaning given by regulation 5;

'DETI' means the Department of Enterprise, Trade and Investment in Northern Ireland;

['the electronic money directive' means Directive 2009/110/EC of the European Parliament and of the Council of 16th September 2009 on the taking up, pursuit and prudential supervision of the business of electronic money institutions;

'electronic money institution' has the meaning given by regulation 2(1) of the Electronic Money Regulations 2011;][7]

['the emission allowance auctioning regulation' means Commission Regulation (EU) No. 1031/2010 of 12 November 2010 on the timing, administration and other aspects of auctioning of greenhouse gas emission allowances pursuant to Directive 2003/87/EC of the European Parliament and of the Council establishing a scheme for greenhouse gas emission allowances trading within the Community;][1]

'estate agent' has the meaning given by regulation 3(11);

'external accountant' has the meaning given by regulation 3(7);

'financial institution' has the meaning given by regulation 3(3);

'firm' means any entity, whether or not a legal person, that is not an individual and includes a body corporate and a partnership or other unincorporated association;

'high value dealer' has the meaning given by regulation 3(12);

'the implementing measures directive' means Commission Directive 2006/70/EC of 1st August 2006 laying down implementing measures for the money laundering directive;

'independent legal professional' has the meaning given by regulation 3(9);

'insolvency practitioner', except in regulation 17(2)(c) and (d), has the meaning given by regulation 3(6);

'the life assurance consolidation directive' means Directive 2002/83/EC of the European Parliament and of the Council of 5th November 2002 concerning life assurance;

'local weights and measures authority' has the meaning given by section 69 of the Weights and Measures Act 1985 (local weights and measures authorities);

'the markets in financial instruments directive' means Directive 2004/39/EC of the European Parliament and of the Council of 12th April 2004 on markets in financial instruments;

'money laundering' means an act which falls within section 340(11) of the Proceeds of Crime Act 2002;

'the money laundering directive' means Directive 2005/60/EC of the European Parliament and of the Council of 26th October 2005 on the prevention of the use of the financial system for the purpose of money laundering and terrorist financing;

'money service business' means an undertaking which by way of business operates a currency exchange office, transmits money (or any representations of monetary value) by any means or cashes cheques which are made payable to customers;

'nominated officer' means a person who is nominated to receive disclosures under Part 7 of the Proceeds of Crime Act 2002 (money laundering) or Part 3 of the Terrorism Act 2000 (terrorist property);

'non-EEA state' means a state that is not an EEA state;

'notice' means a notice in writing;

'occasional transaction' means a transaction (carried out other than as part of a business relationship) amounting to 15,000 euro or more, whether the transaction is carried out in a single operation or several operations which appear to be linked;

...[6]

'ongoing monitoring' has the meaning given by regulation 8(2);

['payment services' has the meaning given by regulation 2(1) of the Payment Services Regulations 2009;][4]

['person who has a qualifying relationship with a PRA-authorised person' is to be read with section 415B(4) of the 2000 Act;

'the PRA' means the Prudential Regulation Authority;

'PRA-authorised person' has the meaning given in section 2B(5) of the 2000 Act;][8]

'regulated market'—

(a)   within the EEA, has the meaning given by point 14 of Article 4(1) of the markets in financial instruments directive; and

(b)   outside the EEA, means a regulated financial market which subjects companies whose securities are admitted to trading to disclosure obligations which are contained in international standards and are equivalent to the specified disclosure obligations;

'relevant person' means a person to whom, in accordance with regulations 3 and 4, these Regulations apply;

'the specified disclosure obligations' means disclosure requirements consistent with—

(a)   Article 6(1) to (4) of Directive 2003/6/EC of the European Parliament and of the Council of 28th January 2003 on insider dealing and market manipulation;

(b)   Articles 3, 5, 7, 8, 10, 14 and 16 of Directive 2003/71/EC of the European Parliament and of the Council of 4th November 2003 on the prospectuses to be published when securities are offered to the public or admitted to trading;

(c)   Articles 4 to 6, 14, 16 to 19 and 30 of Directive 2004/109/EC of the European Parliament and of the Council of 15th December 2004 relating to the harmonisation of transparency requirements in relation to information about issuers whose securities are admitted to trading on a regulated market; or

(d) [EU][9] legislation made under the provisions mentioned in sub-paragraphs (a) to (c);

'supervisory authority' in relation to any relevant person means the supervisory authority specified for such a person by regulation 23;

'tax adviser' (except in regulation 11(3)) has the meaning given by regulation 3(8);

['telecommunication, digital and IT payment service provider' means an undertaking which provides payment services falling within paragraph 1(g) of Schedule 1 to the Payment Services Regulations 2009;][4]

'terrorist financing' means an offence under—

(a) section 15 (fund-raising), 16 (use and possession), 17 (funding arrangements), 18 (money laundering) or 63 (terrorist finance: jurisdiction) of the Terrorism Act 2000;

(b) paragraph 7(2) or (3) of Schedule 3 to the Anti-Terrorism, Crime and Security Act 2001 (freezing orders);

(c) ...[10]

[(d) regulation 10 of the Al-Qaida (Asset-Freezing) Regulations 2011; or][11]

[(e) section 11, 12, 13, 14, 15 or 18 of the Terrorist Asset-Freezing etc. Act 2010 (offences relating to the freezing of funds etc. of designated persons);][12]

'trust or company service provider' has the meaning given by regulation 3(10).

(2) In these Regulations, references to amounts in euro include references to equivalent amounts in another currency.

(3) Unless otherwise defined, expressions used in these Regulations and the money laundering directive have the same meaning as in the money laundering directive and expressions used in these Regulations and in the implementing measures directive have the same meaning as in the implementing measures directive.

Notes

Amendments

1   Inserted by the Recognised Auction Platforms Regulations 2011, SI 2011/2699, reg 11(1), (2). Date in force: 12 December 2011: see the Recognised Auction Platforms Regulations 2011, reg 1(2)(a).
2   Substituted by the Financial Services Act 2012 (Consequential Amendments and Transitional Provisions) Order 2013, SI 2013/472, art 3, Sch 2, para 129(a)(i). Date in force: 1 April 2013; see the Financial Services Act 2012 (Consequential Amendments and Transitional Provisions) Order 2013, art 1(1).
3   Repealed by the Capital Requirements Regulations 2013, SI 2013/3115, reg 46(1), Sch 2, para 68(1), (2)(a). Date in force: 1 January 2014: see the Capital Requirements Regulations 2013, reg 1(2).
4   Inserted by the Payment Services Regulations 2009, SI 2009/209, reg 126, Sch 6, para 6(a). Date in force: 1 November 2009: see the Payment Services Regulations 2009, reg 1(2)(c).
5   Inserted by the Capital Requirements Regulations 2013, SI 2013/3115, reg 46(1), Sch 2, para 68(1), (2)(b). Date in force: 1 January 2014: see the Capital Requirements Regulations 2013, reg 1(2).
6   Repealed by the Financial Services and Markets Act 2000 (Regulated Activities) (Amendment) (No.2) Order 2013, SI 2013/1881, art 28, Schedule, para 31(1), (2). Date in

force: 26 July 2013: see the Financial Services and Markets Act 2000 (Regulated Activities) (Amendment) (No.2) Order 2013, art 1(2), subject to transitional provisions specified in the Financial Services and Markets Act 2000 (Regulated Activities) (Amendment) (No.2) Order 2013, Pt 8, Schedule, para 32.

7   Substituted by the Electronic Money Regulations 2011, SI 2011/99, reg 79, Sch 4, para 19(a). Date in force: 30 April 2011: see the Electronic Money Regulations 2011, reg 1(2)(b).

8   Inserted by the Financial Services Act 2012 (Consequential Amendments and Transitional Provisions) Order 2013, SI 2013/472, art 3, Sch 2, para 129(a)(ii). Date in force: 1 April 2013; see the Financial Services Act 2012 (Consequential Amendments and Transitional Provisions) Order 2013, art 1(1).

9   Substituted by the Treaty of Lisbon (Changes in Terminology) Order 2011, SI 2011/1043, art 6(2)(b). Date in force: 22 April 2011: see the Treaty of Lisbon (Changes in Terminology) Order 2011, art 2.

10   Repealed by the Terrorist Asset-Freezing etc. Act 2010, s 45, Sch 1, para 6(a), Sch 2, Pt 1. Date in force: 17 December 2010: see the Terrorist Asset-Freezing etc. Act 2010, s 55(1).

11   Substituted by the Al-Qaida (Asset-Freezing) Regulations 2011, SI 2011/2742, reg 21, Sch 2, para 2. Date in force: 16 November 2011: see the Al-Qaida (Asset-Freezing) Regulations 2011, reg 1(1).

12   Substituted by the Terrorist Asset-Freezing etc. Act 2010, s 45(1), Sch 1, para 6(b). Date in force: 17 December 2010: see the Terrorist Asset-Freezing etc. Act 2010, s 55(1).

---

3   Application of the Regulations

(1)   Subject to regulation 4, these Regulations apply to the following persons acting in the course of business carried on by them in the United Kingdom ('relevant persons')—

(a)   credit institutions;

(b)   financial institutions;

(c)   auditors, insolvency practitioners, external accountants and tax advisers;

(d)   independent legal professionals;

(e)   trust or company service providers;

(f)   estate agents;

(g)   high value dealers;

(h)   casinos.

[(1A)   Regulations 2, 20, 21, 23, 24, 35 to 42, and 44 to 48 apply to an auction platform acting in the course of business carried on by it in the United Kingdom, and such an auction platform is a relevant person for the purposes of those provisions.][1]

(2)   'Credit institution' means—

(a)   a credit institution as defined in [Article 4(1)(1) of the capital requirements regulation][2]; or

(b)   a branch (within the meaning of [Article 4(1)(17) of that regulation][2]) located in an EEA state of an institution falling within sub-paragraph (a) (or an equivalent institution whose head office is located in a non-EEA state) wherever its head office is located,

when it accepts deposits or other repayable funds from the public or grants credits for its own account (within the meaning of the banking consolidation directive) [, or when it bids directly in auctions in accordance with the emission allowance auctioning regulation on behalf of its clients][3].

(3) 'Financial institution' means—

(a) an undertaking, including a money service business, when it carries out one or more of the activities listed in points 2 to 12[, 14 and 15][4] of Annex 1 to the [capital requirements directive][2] (the relevant text of which is set out in Schedule 1 to these Regulations), other than—

  (i) a credit institution;

  [(ii) an undertaking whose only listed activity is as a creditor under an agreement which—

      (aa) falls within section 12(a) of the Consumer Credit Act 1974 (debtor-creditor-supplier agreements),

      (bb) provides fixed sum credit (within the meaning given in section 10 of the Consumer Credit Act 1974 (running-account credit and fixed-sum credit) 8) in relation to the provision of services, and

      (cc) provides financial accommodation by way of deferred payment or payment by instalments over a period not exceeding 12 months;][5]

  [(iii)][6] an undertaking whose only listed activity is trading for own account in one or more of the products listed in point 7 of Annex 1 to the [capital requirements directive][2] where the undertaking does not have a customer,

  and, for this purpose, 'customer' means a third party which is not a member of the same group as the undertaking;

(b) an insurance company duly authorised in accordance with the life assurance consolidation directive, when it carries out activities covered by that directive;

[(c) a person, other than a person falling within Article 2 of the markets in financial instruments directive, whose regular occupation or business is the provision to other persons of an investment activity on a professional basis, when providing or performing investment services or activities (within the meaning of that directive) or when bidding directly in auctions in accordance with the emission allowance auctioning regulation on behalf of clients;][7]

[(ca) a person falling within Article 2(1)(i) of the markets in financial instruments directive, when bidding directly in auctions in accordance with the emission allowance auctioning regulation on behalf of clients of the person's main business;][3]

(d) a collective investment undertaking, when marketing or otherwise offering its units or shares;

(e) an insurance intermediary as defined in Article 2(5) of Directive 2002/92/EC of the European Parliament and of the Council of 9th December 2002 on insurance mediation, with the exception of a tied insurance intermediary as mentioned in Article 2(7) of that Directive, when it acts in respect of contracts of long-term insurance within the meaning given by article 3(1) of, and Part II of Schedule 1 to, the Financial Services and Markets Act 2000 (Regulated Activities) Order 2001;

(f) a branch located in an EEA state of a person referred to in sub-paragraphs (a) to (e) (or an equivalent person whose head office is located in a non-EEA state), wherever its head office is located, when carrying out any activity mentioned in sub-paragraphs (a) to (e);

(g) the National Savings Bank;

(h) the Director of Savings, when money is raised under the auspices of the Director under the National Loans Act 1968.

(4) 'Auditor' means any firm or individual who is a statutory auditor within the meaning of Part 42 of the Companies Act 2006 (statutory auditors), when carrying out statutory audit work within the meaning of section 1210 of that Act.

(5) Before the entry into force of Part 42 of the Companies Act 2006 the reference in paragraph (4) to—

(a) a person who is a statutory auditor shall be treated as a reference to a person who is eligible for appointment as a company auditor under section 25 of the Companies Act 1989 (eligibility for appointment) or article 28 of the Companies (Northern Ireland) Order 1990; and

(b) the carrying out of statutory audit work shall be treated as a reference to the provision of audit services.

(6) 'Insolvency practitioner' means any person who acts as an insolvency practitioner within the meaning of section 388 of the Insolvency Act 1986 (meaning of 'act as insolvency practitioner') or article 3 of the Insolvency (Northern Ireland) Order 1989.

(7) 'External accountant' means a firm or sole practitioner who by way of business provides accountancy services to other persons, when providing such services.

(8) 'Tax adviser' means a firm or sole practitioner who by way of business provides advice about the tax affairs of other persons, when providing such services.

(9) 'Independent legal professional' means a firm or sole practitioner who by way of business provides legal or notarial services to other persons, when participating in financial or real property transactions concerning—

(a) the buying and selling of real property or business entities;

(b) the managing of client money, securities or other assets;

(c) the opening or management of bank, savings or securities accounts;

(d) the organisation of contributions necessary for the creation, operation or management of companies; or

(e) the creation, operation or management of trusts, companies or similar structures,

and, for this purpose, a person participates in a transaction by assisting in the planning or execution of the transaction or otherwise acting for or on behalf of a client in the transaction.

(10) 'Trust or company service provider' means a firm or sole practitioner who by way of business provides any of the following services to other persons—

(a) forming companies or other legal persons;

(b) acting, or arranging for another person to act—

   (i) as a director or secretary of a company;

   (ii) as a partner of a partnership; or

   (iii) in a similar position in relation to other legal persons;

(c) providing a registered office, business address, correspondence or administrative address or other related services for a company, partnership or any other legal person or arrangement;

(d)   acting, or arranging for another person to act, as—

  (i)   a trustee of an express trust or similar legal arrangement; or

  (ii) a nominee shareholder for a person other than a company whose securities are listed on a regulated market,

  when providing such services.

(11)   'Estate agent' means—

(a)   a firm; or

(b)   sole practitioner,

who, or whose employees, carry out estate agency work ...[8], when in the course of carrying out such work .

[(11A)   For the purposes of paragraph (11) 'estate agency work' is to be read in accordance with section 1 of the Estate Agents Act 1979 (estate agency work), but for those purposes references in that section to disposing of or acquiring an interest in land are (despite anything in section 2 of that Act) to be taken to include references to disposing of or acquiring an estate or interest in land outside the United Kingdom where that estate or interest is capable of being owned or held as a separate interest.][5]

(12)   'High value dealer' means a firm or sole trader who by way of business trades in goods (including an auctioneer dealing in goods), when he receives, in respect of any transaction, a payment or payments in cash of at least 15,000 euros in total, whether the transaction is executed in a single operation or in several operations which appear to be linked.

(13)   'Casino' means the holder of a casino operating licence and, for this purpose, a 'casino operating licence' has the meaning given by section 65(2) of the Gambling Act 2005 (nature of licence).

[(13A)   'Auction platform' means a platform which auctions two-day spot or five-day futures, within the meanings given by Article 3(4) and (5) of the emission allowance auctioning regulation, when it carries out activities covered by that regulation.][1]

(14)   In the application of this regulation to Scotland, for 'real property' in paragraph (9) substitute 'heritable property'.

Notes

Amendments

1   Inserted by the Recognised Auction Platforms Regulations 2011, SI 2011/2699, reg 11(1), (3). Date in force: 12 December 2011: see the Recognised Auction Platforms Regulations 2011, reg 1(2)(a).

2   Substituted by the Capital Requirements Regulations 2013, SI 2013/3115, reg 46(1), Sch 2, para 68(1), (3). Date in force: 1 January 2014: see the Capital Requirements Regulations 2013, reg 1(2).

3   Inserted by the Financial Services and Markets Act 2000 (Regulated Activities) (Amendment) Order 2012, SI 2012/1906, art 7(a), (c). Date in force: 20 July 2012: see the Financial Services and Markets Act 2000 (Regulated Activities) (Amendment) Order 2012, art 1.

4   Substituted by the Electronic Money Regulations 2011, SI 2011/99, reg 79, Sch 4, para 19(b) (ii). Date in force: 30 April 2011: see the Electronic Money Regulations 2011, reg 1(2)(b).

5   Inserted by the Money Laundering (Amendment) Regulations 2012, SI 2012/2298, reg 3(a), (c). Date in force: 1 October 2012: see the Money Laundering (Amendment) Regulations 2012, reg 1.

6   Substituted by the Money Laundering (Amendment) Regulations 2012, SI 2012/2298, reg 3(a). Date in force: 1 October 2012: see the Money Laundering (Amendment) Regulations 2012, reg 1.

7   Substituted by the Financial Services and Markets Act 2000 (Regulated Activities) (Amendment) Order 2012, SI 2012/1906, art 7(b). Date in force: 20 July 2012: see the Financial Services and Markets Act 2000 (Regulated Activities) (Amendment) Order 2012, art 1.

8   Repealed by the Money Laundering (Amendment) Regulations 2012, SI 2012/2298, reg 3(b). Date in force: 1 October 2012: see the Money Laundering (Amendment) Regulations 2012, reg 1.

---

4   Exclusions

(1)   These Regulations do not apply to the following persons when carrying out any of the following activities—

(a)   a society registered under the Industrial and Provident Societies Act 1965, when it—

    (i)   issues withdrawable share capital within the limit set by section 6 of that Act (maximum shareholding in society); or

    (ii)   accepts deposits from the public within the limit set by section 7(3) of that Act (carrying on of banking by societies);

(b)   a society registered under the Industrial and Provident Societies Act (Northern Ireland) 1969, when it—

    (i)   issues withdrawable share capital within the limit set by section 6 of that Act (maximum shareholding in society); or

    (ii)   accepts deposits from the public within the limit set by section 7(3) of that Act (carrying on of banking by societies);

(c)   a person who is (or falls within a class of persons) specified in any of paragraphs 2 to 23, 25 to 38 or 40 to 49 of the Schedule to the Financial Services and Markets Act 2000 (Exemption) Order 2001, when carrying out any activity in respect of which he is exempt;

[(ca) a local authority within the meaning given in article 3 of the Financial Services and Markets Act 2000 (Regulated Activities) Order 2001, when carrying on an activity which would be a regulated activity for the purposes of the Financial Services and Markets Act 2000 but for article 72G of that Order;][1]

(d)   a person who was an exempted person for the purposes of section 45 of the Financial Services Act 1986 (miscellaneous exemptions) immediately before its repeal, when exercising the functions specified in that section;

(e)   a person whose main activity is that of a high value dealer, when he engages in financial activity on an occasional or very limited basis as set out in paragraph 1 of Schedule 2 to these Regulations; or

[(f)   a person, when he prepares a home report.][2]

(2)   These Regulations do not apply to a person who falls within regulation 3 solely as a result of his engaging in financial activity on an occasional or very limited basis as set out in paragraph 1 of Schedule 2 to these Regulations.

(3)   Parts 2 to 5 of these Regulations do not apply to—

(a)   the Auditor General for Scotland;

(b)   the Auditor General for Wales;

(c)   the Bank of England;

(d)   the Comptroller and Auditor General;

(e)   the Comptroller and Auditor General for Northern Ireland;

(f)   the Official Solicitor to the Supreme Court, when acting as trustee in his official capacity;

(g)   the Treasury Solicitor.

[(4)   In paragraph (1)(f), 'home report' means the documents prescribed for the purposes of section 98, 99(1) or 101(2) of the Housing (Scotland) Act 2006.][2]

Notes

Amendments

1   Inserted by the Financial Services and Markets Act 2000 (Consumer Credit) (Miscellaneous Provisions) (No. 2) Order 2014, SI 2014/506, art 4. Date in force: 1 April 2014: see the Financial Services and Markets Act 2000 (Consumer Credit) (Miscellaneous Provisions) (No. 2) Order 2014, art 1(3).
2   Substituted by the Money Laundering (Amendment) Regulations 2012, SI 2012/2298, reg 4. Date in force: 1 October 2012: see the Money Laundering (Amendment) Regulations 2012, reg 1.

Part 2
Customer due diligence

5   Meaning of customer due diligence measures

'Customer due diligence measures' means—

(a)   identifying the customer and verifying the customer's identity on the basis of documents, data or information obtained from a reliable and independent source;

(b)   identifying, where there is a beneficial owner who is not the customer, the beneficial owner and taking adequate measures, on a risk-sensitive basis, to verify his identity so that the relevant person is satisfied that he knows who the beneficial owner is, including, in the case of a legal person, trust or similar legal arrangement, measures to understand the ownership and control structure of the person, trust or arrangement; and

(c)   obtaining information on the purpose and intended nature of the business relationship.

6   Meaning of beneficial owner

(1)   In the case of a body corporate, 'beneficial owner' means any individual who—

(a)   as respects any body other than a company whose securities are listed on a regulated market, ultimately owns or controls (whether through direct or indirect ownership or control, including through bearer share holdings) more than 25% of the shares or voting rights in the body; or

(b)   as respects any body corporate, otherwise exercises control over the management of the body.

(2)   In the case of a partnership (other than a limited liability partnership), 'beneficial owner' means any individual who—

(a) ultimately is entitled to or controls (whether the entitlement or control is direct or indirect) more than a 25% share of the capital or profits of the partnership or more than 25% of the voting rights in the partnership; or

(b) otherwise exercises control over the management of the partnership.

(3)   In the case of a trust, 'beneficial owner' means—

(a) any individual who is entitled to a specified interest in at least 25% of the capital of the trust property;

(b) as respects any trust other than one which is set up or operates entirely for the benefit of individuals falling within sub-paragraph (a), the class of persons in whose main interest the trust is set up or operates;

(c) any individual who has control over the trust.

(4)   In paragraph (3)—

'specified interest' means a vested interest which is—

(a) in possession or in remainder or reversion (or, in Scotland, in fee); and

(b) defeasible or indefeasible;

'control' means a power (whether exercisable alone, jointly with another person or with the consent of another person) under the trust instrument or by law to—

(a) dispose of, advance, lend, invest, pay or apply trust property;

(b) vary the trust;

(c) add or remove a person as a beneficiary or to or from a class of beneficiaries;

(d) appoint or remove trustees;

(e) direct, withhold consent to or veto the exercise of a power such as is mentioned in sub-paragraph (a), (b), (c) or (d).

(5)   For the purposes of paragraph (3)—

(a) where an individual is the beneficial owner of a body corporate which is entitled to a specified interest in the capital of the trust property or which has control over the trust, the individual is to be regarded as entitled to the interest or having control over the trust; and

(b) an individual does not have control solely as a result of—

(i) his consent being required in accordance with section 32(1)(c) of the Trustee Act 1925 (power of advancement);

(ii) any discretion delegated to him under section 34 of the Pensions Act 1995 (power of investment and delegation);

(iii) the power to give a direction conferred on him by section 19(2) of the Trusts of Land and Appointment of Trustees Act 1996 (appointment and retirement of trustee at instance of beneficiaries); or

(iv) the power exercisable collectively at common law to vary or extinguish a trust where the beneficiaries under the trust are of full age and capacity and (taken together) absolutely entitled to the property subject to the trust (or, in Scotland, have a full and unqualified right to the fee).

(6)   In the case of a legal entity or legal arrangement which does not fall within paragraph (1), (2) or (3), 'beneficial owner' means—

(a) where the individuals who benefit from the entity or arrangement have been determined, any individual who benefits from at least 25% of the property of the entity or arrangement;

(b) where the individuals who benefit from the entity or arrangement have yet to be determined, the class of persons in whose main interest the entity or arrangement is set up or operates;

(c) any individual who exercises control over at least 25% of the property of the entity or arrangement.

(7) For the purposes of paragraph (6), where an individual is the beneficial owner of a body corporate which benefits from or exercises control over the property of the entity or arrangement, the individual is to be regarded as benefiting from or exercising control over the property of the entity or arrangement.

(8) In the case of an estate of a deceased person in the course of administration, 'beneficial owner' means—

(a) in England and Wales and Northern Ireland, the executor, original or by representation, or administrator for the time being of a deceased person;

(b) in Scotland, the executor for the purposes of the Executors (Scotland) Act 1900.

(9) In any other case, 'beneficial owner' means the individual who ultimately owns or controls the customer or on whose behalf a transaction is being conducted.

(10) In this regulation—

'arrangement', 'entity' and 'trust' means an arrangement, entity or trust which administers and distributes funds;

'limited liability partnership' has the meaning given by the Limited Liability Partnerships Act 2000.

7 Application of customer due diligence measures

(1) Subject to regulations 9, 10, 12, 13, 14, 16(4) and 17, a relevant person must apply customer due diligence measures when he—

(a) establishes a business relationship;

(b) carries out an occasional transaction;

(c) suspects money laundering or terrorist financing;

(d) doubts the veracity or adequacy of documents, data or information previously obtained for the purposes of identification or verification.

(2) Subject to regulation 16(4), a relevant person must also apply customer due diligence measures at other appropriate times to existing customers on a risk-sensitive basis.

(3) A relevant person must—

(a) determine the extent of customer due diligence measures on a risk-sensitive basis depending on the type of customer, business relationship, product or transaction; and

(b) be able to demonstrate to his supervisory authority that the extent of the measures is appropriate in view of the risks of money laundering and terrorist financing.

(4)   Where—

(a)   a relevant person is required to apply customer due diligence measures in the case of a trust, legal entity (other than a body corporate) or a legal arrangement (other than a trust); and

(b)   the class of persons in whose main interest the trust, entity or arrangement is set up or operates is identified as a beneficial owner,

the relevant person is not required to identify all the members of the class.

(5)   Paragraph (3)(b) does not apply to the National Savings Bank or the Director of Savings.

8   Ongoing monitoring

(1)   A relevant person must conduct ongoing monitoring of a business relationship.

(2)   'Ongoing monitoring' of a business relationship means—

(a)   scrutiny of transactions undertaken throughout the course of the relationship (including, where necessary, the source of funds) to ensure that the transactions are consistent with the relevant person's knowledge of the customer, his business and risk profile; and

(b)   keeping the documents, data or information obtained for the purpose of applying customer due diligence measures up-to-date.

(3)   Regulation 7(3) applies to the duty to conduct ongoing monitoring under paragraph (1) as it applies to customer due diligence measures.

9   Timing of verification

(1)   This regulation applies in respect of the duty under regulation 7(1)(a) and (b) to apply the customer due diligence measures referred to in regulation 5(a) and (b).

(2)   Subject to paragraphs (3) to (5) and regulation 10, a relevant person must verify the identity of the customer (and any beneficial owner) before the establishment of a business relationship or the carrying out of an occasional transaction.

(3)   Such verification may be completed during the establishment of a business relationship if—

(a)   this is necessary not to interrupt the normal conduct of business; and

(b)   there is little risk of money laundering or terrorist financing occurring,

provided that the verification is completed as soon as practicable after contact is first established.

(4)   The verification of the identity of the beneficiary under a life insurance policy may take place after the business relationship has been established provided that it takes place at or before the time of payout or at or before the time the beneficiary exercises a right vested under the policy.

(5)   The verification of the identity of a bank account holder may take place after the bank account has been opened provided that there are adequate safeguards in place to ensure that—

(a)   the account is not closed; and

(b)   transactions are not carried out by or on behalf of the account holder (including any payment from the account to the account holder),

before verification has been completed.

10   Casinos

(1)   A casino must establish and verify the identity of—

(a)   all customers to whom the casino makes facilities for gaming available—

  (i)   before entry to any premises where such facilities are provided; or

  (ii)   where the facilities are for remote gaming, before access is given to such facilities; or

(b)   if the specified conditions are met, all customers who, in the course of any period of 24 hours—

  (i)   purchase from, or exchange with, the casino chips with a total value of 2,000 euro or more;

  (ii)   pay the casino 2,000 [euro][1] or more for the use of gaming machines; or

  (iii)   pay to, or stake with, the casino 2,000 euro or more in connection with facilities for remote gaming.

(2)   The specified conditions are—

(a)   the casino verifies the identity of each customer before or immediately after such purchase, exchange, payment or stake takes place, and

(b)   the Gambling Commission is satisfied that the casino has appropriate procedures in place to monitor and record—

  (i)   the total value of chips purchased from or exchanged with the casino;

  (ii)   the total money paid for the use of gaming machines; or

  (iii)   the total money paid or staked in connection with facilities for remote gaming,

  by each customer.

(3)   In this regulation—

'gaming', 'gaming machine', 'remote operating licence' and 'stake' have the meanings given by, respectively, sections 6(1) (gaming & game of chance), 235 (gaming machine), 67 (remote gambling) and 353(1) (interpretation) of the Gambling Act 2005;

'premises' means premises subject to—

  (a)   a casino premises licence within the meaning of section 150(1)(a) of the Gambling Act 2005 (nature of licence); or

  (b)   a converted casino premises licence within the meaning of paragraph 65 of Part 7 of Schedule 4 to the Gambling Act 2005 (Commencement No. 6 and Transitional Provisions) Order 2006;

'remote gaming' means gaming provided pursuant to a remote operating licence.

Notes

Amendment

1   Inserted by the Money Laundering (Amendment) Regulations 2007, SI 2007/3299, reg 2(a). Date in force: 15 December 2007: see the Money Laundering (Amendment) Regulations 2007, reg 1.

---

11   Requirement to cease transactions etc.

(1)   Where, in relation to any customer, a relevant person is unable to apply customer due diligence measures in accordance with the provisions of this Part, he—

(a)   must not carry out a transaction with or for the customer through a bank account;

(b)   must not establish a business relationship or carry out an occasional transaction with the customer;

(c)   must terminate any existing business relationship with the customer;

(d)   must consider whether he is required to make a disclosure by Part 7 of the Proceeds of Crime Act 2002 or Part 3 of the Terrorism Act 2000.

(2)   Paragraph (1) does not apply where a lawyer or other professional adviser is in the course of ascertaining the legal position for his client or performing his task of defending or representing that client in, or concerning, legal proceedings, including advice on the institution or avoidance of proceedings.

(3)   In paragraph (2), 'other professional adviser' means an auditor, accountant or tax adviser who is a member of a professional body which is established for any such persons and which makes provision for—

(a)   testing the competence of those seeking admission to membership of such a body as a condition for such admission; and

(b)   imposing and maintaining professional and ethical standards for its members, as well as imposing sanctions for non-compliance with those standards.

12   Exception for trustees of debt issues

(1)   A relevant person—

(a)   who is appointed by the issuer of instruments or securities specified in paragraph (2) as trustee of an issue of such instruments or securities; or

(b)   whose customer is a trustee of an issue of such instruments or securities,

is not required to apply the customer due diligence measure referred to in regulation 5(b) in respect of the holders of such instruments or securities.

(2)   The specified instruments and securities are—

(a)   instruments which fall within article 77 [or 77A][1] of the Financial Services and Markets Act 2000 (Regulated Activities) Order 2001; and

(b)   securities which fall within article 78 of that Order.

Notes

Amendment

1   Inserted by the Financial Services and Markets Act 2000 (Regulated Activities) (Amendment) Order 2010, SI 2010/86, art 4, Schedule, para 10. Date in force: 24 February 2010: see the Financial Services and Markets Act 2000 (Regulated Activities) (Amendment) Order 2010, art 1(2).

---

13   Simplified due diligence

(1)   A relevant person is not required to apply customer due diligence measures in the circumstances mentioned in regulation 7(1)(a), (b) or (d) where he has

reasonable grounds for believing that the customer, transaction or product related to such transaction, falls within any of the following paragraphs.

(2)   The customer is—

(a)   a credit or financial institution which is subject to the requirements of the money laundering directive; or

(b)   a credit or financial institution (or equivalent institution) which—

    (i)   is situated in a non-EEA state which imposes requirements equivalent to those laid down in the money laundering directive; and

    (ii)   is supervised for compliance with those requirements.

(3)   The customer is a company whose securities are listed on a regulated market subject to specified disclosure obligations.

(4)   The customer is an independent legal professional and the product is an account into which monies are pooled, provided that—

(a)   where the pooled account is held in a non-EEA state—

    (i)   that state imposes requirements to combat money laundering and terrorist financing which are consistent with international standards; and

    (ii)   the independent legal professional is supervised in that state for compliance with those requirements; and

(b)   information on the identity of the persons on whose behalf monies are held in the pooled account is available, on request, to the institution which acts as a depository institution for the account.

(5)   The customer is a public authority in the United Kingdom.

(6)   The customer is a public authority which fulfils all the conditions set out in paragraph 2 of Schedule 2 to these Regulations.

(7)   The product is—

(a)   a life insurance contract where the annual premium is no more than 1,000 euro or where a single premium of no more than 2,500 euro is paid;

(b)   an insurance contract for the purposes of a pension scheme where the contract contains no surrender clause and cannot be used as collateral;

(c)   a pension, superannuation or similar scheme which provides retirement benefits to employees, where contributions are made by an employer or by way of deduction from an employee's wages and the scheme rules do not permit the assignment of a member's interest under the scheme (other than an assignment permitted by section 44 of the Welfare Reform and Pensions Act 1999 (disapplication of restrictions on alienation) or section 91(5)(a) of the Pensions Act 1995 (inalienability of occupational pension)); or

(d)   electronic money, within the meaning of [Article 2(2)][1] of the electronic money directive, where—

    (i)   if the device cannot be recharged, the maximum amount stored in the device is no more than [250 euro or, in the case of electronic money used to carry out payment transactions within the United Kingdom, 500 euro][1]; or

    (ii)   if the device can be recharged, a limit of 2,500 euro is imposed on the total amount transacted in a calendar year, except when an amount of 1,000 euro or more is redeemed in the same calendar year [by the electronic money holder (within the meaning of Article 11 of the electronic money directive).]¹

(8)   The product and any transaction related to such product fulfils all the conditions set out in paragraph 3 of Schedule 2 to these Regulations.

(9)   The product is a child trust fund within the meaning given by section 1(2) of the Child Trust Funds Act 2004.

[(10)   The product is a junior ISA within the meaning given by regulation 2B of the Individual Savings Account Regulations 1998.]²

Notes

Amendments

1   Substituted by the Electronic Money Regulations 2011, SI 2011/99, reg 79, Sch 4, para 19(c). Date in force: 30 April 2011: see the Electronic Money Regulations 2011, reg 1(2)(b).

2   Inserted by the Money Laundering (Amendment) Regulations 2011, SI 2011/1781, reg 2. Date in force: 1 November 2011: see the Money Laundering (Amendment) Regulations 2011, reg 1.

---

14   Enhanced customer due diligence and ongoing monitoring

(1)   A relevant person must apply on a risk-sensitive basis enhanced customer due diligence measures and enhanced ongoing monitoring—

(a)   in accordance with paragraphs (2) to (4);

(b)   in any other situation which by its nature can present a higher risk of money laundering or terrorist financing.

(2)   Where the customer has not been physically present for identification purposes, a relevant person must take specific and adequate measures to compensate for the higher risk, for example, by applying one or more of the following measures—

(a)   ensuring that the customer's identity is established by additional documents, data or information;

(b)   supplementary measures to verify or certify the documents supplied, or requiring confirmatory certification by a credit or financial institution which is subject to the money laundering directive;

(c)   ensuring that the first payment is carried out through an account opened in the customer's name with a credit institution.

(3)   A credit institution ('the correspondent') which has or proposes to have a correspondent banking relationship with a respondent institution ('the respondent') from a non-EEA state must—

(a)   gather sufficient information about the respondent to understand fully the nature of its business;

(b)   determine from publicly-available information the reputation of the respondent and the quality of its supervision;

(c)   assess the respondent's anti-money laundering and anti-terrorist financing controls;

(d)   obtain approval from senior management before establishing a new correspondent banking relationship;

(e)   document the respective responsibilities of the respondent and correspondent; and

(f)   be satisfied that, in respect of those of the respondent's customers who have direct access to accounts of the correspondent, the respondent—

   (i)   has verified the identity of, and conducts ongoing monitoring in respect of, such customers; and

   (ii) is able to provide to the correspondent, upon request, the documents, data or information obtained when applying customer due diligence measures and ongoing monitoring.

(4)   A relevant person who proposes to have a business relationship or carry out an occasional transaction with a politically exposed person must—

(a)   have approval from senior management for establishing the business relationship with that person;

(b)   take adequate measures to establish the source of wealth and source of funds which are involved in the proposed business relationship or occasional transaction; and

(c)   where the business relationship is entered into, conduct enhanced ongoing monitoring of the relationship.

(5)   In paragraph (4), 'a politically exposed person' means a person who is—

(a)   an individual who is or has, at any time in the preceding year, been entrusted with a prominent public function by—

   (i)   a state other than the United Kingdom;

   (ii)   [an EU]¹ institution; or

   (iii) an international body,

   including a person who falls in any of the categories listed in paragraph 4(1) (a) of Schedule 2;

(b)   an immediate family member of a person referred to in sub-paragraph (a), including a person who falls in any of the categories listed in paragraph 4(1) (c) of Schedule 2; or

(c)   a known close associate of a person referred to in sub-paragraph (a), including a person who falls in either of the categories listed in paragraph 4(1)(d) of Schedule 2.

(6)   For the purpose of deciding whether a person is a known close associate of a person referred to in paragraph (5)(a), a relevant person need only have regard to information which is in his possession or is publicly known.

Notes

Amendment

1   Substituted by the Treaty of Lisbon (Changes in Terminology) Order 2011, SI 2011/1043, art 6(1)(c). Date in force: 22 April 2011: see the Treaty of Lisbon (Changes in Terminology) Order 2011, art 2.

---

15   Branches and subsidiaries

(1)   A credit or financial institution must require its branches and subsidiary undertakings which are located in a non-EEA state to apply, to the extent permitted

by the law of that state, measures at least equivalent to those set out in these Regulations with regard to customer due diligence measures, ongoing monitoring and record-keeping.

(2)   Where the law of a non-EEA state does not permit the application of such equivalent measures by the branch or subsidiary undertaking located in that state, the credit or financial institution must—

(a)   inform its supervisory authority accordingly; and

(b)   take additional measures to handle effectively the risk of money laundering and terrorist financing.

(3)   In this regulation 'subsidiary undertaking'—

(a)   except in relation to an incorporated friendly society, has the meaning given by section 1162 of the Companies Act 2006 (parent and subsidiary undertakings) and, in relation to a body corporate in or formed under the law of an EEA state other than the United Kingdom, includes an undertaking which is a subsidiary undertaking within the meaning of any rule of law in force in that state for purposes connected with implementation of the European Council Seventh Company Law Directive 83/349/EEC of 13th June 1983 on consolidated accounts;

(b)   in relation to an incorporated friendly society, means a body corporate of which the society has control within the meaning of section 13(9)(a) or (aa) of the Friendly Societies Act 1992 (control of subsidiaries and other bodies corporate).

(4)   Before the entry into force of section 1162 of the Companies Act 2006 the reference to that section in paragraph (3)(a) shall be treated as a reference to section 258 of the Companies Act 1985 (parent and subsidiary undertakings).

16   Shell banks, anonymous accounts etc.

(1)   A credit institution must not enter into, or continue, a correspondent banking relationship with a shell bank.

(2)   A credit institution must take appropriate measures to ensure that it does not enter into, or continue, a corresponding banking relationship with a bank which is known to permit its accounts to be used by a shell bank.

(3)   A credit or financial institution carrying on business in the United Kingdom must not set up an anonymous account or an anonymous passbook for any new or existing customer.

(4)   As soon as reasonably practicable on or after 15th December 2007 all credit and financial institutions carrying on business in the United Kingdom must apply customer due diligence measures to, and conduct ongoing monitoring of, all anonymous accounts and passbooks in existence on that date and in any event before such accounts or passbooks are used.

(5)   A 'shell bank' means a credit institution, or an institution engaged in equivalent activities, incorporated in a jurisdiction in which it has no physical presence involving meaningful decision-making and management, and which is not part of a financial conglomerate or third-country financial conglomerate.

(6)   In this regulation, 'financial conglomerate' and 'third-country financial conglomerate' have the meanings given by regulations 1(2) and 7(1) respectively of the Financial Conglomerates and Other Financial Groups Regulations 2004.

17   Reliance

(1)   A relevant person may rely on a person who falls within paragraph (2) (or who the relevant person has reasonable grounds to believe falls within paragraph (2)) to apply any customer due diligence measures provided that—

(a)   the other person consents to being relied on; and

(b)   notwithstanding the relevant person's reliance on the other person, the relevant person remains liable for any failure to apply such measures.

(2)   The persons are—

(a)   a credit or financial institution which is an authorised person;

[(aa) ...¹]²

(b)   a relevant person who is—

  (i)   an auditor, insolvency practitioner, external accountant, tax adviser or independent legal professional; and

  (ii)   supervised for the purposes of these Regulations by one of the bodies listed in ...³ Schedule 3;

(c)   a person who carries on business in another EEA state who is—

  (i)   a credit or financial institution, auditor, insolvency practitioner, external accountant, tax adviser or independent legal professional;

  (ii)   subject to mandatory professional registration recognised by law; and

  (iii)   supervised for compliance with the requirements laid down in the money laundering directive in accordance with section 2 of Chapter V of that directive; or

(d)   a person who carries on business in a non-EEA state who is—

  (i)   a credit or financial institution (or equivalent institution), auditor, insolvency practitioner, external accountant, tax adviser or independent legal professional;

  (ii)   subject to mandatory professional registration recognised by law;

  (iii)   subject to requirements equivalent to those laid down in the money laundering directive; and

  (iv)   supervised for compliance with those requirements in a manner equivalent to section 2 of Chapter V of the money laundering directive.

(3)   In paragraph (2)(c)(i) and (d)(i), 'auditor' and 'insolvency practitioner' includes a person situated in another EEA state or a non-EEA state who provides services equivalent to the services provided by an auditor or insolvency practitioner.

(4)   Nothing in this regulation prevents a relevant person applying customer due diligence measures by means of an outsourcing service provider or agent provided that the relevant person remains liable for any failure to apply such measures.

[(5)   In this regulation, 'financial institution' excludes—

(a)   any money service business;

(b)   any authorised payment institution, EEA authorised payment institution or small payment institution (within the meaning of the Payment Services Regulations 2009) which provides payment services mainly falling within paragraph 1(f) of Schedule 1 to those Regulations[; and

(c) any electronic money institution or EEA authorised electronic money institution (within the meaning of the Electronic Money Regulations 2011) which provides payment services mainly falling within paragraph 1(f) of Schedule 1 to the Payment Services Regulations 2009.][4][5]

Notes

Amendments

1   Repealed by the Financial Services and Markets Act 2000 (Regulated Activities) (Amendment) (No.2) Order 2013, SI 2013/1881, art 28, Schedule, para 31(1), (3). Date in force: 26 July 2013: see the Financial Services and Markets Act 2000 (Regulated Activities) (Amendment) (No.2) Order 2013, art 1(2), subject to transitional provisions specified in the Financial Services and Markets Act 2000 (Regulated Activities) (Amendment) (No.2) Order 2013, Pt 8, Schedule, para 32.
2   Inserted by the Money Laundering (Amendment) Regulations 2012, SI 2012/2298, reg 5(a). Date in force: 1 October 2012: see the Money Laundering (Amendment) Regulations 2012, reg 1.
3   Repealed by the Money Laundering (Amendment) Regulations 2012, SI 2012/2298, reg 5(b). Date in force: 1 October 2012: see the Money Laundering (Amendment) Regulations 2012, reg 1.
4   Inserted by the Electronic Money Regulations 2011, SI 2011/99, reg 79, Sch 4, para 19(d). Date in force: 30 April 2011: see the Electronic Money Regulations 2011, reg 1(2)(b).
5   Substituted by the Payment Services Regulations 2009, SI 2009/209, reg 126, Sch 6, para 6(b). Date in force: 1 November 2009: see the Payment Services Regulations 2009, reg 1(2)(c).

18 ...[1]

...[1]

Notes

Amendment

1   Repealed by the Money Laundering (Amendment) Regulations 2012, SI 2012/2298, reg 6. Date in force: 1 October 2012: see the Money Laundering (Amendment) Regulations 2012, reg 1.

Part 3
Record-keeping, procedures and training

19 Record-keeping

(1) Subject to paragraph (4), a relevant person must keep the records specified in paragraph (2) for at least the period specified in paragraph (3).

(2) The records are—

(a) a copy of, or the references to, the evidence of the customer's identity obtained pursuant to regulation 7, 8, 10, 14 or 16(4);

(b) the supporting records (consisting of the original documents or copies) in respect of a business relationship or occasional transaction which is the subject of customer due diligence measures or ongoing monitoring.

(3) The period is five years beginning on—

(a) in the case of the records specified in paragraph (2)(a), the date on which—

     (i)   the occasional transaction is completed; or

     (ii) the business relationship ends; or

(b) in the case of the records specified in paragraph (2)(b)—

     (i)   where the records relate to a particular transaction, the date on which the transaction is completed;

     (ii) for all other records, the date on which the business relationship ends.

(4)   A relevant person who is relied on by another person must keep the records specified in paragraph (2)(a) for five years beginning on the date on which he is relied on for the purposes of regulation 7, 10, 14 or 16(4) in relation to any business relationship or occasional transaction.

(5)   A person referred to in regulation 17(2)(a) or (b) who is relied on by a relevant person must, if requested by the person relying on him within the period referred to in paragraph (4)—

(a) as soon as reasonably practicable make available to the person who is relying on him any information about the customer (and any beneficial owner) which he obtained when applying customer due diligence measures; and

(b) as soon as reasonably practicable forward to the person who is relying on him copies of any identification and verification data and other relevant documents on the identity of the customer (and any beneficial owner) which he obtained when applying those measures.

(6)   A relevant person who relies on a person referred to in regulation 17(2)(c) or (d) (a 'third party') to apply customer due diligence measures must take steps to ensure that the third party will, if requested by the relevant person within the period referred to in paragraph (4)—

(a) as soon as reasonably practicable make available to him any information about the customer (and any beneficial owner) which the third party obtained when applying customer due diligence measures; and

(b) as soon as reasonably practicable forward to him copies of any identification and verification data and other relevant documents on the identity of the customer (and any beneficial owner) which the third party obtained when applying those measures.

(7)   Paragraphs (5) and (6) do not apply where a relevant person applies customer due diligence measures by means of an outsourcing service provider or agent.

(8)   For the purposes of this regulation, a person relies on another person where he does so in accordance with regulation 17(1).

20 Policies and procedures

(1)   A relevant person must establish and maintain appropriate and risk-sensitive policies and procedures relating to—

(a) customer due diligence measures and ongoing monitoring;

(b) reporting;

(c) record-keeping;

(d) internal control;

(e) risk assessment and management;

(f)   the monitoring and management of compliance with, and the internal communication of, such policies and procedures,

in order to prevent activities related to money laundering and terrorist financing.

(2)   The policies and procedures referred to in paragraph (1) include policies and procedures—

(a)   which provide for the identification and scrutiny of—

    (i)   complex or unusually large transactions;

    (ii)   unusual patterns of transactions which have no apparent economic or visible lawful purpose; and

    (iii)   any other activity which the relevant person regards as particularly likely by its nature to be related to money laundering or terrorist financing;

(b)   which specify the taking of additional measures, where appropriate, to prevent the use for money laundering or terrorist financing of products and transactions which might favour anonymity;

(c)   to determine whether a customer is a politically exposed person;

(d)   under which—

    (i)   an individual in the relevant person's organisation is a nominated officer under Part 7 of the Proceeds of Crime Act 2002 and Part 3 of the Terrorism Act 2000;

    (ii)   anyone in the organisation to whom information or other matter comes in the course of the business as a result of which he knows or suspects or has reasonable grounds for knowing or suspecting that a person is engaged in money laundering or terrorist financing is required to comply with Part 7 of the Proceeds of Crime Act 2002 or, as the case may be, Part 3 of the Terrorism Act 2000; and

    (iii)   where a disclosure is made to the nominated officer, he must consider it in the light of any relevant information which is available to the relevant person and determine whether it gives rise to knowledge or suspicion or reasonable grounds for knowledge or suspicion that a person is engaged in money laundering or terrorist financing.

(3)   Paragraph (2)(d) does not apply where the relevant person is an individual who neither employs nor acts in association with any other person.

(4)   A credit or financial institution [and an auction platform][1] must establish and maintain systems which enable it to respond fully and rapidly to enquiries from financial investigators accredited under section 3 of the Proceeds of Crime Act 2002 (accreditation and training), persons acting on behalf of the Scottish Ministers in their capacity as an enforcement authority under that Act, officers of Revenue and Customs or constables as to—

(a)   whether it maintains, or has maintained during the previous five years, a business relationship with any person; and

(b)   the nature of that relationship.

(5)   A credit or financial institution [and an auction platform][1] must communicate where relevant the policies and procedures which it establishes and maintains in accordance with this regulation to its branches and subsidiary undertakings which are located outside the United Kingdom.

[(5A)   A relevant person who is an issuer of electronic money must appoint an individual to monitor and manage compliance with, and the internal communication of, the policies and procedures relating to the matters referred to in paragraph (1)(a) to (e), and in particular to—

(a)   identify any situations of higher risk of money laundering or terrorist financing;

(b)   maintain a record of its policies and procedures, risk assessment and risk management including the application of such policies and procedures;

(c)   apply measures to ensure that such policies and procedures are taken into account in all relevant functions including in the development of new products, dealing with new customers and in changes to business activities; and

(d)   provide information to senior management about the operation and effectiveness of such policies and procedures at least annually.][2]

(6)   In this regulation—

'politically exposed person' has the same meaning as in regulation 14(4);

'subsidiary undertaking' has the same meaning as in regulation 15.

_____

Notes

Amendments

1   Inserted by the Recognised Auction Platforms Regulations 2011, SI 2011/2699, reg 11(1), (4). Date in force: 12 December 2011: see the Recognised Auction Platforms Regulations 2011, reg 1(2)(a).
2   Inserted by the Electronic Money Regulations 2011, SI 2011/99, reg 79, Sch 4, para 19(e). Date in force: 30 April 2011: see the Electronic Money Regulations 2011, reg 1(2)(b).

_____

21   Training

A relevant person must take appropriate measures so that all relevant employees of his are—

(a)   made aware of the law relating to money laundering and terrorist financing; and

(b)   regularly given training in how to recognise and deal with transactions and other activities which may be related to money laundering or terrorist financing.

Part 4
Supervision and registration

Interpretation

22   Interpretation

(1)   In this Part—

'Annex I financial institution' means any undertaking which falls within regulation 3(3)(a) other than—

(a)   ...[1]

(b)   a money service business; ...[2]

(c)   an authorised person;

[(d) a bill payment service provider; or

(e)   a telecommunication, digital and IT payment service provider;][3]

…[1]

['recognised investment exchange' has the same meaning as in section 285 of the 2000 Act (exemption for recognised investment exchanges and clearing houses).][4]

(2)   …[1]

_____

Notes

Amendments

1   Repealed by the Financial Services and Markets Act 2000 (Regulated Activities) (Amendment) (No.2) Order 2013, SI 2013/1881, art 28, Schedule, para 31(1), (4). Date in force: 26 July 2013: see the Financial Services and Markets Act 2000 (Regulated Activities) (Amendment) (No.2) Order 2013, art 1(2), subject to transitional provisions specified in the Financial Services and Markets Act 2000 (Regulated Activities) (Amendment) (No.2) Order 2013, Pt 8, Schedule, para 32.
2   Repealed by the Payment Services Regulations 2009, SI 2009/209, reg 126, Sch 6, para 6(c)(i). Date in force: 1 November 2009: see the Payment Services Regulations 2009, reg 1(2)(c).
3   Inserted by the Payment Services Regulations 2009, SI 2009/209, reg 126, Sch 6, para 6(c)(i). Date in force: 1 November 2009: see the Payment Services Regulations 2009, reg 1(2)(c).
4   Inserted by the Money Laundering (Amendment) Regulations 2012, SI 2012/2298, reg 7. Date in force: 1 October 2012: see the Money Laundering (Amendment) Regulations 2012, reg 1.

_____

Supervision

23   Supervisory authorities

(1)   Subject to paragraph (2), the following bodies are supervisory authorities—

(a)   the Authority is the supervisory authority for—

(i)   credit and financial institutions which are authorised persons [but not excluded money service businesses][1];

(ii)   trust or company service providers which are authorised persons;

(iii)   Annex I financial institutions;

[(iv)   electronic money institutions;][2]

[(v)   auction platforms;][3]

[(vi)   credit unions in Northern Ireland;][4]

[(vii) recognised investment exchanges;][5]

(b)   …[6]

(c)   each of the professional bodies listed in Schedule 3 is the supervisory authority for relevant persons who are regulated by it;

(d)   the Commissioners are the supervisory authority for—

(i)   high value dealers;

(ii)   money service businesses which are not supervised by the Authority;

(iii)   trust or company service providers which are not supervised by the Authority or one of the bodies listed in Schedule 3;

(iv)   auditors, external accountants and tax advisers who are not supervised by one of the bodies listed in Schedule 3;

[(v)   bill payment service providers which are not supervised by the Authority;

(vi)   telecommunication, digital and IT payment service providers which are not supervised by the Authorit;][7]

[(vii)   estate agents.][8]

(e)   the Gambling Commission is the supervisory authority for casinos;

(f)   DETI is the supervisory authority for—

(i)   ...[9]

(ii)   insolvency practitioners authorised by it under article 351 of the Insolvency (Northern Ireland) Order 1989;

(g)   the Secretary of State is the supervisory authority for insolvency practitioners authorised by him under section 393 of the Insolvency Act 1986 (grant, refusal and withdrawal of authorisation).

(2)   Where under paragraph (1) there is more than one supervisory authority for a relevant person, the supervisory authorities may agree that one of them will act as the supervisory authority for that person.

(3)   Where an agreement has been made under paragraph (2), the authority which has agreed to act as the supervisory authority must notify the relevant person or publish the agreement in such manner as it considers appropriate.

(4)   Where no agreement has been made under paragraph (2), the supervisory authorities for a relevant person must cooperate in the performance of their functions under these Regulations.

[(5)   For the purposes of this regulation, a money service business is an 'excluded money service business' if it is an authorised person who has permission under the 2000 Act which relates to or is connected with a contract of the kind mentioned in paragraph 23 or paragraph 23B of Schedule 2 to that Act (credit agreements and contracts for hire of goods) but does not have permission to carry on any other kind of regulated activity.

(6)   Paragraph (5) must be read with—

(a)   section 22 of the 2000 Act,

(b)   any relevant order under that section, and

(c)   Schedule 2 to that Act.][10]

Notes

Amendments

1   Inserted by the Financial Services and Markets Act 2000 (Regulated Activities) (Amendment) (No.2) Order 2013, SI 2013/1881, art 28, Schedule, para 31(1), (5)(a)(i). Date in force: 26 July 2013: see the Financial Services and Markets Act 2000 (Regulated Activities) (Amendment) (No.2) Order 2013, art 1(2), subject to transitional provisions specified in the Financial Services and Markets Act 2000 (Regulated Activities) (Amendment) (No.2) Order 2013, Pt 8, Schedule, para 32.

2   Inserted by the Electronic Money Regulations 2011, SI 2011/99, reg 79, Sch 4, para 19(f).
     Date in force: 30 April 2011: see the Electronic Money Regulations 2011, reg 1(2)(b).
3   Inserted by the Recognised Auction Platforms Regulations 2011, SI 2011/2699, reg 11(1),
     (5). Date in force: 12 December 2011: see the Recognised Auction Platforms Regulations
     2011, reg 1(2)(a).
4   Inserted by the Money Laundering (Amendment No.2) Regulations 2011, SI 2011/2833,
     reg 2(a)(i). Date in force: 31 March 2012: see the Money Laundering (Amendment No.2)
     Regulations 2011, reg 1.
5   Inserted by the Money Laundering (Amendment) Regulations 2012, SI 2012/2298, reg
     8. Date in force: 1 October 2012: see the Money Laundering (Amendment) Regulations
     2012, reg 1.
6   Repealed by the Financial Services and Markets Act 2000 (Regulated Activities)
     (Amendment) (No.2) Order 2013, SI 2013/1881, art 28, Schedule, para 31(1), (5)(a)(ii).
     Date in force: 26 July 2013: see the Financial Services and Markets Act 2000 (Regulated
     Activities) (Amendment) (No.2) Order 2013, art 1(2), subject to transitional provisions
     specified in the Financial Services and Markets Act 2000 (Regulated Activities)
     (Amendment) (No.2) Order 2013, Pt 8, Schedule, para 32.
7   Inserted by the Payment Services Regulations 2009, SI 2009/209, reg 126, Sch 6, para
     6(d). Date in force: 1 November 2009: see the Payment Services Regulations 2009, reg
     1(2)(c).
8   Inserted by the Public Bodies (Abolition of the National Consumer Council and
     Transfer of the Office of Fair Trading's Functions in relation to Estate Agents etc) Order
     2014, SI 2014/631, art 5(3), Sch 3, para 2(1), (2)(b). Date in force: 31 March 2014: see the
     Public Bodies (Abolition of the National Consumer Council and Transfer of the Office
     of Fair Trading's Functions in relation to Estate Agents etc) Order 2014, art 1(5), subject
     to transitional provisions and savings specified in the Public Bodies (Abolition of the
     National Consumer Council and Transfer of the Office of Fair Trading's Functions in
     relation to Estate Agents etc) Order 2014, art 5(3), Sch 3, paras 3–7.
9   Repealed by the Money Laundering (Amendment No.2) Regulations 2011, SI 2011/2833,
     reg 2(a)(ii). Date in force: 31 March 2012: see the Money Laundering (Amendment No.2)
     Regulations 2011, reg 1.
10   Inserted by the Financial Services and Markets Act 2000 (Regulated Activities)
     (Amendment) (No.2) Order 2013, SI 2013/1881, art 28, Schedule, para 31(1), (5)(b).
     Date in force: 26 July 2013: see the Financial Services and Markets Act 2000 (Regulated
     Activities) (Amendment) (No.2) Order 2013, art 1(2), subject to transitional provisions
     specified in the Financial Services and Markets Act 2000 (Regulated Activities)
     (Amendment) (No.2) Order 2013, Pt 8, Schedule, para 32.

---

24   Duties of supervisory authorities

(1)   A supervisory authority must effectively monitor the relevant persons
for whom it is the supervisory authority and take necessary measures for the
purpose of securing compliance by such persons with the requirements of these
Regulations.

[(1A)   The Authority, when carrying out its supervisory functions in relation to
an auction platform—

(a)   must effectively monitor the auction platform's compliance with—

     (i)   the customer due diligence requirements of Articles 19 and 20(6) of the
           emission allowance auctioning regulation;

     (ii) the monitoring and record keeping requirements of Article 54 of the
           emission allowance auctioning regulation; and

     (iii) the notification requirements of Article 55(2) and (3) of the emission
           allowance auctioning regulation; and

(b)   may monitor the auction platform's compliance with regulations 20 and 21 of
     these Regulations.][1]

(2)   A supervisory authority which, in the course of carrying out any of its functions under these Regulations, knows or suspects that a person is or has engaged in money laundering or terrorist financing must promptly inform [the National Crime Agency][2].

(3)   A disclosure made under paragraph (2) is not to be taken to breach any restriction, however imposed, on the disclosure of information.

(4)   The functions of the Authority under these Regulations shall be treated for the purposes of [Parts 1, 2 and 4 of Schedule 1ZA][3] to the 2000 Act [(the Financial Conduct Authority)][3] as functions conferred on the Authority under that Act.

[(5)   The functions of the PRA under these Regulations shall be treated for the purposes of Parts 1, 2 and 4 of Schedule 1ZB to the 2000 Act (the Prudential Regulation Authority) as functions conferred on the PRA under that Act.][4]

Notes

Amendments

1   Inserted by the Recognised Auction Platforms Regulations 2011, SI 2011/2699, reg 11(1), (6). Date in force: 12 December 2011: see the Recognised Auction Platforms Regulations 2011, reg 1(2)(a).
2   Substituted by the Crime and Courts Act 2013, s 15, Sch 8, para 190(1)(b). Date in force: 7 October 2013: see the Crime and Courts Act 2013 (Commencement No. 2 and Saving Provision) Order 2013, SI 2013/1682, art 3(u), (v), subject to savings and transitional provisions specified in the Crime and Courts Act 2013, s 15, Sch 8.
3   Substituted by the Financial Services Act 2012 (Consequential Amendments and Transitional Provisions) Order 2013, SI 2013/472, art 3, Sch 2, para 129(b)(i). Date in force: 1 April 2013; see the Financial Services Act 2012 (Consequential Amendments and Transitional Provisions) Order 2013, art 1(1).
4   Inserted by the Financial Services Act 2012 (Consequential Amendments and Transitional Provisions) Order 2013, SI 2013/472, art 3, Sch 2, para 129(b)(ii). Date in force: 1 April 2013; see the Financial Services Act 2012 (Consequential Amendments and Transitional Provisions) Order 2013, art 1(1).

[24A   Disclosure by supervisory authorities

(1)   A supervisory authority may disclose to another supervisory authority information it holds relevant to its functions under these Regulations, provided the disclosure is made for purposes connected with the effective exercise of the functions of either supervisory authority under these Regulations.

(2)   Information disclosed to a supervisory authority under paragraph (1) may not be further disclosed by that authority, except—

(a)   in accordance with paragraph (1);

[(aa) by the Authority to the PRA, where the information concerns a PRA-authorised person or a person who has a qualifying relationship with a PRA-authorised person;][1]

(b)   with a view to the institution of, or otherwise for the purposes of, any criminal or other enforcement proceedings; or

(c)   as otherwise required by law.][2]

Notes

Amendments

1   Inserted by the Financial Services Act 2012 (Consequential Amendments and Transitional Provisions) Order 2013, SI 2013/472, art 3, Sch 2, para 129(c). Date in force: 1 April 2013; see the Financial Services Act 2012 (Consequential Amendments and Transitional Provisions) Order 2013, art 1(1).
2   Inserted by the Money Laundering (Amendment) Regulations 2012, SI 2012/2298, reg 9. Date in force: 1 October 2012: see the Money Laundering (Amendment) Regulations 2012, reg 1.

Registration of high value dealers, money service businesses and trust or company service providers

25   Duty to maintain registers

(1)   The Commissioners must maintain registers of—

(a)   high value dealers;

(b)   money service businesses for which they are the supervisory authority; ...[1]

(c)   trust or company service providers for which they are the supervisory authority;

[(d)   bill payment service providers for which they are the supervisory authority; and

(e)   telecommunication, digital and IT payment service providers for which they are the supervisory authority.][2]

(2)   The Commissioners may keep the registers in any form they think fit.

(3)   The Commissioners may publish or make available for public inspection all or part of a register maintained under this regulation.

Notes

Amendments

1   Repealed by the Payment Services Regulations 2009, SI 2009/209, reg 126, Sch 6, para 6(e). Date in force: 1 November 2009: see the Payment Services Regulations 2009, reg 1(2)(c).
2   Inserted by the Payment Services Regulations 2009, SI 2009/209, reg 126, Sch 6, para 6(e). Date in force: 1 November 2009: see the Payment Services Regulations 2009, reg 1(2)(c).

26   Requirement to be registered

(1)   A person in respect of whom the Commissioners are required to maintain a register under regulation 25 must not act as a—

(a)   high value dealer;

(b)   money service business; ...1

(c)   trust or company service provider;

[(d)   bill payment service provider; or

(e)   telecommunication, digital and IT payment service provider,][2]

unless he is included in the register.

(2)   Paragraph (1) and regulation 29 are subject to the transitional provisions set out in regulation 50.

Notes

Amendments

1   Repealed by the Payment Services Regulations 2009, SI 2009/209, reg 126, Sch 6, para 6(f). Date in force: 1 November 2009: see the Payment Services Regulations 2009, reg 1(2)(c).
2   Inserted by the Payment Services Regulations 2009, SI 2009/209, reg 126, Sch 6, para 6(f). Date in force: 1 November 2009: see the Payment Services Regulations 2009, reg 1(2)(c).

---

27   Applications for registration in a register maintained under regulation 25

(1)   An applicant for registration in a register maintained under regulation 25 must make an application in such manner and provide such information as the Commissioners may specify.

(2)   The information which the Commissioners may specify includes—

(a)   the applicant's name and (if different) the name of the business;

(b)   the nature of the business;

(c)   the name of the nominated officer (if any);

(d)   in relation to a money service business or trust or company service provider—

(i)   the name of any person who effectively directs or will direct the business and any beneficial owner of the business; and

(ii)   information needed by the Commissioners to decide whether they must refuse the application pursuant to regulation 28.

(3)   At any time after receiving an application and before determining it, the Commissioners may require the applicant to provide, within 21 days beginning with the date of being requested to do so, such further information as they reasonably consider necessary to enable them to determine the application.

(4)   If at any time after the applicant has provided the Commissioners with any information under paragraph (1) or (3)—

(a)   there is a material change affecting any matter contained in that information; or

(b)   it becomes apparent to that person that the information contains a significant inaccuracy,

he must provide the Commissioners with details of the change or, as the case may be, a correction of the inaccuracy within 30 days beginning with the date of the occurrence of the change (or the discovery of the inaccuracy) or within such later time as may be agreed with the Commissioners.

(5)   The obligation in paragraph (4) applies also to material changes or significant inaccuracies affecting any matter contained in any supplementary information provided pursuant to that paragraph.

(6)   Any information to be provided to the Commissioners under this regulation must be in such form or verified in such manner as they may specify.

28 Fit and proper test

(1) The Commissioners must refuse to register an applicant as a money service business or trust or company service provider if they are satisfied that—

(a) the applicant;

(b) a person who effectively directs, or will effectively direct, the business or service provider;

(c) a beneficial owner of the business or service provider; or

(d) the nominated officer of the business or service provider,

is not a fit and proper person [with regard to the risk of money laundering or terrorist financing][1].

(2) ...[2]

(3) ...[2]

Notes

Amendments

1   Inserted by the Money Laundering (Amendment) Regulations 2012, SI 2012/2298, reg 10(a). Date in force: 1 October 2012: see the Money Laundering (Amendment) Regulations 2012, reg 1.
2   Repealed by the Money Laundering (Amendment) Regulations 2012, SI 2012/2298, reg 10(b). Date in force: 1 October 2012: see the Money Laundering (Amendment) Regulations 2012, reg 1.

---

29 Determination of applications under regulation 27

(1) Subject to regulation 28, the Commissioners may refuse to register an applicant for registration in a register maintained under regulation 25 only if—

(a) any requirement of, or imposed under, regulation 27 has not been complied with;

(b) it appears to the Commissioners that any information provided pursuant to regulation 27 is false or misleading in a material particular; or

(c) the applicant has failed to pay a charge imposed by them under regulation 35(1).

(2) The Commissioners must within 45 days beginning either with the date on which they receive the application or, where applicable, with the date on which they receive any further information required under regulation 27(3), give the applicant notice of—

(a) their decision to register the applicant; or

(b) the following matters—

(i)   their decision not to register the applicant;

(ii)   the reasons for their decision;

[(iii) the right to a review under regulation 43A; and][1]

(iv) the right to appeal under regulation [43][1].

(3)   The Commissioners must, as soon as practicable after deciding to register a person, include him in the relevant register.

Notes

Amendments

1   Substituted by the Transfer of Tribunal Functions and Revenue and Customs Appeals Order 2009, SI 2009/56, art 3(2), Sch 2, paras 168, 169. Date in force: 1 April 2009: see by the Transfer of Tribunal Functions and Revenue and Customs Appeals Order 2009, art 1(2).

---

30   Cancellation of registration in a register maintained under regulation 25

(1)   The Commissioners must cancel the registration of a money service business or trust or company service provider in a register maintained under regulation 25(1) if, at any time after registration, they are satisfied that he or any person mentioned in regulation 28(1)(b), (c) or (d) is not a fit and proper person within the meaning of regulation [28][1].

[(2)   The Commissioners may cancel a person's registration in a register maintained by them under regulation 25 if, at any time after registration—

(a)   it appears to them that that any condition in regulation 29(1) is met; or

(b)   the person has failed to comply with any requirement of a notice given under regulation 37.][1]

[(2A)   The Commissioners may cancel the registration of a money service business in a register maintained under regulation 25(1)(b) where the money service business—

(a)   is providing a payment service in the United Kingdom, or is purporting to do so;

(b)   is not included in the register of payment service providers maintained by the Authority under regulation 4(1) of the Payment Service Regulations 2009; and

(c)   is not a person mentioned in paragraphs (c) to (h) of the definition of a payment service provider in regulation 2(1) of the Payment Services Regulations 2009, or a person to whom regulation 3 or 121 of those Regulations applies.][2]

(3)   Where the Commissioners decide to cancel a person's registration they must give him notice of—

(a)   their decision and, subject to paragraph (4), the date from which the cancellation takes effect;

(b)   the reasons for their decision;

[(c)   the right to a review under regulation 43A; and][3]

(d)   the right to appeal under regulation [43][3].

(4)   If the Commissioners—

(a)   consider that the interests of the public require the cancellation of a person's registration to have immediate effect; and

(b)   include a statement to that effect and the reasons for it in the notice given under paragraph (3),

the cancellation takes effect when the notice is given to the person.

Notes

Amendments

1   Substituted by the Money Laundering (Amendment) Regulations 2012, SI 2012/2298, reg 11. Date in force: 1 October 2012: see the Money Laundering (Amendment) Regulations 2012, reg 1.
2   Inserted by the Payment Services Regulations 2012, SI 2012/1791, reg 2. Date in force: 1 October 2012: see the Payment Services Regulations 2012, reg 1(2)(b)
3   Substituted by the Transfer of Tribunal Functions and Revenue and Customs Appeals Order 2009, SI 2009/56, art 3(2), Sch 2, paras 168, 170. Date in force: 1 April 2009: see by the Transfer of Tribunal Functions and Revenue and Customs Appeals Order 2009, art 1(2).

Requirement to inform the Authority

31   Requirement on authorised person to inform the Authority

(1)   An authorised person whose supervisory authority is the Authority must, before acting as a money service business or a trust or company service provider or within 28 days of so doing, inform the Authority that he intends, or has begun, to act as such.

(2)   Paragraph (1) does not apply to an authorised person who—

(a)   immediately before 15th December 2007 was acting as a money service business or a trust or company service provider and continues to act as such after that date; and

(b)   before 15th January 2008 informs the [Financial Services]¹ Authority that he is or was acting as such.

(3)   Where an authorised person whose supervisory authority is the Authority ceases to act as a money service business or a trust or company service provider, he must immediately inform the Authority.

(4)   Any requirement imposed by this regulation is to be treated as if it were a requirement imposed by or under the 2000 Act.

(5)   Any information to be provided to the Authority under this regulation must be in such form or verified in such manner as it may specify.

Notes

Amendment

1   Inserted by the Financial Services Act 2012 (Consequential Amendments and Transitional Provisions) Order 2013, SI 2013/472, art 3, Sch 2, para 129(d). Date in force: 1 April 2013; see the Financial Services Act 2012 (Consequential Amendments and Transitional Provisions) Order 2013, art 1(1).

Registration of Annex I financial institutions, estate agents etc.

32   Power to maintain registers

(1)   The supervisory authorities mentioned in paragraph (2), (3) or (4) may, in order to fulfil their duties under regulation 24, maintain a register under this regulation.

(2)   The Authority may maintain a register of Annex I financial institutions.

(3)   ...[1]

(4)   The Commissioners may maintain registers of—

(a)   auditors;

(b)   external accountants; and

(c)   tax advisers,

who are not supervised by the Secretary of State, DETI or any of the professional bodies listed in Schedule 3.

[(4A)   The Commissioners may maintain a register of estate agents.][2]

(5)   Where a supervisory authority decides to maintain a register under this regulation, it must take reasonable steps to bring its decision to the attention of those relevant persons in respect of whom the register is to be established.

(6)   A supervisory authority may keep a register under this regulation in any form it thinks fit.

(7)   A supervisory authority may publish or make available to public inspection all or part of a register maintained by it under this regulation.

Notes

Amendments

1   Repealed by the Financial Services and Markets Act 2000 (Regulated Activities) (Amendment) (No.2) Order 2013, SI 2013/1881, art 28, Schedule, para 31(1), (6). Date in force: 26 July 2013: see the Financial Services and Markets Act 2000 (Regulated Activities) (Amendment) (No.2) Order 2013, art 1(2), subject to transitional provisions specified in the Financial Services and Markets Act 2000 (Regulated Activities) (Amendment) (No.2) Order 2013, Pt 8, Schedule, para 32.
2   Inserted by the Public Bodies (Abolition of the National Consumer Council and Transfer of the Office of Fair Trading's Functions in relation to Estate Agents etc) Order 2014, SI 2014/631, art 5(3), Sch 3, para 2(1), (3)(b). Date in force: 31 March 2014: see the Public Bodies (Abolition of the National Consumer Council and Transfer of the Office of Fair Trading's Functions in relation to Estate Agents etc) Order 2014, art 1(5), subject to transitional provisions and savings specified in the Public Bodies (Abolition of the National Consumer Council and Transfer of the Office of Fair Trading's Functions in relation to Estate Agents etc) Order 2014, art 5(3), Sch 3, paras 3–7.

---

33   Requirement to be registered

Where a supervisory authority decides to maintain a register under regulation 32 in respect of any description of relevant persons and establishes a register for that purpose, a relevant person of that description may not carry on the business or profession in question for a period of more than six months beginning on the date on which the supervisory authority establishes the register unless he is included in the register.

34   Applications for and cancellation of registration in a register maintained under regulation 32

(1)   Regulations 27, 29 (with the omission of the words 'Subject to regulation 28' in regulation 29(1)) and 30(2), (3) and (4) apply to registration in a register

maintained by the Commissioners under regulation 32 as they apply to registration in a register maintained under regulation 25.

(2)   Regulation 27 applies to registration in a register maintained by the Authority …[1] under regulation 32 as it applies to registration in a register maintained under regulation 25 and, for this purpose, references to the Commissioners are to be treated as references to the Authority …[1].

(3)   The Authority …[1] may refuse to register an applicant for registration in a register maintained under regulation 32 only if—

(a)   any requirement of, or imposed under, regulation 27 has not been complied with;

(b)   it appears to the Authority …[1] that any information provided pursuant to regulation 27 is false or misleading in a material particular; or

(c)   the applicant has failed to pay a charge imposed by the Authority …[1] under regulation 35(1).

(4)   The Authority …[1] must, within 45 days beginning either with the date on which it receives an application or, where applicable, with the date on which it receives any further information required under regulation 27(3), give the applicant notice of—

(a)   its decision to register the applicant; or

(b)   the following matters—

(i)   that it is minded not to register the applicant;

(ii)   the reasons for being minded not to register him; and

(iii)   the right to make representations to it within a specified period (which may not be less than 28 days).

(5)   The Authority …[1] must then decide, within a reasonable period, whether to register the applicant and it must give the applicant notice of—

(a)   its decision to register the applicant; or

(b)   the following matters—

(i)   its decision not to register the applicant;

(ii)   the reasons for its decision; and

(iii)   the right to appeal under regulation 44(1)(b).

(6)   The Authority …[1] must, as soon as reasonably practicable after deciding to register a person, include him in the relevant register.

[(7)   The Authority …[1] may cancel a person's registration in a register maintained by them under regulation 32 if, at any time after registration—

(a)   it appears to them that any condition in paragraph (3) is met; or

(b)   the person has failed to comply with any requirement of a notice given under regulation 37.][2]

(8)   Where the Authority …[1] proposes to cancel a person's registration, it must give him notice of—

(a)   its proposal to cancel his registration;

(b)   the reasons for the proposed cancellation; and

(c)   the right to make representations to it within a specified period (which may not be less than 28 days).

(9)   The Authority ...[1] must then decide, within a reasonable period, whether to cancel the person's registration and it must give him notice of—

(a)   its decision not to cancel his registration; or

(b)   the following matters—

    (i)   its decision to cancel his registration and, subject to paragraph (10), the date from which cancellation takes effect;

    (ii)   the reasons for its decision; and

    (iii)   the right to appeal under regulation 44(1)(b).

(10)   If the Authority ...[1]—

(a)   considers that the interests of the public require the cancellation of a person's registration to have immediate effect; and

(b)   includes a statement to that effect and the reasons for it in the notice given under paragraph (9)(b),

the cancellation takes effect when the notice is given to the person.

(11)   In paragraphs (3) and (4), references to regulation 27 are to be treated as references to that paragraph as applied by paragraph (2) of this regulation.

Notes

Amendments

1   Repealed by the Financial Services and Markets Act 2000 (Regulated Activities) (Amendment) (No.2) Order 2013, SI 2013/1881, art 28, Schedule, para 31(1), (7). Date in force: 26 July 2013: see the Financial Services and Markets Act 2000 (Regulated Activities) (Amendment) (No.2) Order 2013, art 1(2), subject to transitional provisions specified in the Financial Services and Markets Act 2000 (Regulated Activities) (Amendment) (No.2) Order 2013, Pt 8, Schedule, para 32.

2   Substituted by the Money Laundering (Amendment) Regulations 2012, SI 2012/2298, reg 12. Date in force: 1 October 2012: see the Money Laundering (Amendment) Regulations 2012, reg 1.

Financial provisions

35   Costs of supervision

(1)   The Authority ...[1] and the Commissioners may impose charges—

(a)   on applicants for registration;

(b)   on relevant persons supervised by them.

(2)   Charges levied under paragraph (1) must not exceed such amount as the Authority ...[1] or the Commissioners (as the case may be) consider will enable them to meet any expenses reasonably incurred by them in carrying out their functions under these Regulations or for any incidental purpose.

(3)   Without prejudice to the generality of paragraph (2), a charge may be levied in respect of each of the premises at which a person carries on (or proposes to carry on) business.

[(4)   The Authority must pay to the Treasury any amounts received by the Financial Services Authority during the financial year beginning with 1st April 2012 year by way of penalties imposed under regulation 42 after deducting any amounts the Financial Services Authority has, prior to 1st April 2013, applied towards expenses incurred by it in carrying out its functions under these Regulations or for any incidental purpose.

(4A)   The Authority must in respect of the financial year beginning with 1st April 2013 and each subsequent financial year pay to the Treasury any amounts received by it during the year by way of penalties imposed under regulation 42.

(4B)   The Treasury may give directions to the Authority as to how the Authority is to comply with its duties under paragraphs (4) and (4A).

(4C)   The directions may in particular—

(a)   specify the time when any payment is required to be made to the Treasury, and

(b)   require the Authority to provide the Treasury at specified times with information relating to penalties that the Authority has imposed under regulation 42.

(4D)   The Treasury must pay into the Consolidated Fund any sums received by them under this regulation.]²

(5)   In paragraph (2), 'expenses' in relation to the [Authority]³includes expenses incurred by a local weights and measures authority or DETI pursuant to arrangements made for the purposes of these Regulations with the [Authority]³—

(a)   by or on behalf of the authority; or

(b)   by DETI.

Notes

Amendments

1   Repealed by the Financial Services and Markets Act 2000 (Regulated Activities) (Amendment) (No.2) Order 2013, SI 2013/1881, art 28, Schedule, para 31(1), (8)(a). Date in force: 26 July 2013: see the Financial Services and Markets Act 2000 (Regulated Activities) (Amendment) (No.2) Order 2013, art 1(2), subject to transitional provisions specified in the Financial Services and Markets Act 2000 (Regulated Activities) (Amendment) (No.2) Order 2013, Pt 8, Schedule, para 32.
2   Paragraphs (4)-(4D) substituted for paragraph (4) by the Payment to Treasury of Penalties Regulations 2013, SI 2013/429, reg 2(1). Date in force: 1 April 2013: see the Payment to Treasury of Penalties Regulations 2013, reg 1.
3   Substituted by the Financial Services and Markets Act 2000 (Regulated Activities) (Amendment) (No.2) Order 2013, SI 2013/1881, art 28, Schedule, para 31(1), (8)(b). Date in force: 26 July 2013: see the Financial Services and Markets Act 2000 (Regulated Activities) (Amendment) (No.2) Order 2013, art 1(2), subject to transitional provisions specified in the Financial Services and Markets Act 2000 (Regulated Activities) (Amendment) (No.2) Order 2013, Pt 8, Schedule, para 32.

Part 5
Enforcement

Powers of designated authorities

36   Interpretation

In this Part—

'designated authority' means—

(a)   the Authority; [and]¹

(b)   the Commissioners; [...²]³

(c) ...² ...⁴

(d) ...⁴

'officer', except in regulations 40(3), 41 and 47 means—

(a) an officer of the Authority, including a member of the Authority's staff or an agent of the Authority;

(b) an officer of Revenue and Customs; [or]¹

(c) ...²

(d) a relevant officer; ...⁴

(e) ...⁴

'recorded information' includes information recorded in any form and any document of any nature;

'relevant officer' means—

(a) in Great Britain, an officer of a local weights and measures authority;

(b) in Northern Ireland, an officer of DETI acting pursuant to arrangements made with the [Authority]⁵ for the purposes of these Regulations.

Notes

Amendments

1   Inserted by the Financial Services and Markets Act 2000 (Regulated Activities) (Amendment) (No.2) Order 2013, SI 2013/1881, art 28, Sch 1, para 31(1), (9)(a)(i), (b)(i). Date in force: 26 July 2013: see the Financial Services and Markets Act 2000 (Regulated Activities) (Amendment) (No.2) Order 2013, art 1(2), subject to transitional provisions specified in the Financial Services and Markets Act 2000 (Regulated Activities) (Amendment) (No.2) Order 2013, Sch 1, para 32.

2   Repealed by the Financial Services and Markets Act 2000 (Regulated Activities) (Amendment) (No.2) Order 2013, SI 2013/1881, art 28, Sch 1, para 31(1), (9)(a)(ii), (b)(ii). Date in force: 26 July 2013: see the Financial Services and Markets Act 2000 (Regulated Activities) (Amendment) (No.2) Order 2013, art 1(2), subject to transitional provisions specified in the Financial Services and Markets Act 2000 (Regulated Activities) (Amendment) (No.2) Order 2013, Sch 1, para 32.

3   Inserted by the Money Laundering (Amendment No.2) Regulations 2011, SI 2011/2833, reg 2(b)(i). Date in force: 31 March 2012: see the Money Laundering (Amendment No.2) Regulations 2011, reg 1.

4   Repealed by the Money Laundering (Amendment No.2) Regulations 2011, SI 2011/2833, reg 2(b)(ii), (c)(ii). Date in force: 31 March 2012: see the Money Laundering (Amendment No.2) Regulations 2011, reg 1.

5   Substituted by the Financial Services and Markets Act 2000 (Regulated Activities) (Amendment) (No.2) Order 2013, SI 2013/1881, art 28, Sch 1, para 31(1), (9)(c). Date in force: 26 July 2013: see the Financial Services and Markets Act 2000 (Regulated Activities) (Amendment) (No.2) Order 2013, art 1(2), subject to transitional provisions specified in the Financial Services and Markets Act 2000 (Regulated Activities) (Amendment) (No.2) Order 2013, Sch 1, para 32.

---

37 Power to require information from, and attendance of, relevant and connected persons

(1) An officer may, by notice to a relevant person or to a person connected with a relevant person, require the relevant person or the connected person, as the case may be—

(a) to provide such information as may be specified in the notice;

(b) to produce such recorded information as may be so specified; or

(c) to attend before an officer at a time and place specified in the notice and answer questions.

[(2) For the purposes of paragraph (1)—

(a) 'relevant person' includes a person whom a designated authority believes, or has reasonable grounds to suspect, is or has at any time been a relevant person; and

(b) a person is connected with a relevant person if the person is, or has at any time been, in relation to the relevant person, a person listed in Schedule 4 to these Regulations.]¹

(3) An officer may exercise powers under this regulation only if the information sought to be obtained as a result is reasonably required in connection with the exercise by the designated authority for whom he acts of its functions under these Regulations.

(4) Where an officer requires information to be provided or produced pursuant to paragraph (1)(a) or (b)—

(a) the notice must set out the reasons why the officer requires the information to be provided or produced; and

(b) such information must be provided or produced—

(i) before the end of such reasonable period as may be specified in the notice; and

(ii) at such place as may be so specified.

(5) In relation to information recorded otherwise than in legible form, the power to require production of it includes a power to require the production of a copy of it in legible form or in a form from which it can readily be produced in visible and legible form.

(6) The production of a document does not affect any lien which a person has on the document.

(7) A person may not be required under this regulation to provide or produce information or to answer questions which he would be entitled to refuse to provide, produce or answer on grounds of legal professional privilege in proceedings in the High Court, except that a lawyer may be required to provide the name and address of his client.

(8) Subject to paragraphs (9) and (10), a statement made by a person in compliance with a requirement imposed on him under paragraph (1)(c) is admissible in evidence in any proceedings, so long as it also complies with any requirements governing the admissibility of evidence in the circumstances in question.

(9) In criminal proceedings in which a person is charged with an offence to which this paragraph applies—

(a) no evidence relating to the statement may be adduced; and

(b) no question relating to it may be asked,

by or on behalf of the prosecution unless evidence relating to it is adduced, or a question relating to it is asked, in the proceedings by or on behalf of that person.

(10) Paragraph (9) applies to any offence other than one under—

(a) section 5 of the Perjury Act 1911 (false statements without oath);

(b)   section 44(2) of the Criminal Law (Consolidation)(Scotland) Act 1995 (false statements and declarations); or

(c)   Article 10 of the Perjury (Northern Ireland) Order 1979 (false unsworn statements).

(11)   In the application of this regulation to Scotland, the reference in paragraph (7) to—

(a)   proceedings in the High Court is to be read as a reference to legal proceedings generally; and

(b)   an entitlement on grounds of legal professional privilege is to be read as a reference to an entitlement on the grounds of confidentiality of communications[—

   (i)   between a professional legal adviser and his client; or

   (ii)   made in connection with or in contemplation of legal proceedings and for the purposes of those proceedings.]²

Notes

Amendments

1   Substituted by the Money Laundering (Amendment) Regulations 2012, SI 2012/2298, reg 13. Date in force: 1 October 2012: see the Money Laundering (Amendment) Regulations 2012, reg 1.
2   Inserted by the Money Laundering (Amendment) Regulations 2007, SI 2007/3299, reg 2(b). Date in force: 15 December 2007: see the Money Laundering (Amendment) Regulations 2007, reg 1.

---

38   Entry, inspection without a warrant etc.

(1)   Where an officer has reasonable cause to believe that any premises are being used by a relevant person in connection with his business or professional activities, he may on producing evidence of his authority at any reasonable time—

(a)   enter the premises;

(b)   inspect the premises;

(c)   observe the carrying on of business or professional activities by the relevant person;

(d)   inspect any recorded information found on the premises;

(e)   require any person on the premises to provide an explanation of any recorded information or to state where it may be found;

(f)   in the case of a money service business or a high value dealer, inspect any cash found on the premises.

(2)   An officer may take copies of, or make extracts from, any recorded information found under paragraph (1).

(3)   Paragraphs (1)(d) and (e) and (2) do not apply to recorded information which the relevant person would be entitled to refuse to disclose on grounds of legal professional privilege in proceedings in the High Court, except that a lawyer may be required to provide the name and address of his client and, for this purpose, regulation 37(11) applies to this paragraph as it applies to regulation 37(7).

(4)   An officer may exercise powers under this regulation only if the information sought to be obtained as a result is reasonably required in connection with the

exercise by the designated authority for whom he acts of its functions under these Regulations.

(5)   In this regulation, 'premises' means any premises other than premises used only as a dwelling.

39   Entry to premises under warrant

(1)   A justice may issue a warrant under this paragraph if satisfied on information on oath given by an officer that there are reasonable grounds for believing that the first, second or third set of conditions is satisfied.

(2)   The first set of conditions is—

(a)   that there is on the premises specified in the warrant recorded information in relation to which a requirement could be imposed under regulation 37(1)(b); and

(b)   that if such a requirement were to be imposed—

  (i)   it would not be complied with; or

  (ii)   the recorded information to which it relates would be removed, tampered with or destroyed.

(3)   The second set of conditions is—

(a)   that a person on whom a requirement has been imposed under regulation 37(1)(b) has failed (wholly or in part) to comply with it; and

(b)   that there is on the premises specified in the warrant recorded information which has been required to be produced.

(4)   The third set of conditions is—

(a)   that an officer has been obstructed in the exercise of a power under regulation 38; and

(b)   that there is on the premises specified in the warrant recorded information or cash which could be inspected under regulation 38(1)(d) or (f).

(5)   A justice may issue a warrant under this paragraph if satisfied on information on oath given by an officer that there are reasonable grounds for suspecting that—

(a)   an offence under these Regulations has been, is being or is about to be committed by a relevant person; and

(b)   there is on the premises specified in the warrant recorded information relevant to whether that offence has been, or is being or is about to be committed.

(6)   A warrant issued under this regulation shall authorise an officer—

(a)   to enter the premises specified in the warrant;

(b)   to search the premises and take possession of any recorded information or anything appearing to be recorded information specified in the warrant or to take, in relation to any such recorded information, any other steps which may appear to be necessary for preserving it or preventing interference with it;

(c)   to take copies of, or extracts from, any recorded information specified in the warrant;

(d)   to require any person on the premises to provide an explanation of any recorded information appearing to be of the kind specified in the warrant or to state where it may be found;

(e)   to use such force as may reasonably be necessary.

(7)   Where a warrant is issued by a justice under paragraph (1) or (5) on the basis of information [on oath]¹ given by an officer of the Authority, for 'an officer' in paragraph (6) substitute 'a constable'.

(8)   In paragraphs (1), (5) and (7), 'justice' means—

(a)   in relation to England and Wales, a justice of the peace;

(b)   in relation to Scotland, a justice within the meaning of section 307 of the Criminal Procedure (Scotland) Act 1995 (interpretation);

(c)   in relation to Northern Ireland, a lay magistrate.

(9)   In the application of this regulation to Scotland, the references in paragraphs [(1), (5) and (7)]² to information on oath are to be read as references to evidence on oath.

Notes

Amendments

1   Inserted by the Money Laundering (Amendment) Regulations 2007, SI 2007/3299, reg 2(c)(i). Date in force: 15 December 2007: see the Money Laundering (Amendment) Regulations 2007, reg 1.
2   Substituted by the Money Laundering (Amendment) Regulations 2007, SI 2007/3299, reg 2(c)(ii). Date in force: 15 December 2007: see the Money Laundering (Amendment) Regulations 2007, reg 1.

---

40   Failure to comply with information requirement

(1)   If, on an application made by—

(a)   a designated authority; or

(b)   a local weights and measures authority or DETI pursuant to arrangements made with the [Authority]¹—

   (i)   by or on behalf of the authority; or

   (ii) by DETI,

it appears to the court that a person (the 'information defaulter') has failed to do something that he was required to do under regulation 37(1), the court may make an order under this regulation.

(2)   An order under this regulation may require the information defaulter—

(a)   to do the thing that he failed to do within such period as may be specified in the order;

(b)   otherwise to take such steps to remedy the consequences of the failure as may be so specified.

(3)   If the information defaulter is a body corporate, a partnership or an unincorporated body of persons which is not a partnership, the order may require any officer of the body corporate, partnership or body, who is (wholly or partly) responsible for the failure to meet such costs of the application as are specified in the order.

(4)   In this regulation, 'court' means—

(a)   in England and Wales and Northern Ireland, the High Court or the county court;

(b)   in Scotland, the Court of Session or the sheriff [court]².

Notes

Amendments

1   Substituted by the Financial Services and Markets Act 2000 (Regulated Activities) (Amendment) (No.2) Order 2013, SI 2013/1881, art 28, Sch 1, para 31(1), (10). Date in force: 26 July 2013: see the Financial Services and Markets Act 2000 (Regulated Activities) (Amendment) (No.2) Order 2013, art 1(2), subject to transitional provisions specified in the Financial Services and Markets Act 2000 (Regulated Activities) (Amendment) (No.2) Order 2013, Sch 1, para 32.

2   Inserted by the Money Laundering (Amendment) Regulations 2007, SI 2007/3299, reg 2(d). Date in force: 15 December 2007: see the Money Laundering (Amendment) Regulations 2007, reg 1.

41   Powers of relevant officers

(1)   A relevant officer may only exercise powers under regulations 37 to 39 pursuant to arrangements made with the [Authority][1]—

(a)   by or on behalf of the local weights and measures authority of which he is an officer ('his authority'); or

(b)   by DETI.

(2)   Anything done or omitted to be done by, or in relation to, a relevant officer in the exercise or purported exercise of a power in this Part shall be treated for all purposes as having been done or omitted to be done by, or in relation to, an officer of the [Authority][1].

(3)   Paragraph (2) does not apply for the purposes of any criminal proceedings brought against the relevant officer, his authority, DETI or the [Authority][1], in respect of anything done or omitted to be done by the officer.

(4)   A relevant officer shall not disclose to any person other than the [Authority][1] and his authority or, as the case may be, DETI information obtained by him in the exercise of such powers unless—

(a)   he has the approval of the [Authority][1] to do so; or

(b)   he is under a duty to make the disclosure.

Notes

Amendments

1   Substituted by the Financial Services and Markets Act 2000 (Regulated Activities) (Amendment) (No.2) Order 2013, SI 2013/1881, art 28, Sch 1, para 31(1), (11). Date in force: 26 July 2013: see the Financial Services and Markets Act 2000 (Regulated Activities) (Amendment) (No.2) Order 2013, art 1(2), subject to transitional provisions specified in the Financial Services and Markets Act 2000 (Regulated Activities) (Amendment) (No.2) Order 2013, Sch 1, para 32.

Civil penalties, review and appeals

42   Power to impose civil penalties

(1)   A designated authority may impose a penalty of such amount as it considers appropriate on a ...[1] person [(except an auction platform)][2] who fails to comply with any requirement in regulation 7(1), (2) or (3), 8(1) or (3), 9(2), 10(1), 11(1),

14(1), 15(1) or (2), 16(1), (2), (3) or (4), 19(1), (4), (5) or (6), 20(1), (4) or (5), 21, 26, 27(4) or 33 ...¹.

[(1A)   A designated authority may impose a penalty of such amount as it considers appropriate on an auction platform which fails to comply with—

(a)   the customer due diligence requirements of Article 19 or 20(6) of the emission allowance auctioning regulation;

(b)   the monitoring and record keeping requirements of Article 54 of the emission allowance auctioning regulation; or

(c)   regulation 20(1), (4) or (5) or 21 of these Regulations

...¹]²

[(1B)   A designated authority may impose a penalty of such amount as it considers appropriate on a person who fails to comply with any requirement of a notice given under regulation 37(1).

(1C)   In paragraphs (1), (1A) and (1B), 'appropriate' means effective, proportionate and dissuasive.]³

(2)   The designated authority must not impose a penalty on a person under paragraph (1)[, (1A) or (1B)]⁴ where there are reasonable grounds for it to be satisfied that the person took all reasonable steps and exercised all due diligence to ensure that the requirement would be complied with.

(3)   In deciding whether a person has failed to comply with a requirement of these Regulations, the designated authority must consider whether he followed any relevant guidance which was at the time—

(a)   issued by a supervisory authority or any other appropriate body;

(b)   approved by the Treasury; and

(c)   published in a manner approved by the Treasury as suitable in their opinion to bring the guidance to the attention of persons likely to be affected by it.

(4)   In paragraph (3), an 'appropriate body' means any body which regulates or is representative of any trade, profession, business or employment carried on by the [person]⁵.

[(4A)   Where the Authority proposes to impose a penalty under this regulation on a PRA-authorised person or on a person who has a qualifying relationship with a PRA-authorised person, it must consult the PRA.]⁶

(5)   Where the Commissioners decide to impose a penalty under this regulation, they must give the person notice of—

(a)   their decision to impose the penalty and its amount;

(b)   the reasons for imposing the penalty;

(c)   the right to a review under [regulation 43A]⁷; and

(d)   the right to appeal under [regulation 43]⁷.

(6)   Where the Authority ...⁸ or DETI proposes to impose a penalty under this regulation, it must give the person notice of—

(a)   its proposal to impose the penalty and the proposed amount;

(b)   the reasons for imposing the penalty; and

(c)   the right to make representations to it within a specified period (which may not be less than 28 days).

(7)   The Authority ...[8] or DETI, as the case may be, must then decide, within a reasonable period, whether to impose a penalty under this regulation and it must give the person notice of—

(a)   its decision not to impose a penalty; or

(b)   the following matters—

   (i)   its decision to impose a penalty and the amount;

   (ii)   the reasons for its decision; and

   (iii)   the right to appeal under regulation 44(1)(b).

(8)   A penalty imposed under this regulation is payable to the designated authority which imposes it.

Notes

Amendments

1   Repealed by the Money Laundering (Amendment) Regulations 2012, SI 2012/2298, reg 14(a), (b). Date in force: 1 October 2012: see the Money Laundering (Amendment) Regulations 2012, reg 1.
2   Inserted by the Recognised Auction Platforms Regulations 2011, SI 2011/2699, reg 11(1), (7). Date in force: 12 December 2011: see the Recognised Auction Platforms Regulations 2011, reg 1(2)(a).
3   Inserted by the Money Laundering (Amendment) Regulations 2012, SI 2012/2298, reg 14(c). Date in force: 1 October 2012: see the Money Laundering (Amendment) Regulations 2012, reg 1.
4   Substituted by the Money Laundering (Amendment) Regulations 2012, SI 2012/2298, reg 14(d). Date in force: 1 October 2012: see the Money Laundering (Amendment) Regulations 2012, reg 1.
5   Substituted by the Money Laundering (Amendment) Regulations 2007, SI 2007/3299, reg 2(e). Date in force: 15 December 2007: see the Money Laundering (Amendment) Regulations 2007, reg 1.
6   Inserted by the Financial Services Act 2012 (Consequential Amendments and Transitional Provisions) Order 2013, SI 2013/472, art 3, Sch 2, para 129(e). Date in force: 1 April 2013: see the Financial Services Act 2012 (Consequential Amendments and Transitional Provisions) Order 2013, art 1(1).
7   Substituted by the Transfer of Tribunal Functions and Revenue and Customs Appeals Order 2009, SI 2009/56, art 3(2), Sch 2, paras 168, 171. Date in force: 1 April 2009: see by the Transfer of Tribunal Functions and Revenue and Customs Appeals Order 2009, art 1(2).
8   Repealed by the Financial Services and Markets Act 2000 (Regulated Activities) (Amendment) (No.2) Order 2013, SI 2013/1881, art 28, Sch 1, para 31(1), (12). Date in force: 26 July 2013: see the Financial Services and Markets Act 2000 (Regulated Activities) (Amendment) (No.2) Order 2013, art 1(2), subject to transitional provisions specified in the Financial Services and Markets Act 2000 (Regulated Activities) (Amendment) (No.2) Order 2013, Sch 1, para 32.

---

43   [Appeals against decisions of the Commissioners][1]

(1)   This regulation applies to decisions of the Commissioners made under—

[(za)   regulation 28, to the effect that a person is not a fit and proper person;][2]

(a)   regulation 29, to refuse to register an applicant;

(b)   regulation 30, to cancel the registration of a registered person; and

(c)   regulation 42, to impose a penalty.

(2)   Any person who is the subject of a decision to which this regulation applies may [appeal to the tribunal in accordance with regulation 43F][1].

[(3)   The provisions of Part 5 of the Value Added Tax Act 1994 (appeals), subject to the modifications set out in paragraph 1 of Schedule 5 to these Regulations, apply in respect of appeals to a tribunal made under this regulation as they apply in respect of appeals made to the tribunal under section 83 (appeals) of that Act.

(4)   A tribunal hearing an appeal under paragraph (2) has the power to—

(a)   quash or vary any decision of the supervisory authority, including the power to reduce any penalty to such amount (including nil) as it thinks proper, and

(b)   substitute its own decision for any decision quashed on appeal.

(5)   The modifications in Schedule 5 have effect for the purposes of appeals made under this regulation.

(6)   For the purposes of appeals under this regulation, the meaning of 'tribunal' is as defined in section 82 of the Value Added Tax Act 1994.][3]

Notes

Amendments

1   Substituted by the Transfer of Tribunal Functions and Revenue and Customs Appeals Order 2009, SI 2009/56, art 3(2), Sch 2, paras 168, 172(1)-(3). Date in force: 1 April 2009: see by the Transfer of Tribunal Functions and Revenue and Customs Appeals Order 2009, art 1(2).
2   Inserted by the Money Laundering (Amendment) Regulations 2012, SI 2012/2298, reg 15. Date in force: 1 October 2012: see the Money Laundering (Amendment) Regulations 2012, reg 1.
3   Paragraphs (3)-(6) substituted for paras (3)-(5) by the Transfer of Tribunal Functions and Revenue and Customs Appeals Order 2009, SI 2009/56, art 3(2), Sch 2, paras 168, 172(1), (4). Date in force: 1 April 2009: see by the Transfer of Tribunal Functions and Revenue and Customs Appeals Order 2009, art 1(2).

[43A   Offer of review

(1)   The Commissioners must offer a person (P) a review of a decision that has been notified to P if an appeal lies under regulation 43 in respect of the decision.

(2)   The offer of the review must be made by notice given to P at the same time as the decision is notified to P.

(3)   This regulation does not apply to the notification of the conclusions of a review.][1]

Notes

Amendment

1   Inserted by the Transfer of Tribunal Functions and Revenue and Customs Appeals Order 2009, SI 2009/56, art 3(2), Sch 2, paras 168, 173. Date in force: 1 April 2009: see by the Transfer of Tribunal Functions and Revenue and Customs Appeals Order 2009, art 1(2).

[43B Review by the Commissioners

(1) The Commissioners must review a decision if—

(a) they have offered a review of the decision under regulation 43A, and

(b) P notifies the Commissioners accepting the offer within 30 days from the date of the document containing the notification of the offer.

(2) But P may not notify acceptance of the offer if P has already appealed to the tribunal under regulation 43F.

(3) The Commissioners shall not review a decision if P has appealed to the tribunal under regulation 43F in respect of the decision.][1]

Notes

Amendment

1   Inserted by the Transfer of Tribunal Functions and Revenue and Customs Appeals Order 2009, SI 2009/56, art 3(2), Sch 2, paras 168, 173. Date in force: 1 April 2009: see by the Transfer of Tribunal Functions and Revenue and Customs Appeals Order 2009, art 1(2).

[43C Extensions of time

(1) If under regulation 43A, the Commissioners have offered P a review of a decision, the Commissioners may within the relevant period notify P that the relevant period is extended.

(2) If notice is given the relevant period is extended to the end of 30 days from—

(a) the date of the notice, or

(b) any other date set out in the notice or a further notice.

(3) In this regulation 'relevant period' means—

(a) the period of 30 days referred to in regulation 43B(1)(b), or

(b) if notice has been given under paragraph (1) that period as extended (or as most recently extended) in accordance with paragraph (2).][1]

Notes

Amendment

1   Inserted by the Transfer of Tribunal Functions and Revenue and Customs Appeals Order 2009, SI 2009/56, art 3(2), Sch 2, paras 168, 173. Date in force: 1 April 2009: see by the Transfer of Tribunal Functions and Revenue and Customs Appeals Order 2009, art 1(2).

[43D Review out of time

(1) This regulation applies if—

(a) the Commissioners have offered a review of a decision under regulation 43A, and

(b) P does not accept the offer within the time allowed under regulation 43B(1)(b) or 43C(2).

(2)   The Commissioners must review the decision under regulation 43B if—

(a)   after the time allowed, P notifies the Commissioners in writing requesting a review out of time,

(b)   the Commissioners are satisfied that P had a reasonable excuse for not accepting the offer or requiring review within the time allowed, and

(c)   the Commissioners are satisfied that P made the request without unreasonable delay after the excuse had ceased to apply.

(3)   The Commissioners shall not review a decision if P has appealed to the tribunal under regulation 43F in respect of the decision.][1]

_____

Notes

Amendment

1   Inserted by the Transfer of Tribunal Functions and Revenue and Customs Appeals Order 2009, SI 2009/56, art 3(2), Sch 2, paras 168, 173. Date in force: 1 April 2009: see by the Transfer of Tribunal Functions and Revenue and Customs Appeals Order 2009, art 1(2).

_____

[43E   Nature of review etc

(1)   This regulation applies if the Commissioners are required to undertake a review under regulation 43B or 43D.

(2)   The nature and extent of the review are to be such as appear appropriate to the Commissioners in the circumstances.

(3)   For the purpose of paragraph (2), the Commissioners must, in particular, have regard to steps taken before the beginning of the review—

(a)   by the Commissioners in reaching the decision, and

(b)   by any person in seeking to resolve disagreement about the decision.

(4)   The review must take account of any representations made by P at a stage which gives the Commissioners a reasonable opportunity to consider them.

(5)   The review may conclude that the decision is to be—

(a)   upheld,

(b)   varied, or

(c)   cancelled.

(6)   The Commissioners must give P notice of the conclusions of the review and their reasoning within—

(a)   a period of 45 days beginning with the relevant date, or

(b)   such other period as the Commissioners and P may agree.

(7)   In paragraph (6) 'relevant date' means—

(a)   the date the Commissioners received P's notification accepting the offer of a review (in a case falling within regulation 43A), or

(b)   the date on which the Commissioners decided to undertake the review (in a case falling within regulation 43D).

(8)   Where the Commissioners are required to undertake a review but do not give notice of the conclusions within the time period specified in paragraph (6), the review is to be treated as having concluded that the decision is upheld.

(9)   If paragraph (8) applies, the Commissioners must notify P of the conclusion which the review is treated as having reached.]¹

Notes

Amendment

1   Inserted by the Transfer of Tribunal Functions and Revenue and Customs Appeals Order 2009, SI 2009/56, art 3(2), Sch 2, paras 168, 173. Date in force: 1 April 2009: see by the Transfer of Tribunal Functions and Revenue and Customs Appeals Order 2009, art 1(2).

[43F   Bringing of appeals against decisions of the Commissioners

(1)   An appeal under regulation 43 is to be made to the tribunal before—

(a)   the end of the period of 30 days beginning with the date of the document notifying the decision to which the appeal relates, or

(b)   if later, the end of the relevant period (within the meaning of regulation 43C).

(2)   But that is subject to paragraphs (3) to (5).

(3)   In a case where the Commissioners are required to undertake a review under regulation 43B—

(a)   an appeal may not be made until the conclusion date, and

(b)   any appeal is to be made within the period of 30 days beginning with the conclusion date.

[(4)   In a case where the Commissioners are requested to undertake a review in accordance with regulation 43D—

(a)   an appeal may not be made—

   (i)   unless the Commissioners have notified P as to whether or not a review will be undertaken, and

   (ii)   if the Commissioners have notified P that a review will be undertaken, until the conclusion date;

(b)   any appeal where sub-paragraph (a)(ii) applies is to be made within the period of 30 days beginning with the conclusion date;

(c)   if the Commissioners have notified P that a review will not be undertaken, an appeal may be made only if the tribunal gives permission to do so.]¹

(5)   In a case where regulation 43E(8) applies, an appeal may be made at any time from the end of the period specified in regulation 43E(6) to the date 30 days after the conclusion date.

(6)   An appeal may be made after the end of the period specified in paragraph (1), (3)(b), (4)(b) or (5) if the tribunal gives permission to do so.

(7)   In this regulation 'conclusion date' means the date of the document notifying the conclusions of the review.]²

Notes

Amendments

1   Substituted by the Revenue and Customs (Amendment of Appeal Provisions for Out of Time Reviews) Order 2014, SI 2014/1264, art 11. Date in force: 1 June 2014: see the Revenue and Customs (Amendment of Appeal Provisions for Out of Time Reviews) Order 2014, art 1(2), subject to the Revenue and Customs (Amendment of Appeal Provisions for Out of Time Reviews) Order 2014, art 1(3).
2   Inserted by the Transfer of Tribunal Functions and Revenue and Customs Appeals Order 2009, SI 2009/56, art 3(2), Sch 2, paras 168, 173. Date in force: 1 April 2009: see by the Transfer of Tribunal Functions and Revenue and Customs Appeals Order 2009, art 1(2).

---

44   Appeals

(1)   A person may appeal from a decision by—

(a)   ...[1]

(b)   the Authority ...[2] or DETI under regulation 34 or 42.

(2)   An appeal from a decision by—

(a)   ...[1]

(b)   the Authority is to the [Upper Tribunal][3]; [and][4]

(c)   ...[2]

(d)   DETI is to the High Court.

(3)   ...[1]

(4)   The provisions of Part 9 of the 2000 Act (hearings and appeals), subject to the modifications set out in paragraph 2 of Schedule 5 , apply in respect of appeals to the [Upper Tribunal][3] made under this regulation as they apply in respect of references made to that Tribunal under that Act.

(5)   ...[4]

(6)   ...[1]

(7)   ...[2]

(8)   The modifications in Schedule 5 have effect for the purposes of appeals made under this regulation.

Notes

Amendments

1   Repealed by the Transfer of Tribunal Functions and Revenue and Customs Appeals Order 2009, SI 2009/56, art 3(2), Sch 2, paras 168, 174. Date in force: 1 April 2009: see by the Transfer of Tribunal Functions and Revenue and Customs Appeals Order 2009, art 1(2).
2   Repealed by the Financial Services and Markets Act 2000 (Regulated Activities) (Amendment) (No.2) Order 2013, SI 2013/1881, art 28, Sch 1, para 31(1), (13). Date in force: 26 July 2013: see the Financial Services and Markets Act 2000 (Regulated Activities) (Amendment) (No.2) Order 2013, art 1(2), subject to transitional provisions specified in the Financial Services and Markets Act 2000 (Regulated Activities) (Amendment) (No.2) Order 2013, Sch 1, para 32.

3   Substituted by the Transfer of Tribunal Functions Order 2010, SI 2010/22, art 5(2), Sch 3, paras 140, 141. Date in force: 6 April 2010: see the Transfer of Tribunal Functions Order 2010, art 1(2)(f).
4   Repealed by the Transfer of Functions of the Consumer Credit Appeals Tribunal Order 2009, SI 2009/1835, art 4(2), Sch 2, para 1(b). Date in force: 1 September 2009: see the Transfer of Functions of the Consumer Credit Appeals Tribunal Order 2009, art 1, subject to transitional provisions and savings specified in the Transfer of Functions of the Consumer Credit Appeals Tribunal Order 2009, Sch 4.

Criminal offences

45   Offences

(1)   A person [(except an auction platform)]¹ who fails to comply with any requirement in regulation 7(1), (2) or (3), 8(1) or (3), 9(2), 10(1), 11(1)(a), (b) or (c), 14(1), 15(1) or (2), 16(1), (2), (3) or (4), 19(1), (4), (5) or (6), 20(1), (4) or (5), 21, 26, 27(4) or 33 …² is guilty of an offence and liable—

(a)   on summary conviction, to a fine not exceeding the statutory maximum;

(b)   on conviction on indictment, to imprisonment for a term not exceeding two years, to a fine or to both.

[(1A)   An auction platform which fails to comply with the customer due diligence requirements of Article 19 or 20(6) of the emission allowance auctioning regulation, the monitoring and record keeping requirements of Article 54 of that regulation, or regulation 20(1), (4) or (5) or 21 of these Regulations, is guilty of an offence and liable—

(a)   on summary conviction, to a fine not exceeding the statutory maximum;

(b)   on conviction on indictment, to imprisonment for a term not exceeding two years, to a fine or to both.]¹

(2)   In deciding whether a person has committed an offence under paragraph (1) [or (1A)]¹, the court must consider whether he followed any relevant guidance which was at the time—

(a)   issued by a supervisory authority or any other appropriate body;

(b)   approved by the Treasury; and

(c)   published in a manner approved by the Treasury as suitable in their opinion to bring the guidance to the attention of persons likely to be affected by it.

(3)   In paragraph (2), an 'appropriate body' means any body which regulates or is representative of any trade, profession, business or employment carried on by the alleged offender.

(4)   A person is not guilty of an offence under this regulation if he took all reasonable steps and exercised all due diligence to avoid committing the offence.

(5)   Where a person is convicted of an offence under this regulation, he shall not also be liable to a penalty under regulation 42.

Notes

Amendments

1   Inserted by the Recognised Auction Platforms Regulations 2011, SI 2011/2699, reg 11(1), (8). Date in force: 12 December 2011: see the Recognised Auction Platforms Regulations 2011, reg 1(2)(a).
2   Repealed by the Money Laundering (Amendment) Regulations 2012, SI 2012/2298, reg 16. Date in force: 1 October 2012: see the Money Laundering (Amendment) Regulations 2012, reg 1.

46   Prosecution of offences

(1)   Proceedings for an offence under regulation 45 may be instituted by—

(a)   ...[1] order of the Commissioners;

(b)   ...[2]

(c)   a local weights and measures authority;

(d)   DETI;

(e)   the Director of Public Prosecutions; or

(f)   the Director of Public Prosecutions for Northern Ireland.

(2)   Proceedings for an offence under regulation 45 may be instituted only against a relevant person or, where such a person is a body corporate, a partnership or an unincorporated association, against any person who is liable to be proceeded against under regulation 47.

(3)   Where proceedings under paragraph (1) are instituted by order of the Commissioners, the proceedings must be brought in the name of an officer of Revenue and Customs.

(4)   ...[2]

(5)   ...[2]

(6)   A local weights and measures authority must, whenever the [Authority][3] requires, report in such form and with such particulars as the [Authority][3] requires on the exercise of its functions under these Regulations.

(7)   Where the Commissioners investigate, or propose to investigate, any matter with a view to determining—

(a)   whether there are grounds for believing that an offence under regulation 45 has been committed by any person; or

(b)   whether such a person should be prosecuted for such an offence,

that matter is to be treated as an assigned matter within the meaning of section 1(1) of the Customs and Excise Management Act 1979.

(8)   Paragraphs (1) and (3) to (6) do not extend to Scotland.

[(9)   In its application to the Commissioners acting in Scotland, paragraph (7) (b) shall be read as referring to the Commissioners determining whether to refer the matter to the Crown Office and Procurator Fiscal Service with a view to the Procurator Fiscal determining whether a person should be prosecuted for such an offence.][4]

Notes

Amendments

1   Repealed by the Public Bodies (Merger of the Director of Public Prosecutions and the Director of Revenue and Customs Prosecutions) Order 2014, SI 2014/834, art 3(3)(a), Sch 3, para 21. Date in force: 27 March 2014: see the Public Bodies (Merger of the Director of Public Prosecutions and the Director of Revenue and Customs Prosecutions) Order 2014, art 1(1).
2   Repealed by the Financial Services and Markets Act 2000 (Regulated Activities) (Amendment) (No.2) Order 2013, SI 2013/1881, art 28, Sch 1, para 31(1), (14)(a), (b). Date in force: 26 July 2013: see the Financial Services and Markets Act 2000 (Regulated Activities) (Amendment) (No.2) Order 2013, art 1(2), subject to transitional provisions specified in the Financial Services and Markets Act 2000 (Regulated Activities) (Amendment) (No.2) Order 2013, Sch 1, para 32.
3   Substituted by the Financial Services and Markets Act 2000 (Regulated Activities) (Amendment) (No.2) Order 2013, SI 2013/1881, art 28, Sch 1, para 31(1), (14)(c). Date in force: 26 July 2013: see the Financial Services and Markets Act 2000 (Regulated Activities) (Amendment) (No.2) Order 2013, art 1(2), subject to transitional provisions specified in the Financial Services and Markets Act 2000 (Regulated Activities) (Amendment) (No.2) Order 2013, Sch 1, para 32.
4   Inserted by the Money Laundering (Amendment) Regulations 2007, SI 2007/3299, reg 2(f). Date in force: 15 December 2007: see the Money Laundering (Amendment) Regulations 2007, reg 1.

47   Offences by bodies corporate etc.

(1)   If an offence under regulation 45 committed by a body corporate is shown—

(a)   to have been committed with the consent or the connivance of an officer of the body corporate; or

(b)   to be attributable to any neglect on his part,

the officer as well as the body corporate is guilty of an offence and liable to be proceeded against and punished accordingly.

(2)   If an offence under regulation 45 committed by a partnership is shown—

(a)   to have been committed with the consent or the connivance of a partner; or

(b)   to be attributable to any neglect on his part,

the partner as well as the partnership is guilty of an offence and liable to be proceeded against and punished accordingly.

(3)   If an offence under regulation 45 committed by an unincorporated association (other than a partnership) is shown—

(a)   to have been committed with the consent or the connivance of an officer of the association; or

(b)   to be attributable to any neglect on his part,

that officer as well as the association is guilty of an offence and liable to be proceeded against and punished accordingly.

(4)   If the affairs of a body corporate are managed by its members, paragraph (1) applies in relation to the acts and defaults of a member in connection with his functions of management as if he were a director of the body.

(5)   Proceedings for an offence alleged to have been committed by a partnership or an unincorporated association must be brought in the name of the partnership or association (and not in that of its members).

(6)   A fine imposed on the partnership or association on its conviction of an offence is to be paid out of the funds of the partnership or association.

(7)   Rules of court relating to the service of documents are to have effect as if the partnership or association were a body corporate.

(8)   In proceedings for an offence brought against the partnership or association—

(a)   section 33 of the Criminal Justice Act 1925 (procedure on charge of offence against corporation) and Schedule 3 to the Magistrates' Courts Act 1980 (corporations) apply as they do in relation to a body corporate;

(b)   section 70 (proceedings against bodies corporate) of the Criminal Procedure (Scotland) Act 1995 applies as it does in relation to a body corporate;

(c)   section 18 of the Criminal Justice (Northern Ireland) Act 1945 (procedure on charge) and Schedule 4 to the Magistrates' Courts (Northern Ireland) Order 1981 (corporations) apply as they do in relation to a body corporate.

(9)   In this regulation—

'officer'—

(a)   in relation to a body corporate, means a director, manager, secretary, chief executive, member of the committee of management, or a person purporting to act in such a capacity; and

(b)   in relation to an unincorporated association, means any officer of the association or any member of its governing body, or a person purporting to act in such capacity; and

'partner' includes a person purporting to act as a partner.

Part 6
Miscellaneous

48   Recovery of charges and penalties through the court

Any charge or penalty imposed on a person by a supervisory authority under regulation 35(1) or 42(1) is a debt due from that person to the authority, and is recoverable accordingly.

49   Obligations on public authorities

(1)   The following bodies and persons must, if they know or suspect or have reasonable grounds for knowing or suspecting that a person is or has engaged in money laundering or terrorist financing, as soon as reasonably practicable inform [the National Crime Agency][1]—

(a)   the Auditor General for Scotland;

(b)   the Auditor General for Wales;

(c)   the Authority;

(d)   the Bank of England;

(e)   the Comptroller and Auditor General;

(f)   the Comptroller and Auditor General for Northern Ireland;

(g)   the Gambling Commission;

(h)   ...[2]

(i)   the Official Solicitor to the Supreme Court;

(j)   the Pensions Regulator;

[(ja) the PRA;][3]

(k)   the Public Trustee;

(l)   the Secretary of State, in the exercise of his functions under enactments relating to companies and insolvency;

(m) the Treasury, in the exercise of their functions under the 2000 Act;

(n)   the Treasury Solicitor;

(o)   a designated professional body for the purposes of Part 20 of the 2000 Act (provision of financial services by members of the professions);

(p)   a person or inspector appointed under section 65 (investigations on behalf of Authority) or 66 (inspections and special meetings) of the Friendly Societies Act 1992;

(q)   an inspector appointed under section 49 of the Industrial and Provident Societies Act 1965 (appointment of inspectors) or section 18 of the Credit Unions Act 1979 (power to appoint inspector);

(r)   an inspector appointed under section 431 (investigation of a company on its own application), 432 (other company investigations), 442 (power to investigate company ownership) or [446D (appointment of replacement inspectors)][4] of the Companies Act 1985 …[5];

(s)   a person or inspector appointed under section 55 (investigations on behalf of Authority) or 56 (inspections and special meetings) of the Building Societies Act 1986;

(t)   a person appointed under section 167 (appointment of persons to carry out investigations), 168(3) or (5) (appointment of persons to carry out investigations in particular cases), 169(1)(b) (investigations to support overseas regulator) or 284 (power to investigate affairs of a scheme) of the 2000 Act, or under regulations made under section 262(2)(k) (open-ended investment companies) of that Act, to conduct an investigation; and

(u)   a person authorised to require the production of documents under section 447 of the Companies Act 1985 (Secretary of State's power to require production of documents), Article 440 of the Companies (Northern Ireland) Order 1986 or section 84 of the Companies Act 1989 (exercise of powers by officer).

(2)   A disclosure made under paragraph (1) is not to be taken to breach any restriction on the disclosure of information however imposed.

Notes

Amendments

1   Substituted by the Crime and Courts Act 2013, s 15, Sch 8, para 190(1)(b). Date in force: 7 October 2013: see the Crime and Courts Act 2013 (Commencement No. 2 and Saving Provision) Order 2013, SI 2013/1682, art 3(u), (v), subject to savings and transitional provisions specified in the Crime and Courts Act 2013, s 15, Sch 8.
2   Repealed by the Financial Services and Markets Act 2000 (Regulated Activities) (Amendment) (No.2) Order 2013, SI 2013/1881, art 28, Sch 1, para 31(1), (15). Date in force: 26 July 2013: see the Financial Services and Markets Act 2000 (Regulated Activities) (Amendment) (No.2) Order 2013, art 1(2), subject to transitional provisions specified in the Financial Services and Markets Act 2000 (Regulated Activities) (Amendment) (No.2) Order 2013, Sch 1, para 32.
3   Inserted by the Financial Services Act 2012 (Consequential Amendments and Transitional Provisions) Order 2013, SI 2013/472, art 3, Sch 2, para 129(f). Date in force: 1 April 2013: see the Financial Services Act 2012 (Consequential Amendments and Transitional Provisions) Order 2013, art 1(1).

4   Substituted by the Companies Act 2006 (Consequential Amendments and Transitional Provisions) Order 2011, SI 2011/1265, art 30. Date in force: 12 May 2011: see the Companies Act 2006 (Consequential Amendments and Transitional Provisions) Order 2011, art 1(2).
5   Repealed by the Companies Act 2006 (Consequential Amendments and Transitional Provisions) Order 2011, SI 2011/1265, art 30. Date in force: 12 May 2011: see the Companies Act 2006 (Consequential Amendments and Transitional Provisions) Order 2011, art 1(2).

[49A   Disclosure by the Commissioners

(1)   The Commissioners may disclose to the Authority information held in connection with their functions under these Regulations if the disclosure is made for the purpose of enabling or assisting the Authority to discharge any of its functions under the Payment Services Regulations 2009 [or the Electronic Money Regulations 2011][1].

(2)   Information disclosed to the Authority under subsection (1) may not be disclosed by the Authority or any person who receives the information directly or indirectly from the Authority except—

(a)   to, or in accordance with authority given by, the Commissioners;

(b)   with a view to the institution of, or otherwise for the purposes of, any criminal proceedings;

(c)   with a view to the institution of any other proceedings by the Authority, for the purposes of any such proceedings instituted by the Authority, or for the purposes of any reference to the Tribunal under the Payment Services Regulations 2009; or

(d)   in the form of a summary or collection of information so framed as not to enable information relating to any particular person to be ascertained from it.

(3)   Any person who discloses information in contravention of subsection (2) is guilty of an offence and liable—

(a)   on summary conviction, to imprisonment for a term not exceeding three months, to a fine not exceeding the statutory maximum, or to both;

(b)   on conviction on indictment, to imprisonment for a term not exceeding two years to a fine, or to both.

(4)   It is a defence for a person charged with an offence under this regulation of disclosing information to prove that they reasonably believed

(a)   that the disclosure was lawful; or

(b)   that the information had already and lawfully been made available to the public.][2]

Notes

Amendments

1   Inserted by the Electronic Money Regulations 2011, SI 2011/99, reg 79, Sch 4, para 19(g). Date in force: 9 February 2011: see the Electronic Money Regulations 2011, reg 1(2)(a) (xv).
2   Inserted by the Payment Services Regulations 2009, SI 2009/209, reg 126, Sch 6, para 6(g). Date in force: 2 March 2009: see the Payment Services Regulations 2009, reg 1(2)(a).

---

50   Transitional provisions: requirement to be registered

(1)   Regulation 26 does not apply to an existing money service business, an existing trust or company service provider[, an existing high value dealer, an existing bill payment service provider or an existing telecommunication, digital and IT payment service provider]¹ until—

(a)   where it has applied in accordance with regulation 27 before the specified date for registration in a register maintained under regulation 25(1) (a 'new register')—

  (i)   the date it is included in a new register following the determination of its application by the Commissioners; or

  (ii)   where the Commissioners give it notice under regulation 29(2)(b) of their decision not to register it, the date on which the Commissioners state that the decision takes effect or, where a statement is included in accordance with paragraph (3)(b), the time at which the Commissioners give it such notice;

(b)   in any other case, the specified date.

(2)   The specified date is—

(a)   in the case of an existing money service business, 1st February 2008;

(b)   in the case of an existing trust or company service provider, 1st April 2008;

(c)   in the case of an existing high value dealer, the first anniversary which falls on or after 1st January 2008 of the date of its registration in a register maintained under regulation 10 of the Money Laundering Regulations 2003;

[(d)   in the case of an existing bill payment service provider or an existing telecommunication, digital and IT payment service provider, 1st March 2010.]²

(3)   In the case of an application for registration in a new register made before the specified date by an existing money service business, an existing trust or company service provider[, an existing high value dealer, an existing bill payment service provider or an existing telecommunication, digital and IT payment service provider]¹, the Commissioners must include in a notice given to it under regulation 29(2)(b)—

(a)   the date on which their decision is to take effect; or

(b)   if the Commissioners consider that the interests of the public require their decision to have immediate effect, a statement to that effect and the reasons for it.

(4)   In the case of an application for registration in a new register made before the specified date by an existing money services business or an existing trust or company service provider, the Commissioners must give it a notice under regulation 29(2) by—

(a)   in the case of an existing money service business, 1st June 2008;

(b)   in the case of an existing trust or company service provider, 1st July 2008; or

(c)   where applicable, 45 days beginning with the date on which they receive any further information required under regulation 27(3).

(5)   In this regulation—

['existing bill payment service provider' and 'existing telecommunication, digital and IT payment service provider' mean a bill payment service provider or a telecommunication, digital and IT payment service provider carrying on business in the United Kingdom immediately before 1st November 2009;]²

'existing money service business' and an 'existing high value dealer' mean a money service business or a high value dealer which, immediately before 15th December 2007, was included in a register maintained under regulation 10 of the Money Laundering Regulations 2003;

'existing trust or company service provider' means a trust or company service provider carrying on business in the United Kingdom immediately before 15th December 2007.

Notes

Amendments

1   Substituted by the Payment Services Regulations 2009, SI 2009/209, reg 126, Sch 6, para 6(h)(i), (iii). Date in force: 1 November 2009: see the Payment Services Regulations 2009, reg 1(2)(c).
2   Inserted by the Payment Services Regulations 2009, SI 2009/209, reg 126, Sch 6, para 6(h)(ii), (iv). Date in force: 1 November 2009: see the Payment Services Regulations 2009, reg 1(2)(c).

---

51   Minor and consequential amendments

Schedule 6, which contains minor and consequential amendments to primary and secondary legislation, has effect.

Schedule 1
Activities listed in points 2 to 12[, 14 and 15][1] of Annex 1 to the capital requirements directive

2.

Lending including, inter alia: consumer credit, mortgage credit, factoring, with or without recourse, financing of commercial transactions (including forfeiting).

3.

Financial leasing.

[4.

Payment services as defined in Article 4(3) of Directive 2007/64/EC of the European Parliament and of the Council of 13 November 2007 on payment services in the internal market.

5.

Issuing and administering other means of payment (including travellers' cheques and bankers' drafts) insofar as this activity is not covered by point 4.][2]

6.

Guarantees and commitments.

7.

Trading for own account or for account of customers in:

(a)   money market instruments (cheques, bills, certificates of deposit, etc.);

(b)   foreign exchange;

(c)   financial futures and options;

(d)   exchange and interest-rate instruments; or

(e)   transferable securities.

8.

Participation in securities issues and the provision of services related to such issues.

9.

Advice to undertakings on capital structure, industrial strategy and related questions and advice as well as services relating to mergers and the purchase of undertakings.

10.

Money broking.

11.

Portfolio management and advice.

12.

Safekeeping and administration of securities.

14.

Safe custody services.

[15.

Issuing electronic money.]³

Notes

Amendments

1   Substituted by the Electronic Money Regulations 2011, SI 2011/99, reg 79, Sch 4, para 19(h)(i). Date in force: 30 April 2011: see the Electronic Money Regulations 2011, reg 1(2) (b).

2   Substituted by the Payment Services Regulations 2009, SI 2009/209, reg 126, Sch 6, para 6(i). Date in force: 1 November 2009: see the Payment Services Regulations 2009, reg 1(2)(c).

3   Inserted by the Electronic Money Regulations 2011, SI 2011/99, reg 79, Sch 4, para 19(h) (ii). Date in force: 30 April 2011: see the Electronic Money Regulations 2011, reg 1(2)(b).

Schedule 2
Financial activity, simplified due diligence and politically exposed persons

Financial activity on an occasional or very limited basis

1.

For the purposes of regulation 4(1)(e) and (2), a person is to be considered as engaging in financial activity on an occasional or very limited basis if all the following conditions are fulfilled—

(a)   the person's total annual turnover in respect of the financial activity does not exceed £64,000;

(b)   the financial activity is limited in relation to any customer to no more than one transaction exceeding 1,000 euro, whether the transaction is carried out in a single operation, or a series of operations which appear to be linked;

(c)   the financial activity does not exceed 5% of the person's total annual turnover;

(d)   the financial activity is ancillary and directly related to the person's main activity;

(e)   the financial activity is not the transmission or remittance of money (or any representation of monetary value) by any means;

(f)   the person's main activity is not that of a person falling within regulation 3(1) (a) to (f) or (h);

(g)   the financial activity is provided only to customers of the person's main activity and is not offered to the public.

Simplified due diligence

2.

For the purposes of regulation 13(6), the conditions are—

(a)   the authority has been entrusted with public functions pursuant to the [Treaty on European Union, the Treaty on the Functioning of the European Union or EU secondary legislation][1];

(b)   the authority's identity is publicly available, transparent and certain;

(c)   the activities of the authority and its accounting practices are transparent;

(d)   either the authority is accountable to [an EU][2] institution or to the authorities of an EEA state, or otherwise appropriate check and balance procedures exist ensuring control of the authority's activity.

Notes

Amendments

1   Substituted by the Treaty of Lisbon (Changes in Terminology or Numbering) Order 2012, SI 2012/1809, art 3(1), Sch 1, Pt 2. Date in force: 1 August 2012: see the Treaty of Lisbon (Changes in Terminology or Numbering) Order 2012, art 2(1), subject to savings specified in the Treaty of Lisbon (Changes in Terminology or Numbering) Order 2012, art 2(2).
2   Substituted by the Treaty of Lisbon (Changes in Terminology) Order 2011, SI 2011/1043, art 6(1)(c), (3). Date in force: 22 April 2011: see the Treaty of Lisbon (Changes in Terminology) Order 2011, art 2.

3.

For the purposes of regulation 13(8), the conditions are—

(a)   the product has a written contractual base;

(b)   any related transaction is carried out through an account of the customer with a credit institution which is subject to the money laundering directive or with a credit institution situated in a non-EEA state which imposes requirements equivalent to those laid down in that directive;

(c)   the product or related transaction is not anonymous and its nature is such that it allows for the timely application of customer due diligence measures where there is a suspicion of money laundering or terrorist financing;

(d)   the product is within the following maximum threshold—

    (i)   in the case of insurance policies or savings products of a similar nature, the annual premium is no more than 1,000 euro or there is a single premium of no more than 2,500 euro;

    (ii) in the case of products which are related to the financing of physical assets where the legal and beneficial title of the assets is not transferred to the customer until the termination of the contractual relationship (whether the transaction is carried out in a single operation or in several operations which appear to be linked), the annual payments do not exceed 15,000 euro;

    (iii) in all other cases, the maximum threshold is 15,000 euro;

(e)   the benefits of the product or related transaction cannot be realised for the benefit of third parties, except in the case of death, disablement, survival to a predetermined advanced age, or similar events;

(f)   in the case of products or related transactions allowing for the investment of funds in financial assets or claims, including insurance or other kinds of contingent claims—

    (i)   the benefits of the product or related transaction are only realisable in the long term;

    (ii) the product or related transaction cannot be used as collateral; and

    (iii) during the contractual relationship, no accelerated payments are made, surrender clauses used or early termination takes place.

Politically exposed persons

4.

(1)   For the purposes of regulation 14(5)—

(a)   individuals who are or have been entrusted with prominent public functions include the following—

    (i)   heads of state, heads of government, ministers and deputy or assistant ministers;

    (ii) members of parliaments;

    (iii) members of supreme courts, of constitutional courts or of other high-level judicial bodies whose decisions are not generally subject to further appeal, other than in exceptional circumstances;

    (iv) members of courts of auditors or of the boards of central banks;

    (v) ambassadors, chargés d'affaires and high-ranking officers in the armed forces; and

    (vi) members of the administrative, management or supervisory bodies of state-owned enterprises;

(b)   the categories set out in paragraphs (i) to (vi) of sub-paragraph (a) do not include middle-ranking or more junior officials;

(c)   immediate family members include the following—

    (i)   a spouse;

    (ii) a partner;

    (iii) children and their spouses or partners; and

    (iv) parents;

(d)   persons known to be close associates include the following—

   (i)   any individual who is known to have joint beneficial ownership of a legal entity or legal arrangement, or any other close business relations, with a person referred to in regulation 14(5)(a); and

   (ii)   any individual who has sole beneficial ownership of a legal entity or legal arrangement which is known to have been set up for the benefit of a person referred to in regulation 14(5)(a).

(2)   In paragraph (1)(c), 'partner' means a person who is considered by his national law as equivalent to a spouse.

[Schedule 3
Professional bodies][1]

[1.

Association of Accounting Technicians][1]

Notes

Amendment

1   Existing Sch 3 substituted for a new Sch 3 consisting of paras 1–22 by the Money Laundering (Amendment) Regulations 2012, SI 2012/2298, reg 17, Schedule. Date in force: 1 October 2012: see the Money Laundering (Amendment) Regulations 2012, reg 1.

[2.

Association of Chartered Certified Accountants][1]

Notes

Amendment

1   Existing Sch 3 substituted for a new Sch 3 consisting of paras 1–22 by the Money Laundering (Amendment) Regulations 2012, SI 2012/2298, reg 17, Schedule. Date in force: 1 October 2012: see the Money Laundering (Amendment) Regulations 2012, reg 1.

[3.

Association of International Accountants][1]

Notes

Amendment

1   Existing Sch 3 substituted for a new Sch 3 consisting of paras 1–22 by the Money Laundering (Amendment) Regulations 2012, SI 2012/2298, reg 17, Schedule. Date in force: 1 October 2012: see the Money Laundering (Amendment) Regulations 2012, reg 1.

[4.

Association of Taxation Technicians][1]

Notes

Amendment

1   Existing Sch 3 substituted for a new Sch 3 consisting of paras 1–22 by the Money Laundering (Amendment) Regulations 2012, SI 2012/2298, reg 17, Schedule. Date in force: 1 October 2012: see the Money Laundering (Amendment) Regulations 2012, reg 1.

[5.

Chartered Institute of Management Accountants][1]

Notes

Amendment

1   Existing Sch 3 substituted for a new Sch 3 consisting of paras 1–22 by the Money Laundering (Amendment) Regulations 2012, SI 2012/2298, reg 17, Schedule. Date in force: 1 October 2012: see the Money Laundering (Amendment) Regulations 2012, reg 1.

[6.

Chartered Institute of Public Finance and Accountancy][1]

Notes

Amendment

1   Existing Sch 3 substituted for a new Sch 3 consisting of paras 1–22 by the Money Laundering (Amendment) Regulations 2012, SI 2012/2298, reg 17, Schedule. Date in force: 1 October 2012: see the Money Laundering (Amendment) Regulations 2012, reg 1.

[7.

Chartered Institute of Taxation][1]

Notes

Amendment

1   Existing Sch 3 substituted for a new Sch 3 consisting of paras 1–22 by the Money Laundering (Amendment) Regulations 2012, SI 2012/2298, reg 17, Schedule. Date in force: 1 October 2012: see the Money Laundering (Amendment) Regulations 2012, reg 1.

[8.

Council for Licensed Conveyancers][1]

Notes

Amendment

1   Existing Sch 3 substituted for a new Sch 3 consisting of paras 1–22 by the Money Laundering (Amendment) Regulations 2012, SI 2012/2298, reg 17, Schedule. Date in force: 1 October 2012: see the Money Laundering (Amendment) Regulations 2012, reg 1.

[9.

Faculty of Advocates][1]

Notes

Amendment

1   Existing Sch 3 substituted for a new Sch 3 consisting of paras 1–22 by the Money Laundering (Amendment) Regulations 2012, SI 2012/2298, reg 17, Schedule. Date in force: 1 October 2012: see the Money Laundering (Amendment) Regulations 2012, reg 1.

[10.

Faculty Office of the Archbishop of Canterbury][1]

Notes

Amendment

1   Existing Sch 3 substituted for a new Sch 3 consisting of paras 1–22 by the Money Laundering (Amendment) Regulations 2012, SI 2012/2298, reg 17, Schedule. Date in force: 1 October 2012: see the Money Laundering (Amendment) Regulations 2012, reg 1.

[11.

General Council of the Bar][1]

Notes

Amendment

1   Existing Sch 3 substituted for a new Sch 3 consisting of paras 1–22 by the Money Laundering (Amendment) Regulations 2012, SI 2012/2298, reg 17, Schedule. Date in force: 1 October 2012: see the Money Laundering (Amendment) Regulations 2012, reg 1.

[12.

General Council of the Bar of Northern Ireland][1]

Notes

Amendment

1   Existing Sch 3 substituted for a new Sch 3 consisting of paras 1–22 by the Money Laundering (Amendment) Regulations 2012, SI 2012/2298, reg 17, Schedule. Date in force: 1 October 2012: see the Money Laundering (Amendment) Regulations 2012, reg 1.

[13.

Insolvency Practitioners Association][1]

Notes

Amendment

1   Existing Sch 3 substituted for a new Sch 3 consisting of paras 1–22 by the Money Laundering (Amendment) Regulations 2012, SI 2012/2298, reg 17, Schedule. Date in force: 1 October 2012: see the Money Laundering (Amendment) Regulations 2012, reg 1.

[14.

Institute of Certified Bookkeepers]¹

Notes

Amendment

1   Existing Sch 3 substituted for a new Sch 3 consisting of paras 1–22 by the Money
     Laundering (Amendment) Regulations 2012, SI 2012/2298, reg 17, Schedule. Date in
     force: 1 October 2012: see the Money Laundering (Amendment) Regulations 2012, reg 1.

[15.

Institute of Chartered Accountants in England and Wales]¹

Notes

Amendment

1   Existing Sch 3 substituted for a new Sch 3 consisting of paras 1–22 by the Money
     Laundering (Amendment) Regulations 2012, SI 2012/2298, reg 17, Schedule. Date in
     force: 1 October 2012: see the Money Laundering (Amendment) Regulations 2012, reg 1.

[16.

Institute of Chartered Accountants in Ireland]¹

Notes

Amendment

1   Existing Sch 3 substituted for a new Sch 3 consisting of paras 1–22 by the Money
     Laundering (Amendment) Regulations 2012, SI 2012/2298, reg 17, Schedule. Date in
     force: 1 October 2012: see the Money Laundering (Amendment) Regulations 2012, reg 1.

[17.

Institute of Chartered Accountants of Scotland]¹

Notes

Amendment

1   Existing Sch 3 substituted for a new Sch 3 consisting of paras 1–22 by the Money
     Laundering (Amendment) Regulations 2012, SI 2012/2298, reg 17, Schedule. Date in
     force: 1 October 2012: see the Money Laundering (Amendment) Regulations 2012, reg 1.

[18.

Institute of Financial Accountants]¹

Notes

Amendment

1   Existing Sch 3 substituted for a new Sch 3 consisting of paras 1–22 by the Money
     Laundering (Amendment) Regulations 2012, SI 2012/2298, reg 17, Schedule. Date in
     force: 1 October 2012: see the Money Laundering (Amendment) Regulations 2012, reg 1.

[19.

International Association of Book-keepers][1]

Notes

Amendment

1   Existing Sch 3 substituted for a new Sch 3 consisting of paras 1–22 by the Money Laundering (Amendment) Regulations 2012, SI 2012/2298, reg 17, Schedule. Date in force: 1 October 2012: see the Money Laundering (Amendment) Regulations 2012, reg 1.

[20.

Law Society][1]

Notes

Amendment

1   Existing Sch 3 substituted for a new Sch 3 consisting of paras 1–22 by the Money Laundering (Amendment) Regulations 2012, SI 2012/2298, reg 17, Schedule. Date in force: 1 October 2012: see the Money Laundering (Amendment) Regulations 2012, reg 1.

[21.

Law Society of Northern Ireland][1]

Notes

Amendment

1   Existing Sch 3 substituted for a new Sch 3 consisting of paras 1–22 by the Money Laundering (Amendment) Regulations 2012, SI 2012/2298, reg 17, Schedule. Date in force: 1 October 2012: see the Money Laundering (Amendment) Regulations 2012, reg 1.

[22.

Law Society of Scotland][1]

Notes

Amendment

1   Existing Sch 3 substituted for a new Sch 3 consisting of paras 1–22 by the Money Laundering (Amendment) Regulations 2012, SI 2012/2298, reg 17, Schedule. Date in force: 1 October 2012: see the Money Laundering (Amendment) Regulations 2012, reg 1.

Schedule 4
Connected persons

Corporate bodies

1.

If the relevant person is a body corporate ('BC'), a person who is or has been—

(a)   an officer or manager of BC or of a parent undertaking of BC;

(b)   an employee of BC;

(c)   an agent of BC or of a parent undertaking of BC.

Partnerships

2.

If the relevant person is a partnership, a person who is or has been a member, manager, employee or agent of the partnership.

Unincorporated associations

3.

If the relevant person is an unincorporated association of persons which is not a partnership, a person who is or has been an officer, manager, employee or agent of the association.

Individuals

4.

If the relevant person is an individual, a person who is or has been an employee or agent of that individual.

Appendix 1.6   Extracts from the Joint Money Laundering Steering Group ('JMLSG') Prevention of money laundering/combating terrorist financing 2013 revised version[1]

PART 1: GUIDANCE FOR THE UK FINANCIAL SECTOR (JUNE 2013, REVISED NOVEMBER 2013)

POCA, s 330 (2),(3), s 331 (2), (3) Terrorism Act ss 21A, 21ZA, 21ZB

6.10   Having <u>knowledge</u> means actually knowing something to be true. In a criminal court, it must be proved that the individual *in fact* knew that a person was engaged in money laundering. That said, knowledge can be *inferred* from the surrounding circumstances; so, for example, a failure to ask obvious questions may be relied upon by a jury to imply knowledge. The knowledge must, however, have come to the firm (or to the member of staff) in the course of business, or (in the case of a nominated officer) as a consequence of a disclosure under s 330 of POCA or s 21A of the Terrorism Act. Information that comes to the firm or staff member in other circumstances does not come within the scope of the regulated sector obligation to make a report. This does not preclude a report being made should staff choose to do so, or are obligated to do so by other parts of these Acts.

6.11   <u>Suspicion</u> is more subjective and falls short of proof based on firm evidence. Suspicion has been defined by the courts as being beyond mere speculation and based on some foundation, for example:

> *"A degree of satisfaction and not necessarily amounting to belief but at least extending beyond speculation as to whether an event has occurred or not"*; and

> *"Although the creation of suspicion requires a lesser factual basis than the creation of a belief, it must nonetheless be built upon some foundation."*

6.12   A transaction which appears unusual is not necessarily suspicious. Even customers with a stable and predictable transactions profile will have periodic transactions that are unusual for them. Many customers will, for perfectly good reasons, have an erratic pattern of transactions or account activity. So the unusual is, in the first instance, only a basis for further enquiry, which may in turn

1 © Joint Money Laundering Steering Group ('JMLSG'). Reproduced by kind permission of the JMLSG. For further information please visit www.jmlsg.org.uk.

6.12   require judgement as to whether it is suspicious. A transaction or activity may not be suspicious at the time, but if suspicions are raised later, an obligation to report then arises.

6.13   A member of staff, including the nominated officer, who considers a transaction or activity to be suspicious, would not necessarily be expected either to know or to establish the exact nature of any underlying criminal offence, or that the particular funds or property were definitely those arising from a crime or terrorist financing.

6.14   Transactions, or proposed transactions, as part of '419' scams are attempted advance fee frauds, and not money laundering; they are therefore not reportable under POCA or the Terrorism Act, unless the fraud is successful, and the firm is aware of resulting criminal property.

What is meant by "reasonable grounds to know or suspect"?

POCA, s 330 (2)(b), s 331 (2)(b) Terrorism Act s 21A

6.15   In addition to establishing a criminal offence when suspicion or actual knowledge of money laundering/terrorist financing is proved, POCA and the Terrorism Act introduce criminal liability for failing to disclose information when reasonable grounds exist for knowing or suspecting that a person is engaged in money laundering/terrorist financing. This introduces an objective test of suspicion. The test would likely be met when there are demonstrated to be facts or circumstances, known to the member of staff, from which a reasonable person engaged in a business subject to the ML Regulations would have inferred knowledge, or formed the suspicion, that another person was engaged in money laundering or terrorist financing.

6.16   To defend themselves against a charge that they failed to meet the objective test of suspicion, staff within financial sector firms would need to be able to demonstrate that they took reasonable steps in the particular circumstances, in the context of a risk-based approach, to know the customer and the rationale for the transaction, activity or instruction. It is important to bear in mind that, in practice, members of a jury may decide, with the benefit of hindsight, whether the objective test has been met.

6.17   Depending on the circumstances, a firm being served with a court order in relation to a customer may give rise to reasonable grounds for suspicion in relation to that customer. In such an event, firms should review the information it holds about that customer across the firm, in order to determine whether or not such grounds exist.

Internal reporting

Regulation 20(2)(d)(ii) POCA s 330(5)	6.18	The obligation to report to the nominated officer within the firm where they have grounds for knowledge or suspicion of money laundering or terrorist financing is placed on all relevant employees in the regulated sector. All financial sector firms therefore need to ensure that all relevant employees know who they should report suspicions to.

6.19 Firms may wish to set up internal systems that allow staff to consult with their line manager before sending a report to the nominated officer. The obligation under POCA is to report 'as soon as is reasonably practicable', and so any such consultations should take this into account. Where a firm sets up such systems it should ensure that they are not used to prevent reports reaching the nominated officer whenever staff have stated that they have knowledge or suspicion that a transaction or activity may involve money laundering or terrorist financing.

6.20 Whether or not a member of staff consults colleagues, the legal obligation remains with the staff member to decide for himself whether a report should be made; he must not allow colleagues to decide for him. Where a colleague has been consulted, he himself will then have knowledge on the basis of which he must consider whether a report to the nominated officer is necessary. In such circumstances, firms should make arrangements such that the nominated officer only receives one report in respect of the same information giving rise to knowledge or suspicion.

6.21 Short reporting lines, with a minimum number of people between the person with the knowledge or suspicion and the nominated officer, will ensure speed, confidentiality and swift access to the nominated officer.

6.22 All suspicions reported to the nominated officer should be documented, or recorded electronically. The report should include full details of the customer who is the subject of concern and as full a statement as possible of the information giving rise to the knowledge or suspicion. All internal enquiries made in relation to the report should also be documented, or recorded electronically. This information may be required to supplement the initial report or as evidence of good practice and best endeavours if, at some future date, there is an investigation and the suspicions are confirmed or disproved.

6.23   Once an employee has reported his suspicion in an appropriate manner to the nominated officer, or to an individual to whom the nominated officer has delegated the responsibility to receive such internal reports, he has fully satisfied his statutory obligation.

6.24   Until the nominated officer advises the member of staff making an internal report that no report to the NCA is to be made, further transactions or activity in respect of that customer, whether of the same nature or different from that giving rise to the previous suspicion, should be reported to the nominated officer as they arise.

Non-UK offences

POCA, s 340 (2), (11) SOCPA, s 102	6.25	The offence of money laundering, and the duty to report under POCA, apply in relation to the proceeds of any criminal activity, wherever conducted (including abroad), that would constitute an offence if it took place in the UK. This broad scope excludes offences (other than those referred to in paragraph 6.26) which the firm, staff member or nominated officer knows, or believes on reasonable grounds, to have been committed in a country or territory outside the UK and not to be unlawful under the criminal law then applying in the country or territory concerned.
SI 2006/1070 1968 c 65 1976 c 32 2000 c 8	6.26	Offences committed overseas which the Secretary of State has prescribed by order as remaining within the scope of the duty to report under POCA are those which are punishable by imprisonment for a maximum term in excess of 12 months in any part of the United Kingdom if they occurred there, other than: • an offence under the Gaming Act 1968; • an offence under the Lotteries and Amusements Act 1976; or • an offence under ss 23 or 25 of FSMA
Terrorism Act s 21A(11)	6.27	The duty to report under the Terrorism Act applies in relation to taking any action, or being in possession of a thing, that is unlawful under ss 15–18 of that Act, that would have been an offence under these sections of the Act had it occurred in the UK.

POCA s 331 POCA ss 327–329 Terrorism Act s 21A	6.28	The obligation to consider reporting to the NCA applies only when the nominated officer has received a report made by someone working within the UK regulated sector, or when he himself becomes aware of such a matter in the course of relevant business (which may come from overseas, or from a person overseas). The nominated officer is not, therefore, obliged to report everything that comes to his attention from outside of the UK, although he would be prudent to exercise his judgement in relation to information that comes to his attention from non-business sources. In reaching a decision on whether to make a disclosure, the nominated officer must bear in mind the need to avoid involvement in an offence under ss 327–329 of POCA.

PART II: SECTORAL GUIDANCE (2013 REVIEW VERSION, AMENDED JUNE 2013)

2: Equivalent jurisdictions

This guidance is issued to assist firms by setting out how they might approach their assessment of other jurisdictions, to determine whether they are 'equivalent'. Although it is not formal guidance that has been given Ministerial approval, it has been discussed with RM Treasury and reflects their input.

The guidance discusses jurisdictions where there may be a presumption of equivalence, and those where such a presumption may not be appropriate without further investigation. It then discusses issues that a firm should consider in all cases when coming to a judgement on whether a particular jurisdiction is, in its view, equivalent.

2.1 What is an "equivalent jurisdiction" and why does it matter?

The 3rd European Council Directive on prevention of the use of the financial system for the purpose of money laundering and terrorist financing (the money laundering directive), whilst setting out (in articles 6–9) the obligation on firms to carry out specific customer due diligence (CDD) measures, allows firms (article 11) to carry out simplified due diligence (SDD) in respect of other firms which are subject to the provisions of the directive, and to rely (article 16) on other firms that are subject to the provisions of the directive to carry out CDD measures on their behalf. The money laundering directive also extends these derogations to firms in third countries, in those jurisdictions where they are subject to legal obligations that are 'equivalent' to those laid down in the directive, and where they are supervised for compliance with those obligations.

The Money Laundering Regulations 2007 (the 2007 Regulations) implement the provisions of the money laundering directive into UK law. The 2007 Regulations provide (Regulation 13) that firms may apply SDD where the customer is itself a credit or financial institution which is subject to the requirements of the money laundering directive, or is situated in a non-EEA state which imposes requirements equivalent to those laid down in the money laundering directive. The Regulations also permit (Regulation 17) reliance on firms which carry on business in a non-EEA state which is subject to requirements equivalent to those laid down in the money laundering directive, and which are supervised for compliance with those requirements, to carry out CDD on the relying firm's behalf.

It should be noted that the basis for the exemption in the directive and the Regulations is focused on the provisions of the legislation in a particular jurisdiction, rather than what actually happens in practice (although firms have to be supervised for compliance with the relevant legislation). This applies to both EU Member States and non-EEA states which are "equivalent jurisdictions".

Countries that meet the provisions in Regulations 13 and 17 are described as "equivalent jurisdictions". UK firms therefore need to determine whether a particular jurisdiction is 'equivalent', in order that it may take advantage of the SDD derogation, and/or to determine whether they may rely, for the purposes of carrying out CDD measures, on firms situated in a non-EEA state.

However, 'equivalence' only provides an exemption from the application of CDD measures, in respect of customer identification. It does not exempt the firm from carrying out ongoing monitoring of the business relationship with the customer, nor from the need for such other procedures (such as monitoring) as may be necessary to enable a firm to fulfil its responsibilities under the Proceeds of Crime Act 2002.

Although the judgement on equivalence is one to be made by each firm in the light of the particular circumstances, senior management is accountable for this judgement – either to its regulator, or, if necessary, to a court. It is therefore important that the reasons for concluding that a particular jurisdiction is equivalent (other than those in respect of which a presumption of equivalence may be made) are documented at the time the decision is made, and that it is made on relevant and up to date data or information.

2.2 Categories of country

(a) Countries for which equivalence may be presumed

Jurisdictions where a presumption of equivalence may be made are:

- EU/EEA member states, through the implementation of the money laundering directive

- Countries on a list of equivalent jurisdictions issued by the EU, or by HMT

EU/EEA member states

Member States of the EU/EEA benefit de jure from mutual recognition through the implementation of the money laundering directive.

All Member States of the EU (which, for this purpose, includes Gibraltar as part of the UK, and Aruba as part of the Kingdom of the Netherlands) are required to enact legislation and financial sector procedures in accordance with the money laundering directive. In addition, EU Member States that are part of the Financial Action Task Force (FATF) have committed themselves to implementing the Forty Recommendations, and the Nine Special Recommendations to Combat Terrorist Financing.

All EEA countries have undertaken to implement the money laundering directive, and some are also FATF member countries.

EU members of FATF:		*Other EU member states:*	
Austria	Ireland	Bulgaria	Lithuania
Belgium	Italy	Cyprus	Malta
Denmark	Luxembourg	Czech Republic	Poland
Finland	Netherlands	Estonia	Romania
France	Portugal	Hungary	Slovakia
Germany	Spain	Latvia	Slovenia
Greece	Sweden		

EEA states:
Iceland – Member of FATF
Liechtenstein
Norway – Member of FATF

Although firms may initially presume equivalence, significant variations may exist in the precise measures (and in the timing of their introduction) that have been taken to transpose the money laundering directive (and its predecessors) into national laws and regulations. Moreover, the standards of compliance monitoring in respect of credit and financial institutions will also vary. Where firms have substantive information which indicates that a presumption of equivalence cannot be sustained, either in general or for particular products, they will need to consider whether their procedures should be enhanced to take account of this information.

The status of implementation of the money laundering directive across the EU is available a http://ec.europa.eu/internal market/company/docs/official/080522web en.pdf

EU agreed list

Member states participating in the EU Committee on the Prevention of Money Laundering and Terrorist Financing have agreed a list of equivalent third countries, for the purposes of the relevant parts of the money laundering directive. The list is a voluntary, non-binding measure that nevertheless represents the common understanding of Member States. The text of the statement on equivalence and the list of equivalent jurisdictions are available at http://ec.europa.eu/internal_market/company/financialcrime/index_en.htm#3rdcountry.

The following third countries are currently considered as having equivalent AML/CTF systems to the EU. The list may be reviewed, in particular in the light of public evaluation reports adopted by the FATF, FSRBs, the IMF or the World Bank according to the revised 2003 FATF Recommendations and Methodology.

Australia	Mexico
Brazil	The Russian Federation
Canada	Singapore
Hong Kong	South Africa
India	Switzerland
Japan	The United States
Republic of Korea	

All of the above are members of the FATF.

The list also includes certain **French overseas territories** (Mayotte, New Caledonia, French Polynesia Saint Pierre and Miquelon and Wallis and Futuna) and the **Dutch overseas territories** (Aruba). Those overseas territories are not members of the EU/EEA but are part of the membership of France and the Kingdom of the Netherlands of the FATF.

The **UK Crown Dependencies** (Jersey, Guernsey, Isle of Man) may also be considered as equivalent by Member States. **Gibraltar** is also directly subject to the requirements of the money laundering directive, which it has implemented. It is therefore considered to be equivalent for these purposes.

Firms should note that inclusion on the EU list does not override the need for firms to continue to operate risk-based procedures when dealing with customers based in an equivalent jurisdiction.

(b) Countries for which equivalence should not be presumed

It would not normally be appropriate to make a presumption of equivalence in respect of other countrie without further investigation, notwithstanding that they might be members of other AML/CTF-related bodies.

FATF members

All FATF members (those which are not EU/EEA member states/countries are listed below) undertake to implement the FATF anti-money laundering and counter-terrorism Recommendations as part of thei membership obligations.

However, unlike the transposition of the money laundering directive by EU Member States, implementation cannot be mandatory, and all members will approach their obligations in different ways, and under different timetables. Only those countries listed above under the EU agreed list may be presumed to be equivalent. The others are as follows:

Argentina
China
New Zealand
Turkey

Information on the effectiveness of implementation in these jurisdictions may be obtained through scrutiny of Mutual Evaluation reports, which are published on the FATF website.

Gulf Co-operation Council

The Gulf Co-operation Council (GCC) is in the unique position of being a member of FATF but with non-FATF countries as its members. However, whilst the GCC countries – Bahrain, Kuwait, Oman, Qatar, Saudi Arabia and the United Arab Emirates – have all undergone FATF-style mutual evaluations, few of these reports are publicly available. Moreover, few GCC countries have yet enacted legislation that contains equivalent provisions to the Money Laundering Directive, and so there is unevenness in the position of relevant regulation across GCC member countries. Individual GCC member countries should therefore by assessed in the same way as for other non-EU/FATF jurisdictions.

None of the GCC members is included on the EU agreed lists, so there can be no presumption of equivalence.

Other jurisdictions

A majority of countries and territories do not fall within the lists of countries that can be presumed to be "equivalent jurisdictions". This does not necessarily mean that the AML/CTF legislation, and standards of due diligence, in those countries are lower than those in "equivalent jurisdictions". However, standards vary significantly, and firms will need to carry out their own assessment of particular countries. In addition to a firm's own knowledge and experience of the country concerned, particular attention should be paid to any FATF-style or IMF/World Bank evaluations that have been undertaken.

As a result of due diligence carried out, therefore, jurisdictions may be added to those on the EU agreed list, for the purposes of determining those jurisdictions which, in the firm's judgement, are equivalent, for the purposes of the SDD derogation, and/or determining whether firms may rely, for the purposes of carrying out CDD measures, on other firms situated in such a jurisdiction.

2.3 Factors to be taken into account when assessing other jurisdictions

Factors include:

- embership of groups that only admit those meeting a certain benchmark
- Contextual factors – political stability; level of (endemic) corruption etc
- Evidence of relevant (public) criticism of a jurisdiction, including HMT/FATF advisory notices
- Independent and public assessment of the jurisdiction's overall AML regime
- Need for any assessment to be recent
- Implementation standards (inc quality and effectiveness of supervision)
- ncidence of trade with the jurisdiction – need to be proportionate especially where very small

Membership of an international or regional 'group'

There are a number of international and regional 'groups' of jurisdictions that admit to membership only those jurisdictions that have demonstrated a commitment to the fight against money laundering and terrorist financing, and which have an appropriate legal and regulatory regime to back up thi commitment.

Contextual factors

Such factors as the political stability of a jurisdiction, and where it stands in tables of corruption are relevant to whether it is likely that a jurisdiction will be 'equivalent'. It will, however, seldom be easy for firms to make their own assessments of such matters, and it is likely that they will have to rely on external agencies for such evidence – whether prepared for general consumption, or specifically for the firm. Where the firm looks to publicly available evidence, it will be important that it has some knowledge of the criteria that were used in making the assessment; the firm cannot rely solely on the fact that such a list has been independently prepared, even if by a respected third party agency.

Evidence of relevant (public) criticism

The FATF from time to time issues statements on its concerns about the lack of comprehensive AML/CFT systems in a number of jurisdictions (see section 2.4 below). When constructing thei internal procedures, therefore, financial sector firms should have regard to the need for additiona monitoring procedures for transactions from any country that is listed on these statements of concern Additional monitoring procedures will also be required in respect of correspondent relationships with financial institutions from such countries.

Other, commercial agencies also produce reports and lists of jurisdictions, entities and individuals tha are involved, or that are alleged to be involved, in activities that cast doubt on their integrity in the AML/CTF area. Such reports lists can provide some useful and relevant evidence – which may or may not be conclusive – on whether or not a particular jurisdiction is likely to be equivalent.

Mutual evaluation reports

Particular attention should be paid to assessments that have been undertaken by standard setting bodie such as FATF, and by international financial institutions such as the IMF.

FATF

FATF member countries monitor their own progress in the fight against money laundering and terrorist financing through regular mutual evaluation by their peers. In 1998, FATF extended the concept of mutual evaluation beyond its own membership through its endorsement of FATF-style mutual evaluation programmes of a number of regional groups which contain non-FATF members. The groups undertaking FATF-style mutual evaluations are

- he Offshore Group of Banking Supervisors (OGBS) see www.ogbs.net

- the Caribbean Financial Action Task Force (CFATF) see www.cfatf.org

- the Asia/Pacific Group on Money Laundering (APG) see www.apgml.org

- MONEYVAL, covering the Council of Europe countries which are not members of FATF see www.coe.int/moneyval

- the Financial Action Task Force on Money Laundering in South America (GAFISUD) see www.gafisud.org

- the Middle East and North Africa Financial Action Task Force (MENAFATF) see www.menafatf.org

- the Eurasian Group (EAG) see www.eurasiangroup.org,

- the Eastern and Southern Africa Anti-Money Laundering Group (ESAAMLG) see www.esaamlg.org

- the Intergovernmental Action Group against Money-Laundering in Africa (GIABA) see www.giabasn.org

Firms should bear in mind that mutual evaluation reports are at a 'point in time', and should be interpreted as such. Although follow up actions are usually reviewed after two years, there can be quite long intervals between evaluation reports in respect of a particular jurisdiction. Even at the point an evaluation is carried out there can be changes in train to the jurisdiction's AML/CTF regime, but these will not be reflected in the evaluation report. There can also be subsequent changes to the regime (whether to respond to criticisms by the evaluators or otherwise) which firms should seek to understand and to factor into their assessment of whether the jurisdiction is equivalent.

In assessing the conclusions of a mutual evaluation report, firms may find it difficult to give appropriate weighting to findings and conclusions in respect of the jurisdiction's compliance with particular Recommendations. For the purposes of assessing equivalence, compliance (or otherwise) with certain Recommendations may have more relevance than others. The extent to which a jurisdiction complies with the following Recommendations may be particularly relevant (these are the old Recommendation numbers, as no mutual evaluations have yet been carried out using the revised numbering):

Legal framework:
    Recommendation 1
    Special Recommendation II
Measures to be taken by firms:
    Recommendations 4, 5, 6, 9, 10, 11, and 13,
    Special Recommendation IV
Supervisory regime:
    Recommendations 17, 23, 29 and 30
International co-operation:
    Recommendation 40

Summaries of FATF and FATF-style evaluations are published in FATF Annual Reports and can be accessed at www.fatf-gafi.org. However, mutual evaluation reports prepared by some FATF-style regional bodies may not be carried out fully to FATF standards, and firms should bear this in mind if a decisions on whether a jurisdiction is equivalent is based on such reports.

IMF/World bank

As part of their financial stability assessments of countries and territories, the IMF and the World Bank have agreed with FATF a detailed methodology for assessing compliance with AML/CTF standards, using the FATF Recommendations as the base. A number of countries have already undergone IMF/World Bank assessments in addition to those carried out by FATF, and some of the results can be accessed at www.imf.org. Where IMF/World Bank assessments relate to FATF members, the assessments are formally adopted by the FATF and appear on the FATF website.

Implementation standards (including effectiveness of supervision)

Information on the extent and quality of supervision of AML/CTF standards may be obtained from the extent to which a jurisdiction complies with Recommendations 17, 23, 29 and 30.

Incidence of trade with the jurisdiction

In respect of any particular jurisdiction, the level and extent of due diligence that needs to be carried out in making a judgement on equivalence will be influenced by the volume and size of the firm's business with that jurisdiction in relation to the firm's overall business.

2.4 UK prohibition notices and advisory notices

Prohibition notices

> As at December 2011, no prohibition notices have been issued by HM Treasury under Regulation 18 of the 2007 Regulations.

Advisory notices

HM Treasury

HM Treasury issues press notices in which it expresses the UK's full support of the work of the FATF on jurisdictions of concern. The HM Treasury press notices are available at http://www.hmtreasury.gov.uk/press
    The FATF issues periodic announcements about its concerns regarding the lack of comprehensive AML/CFT systems in various jurisdictions.
    The FATF maintains a Public Statement which lists jurisdictions of concern in three categories:

1. isdictions subject to a FATF call on its members and other jurisdictions to apply countermeasures to protect the international financial system from the ongoing and substantial money laundering and terrorist financing (ML/TF) risks emanating from the jurisdiction.

2   Jurisdictions with strategic AML/CFT deficiencies that have not committed to an action plan developed with the FATF to address key deficiencies. The FATF calls on its members to consider the risks arising from the deficiencies associated with each jurisdiction, as described below.

3   Jurisdictions previously publicly identified by the FATF as having strategic AML/CFT deficiencies, which remain to be addressed.

The FATF also maintains a statement Improving Global AML/CFT Compliance: On-going Process, which lists jurisdictions identified as having strategic AML/

CFT deficiencies for which they have developed an action plan with the FATF. While the situations differ among jurisdictions, each has provided a written high-level political commitment to address the identified deficiencies. The FATF will closely monitor the implementation of these action plans and encourages its members to consider the information set out in the statement.

The latest versions of these FATF Statements are available at http://www.fatf-gafi.org.

FCA

The FCA has set out how it expects firms to use information contained in the FATF Public Statements:

> *"The FCA expects authorised firms to establish and maintain systems and controls to counter the risk that they might be used to further financial crime. All firms must also comply with their legal obligations under the Money Laundering Regulations 2007. We would therefore expect all firms to actively consider the risks associated with transactions and business relationships linked to urisdictions included within these statements. Policies and procedures must be adapted where necessary to reflect this.*

"We also expect firms supervised by the FCA for money laundering purposes to consider the impact of these statements on their policies and procedures in relation to simplified due diligence under section 13 and reliance under section 17 of the Money Laundering Regulations 2007".

Appendix 1.7 Draft of the 4th EU Anti-Money Laundering Directive

Proposal for a Directive of the European Parliament and of the Council

on the prevention of the use of the financial system for the purpose of money laundering and terrorist financing

Explanatory memorandum

1 Context of the proposal

Grounds for and objectives of the proposal

The main objectives of the measures proposed are to strengthen the Internal Market by reducing complexity across borders, to safeguard the interests of society from criminality and terrorist acts, to safeguard the economic prosperity of the European Union by ensuring an efficient business environment, to contribute to financial stability by protecting the soundness, proper functioning and integrity of the financial system.

These objectives will be achieved by ensuring consistency between the EU approach and the international one; ensuring consistency between national rules, as well as flexibility in their implementation; ensuring that the rules are risk-focused and adjusted to address new emerging threats.

In addition, this proposal incorporates and repeals Commission Directive 2006/70/EC of 1 August 2006 laying down implementing measures for Directive 2005/60/EC[1], thus improving the comprehensibility and accessibility of the anti-money laundering (AML) legislative framework for all stakeholders.

The Commission intends to complement the current proposal by strengthening the EU's repressive response to money laundering. Consequently it is planned to propose criminal law harmonisation for this offence based on Article 83(1) of the Treaty on the Functioning of the European Union (TFEU) in 2013[2].

Notes
1   OJ L 214, 4.8.2006, p. 29.
2   http://ec.europa.eu/governance/impact/planned_ia/docs/2013_home_006_money_laundering_en.pdf

---

General context

The breaking down of barriers within the Internal Market facilitates not only the establishment or development of legitimate businesses across the EU, but may

304

also provide increased opportunities for money laundering and terrorist financing. Criminals engaged in money laundering could therefore attempt to conceal or disguise the true nature, source or ownership of the assets in question and transform them into seemingly legitimate proceeds. Moreover, terrorist financing can be funded through both legitimate and criminal activities, as terrorist organisations engage in revenue-generating activities which in themselves may be, or at least appear to be, legitimate. Money laundering and terrorism financing create thus a high risk to the integrity, proper functioning, reputation and stability of the financial system, with potentially devastating consequences for the broader society.

European legislation has been adopted to protect the proper functioning of the financial system and of the Internal Market. However, the changing nature of money laundering and terrorist financing threats, facilitated by a constant evolution of technology and of the means at the disposal of criminals, requires a permanent adaptation of the legal framework to counter such threats.

At the EU level, Directive 2005/60/EC of 26 October 2005 on the prevention of the use of the financial system for the purpose of money laundering and terrorist financing[3] (hereinafter referred to as the Third AMLD) sets out the framework designed to protect the soundness, integrity and stability of credit and financial institutions and confidence in the financial system as a whole, against the risks of money laundering and terrorist financing. The EU rules are to a large extent based on international standards adopted by the Financial Action Task Force (FATF) and, as the Directive follows a minimum harmonisation approach, the framework is completed by rules adopted at national level.

At international level, the FATF has undertaken a fundamental review of the international standards and adopted a new set of Recommendations in February 2012.

In parallel to the international process, the European Commission has been undertaking its own review of the European framework. A revision of the Directive at this time is complementary to the revised FATF Recommendations, which in themselves represent a substantial strengthening of the anti-money laundering and combating terrorist financing framework. The Directive itself further strengthens elements of the revised Recommendations, in particular in relation to scope (by including providers of gambling services and dealers in goods with a threshold of EUR 7 500), beneficial ownership information (which is to be made available to obliged entities and competent authorities), and in the provisions on sanctions. It takes into account the necessity to increase effectiveness of AML measures by adapting the legal framework to ensure that risk assessments are carried out at the appropriate level and with the necessary degree of flexibility to allow adaptation to the different situations and actors. As a consequence of this, the Directive, while setting a high level of common standards, requires Member States, supervisory authorities and obliged entities to assess risk and take adequate mitigating measures commensurate to such risk. This results in the Directive being less detailed as regards concrete measures to be taken.

Notes
3   OJ L 309, 25.11.2005, p.15.

Existing provisions in this area

Various legal instruments have been adopted to ensure an effective anti-money laundering and combating terrorist financing framework at EU level. The most important ones are:

- The Third AML Directive, which covers most of the 40 FATF Recommendations and some of the 9 FATF Special Recommendations;

- Regulation (EC) No 1781/2006 of 15 November 2006 on information on the payer accompanying transfers of funds[4], which implements FATF SR VII on wire transfers;

- Regulation (EC) No 1889/2005 of 26 October 2005 on controls of cash entering or leaving the Community[5], which implements FATF SR IX on cash couriers;

- Directive 2007/64/EC of 13 December 2007 on payment services in the internal market[6] (Payment Services Directive) which, in combination with the Third AMLD, implements FATF SR VI on alternative remittance;

- Regulation (EC) No 2580/2001 of 27 December 2001 on specific restrictive measures directed against certain persons and entities with a view to combating terrorism[7] which, together with Regulation (EC) No 881/2002 of 27 May 2002 implementing UN Al Qai'da and Taliban sanctions, implements part of FATF SR III on freezing terrorist assets.

Notes
4   OJ L 345, 8.12.2006, p. 1.
5   OJ L 309, 25.11.2005, p. 9.
6   OJ L 319, 5.12.2007, p. 1.
7   OJ L 344, 28.12.2001, p. 70.

Consistency with other policies and objectives of the Union

The proposed adaptation of the anti-money laundering and combating terrorist financing framework is fully coherent with EU policies in other areas. In particular:

- the Stockholm Programme[9], which aims at achieving an open and secure Europe serving and protecting citizens, calls on Member States and the Commission to further develop information exchange between the FIUs, in the fight against money laundering;

- the EU's Internal Security Strategy[10] identifies the most urgent challenges to EU security in the years to come and proposes five strategic objectives and specific actions for 2011–2014 to help make the EU more secure. This includes tackling money laundering and preventing terrorism. The need to update the EU anti-money laundering and combating terrorist financing framework with a view to enhancing the transparency of legal persons and legal arrangements has been specifically recognised;

- the potential for misuse of new technologies to conceal transactions and hide identity makes it important for Member States to be aware of technological developments and simulate the use of electronic identification, electronic signature and trust services for electronic transactions, in line with Commission's proposal for a Regulation on electronic identification and trust services for electronic transactions in the internal market[11];

- in March 2012, the European Commission adopted a proposal on the freezing and confiscation of proceeds of crime in the EU[12] which seeks to ensure that Member States have in place an efficient system to freeze, manage and confiscate criminal assets, backed by the necessary institutional setup, financial and human resources;

- with respect to data protection, the proposed clarifications to the Third AMLD are fully in line with the approach set out in the Commission's recent data protection proposals[13], whereby a specific provision[14] empowers EU or national legislation to restrict the scope of the obligations and rights provided for in the draft regulation on a number of specified grounds, including the prevention, investigation, detection and prosecution of criminal offences;

– with respect to sanctions, the proposal to introduce a set of minimum principles-based rules to strengthen administrative sanctions is fully in line with the Commission's policy as outlined in its Communication 'Reinforcing sanctioning regimes in the financial services sector'[15];

– with respect to financial inclusion, the fact that applying an overly cautious approach to anti-money laundering and combating terrorist financing safeguards might have the unintended consequence of excluding legitimate businesses and consumers from the financial system has been recognised. Work has been carried out on this issue at international level[16] to provide guidance to support countries and their financial institutions in designing anti-money laundering and combating terrorist financing measures that meet the national goal of financial inclusion, without compromising the measures that exist for the purpose of combating crime. At EU level, the issue of financial inclusion is currently under consideration as part of the work on a Bank Accounts package;

– with respect to the cooperation with persons or authorities (including courts and administrative bodies) concerned with the assessment of, collection of, the enforcement or prosecution in respect of, or the determination of appeals in relation to taxes and any other public levy, the proposal is consistent with the approach for fighting against tax fraud and tax evasion[17] followed at international level in including a specific reference to tax crimes within the serious crimes which can be considered as predicate offences to money laundering. The enhancement of the customer due diligence procedures for AML purposes will also assist the fight against tax fraud and tax evasion.

Notes

9   OJ L 139, 29.5.2002, p. 9.
10   OJ C 115, 4.5.2010, p. 1.
11   Communication from the Commission to the European Parliament and the Council 'The EU Internal Security Strategy in Action: Five steps towards a more secure Europe' (COM(2010)673 final).
12   COM(2012)238/2
13   Proposal for a Directive of the European Parliament and of the Council on the freezing and confiscation of proceeds of crime in the European Union (COM(2012)085 final).
14   Proposal for a Directive of the European Parliament and of the Council on the protection of individuals with regard to the processing of personal data by competent authorities for the purposes of prevention, investigation, detection or prosecution of criminal offences or the execution of criminal penalties, and the free movement of such data (COM(2012)010 final) and Proposal for a Regulation of the European Parliament and of the Council on the protection of individuals with regard to the processing of personal data and on the free movement of such data (General Data Protection Regulation) (COM(2012)011 final).
15   Article 21 of the General Data Protection Regulation.
16   COM(2010)716 final.
17   'Anti-money laundering and terrorist financing measures and Financial Inclusion', FATF, June 2011.

---

2 Results of consultations with the interested parties and impact assessment

Consultation of interested parties

The Commission adopted in April 2012 a report on the application of the Third AMLD and solicited comments from all stakeholders. The report focused on a number of identified key themes (e.g. including application of a risk-based approach, extending the scope of the existing framework, adjusting the approach to customer due diligence, clarifying reporting obligations and supervisory powers, enhancing FIU co-operation etc.), which were essential for the review of the Third AMLD.

The Commission received 77 contributions from public authorities, civil society, business federations and companies in several fields (including financial services, gambling sector, liberal professions, real estate sector, trust and company service providers), representing a broad variety of stakeholders. An additional number of comments, position papers and contributions were received outside the consultation.

The overall results of the consultation[18] point to a general confirmation of the issues and problems highlighted by the Commission's Report, as well as broad support for the proposed alignment to the revised FATF standards and for greater clarification in certain areas (i.e. data protection and how to apply the rules in cross-border situations).

Notes
18   The feedback statement is available at http://ec.europa.eu/internal_market/ company/financial-crime/index_en.htm

---

Use of expertise

Substantial efforts have been made to obtain evidence in this field and to ensure full engagement of the different stakeholders.

In particular, over the course of 2010, a study by external consultants Deloitte[19] was carried out on behalf of the Commission to look into the application of the Third AML Directive.

Notes
19   The study is available at http://ec.europa.eu/internal_market/company/financial-crime/index_en.htm

---

Impact assessment

The Commission has undertaken an Impact Assessment[20], where it analysed the potential consequences of money laundering and terrorism financing. In particular, the financial system failing to prevent money laundering and terrorist financing can lead to negative economic impacts (arising from disruptions to international capital flows, reduced investment and lower economic growth) and financial market instability (resulting from reluctance of other financial intermediaries to engage in business, loss of reputation, drop in confidence and prudential risks).

The following problem drivers were examined:

−   the different application of existing EU rules across Member States, leading to reduced legal certainty;

−   the inadequacies and loopholes with respect to the current EU rules;

−   the inconsistency of the current rules with the recently revised international standards.

This requires the achievement of the following operational objectives:

- ensure consistency between national rules and, where appropriate, flexibility in their implementation by strengthening and clarifying current requirements;

- ensure that the rules are risk-focused and adjusted to address new emerging threats, by strengthening and clarifying current requirements;

- ensure that the EU approach is consistent with the approach followed at international level by extending the scope of application, strengthening and clarifying the current requirements.

The impact assessment concluded that the best options to improve the existing situation would be:

- *Broadening scope to cover gambling*: broaden the scope of the Directive beyond 'casinos' to cover the gambling sector;

- *Thresholds for traders in goods*: reduce the scope and customer due diligence thresholds for traders in high value goods from EUR 15 000 to EUR 7 500 for cash transactions;

- *Sanctions regimes*: introduce a set of minimum principles-based rules to strengthen administrative sanctions;

- *Comparability of statistical data*: reinforce and make more precise the requirement regarding the collecting and reporting of statistical data;

- *Data protection*: introduce provisions in the Directive to clarify the interaction between anti-money laundering/combating terrorist financing and data protection requirements;

- *Inclusion of tax crimes in the scope*: include an explicit reference to tax crimes as a predicate offence;

- *Availability of beneficial owner information*: require all companies to hold information on their beneficial owners;

- *Identification of Beneficial Owner (BO)*: maintain the approach which requires identification of the BO as of a 25% ownership threshold, but clarify what the '25% threshold' refers to;

- *Home and host supervisory responsibilities for AML*: introduce new rules clarifying that branches and subsidiaries situated in other Member States than the head office apply host state AML rules and reinforce cooperation arrangements between home and host supervisors;

- *Cross-border cooperation between Financial Intelligence Units (FIUs)*: introduce new requirements that would strengthen FIU powers and cooperation;

- *National Risk Assessments*: introduce a requirement for Member States to carry out a risk assessment at national level and take measures to mitigate risks;

- *Customer Due Diligence*: Member States to ensure that enhanced due diligence must be conducted in certain situations of high risk, while allowing them to permit simplified due diligence in lower risk situations;

- *Equivalence of third country regimes*: remove the 'white list' process;

- *Risk-Sensitive Approach to supervision*: specific recognition in the Directive that supervision can be carried out on a risk-sensitive basis;

- *Treatment of Politically Exposed Persons (PEPs)*: introduce new requirements for domestic PEPs/PEPs working in international organisations, with risk-sensitive measures to be applied.

In addition, the impact assessment analysed the impact of the legislative proposals on Fundamental Rights. In line with the Charter of Fundamental rights, the proposals seek in particular to ensure protection of personal data (Article 8 of the Charter) by clarifying the conditions under which personal data can be stored and transferred. The proposals will bring no change and therefore have no impact on the right to an effective remedy and to a fair trial (Article 47 of the Charter) which are not infringed by the Directive as confirmed by the European Court of Justice (case C-305/05). The respect for private life (Article 7), the freedom to conduct a business (Article 16) and the prohibition of discrimination (Article 21) have been duly taken into account. Finally, the proposal will indirectly help to protect the right to life (Article 2 of the Charter).

Notes

20   The impact assessment is available at http://ec.europa.eu/internal_market/company/financial-crime/index_en.htm

---

3 Legal elements of the proposal

Legal basis

The current proposal is based on Article 114 TFEU.

Subsidiarity and proportionality

In accordance with the principles of subsidiarity and proportionality as set out in Article 5 of the Treaty on European Union, the objectives of the proposal cannot be sufficiently achieved by Member States and can therefore be better achieved at the Union level. The proposal does not go beyond what is necessary to achieve those objectives.

Recital 2 of the Third AMLD underlines the necessity of having measures at the EU level aiming at protecting the soundness, integrity and stability of credit and financial institutions and confidence in the financial system as a whole, 'in order to avoid Member States adopting measures to protect their financial systems which could be inconsistent with the functioning of the internal market and with the prescriptions of the rule of law and Community public policy, Community action in this area is necessary'.

As massive flows of dirty money and terrorist financing can damage the stability and reputation of the financial sector and threaten the internal market, any measures adopted solely at national level could have adverse effects on the EU Single Market: an absence of coordinated rules across Member States aimed at protecting their financial systems could be inconsistent with the functioning of the internal market and result in fragmentation. EU action is also justified in order to maintain a level playing field across the EU – with entities in all Member States subject to a consistent set of anti-money laundering and combating terrorist financing obligations.

The Commission considers that the proposed rule changes are proportionate to the objectives. By imposing thresholds on scope and customer due diligence, the Commission has taken proportionate steps to limit the applicability of the Directive, where appropriate. In addition, the Directive allows certain of the preventative measures to be taken by SMEs to be proportionate to the size and nature of the obliged entity. At the same time, by ensuring a tailored and flexible risk-based approach, Member States should not be constrained from adopting measures and taking actions as necessary to counter important threats they may confront at national level. These measures are better suited to a Directive than a fully harmonised Regulation, with the inclusion of processes at EU level to ensure greater coordination and the development of supranational approaches, together with further harmonisation in specific areas ensuring that EU objectives are also met. Although ensuring an effective AML/counter terrorism financing system entails some cost for obliged entities (these costs have been analysed in the Impact Assessment), the Commission considers that the benefits associated with preventing money laundering and terrorist financing will continue to outweigh the costs.

The evaluation of the new international standards will begin in the fourth quarter of 2013. Unless the Commission provides clear and early indications of the desired EU approach to their implementation, there is a risk that those EU Member States who will be evaluated first will opt for solutions which may not coincide with the proposed EU approach, thus rendering agreement of common EU rules more difficult.

Finally, with the adoption of revised international standards, commitments have been taken by the Commission as well as all EU Member States (either directly or via their membership of FATF or Moneyval) to ensure their implementation.

4 Budgetary implication

The proposal has no implication for the budget of the European Union.

5 Additional information

Detailed explanation of the proposal

The main modifications to the Third AMLD are:

– *Extension of the scope of the Directive*: two main changes are proposed to the scope:

(a) the threshold for traders in high value goods dealing with cash payments be reduced from EUR 15 000 to EUR 7 500. Currently traders in goods are included in the scope of the Directive if they deal with cash payments of EUR 15 000 or more. After receiving information from Member States that this relatively high threshold was being exploited by criminals it is proposed to lower it to EUR 7 500. In addition, the new proposal requires traders to carry out customer due diligence when carrying out an occasional transaction of at least EUR 7 500, a reduction from the previous threshold of EUR 15 000. Both the definition and the threshold show a tightening of measures against the use of these traders for money laundering purposes across the EU;

(b) the scope of the Directive includes 'providers of gambling services' (in accordance with Directive 2000/31/EC of 8 June 2000 on certain legal aspects of information society services, in particular electronic commerce, in the Internal Market[21]). The current Third AMLD and the revised FATF Recommendations require that only casinos be included in the scope of anti-money laundering/combating terrorist financing legislation. Evidence in the EU suggests that this leaves other areas of gambling vulnerable to miss-use by criminals.

– *Risk-based approach*: The Directive recognises that the use of a risk-based approach is an effective way to identify and mitigate risks to the financial system and wider economic stability in the internal market area. The new measures proposed would require evidence-based measures to be implemented in three main areas, each of which would be supplemented with a minimum list of factors to be taken into consideration or guidance to be developed by the European Supervisory Authorities:

(a) Member States will be required to identify, understand and mitigate the risks facing them. This can be supplemented by risk assessment work carried out at a supra-national level (e.g. by the European Supervisory Authorities or Europol) and the results should be shared with other Member States and obliged entities. This would be the starting point for the risk-based approach, and would recognise that an EU-wide response can be informed by Member States' national experience;

(b) Obliged entities operating within the scope of the Directive would be required to identify, understand and mitigate their risks, and to document and update the assessments of risk that they undertake. This is a key element of the risk-based approach, allowing competent authorities (such as supervisors) within Member States to thoroughly review and understand the decisions made by obliged entities under their supervision. Ultimately, those adopting a risk-based approach would be fully accountable for the decisions they make;

(c) The proposal would recognise that the resources of supervisors can be used to concentrate on areas where the risks of money laundering and terrorist financing are greater. The use of a risk-based approach would mean that evidence is used to better target the risks.

–   *Simplified and Enhanced Customer Due Diligence*: in the proposal, obliged entities would be required to take enhanced measures where risks are greater and may be permitted to take simplified measures where risks are demonstrated to be less. With regard to the current (Third) AMLD, the provisions on simplified due diligence were found to be overly permissive, with certain categories of client or transaction being given outright exemptions from due diligence requirements. The revised Directive would therefore tighten the rules on simplified due diligence and would not permit situations where exemptions apply. Instead, decisions on when and how to undertake simplified due diligence would have to be justified on the basis of risk, while minimum requirements of the factors to be taken into consideration would be given. In one of the situations where enhanced due diligence should always be conducted, namely for politically exposed persons, the Directive has been strengthened to include politically exposed persons who are entrusted with prominent public functions domestically, as well as those who work for international organisations.

–   *Information on the beneficial owner*: the revised Directive proposes new measures in order to provide enhanced clarity and accessibility of beneficial ownership information. It requires legal persons to hold information on their own beneficial ownership. This information should be made available to both competent authorities and obliged entities. For legal arrangements, trustees are required to declare their status when becoming a customer and information on beneficial ownership is similarly required to be made available to competent authorities and obliged entities.

–   *Third country equivalence*: the revised Directive will remove the provisions relating to positive 'equivalence', as the customer due diligence regime is becoming more strongly risk-based and the use of exemptions on the grounds of purely geographical factors is less relevant. The current provisions of the Third AMLD require decisions to be made on whether third countries have anti-money laundering/combating terrorist financing systems that are 'equivalent' to those in the EU. This information was then used to allow exemptions for certain aspects of customer due diligence.

- *Administrative sanctions*: in line with Commission policy to align administrative sanctions, the revised Directive contains a range of sanctions that Member States should ensure are available for systematic breaches of key requirements of the Directive, namely customer due diligence, record keeping, suspicious transaction reporting and internal controls.

- *Financial Intelligence Units*: the proposal would bring in the provisions of Council Decision 2000/642/JHA of 17 October 2000 concerning arrangements for cooperation between financial intelligence units of the Member States in respect of exchanging information and further extend and strengthen cooperation.

- *European Supervisory Authorities (ESA)*: the proposal contains several areas where work by the ESA is envisaged. In particular, EBA, EIOPA and ESMA are asked to carry out an assessment and provide an opinion on the money laundering and terrorist financing risks facing the EU. In addition, the greater emphasis on the risk-based approach requires an enhanced degree of guidance for Member States and financial institutions on what factors should be taken into account when applying simplified customer due diligence and enhanced customer due diligence and when applying a risk-based approach to supervision. In addition, the ESAs have been tasked with providing regulatory technical standards for certain issues where financial institutions have to adapt their internal controls to deal with specific situations.

- *Data Protection*: the need to strike a balance between allowing robust systems and controls and preventative measures against money laundering and terrorist financing on the one hand, and protecting the rights of data subjects on the other is reflected in the proposal.

- *Transposition measures*: Due to the complexity and scope of the proposal, Member States are required to transmit a correlation table of the provisions of their national law and the Directive.

Notes
21   OJ L 178, 17.7.2000, p. 1.

European Economic Area

The proposal is relevant for the EEA countries.

Proposal for a Directive of the European Parliament and of the Council

on the prevention of the use of the financial system for the purpose of money laundering and terrorist financing

The European Parliament and the Council of the European Union,

Having regard to the Treaty on the Functioning of the European Union, and in particular Article 114 thereof,
  Having regard to the proposal from the European Commission,
  After transmission of the draft legislative act to the national Parliaments,
  Having regard to the opinion of the European Economic and Social Committee,
  Having regard to the opinion of the European Central Bank,
  After consulting the European Data Protection Supervisor,
  Acting in accordance with the ordinary legislative procedure,

Whereas:

(1) Massive flows of dirty money can damage the stability and reputation of the financial sector and threaten the single market, and terrorism shakes the very foundations of our society. In addition to the criminal law approach, a preventive effort via the financial system can produce results.

(2) The soundness, integrity and stability of credit and financial institutions and confidence in the financial system as a whole could be seriously jeopardised by the efforts of criminals and their associates either to disguise the origin of criminal proceeds or to channel lawful or unlawful money for terrorist purposes. In order to facilitate their criminal activities, money launderers and terrorist financers could try to take advantage of the freedom of capital movements and the freedom to supply financial services which the integrated financial area entails, if certain coordinating measures are not adopted at Union level.

(3) The current proposal is the fourth Directive to deal with the threat of money laundering. Council Directive 91/308/EEC of 10 June 1991 on prevention of the use of the financial system for the purpose of money laundering[1] defined money laundering in terms of drugs offences and imposed obligations solely on the financial sector. Directive 2001/97/EC of the European Parliament and of the Council of December 2001 amending Council Directive 91/308/EEC[2] extended the scope both in terms of the crimes covered and the range of professions and activities covered. In June 2003 the Financial Action Task Force (hereinafter referred to as the FATF) revised its Recommendations to cover terrorist financing, and provided more detailed requirements in relation to customer identification and verification, the situations where a higher risk of money laundering may justify enhanced measures and also situations where a reduced risk may justify less rigorous controls. These changes were reflected in Directive 2005/60/EC of the European Parliament and of the Council of 26 October 2005 on the prevention of the use of the financial system for the purpose of money laundering and terrorist financing[3] and Commission Directive 2006/70/EC of 1 August 2006 laying down implementing measures for Directive 2005/60/EC of the European Parliament and of the Council as regards the definition of politically exposed person and the technical criteria for simplified customer due diligence procedures and for exemption on grounds of a financial activity conducted on an occasional or very limited basis[4].

(4) Money laundering and terrorist financing are frequently carried out in an international context. Measures adopted solely at national or even European Union level, without taking account of international coordination and cooperation, would have very limited effects. The measures adopted by the European Union in this field should therefore be consistent with other action undertaken in other international fora. The European Union action should continue to take particular account of the Recommendations of the FATF, which constitutes the foremost international body active in the fight against money laundering and terrorist financing. With the view to reinforce the efficacy of the fight against money laundering and terrorist financing, Directives 2005/60/EC and 2006/70/EC should be aligned with the new FATF Recommendations adopted and expanded in February 2012.

(5) Furthermore, the misuse of the financial system to channel criminal or even clean money to terrorist purposes poses a clear risk to the integrity, proper functioning, reputation and stability of the financial system. Accordingly, the preventive measures of this Directive should cover not only the manipulation of money derived from crime but also the collection of money or property for terrorist purposes.

(6) The use of large cash payments is vulnerable to money laundering and terrorist financing. In order to increase vigilance and mitigate the risks posed

by cash payments natural or legal persons trading in goods should be covered by this Directive to the extent that they make or receive cash payments of EUR 7 500 or more. Member States may decide to adopt stricter provisions including a lower threshold.

(7) Legal professionals, as defined by the Member States, should be subject to the provisions of this Directive when participating in financial or corporate transactions, including providing tax advice, where there is the greatest risk of the services of those legal professionals being misused for the purpose of laundering the proceeds of criminal activity or for the purpose of terrorist financing. There should, however, be exemptions from any obligation to report information obtained either before, during or after judicial proceedings, or in the course of ascertaining the legal position of a client. Thus, legal advice should remain subject to the obligation of professional secrecy unless the legal counsellor is taking part in money laundering or terrorist financing, the legal advice is provided for money laundering or terrorist financing purposes or the lawyer knows that the client is seeking legal advice for money laundering or terrorist financing purposes.

(8) Directly comparable services should be treated in the same manner when provided by any of the professionals covered by this Directive. In order to ensure the respect of the rights guaranteed by the Charter of Fundamental Rights of the European Union, in the case of auditors, external accountants and tax advisors, who, in some Member States, may defend or represent a client in the context of judicial proceedings or ascertain a client's legal position, the information they obtain in the performance of those tasks should not be subject to the reporting obligations in accordance with this Directive.

(9) It is important to expressly highlight that 'tax crimes' related to direct and indirect taxes are included in the broad definition of 'criminal activity' under this Directive in line with the revised FATF Recommendations.

(10) There is a need to identify any natural person who exercises ownership or control over a legal person. While finding a percentage shareholding will not automatically result in finding the beneficial owner, it is an evidential factor to be taken into account. Identification and verification of beneficial owners should, where relevant, extend to legal entities that own other legal entities, and should follow the chain of ownership until the natural person who exercises ownership or control of the legal person that is the customer is found.

(11) The need for accurate and up-to-date information on the beneficial owner is a key factor in tracing criminals who might otherwise hide their identity behind a corporate structure. Member States should therefore ensure that companies retain information on their beneficial ownership and make this information available to competent authorities and obliged entities. In addition, trustees should declare their status to obliged entities.

(12) This Directive should also apply to those activities of the obliged entities covered by this Directive which are performed on the internet.

(13) The use of the gambling sector to launder the proceeds of criminal activity is of concern. In order to mitigate the risks related to the sector and to provide parity amongst the providers of gambling services, an obligation for all providers of gambling services to conduct customer due diligence for single transactions of EUR 2 000 or more should be laid down. Member States should consider applying this threshold to the collection of winnings as well as wagering a stake. Providers of gambling services with physical premises (e.g. casinos and gaming houses) should ensure that customer due diligence, if it is taken at the point of entry to the premises, can be linked to the transactions conducted by the customer on those premises.

(14) The risk of money laundering and terrorist financing is not the same in every case. Accordingly, a risk-based approach should be used. The risk-based approach is not an unduly permissive option for Member States and obliged entities. It involves the use of evidence-based decision making to better target the money laundering and terrorist financing risks facing the European Union and those operating within it.

(15) Underpinning the risk-based approach is a need for Member States to identify, understand and mitigate the money laundering and terrorist financing risks it faces. The importance of a supra-national approach to risk identification has been recognised at international level, and the European Supervisory Authority (European Banking Authority) (hereinafter 'EBA'), established by Regulation (EU) No 1093/2010 of the European Parliament and of the Council of 24 November 2010 establishing a European Supervisory Authority (European Banking Authority), amending Decision No 716/2009/EC and repealing Commission Decision 2009/78/EC[5]; the European Supervisory Authority (European Insurance and Occupational Pensions Authority) (hereinafter 'EIOPA'), established by Regulation (EU) No 1094/2010 of the European Parliament and of the Council of 24 November 2010 establishing a European Supervisory Authority (European Insurance and Occupational Pensions Authority), amending Decision No 716/2009/EC and repealing Commission Decision 2009/79/EC[6]; and the European Supervisory Authority (European Securities and Markets Authority) (hereinafter 'ESMA'), established by Regulation (EU) No 1095/2010 of the European Parliament and of the Council of 24 November 2010 establishing a European Supervisory Authority (European Securities and Markets Authority), amending Decision No 716/2009/EC and repealing Commission Decision 2009/77/EC[7], should be tasked with issuing an opinion on the risks affecting the financial sector.

(16) The results of risk assessments at Member State level should, where appropriate, be made available to obliged entities to enable them to identify, understand and mitigate their own risks.

(17) In order to better understand and mitigate risks at European Union level, Member States should share the results of their risk assessments with each other, the Commission and EBA, EIOPA and ESMA, where appropriate.

(18) When applying the provisions of this Directive, it is appropriate to take account of the characteristics and needs of small obliged entities which fall under its scope, and to ensure a treatment which is appropriate to the specific needs of small obliged entities, and the nature of the business.

(19) Risk itself is variable in nature, and the variables, either on their own or in combination, may increase or decrease the potential risk posed, thus having an impact on the appropriate level of preventative measures, such as customer due diligence measures. Thus, there are circumstances in which enhanced due diligence should be applied and others in which simplified due diligence may be appropriate.

(20) It should be recognised that certain situations present a greater risk of money laundering or terrorist financing. Although the identity and business profile of all customers should be established, there are cases where particularly rigorous customer identification and verification procedures are required.

(21) This is particularly true of business relationships with individuals holding, or having held, important public positions, particularly those from countries where corruption is widespread. Such relationships may expose the financial sector in particular to significant reputational and legal risks. The international effort to combat corruption also justifies the need to pay special attention to such cases and to apply appropriate enhanced customer due diligence measures in respect of persons who hold or have held prominent functions domestically or abroad and senior figures in international organisations.

(22) Obtaining approval from senior management for establishing business relationships need not, in all cases, imply obtaining approval from the board of directors. Granting of such approval should be possible by someone with sufficient knowledge of the institution's money laundering and terrorist financing risk exposure and sufficient seniority to make decisions affecting its risk exposure.

(23) In order to avoid repeated customer identification procedures, leading to delays and inefficiency in business, it is appropriate, subject to suitable safeguards, to allow customers whose identification has been carried out elsewhere to be introduced to the obliged entities. Where an obliged entity relies on a third party, the ultimate responsibility for the customer due diligence procedure remains with the obliged entity to whom the customer is introduced. The third party, or the person that has introduced the customer, should also retain his own responsibility for compliance with the requirements in this Directive, including the requirement to report suspicious transactions and maintain records, to the extent that he has a relationship with the customer that is covered by this Directive.

(24) In the case of agency or outsourcing relationships on a contractual basis between obliged entities and external natural or legal persons not covered by this Directive, any anti money laundering and anti-terrorist financing obligations for those agents or outsourcing service providers as part of the obliged entities, may only arise from contract and not from this Directive. The responsibility for complying with this Directive should remain with the obliged entity covered hereby.

(25) All Member States have, or should, set up financial intelligence units (hereinafter referred to as FIUs) to collect and analyse the information which they receive with the aim of establishing links between suspicious transactions and underlying criminal activity in order to prevent and combat money laundering and terrorist financing. Suspicious transactions should be reported to the FIUs, which should serve as a national centre for receiving, analysing and disseminating to the competent authorities suspicious transaction reports and other information regarding potential money laundering or terrorist financing. This should not compel Member States to change their existing reporting systems where the reporting is done through a public prosecutor or other law enforcement authorities, as long as the information is forwarded promptly and unfiltered to FIUs, allowing them to perform their tasks properly, including international cooperation with other FIUs.

(26) By way of derogation from the general prohibition on executing suspicious transactions, obliged entities may execute suspicious transactions before informing the competent authorities, where refraining from the execution thereof is impossible or likely to frustrate efforts to pursue the beneficiaries of a suspected money laundering or terrorist financing operation. This, however, should be without prejudice to the international obligations accepted by the Member States to freeze without delay funds or other assets of terrorists, terrorist organisations or those who finance terrorism, in accordance with the relevant United Nations Security Council resolutions.

(27) Member States should have the possibility to designate an appropriate self-regulatory body of the professions referred to in Article 2(1)(3)(a),(b), and (d) as the authority to be informed in the first instance in place of the FIU. In line with the case law of the European Court of Human Rights, a system of first instance reporting to a self-regulatory body constitutes an important safeguard to uphold the protection of fundamental rights as concerns the reporting obligations applicable to lawyers.

(28) Where a Member State decides to make use of the exemptions provided for in Article 33(2), it may allow or require the self-regulatory body representing

the persons referred to therein not to transmit to the FIU any information obtained from those persons in the circumstances referred to in that Article.

(29) There have been a number of cases of employees who report their suspicions of money laundering being subjected to threats or hostile action. Although this Directive cannot interfere with Member States' judicial procedures, this is a crucial issue for the effectiveness of the anti-money laundering and anti-terrorist financing system. Member States should be aware of this problem and should do whatever they can to protect employees from such threats or hostile action.

(30) Directive 95/46/EC of the European Parliament and of the Council of 24 October 1995 on the protection of individuals with regard to the processing of personal data and on the free movement of such data[8], as implemented in national law, is applicable to the processing of personal data for the purposes of this Directive.

(31) Certain aspects of the implementation of this Directive involve the collection, analysis, storage and sharing of data. The processing of personal data should be permitted in order to comply with the obligations laid down in this Directive, including carrying out of customer due diligence, ongoing monitoring, investigation and reporting of unusual and suspicious transactions, identification of the beneficial owner of a legal person or legal arrangement, sharing of information by competent authorities and sharing of information by financial institutions. The personal data collected should be limited to what is strictly necessary for the purpose of complying with the requirements of this Directive and not further processed in a way inconsistent with Directive 95/46/EC. In particular, further processing of personal data for commercial purposes should be strictly prohibited.

(32) The fight against money-laundering and terrorist financing is recognised as an important public interest ground by all Member States.

(33) This Directive is without prejudice to the protection of personal data processed in the framework of police and judicial cooperation in criminal matters, including the provisions of Framework decision 977/2008/JHA.

(34) The rights of access of the data subject are applicable to the personal data processed for the purpose of this Directive. However, access by the data subject to information contained in a suspicious transaction report would seriously undermine the effectiveness of the fight against money laundering and terrorist financing. Limitations to this right in accordance with the rules laid down in Article 13 of Directive 95/46/EC may therefore be justified.

(35) Persons who merely convert paper documents into electronic data and are acting under a contract with a credit institution or a financial institution do not fall within the scope of this Directive, nor does any natural or legal person that provides credit or financial institutions solely with a message or other support systems for transmitting funds or with clearing and settlement systems.

(36) Money laundering and terrorist financing are international problems and the effort to combat them should be global. Where Union credit and financial institutions have branches and subsidiaries located in third countries where the legislation in this area is deficient, they should, in order to avoid the application of very different standards within the institution or group of institutions, apply Union standards or notify the competent authorities of the home Member State if application of such standards is impossible.

(37) Feedback should, where practicable, be made available to obliged entities on the usefulness and follow-up of the suspicious transactions reports they present. To make this possible, and to be able to review the effectiveness of

their systems to combat money laundering and terrorist financing Member States should keep and improve the relevant statistics. To further enhance the quality and consistency of the statistical data collected at Union level, the Commission should keep track of the EU-wide situation with respect to the fight against money laundering and terrorist financing and publish regular overviews.

(38) Competent authorities should ensure that, in regard to currency exchange offices, trust and company service providers or gambling service providers, the persons who effectively direct the business of such entities and the beneficial owners of such entities are fit and proper persons. The criteria for determining whether or not a person is fit and proper should, as a minimum, reflect the need to protect such entities from being misused by their managers or beneficial owners for criminal purposes.

(39) Taking into account the transnational character of money laundering and terrorist financing, co-ordination and co-operation between EU FIUs are extremely important. This co-operation has so far only been addressed by Council Decision 2000/642/JHA of 17 October 2000 concerning arrangements for cooperation between financial intelligence units of the Member States in respect of exchanging information[9]. In order to ensure better co-ordination and cooperation between FUIs, and in particular to ensure that suspicious transactions reports reach the FIU of the Member State where the report would be of most use, more detailed, further going and up-dated rules should be included in this Directive.

(40) Improving the exchange of information between FIUs within the EU is of particular importance to face the transnational character of money laundering and terrorist financing. The use of secure facilities for the exchange of information, especially the decentralised computer network FIU.net and the techniques offered by that network should be encouraged by Member States.

(41) The importance of combating money laundering and terrorist financing should lead Member States to lay down effective, proportionate and dissuasive sanctions in national law for failure to respect the national provisions adopted pursuant to this Directive. Member States currently have a diverse range of administrative measures and sanctions for breaches of the key preventative measures. This diversity could be detrimental to the efforts put in combating money laundering and terrorist financing and the Union's response is at risk of being fragmented. This Directive should therefore include a range of administrative measures and sanctions that Member States shall have available for systematic breaches of the requirements relating to customer due diligence measures, record keeping, reporting of suspicious transactions and internal controls of obliged entities. This range should be sufficiently broad to allow Member States and competent authorities to take account of the differences between obliged entities, in particular between financial institutions and other obliged entities, as regards their size, characteristics and areas of activity. In the application of this Directive, Member States should ensure that the imposition of administrative measures and sanctions in accordance with this Directive and of criminal sanctions in accordance with national law does not breach the principle of ne bis in idem.

(42) Technical standards in financial services should ensure consistent harmonisation and adequate protection of depositors, investors and consumers across the Union. As bodies with highly specialised expertise, it would be efficient and appropriate to entrust EBA, EIOPA and ESMA with the elaboration of draft regulatory technical standards which do not involve policy choices, for submission to the Commission.

(43) The Commission should adopt the draft regulatory technical standards developed by EBA, EIOPA and ESMA pursuant to Article 42 of this Directive

by means of delegated acts pursuant to Article 290 of the Treaty on the Functioning of the European Union and in accordance with Articles 10 to 14 of Regulation (EU) No 1093/2010, Regulation (EU) No 1094/2010 and Regulation (EU) No 1095/2010.

(44) In view of the very substantial amendments that would need to be made to Directive 2005/60/EC and Directive 2006/70/EC, they should be merged and replaced for reasons of clarity and consistency.

(45) Since the objective of this Directive, namely the protection of the financial system by means of prevention, investigation and detection of money laundering and terrorist financing, cannot be sufficiently achieved by the Member States, as individual measures adopted by Member States to protect their financial systems could be inconsistent with the functioning of the internal market and with the prescriptions of the rule of law and Union public policy and can therefore, by reason of the scale and effects of the action, be better achieved at Union level, the Union may adopt measures, in accordance with the principle of subsidiarity as set out in Article 5 of the Treaty on European Union. In accordance with the principle of proportionality, as set out in that Article, this Directive does not go beyond what is necessary in order to achieve that objective.

(46) This Directive respects the fundamental rights and observes the principles recognised by the Charter of Fundamental Rights of the European Union, in particular, the respect for private and family life, the right to protection of personal data, the freedom to conduct a business, the prohibition of discrimination, the right to an effective remedy and to a fair trial, and the right of defence.

(47) In line with Article 21 of the EU Charter of Fundamental Rights prohibiting any discrimination based on any ground, Member States have to ensure that this Directive is implemented, as regards risk assessments in the context of customer due diligence, without discrimination.

(48) In accordance with the Joint Political Declaration of Member States and the Commission of 28 September 2011 on explanatory documents, Member States have undertaken to accompany, in justified cases, the notification of their transposition measures with one or more documents explaining the relationship between the components of a directive and the corresponding parts of national transposition instruments. With regard to this Directive, the legislator considers the transmission of such documents to be justified,

---

Notes

1   OJ L 166, 28.6.1991, p. 77.
2   OJ L 344, 28.12.2001, p. 76.
3   OJ L 309, 25.11.2005, p. 15.
4   OJ L 214, 4.8.2006, p. 29.
5   OJ L 331, 15.12.2010, p. 12.
6   OJ L 331, 15.12.2010, p. 48.
7   OJ L 331, 15.12.2010, p. 84.
8   OJ L 281, 23.11.1995, p. 31.
9   OJ L 271, 24.10.2000, p. 4.

Have adopted this Directive:

Chapter I
General provisions

Section 1
Scope and definitions

Article 1

1.   Member States shall ensure that money laundering and terrorist financing are prohibited.

2.   For the purposes of this Directive, the following conduct, when committed intentionally, shall be regarded as money laundering:

(a)   the conversion or transfer of property, knowing that such property is derived from criminal activity or from an act of participation in such activity, for the purpose of concealing or disguising the illicit origin of the property or of assisting any person who is involved in the commission of such activity to evade the legal consequences of his action;

(b)   the concealment or disguise of the true nature, source, location, disposition, movement, rights with respect to, or ownership of property, knowing that such property is derived from criminal activity or from an act of participation in such activity;

(c)   the acquisition, possession or use of property, knowing, at the time of receipt, that such property was derived from criminal activity or from an act of participation in such activity;

(d)   participation in, association to commit, attempts to commit and aiding, abetting, facilitating and counselling the commission of any of the actions referred to in points (a), (b) and (c).

3.   Money laundering shall be regarded as such even where the activities which generated the property to be laundered were carried out in the territory of another Member State or in that of a third country.

4.   For the purposes of this Directive, 'terrorist financing' means the provision or collection of funds, by any means, directly or indirectly, with the intention that they should be used or in the knowledge that they are to be used, in full or in part, in order to carry out any of the offences within the meaning of Articles 1 to 4 of Council Framework Decision 2002/475/JHA of 13 June 2002 on combating terrorism[10], as amended by Council Framework Decision 2008/919/JHA of 28 November 2008[11].

5.   Knowledge, intent or purpose required as an element of the activities referred to in paragraphs 2 and 4 may be inferred from objective factual circumstances.

Notes
10   OJ L 164, 22.6.2002, p. 3.
11   OJ L 330, 9.12.2008, p. 21–23.

Article 2

1.   This Directive shall apply to the following obliged entities:

(1) credit institutions;

(2) financial institutions;

(3) the following legal or natural persons acting in the exercise of their professional activities:

  (a) auditors, external accountants and tax advisors;

  (b) notaries and other independent legal professionals, when they participate, whether by acting on behalf of and for their client in any financial or real estate transaction, or by assisting in the planning or execution of transactions for their client concerning the:

    (i)   buying and selling of real property or business entities;

    (ii) managing of client money, securities or other assets;

    (iii) opening or management of bank, savings or securities accounts;

    (iv) organisation of contributions necessary for the creation, operation or management of companies;

    (v) creation, operation or management of trusts, companies or similar structures;

  (c) trust or company service providers not already covered under points (a) or (b);

  (d) real estate agents, including letting agents;

  (e) other natural or legal persons trading in goods, only to the extent that payments are made or received in cash in an amount of EUR 7 500 or more, whether the transaction is executed in a single operation or in several operations which appear to be linked;

  (f) providers of gambling services.

2.   Member States may decide that legal and natural persons, who engage in a financial activity on an occasional or very limited basis where there is little risk of money laundering or terrorist financing occurring, do not fall within the scope of this Directive provided that the legal or natural person fulfils all of the following criteria:

(a) the financial activity is limited in absolute terms;

(b) the financial activity is limited on a transaction basis;

(c) the financial activity is not the main activity;

(d) the financial activity is ancillary and directly related to the main activity;

(e) the main activity is not an activity mentioned in paragraph 1, with the exception of the activity referred to in point (3)(e) of paragraph 1;

(f) the financial activity is provided only to the customers of the main activity and is not generally offered to the public.

The previous subparagraph shall not apply to the legal and natural persons engaged in the activity of money remittance within the meaning of Article 4(13) of Directive 2007/64/EC of the European Parliament and of the Council of 13 November 2007 on payment services in the internal market amending Directives 97/7/EC, 2002/65/EC, 2005/60/EC and 2006/48/EC and repealing Directive 97/5/EC[12].

3.   For the purposes of point (a) of paragraph 2, Member States shall require that the total turnover of the financial activity may not exceed a threshold which must

be sufficiently low. That threshold shall be established at national level, depending on the type of financial activity.

4.   For the purposes of point (b) of paragraph 2, Member States shall apply a maximum threshold per customer and single transaction, whether the transaction is carried out in a single operation or in several operations which appear to be linked. That threshold shall be established at national level, depending on the type of financial activity. It shall be sufficiently low in order to ensure that the types of transactions in question are an impractical and inefficient method for laundering money or for terrorist financing, and shall not exceed EUR 1 000.

5.   For the purposes of point (c) of paragraph 2, Member States shall require that the turnover of the financial activity does not exceed 5 % of the total turnover of the legal or natural person concerned.

6.   In assessing the risk of money laundering or terrorist financing occurring for the purposes of this Article, Member States shall pay special attention to any financial activity which is regarded as particularly likely, by its nature, to be used or abused for money laundering or terrorist financing purposes.

7.   Any decision pursuant to this Article shall state the reasons on which it is based. Member States shall provide for the possibility of withdrawing that decision should circumstances change.

8.   Member States shall establish risk-based monitoring activities or take any other adequate measures to ensure that the exemption granted by decisions pursuant to this Article is not abused.

Notes
12   OJ L 319, 5.12.2007, p. 1.

Article 3

For the purposes of this Directive the following definitions shall apply:

(1)   'credit institution' means a credit institution, as defined in Article 4(1) of Directive 2006/48/EC of the European Parliament and of the Council of 14 June 2006 relating to the taking up and pursuit of the business of credit institutions[13], including branches within the meaning of Article 4(3) of that Directive located in the European Union of credit institutions having their head offices inside or outside the European Union;

(2)   'financial institution' means:

(a)   an undertaking, other than a credit institution, which carries out one or more of the operations included in points 2 to 12 and points 14 and 15 of Annex I to Directive 2006/48/EC, including the activities of currency exchange offices (bureaux de change);

(b)   an insurance company duly authorised in accordance with Directive 2002/83/EC of the European Parliament and of the Council of 5 November 2002 concerning life assurance[14], insofar as it carries out activities covered by that Directive;

(c)   an investment firm as defined in point 1 of Article 4(1) of Directive 2004/39/EC of the European Parliament and of the Council of 21 April 2004 on markets in financial instruments[15];

(d)   a collective investment undertaking marketing its units or shares;

(e) an insurance intermediary as defined in Article 2(5) of Directive 2002/92/EC of the European Parliament and of the Council of 9 December 2002 on insurance mediation[16], with the exception of intermediaries as mentioned in Article 2(7) of that Directive, when they act in respect of life insurance and other investment related services;

(f) branches, when located in the European Union, of financial institutions as referred to in points (a) to (e), whose head offices are inside or outside the European Union;

(3) 'property' means assets of every kind, whether corporeal or incorporeal, movable or immovable, tangible or intangible, and legal documents or instruments in any form including electronic or digital, evidencing title to or an interest in such assets;

(4) 'criminal activity' means any kind of criminal involvement in the commission of the following serious crimes:

(a) acts as defined in Articles 1 to 4 of Framework Decision 2002/475/JHA on combatting terrorism, as amended by Council Framework Decision 2008/919/JHA of 28 November 2008;

(b) any of the offences referred in Article 3(1)(a) of the 1988 United Nations Convention against Illicit Traffic in Narcotic Drugs and Psychotropic Substances;

(c) the activities of criminal organisations as defined in Article 1 of Council Joint Action 98/733/JHA of 21 December 1998 on making it a criminal offence to participate in a criminal organisation in the Member States of the European Union[17];

(d) fraud affecting the Union's financial interests, at least serious, as defined in Article 1(1) and Article 2 of the Convention on the Protection of the European Communities' Financial Interests[18];

(e) corruption;

(f) all offences, including tax crimes related to direct taxes and indirect taxes, which are punishable by deprivation of liberty or a detention order for a maximum of more than one year or, as regards those States which have a minimum threshold for offences in their legal system, all offences punishable by deprivation of liberty or a detention order for a minimum of more than six months;

(5) 'beneficial owner' means any natural person(s) who ultimately owns or controls the customer and/or the natural person on whose behalf a transaction or activity is being conducted. The beneficial owner shall at least include:

(a) in the case of corporate entities:

(i) the natural person(s) who ultimately owns or controls a legal entity through direct or indirect ownership or control over a sufficient percentage of the shares or voting rights in that legal entity, including through bearer share holdings, other than a company listed on a regulated market that is subject to disclosure requirements consistent with European Union legislation or subject to equivalent international standards.

A percentage of 25% plus one share shall be evidence of ownership or control through shareholding and applies to every level of direct and indirect ownership;

(ii) if there is any doubt that the person(s) identified in point (i) are the beneficial owner(s), the natural person(s) who exercises control over the management of a legal entity through other means;

(b) in the case of legal entities, such as foundations, and legal arrangements, such as trusts, which administer and distribute funds:

    (i) the natural person(s) who exercises control over 25 % or more of the property of a legal arrangement or entity; and

    (ii) where the future beneficiaries have already been determined, the natural person(s) who is the beneficiary of 25 % or more of the property of a legal arrangement or entity; or

    (iii) where the individuals that benefit from the legal arrangement or entity have yet to be determined, the class of persons in whose main interest the legal arrangement or entity is set up or operates. For beneficiaries of trusts that are designated by characteristics or by class, obliged entities shall obtain sufficient information concerning the beneficiary to satisfy itself that it will be able to establish the identity of the beneficiary at the time of the payout or when the beneficiary intends to exercise vested rights;

(6) 'trust or company service providers' means any natural or legal person which by way of business provides any of the following services to third parties:

(a) forming companies or other legal persons;

(b) acting as or arranging for another person to act as a director or secretary of a company, a partner of a partnership, or a similar position in relation to other legal persons;

(c) providing a registered office, business address, correspondence or administrative address and other related services for a company, a partnership or any other legal person or arrangement;

(d) acting as or arranging for another person to act as a trustee of an express trust or a similar legal arrangement;

(e) acting as or arranging for another person to act as a nominee shareholder for another person other than a company listed on a regulated market that is subject to disclosure requirements in conformity with European Union legislation or subject to equivalent international standards;

(7)

(a) 'foreign politically exposed persons' means natural persons who are or have been entrusted with prominent public functions by a third country;

(b) 'domestic politically exposed persons' means natural persons who are or who have been entrusted by a Member State with prominent public functions;

(c) 'persons who are or who have been entrusted with a prominent function by an international organisation' means directors, deputy directors and members of the board or equivalent function of an international organisation;

(d) 'natural persons who are or have been entrusted with prominent public functions' shall include the following:

    (i) heads of State, heads of government, ministers and deputy or assistant ministers;

    (ii) members of parliaments;

    (iii) members of supreme courts, of constitutional courts or of other high-level judicial bodies whose decisions are not subject to further appeal, except in exceptional circumstances;

    (iv) members of courts of auditors or of the boards of central banks;

> > (v) ambassadors, chargés d'affaires and high-ranking officers in the armed forces;
>
> > (vi) members of the administrative, management or supervisory bodies of State owned enterprises.
>
> None of the categories set out in points (i) to (vi) shall be understood as covering middle ranking or more junior officials;
>
> (e) 'family members' shall include the following:
>
> > (i) the spouse;
> >
> > (ii) any partner considered as equivalent to the spouse;
> >
> > (iii) the children and their spouses or partners;
> >
> > (iv) the parents;
>
> (f) 'persons known to be close associates' shall include the following:
>
> > (i) any natural person who is known to have joint beneficial ownership of legal entities or legal arrangements, or any other close business relations, with a person referred to in points (7)(a) to (7)(d) above;
> >
> > (ii) any natural person who has sole beneficial ownership of a legal entity or legal arrangement which is known to have been set up for the benefit de facto of the person referred to in points (7)(a) to (7)(d) above;

(8) 'senior management' means an officer or employee with sufficient knowledge of the institution's money laundering and terrorist financing risk exposure and sufficient seniority to make decisions affecting its risk exposure. It need not, in all cases, involve a member of the board of directors;

(9) 'business relationship' means a business, professional or commercial relationship which is connected with the professional activities of the obliged entities and which is expected, at the time when the contact is established, to have an element of duration;

(10) 'gambling services' means any service which involves wagering a stake with monetary value in games of chance including those with an element of skill such as lotteries, casino games, poker games and betting transactions that are provided at a physical location, or by any means at a distance, by electronic means or any other technology for facilitating communication, and at the individual request of a recipient of services;

(11) 'group' has the meaning given to it in Article 2(12) of Directive 2002/87/EC of the European Parliament and of the Council of 16 December 2002 on the supplementary supervision of credit institutions, insurance undertakings and investment firms in a financial conglomerate[19].

Notes
13   OJ L 177, 30.6.2006, p. 1.
14   OJ L 345, 19.12.2002, p. 1.
15   OJ L 145, 30.4.2004, p. 1.
16   OJ L 9, 15.1.2003, p. 3.
17   OJ L 351, 29.12.1998, p. 1.
18   OJ C 316, 27.11.1995, p. 49.
19   OJ L 35, 11.2.2003, p. 1.

Article 4

1.   Member States shall ensure that the provisions of this Directive are extended in whole or in part to professions and to categories of undertakings, other than the obliged entities referred to in Article 2(1), which engage in activities which are particularly likely to be used for money laundering or terrorist financing purposes.

2.   Where a Member State decides to extend the provisions of this Directive to professions and to categories of undertakings other than those referred to in Article 2(1), it shall inform the Commission thereof.

Article 5

The Member States may adopt or retain in force stricter provisions in the field covered by this Directive to prevent money laundering and terrorist financing.

Section 2
Risk assessment

Article 6

1.   The European Banking Authority (hereinafter 'EBA'), European Insurance and Occupational Pensions Authority (hereinafter 'EIOPA') and European Securities and Markets Authority (hereinafter 'ESMA') shall provide a joint opinion on the money laundering and terrorist financing risks affecting the internal market.

The opinion shall be provided within 2 years from the date of entry into force of this Directive.

2.   The Commission shall make the opinion available to assist Member States and obliged entities to identify, manage and mitigate the risk of money laundering and terrorist financing.

Article 7

1.   Each Member State shall take appropriate steps to identify, assess, understand and mitigate the money laundering and terrorist financing risks affecting it, and keep the assessment up-to-date.

2.   Each Member State shall designate an authority to co-ordinate the national response to the risks referred to in paragraph 1. The identity of that authority shall be notified to the Commission, EBA, EIOPA and ESMA and other Member States.

3.   In carrying out the assessments referred to in paragraph 1, Member States may make use of the opinion referred to in Article 6(1).

4.   Each Member State shall carry out the assessment referred to in paragraph 1 and:

(a)   use the assessment(s) to improve its anti-money laundering and combating terrorist financing regime, in particular by identifying any areas where obliged entities shall apply enhanced measures and, where appropriate, specifying the measures to be taken;

(b)   use the assessment(s) to assist it in the allocation and prioritisation of resources to combat money laundering and terrorist financing;

(c)   make appropriate information available to obliged entities to carry out their own money laundering and terrorist financing risk assessments.

5.   Member States shall make the results of their risk assessments available to the other Member States, the Commission, and EBA, EIOPA and ESMA upon request.

Article 8

1.   Member States shall ensure that obliged entities take appropriate steps to identify and assess their money laundering and terrorist financing risks taking into account risk factors including customers, countries or geographic areas, products, services, transactions or delivery channels. These steps shall be proportionate to the nature and size of the obliged entities.

2.   The assessments referred to in paragraph 1 shall be documented, kept up to date and be made available to competent authorities and self-regulatory bodies.

3.   Member States shall ensure that obliged entities have policies, controls and procedures to mitigate and manage effectively the money laundering and terrorist financing risks identified at Union level, Member State level, and at the level of obliged entities. Policies, controls and procedures should be proportionate to the nature and size of those obliged entities.

4.   The policies and procedures referred to in paragraph 3 shall at least include:

(a) the development of internal policies, procedures and controls, including customer due diligence, reporting, record keeping, internal control, compliance management (including, when appropriate to the size and nature of the business, the appointment of a compliance officer at management level) and employee screening;

(b) when appropriate with regard to the size and nature of the business, an independent audit function to test internal policies, procedures and controls referred to in point (a).

5.   Member States shall require obliged entities to obtain approval from senior management for the policies and procedures they put in place, and shall monitor and enhance the measures taken, where appropriate.

Chapter II
Customer due diligence

Section 1
General provisions

Article 9

Member States shall prohibit their credit and financial institutions from keeping anonymous accounts or anonymous passbooks. Member States shall in all cases require that the owners and beneficiaries of existing anonymous accounts or anonymous passbooks be made the subject of customer due diligence measures as soon as possible and in any event before such accounts or passbooks are used in any way.

Article 10

Member States shall ensure that obliged entities apply customer due diligence measures in the following cases:

(a) when establishing a business relationship;

(b)   when carrying out occasional transactions amounting to EUR 15 000 or more, whether the transaction is carried out in a single operation or in several operations which appear to be linked;

(c)   for natural or legal persons trading in goods, when carrying out occasional transactions in cash amounting to EUR 7 500 or more, whether the transaction is carried out in a single operation or in several operations which appear to be linked;

(d)   for providers of gambling services, when carrying out occasional transactions amounting to EUR 2 000 or more, whether the transaction is carried out in a single operation or in several operations which appear to be linked;

(e)   when there is a suspicion of money laundering or terrorist financing, regardless of any derogation, exemption or threshold;

(f)   when there are doubts about the veracity or adequacy of previously obtained customer identification data.

Article 11

1.   Customer due diligence measures shall comprise:

(a)   identifying the customer and verifying the customer's identity on the basis of documents, data or information obtained from a reliable and independent source;

(b)   identifying the beneficial owner and taking reasonable measures to verify his identity so that the institution or person covered by this Directive is satisfied that it knows who the beneficial owner is, including, as regards legal persons, trusts and similar legal arrangements, taking reasonable measures to understand the ownership and control structure of the customer;

(c)   assessing and, as appropriate, obtaining information on the purpose and intended nature of the business relationship;

(d)   conducting ongoing monitoring of the business relationship including scrutiny of transactions undertaken throughout the course of that relationship to ensure that the transactions being conducted are consistent with the institution's or person's knowledge of the customer, the business and risk profile, including, where necessary, the source of funds and ensuring that the documents, data or information held are kept up-to-date.

2.   Member States shall ensure that obliged entities apply each of the customer due diligence requirements set out in paragraph 1, but may determine the extent of such measures on a risk-sensitive basis.

3.   When assessing money laundering and terrorist financing risks, Member States shall require obliged entities to take into account at least the variables set out in Annex I.

4.   Member States shall ensure that obliged entities are able to demonstrate to competent authorities or self-regulatory bodies that the measures are appropriate in view of the risks of money laundering and terrorist financing that have been identified.

5.   For life or other investment-related insurance business, Member States shall ensure that financial institutions shall, in addition to the customer due diligence measures required for the customer and the beneficial owner, conduct the following customer due diligence measures on the beneficiaries of life insurance and other investment related insurance policies, as soon as the beneficiaries are identified or designated:

(a) for beneficiaries that are identified as specifically named natural or legal persons or legal arrangements, taking the name of the person;

(b) for beneficiaries that are designated by characteristics or by class or by other means, obtaining sufficient information concerning those beneficiaries to satisfy the financial institution that it will be able to establish the identity of the beneficiary at the time of the payout.

For both the cases referred to in points (a) and (b), the verification of the identity of the beneficiaries shall occur at the time of the payout. In case of assignment, in whole or in part, of the life or other investment related insurance to a third party, financial institutions aware of the assignment shall identify the beneficial owner at the time of the assignment to the natural or legal person or legal arrangement receiving for own benefit the value of the policy assigned.

Article 12

1.   Member States shall require that the verification of the identity of the customer and the beneficial owner takes place before the establishment of a business relationship or the carrying-out of the transaction.

2.   By way of derogation from paragraph 1, Member States may allow the verification of the identity of the customer and the beneficial owner to be completed during the establishment of a business relationship if this is necessary not to interrupt the normal conduct of business and where there is little risk of money laundering or terrorist financing occurring. In such situations these procedures shall be completed as soon as practicable after the initial contact.

3.   By way of derogation from paragraphs 1 and 2, Member States may allow the opening of a bank account provided that there are adequate safeguards in place to ensure that transactions are not carried out by the customer or on its behalf until full compliance with paragraphs 1 and 2 is obtained.

4.   Member States shall require that, where the institution or person concerned is unable to comply with points (a), (b) and (c) of Article 11(1), it shall not carry out a transaction through a bank account, establish a business relationship or carry out the transaction, and shall consider terminating the business relationship and making a suspicious transaction report to the financial intelligence unit (FIU) in accordance with Article 32 in relation to the customer.

Member States shall not apply the previous subparagraph to, notaries, other independent legal professionals, auditors, external accountants and tax advisors only to the strict extent that such exemption relates to ascertaining the legal position for their client or performing their task of defending or representing that client in, or concerning judicial proceedings, including advice on instituting or avoiding proceedings.

5.   Member States shall require that obliged entities apply the customer due diligence procedures not only to all new customers but also at appropriate times to existing customers on a risk-sensitive basis, including at times when the relevant circumstances of a customer change.

Section 2
Simplified customer due diligence

Article 13

1.   Where a Member State or an obliged entity identifies areas of lower risk, that Member State may allow obliged entities to apply simplified customer due diligence measures.

2. Before applying simplified customer due diligence measures obliged entities shall ascertain that the customer relationship or transaction presents a lower degree of risk.

3. Member States shall ensure that obliged entities carry out sufficient monitoring of the transaction or business relationship to enable the detection of unusual or suspicious transactions.

Article 14

When assessing the money laundering and terrorist financing risks relating to types of customers, countries or geographic areas, and particular products, services, transactions or delivery channels, Member States and obliged entities shall take into account at least the factors of potentially lower risk situations set out in Annex II.

Article 15

EBA, EIOPA and ESMA shall issue guidelines addressed to competent authorities and the obliged entities referred to in Article 2(1)(1) and (2) in accordance with Article 16 of Regulation (EU) No 1093/2010, of Regulation (EU) No 1094/2010, and of Regulation (EU) No 1095/2010, on the risk factors to be taken into consideration and/or the measures to be taken in situations where simplified due diligence measures are appropriate. Specific account should be taken of the nature and size of the business, and where appropriate and proportionate, specific measures should be foreseen. These guidelines shall be issued within 2 years of the date of entry into force of this Directive.

Section 3
Enhanced customer due diligence

Article 16

1. In cases identified in Articles 17 to 23 of this Directive and in other cases of higher risks that are identified by Member States or obliged entities, Member States shall require obliged entities to apply enhanced customer due diligence measures to manage and mitigate those risks appropriately.

2. Member States shall require obliged entities to examine, as far as reasonably possible, the background and purpose of all complex, unusual large transactions, and all unusual patterns of transactions, which have no apparent economic or lawful purpose. In particular, they shall increase the degree and nature of monitoring of the business relationship, in order to determine whether those transactions or activities appear unusual or suspicious.

3. When assessing the money laundering and terrorist financing risks, Member States and obliged entities shall take into account at least the factors of potentially higher-risk situations set out in Annex III.

4. EBA, EIOPA and ESMA shall issue guidelines addressed to competent authorities and the obliged entities referred to Article 2(1)(1) and (2) in accordance with Article 16 of Regulation (EU) No 1093/2010, of Regulation (EU) No 1094/2010, and of Regulation (EU) No 1095/2010 on the risk factors to be taken into consideration and/or the measures to be taken in situations where enhanced due diligence measures need to be applied. Those guidelines shall be issued within 2 years of the date of entry into force of this Directive.

Article 17

In respect of cross-frontier correspondent banking relationships with respondent institutions from third countries, Member States shall, in addition to the customer due diligence measures as set out in Article 11, require their credit institutions to:

(a) gather sufficient information about a respondent institution to understand fully the nature of the respondent's business and to determine from publicly available information the reputation of the institution and the quality of supervision;

(b) assess the respondent institution's anti-money laundering and anti-terrorist financing controls;

(c) obtain approval from senior management before establishing new correspondent banking relationships;

(d) document the respective responsibilities of each institution;

(e) with respect to payable-through accounts, be satisfied that the respondent credit institution has verified the identity of and performed ongoing due diligence on the customers having direct access to accounts of the correspondent and that it is able to provide relevant customer due diligence data to the correspondent institution, upon request.

Article 18

In respect of transactions or business relationships with foreign politically exposed persons, Member States shall, in addition to the customer due diligence measures set out in Article 11, require obliged entities to:

(a) have appropriate risk-based procedures to determine whether the customer or the beneficial owner of the customer is such a person;

(b) obtain senior management approval for establishing or continuing business relationships with such customers;

(c) take adequate measures to establish the source of wealth and source of funds that are involved in the business relationship or transaction;

(d) conduct enhanced ongoing monitoring of the business relationship.

Article 19

In respect of transactions or business relationships with domestic politically exposed persons or a person who is or has been entrusted with a prominent function by an international organisation, Member States shall, in addition to the customer due diligence measures set out in Article 11, require obliged entities:

(a) to have appropriate risk-based procedures to determine whether the customer or the beneficial owner of the customer is such a person;

(b) in cases of higher risk business relationships with such persons, to apply the measures referred to in points (b), (c) and (d) of Article 18.

Article 20

Obliged entities shall take reasonable measures to determine whether the beneficiaries of a life or other investment related insurance policy and/or, where required, the beneficial owner of the beneficiary are politically exposed persons. Those measures shall be taken at the latest at the time of the payout or at the time of the assignment, in whole or in part, of the policy. Where there are higher risks identified, in addition to taking normal customer due diligence measures, Member States shall require obliged entities to:

(a) inform senior management before the payout of the policy proceeds;

(b) conduct enhanced scrutiny on the whole business relationship with the policyholder.

Article 21

The measures referred to in Articles 18, 19 and 20 shall also apply to family members or persons known to be close associates of such politically exposed persons.

Article 22

Where a person referred to in Articles 18, 19 and 20 has ceased to be entrusted with a prominent public function by a Member State or a third country or with a prominent function by an international organisation, obliged entities shall be required to consider the continuing risk posed by that person and to apply such appropriate and risk-sensitive measures until such time as that person is deemed to pose no further risk. This period of time shall not be less than 18 months.

Article 23

1. Member States shall prohibit credit institutions from entering into or continuing a correspondent banking relationship with a shell bank and shall require that credit institutions take appropriate measures to ensure that they do not engage in or continue correspondent banking relationships with a bank that is known to permit its accounts to be used by a shell bank.

2. For the purposes of paragraph 1, 'shell bank' shall mean a credit institution, or an institution engaged in equivalent activities, incorporated in a jurisdiction in which it has no physical presence, involving meaningful mind and management, and which is unaffiliated with a regulated financial group.

Section 4
Performance by third parties

Article 24

Member States may permit the obliged entities to rely on third parties to meet the requirements laid down in Article 11(1)(a), (b) and (c). However, the ultimate responsibility for meeting those requirements shall remain with the obliged entity which relies on the third party.

Article 25

1. For the purposes of this Section, 'third parties' shall mean obliged entities who are listed in Article 2, or other institutions and persons situated in Member States or a third country, who apply customer due diligence requirements and record keeping requirements equivalent to those laid down in this Directive and their compliance with the requirements of this Directive is supervised in accordance with Section 2 of Chapter VI.

2. The Member States shall consider information available on the level of geographical risk when deciding if a third country meets the conditions laid down in paragraph 1 and shall inform each other, the Commission and EBA, EIOPA and ESMA to the extent relevant for the purposes of this Directive and in accordance with the relevant provisions of Regulation (EU) No 1093/2010, of Regulation (EU) No 1094/2010, and of Regulation (EU) No 1095/2010, of cases where they consider that a third country meets such conditions.

Article 26

1.   Member States shall ensure that obliged entities obtain from the third party being relied upon the necessary information concerning the requirements laid down in Article 11(1)(a), (b) and (c).

2.   Member States shall ensure that obliged entities to which the customer is being referred take adequate steps to ensure that relevant copies of identification and verification data and other relevant documentation on the identity of the customer or the beneficial owner are immediately forwarded, on request, by the third party.

Article 27

Member States shall ensure that the home competent authority (for group-wide policies and controls) and the host competent authority (for branches and subsidiaries) may consider that an obliged entity applies the measures contained in Article 25(1) and 26 through its group programme, where the following conditions are fulfilled:

(a)   an obliged entity relies on information provided by a third party that is part of the same group;

(b)   that group applies customer due diligence measures, rules on record keeping and programmes against money laundering and terrorist financing in accordance with this Directive or equivalent rules;

(c)   the effective implementation of requirements referred to in point (b) is supervised at group level by a competent authority.

Article 28

This Section shall not apply to outsourcing or agency relationships where, on the basis of a contractual arrangement, the outsourcing service provider or agent is to be regarded as part of the obliged entity.

Chapter III
Beneficial ownership information

Article 29

1.   Member States shall ensure that corporate or legal entities established within their territory obtain and hold adequate, accurate and current information on their beneficial ownership.

2.   Member States shall ensure that the information referred to in paragraph 1 of this Article can be accessed in a timely manner by competent authorities and by obliged entities.

Article 30

1.   Member States shall ensure that trustees of any express trust governed under their law obtain and hold adequate, accurate and current information on beneficial ownership regarding the trust. This information shall include the identity of the settlor, of the trustee(s), of the protector (if relevant), of the beneficiaries or class of beneficiaries, and of any other natural person exercising effective control over the trust.

2.   Member States shall ensure that trustees disclose their status to obliged entities when, as a trustee, the trustee forms a business relationship or carries out

an occasional transaction above the threshold set out in points (b), (c) and (d) of Article 10.

3. Member States shall ensure that the information referred to in paragraph 1 of this Article can be accessed in a timely manner by competent authorities and by obliged entities.

4. Member States shall ensure that measures corresponding to those in paragraphs 1, 2 and 3 apply to other types of legal entity and arrangement with a similar structure and function to trusts.

Chapter IV
Reporting obligations

Section 1
General provisions

Article 31

1. Each Member State shall establish an FIU in order to prevent, detect and investigate money laundering and terrorist financing.

2. Member States shall notify the Commission in writing of the name and address of the respective FIUs.

3. The FIU shall be established as a central national unit. It shall be responsible for receiving (and to the extent permitted, requesting), analysing and disseminating to the competent authorities, disclosures of information which concern potential money laundering or associated predicate offences, potential terrorist financing or are required by national legislation or regulation. The FIU shall be provided with adequate resources in order to fulfil its tasks.

4. Member States shall ensure that the FIU has access, directly or indirectly, on a timely basis, to the financial, administrative and law enforcement information that it requires to properly fulfil its tasks. In addition, FIUs shall respond to requests for information by law enforcement authorities in their Member State unless there are factual reasons to assume that the provision of such information would have a negative impact on ongoing investigations or analyses, or, in exceptional circumstances, where divulgation of the information would be clearly disproportionate to the legitimate interests of a natural or legal person or irrelevant with regard to the purposes for which it has been requested.

5. Member States shall ensure that the FIU is empowered to take urgent action, either directly or indirectly, when there is a suspicion that a transaction is related to money laundering or terrorist financing, to suspend or withhold consent to a transaction going ahead in order to analyse the transaction and confirm the suspicion.

6. The FIU's analysis function shall consist of an operational analysis which focusses on individual cases and specific targets and a strategic analysis addressing money laundering and terrorist financing trends and patterns.

Article 32

1. Member States shall require obliged entities, and where applicable their directors and employees, to cooperate fully:

(a) by promptly informing the FIU, on their own initiative, where the institution or person covered by this Directive knows, suspects or has reasonable grounds to suspect that funds are the proceeds of criminal activity or are related to terrorist financing and by promptly responding to requests by the FIU for additional information in such cases;

(b) by promptly furnishing the FIU, at its request, with all necessary information, in accordance with the procedures established by the applicable legislation.

2.   The information referred to in paragraph 1 of this Article shall be forwarded to the FIU of the Member State in whose territory the institution or person forwarding the information is situated. The person or persons designated in accordance with the procedures provided for in Article 8(4) shall forward the information.

Article 33

1.   By way of derogation from Article 32(1), Member States may, in the case of the persons referred to in Article 2(1)(3)(a), (b), and (d) designate an appropriate self-regulatory body of the profession concerned as the authority to receive the information referred to in Article 32(1).

Without prejudice to paragraph 2, the designated self-regulatory body shall in cases referred to in the first subparagraph forward the information to the FIU promptly and unfiltered.

2.   Member States shall not apply the obligations laid down in Article 32(1) to notaries, other independent legal professionals, auditors, external accountants and tax advisors only to the strict extent that such exemption relates to information they receive from or obtain on one of their clients, in the course of ascertaining the legal position for their client or performing their task of defending or representing that client in, or concerning judicial proceedings, including advice on instituting or avoiding proceedings, whether such information is received or obtained before, during or after such proceedings.

Article 34

1.   Member States shall require obliged entities to refrain from carrying out transactions which they know or suspect to be related to money laundering or terrorist financing until they have completed the necessary action in accordance with Article 32(1)(a).

In conformity with the legislation of the Member States, instructions may be given not to carry out the transaction.

2.   Where such a transaction is suspected of giving rise to money laundering or terrorist financing and where to refrain in such manner is impossible or is likely to frustrate efforts to pursue the beneficiaries of a suspected money laundering or terrorist financing operation, the obliged entities concerned shall inform the FIU immediately afterwards.

Article 35

1.   Member States shall ensure that if, in the course of inspections carried out in the obliged entities by the competent authorities referred to in Article 45, or in any other way, those authorities discover facts that could be related to money laundering or terrorist financing, they shall promptly inform the FIU.

2.   Member States shall ensure that supervisory bodies empowered by law or regulation to oversee the stock, foreign exchange and financial derivatives markets inform the FIU if they discover facts that could be related to money laundering or terrorist financing.

Article 36

The disclosure in good faith as foreseen in Articles 32 (1) and 33 by an obliged entity or by an employee or director of such an obliged entity of the information referred to in Articles 32 and 33 shall not constitute a breach of any restriction on disclosure of information imposed by contract or by any legislative, regulatory or administrative provision, and shall not involve the obliged entity or its directors or employees in liability of any kind.

Article 37

Member States shall take all appropriate measures in order to protect employees of the obliged entity who report suspicions of money laundering or terrorist financing either internally or to the FIU from being exposed to threats or hostile action.

Section 2
Prohibition of disclosure

Article 38

1.   Obliged entities and their directors and employees shall not disclose to the customer concerned or to other third persons the fact that information has been transmitted in accordance with Articles 32 and 33 or that a money laundering or terrorist financing investigation is being or may be carried out.

2.   The prohibition laid down in paragraph 1 shall not include disclosure to the competent authorities of Member States, including the self-regulatory bodies, or disclosure for law enforcement purposes.

3.   The prohibition laid down in paragraph 1 shall not prevent disclosure between institutions from Member States, or from third countries which impose requirements equivalent to those laid down in this Directive provided that they belong to the same group.

4.   The prohibition laid down in paragraph 1 shall not prevent disclosure between persons referred to in Article 2(1)(3)(a) and (b) from Member States, or from third countries which impose requirements equivalent to those laid down in this Directive, who perform their professional activities, whether as employees or not, within the same legal person or a network.

For the purposes of the first subparagraph, a 'network' shall mean the larger structure to which the person belongs and which shares common ownership, management or compliance control.

5.   For entities or persons referred to in Article 2(1)(1), (2) and (3)(a) and (b) in cases related to the same customer and the same transaction involving two or more institutions or persons, the prohibition laid down in paragraph 1 of this Article shall not prevent disclosure between the relevant institutions or persons provided that they are situated in a Member State, or in a third country which imposes requirements equivalent to those laid down in this Directive, and that they are from the same professional category and are subject to obligations as regards professional secrecy and personal data protection.

6.   Where the persons referred to in Article 2(1)(3)(a) and (b) seek to dissuade a client from engaging in illegal activity, this shall not constitute a disclosure within the meaning of paragraph 1.

Chapter V
Record keeping and statistical data

Article 39

Member States shall require obliged entities to store the following documents and information in accordance with national law for the purpose of the prevention, detection and investigation of possible money laundering or terrorist financing by the FIU or by other competent authorities:

(a) in the case of the customer due diligence, a copy or the references of the evidence required, for a period of five years after the business relationship with their customer has ended. Upon expiration of this period, personal data shall be deleted unless otherwise provided for by national law, which shall determine under which circumstances obliged entities may or shall further retain data. Member States may allow or require further retention only if necessary for the prevention, detection or investigation of money laundering and terrorist financing. The maximum retention period after the business relationship has ended shall not exceed ten years;

(b) in the case of business relationships and transactions, the supporting evidence and records, consisting of the original documents or copies admissible in court proceedings under the applicable national legislation for a period of five years following either the carrying-out of the transactions or the end of the business relationship, whichever period is the shortest. Upon expiration of this period, personal data shall be deleted, unless otherwise provided for by national law, which shall determine under which circumstances obliged entities may or shall further retain data. Member States may allow or require further retention only if necessary for the prevention, detection or investigation of money laundering and terrorist financing. The maximum retention period following either the carrying-out of the transactions or the end of the business relationship, whichever period ends first, shall not exceed ten years.

Article 40

Member States shall require that their obliged entities have systems in place that enable them to respond fully and rapidly to enquiries from the FIU, or from other authorities, in accordance with their national law, as to whether they maintain or have maintained during the previous five years a business relationship with specified natural or legal persons and on the nature of that relationship.

Article 41

1. Member States shall, for the purposes of the preparation of national risk assessments pursuant to Article 7, ensure that they are able to review the effectiveness of their systems to combat money laundering or terrorist financing by maintaining comprehensive statistics on matters relevant to the effectiveness of such systems.

2. Statistics referred to in paragraph 1 shall include:

(a) data measuring the size and importance of the different sectors which fall under the scope of this Directive, including the number of entities and persons and the economic importance of each sector;

(b) data measuring the reporting, investigation and judicial phases of the national anti-money laundering and terrorist financing regime, including the number of suspicious transaction reports made to the FIU, the follow-up given to these reports and, on an annual basis, the number of cases investigated, the number of persons prosecuted, the number of persons convicted for money laundering or terrorist financing offences and the value in euro of property that has been frozen, seized or confiscated.

3. Member States shall ensure that a consolidated review of their statistical reports is published and shall transmit to the Commission the statistics referred to in paragraph 2.

Chapter VI
Policies, procedures and supervision

Section 1
Internal procedures, training and feedback

Article 42

1. Member States shall require obliged entities that are part of a group to implement group-wide policies and procedures, including data protection policies and policies and procedures for sharing information within the group for anti-money laundering and combating terrorist financing purposes. Those policies and procedures shall be implemented effectively at the level of branches and majority-owned subsidiaries in Member States and third countries.

2. Member States shall ensure that where obliged entities have branches or majority-owned subsidiaries located in third countries where the minimum anti-money laundering and combating terrorist financing requirements are less strict than those of the Member State, their branches and majority-owned subsidiaries located in the third country implement the requirements of the Member State, including data protection, to the extent that the third country's laws and regulations so allow.

3. The Member States, EBA, EIOPA and ESMA shall inform each other of cases where the legislation of the third country does not permit application of the measures required under paragraph 1 and coordinated action could be taken to pursue a solution.

4. Member States shall require that, where the legislation of the third country does not permit application of the measures required under the first subparagraph of paragraph 1, obliged entities take additional measures to effectively handle the risk of money laundering or terrorist financing, and inform their home supervisors. If the additional measures are not sufficient, competent authorities in the home country shall consider additional supervisory actions, including, as appropriate, requesting the financial group to close down its operations in the host country.

5. EBA, EIOPA and ESMA shall develop draft regulatory technical standards specifying the type of additional measures referred to in paragraph 4 of this Article and the minimum action to be taken by obliged entities referred to Article 2(1)(1) and (2) where the legislation of the third country does not permit application of the measures required under paragraphs 1 and 2. EBA, EIOPA and ESMA shall submit those draft regulatory technical standards to the Commission within two years of the date of entry into force of this Directive.

6. Power is delegated to the Commission to adopt the regulatory technical standards referred to in paragraph 5 in accordance with the procedure laid down in Articles 10 to 14 of Regulation (EU) No 1093/2010, of Regulation (EU) No 1094/2010 and of Regulation (EU) No 1095/2010.

7. Member States shall ensure that sharing of information within the group is allowed provided that it does not prejudice investigation into, or analysis of, possible money laundering or terrorist financing by the FIU or by other competent authorities in accordance with national law.

8.   Member States may require issuers of electronic money as defined by Directive 2009/110/EC of the European Parliament and of the Council[20] and payment providers as defined by Directive 2007/64/EC of the European Parliament and of the Council[21] established on their territory, and whose head office is situated in another Member State or outside the Union, to appoint a central contact point in their territory to oversee the compliance with anti-money laundering and terrorist financing rules.

9.   EBA, EIOPA and ESMA shall develop draft regulatory technical standards on the criteria for determining the circumstances when the appointment of a central contact point pursuant to paragraph 8 above is appropriate, and what the functions of central contact points should be. EBA, ESMA and EIOPA shall submit these draft regulatory technical standards to the Commission within two years of the date of entry into force of this Directive.

10.   Power is delegated to the Commission to adopt the regulatory technical standards referred to in paragraph 9 in accordance with the procedure laid down in Articles 10 to 14 of Regulation (EU) No 1093/2010, of Regulation (EU) No 1094/2010 and of Regulation (EU) No 1095/2010.

Notes
20   OJ L 267, 10.10.2009, p. 7.
21   OJ L 319, 5.12.2007, p. 1.

Article 43

1.   Member States shall require that obliged entities take measures proportionate to their risks, nature and size so that their relevant employees are aware of the provisions adopted pursuant to this Directive, including relevant data protection requirements.

These measures shall include participation of their relevant employees in special ongoing training programmes to help them recognise operations which may be related to money laundering or terrorist financing and to instruct them as to how to proceed in such cases.

Where a natural person falling within any of the categories listed in Article 2(1) (3) performs his professional activities as an employee of a legal person, the obligations in this Section shall apply to that legal person rather than to the natural person.

2.   Member States shall ensure that obliged entities have access to up-to-date information on the practices of money launderers and terrorist financers and on indications leading to the recognition of suspicious transactions.

3.   Member States shall ensure that, wherever practicable, timely feedback on the effectiveness of and follow-up to reports of suspected money laundering or terrorist financing is provided.

Section 2
Supervision

Article 44

1.   Member States shall provide that currency exchange offices and trust or company service providers shall be licensed or registered and providers of gambling services be authorised.

2.   In respect of the entities referred to in paragraph 1, Member States shall require competent authorities to ensure that the persons who effectively direct or will direct the business of such entities or the beneficial owners of such entities are fit and proper persons.

3.   In respect of the obliged entities referred to in Article 2(1)(3) (a), (b), (d) and (e), Member States shall ensure that competent authorities take the necessary measures to prevent criminals or their associates from holding or being the beneficial owner of a significant or controlling interest, or holding a management function in those obliged entities.

Article 45

1.   Member States shall require the competent authorities to effectively monitor and to take the necessary measures with a view to ensure compliance with the requirements of this Directive.

2.   Member States shall ensure that the competent authorities have adequate powers, including the power to compel the production of any information that is relevant to monitoring compliance and perform checks, and have adequate financial, human and technical resources to perform their functions. Member States shall ensure that staff of these authorities maintain high professional standards, including standards of confidentiality and data protection, they shall be of high integrity and be appropriately skilled.

3.   In the case of credit and financial institutions and providers of gambling services, competent authorities shall have enhanced supervisory powers, notably the possibility to conduct on-site inspections.

4.   Member States shall ensure that obliged entities that operate branches or subsidiaries in other Member States respect the national provisions of that other Member State pertaining to this Directive.

5.   Member States shall ensure that the competent authorities of the Member State in which the branch or subsidiary is established shall cooperate with the competent authorities of the Member State in which the obliged entity has its head office, to ensure effective supervision of the requirements of this Directive.

6.   Member States shall ensure that competent authorities that apply a risk-sensitive approach to supervision:

(a)   have a clear understanding of the money laundering and terrorist financing risks present in their country;

(b)   have on-site and off-site access to all relevant information on the specific domestic and international risks associated with customers, products and services of the obliged entities; and

(c)   base the frequency and intensity of on-site and off-site supervision on the risk profile of the obliged entity, and on the money laundering and terrorist financing risks present in the country.

7.   The assessment of the money laundering and terrorist financing risk profile of obliged entities, including the risks of non-compliance, shall be reviewed both periodically and when there are major events or developments in the management and operations of the obliged entity.

8.   Member States shall ensure that competent authorities take into account the degree of discretion allowed to the obliged entity, and appropriately review the

risk assessments underlying this discretion, and the adequacy and implementation of its policies, internal controls and procedures.

9.   In the case of the obliged entities referred to in Article 2(1)(3)(a), (b) and (d) Member States may allow the functions referred to in paragraph 1 to be performed by self-regulatory bodies, provided that they comply with paragraph 2 of this Article.

10.   EBA, EIOPA and ESMA shall issue guidelines addressed to competent authorities in accordance with Article 16 of Regulation (EU) No 1093/2010, of Regulation (EU) No 1094/2010 and of Regulation (EU) No 1095/2010 on the factors to be applied when conducting supervision on a risk-sensitive basis. Specific account should be taken of the nature and size of the business, and where appropriate and proportionate, specific measures should be foreseen. These guidelines shall be issued within 2 years of the date of entry into force of this Directive.

Section 3
Co-operation

Subsection I
National co-operation

Article 46

Member States shall ensure that policy makers, the FIU, law enforcement authorities, supervisors and other competent authorities involved in anti-money laundering and combating terrorist financing have effective mechanisms to enable them to co-operate and co-ordinate domestically concerning the development and implementation of policies and activities to combat money laundering and terrorist financing.

Subsection II
Co-operation with EBA, EIOPA and ESMA

Article 47

The competent authorities shall provide EBA, EIOPA and ESMA with all the information necessary to carry out their duties under this Directive.

Subsection III
Co-operation between FIUs and with the European Commission

Article 48

The Commission may lend such assistance as may be needed to facilitate coordination, including the exchange of information between FIUs within the Union. It may regularly convene meetings with representatives from Member States' FIUs to facilitate co-operation and to exchange views on co-operation related issues.

Article 49

Member States shall ensure that their FIUs co-operate with each other to the greatest extent possible irrespective of whether they are administrative, law enforcement or judicial or hybrid authorities.

Article 50

1.   Member States shall ensure that FIUs exchange, spontaneously or upon request, any information that may be relevant for the processing or analysis of information or investigation by the FIU regarding financial transactions related to money laundering or terrorist financing and the natural or legal person involved. A request shall contain the relevant facts, background information, reasons for the request and how the information sought will be used.

2.   Member States shall ensure that the FIU to whom the request is made is required to use the whole range of its powers which it has domestically available for receiving and analysing information when it replies to a request for information referred to in paragraph 1 from another FIU based in the Union. The FIU to whom the request is made shall respond in a timely manner and both the requesting and requested FIU shall use secure digital means to exchange information, wherever possible.

3.   An FIU may refuse to divulge information which could lead to impairment of a criminal investigation being conducted in the requested Member State or, in exceptional circumstances, where divulgation of the information would be clearly disproportionate to the legitimate interests of a natural or legal person or the Member State or irrelevant to the purposes for which it has been collected. Any such refusal shall be appropriately justified to the FIU requesting the information.

Article 51

Information and documents received pursuant to Articles 49 and 50 shall be used for the accomplishment of the FIU's tasks as laid down in this Directive. When transmitting information and documents pursuant to Articles 49 and 50, the transmitting FIU may impose restrictions and conditions for the use of that information. The receiving FIU shall comply with those restrictions and conditions. This does not affect the use for criminal investigations and prosecutions linked to the FIU's tasks to prevent, detect and investigate money laundering and terrorist financing.

Article 52

Member States shall ensure that FIUs undertake all necessary measures, including security measures, to ensure that information submitted pursuant to Articles 49 and 50 is not accessible by any other authority, agency or department, unless prior approval is given by the FIU providing the information.

Article 53

1.   Member States shall encourage their FIUs to use protected channels of communication between FIUs and to use the decentralised computer network FIU.net.

2.   Member States shall ensure that, in order to fulfil their tasks as laid down in this Directive, their FIUs co-operate to apply sophisticated technologies. These technologies shall allow FIUs to match their data with other FIUs in an anonymous way by ensuring full protection of personal data with the aim to detect subjects of the FIU's interests in other Member States and identify their proceeds and funds.

Article 54

Member States shall ensure that their FIUs cooperate with Europol regarding analyses carried out having a cross-border dimension concerning at least two Member States.

Section 4
Sanctions

Article 55

1.   Member States shall ensure that obliged entities can be held liable for breaches of the national provisions adopted pursuant to this Directive.

2.   Without prejudice to the right of Member States to impose criminal penalties, Member States shall ensure that competent authorities may take appropriate administrative measures and impose administrative sanctions where obliged entities breach the national provisions, adopted in the implementation of this Directive, and shall ensure that they are applied. Those measures and sanctions shall be effective, proportionate and dissuasive.

3.   Member States shall ensure that where obligations apply to legal persons, sanctions can be applied to the members of the management body or to any other individuals who under national law are responsible for the breach.

4.   Member States shall ensure that the competent authorities have all the investigatory powers that are necessary for the exercise of their functions. In the exercise of their sanctioning powers, competent authorities shall cooperate closely to ensure that administrative measures or sanctions produce the desired results and coordinate their action when dealing with cross border cases.

Article 56

1.   This Article shall at least apply to situations where obliged entities demonstrate systematic failings in relation to the requirements of the following Articles:

(a)   9 to 23 (customer due diligence);

(b)   32, 33 and 34 (suspicious transaction reporting);

(c)   39 (record keeping); and

(d)   42 and 43 (internal controls).

2.   Member States shall ensure that in the cases referred to in paragraph 1, the administrative measures and sanctions that can be applied include at least the following:

(a)   a public statement which indicates the natural or legal person and the nature of the breach;

(b)   an order requiring the natural or legal person to cease the conduct and to desist from a repetition of that conduct;

(c)   in case of an obliged entity subject to an authorisation, withdrawal of the authorisation;

(d)   a temporary ban against any member of the obliged entity's management body, who is held responsible, to exercise functions in institutions;

(e)   in case of a legal person, administrative pecuniary sanctions of up to 10% of the total annual turnover of that legal person in the preceding business year;

(f)   in case of a natural person, administrative pecuniary sanctions of up to EUR 5 000 000, or in the Member States where the euro is not the official currency, the corresponding value in the national currency on the date of entry into force of this Directive;

(g)   administrative pecuniary sanctions of up to twice the amount of the profits gained or losses avoided because of the breach where those can be determined.

For the purpose of point (e), where the legal person is a subsidiary of a parent undertaking, the relevant total annual turnover shall be the total annual turnover resulting from the consolidated account of the ultimate parent undertaking in the preceding business year.

Article 57

1.   Member States shall ensure that competent authorities publish any sanction or measure imposed for breach of the national provisions adopted in the implementation of this Directive without undue delay including information on the type and nature of the breach and the identity of persons responsible for it, unless such publication would seriously jeopardise the stability of financial markets. Where publication would cause a disproportionate damage to the parties involved, competent authorities shall publish the sanctions on an anonymous basis.

2.   Member States shall ensure that when determining the type of administrative sanctions or measures and the level of administrative pecuniary sanctions, the competent authorities shall take into account all relevant circumstances, including:

(a)   the gravity and the duration of the breach;

(b)   the degree of responsibility of the responsible natural or legal person;

(c)   the financial strength of the responsible natural or legal person, as indicated by the total turnover of that person or the annual income of that person;

(d)   the importance of profits gained or losses avoided by the responsible natural or legal person, insofar as they can be determined;

(e)   the losses for third parties caused by the breach, insofar as they can be determined;

(f)   the level of cooperation of the responsible natural or legal person with the competent authority;

(g)   previous breaches by the responsible natural or legal person.

3.   EBA, EIOPA, and ESMA shall issue guidelines addressed to competent authorities in accordance with Article 16 of Regulation (EU) No 1093/2010, of Regulation (EU) No 1094/2010 and of Regulation (EU) No 1095/2010 on types of administrative measures and sanctions and level of administrative pecuniary sanctions applicable to obliged entities referred to in Article 2(1)(1) and (2). These guidelines shall be issued within 2 years of the date of entry into force of this Directive.

4.   In the case of legal persons, Member States shall ensure that they may be held liable for infringements referred to in paragraph 1 of Article 56 which are committed for their benefit by any person, acting either individually or as part of an organ of the legal person, who has a leading position within the legal person, based on any of the following:

(a)   a power of representation of the legal person;

(b)   an authority to take decisions on behalf of the legal person; or

(c)   an authority to exercise control within the legal person.

5.   In addition to the cases referred to in paragraph 4, Member States shall ensure that legal persons can be held liable where the lack of supervision or control by a person referred to in paragraph 4 has made possible the commission of the infringements referred to in paragraph 1 of Article 56 for the benefit of a legal person by a person under its authority.

Article 58

1.   Member States shall ensure that competent authorities establish effective mechanisms to encourage reporting of breaches of the national provisions implementing this Directive to competent authorities.

2.   The mechanisms referred to in paragraph 1 shall include at least:

(a)   specific procedures for the receipt of reports on breaches and their follow-up;

(b)   appropriate protection for employees of institutions who report breaches committed within the institution;

(c)   protection of personal data concerning both the person who reports the breaches and the natural person who is allegedly responsible for a breach, in compliance with the principles laid down in Directive 95/46/EC.

3.   Member States shall require obliged entities to have in place appropriate procedures for their employees to report breaches internally through a specific, independent and anonymous channel.

Chapter VII
Final provisions

Article 59

Within four years after the date of entry into force of this Directive, the Commission shall draw up a report on the implementation of this Directive and submit it to the European Parliament and the Council.

Article 60

Directives 2005/60/EC and 2006/70/EC are repealed with effect from [insert date – day after the date set out in the first subparagraph of Article 61].

References to the repealed Directives shall be construed as being made to this Directive and should be read in accordance with the correlation table in Annex IV.

Article 61

1.   Member States shall bring into force the laws, regulations and administrative provisions necessary to comply with this Directive by [two years after adoption] at the latest. They shall forthwith communicate to the Commission the text of those provisions.

When Member States adopt those provisions, they shall contain a reference to this Directive or be accompanied by such a reference on the occasion of their official publication. Member States shall determine how such reference is to be made.

2.   Member States shall communicate to the Commission the text of the main provisions of national law which they adopt in the field covered by this Directive.

Article 62

This Directive shall enter into force on the twentieth day following that of its publication in the Official Journal of the European Union.

Article 63

This Directive is addressed to the Member States.

Done at Strasbourg,

For the European Parliament

The President

For the Council

The President

Annex I

The following is a non-exhaustive list of risk variables that obliged entities shall consider when determining to what extent to apply customer due diligence measures in accordance with Article 11(3):

(i)   The purpose of an account or relationship;

(ii)   The level of assets to be deposited by a customer or the size of transactions undertaken;

(iii)   The regularity or duration of the business relationship.

Annex II

The following is a non-exhaustive list of factors and types of evidence of potentially lower risk referred to in Article 14:

(1)   Customer risk factors:

(a)   public companies listed on a stock exchange and subject to disclosure requirements (either by stock exchange rules or through law or enforceable means), which impose requirements to ensure adequate transparency of beneficial ownership;

(b)   public administrations or enterprises;

(c)   customers resident in lower risk geographical areas as set out in paragraph (3).

(2)   Product, service, transaction or delivery channel risk factors:

(a)   life insurance policies where the premium is low;

(b)   insurance policies for pension schemes if there is no early surrender option and the policy cannot be used as collateral;

(c)   a pension, superannuation or similar scheme that provides retirement benefits to employees, where contributions are made by way of deduction from wages, and the scheme rules do not permit the assignment of a member's interest under the scheme;

(d)   financial products or services that provide appropriately defined and limited services to certain types of customers, so as to increase access for financial inclusion purposes;

    (e) products where the risk of money laundering/terrorist financing are managed by other factors such as purse limits or transparency of ownership (e.g. certain types of electronic money as defined in Directive 2009/110/EC on the taking up, pursuit and prudential supervision of the business of electronic money institutions).

(3) Geographical risk factors:

    (a) other EU Member States;

    (b) third countries having effective anti-money laundering/combating terrorist financing systems;

    (c) third countries identified by credible sources as having a low level of corruption or other criminal activity;

    (d) third countries which are subject to requirements to combat money laundering and terrorist financing consistent with the FATF Recommendations, have effectively implemented those requirements, and are effectively supervised or monitored in accordance with the Recommendations to ensure compliance with those requirements.

Annex III

The following is a non-exhaustive list of factors and types of evidence of potentially higher risk referred to in Article 16(3):

(1) Customer risk factors:

    (a) the business relationship is conducted in unusual circumstances;

    (b) customers resident in countries set out in (3);

    (c) legal persons or arrangements that are personal asset-holding vehicles;

    (d) companies that have nominee shareholders or shares in bearer form;

    (e) businesses that are cash-intensive;

    (f) the ownership structure of the company appears unusual or excessively complex given the nature of the company's business.

(2) Product, service, transaction or delivery channel risk factors:

    (a) private banking;

    (b) products or transactions that might favour anonymity;

    (c) non-face-to-face business relationships or transactions;

    (d) payment received from unknown or un-associated third parties;

    (e) new products and new business practices, including new delivery mechanism, and the use of new or developing technologies for both new and pre-existing products.

(3) Geographical risk factors:

    (a) countries identified by credible sources, such FATF public statements, mutual evaluation or detailed assessment reports or published follow-up reports, as not having effective anti-money laundering/combating terrorist financing systems;

    (b) countries identified by credible sources as having significant levels of corruption or other criminal activity;

    (c) countries subject to sanctions, embargos or similar measures issued by, for example, the United Nations;

    (d) countries providing funding or support for terrorist activities, or that have designated terrorist organisations operating within their country.

Annex IV
Correlation table referred to in Article 60.

Directive 2005/60/EC	This Directive
Article 1	Article 1
Article 2	Article 2
Article 3	Article 3
Article 4	Article 4
Article 5	Article 5
	Articles 6 to 8
Article 6	Article 9
Article 7	Article 10
Article 8	Article 11
Article 9	Article 12
Article 10(1)	Article 10(d)
Article 10(2)	–
Article 11	Articles 13, 14 and 15
Article 12	–
Article 13	Articles 16 to 23
Article 14	Article 24
Article 15	–
Article 16	Article 25
Article 17	–
Article 18	Article 26
	Article 27
Article 19	Article 28
	Article 29
	Article 30
Article 20	–
Article 21	Article 31
Article 22	Article 32
Article 23	Article 33
Article 24	Article 34
Article 25	Article 35
Article 26	Article 36
Article 27	Article 37
Article 28	Article 38
Article 29	–
Article 30	Article 39
Article 31	Article 42
Article 32	Article 40

Article 33	Article 41
Article 34	Article 42
Article 35	Article 43
Article 36	Article 44
Article 37	Article 45
	Article 46
Article 37a	Article 47
Article 38	Article 48
	Articles 49 to 54
Article 39	Articles 55 to 58
Article 40	–
Article 41	–
Article 41a	–
Article 41b	–
Article 42	Article 59
Article 43	–
Article 44	Article 60
Article 45	Article 61
Article 46	Article 62
Article 47	Article 63
Directive 2006/70/EC	This Directive
Article 1	–
Article 2(1), (2) and (3)	Article 3(7)(d), (e) and (f)
Article 2(4)	–
Article 3	–
Article 4	Article 2(2) to (8)
Article 5	–
Article 6	–
Article 7	–

Appendix 1.8   Third Money Laundering Directive

Directive 2005/60/EC of the European Parliament and of the Council

of 26 October 2005

on the prevention of the use of the financial system for the purpose of money laundering and terrorist financing

The European Parliament and the Council of the European Union,

Having regard to the Treaty establishing the European Community, and in particular Article 47(2), first and third sentences, and Article 95 thereof,
Having regard to the proposal from the Commission,
Having regard to the opinion of the European Economic and Social Committee[1],
Having regard to the opinion of the European Central Bank[2],
Acting in accordance with the procedure laid down in Article 251 of the Treaty[3],

Whereas:

(1) Massive flows of dirty money can damage the stability and reputation of the financial sector and threaten the single market, and terrorism shakes the very foundations of our society. In addition to the criminal law approach, a preventive effort via the financial system can produce results.

(2) The soundness, integrity and stability of credit and financial institutions and confidence in the financial system as a whole could be seriously jeopardised by the efforts of criminals and their associates either to disguise the origin of criminal proceeds or to channel lawful or unlawful money for terrorist purposes. In order to avoid Member States' adopting measures to protect their financial systems which could be inconsistent with the functioning of the internal market and with the prescriptions of the rule of law and Community public policy, Community action in this area is necessary.

(3) In order to facilitate their criminal activities, money launderers and terrorist financers could try to take advantage of the freedom of capital movements and the freedom to supply financial services which the integrated financial area entails, if certain coordinating measures are not adopted at Community level.

(4) In order to respond to these concerns in the field of money laundering, Council Directive 91/308/EEC of 10 June 1991 on prevention of the use of the financial system for the purpose of money laundering[4] was adopted. It required Member States to prohibit money laundering and to oblige the financial sector, comprising credit institutions and a wide range of other financial institutions, to identify their customers, keep appropriate records, establish internal procedures to train staff and guard against money laundering and to report any indications of money laundering to the competent authorities.

(5) Money laundering and terrorist financing are frequently carried out in an international context. Measures adopted solely at national or even Community level, without taking account of international coordination and cooperation, would have very limited effects. The measures adopted by the Community in this field should therefore be consistent with other action undertaken in other international fora. The Community action should continue to take particular account of the Recommendations of the Financial Action Task Force (hereinafter referred to as the FATF), which constitutes the foremost international body active in the fight against money laundering and terrorist financing. Since the FATF Recommendations were substantially revised and expanded in 2003, this Directive should be in line with that new international standard.

(6) The General Agreement on Trade in Services (GATS) allows Members to adopt measures necessary to protect public morals and prevent fraud and adopt measures for prudential reasons, including for ensuring the stability and integrity of the financial system.

(7) Although initially limited to drugs offences, there has been a trend in recent years towards a much wider definition of money laundering based on a broader range of predicate offences. A wider range of predicate offences facilitates the reporting of suspicious transactions and international cooperation in this area. Therefore, the definition of serious crime should be brought into line with the definition of serious crime in Council Framework Decision 2001/500/JHA of 26 June 2001 on money laundering, the identification, tracing, freezing, seizing and confiscation of instrumentalities and the proceeds of crime[5].

(8) Furthermore, the misuse of the financial system to channel criminal or even clean money to terrorist purposes poses a clear risk to the integrity, proper functioning, reputation and stability of the financial system. Accordingly, the preventive measures of this Directive should cover not only the manipulation of money derived from crime but also the collection of money or property for terrorist purposes.

(9) Directive 91/308/EEC, though imposing a customer identification obligation, contained relatively little detail on the relevant procedures. In view of the crucial importance of this aspect of the prevention of money laundering and terrorist financing, it is appropriate, in accordance with the new international standards, to introduce more specific and detailed provisions relating to the identification of the customer and of any beneficial owner and the verification of their identity. To that end a precise definition of 'beneficial owner' is essential. Where the individual beneficiaries of a legal entity or arrangement such as a foundation or trust are yet to be determined, and it is therefore impossible to identify an individual as the beneficial owner, it would suffice to identify the class of persons intended to be the beneficiaries of the foundation or trust. This requirement should not include the identification of the individuals within that class of persons.

(10) The institutions and persons covered by this Directive should, in conformity with this Directive, identify and verify the identity of the beneficial owner. To fulfil this requirement, it should be left to those institutions and persons whether they make use of public records of beneficial owners, ask their clients for relevant data or obtain the information otherwise, taking into account the fact that the extent of such customer due diligence measures relates to the risk of money laundering and terrorist financing, which depends on the type of customer, business relationship, product or transaction.

(11) Credit agreements in which the credit account serves exclusively to settle the loan and the repayment of the loan is effected from an account which was opened in the name of the customer with a credit institution covered by this Directive pursuant to Article 8(1)(a) to (c) should generally be considered as an example of types of less risky transactions.

(12) To the extent that the providers of the property of a legal entity or arrangement have significant control over the use of the property they should be identified as a beneficial owner.

(13) Trust relationships are widely used in commercial products as an internationally recognised feature of the comprehensively supervised wholesale financial markets. An obligation to identify the beneficial owner does not arise from the fact alone that there is a trust relationship in this particular case.

(14) This Directive should also apply to those activities of the institutions and persons covered hereunder which are performed on the Internet.

(15) As the tightening of controls in the financial sector has prompted money launderers and terrorist financers to seek alternative methods for concealing the origin of the proceeds of crime and as such channels can be used for terrorist financing, the anti-money laundering and anti-terrorist financing obligations should cover life insurance intermediaries and trust and company service providers.

(16) Entities already falling under the legal responsibility of an insurance undertaking, and therefore falling within the scope of this Directive, should not be included within the category of insurance intermediary.

(17) Acting as a company director or secretary does not of itself make someone a trust and company service provider. For that reason, the definition covers only those persons that act as a company director or secretary for a third party and by way of business.

(18) The use of large cash payments has repeatedly proven to be very vulnerable to money laundering and terrorist financing. Therefore, in those Member States that allow cash payments above the established threshold, all natural or legal persons trading in goods by way of business should be covered by this Directive when accepting such cash payments. Dealers in high-value goods, such as precious stones or metals, or works of art, and auctioneers are in any event covered by this Directive to the extent that payments to them are made in cash in an amount of EUR 15 000 or more. To ensure effective monitoring of compliance with this Directive by that potentially wide group of institutions and persons, Member States may focus their monitoring activities in particular on those natural and legal persons trading in goods that are exposed to a relatively high risk of money laundering or terrorist financing, in accordance with the principle of risk-based supervision. In view of the different situations in the various Member States, Member States may decide to adopt stricter provisions, in order to properly address the risk involved with large cash payments.

(19) Directive 91/308/EEC brought notaries and other independent legal professionals within the scope of the Community anti-money laundering regime; this coverage should be maintained unchanged in this Directive; these legal professionals, as defined by the Member States, are subject to the provisions of this Directive when participating in financial or corporate transactions, including providing tax advice, where there is the greatest risk of the services of those legal professionals being misused for the purpose of laundering the proceeds of criminal activity or for the purpose of terrorist financing.

(20) Where independent members of professions providing legal advice which are legally recognised and controlled, such as lawyers, are ascertaining the legal position of a client or representing a client in legal proceedings, it would not be appropriate under this Directive to put those legal professionals in respect of these activities under an obligation to report suspicions of money laundering or terrorist financing. There must be exemptions from any obligation to report information obtained either before, during or after judicial proceedings, or

in the course of ascertaining the legal position for a client. Thus, legal advice shall remain subject to the obligation of professional secrecy unless the legal counsellor is taking part in money laundering or terrorist financing, the legal advice is provided for money laundering or terrorist financing purposes or the lawyer knows that the client is seeking legal advice for money laundering or terrorist financing purposes.

(21) Directly comparable services need to be treated in the same manner when provided by any of the professionals covered by this Directive. In order to ensure the respect of the rights laid down in the European Convention for the Protection of Human Rights and Fundamental Freedoms and the Treaty on European Union, in the case of auditors, external accountants and tax advisors, who, in some Member States, may defend or represent a client in the context of judicial proceedings or ascertain a client's legal position, the information they obtain in the performance of those tasks should not be subject to the reporting obligations in accordance with this Directive.

(22) It should be recognised that the risk of money laundering and terrorist financing is not the same in every case. In line with a risk-based approach, the principle should be introduced into Community legislation that simplified customer due diligence is allowed in appropriate cases.

(23) The derogation concerning the identification of beneficial owners of pooled accounts held by notaries or other independent legal professionals should be without prejudice to the obligations that those notaries or other independent legal professionals have pursuant to this Directive. Those obligations include the need for such notaries or other independent legal professionals themselves to identify the beneficial owners of the pooled accounts held by them.

(24) Equally, Community legislation should recognise that certain situations present a greater risk of money laundering or terrorist financing. Although the identity and business profile of all customers should be established, there are cases where particularly rigorous customer identification and verification procedures are required.

(25) This is particularly true of business relationships with individuals holding, or having held, important public positions, particularly those from countries where corruption is widespread. Such relationships may expose the financial sector in particular to significant reputational and/or legal risks. The international effort to combat corruption also justifies the need to pay special attention to such cases and to apply the complete normal customer due diligence measures in respect of domestic politically exposed persons or enhanced customer due diligence measures in respect of politically exposed persons residing in another Member State or in a third country.

(26) Obtaining approval from senior management for establishing business relationships should not imply obtaining approval from the board of directors but from the immediate higher level of the hierarchy of the person seeking such approval.

(27) In order to avoid repeated customer identification procedures, leading to delays and inefficiency in business, it is appropriate, subject to suitable safeguards, to allow customers to be introduced whose identification has been carried out elsewhere. Where an institution or person covered by this Directive relies on a third party, the ultimate responsibility for the customer due diligence procedure remains with the institution or person to whom the customer is introduced. The third party, or introducer, also retains his own responsibility for all the requirements in this Directive, including the requirement to report suspicious transactions and maintain records, to the extent that he has a relationship with the customer that is covered by this Directive.

(28) In the case of agency or outsourcing relationships on a contractual basis between institutions or persons covered by this Directive and external natural or legal persons not covered hereby, any anti-money laundering and anti-terrorist financing obligations for those agents or outsourcing service providers as part of the institutions or persons covered by this Directive, may only arise from contract and not from this Directive. The responsibility for complying with this Directive should remain with the institution or person covered hereby.

(29) Suspicious transactions should be reported to the financial intelligence unit (FIU), which serves as a national centre for receiving, analysing and disseminating to the competent authorities suspicious transaction reports and other information regarding potential money laundering or terrorist financing. This should not compel Member States to change their existing reporting systems where the reporting is done through a public prosecutor or other law enforcement authorities, as long as the information is forwarded promptly and unfiltered to FIUs, allowing them to conduct their business properly, including international cooperation with other FIUs.

(30) By way of derogation from the general prohibition on executing suspicious transactions, the institutions and persons covered by this Directive may execute suspicious transactions before informing the competent authorities, where refraining from the execution thereof is impossible or likely to frustrate efforts to pursue the beneficiaries of a suspected money laundering or terrorist financing operation. This, however, should be without prejudice to the international obligations accepted by the Member States to freeze without delay funds or other assets of terrorists, terrorist organisations or those who finance terrorism, in accordance with the relevant United Nations Security Council resolutions.

(31) Where a Member State decides to make use of the exemptions provided for in Article 23(2), it may allow or require the self-regulatory body representing the persons referred to therein not to transmit to the FIU any information obtained from those persons in the circumstances referred to in that Article.

(32) There has been a number of cases of employees who report their suspicions of money laundering being subjected to threats or hostile action. Although this Directive cannot interfere with Member States' judicial procedures, this is a crucial issue for the effectiveness of the anti-money laundering and anti-terrorist financing system. Member States should be aware of this problem and should do whatever they can to protect employees from such threats or hostile action.

(33) Disclosure of information as referred to in Article 28 should be in accordance with the rules on transfer of personal data to third countries as laid down in Directive 95/46/EC of the European Parliament and of the Council of 24 October 1995 on the protection of individuals with regard to the processing of personal data and on the free movement of such data[6]. Moreover, Article 28 cannot interfere with national data protection and professional secrecy legislation.

(34) Persons who merely convert paper documents into electronic data and are acting under a contract with a credit institution or a financial institution do not fall within the scope of this Directive, nor does any natural or legal person that provides credit or financial institutions solely with a message or other support systems for transmitting funds or with clearing and settlement systems.

(35) Money laundering and terrorist financing are international problems and the effort to combat them should be global. Where Community credit and financial institutions have branches and subsidiaries located in third

countries where the legislation in this area is deficient, they should, in order to avoid the application of very different standards within an institution or group of institutions, apply the Community standard or notify the competent authorities of the home Member State if this application is impossible.

(36) It is important that credit and financial institutions should be able to respond rapidly to requests for information on whether they maintain business relationships with named persons. For the purpose of identifying such business relationships in order to be able to provide that information quickly, credit and financial institutions should have effective systems in place which are commensurate with the size and nature of their business. In particular it would be appropriate for credit institutions and larger financial institutions to have electronic systems at their disposal. This provision is of particular importance in the context of procedures leading to measures such as the freezing or seizing of assets (including terrorist assets), pursuant to applicable national or Community legislation with a view to combating terrorism.

(37) This Directive establishes detailed rules for customer due diligence, including enhanced customer due diligence for high-risk customers or business relationships, such as appropriate procedures to determine whether a person is a politically exposed person, and certain additional, more detailed requirements, such as the existence of compliance management procedures and policies. All these requirements are to be met by each of the institutions and persons covered by this Directive, while Member States are expected to tailor the detailed implementation of those provisions to the particularities of the various professions and to the differences in scale and size of the institutions and persons covered by this Directive.

(38) In order to ensure that the institutions and others subject to Community legislation in this field remain committed, feedback should, where practicable, be made available to them on the usefulness and follow-up of the reports they present. To make this possible, and to be able to review the effectiveness of their systems to combat money laundering and terrorist financing Member States should keep and improve the relevant statistics.

(39) When registering or licensing a currency exchange office, a trust and company service provider or a casino nationally, competent authorities should ensure that the persons who effectively direct or will direct the business of such entities and the beneficial owners of such entities are fit and proper persons. The criteria for determining whether or not a person is fit and proper should be established in conformity with national law. As a minimum, such criteria should reflect the need to protect such entities from being misused by their managers or beneficial owners for criminal purposes.

(40) Taking into account the international character of money laundering and terrorist financing, coordination and cooperation between FIUs as referred to in Council Decision 2000/642/JHA of 17 October 2000 concerning arrangements for cooperation between financial intelligence units of the Member States in respect of exchanging information[7], including the establishment of an EU FIU-net, should be encouraged to the greatest possible extent. To that end, the Commission should lend such assistance as may be needed to facilitate such coordination, including financial assistance.

(41) The importance of combating money laundering and terrorist financing should lead Member States to lay down effective, proportionate and dissuasive penalties in national law for failure to respect the national provisions adopted pursuant to this Directive. Provision should be made for penalties in respect of natural and legal persons. Since legal persons are often involved in complex money laundering or terrorist financing operations, sanctions should also be adjusted in line with the activity carried on by legal persons.

(42) Natural persons exercising any of the activities referred to in Article 2(1)(3)(a) and (b) within the structure of a legal person, but on an independent basis, should be independently responsible for compliance with the provisions of this Directive, with the exception of Article 35.

(43) Clarification of the technical aspects of the rules laid down in this Directive may be necessary to ensure an effective and sufficiently consistent implementation of this Directive, taking into account the different financial instruments, professions and risks in the different Member States and the technical developments in the fight against money laundering and terrorist financing. The Commission should accordingly be empowered to adopt implementing measures, such as certain criteria for identifying low and high risk situations in which simplified due diligence could suffice or enhanced due diligence would be appropriate, provided that they do not modify the essential elements of this Directive and provided that the Commission acts in accordance with the principles set out herein, after consulting the Committee on the Prevention of Money Laundering and Terrorist Financing.

(44) The measures necessary for the implementation of this Directive should be adopted in accordance with Council Decision 1999/468/EC of 28 June 1999 laying down the procedures for the exercise of implementing powers conferred on the Commission[8]. To that end a new Committee on the Prevention of Money Laundering and Terrorist Financing, replacing the Money Laundering Contact Committee set up by Directive 91/308/EEC, should be established.

(45) In view of the very substantial amendments that would need to be made to Directive 91/308/EEC, it should be repealed for reasons of clarity.

(46) Since the objective of this Directive, namely the prevention of the use of the financial system for the purpose of money laundering and terrorist financing, cannot be sufficiently achieved by the Member States and can therefore, by reason of the scale and effects of the action, be better achieved at Community level, the Community may adopt measures, in accordance with the principle of subsidiarity as set out in Article 5 of the Treaty. In accordance with the principle of proportionality, as set out in that Article, this Directive does not go beyond what is necessary in order to achieve that objective.

(47) In exercising its implementing powers in accordance with this Directive, the Commission should respect the following principles: the need for high levels of transparency and consultation with institutions and persons covered by this Directive and with the European Parliament and the Council; the need to ensure that competent authorities will be able to ensure compliance with the rules consistently; the balance of costs and benefits to institutions and persons covered by this Directive on a long-term basis in any implementing measures; the need to respect the necessary flexibility in the application of the implementing measures in accordance with a risk-sensitive approach; the need to ensure coherence with other Community legislation in this area; the need to protect the Community, its Member States and their citizens from the consequences of money laundering and terrorist financing.

(48) This Directive respects the fundamental rights and observes the principles recognised in particular by the Charter of Fundamental Rights of the European Union. Nothing in this Directive should be interpreted or implemented in a manner that is inconsistent with the European Convention on Human Rights,

---

Notes
1   Opinion delivered on 11 May 2005 (not yet published in the Official Journal).
2   OJ C 40, 17.2.2005, p. 9.
3   Opinion of the European Parliament of 26 May 2005 (not yet published in the Official Journal) and Council Decision of 19 September 2005.

4   OJ L 166, 28.6.1991, p. 77. Directive as amended by Directive 2001/97/EC of the
    European Parliament and of the Council (OJ L 344, 28.12.2001, p. 76).
5   OJ L 182, 5.7.2001, p. 1.
6   OJ L 281, 23.11.1995, p. 31. Directive as amended by Regulation (EC) No 1882/2003 (OJ
    L 284, 31.10.2003, p. 1).
7   OJ L 271, 24.10.2000, p. 4.
8   OJ L 184, 17.7.1999, p. 23.

Have adopted this Directive:

Chapter I
Subject matter, scope and definitions

Article 1

1.   Member States shall ensure that money laundering and terrorist financing are
prohibited.

2.   For the purposes of this Directive, the following conduct, when committed
intentionally, shall be regarded as money laundering:

(a)   the conversion or transfer of property, knowing that such property is derived
      from criminal activity or from an act of participation in such activity, for the
      purpose of concealing or disguising the illicit origin of the property or of
      assisting any person who is involved in the commission of such activity to
      evade the legal consequences of his action;

(b)   the concealment or disguise of the true nature, source, location, disposition,
      movement, rights with respect to, or ownership of property, knowing that
      such property is derived from criminal activity or from an act of participation
      in such activity;

(c)   the acquisition, possession or use of property, knowing, at the time of receipt,
      that such property was derived from criminal activity or from an act of
      participation in such activity;

(d)   participation in, association to commit, attempts to commit and aiding,
      abetting, facilitating and counselling the commission of any of the actions
      mentioned in the foregoing points.

3.   Money laundering shall be regarded as such even where the activities which
generated the property to be laundered were carried out in the territory of another
Member State or in that of a third country.

4.   For the purposes of this Directive, 'terrorist financing' means the provision
or collection of funds, by any means, directly or indirectly, with the intention that
they should be used or in the knowledge that they are to be used, in full or in
part, in order to carry out any of the offences within the meaning of Articles 1 to
4 of Council Framework Decision 2002/475/JHA of 13 June 2002 on combating
terrorism[9].

5.   Knowledge, intent or purpose required as an element of the activities mentioned
in paragraphs 2 and 4 may be inferred from objective factual circumstances.

Notes
9   OJ L 164, 22.6.2002, p. 3.

Article 2

1. This Directive shall apply to:

(1) credit institutions;

(2) financial institutions;

(3) the following legal or natural persons acting in the exercise of their professional activities:

   (a) auditors, external accountants and tax advisors;

   (b) notaries and other independent legal professionals, when they participate, whether by acting on behalf of and for their client in any financial or real estate transaction, or by assisting in the planning or execution of transactions for their client concerning the:

   (i) buying and selling of real property or business entities;

   (ii) managing of client money, securities or other assets;

   (iii) opening or management of bank, savings or securities accounts;

   (iv) organisation of contributions necessary for the creation, operation or management of companies;

   (v) creation, operation or management of trusts, companies or similar structures;

   (c) trust or company service providers not already covered under points (a) or (b);

   (d) real estate agents;

   (e) other natural or legal persons trading in goods, only to the extent that payments are made in cash in an amount of EUR 15 000 or more, whether the transaction is executed in a single operation or in several operations which appear to be linked;

   (f) casinos.

2. Member States may decide that legal and natural persons who engage in a financial activity on an occasional or very limited basis and where there is little risk of money laundering or terrorist financing occurring do not fall within the scope of Article 3(1) or (2).

Article 3

For the purposes of this Directive the following definitions shall apply:

(1) 'credit institution' means a credit institution, as defined in the first subparagraph of Article 1(1) of Directive 2000/12/EC of the European Parliament and of the Council of 20 March 2000 relating to the taking up and pursuit of the business of credit institutions[10], including branches within the meaning of Article 1(3) of that Directive located in the Community of credit institutions having their head offices inside or outside the Community;

(2) 'financial institution' means:

   (a) an undertaking other than a credit institution which carries out one or more of the operations included in points 2 to 12 and 14 of Annex I to Directive 2000/12/EC, including the activities of currency exchange offices (bureaux de change) and of money transmission or remittance offices;

(b)   an insurance company duly authorised in accordance with Directive 2002/83/EC of the European Parliament and of the Council of 5 November 2002 concerning life assurance[11], insofar as it carries out activities covered by that Directive;

(c)   an investment firm as defined in point 1 of Article 4(1) of Directive 2004/39/EC of the European Parliament and of the Council of 21 April 2004 on markets in financial instruments[12];

(d)   a collective investment undertaking marketing its units or shares;

(e)   an insurance intermediary as defined in Article 2(5) of Directive 2002/92/EC of the European Parliament and of the Council of 9 December 2002 on insurance mediation[13], with the exception of intermediaries as mentioned in Article 2(7) of that Directive, when they act in respect of life insurance and other investment related services;

(f)   branches, when located in the Community, of financial institutions as referred to in points (a) to (e), whose head offices are inside or outside the Community;

(3)   'property' means assets of every kind, whether corporeal or incorporeal, movable or immovable, tangible or intangible, and legal documents or instruments in any form including electronic or digital, evidencing title to or an interest in such assets;

(4)   'criminal activity' means any kind of criminal involvement in the commission of a serious crime;

(5)   'serious crimes' means, at least:

(a)   acts as defined in Articles 1 to 4 of Framework Decision 2002/475/JHA;

(b)   any of the offences defined in Article 3(1)(a) of the 1988 United Nations Convention against Illicit Traffic in Narcotic Drugs and Psychotropic Substances;

(c)   the activities of criminal organisations as defined in Article 1 of Council Joint Action 98/733/JHA of 21 December 1998 on making it a criminal offence to participate in a criminal organisation in the Member States of the European Union[14];

(d)   fraud, at least serious, as defined in Article 1(1) and Article 2 of the Convention on the Protection of the European Communities' Financial Interests[15];

(e)   corruption;

(f)   all offences which are punishable by deprivation of liberty or a detention order for a maximum of more than one year or, as regards those States which have a minimum threshold for offences in their legal system, all offences punishable by deprivation of liberty or a detention order for a minimum of more than six months;

(6)   'beneficial owner' means the natural person(s) who ultimately owns or controls the customer and/or the natural person on whose behalf a transaction or activity is being conducted. The beneficial owner shall at least include:

(a)   in the case of corporate entities:

(i)   the natural person(s) who ultimately owns or controls a legal entity through direct or indirect ownership or control over a sufficient percentage of the shares or voting rights in that legal entity, including through bearer share holdings, other than a company listed on a regulated market that is subject to disclosure requirements consistent with Community legislation or subject to equivalent international standards; a percentage of 25 % plus one share shall be deemed sufficient to meet this criterion;

   (ii) the natural person(s) who otherwise exercises control over the management of a legal entity:

  (b) in the case of legal entities, such as foundations, and legal arrangements, such as trusts, which administer and distribute funds:

     (i) where the future beneficiaries have already been determined, the natural person(s) who is the beneficiary of 25 % or more of the property of a legal arrangement or entity;

    (ii) where the individuals that benefit from the legal arrangement or entity have yet to be determined, the class of persons in whose main interest the legal arrangement or entity is set up or operates;

   (iii) the natural person(s) who exercises control over 25 % or more of the property of a legal arrangement or entity;

(7) 'trust and company service providers' means any natural or legal person which by way of business provides any of the following services to third parties:

  (a) forming companies or other legal persons;

  (b) acting as or arranging for another person to act as a director or secretary of a company, a partner of a partnership, or a similar position in relation to other legal persons;

  (c) providing a registered office, business address, correspondence or administrative address and other related services for a company, a partnership or any other legal person or arrangement;

  (d) acting as or arranging for another person to act as a trustee of an express trust or a similar legal arrangement;

  (e) acting as or arranging for another person to act as a nominee shareholder for another person other than a company listed on a regulated market that is subject to disclosure requirements in conformity with Community legislation or subject to equivalent international standards;

(8) 'politically exposed persons' means natural persons who are or have been entrusted with prominent public functions and immediate family members, or persons known to be close associates, of such persons;

(9) 'business relationship' means a business, professional or commercial relationship which is connected with the professional activities of the institutions and persons covered by this Directive and which is expected, at the time when the contact is established, to have an element of duration;

(10) 'shell bank' means a credit institution, or an institution engaged in equivalent activities, incorporated in a jurisdiction in which it has no physical presence, involving meaningful mind and management, and which is unaffiliated with a regulated financial group.

Notes
10 OJ L 126, 26.5.2000, p. 1. Directive as last amended by Directive 2005/1/EC (OJ L 79, 24.3.2005, p. 9).
11 OJ L 345, 19.12.2002, p. 1. Directive as last amended by Directive 2005/1/EC.
12 OJ L 145, 30.4.2004, p. 1.
13 OJ L 9, 15.1.2003, p. 3.
14 OJ L 351, 29.12.1998, p. 1.
15 OJ C 316, 27.11.1995, p. 49.

Article 4

1.   Member States shall ensure that the provisions of this Directive are extended in whole or in part to professions and to categories of undertakings, other than the institutions and persons referred to in Article 2(1), which engage in activities which are particularly likely to be used for money laundering or terrorist financing purposes.

2.   Where a Member State decides to extend the provisions of this Directive to professions and to categories of undertakings other than those referred to in Article 2(1), it shall inform the Commission thereof.

Article 5

The Member States may adopt or retain in force stricter provisions in the field covered by this Directive to prevent money laundering and terrorist financing.

Chapter II
Customer due diligence

Section 1
General provisions

Article 6

Member States shall prohibit their credit and financial institutions from keeping anonymous accounts or anonymous passbooks. By way of derogation from Article 9(6), Member States shall in all cases require that the owners and beneficiaries of existing anonymous accounts or anonymous passbooks be made the subject of customer due diligence measures as soon as possible and in any event before such accounts or passbooks are used in any way.

Article 7

The institutions and persons covered by this Directive shall apply customer due diligence measures in the following cases:

(a) when establishing a business relationship;

(b) when carrying out occasional transactions amounting to EUR 15 000 or more, whether the transaction is carried out in a single operation or in several operations which appear to be linked;

(c) when there is a suspicion of money laundering or terrorist financing, regardless of any derogation, exemption or threshold;

(d) when there are doubts about the veracity or adequacy of previously obtained customer identification data.

Article 8

1.   Customer due diligence measures shall comprise:

(a) identifying the customer and verifying the customer's identity on the basis of documents, data or information obtained from a reliable and independent source;

(b) identifying, where applicable, the beneficial owner and taking risk-based and adequate measures to verify his identity so that the institution or person covered by this Directive is satisfied that it knows who the beneficial owner is, including, as regards legal persons, trusts and similar legal arrangements, taking risk-based and adequate measures to understand the ownership and control structure of the customer;

(c) obtaining information on the purpose and intended nature of the business relationship;

(d) conducting ongoing monitoring of the business relationship including scrutiny of transactions undertaken throughout the course of that relationship to ensure that the transactions being conducted are consistent with the institution's or person's knowledge of the customer, the business and risk profile, including, where necessary, the source of funds and ensuring that the documents, data or information held are kept up-to-date.

2.   The institutions and persons covered by this Directive shall apply each of the customer due diligence requirements set out in paragraph 1, but may determine the extent of such measures on a risk-sensitive basis depending on the type of customer, business relationship, product or transaction. The institutions and persons covered by this Directive shall be able to demonstrate to the competent authorities mentioned in Article 37, including self-regulatory bodies, that the extent of the measures is appropriate in view of the risks of money laundering and terrorist financing.

Article 9

1.   Member States shall require that the verification of the identity of the customer and the beneficial owner takes place before the establishment of a business relationship or the carrying-out of the transaction.

2.   By way of derogation from paragraph 1, Member States may allow the verification of the identity of the customer and the beneficial owner to be completed during the establishment of a business relationship if this is necessary not to interrupt the normal conduct of business and where there is little risk of money laundering or terrorist financing occurring. In such situations these procedures shall be completed as soon as practicable after the initial contact.

3.   By way of derogation from paragraphs 1 and 2, Member States may, in relation to life insurance business, allow the verification of the identity of the beneficiary under the policy to take place after the business relationship has been established. In that case, verification shall take place at or before the time of payout or at or before the time the beneficiary intends to exercise rights vested under the policy.

4.   By way of derogation from paragraphs 1 and 2, Member States may allow the opening of a bank account provided that there are adequate safeguards in place to ensure that transactions are not carried out by the customer or on its behalf until full compliance with the aforementioned provisions is obtained.

5.   Member States shall require that, where the institution or person concerned is unable to comply with points (a), (b) and (c) of Article 8(1), it may not carry out a transaction through a bank account, establish a business relationship or carry out the transaction, or shall terminate the business relationship, and shall consider making a report to the financial intelligence unit (FIU) in accordance with Article 22 in relation to the customer.

Member States shall not be obliged to apply the previous subparagraph in situations when notaries, independent legal professionals, auditors, external accountants and tax advisors are in the course of ascertaining the legal position for their client or performing their task of defending or representing that client in, or concerning judicial proceedings, including advice on instituting or avoiding proceedings.

6.   Member States shall require that institutions and persons covered by this Directive apply the customer due diligence procedures not only to all new customers but also at appropriate times to existing customers on a risk-sensitive basis.

Article 10

1.   Member States shall require that all casino customers be identified and their identity verified if they purchase or exchange gambling chips with a value of EUR 2 000 or more.

2.   Casinos subject to State supervision shall be deemed in any event to have satisfied the customer due diligence requirements if they register, identify and verify the identity of their customers immediately on or before entry, regardless of the amount of gambling chips purchased.

Section 2
Simplified customer due diligence

Article 11

1.   By way of derogation from Articles 7(a), (b) and (d), 8 and 9(1), the institutions and persons covered by this Directive shall not be subject to the requirements provided for in those Articles where the customer is a credit or financial institution covered by this Directive, or a credit or financial institution situated in a third country which imposes requirements equivalent to those laid down in this Directive and supervised for compliance with those requirements.

2.   By way of derogation from Articles 7(a), (b) and (d), 8 and 9(1) Member States may allow the institutions and persons covered by this Directive not to apply customer due diligence in respect of:

(a)   listed companies whose securities are admitted to trading on a regulated market within the meaning of Directive 2004/39/EC in one or more Member States and listed companies from third countries which are subject to disclosure requirements consistent with Community legislation;

(b)   beneficial owners of pooled accounts held by notaries and other independent legal professionals from the Member States, or from third countries provided that they are subject to requirements to combat money laundering or terrorist financing consistent with international standards and are supervised for compliance with those requirements and provided that the information on the identity of the beneficial owner is available, on request, to the institutions that act as depository institutions for the pooled accounts;

(c)   domestic public authorities,

or in respect of any other customer representing a low risk of money laundering or terrorist financing which meets the technical criteria established in accordance with Article 40(1)(b).

3.   In the cases mentioned in paragraphs 1 and 2, institutions and persons covered by this Directive shall in any case gather sufficient information to establish if the customer qualifies for an exemption as mentioned in these paragraphs.

4.   The Member States shall inform each other and the Commission of cases where they consider that a third country meets the conditions laid down in paragraphs 1 or 2 or in other situations which meet the technical criteria established in accordance with Article 40(1)(b).

5.   By way of derogation from Articles 7(a), (b) and (d), 8 and 9(1), Member States may allow the institutions and persons covered by this Directive not to apply customer due diligence in respect of:

(a)   life insurance policies where the annual premium is no more than EUR 1 000 or the single premium is no more than EUR 2 500;

(b)   insurance policies for pension schemes if there is no surrender clause and the policy cannot be used as collateral;

(c)   a pension, superannuation or similar scheme that provides retirement benefits to employees, where contributions are made by way of deduction from wages and the scheme rules do not permit the assignment of a member's interest under the scheme;

(d)   electronic money, as defined in Article 1(3)(b) of Directive 2000/46/EC of the European Parliament and of the Council of 18 September 2000 on the taking up, pursuit of and prudential supervision of the business of electronic money institutions[16], where, if the device cannot be recharged, the maximum amount stored in the device is no more than EUR 150, or where, if the device can be recharged, a limit of EUR 2 500 is imposed on the total amount transacted in a calendar year, except when an amount of EUR 1 000 or more is redeemed in that same calendar year by the bearer as referred to in Article 3 of Directive 2000/46/EC,

or in respect of any other product or transaction representing a low risk of money laundering or terrorist financing which meets the technical criteria established in accordance with Article 40(1)(b).

Notes
16   OJ L 275, 27.10.2000, p. 39.

Article 12

Where the Commission adopts a decision pursuant to Article 40(4), the Member States shall prohibit the institutions and persons covered by this Directive from applying simplified due diligence to credit and financial institutions or listed companies from the third country concerned or other entities following from situations which meet the technical criteria established in accordance with Article 40(1)(b).

Section 3
Enhanced customer due diligence

Article 13

1.   Member States shall require the institutions and persons covered by this Directive to apply, on a risk-sensitive basis, enhanced customer due diligence measures, in addition to the measures referred to in Articles 7, 8 and 9(6), in situations which by their nature can present a higher risk of money laundering or terrorist financing, and at least in the situations set out in paragraphs 2, 3, 4 and in other situations representing a high risk of money laundering or terrorist financing which meet the technical criteria established in accordance with Article 40(1)(c).

2.   Where the customer has not been physically present for identification purposes, Member States shall require those institutions and persons to take specific and adequate measures to compensate for the higher risk, for example by applying one or more of the following measures:

(a)   ensuring that the customer's identity is established by additional documents, data or information;

(b) supplementary measures to verify or certify the documents supplied, or requiring confirmatory certification by a credit or financial institution covered by this Directive;

(c) ensuring that the first payment of the operations is carried out through an account opened in the customer's name with a credit institution.

3.   In respect of cross-frontier correspondent banking relationships with respondent institutions from third countries, Member States shall require their credit institutions to:

(a) gather sufficient information about a respondent institution to understand fully the nature of the respondent's business and to determine from publicly available information the reputation of the institution and the quality of supervision;

(b) assess the respondent institution's anti-money laundering and anti-terrorist financing controls;

(c) obtain approval from senior management before establishing new correspondent banking relationships;

(d) document the respective responsibilities of each institution;

(e) with respect to payable-through accounts, be satisfied that the respondent credit institution has verified the identity of and performed ongoing due diligence on the customers having direct access to accounts of the correspondent and that it is able to provide relevant customer due diligence data to the correspondent institution, upon request.

4.   In respect of transactions or business relationships with politically exposed persons residing in another Member State or in a third country, Member States shall require those institutions and persons covered by this Directive to:

(a) have appropriate risk-based procedures to determine whether the customer is a politically exposed person;

(b) have senior management approval for establishing business relationships with such customers;

(c) take adequate measures to establish the source of wealth and source of funds that are involved in the business relationship or transaction;

(d) conduct enhanced ongoing monitoring of the business relationship.

5.   Member States shall prohibit credit institutions from entering into or continuing a correspondent banking relationship with a shell bank and shall require that credit institutions take appropriate measures to ensure that they do not engage in or continue correspondent banking relationships with a bank that is known to permit its accounts to be used by a shell bank.

6.   Member States shall ensure that the institutions and persons covered by this Directive pay special attention to any money laundering or terrorist financing threat that may arise from products or transactions that might favour anonymity, and take measures, if needed, to prevent their use for money laundering or terrorist financing purposes.

Section 4
Performance by third parties

Article 14

Member States may permit the institutions and persons covered by this Directive to rely on third parties to meet the requirements laid down in Article 8(1)(a) to (c).

However, the ultimate responsibility for meeting those requirements shall remain with the institution or person covered by this Directive which relies on the third party.

Article 15

1.   Where a Member State permits credit and financial institutions referred to in Article 2(1)(1) or (2) situated in its territory to be relied on as a third party domestically, that Member State shall in any case permit institutions and persons referred to in Article 2(1) situated in its territory to recognise and accept, in accordance with the provisions laid down in Article 14, the outcome of the customer due diligence requirements laid down in Article 8(1)(a) to (c), carried out in accordance with this Directive by an institution referred to in Article 2(1)(1) or (2) in another Member State, with the exception of currency exchange offices and money transmission or remittance offices, and meeting the requirements laid down in Articles 16 and 18, even if the documents or data on which these requirements have been based are different to those required in the Member State to which the customer is being referred.

2.   Where a Member State permits currency exchange offices and money transmission or remittance offices referred to in Article 3(2)(a) situated in its territory to be relied on as a third party domestically, that Member State shall in any case permit them to recognise and accept, in accordance with Article 14, the outcome of the customer due diligence requirements laid down in Article 8(1) (a) to (c), carried out in accordance with this Directive by the same category of institution in another Member State and meeting the requirements laid down in Articles 16 and 18, even if the documents or data on which these requirements have been based are different to those required in the Member State to which the customer is being referred.

3.   Where a Member State permits persons referred to in Article 2(1)(3)(a) to (c) situated in its territory to be relied on as a third party domestically, that Member State shall in any case permit them to recognise and accept, in accordance with Article 14, the outcome of the customer due diligence requirements laid down in Article 8(1)(a) to (c), carried out in accordance with this Directive by a person referred to in Article 2(1)(3)(a) to (c) in another Member State and meeting the requirements laid down in Articles 16 and 18, even if the documents or data on which these requirements have been based are different to those required in the Member State to which the customer is being referred.

Article 16

1.   For the purposes of this Section, 'third parties' shall mean institutions and persons who are listed in Article 2, or equivalent institutions and persons situated in a third country, who meet the following requirements:

(a) they are subject to mandatory professional registration, recognised by law;

(b) they apply customer due diligence requirements and record keeping requirements as laid down or equivalent to those laid down in this Directive and their compliance with the requirements of this Directive is supervised in accordance with Section 2 of Chapter V, or they are situated in a third country which imposes equivalent requirements to those laid down in this Directive.

2.   Member States shall inform each other and the Commission of cases where they consider that a third country meets the conditions laid down in paragraph 1(b).

Article 17

Where the Commission adopts a decision pursuant to Article 40(4), Member States shall prohibit the institutions and persons covered by this Directive from relying on third parties from the third country concerned to meet the requirements laid down in Article 8(1)(a) to (c).

Article 18

1. Third parties shall make information requested in accordance with the requirements laid down in Article 8(1)(a) to (c) immediately available to the institution or person covered by this Directive to which the customer is being referred.

2. Relevant copies of identification and verification data and other relevant documentation on the identity of the customer or the beneficial owner shall immediately be forwarded, on request, by the third party to the institution or person covered by this Directive to which the customer is being referred.

Article 19

This Section shall not apply to outsourcing or agency relationships where, on the basis of a contractual arrangement, the outsourcing service provider or agent is to be regarded as part of the institution or person covered by this Directive.

Chapter III
Reporting obligations

Section 1
General provisions

Article 20

Member States shall require that the institutions and persons covered by this Directive pay special attention to any activity which they regard as particularly likely, by its nature, to be related to money laundering or terrorist financing and in particular complex or unusually large transactions and all unusual patterns of transactions which have no apparent economic or visible lawful purpose.

Article 21

1. Each Member State shall establish a FIU in order effectively to combat money laundering and terrorist financing.

2. That FIU shall be established as a central national unit. It shall be responsible for receiving (and to the extent permitted, requesting), analysing and disseminating to the competent authorities, disclosures of information which concern potential money laundering, potential terrorist financing or are required by national legislation or regulation. It shall be provided with adequate resources in order to fulfil its tasks.

3. Member States shall ensure that the FIU has access, directly or indirectly, on a timely basis, to the financial, administrative and law enforcement information that it requires to properly fulfil its tasks.

Article 22

1. Member States shall require the institutions and persons covered by this Directive, and where applicable their directors and employees, to cooperate fully:

(a) by promptly informing the FIU, on their own initiative, where the institution or person covered by this Directive knows, suspects or has reasonable grounds to suspect that money laundering or terrorist financing is being or has been committed or attempted;

(b) by promptly furnishing the FIU, at its request, with all necessary information, in accordance with the procedures established by the applicable legislation.

2. The information referred to in paragraph 1 shall be forwarded to the FIU of the Member State in whose territory the institution or person forwarding the information is situated. The person or persons designated in accordance with the procedures provided for in Article 34 shall normally forward the information.

Article 23

1. By way of derogation from Article 22(1), Member States may, in the case of the persons referred to in Article 2(1)(3)(a) and (b), designate an appropriate self-regulatory body of the profession concerned as the authority to be informed in the first instance in place of the FIU. Without prejudice to paragraph 2, the designated self-regulatory body shall in such cases forward the information to the FIU promptly and unfiltered.

2. Member States shall not be obliged to apply the obligations laid down in Article 22(1) to notaries, independent legal professionals, auditors, external accountants and tax advisors with regard to information they receive from or obtain on one of their clients, in the course of ascertaining the legal position for their client or performing their task of defending or representing that client in, or concerning judicial proceedings, including advice on instituting or avoiding proceedings, whether such information is received or obtained before, during or after such proceedings.

Article 24

1. Member States shall require the institutions and persons covered by this Directive to refrain from carrying out transactions which they know or suspect to be related to money laundering or terrorist financing until they have completed the necessary action in accordance with Article 22(1)(a). In conformity with the legislation of the Member States, instructions may be given not to carry out the transaction.

2. Where such a transaction is suspected of giving rise to money laundering or terrorist financing and where to refrain in such manner is impossible or is likely to frustrate efforts to pursue the beneficiaries of a suspected money laundering or terrorist financing operation, the institutions and persons concerned shall inform the FIU immediately afterwards.

Article 25

1. Member States shall ensure that if, in the course of inspections carried out in the institutions and persons covered by this Directive by the competent authorities referred to in Article 37, or in any other way, those authorities discover facts that could be related to money laundering or terrorist financing, they shall promptly inform the FIU.

2.   Member States shall ensure that supervisory bodies empowered by law or regulation to oversee the stock, foreign exchange and financial derivatives markets inform the FIU if they discover facts that could be related to money laundering or terrorist financing.

Article 26

The disclosure in good faith as foreseen in Articles 22(1) and 23 by an institution or person covered by this Directive or by an employee or director of such an institution or person of the information referred to in Articles 22 and 23 shall not constitute a breach of any restriction on disclosure of information imposed by contract or by any legislative, regulatory or administrative provision, and shall not involve the institution or person or its directors or employees in liability of any kind.

Article 27

Member States shall take all appropriate measures in order to protect employees of the institutions or persons covered by this Directive who report suspicions of money laundering or terrorist financing either internally or to the FIU from being exposed to threats or hostile action.

Section 2
Prohibition of disclosure

Article 28

1.   The institutions and persons covered by this Directive and their directors and employees shall not disclose to the customer concerned or to other third persons the fact that information has been transmitted in accordance with Articles 22 and 23 or that a money laundering or terrorist financing investigation is being or may be carried out.

2.   The prohibition laid down in paragraph 1 shall not include disclosure to the competent authorities referred to in Article 37, including the self-regulatory bodies, or disclosure for law enforcement purposes.

3.   The prohibition laid down in paragraph 1 shall not prevent disclosure between institutions from Member States, or from third countries provided that they meet the conditions laid down in Article 11(1), belonging to the same group as defined by Article 2(12) of Directive 2002/87/EC of the European Parliament and of the Council of 16 December 2002 on the supplementary supervision of credit institutions, insurance undertakings and investment firms in a financial conglomerate[17].

4.   The prohibition laid down in paragraph 1 shall not prevent disclosure between persons referred to in Article 2(1)(3)(a) and (b) from Member States, or from third countries which impose requirements equivalent to those laid down in this Directive, who perform their professional activities, whether as employees or not, within the same legal person or a network. For the purposes of this Article, a 'network' means the larger structure to which the person belongs and which shares common ownership, management or compliance control.

5.   For institutions or persons referred to in Article 2(1)(1), (2) and (3)(a) and (b) in cases related to the same customer and the same transaction involving two or more institutions or persons, the prohibition laid down in paragraph 1 shall not prevent disclosure between the relevant institutions or persons provided that they are situated in a Member State, or in a third country which imposes requirements

equivalent to those laid down in this Directive, and that they are from the same professional category and are subject to equivalent obligations as regards professional secrecy and personal data protection. The information exchanged shall be used exclusively for the purposes of the prevention of money laundering and terrorist financing.

6.   Where the persons referred to in Article 2(1)(3)(a) and (b) seek to dissuade a client from engaging in illegal activity, this shall not constitute a disclosure within the meaning of the paragraph 1.

7.   The Member States shall inform each other and the Commission of cases where they consider that a third country meets the conditions laid down in paragraphs 3, 4 or 5.

Notes
17   OJ L 35, 11.2.2003, p. 1.

Article 29

Where the Commission adopts a decision pursuant to Article 40(4), the Member States shall prohibit the disclosure between institutions and persons covered by this Directive and institutions and persons from the third country concerned.

Chapter IV
Record keeping and statistical data

Article 30

Member States shall require the institutions and persons covered by this Directive to keep the following documents and information for use in any investigation into, or analysis of, possible money laundering or terrorist financing by the FIU or by other competent authorities in accordance with national law:

(a)   in the case of the customer due diligence, a copy or the references of the evidence required, for a period of at least five years after the business relationship with their customer has ended;

(b)   in the case of business relationships and transactions, the supporting evidence and records, consisting of the original documents or copies admissible in court proceedings under the applicable national legislation for a period of at least five years following the carrying-out of the transactions or the end of the business relationship.

Article 31

1.   Member States shall require the credit and financial institutions covered by this Directive to apply, where applicable, in their branches and majority-owned subsidiaries located in third countries measures at least equivalent to those laid down in this Directive with regard to customer due diligence and record keeping.

Where the legislation of the third country does not permit application of such equivalent measures, the Member States shall require the credit and financial institutions concerned to inform the competent authorities of the relevant home Member State accordingly.

2.   Member States and the Commission shall inform each other of cases where the legislation of the third country does not permit application of the measures

required under the first subparagraph of paragraph 1 and coordinated action could be taken to pursue a solution.

3.   Member States shall require that, where the legislation of the third country does not permit application of the measures required under the first subparagraph of paragraph 1, credit or financial institutions take additional measures to effectively handle the risk of money laundering or terrorist financing.

Article 32

Member States shall require that their credit and financial institutions have systems in place that enable them to respond fully and rapidly to enquiries from the FIU, or from other authorities, in accordance with their national law, as to whether they maintain or have maintained during the previous five years a business relationship with specified natural or legal persons and on the nature of that relationship.

Article 33

1.   Member States shall ensure that they are able to review the effectiveness of their systems to combat money laundering or terrorist financing by maintaining comprehensive statistics on matters relevant to the effectiveness of such systems.

2.   Such statistics shall as a minimum cover the number of suspicious transaction reports made to the FIU, the follow-up given to these reports and indicate on an annual basis the number of cases investigated, the number of persons prosecuted, the number of persons convicted for money laundering or terrorist financing offences and how much property has been frozen, seized or confiscated.

3.   Member States shall ensure that a consolidated review of these statistical reports is published.

Chapter V
Enforcement measures

Section 1
Internal procedures, training and feedback

Article 34

1.   Member States shall require that the institutions and persons covered by this Directive establish adequate and appropriate policies and procedures of customer due diligence, reporting, record keeping, internal control, risk assessment, risk management, compliance management and communication in order to forestall and prevent operations related to money laundering or terrorist financing.

2.   Member States shall require that credit and financial institutions covered by this Directive communicate relevant policies and procedures where applicable to branches and majority-owned subsidiaries in third countries.

Article 35

1.   Member States shall require that the institutions and persons covered by this Directive take appropriate measures so that their relevant employees are aware of the provisions in force on the basis of this Directive.

These measures shall include participation of their relevant employees in special ongoing training programmes to help them recognise operations which may be related to money laundering or terrorist financing and to instruct them as to how to proceed in such cases.

Where a natural person falling within any of the categories listed in Article 2(1) (3) performs his professional activities as an employee of a legal person, the obligations in this Section shall apply to that legal person rather than to the natural person.

2.   Member States shall ensure that the institutions and persons covered by this Directive have access to up-to-date information on the practices of money launderers and terrorist financers and on indications leading to the recognition of suspicious transactions.

3.   Member States shall ensure that, wherever practicable, timely feedback on the effectiveness of and follow-up to reports of suspected money laundering or terrorist financing is provided.

Section 2
Supervision

Article 36

1.   Member States shall provide that currency exchange offices and trust and company service providers shall be licensed or registered and casinos be licensed in order to operate their business legally. Without prejudice to future Community legislation, Member States shall provide that money transmission or remittance offices shall be licensed or registered in order to operate their business legally.

2.   Member States shall require competent authorities to refuse licensing or registration of the entities referred to in paragraph 1 if they are not satisfied that the persons who effectively direct or will direct the business of such entities or the beneficial owners of such entities are fit and proper persons.

Article 37

1.   Member States shall require the competent authorities at least to effectively monitor and to take the necessary measures with a view to ensuring compliance with the requirements of this Directive by all the institutions and persons covered by this Directive.

2.   Member States shall ensure that the competent authorities have adequate powers, including the power to compel the production of any information that is relevant to monitoring compliance and perform checks, and have adequate resources to perform their functions.

3.   In the case of credit and financial institutions and casinos, competent authorities shall have enhanced supervisory powers, notably the possibility to conduct on-site inspections.

4.   In the case of the natural and legal persons referred to in Article 2(1)(3)(a) to (e), Member States may allow the functions referred to in paragraph 1 to be performed on a risk-sensitive basis.

5.   In the case of the persons referred to in Article 2(1)(3)(a) and (b), Member States may allow the functions referred to in paragraph 1 to be performed by self-regulatory bodies, provided that they comply with paragraph 2.

Section 3
Cooperation

Article 38

The Commission shall lend such assistance as may be needed to facilitate coordination, including the exchange of information between FIUs within the Community.

Section 4
Penalties

Article 39

1.   Member States shall ensure that natural and legal persons covered by this Directive can be held liable for infringements of the national provisions adopted pursuant to this Directive. The penalties must be effective, proportionate and dissuasive.

2.   Without prejudice to the right of Member States to impose criminal penalties, Member States shall ensure, in conformity with their national law, that the appropriate administrative measures can be taken or administrative sanctions can be imposed against credit and financial institutions for infringements of the national provisions adopted pursuant to this Directive. Member States shall ensure that these measures or sanctions are effective, proportionate and dissuasive.

3.   In the case of legal persons, Member States shall ensure that at least they can be held liable for infringements referred to in paragraph 1 which are committed for their benefit by any person, acting either individually or as part of an organ of the legal person, who has a leading position within the legal person, based on:

(a)   a power of representation of the legal person;

(b)   an authority to take decisions on behalf of the legal person, or

(c)   an authority to exercise control within the legal person.

4.   In addition to the cases already provided for in paragraph 3, Member States shall ensure that legal persons can be held liable where the lack of supervision or control by a person referred to in paragraph 3 has made possible the commission of the infringements referred to in paragraph 1 for the benefit of a legal person by a person under its authority.

Chapter VI
Implementing measures

Article 40

1.   In order to take account of technical developments in the fight against money laundering or terrorist financing and to ensure uniform implementation of this Directive, the Commission may, in accordance with the procedure referred to in Article 41(2), adopt the following implementing measures:

(a)   clarification of the technical aspects of the definitions in Article 3(2)(a) and (d), (6), (7), (8), (9) and (10);

(b)   establishment of technical criteria for assessing whether situations represent a low risk of money laundering or terrorist financing as referred to in Article 11(2) and (5);

374

(c) establishment of technical criteria for assessing whether situations represent a high risk of money laundering or terrorist financing as referred to in Article 13;

(d) establishment of technical criteria for assessing whether, in accordance with Article 2(2), it is justified not to apply this Directive to certain legal or natural persons carrying out a financial activity on an occasional or very limited basis.

2. In any event, the Commission shall adopt the first implementing measures to give effect to paragraphs 1(b) and 1(d) by 15 June 2006.

3. The Commission shall, in accordance with the procedure referred to in Article 41(2), adapt the amounts referred to in Articles 2(1)(3)(e), 7(b), 10(1) and 11(5) (a) and (d) taking into account Community legislation, economic developments and changes in international standards.

4. Where the Commission finds that a third country does not meet the conditions laid down in Article 11(1) or (2), Article 28(3), (4) or (5), or in the measures established in accordance with paragraph 1(b) of this Article or in Article 16(1) (b), or that the legislation of that third country does not permit application of the measures required under the first subparagraph of Article 31(1), it shall adopt a decision so stating in accordance with the procedure referred to in Article 41(2).

Article 41

1. The Commission shall be assisted by a Committee on the Prevention of Money Laundering and Terrorist Financing, hereinafter 'the Committee'.

2. Where reference is made to this paragraph, Articles 5 and 7 of Decision 1999/468/EC shall apply, having regard to the provisions of Article 8 thereof and provided that the implementing measures adopted in accordance with this procedure do not modify the essential provisions of this Directive.

The period laid down in Article 5(6) of Decision 1999/468/EC shall be set at three months.

3. The Committee shall adopt its Rules of Procedure.

4. Without prejudice to the implementing measures already adopted, the implementation of the provisions of this Directive concerning the adoption of technical rules and decisions in accordance with the procedure referred to in paragraph 2 shall be suspended four years after the entry into force of this Directive. On a proposal from the Commission, the European Parliament and the Council may renew the provisions concerned in accordance with the procedure laid down in Article 251 of the Treaty and, to that end, shall review them prior to the expiry of the four-year period.

Chapter VII
Final provisions

Article 42

By 15 December 2009, and at least at three-yearly intervals thereafter, the Commission shall draw up a report on the implementation of this Directive and submit it to the European Parliament and the Council. For the first such report, the Commission shall include a specific examination of the treatment of lawyers and other independent legal professionals.

Article 43

By 15 December 2010, the Commission shall present a report to the European Parliament and to the Council on the threshold percentages in Article 3(6), paying particular attention to the possible expediency and consequences of a reduction of the percentage in points (a)(i), (b)(i) and (b)(iii) of Article 3(6) from 25 % to 20 %. On the basis of the report the Commission may submit a proposal for amendments to this Directive.

Article 44

Directive 91/308/EEC is hereby repealed.

References made to the repealed Directive shall be construed as being made to this Directive and should be read in accordance with the correlation table set out in the Annex.

Article 45

1.   Member States shall bring into force the laws, regulations and administrative provisions necessary to comply with this Directive by 15 December 2007. They shall forthwith communicate to the Commission the text of those provisions together with a table showing how the provisions of this Directive correspond to the national provisions adopted.

When Member States adopt those measures, they shall contain a reference to this Directive or be accompanied by such a reference on the occasion of their official publication. The methods of making such reference shall be laid down by Member States.

2.   Member States shall communicate to the Commission the text of the main provisions of national law which they adopt in the field covered by this Directive.

Article 46

This Directive shall enter into force on the 20th day after its publication in the Official Journal of the European Union.

Article 47

This Directive is addressed to the Member States.

Done at Strasbourg, 26 October 2005.

For the European Parliament

The President

J. Borrell Fontelles

For the Council

The President

D. Alexander

Annex
Correlation table

This Directive	Directive 91/308/EEC
Article 1(1)	Article 2
Article 1(2)	Article 1(C)
Article 1(2)(a)	Article 1(C) first point
Article 1(2)(b)	Article 1(C) second point
Article 1(2)(c)	Article 1(C) third point
Article 1(2)(d)	Article 1(C) fourth point
Article 1(3)	Article 1(C), third paragraph
Article 1(4)	
Article 1(5)	Article 1(C), second paragraph
Article 2(1)(1)	Article 2a(1)
Article 2(1)(2)	Article 2a(2)
Article 2(1)(3)(a), (b) and (d) to (f)	Article 2a(3) to (7)
Article 2(1)(3)(c)	
Article 2(2)	
Article 3(1)	Article 1(A)
Article 3(2)(a)	Article 1(B)(1)
Article 3(2)(b)	Article 1(B)(2)
Article 3(2)(c)	Article 1(B)(3)
Article 3(2)(d)	Article 1(B)(4)
Article 3(2)(e)	
Article 3(2)(f)	Article 1(B), second paragraph
Article 3(3)	Article 1(D)
Article 3(4)	Article 1(E), first paragraph
Article 3(5)	Article 1(E), second paragraph
Article 3(5)(a)	
Article 3(5)(b)	Article 1(E), first indent
Article 3(5)(c)	Article 1(E), second indent
Article 3(5)(d)	Article 1(E), third indent
Article 3(5)(e)	Article 1(E), fourth indent
Article 3(5)(f)	Article 1(E), fifth indent, and third paragraph
Article 3(6)	
Article 3(7)	
Article 3(8)	
Article 3(9)	
Article 3(10)	
Article 4	Article 12

Appendix 1   Statutory and EU Provisions

This Directive	Directive 91/308/EEC
Article 5	Article 15
Article 6	
Article 7(a)	Article 3(1)
Article 7(b)	Article 3(2)
Article 7(c)	Article 3(8)
Article 7(d)	Article 3(7)
Article 8(1)(a)	Article 3(1)
Article 8(1)(b) to (d)	
Article 8(2)	
Article 9(1)	Article 3(1)
Article 9(2) to (6)	
Article 10	Article 3(5) and (6)
Article 11(1)	Article 3(9)
Article 11(2)	
Article 11(3) and (4)	
Article 11(5)(a)	Article 3(3)
Article 11(5)(b)	Article 3(4)
Article 11(5)(c)	Article 3(4)
Article 11(5)(d)	
Article 12	
Article 13(1) and (2)	Article 3(10) and (11)
Article 13(3) to (5)	
Article 13(6)	Article 5
Article 14	
Article 15	
Article 16	
Article 17	
Article 18	
Article 19	
Article 20	Article 5
Article 21	
Article 22	Article 6(1) and (2)
Article 23	Article 6(3)
Article 24	Article 7
Article 25	Article 10
Article 26	Article 9
Article 27	
Article 28(1)	Article 8(1)

This Directive	Directive 91/308/EEC
Article 28(2) to (7)	
Article 29	
Article 30(a)	Article 4, first indent
Article 30(b)	Article 4, second indent
Article 31	
Article 32	
Article 33	
Article 34(1)	Article 11(1) (a)
Article 34(2)	
Article 35(1), first paragraph	Article 11(1)(b), first sentence
Article 35(1), second paragraph	Article 11(1)(b) second sentence
Article 35(1), third paragraph	Article 11(1), second paragraph
Article 35(2)	
Article 35(3)	
Article 36	
Article 37	
Article 38	
Article 39(1)	Article 14
Article 39(2) to (4)	
Article 40	
Article 41	
Article 42	Article 17
Article 43	
Article 44	
Article 45	Article 16
Article 46	Article 16

Appendix 1.9 Commission Directive 2006/70/EC

Commission Directive 2006/70/EC

of 1 August 2006

laying down implementing measures for Directive 2005/60/EC of the European Parliament and of the Council as regards the definition of 'politically exposed person' and the technical criteria for simplified customer due diligence procedures and for exemption on grounds of a financial activity conducted on an occasional or very limited basis

The Commission of the European Communities,

Having regard to the Treaty establishing the European Community,

Having regard to Directive 2005/60/EC of the European Parliament and of the Council of 26 October 2005 on the prevention of the use of the financial system for the purpose of money laundering and terrorist financing[1], and in particular points (a), (b) and (d) of Article 40(1) thereof,

Whereas:

(1) Directive 2005/60/EC requires institutions and persons covered to apply, on a risk-sensitive basis, enhanced customer due diligence measures in respect of transactions or business relationships with politically exposed persons residing in another Member State or in a third country. In the context of this risk analysis, it is appropriate for the resources of the institutions and persons covered to be focused in particular on products and transactions that are characterised by a high risk of money laundering. Politically exposed persons are understood to be persons entrusted with prominent public functions, their immediate family members or persons known to be close associates of such persons. In order to provide for a coherent application of the concept of politically exposed person, when determining the groups of persons covered, it is essential to take into consideration the social, political and economic differences between countries concerned.

(2) Institutions and persons covered by Directive 2005/60/EC may fail to identify a customer as falling within one of the politically exposed person categories, despite having taken reasonable and adequate measures in this regard. In those circumstances, Member States, when exercising their powers in relation to the application of that Directive, should give due consideration to the need to ensure that those persons do not automatically incur liability for such failure. Member States should also consider facilitating compliance with that Directive by providing the necessary guidance to institutions and persons in this connection.

(3) Public functions exercised at levels lower than national should normally not be considered prominent. However, where their political exposure is comparable to that of similar positions at national level, institutions and persons covered by this Directive should consider, on a risk-sensitive basis, whether persons exercising those public functions should be considered as politically exposed persons.

(4) Where Directive 2005/60/EC requires institutions and persons covered to identify close associates of natural persons who are entrusted with prominent public functions, this requirement applies to the extent that the relation with the associate is publicly known or that the institution or person has reasons to believe that such relation exists. Thus it does not presuppose active research on the part of the institutions and persons covered by the Directive.

(5) Persons falling under the concept of politically exposed persons should not be considered as such after they have ceased to exercise prominent public functions, subject to a minimum period.

(6) Since the adaptation, on a risk-sensitive basis, of the general customer due diligence procedures to low-risk situations is the normal tool under Directive 2005/60/EC, and given the fact that simplified customer due diligence procedures require adequate checks and balances elsewhere in the system aiming at preventing money laundering and terrorist financing, the application of simplified customer due diligence procedures should be restricted to a limited number of cases. In these cases, the requirements for institutions and persons covered by that Directive do not disappear, and these are expected to, inter alia, conduct ongoing monitoring of the business relations, in order to be able to detect complex or unusually large transactions which have no apparent economic or visible lawful purpose.

(7) Domestic public authorities are generally considered as low-risk customers within their own Member State and, in accordance with Directive 2005/60/EC, may be subject to simplified customer due diligence procedures. However, none of the Community institutions, bodies, offices or agencies, including the European Central Bank (ECB), directly qualify in the Directive for simplified customer due diligence under the 'domestic public authority' category or, in the case of the ECB, under the 'credit and financial institution' category. However, since these entities do not appear to present a high risk of money laundering or terrorist financing, they should be recognised as low-risk customers and benefit from the simplified customer due diligence procedures provided that appropriate criteria are fulfilled.

(8) Furthermore, it should be possible to apply simplified customer due diligence procedures in the case of legal entities undertaking financial activities which do not fall under the definition of financial institution under Directive 2005/60/EC but which are subject to national legislation pursuant to that Directive and comply with requirements concerning sufficient transparency as to their identity and adequate control mechanisms, in particular enhanced supervision. This could be the case for undertakings providing general insurance services.

(9) It should be possible to apply simplified customer due diligence procedures to products and related transactions in limited circumstances, for example where the benefits of the financial product in question cannot generally be realised for the benefit of third parties and those benefits are only realisable in the long term, such as some investment insurance policies or savings products, or where the financial product aims at financing physical assets in the form of leasing agreements in which the legal and beneficial title of the underlying asset remains with the leasing company or in the form of low value consumer credit, provided the transactions are carried out through bank accounts and are below an appropriate threshold. State controlled

products which are generally addressed to specific categories of clients, such as savings products for the benefit of children, should benefit from simplified customer due diligence procedures even if not all the criteria are fulfilled. State control should be understood as an activity beyond normal supervision on financial markets and should not be construed as covering products, such as debt securities, issued directly by the State.

(10) Before allowing use of simplified customer due diligence procedures, Member States should assess whether the customers or the products and related transactions represent a low-risk of money laundering or terrorist financing, notably by paying special attention to any activity of these customers or to any type of products or transactions which may be regarded as particularly likely, by their nature, to be used or abused for money laundering or terrorist financing purposes. In particular, any attempt by customers in relation to low-risk products to act anonymously or hide their identity should be considered as a risk factor and as potentially suspicious.

(11) In certain circumstances, natural persons or legal entities may conduct financial activities on an occasional or very limited basis, as a complement to other non-financial activities, such as hotels that provide currency exchange services to their clients. Directive 2005/60/EC allows Member States to decide that financial activities of that kind fall outside its scope. The assessment of the occasional or very limited nature of the activity should be made by reference to quantitative thresholds in relation to the transactions and the turnover of the business concerned. These thresholds should be decided at national level, depending on the type of financial activity, in order to take account of differences between countries.

(12) Moreover, a person engaging in a financial activity on an occasional or very limited basis should not provide a full range of financial services to the public but only those needed for improving the performance of its main business. When the main business of the person relates to an activity covered by Directive 2005/60/EC, the exemption for occasional or limited financial activities should not be granted, except in relation to traders in goods.

(13) Some financial activities, such as money transmission or remittance services, are more likely to be used or abused for money laundering or terrorist financing purposes. It is therefore necessary to ensure that these or similar financial activities are not exempted from the scope of Directive 2005/60/EC.

(14) Provision should be made for decisions pursuant to Article 2(2) of Directive 2005/60/EC to be withdrawn as quickly as possible if necessary.

(15) Member States should ensure that the exemption decisions are not abused for money laundering or terrorist financing purposes. They notably should avoid adopting decisions under Article 2(2) of Directive 2005/60/EC in cases where monitoring or enforcement activities by national authorities present special difficulties as a result of overlapping competences between more than one Member State, such as the provision of financial services on board ships providing transport services between ports situated in different Member States.

(16) The application of this Directive is without prejudice to the application of Council Regulation (EC) No 2580/2001 of 27 December 2001 on specific restrictive measures directed against certain persons and entities with a view to combating terrorism[2] and Council Regulation (EC) No 881/2002 of 27 May 2002 imposing certain specific restrictive measures directed against certain persons and entities associated with Usama bin Laden, the Al-Qaida network and the Taliban, and repealing Council Regulation (EC) No 467/2001 prohibiting the export of certain goods and services to Afghanistan, strengthening the flight ban and extending the freeze of funds and other financial resources in respect of the Taliban of Afghanistan[3].

(17) The measures provided for in this Directive are in accordance with the opinion of the Committee on the Prevention of Money Laundering and Terrorist Financing,

---

Notes
1 OJ L 309, 25.11.2005, p. 15.
2 OJ L 344, 28.12.2001, p. 70. Regulation as last amended by Decision 2006/379/EC (OJ L 144, 31.5.2006, p. 21).
3 OJ L 139, 29.5.2002, p. 9. Regulation as last amended by Commission Regulation (EC) No 674/2006 (OJ L 116, 29.4.2006, p. 58).

Has adopted this Directive:

Article 1

Subject-matter

This Directive lays down implementing measures for Directive 2005/60/EC as regards the following:

1. the technical aspects of the definition of politically exposed persons set out in Article 3(8) of that Directive;

2. technical criteria for assessing whether situations represent a low risk of money laundering or terrorist financing as referred to in Article 11(2) and (5) of that Directive;

3. technical criteria for assessing whether, in accordance with Article 2(2) of Directive 2005/60/EC, it is justified not to apply that Directive to certain legal or natural persons carrying out a financial activity on an occasional or very limited basis.

Article 2

Politically exposed persons

1. For the purposes of Article 3(8) of Directive 2005/60/EC, 'natural persons who are or have been entrusted with prominent public functions' shall include the following:

(a) heads of State, heads of government, ministers and deputy or assistant ministers;

(b) members of parliaments;

(c) members of supreme courts, of constitutional courts or of other high-level judicial bodies whose decisions are not subject to further appeal, except in exceptional circumstances;

(d) members of courts of auditors or of the boards of central banks;

(e) ambassadors, chargés d'affaires and high-ranking officers in the armed forces;

(f) members of the administrative, management or supervisory bodies of State-owned enterprises.

None of the categories set out in points (a) to (f) of the first subparagraph shall be understood as covering middle ranking or more junior officials.

The categories set out in points (a) to (e) of the first subparagraph shall, where applicable, include positions at Community and international level.

2.   For the purposes of Article 3(8) of Directive 2005/60/EC, 'immediate family members' shall include the following:

(a)   the spouse;

(b)   any partner considered by national law as equivalent to the spouse;

(c)   the children and their spouses or partners;

(d)   the parents.

3.   For the purposes of Article 3(8) of Directive 2005/60/EC, 'persons known to be close associates' shall include the following:

(a)   any natural person who is known to have joint beneficial ownership of legal entities or legal arrangements, or any other close business relations, with a person referred to in paragraph 1;

(b)   any natural person who has sole beneficial ownership of a legal entity or legal arrangement which is known to have been set up for the benefit de facto of the person referred to in paragraph 1.

4.   Without prejudice to the application, on a risk-sensitive basis, of enhanced customer due diligence measures, where a person has ceased to be entrusted with a prominent public function within the meaning of paragraph 1 of this Article for a period of at least one year, institutions and persons referred to in Article 2(1) of Directive 2005/60/EC shall not be obliged to consider such a person as politically exposed.

Article 3

Simplified customer due diligence

1.   For the purposes of Article 11(2) of Directive 2005/60/EC, Member States may, subject to paragraph 4 of this Article, consider customers who are public authorities or public bodies and who fulfil all the following criteria as customers representing a low risk of money laundering or terrorist financing:

(a)   the customer has been entrusted with public functions pursuant to the Treaty on European Union, the Treaties on the Communities or Community secondary legislation;

(b)   the customer's identity is publicly available, transparent and certain;

(c)   the activities of the customer, as well as its accounting practices, are transparent;

(d)   either the customer is accountable to a Community institution or to the authorities of a Member State, or appropriate check and balance procedures exist ensuring control of the customer's activity.

2.   For the purposes of Article 11(2) of Directive 2005/60/EC, Member States may, subject to paragraph 4 of this Article, consider customers who are legal entities which do not enjoy the status of public authority or public body but which fulfil all the following criteria as customers representing a low risk of money laundering or terrorist financing:

(a)   the customer is an entity that undertakes financial activities outside the scope of Article 2 of Directive 2005/60/EC but to which national legislation has extended the obligations of that Directive pursuant to Article 4 thereof;

(b)   the identity of the customer is publicly available, transparent and certain;

(c)   the customer is subject to a mandatory licensing requirement under national law for the undertaking of financial activities and licensing may be refused if the competent authorities are not satisfied that the persons who effectively direct or will direct the business of such an entity, or its beneficial owner, are fit and proper persons;

(d) the customer is subject to supervision, within the meaning of Article 37(3) of Directive 2005/60/EC, by competent authorities as regards compliance with the national legislation transposing that Directive and, where applicable, additional obligations under national legislation;

(e) failure by the customer to comply with the obligations referred to in point (a) is subject to effective, proportionate and dissuasive sanctions including the possibility of appropriate administrative measures or the imposition of administrative sanctions.

Entity, as referred to in point (a) of the first subparagraph, shall include subsidiaries only in so far as the obligations of Directive 2005/60/EC have been extended to them on their own account.

For the purposes of point (c) of the first subparagraph, the activity conducted by the customer shall be supervised by competent authorities. Supervision is to be understood in this context as meaning the type of supervisory activity with the highest supervisory powers, including the possibility of conducting on-site inspections. Such inspections shall include the review of policies, procedures, books and records, and shall extend to sample testing.

3. For the purposes of Article 11(5) of Directive 2005/60/EC, Member States may, subject to paragraph 4 of this Article, allow the institutions and persons covered by that Directive to consider products which fulfil all the following criteria, or transactions related to such products, as representing a low risk of money laundering or terrorist financing:

(a) the product has a written contractual base;

(b) the related transactions are carried out through an account of the customer with a credit institution covered by Directive 2005/60/EC or a credit institution situated in a third country which imposes requirements equivalent to those laid down in that Directive;

(c) the product or related transactions are not anonymous and their nature is such that it allows for the timely application of Article 7(c) of Directive 2005/60/EC;

(d) the product is subject to a predetermined maximum threshold;

(e) the benefits of the product or related transactions cannot be realised for the benefit of third parties, except in the case of death, disablement, survival to a predetermined advanced age, or similar events;

(f) in the case of products or related transactions allowing for the investment of funds in financial assets or claims, including insurance or other kind of contingent claims:

   (i) the benefits of the product or related transactions are only realisable in the long term;

   (ii) the product or related transactions cannot be used as collateral;

   (iii) during the contractual relationship, no accelerated payments are made, no surrender clauses are used and no early termination takes place.

For the purposes of point (d) of the first subparagraph, the thresholds established in Article 11(5)(a) of Directive 2005/60/EC shall apply in the case of insurance policies or savings products of similar nature. Without prejudice to the third subparagraph, in the other cases the maximum threshold shall be EUR 15 000.

Member States may derogate from that threshold in the case of products which are related to the financing of physical assets and where the legal and beneficial title of the assets is not transferred to the customer until termination of the contractual relationship, provided that the threshold established by the Member State for the transactions related to this type of product, whether the transaction is carried out in a single operation or in several operations which appear to be linked, does not exceed EUR 15 000 per year.

Member States may derogate from the criteria set out in points (e) and (f) of the first subparagraph in the case of products the characteristics of which are determined by their relevant domestic public authorities for purposes of general interest, which benefit from specific advantages from the State in the form of direct grants or tax rebates, and the use of which is subject to control by those authorities, provided that the benefits of the product are realisable only in the long term and that the threshold established for the purposes of point (d) of the first subparagraph is sufficiently low. Where appropriate, that threshold may be set as a maximum annual amount.

4.   In assessing whether the customers or products and transactions referred to in paragraphs 1, 2 and 3 represent a low risk of money laundering or terrorist financing, Member States shall pay special attention to any activity of those customers or to any type of product or transaction which may be regarded as particularly likely, by its nature, to be used or abused for money laundering or terrorist financing purposes.

Member States shall not consider that customers or products and transactions referred to in paragraphs 1, 2 and 3 represent a low risk of money laundering or terrorist financing if there is information available to suggest that the risk of money laundering or terrorist financing may not be low.

Article 4

Financial activity on an occasional or very limited basis

1.   For the purposes of Article 2(2) of Directive 2005/60/EC, Member States may, subject to paragraph 2 of this Article, consider legal or natural persons who engage in a financial activity which fulfils all the following criteria as not falling within the scope of Article 3(1) or (2) of that Directive:

(a)   the financial activity is limited in absolute terms;

(b)   the financial activity is limited on a transaction basis;

(c)   the financial activity is not the main activity;

(d)   the financial activity is ancillary and directly related to the main activity;

(e)   with the exception of the activity referred to in point (3)(e) of Article 2(1) of Directive 2005/60/EC, the main activity is not an activity mentioned in Article 2(1) of that Directive;

(f)   the financial activity is provided only to the customers of the main activity and is not generally offered to the public.

For the purposes of point (a) of the first subparagraph, the total turnover of the financial activity may not exceed a threshold which must be sufficiently low. That threshold shall be established at national level, depending on the type of financial activity.

For the purposes of point (b) of the first subparagraph, Member States shall apply a maximum threshold per customer and single transaction, whether the transaction is carried out in a single operation or in several operations which appear to be linked. That threshold shall be established at national level, depending on the type of financial activity. It shall be sufficiently low in order to ensure that the types of transactions in question are an impractical and inefficient method for laundering money or for terrorist financing, and shall not exceed EUR 1 000.

For the purposes of point (c) of the first subparagraph, Member States shall require that the turnover of the financial activity does not exceed 5 % of the total turnover of the legal or natural person concerned.

2.   In assessing the risk of money laundering or terrorist financing occurring for the purposes of Article 2(2) of Directive 2005/60/EC, Member States shall pay special attention to any financial activity which is regarded as particularly likely, by its nature, to be used or abused for money laundering or terrorist financing purposes.

Member States shall not consider that the financial activities referred to in paragraph 1 represent a low risk of money laundering or terrorist financing if there is information available to suggest that the risk of money laundering or terrorist financing may not be low.

3.   Any decision pursuant to Article 2(2) of Directive 2005/60/EC shall state the reasons on which it is based. Member States shall provide for the possibility of withdrawing that decision should circumstances change.

4.   Member States shall establish risk-based monitoring activities or take any other adequate measures to ensure that the exemption granted by decisions pursuant to Article 2(2) of Directive 2005/60/EC is not abused by possible money launderers or financers of terrorism.

Article 5

Transposition

1.   Member States shall bring into force the laws, regulations and administrative provisions necessary to comply with this Directive by 15 December 2007 at the latest. They shall forthwith communicate to the Commission the text of those provisions and a correlation table between those provisions and this Directive.

When Member States adopt those provisions, they shall contain a reference to this Directive or be accompanied by such a reference on the occasion of their official publication. Member States shall determine how such reference is to be made.

2.   Member States shall communicate to the Commission the text of the main provisions of national law which they adopt in the field covered by this Directive.

Article 6

This Directive shall enter into force on the 20th day following its publication in the Official Journal of the European Union.

Article 7

This Directive is addressed to the Member States.
Done at Brussels, 1 August 2006.
For the Commission
Charlie McCreevy
Member of the Commission

Appendix 1.10   Directive 2014/42/EU

Directive 2014/42/EU of the European Parliament and of the Council

of 3 April 2014

on the freezing and confiscation of instrumentalities and proceeds of crime in the European Union

The European Parliament and the Council of the European Union,

Having regard to the Treaty on the Functioning of the European Union, and in particular Article 82(2) and Article 83(1) thereof,
    Having regard to the proposal from the European Commission,
    After transmission of the draft legislative act to the national parliaments,
    Having regard to the opinion of the European Economic and Social Committee[1],
    Having regard to the opinion of the Committee of the Regions[2],
    Acting in accordance with the ordinary legislative procedure[3],

Whereas:

(1) The main motive for cross-border organised crime, including mafia-type criminal organisation, is financial gain. As a consequence, competent authorities should be given the means to trace, freeze, manage and confiscate the proceeds of crime. However, the effective prevention of and fight against organised crime should be achieved by neutralising the proceeds of crime and should be extended, in certain cases, to any property deriving from activities of a criminal nature.

(2) Organised criminal groups operate without borders and increasingly acquire assets in Member States other than those in which they are based and in third countries. There is an increasing need for effective international cooperation on asset recovery and mutual legal assistance.

(3) Among the most effective means of combating organised crime is providing for severe legal consequences for committing such crime, as well as effective detection and the freezing and confiscation of the instrumentalities and proceeds of crime.

(4) Although existing statistics are limited, the amounts recovered from proceeds of crime in the Union seem insufficient compared to the estimated proceeds. Studies have shown that, although regulated by Union and national law, confiscation procedures remain underused.

(5) The adoption of minimum rules will approximate the Member States' freezing and confiscation regimes, thus facilitating mutual trust and effective cross-border cooperation.

(6) The Stockholm Programme and the Justice and Home Affairs Council Conclusions on confiscation and asset recovery adopted in June 2010

emphasise the importance of a more effective identification, confiscation and re-use of criminal assets.

(7) The current Union legal framework on freezing, seizure and confiscation of assets consists of Joint Action 98/699/JHA[4], Council Framework Decision 2001/500/JHA[5], Council Framework Decision 2003/577/JHA[6], Council Framework Decision 2005/212/JHA[7] and Council Framework Decision 2006/783/JHA[8].

(8) The Commission implementation reports on Framework Decisions 2003/577/JHA, 2005/212/JHA and 2006/783/JHA show that existing regimes for extended confiscation and for the mutual recognition of freezing and confiscation orders are not fully effective. Confiscation is hindered by differences between Member States' law.

(9) This Directive aims to amend and expand the provisions of Framework Decisions 2001/500/JHA and 2005/212/JHA. Those Framework Decisions should be partially replaced for the Member States bound by this Directive.

(10) Member States are free to bring confiscation proceedings which are linked to a criminal case before any competent court.

(11) There is a need to clarify the existing concept of proceeds of crime to include the direct proceeds from criminal activity and all indirect benefits, including subsequent reinvestment or transformation of direct proceeds. Thus proceeds can include any property including that which has been transformed or converted, fully or in part, into other property, and that which has been intermingled with property acquired from legitimate sources, up to the assessed value of the intermingled proceeds. It can also include the income or other benefits derived from proceeds of crime, or from property into or with which such proceeds have been transformed, converted or intermingled.

(12) This Directive provides for a broad definition of property that can be subject to freezing and confiscation. That definition includes legal documents or instruments evidencing title or interest in such property. Such documents or instruments could include, for example, financial instruments, or documents that may give rise to creditor claims and are normally found in the possession of the person affected by the relevant procedures. This Directive is without prejudice to the existing national procedures for keeping legal documents or instruments evidencing title or interest in property, as they are applied by the competent national authorities or public bodies in accordance with national law.

(13) Freezing and confiscation under this Directive are autonomous concepts, which should not prevent Member States from implementing this Directive using instruments which, in accordance with national law, would be considered as sanctions or other types of measures.

(14) In the confiscation of instrumentalities and proceeds of crime following a final decision of a court and of property of equivalent value to those instrumentalities and proceeds, the broad concept of criminal offences covered by this Directive should apply. Framework Decision 2001/500/JHA requires Member States to enable the confiscation of instrumentalities and proceeds of crime following a final conviction and to enable the confiscation of property the value of which corresponds to such instrumentalities and proceeds. Such obligations should be maintained for the criminal offences not covered by this Directive, and the concept of proceeds as defined in this Directive should be interpreted in the similar way as regards criminal offences not covered by this Directive. Member States are free to define the confiscation of property of equivalent value as subsidiary or alternative to direct confiscation, as appropriate in accordance with national law.

(15) Subject to a final conviction for a criminal offence, it should be possible to confiscate instrumentalities and proceeds of crime, or property the value of which corresponds to such instrumentalities or proceeds. Such final conviction can also result from proceedings in absentia. When confiscation on the basis of a final conviction is not possible, it should nevertheless under certain circumstances still be possible to confiscate instrumentalities and proceeds, at least in the cases of illness or absconding of the suspected or accused person. However, in such cases of illness and absconding, the existence of proceedings in absentia in Member States would be sufficient to comply with this obligation. When the suspected or accused person has absconded, Member States should take all reasonable steps and may require that the person concerned be summoned to or made aware of the confiscation proceedings.

(16) For the purposes of this Directive, illness should be understood to mean the inability of the suspected or accused person to attend the criminal proceedings for an extended period, as a result of which the proceedings cannot continue under normal conditions. Suspected or accused persons may be requested to prove illness, for example by a medical certificate, which the court should be able to disregard if it finds it unsatisfactory. The right of that person to be represented in the proceedings by a lawyer should not be affected.

(17) When implementing this Directive in respect of confiscation of property the value of which corresponds to instrumentalities, the relevant provisions could be applicable where, in view of the particular circumstances of the case at hand, such a measure is proportionate, having regard in particular to the value of the instrumentalities concerned. Member States may also take into account whether and to what extent the convicted person is responsible for making the confiscation of the instrumentalities impossible.

(18) When implementing this Directive, Member States may provide that, in exceptional circumstances, confiscation should not be ordered, insofar as it would, in accordance with national law, represent undue hardship for the affected person, on the basis of the circumstances of the respective individual case which should be decisive. Member States should make a very restricted use of this possibility, and should only be allowed to provide that confiscation is not to be ordered in cases where it would put the person concerned in a situation in which it would be very difficult for him to survive.

(19) Criminal groups engage in a wide range of criminal activities. In order to effectively tackle organised criminal activities there may be situations where it is appropriate that a criminal conviction be followed by the confiscation not only of property associated with a specific crime, but also of additional property which the court determines constitutes the proceeds of other crimes. This approach is referred to as extended confiscation. Framework Decision 2005/212/JHA provides for three different sets of minimum requirements that Member States can choose from in order to apply extended confiscation. As a result, in the process of transposition of that Framework Decision, Member States have chosen different options which resulted in divergent concepts of extended confiscation in national jurisdictions. That divergence hampers cross-border cooperation in relation to confiscation cases. It is therefore necessary to further harmonise the provisions on extended confiscation by setting a single minimum standard.

(20) When determining whether a criminal offence is liable to give rise to economic benefit, Member States may take into account the modus operandi, for example if a condition of the offence is that it was committed in the context of organised crime or with the intention of generating regular profits from criminal offences. However, this should not, in general, prejudice the possibility to resort to extended confiscation.

(21) Extended confiscation should be possible where a court is satisfied that the property in question is derived from criminal conduct. This does not mean that it must be established that the property in question is derived from criminal conduct. Member States may provide that it could, for example, be sufficient for the court to consider on the balance of probabilities, or to reasonably presume that it is substantially more probable, that the property in question has been obtained from criminal conduct than from other activities. In this context, the court has to consider the specific circumstances of the case, including the facts and available evidence based on which a decision on extended confiscation could be issued. The fact that the property of the person is disproportionate to his lawful income could be among those facts giving rise to a conclusion of the court that the property derives from criminal conduct. Member States could also determine a requirement for a certain period of time during which the property could be deemed to have originated from criminal conduct.

(22) This Directive lays down minimum rules. It does not prevent Member States from providing more extensive powers in their national law, including, for example, in relation to their rules on evidence.

(23) This Directive applies to criminal offences which fall within the scope of the instruments listed herein. Within the scope of those instruments, Member States should apply extended confiscation at least to certain criminal offences as defined in this Directive.

(24) The practice by a suspected or accused person of transferring property to a knowing third party with a view to avoiding confiscation is common and increasingly widespread. The current Union legal framework does not contain binding rules on the confiscation of property transferred to third parties. It is therefore becoming increasingly necessary to allow for the confiscation of property transferred to or acquired by third parties. Acquisition by a third party refers to situations where, for example, property has been acquired, directly or indirectly, for example through an intermediary, by the third party from a suspected or accused person, including when the criminal offence has been committed on their behalf or for their benefit, and when an accused person does not have property that can be confiscated. Such confiscation should be possible at least in cases where third parties knew or ought to have known that the purpose of the transfer or acquisition was to avoid confiscation, on the basis of concrete facts and circumstances, including that the transfer was carried out free of charge or in exchange for an amount significantly lower than the market value. The rules on third party confiscation should extend to both natural and legal persons. In any event the rights of bona fide third parties should not be prejudiced.

(25) Member States are free to define third party confiscation as subsidiary or alternative to direct confiscation, as appropriate in accordance with national law.

(26) Confiscation leads to the final deprivation of property. However, preservation of property can be a prerequisite to confiscation and can be of importance for the enforcement of a confiscation order. Property is preserved by means of freezing. In order to prevent the dissipation of property before a freezing order can be issued, the competent authorities in the Member States should be empowered to take immediate action in order to secure such property.

(27) Since property is often preserved for the purposes of confiscation, freezing and confiscation are closely linked. In some legal systems freezing for the purposes of confiscation is regarded as a separate procedural measure of a provisional nature, which may be followed by a confiscation order. Without prejudice to different national legal systems and to Framework Decision 2003/577/JHA, this Directive should approximate some aspects of the national systems of freezing for the purposes of confiscation.

(28) Freezing measures are without prejudice to the possibility for a specific property to be considered evidence throughout the proceedings, provided that it would ultimately be made available for effective execution of the confiscation order.

(29) In the context of criminal proceedings, property may also be frozen with a view to its possible subsequent restitution or in order to safeguard compensation for the damage caused by a criminal offence.

(30) Suspected or accused persons often hide property throughout the entire duration of criminal proceedings. As a result confiscation orders cannot be executed, leaving those subject to confiscation orders to benefit from their property once they have served their sentences. It is therefore necessary to enable the determination of the precise extent of the property to be confiscated even after a final conviction for a criminal offence, in order to permit the full execution of confiscation orders when no property or insufficient property was initially identified and the confiscation order remains unexecuted.

(31) Given the limitation of the right to property by freezing orders, such provisional measures should not be maintained longer than necessary to preserve the availability of the property with a view to possible subsequent confiscation. This may require a review by the court in order to ensure that the purpose of preventing the dissipation of property remains valid.

(32) Property frozen with a view to possible subsequent confiscation should be managed adequately in order not to lose its economic value. Member States should take the necessary measures, including the possibility of selling or transferring the property to minimise such losses. Member States should take relevant measures, for example the establishment of national centralised Asset Management Offices, a set of specialised offices or equivalent mechanisms, in order to effectively manage the assets frozen before confiscation and preserve their value, pending judicial determination.

(33) This Directive substantially affects the rights of persons, not only of suspected or accused persons, but also of third parties who are not being prosecuted. It is therefore necessary to provide for specific safeguards and judicial remedies in order to guarantee the preservation of their fundamental rights in the implementation of this Directive. This includes the right to be heard for third parties who claim that they are the owner of the property concerned, or who claim that they have other property rights ('real rights', 'ius in re'), such as the right of usufruct. The freezing order should be communicated to the affected person as soon as possible after its execution. Nevertheless, the competent authorities may postpone communicating such orders to the affected person due to the needs of the investigation.

(34) The purpose of communicating the freezing order is, inter alia, to allow the affected person to challenge the order. Therefore, such communication should indicate, at least briefly, the reason or reasons for the order concerned, it being understood that such indication can be very succinct.

(35) Member States should consider taking measures allowing confiscated property to be used for public interest or social purposes. Such measures could, inter alia, comprise earmarking property for law enforcement and crime prevention projects, as well as for other projects of public interest and social utility. That obligation to consider taking measures entails a procedural obligation for Member States, such as conducting a legal analysis or discussing the advantages and disadvantages of introducing measures. When managing frozen property and when taking measures concerning the use of confiscated property, Member States should take appropriate action to prevent criminal or illegal infiltration.

(36) Reliable data sources on the freezing and confiscation of the proceeds of crime are scarce. In order to allow for the evaluation of this Directive, it is necessary to collect a comparable minimum set of appropriate statistical data on freezing and confiscation of property, asset tracing, judicial and asset disposal activities.

(37) Member States should endeavour to collect data for certain statistics at a central level, with a view to sending them to the Commission. This means that the Member States should make reasonable efforts to collect the data concerned. It does not mean, however, that the Member States are under an obligation to achieve the result of collecting the data where there is a disproportionate administrative burden or when there are high costs for the Member State concerned.

(38) This Directive respects the fundamental rights and observes the principles recognised by the Charter of Fundamental Rights of the European Union ('the Charter') and the European Convention for the Protection of Human Rights and Fundamental Freedoms ('the ECHR'), as interpreted in the case-law of the European Court of Human Rights. This Directive should be implemented in accordance with those rights and principles. This Directive should be without prejudice to national law in relation to legal aid and does not create any obligations for Member States' legal aid systems, which should apply in accordance with the Charter and the ECHR.

(39) Specific safeguards should be put in place, so as to ensure that as a general rule reasons are given for confiscation orders, unless when, in simplified criminal proceedings in minor cases, the affected person has waived his or her right to be given reasons.

(40) This Directive should be implemented taking account of the provisions of Directive 2010/64/EU of the European Parliament and of the Council[9], Directive 2012/13/EU of the European Parliament and of the Council[10] and Directive 2013/48/EU of the European Parliament and of the Council[11] which concern procedural rights in criminal proceedings.

(41) Since the objective of this Directive, namely facilitating confiscation of property in criminal matters, cannot be sufficiently achieved by the Member States but can rather be better achieved at Union level, the Union may adopt measures, in accordance with the principle of subsidiarity as set out in Article 5 of the Treaty on European Union (TEU). In accordance with the principle of proportionality, as set out in that Article, this Directive does not go beyond what is necessary in order to achieve that objective.

(42) In accordance with Articles 3 and 4a(1) of Protocol (No 21) on the position of the United Kingdom and Ireland in respect of the Area of Freedom, Security and Justice, annexed to the TEU and to the Treaty on the Functioning of the European Union (TFEU), Ireland has notified its wish to take part in the adoption and application of this Directive. In accordance with that Protocol, Ireland is to be bound by this Directive only in respect of the offences covered by the instruments by which it is bound.

(43) In accordance with Articles 1, 2 and 4a(1) of Protocol (No 21) on the position of the United Kingdom and Ireland in respect of the Area of Freedom, Security and Justice, annexed to the TEU and to the TFEU, and without prejudice to Article 4 of that Protocol, the United Kingdom is not taking part in the adoption of this Directive and is not bound by it or subject to its application. Subject to its participation in accordance with Article 4 of that Protocol, the United Kingdom is to be bound by this Directive only in respect of the offences covered by the instruments by which it is bound.

(44) In accordance with Articles 1 and 2 of Protocol (No 22) on the position of Denmark annexed to the TEU and to the TFEU, Denmark is not taking

part in the adoption of this Directive and is not bound by it or subject to its application,

---

Notes

1   OJ C 299, 4.10.2012, p. 128.
2   OJ C 391, 18.12.2012, p. 134.
3   Position of the European Parliament of 25 February 2014 (not yet published in the Official Journal) and Council decision of 14 March 2014.
4   Joint Action 98/699/JHA of 3 December 1998 adopted by the Council on the basis of Article K.3 of the Treaty on European Union, on money laundering, the identification, tracing, freezing, seizing and confiscation of instrumentalities and the proceeds from crime (OJ L 333, 9.12.1998, p. 1).
5   Council Framework Decision 2001/500/JHA of 26 June 2001 on money laundering, the identification, tracing, freezing, seizing and confiscation of instrumentalities and the proceeds of crime (OJ L 182, 5.7.2001, p. 1).
6   Council Framework Decision 2003/577/JHA of 22 July 2003 on the execution in the European Union of orders freezing property or evidence (OJ L 196, 2.8.2003, p. 45).
7   Council Framework Decision 2005/212/JHA of 24 February 2005 on confiscation of crime-related proceeds, instrumentalities and property (OJ L 68, 15.3.2005, p. 49).
8   Council Framework Decision 2006/783/JHA of 6 October 2006 on the application of the principle of mutual recognition to confiscation orders (OJ L 328, 24.11.2006, p. 59).
9   Directive 2010/64/EU of the European Parliament and of the Council of 20 October 2010 on the right to interpretation and translation in criminal proceedings (OJ L 280, 26.10.2010, p. 1).
10   Directive 2012/13/EU of the European Parliament and of the Council of 22 May 2012 on the right to information in criminal proceedings (OJ L 142, 1.6.2012, p. 1).
11   Directive 2013/48/EU of the European Parliament and of the Council of 22 October 2013 on the right of access to a lawyer in criminal proceedings and in European arrest warrant proceedings, and on the right to have a third party informed upon deprivation of liberty and to communicate with third persons and with consular authorities while deprived of liberty (OJ L 294, 6.11.2013, p. 1).

Have adopted this Directive:

Article 1

Subject matter

1.   This Directive establishes minimum rules on the freezing of property with a view to possible subsequent confiscation and on the confiscation of property in criminal matters.

2.   This Directive is without prejudice to the procedures that Member States may use to confiscate the property in question.

Article 2

Definitions

For the purpose of this Directive, the following definitions apply:

(1)   'proceeds' means any economic advantage derived directly or indirectly from a criminal offence; it may consist of any form of property and includes any subsequent reinvestment or transformation of direct proceeds and any valuable benefits;

(2)   'property' means property of any description, whether corporeal or incorporeal, movable or immovable, and legal documents or instruments evidencing title or interest in such property;

(3) 'instrumentalities' means any property used or intended to be used, in any manner, wholly or in part, to commit a criminal offence or criminal offences;

(4) 'confiscation' means a final deprivation of property ordered by a court in relation to a criminal offence;

(5) 'freezing' means the temporary prohibition of the transfer, destruction, conversion, disposal or movement of property or temporarily assuming custody or control of property;

(6) 'criminal offence' means an offence covered by any of the instruments listed in Article 3.

Article 3

Scope

This Directive shall apply to criminal offences covered by:

(a) Convention drawn up on the basis of Article K.3(2)(c) of the Treaty on European Union on the fight against corruption involving officials of the European Communities or officials of the Member States of the European Union[12] ('Convention on the fight against corruption involving officials');

(b) Council Framework Decision 2000/383/JHA of 29 May 2000 on increasing protection by criminal penalties and other sanctions against counterfeiting in connection with the introduction of the euro[13];

(c) Council Framework Decision 2001/413/JHA of 28 May 2001 on combating fraud and counterfeiting on non-cash means of payment[14];

(d) Council Framework Decision 2001/500/JHA of 26 June 2001 on money laundering, the identification, tracing, freezing, seizing and confiscation of instrumentalities and the proceeds of crime[15];

(e) Council Framework Decision 2002/475/JHA of 13 June 2002 on combating terrorism[16];

(f) Council Framework Decision 2003/568/JHA of 22 July 2003 on combating corruption in the private sector[17];

(g) Council Framework Decision 2004/757/JHA of 25 October 2004 laying down minimum provisions on the constituent elements of criminal acts and penalties in the field of illicit drug trafficking[18];

(h) Council Framework Decision 2008/841/JHA of 24 October 2008 on the fight against organised crime[19];

(i) Directive 2011/36/EU of the European Parliament and of the Council of 5 April 2011 on preventing and combating trafficking in human beings and protecting its victims, and replacing Council Framework Decision 2002/629/JHA[20];

(j) Directive 2011/93/EU of the European Parliament and of the Council of 13 December 2011 on combating the sexual abuse and sexual exploitation of children and child pornography, and replacing Council Framework Decision 2004/68/JHA[21];

(k) Directive 2013/40/EU of the European Parliament and of the Council of 12 August 2013 on attacks against information systems and replacing Council Framework Decision 2005/222/JHA[22],

as well as other legal instruments if those instruments provide specifically that this Directive applies to the criminal offences harmonised therein.

Notes
12   OJ C 195, 25.6.1997, p. 1.

13   OJ L 140, 14.6.2000, p. 1.
14   OJ L 149, 2.6.2001, p. 1.
15   OJ L 182, 5.7.2001, p. 1.
16   OJ L 164, 22.6.2002, p. 3.
17   OJ L 192, 31.7.2003, p. 54.
18   OJ L 335, 11.11.2004, p. 8.
19   OJ L 300, 11.11.2008, p. 42.
20   OJ L 101, 15.4.2011, p. 1.
21   OJ L 335, 17.12.2011, p. 1.
22   OJ L 218, 14.8.2013, p. 8.

Article 4

Confiscation

1.   Member States shall take the necessary measures to enable the confiscation, either in whole or in part, of instrumentalities and proceeds or property the value of which corresponds to such instrumentalities or proceeds, subject to a final conviction for a criminal offence, which may also result from proceedings in absentia.

2.   Where confiscation on the basis of paragraph 1 is not possible, at least where such impossibility is the result of illness or absconding of the suspected or accused person, Member States shall take the necessary measures to enable the confiscation of instrumentalities and proceeds in cases where criminal proceedings have been initiated regarding a criminal offence which is liable to give rise, directly or indirectly, to economic benefit, and such proceedings could have led to a criminal conviction if the suspected or accused person had been able to stand trial.

Article 5

Extended confiscation

1.   Member States shall adopt the necessary measures to enable the confiscation, either in whole or in part, of property belonging to a person convicted of a criminal offence which is liable to give rise, directly or indirectly, to economic benefit, where a court, on the basis of the circumstances of the case, including the specific facts and available evidence, such as that the value of the property is disproportionate to the lawful income of the convicted person, is satisfied that the property in question is derived from criminal conduct.

2.   For the purpose of paragraph 1 of this Article, the notion of 'criminal offence' shall include at least the following:

(a)   active and passive corruption in the private sector, as provided for in Article 2 of Framework Decision 2003/568/JHA, as well as active and passive corruption involving officials of institutions of the Union or of the Member States, as provided for in Articles 2 and 3 respectively of the Convention on the fight against corruption involving officials;

(b)   offences relating to participation in a criminal organisation, as provided for in Article 2 of Framework Decision 2008/841/JHA, at least in cases where the offence has led to economic benefit;

(c)   causing or recruiting a child to participate in pornographic performances, or profiting from or otherwise exploiting a child for such purposes if the child is over the age of sexual consent, as provided for in Article 4(2) of Directive 2011/93/EU; distribution, dissemination or transmission of child pornography, as provided for in Article 5(4) of that Directive; offering, supplying or making available child pornography, as provided for in Article

5(5) of that Directive; production of child pornography, as provided for in Article 5(6) of that Directive;

(d) illegal system interference and illegal data interference, as provided for in Articles 4 and 5 respectively of Directive 2013/40/EU, where a significant number of information systems have been affected through the use of a tool, as provided for in Article 7 of that Directive, designed or adapted primarily for that purpose; the intentional production, sale, procurement for use, import, distribution or otherwise making available of tools used for committing offences, at least for cases which are not minor, as provided for in Article 7 of that Directive;

(e) a criminal offence that is punishable, in accordance with the relevant instrument in Article 3 or, in the event that the instrument in question does not contain a penalty threshold, in accordance with the relevant national law, by a custodial sentence of a maximum of at least four years.

Article 6

Confiscation from a third party

1. Member States shall take the necessary measures to enable the confiscation of proceeds, or other property the value of which corresponds to proceeds, which, directly or indirectly, were transferred by a suspected or accused person to third parties, or which were acquired by third parties from a suspected or accused person, at least if those third parties knew or ought to have known that the purpose of the transfer or acquisition was to avoid confiscation, on the basis of concrete facts and circumstances, including that the transfer or acquisition was carried out free of charge or in exchange for an amount significantly lower than the market value.

2. Paragraph 1 shall not prejudice the rights of bona fide third parties.

Article 7

Freezing

1. Member States shall take the necessary measures to enable the freezing of property with a view to possible subsequent confiscation. Those measures, which shall be ordered by a competent authority, shall include urgent action to be taken when necessary in order to preserve property.

2. Property in the possession of a third party, as referred to under Article 6, can be subject to freezing measures for the purposes of possible subsequent confiscation.

Article 8

Safeguards

1. Member States shall take the necessary measures to ensure that the persons affected by the measures provided for under this Directive have the right to an effective remedy and a fair trial in order to uphold their rights.

2. Member States shall take the necessary measures to ensure that the freezing order is communicated to the affected person as soon as possible after its execution. Such communication shall indicate, at least briefly, the reason or reasons for the order concerned. When it is necessary to avoid jeopardising a criminal investigation, the competent authorities may postpone communicating the freezing order to the affected person.

3.   The freezing order shall remain in force only for as long as it is necessary to preserve the property with a view to possible subsequent confiscation.

4.   Member States shall provide for the effective possibility for the person whose property is affected to challenge the freezing order before a court, in accordance with procedures provided for in national law. Such procedures may provide that when the initial freezing order has been taken by a competent authority other than a judicial authority, such order shall first be submitted for validation or review to a judicial authority before it can be challenged before a court.

5.   Frozen property which is not subsequently confiscated shall be returned immediately. The conditions or procedural rules under which such property is returned shall be determined by national law.

6.   Member States shall take the necessary measures to ensure that reasons are given for any confiscation order and that the order is communicated to the person affected. Member States shall provide for the effective possibility for a person in respect of whom confiscation is ordered to challenge the order before a court.

7.   Without prejudice to Directive 2012/13/EU and Directive 2013/48/EU, persons whose property is affected by a confiscation order shall have the right of access to a lawyer throughout the confiscation proceedings relating to the determination of the proceeds and instrumentalities in order to uphold their rights. The persons concerned shall be informed of that right.

8.   In proceedings referred to in Article 5, the affected person shall have an effective possibility to challenge the circumstances of the case, including specific facts and available evidence on the basis of which the property concerned is considered to be property that is derived from criminal conduct.

9.   Third parties shall be entitled to claim title of ownership or other property rights, including in the cases referred to in Article 6.

10.   Where, as a result of a criminal offence, victims have claims against the person who is subject to a confiscation measure provided for under this Directive, Member States shall take the necessary measures to ensure that the confiscation measure does not prevent those victims from seeking compensation for their claims.

Article 9

Effective confiscation and execution

Member States shall take the necessary measures to enable the detection and tracing of property to be frozen and confiscated even after a final conviction for a criminal offence or following proceedings in application of Article 4(2) and to ensure the effective execution of a confiscation order, if such an order has already been issued.

Article 10

Management of frozen and confiscated property

1.   Member States shall take the necessary measures, for example by establishing centralised offices, a set of specialised offices or equivalent mechanisms, to ensure the adequate management of property frozen with a view to possible subsequent confiscation.

2.   Member States shall ensure that the measures referred to in paragraph 1 include the possibility to sell or transfer property where necessary.

3.   Member States shall consider taking measures allowing confiscated property to be used for public interest or social purposes.

Article 11

Statistics

1.   Member States shall regularly collect and maintain comprehensive statistics from the relevant authorities. The statistics collected shall be sent to the Commission each year and shall include:

(a)   the number of freezing orders executed;

(b)   the number of confiscation orders executed;

(c)   the estimated value of property frozen, at least of property frozen with a view to possible subsequent confiscation at the time of freezing;

(d)   the estimated value of property recovered at the time of confiscation.

2.   Member States shall also send each year the following statistics to the Commission, if they are available at a central level in the Member State concerned:

(a)   the number of requests for freezing orders to be executed in another Member State;

(b)   the number of requests for confiscation orders to be executed in another Member State;

(c)   the value or estimated value of the property recovered following execution in another Member State.

3.   Member States shall endeavour to collect data referred to in paragraph 2 at a central level.

Article 12

Transposition

1.   Member States shall bring into force the laws, regulations and administrative provisions necessary to comply with this Directive by 4 October 2015. They shall forthwith transmit to the Commission the text of those provisions.

2.   When Member States adopt those provisions, they shall contain a reference to this Directive or be accompanied by such a reference on the occasion of their official publication. The methods of making such reference shall be laid down by Member States.

3.   Member States shall communicate to the Commission the text of the main provisions of national law which they adopt in the field covered by this Directive.

Article 13

Reporting

The Commission shall, by 4 October 2018 submit a report to the European Parliament and the Council, assessing the impact of existing national law on confiscation and asset recovery, accompanied, if necessary, by adequate proposals.

In that report, the Commission shall also assess whether there is any need to revise the list of offences in Article 5(2).

Article 14

Replacement of Joint Action 98/699/JHA and of certain provisions of Framework Decisions 2001/500/JHA and 2005/212/JHA

1.   Joint Action 98/699/JHA, point (a) of Article 1 and Articles 3 and 4 of Framework Decision 2001/500/JHA, and the first four indents of Article 1 and Article 3 of Framework Decision 2005/212/JHA, are replaced by this Directive for the Member States bound by this Directive, without prejudice to the obligations of those Member States relating to the time limits for transposition of those Framework Decisions into national law.

2.   For the Member States bound by this Directive, references to Joint Action 98/699/JHA and to the provisions of Framework Decisions 2001/500/JHA and 2005/212/JHA referred to in paragraph 1 shall be construed as references to this Directive.

Article 15

Entry into force

This Directive shall enter into force on the twentieth day following that of its publication in the Official Journal of the European Union.

Article 16

Addressees

This Directive is addressed to Member States in accordance with the Treaties.

Done at Brussels, 3 April 2014.
For the European Parliament
The President
M. Schulz
For the Council
The President
D. Kourkoulas

Appendix 1.11   Equivalent jurisdictions

COMMON UNDERSTANDING BETWEEN MEMBER STATES ON THIRD COUNTRY EQUIVALENCE[12] UNDER THE ANTI-MONEY LAUNDERING DIRECTIVE (DIRECTIVE 2005/60/EC) JUNE 2012

These third countries are currently considered as having equivalent AML/CFT systems to the EU. **The list may be reviewed**, in particular in the light of public evaluation reports adopted by the FATF, FSRBs, the IMF or the World Bank according to the revised 2003 FATF Recommendations and Methodology.

It should be noted that the list does not override the need to continue to operate the risk-based approach. The fact that a financial institution is based in a 3rd country featuring on the list only constitutes a refutable presumption of the application of simplified CDD. Moreover, the list does not override the obligation under article 13 of the Directive to apply enhanced customer due diligence measures in all situations which by their nature can present a higher risk of money laundering or terrorist financing, when dealing with credit and financial institutions, as customers, based in an equivalent jurisdiction.

List after the Meeting on 26 June 2012

Australia

Brazil

Canada

Hong Kong

India

Japan

South Korea

Mexico

Singapore

Switzerland

South Africa

The United States of America

1 Directive 2005/60/EC does not grant the European Commission a mandate to establish a positive list of equivalent third countries. The Common Understanding between EU Member States on Third Country Equivalence is drafted, managed and agreed by the EU Member States.

2 The list does not apply to Member States of the EU/EEA which benefit de jure from mutual recognition through the implementation of the 3rd AML Directive. The list also includes the French overseas territories (Mayotte, New Caledonia, French Polynesia, Saint Pierre and Miquelon and Wallis and Futuna) and Aruba, Curacao, Sint Maarten, Bonaire, Sint Eustatius and Saba. Those countries and territories are not members of the EU/EEA but are part of the membership of France and the Kingdom of the Netherlands of the FATF. The UK Crown Dependencies (Jersey, Guernsey, Isle of Man) may also be considered as equivalent by Member States.

Appendix 1.12   Guernsey Financial Services Commission Handbook for Financial Services Businesses on Countering Financial Crime and Terrorist Financing 15 December 2007 (updated March and April 2013)[1]

APPENDIX C   COUNTRIES OR TERRITORIES WHOSE REGULATED FINANCIAL SERVICES BUSINESSES MAY BE TREATED AS IF THEY WERE LOCAL FINANCIAL SERVICES BUSINESSES.

Austria	Japan
Australia	Jersey
Belgium	Latvia
Bulgaria	Liechtenstein
Canada	Lithuania
Cayman Islands	Luxembourg
Cyprus	Malta
Denmark	Netherlands
Estonia	New Zealand
Finland	Norway
France	Portugal
Germany	Singapore
Gibraltar	South Africa
Greece	Spain
Hong Kong	Sweden
Iceland	Switzerland
Ireland	United Kingdom
Isle of Man	United States of America
Italy	

Appendix C to the Handbook was established to reflect those countries or territories which the Commission considers require regulated financial services businesses to have in place standards to combat money laundering and terrorist financing consistent with the FATF

Recommendations and where such financial services businesses are supervised for compliance with those requirements. It was also designed as a mechanism

---

1 Reproduced with kind permission of the Guernsey Financial Services Commission. For more information and updates, please contact the Guernsey Financial Services Commission or visit www.gfsc.org.

to recognise the geographic spread of the customers of the Guernsey finance sector and is reviewed periodically with countries or territories being added as appropriate.

The fact that a country or territory has requirements to combat money laundering and terrorist financing that are consistent with the FATF Recommendations means only that the necessary legislation and other means of ensuring compliance with the Recommendations is in force in that country or territory. It does not provide assurance that a particular overseas financial services business is subject to that legislation, or that it has implemented the necessary measures to ensure compliance with that legislation.

Guernsey financial services businesses are not obliged to deal with regulated financial services businesses in the jurisdictions listed above as if they were local, notwithstanding that they meet the requirements identified in this Appendix. Guernsey financial services businesses should use their commercial judgement in considering whether or not to deal with a regulated financial services business and may, if they wish, impose higher standards than the minimum standards identified in the Handbook.

In accordance with the definition provided for in the Regulations an "**Appendix C business**" means –

(a) a financial services business supervised by the Commission; or

(b) a business which is carried on from –

    (i) a country or territory listed in Appendix C to the Handbook and which would, if it were carried on in the Bailiwick, be a financial services business; or

    (ii) the United Kingdom, the Bailiwick of Jersey, the Bailiwick of Guernsey or the Isle of Man by a lawyer or accountant;

and, in either case is a business –

(A) which may only be carried on in that country or territory by a person regulated for that purpose under the law of that country or territory;

(B) the conduct of which is subject to requirements to forestall, prevent and detect money laundering and terrorist financing that are consistent with those in the Financial Action Task Force Recommendations on Money Laundering in respect of such a business; and

(C) the conduct of which is supervised for compliance with the requirements referred to in subparagraph (B), by the Commission or an overseas regulatory authority.

The absence of a country or territory from the above list does not prevent the application of section 4.10.1 of the Handbook (reliable introductions by an overseas branch or member of the same group, subject to satisfactory terms of business).

Appendix 2

FATF and Supranational reports

Contents

Appendix 2.1 FATF Members

As of 2014, FATF membership consists of 36 countries and territories and two regional organizations. FATF has developed 40 AML-CFT recommendations and assesses each member country against these recommendations in published reports: countries seen as not being sufficiently compliant with such recommendations are subjected to financial sanctions

FATF's three primary functions with regard to money laundering are:

1. Monitoring members' progress in implementing anti-money laundering measures.

2. Reviewing and reporting on laundering trends, techniques, and countermeasures.

3. Promoting the adoption and implementation of FATF anti-money laundering standards globally.

FATF currently comprises 34 member jurisdictions and 2 regional organisations, representing most major financial centres in all parts of the globe:

- Argentina
- Australia
- Austria
- Belgium
- Brazil
- Canada
- China
- Denmark
- European Commission
- Finland
- France
- Germany
- Greece
- Gulf Cooperation Council
- Hong Kong
- Iceland
- India
- Ireland
- Italy
- Japan
- Luxembourg

- Mexico
- Netherlands
- New Zealand
- Norway
- Portugal
- Russia
- Singapore
- South Africa
- South Korea
- Spain
- Sweden
- Switzerland
- Turkey
- United Kingdom
- United States

Appendix 2.2   The FATF Blacklist

In November 2013, FATF identified the following 15 countries as jurisdictions that have strategic deficiencies that pose a risk to the international financial system.

1.   Iran
2.   North Korea
3.   Guyana
4.   Ecuador
5.   Ethiopia
6.   Indonesia
7.   Kenya*
8.   Myanmar
9.   Pakistan
10. São Tomé and Príncipe
11. Syria
12. Tanzania*
13. Turkey
14. Vietnam
15. Yemen

In June 2014 the FATF removed Kenya* and Tanzania* from the above list. At the same time the FATFA highlighted two jurisdictions where FATF members need to apply counter-measures to protect the international financial system from the on-going and substantial AML-CFT risks emanating from these jurisdictions.

1.   Iran
2.   Democratic People's Republic of Korea ("DPRK")

The FATF also added Algeria to the list of jurisdictions with strategic AML/CFT deficiencies that have not made sufficient progress in addressing the deficiencies or have not committed to an action plan developed with the FATF to address the deficiencies

The FATF official link to the black list is at http://www.fatf-gafi.org/topics/high-riskandnon-cooperativejurisdictions/documents/public-statement-june-2014.html   and   http://www.fatf-gafi.org/topics/high-riskandnon-cooperative jurisdictions/documents/public-statement-feb-2014.html

Appendix 2.3 International standards on combating money laundering and the financing of terrorism and proliferation: the FATF recommendations

Number	Old Number[1]	
		A – AML/CFT POLICIES AND COORDINATION
1	–	Assessing risks & applying a risk-based approach *
2	R.31	National cooperation and coordination
		B – MONEY LAUNDERING AND CONFISCATION
3	R.1 & R.2	Money laundering offence *
4	R.3	Confiscation and provisional measures *
		C – TERRORIST FINANCING AND FINANCING OF PROLIFERATION
5	SRII	Terrorist financing offence *
6	SRIII	Targeted financial sanctions related to terrorism & terrorist financing *
7		Targeted financial sanctions related to proliferation *
8	SRVIII	Non-profit organisations *
		D – PREVENTIVE MEASURES
9	R.4	Financial institution secrecy laws
		Customer due diligence and record keeping
10	R.5	Customer due diligence *
11	R.10	Record keeping
		Additional measures for specific customers and activities
12	R.6	Politically exposed persons *
13	R.7	Correspondent banking *
14	SRVI	Money or value transfer services *
15	R.8	New technologies
16	SRVII	Wire transfers *
		Reliance, Controls and Financial Groups
17	R.9	Reliance on third parties *
18	R.15 & R.22	Internal controls and foreign branches and subsidiaries *

Number	Old Number[1]	
19	R.21	Higher-risk countries *
		Reporting of suspicious transactions
20	R.13 & SRIV	Reporting of suspicious transactions *
21	R.14	Tipping-off and confidentiality
		Designated non-financial Businesses and Professions (DNFBPs)
22	R.12	DNFBPs: Customer due diligence *
23	R.16	DNFBPs: Other measures *
		E – TRANSPARENCY AND BENEFICIAL OWNERSHIP OF LEGAL PERSONS AND ARRANGEMENTS
24	R.33	Transparency and beneficial ownership of legal persons *
25	R.34	Transparency and beneficial ownership of legal arrangements *
		F – POWERS AND RESPONSIBILITIES OF COMPETENT AUTHORITIES AND OTHER INSTITUTIONAL MEASURES
		Regulation and Supervision
26	R.23	Regulation and supervision of financial institutions *
27	R.29	Powers of supervisors
28	R.24	Regulation and supervision of DNFBPs
		Operational and Law Enforcement
29	R.26	Financial intelligence units *
30	R.27	Responsibilities of law enforcement and investigative authorities *
31	R.28	Powers of law enforcement and investigative authorities
32	SRIX	Cash couriers *
		General Requirements
33	R.32	Statistics
34	R.25	Guidance and feedback
		Sanctions
35	R.17	Sanctions
		G – INTERNATIONAL COOPERATION
36	R.35 & SRI	International instruments
37	R.36 & SRV	Mutual legal assistance
38	R.38	Mutual legal assistance: freezing and confiscation *
39	R.39	Extradition
40	R.40	Other forms of international cooperation *

1. *The 'old number' column refers to the corresponding 2003 FATF Recommendation.*

* *Recommendations marked with an asterisk have interpretive notes, which should be read in conjunction with the Recommendation.*

Version as adopted on 15 February 2012.

THE FATF RECOMMENDATIONS

A.   AML/CFT POLICIES AND COORDINATION

1.   Assessing risks and applying a risk-based approach *

Countries should identify, assess, and understand the money laundering and terrorist financing risks for the country, and should take action, including designating an authority or mechanism to coordinate actions to assess risks, and apply resources, aimed at ensuring the risks are mitigated effectively. Based on that assessment, countries should apply a risk-based approach (RBA) to ensure that measures to prevent or mitigate money laundering and terrorist financing are commensurate with the risks identified. This approach should be an essential foundation to efficient allocation of resources across the anti-money laundering and countering the financing of terrorism (AML/CFT) regime and the implementation of risk- based measures throughout the FATF Recommendations. Where countries identify higher risks, they should ensure that their AML/CFT regime adequately addresses such risks. Where countries identify lower risks, they may decide to allow simplified measures for some of the FATF Recommendations under certain conditions.

Countries should require financial institutions and designated non-financial businesses and professions (DNFBPs) to identify, assess and take effective action to mitigate their money laundering and terrorist financing risks.

2.   National cooperation and coordination

Countries should have national AML/CFT policies, informed by the risks identified, which should be regularly reviewed, and should designate an authority or have a coordination or other mechanism that is responsible for such policies.

Countries should ensure that policy-makers, the financial intelligence unit (FIU), law enforcement authorities, supervisors and other relevant competent authorities, at the policy- making and operational levels, have effective mechanisms in place which enable them to cooperate, and, where appropriate, coordinate domestically with each other concerning the development and implementation of policies and activities to combat money laundering, terrorist financing and the financing of proliferation of weapons of mass destruction.

B.   MONEY LAUNDERING AND CONFISCATION

3.   Money laundering offence *

Countries should criminalise money laundering on the basis of the Vienna Convention and the Palermo Convention. Countries should apply the crime of money laundering to all serious offences, with a view to including the widest range of predicate offences.

4.   Confiscation and provisional measures *

Countries should adopt measures similar to those set forth in the Vienna Convention, the Palermo Convention, and the Terrorist Financing Convention, including legislative measures, to enable their competent authorities to freeze or seize and confiscate the following, without prejudicing the rights of *bona fide* third parties: (a) property laundered, (b) proceeds from, or instrumentalities used in or intended for use in money laundering or predicate offences, (c) property that is the proceeds of, or used in, or intended or allocated for use in, the financing of terrorism, terrorist acts or terrorist organisations, or (d) property of corresponding value.

Such measures should include the authority to: (a) identify, trace and evaluate property that is subject to confiscation; (b) carry out provisional measures, such as freezing and seizing, to prevent any dealing, transfer or disposal of such property; (c) take steps that will prevent or void actions that prejudice the country's ability to freeze or seize or recover property that is subject to confiscation; and (d) take any appropriate investigative measures.

Countries should consider adopting measures that allow such proceeds or instrumentalities to be confiscated without requiring a criminal conviction (non-conviction based confiscation), or which require an offender to demonstrate the lawful origin of the property alleged to be liable to confiscation, to the extent that such a requirement is consistent with the principles of their domestic law.

C.   TERRORIST FINANCING AND FINANCING OF   *PROLIFERATION*

5.   Terrorist financing offence *

Countries should criminalise terrorist financing on the basis of the Terrorist Financing Convention, and should criminalise not only the financing of terrorist acts but also the financing of terrorist organisations and individual terrorists even in the absence of a link to a specific terrorist act or acts. Countries should ensure that such offences are designated as money laundering predicate offences.

6.   Targeted financial sanctions related to terrorism and terrorist financing *

Countries should implement targeted financial sanctions regimes to comply with United Nations Security Council resolutions relating to the prevention and suppression of terrorism and terrorist financing. The resolutions require countries to freeze without delay the funds or other assets of, and to ensure that no funds or other assets are made available, directly or indirectly, to or for the benefit of, any person or entity either (i) designated by, or under the authority of, the United Nations Security Council under Chapter VII of the Charter of the United Nations, including in accordance with resolution 1267 (1999) and its successor resolutions; or (ii) designated by that country pursuant to resolution 1373 (2001).

7.   Targeted financial sanctions related to proliferation *

Countries should implement targeted financial sanctions to comply with United Nations Security Council resolutions relating to the prevention, suppression and disruption of proliferation of weapons of mass destruction and its financing. These resolutions require countries to freeze without delay the funds or other assets of, and to ensure that no funds and other assets are made available, directly or indirectly, to or for the benefit of, any person or entity designated by, or under the authority of, the United Nations Security Council under Chapter VII of the Charter of the United Nations.

8.   Non-profit organisations *

Countries should review the adequacy of laws and regulations that relate to entities that can be abused for the financing of terrorism. Non-profit organisations are particularly vulnerable, and countries should ensure that they cannot be misused:

(a) by terrorist organisations posing as legitimate entities;

(b) to exploit legitimate entities as conduits for terrorist financing, including for the purpose of escaping asset-freezing measures; and

(c) to conceal or obscure the clandestine diversion of funds intended for legitimate purposes to terrorist organisations.

D.   PREVENTIVE MEASURES

9.   Financial institution secrecy laws

Countries should ensure that financial institution secrecy laws do not inhibit implementation of the FATF Recommendations.

CUSTOMER DUE DILIGENCE AND RECORD-KEEPING

10.   Customer due diligence *

Financial institutions should be prohibited from keeping anonymous accounts or accounts in obviously fictitious names.

Financial institutions should be required to undertake customer due diligence (CDD) measures when:

(i)   establishing business relations;

(ii)   carrying out occasional transactions: (i) above the applicable designated threshold (USD/EUR 15,000); or (ii) that are wire transfers in the circumstances covered by the Interpretive Note to Recommendation 16;

(iii)   there is a suspicion of money laundering or terrorist financing; or

(iv)   the financial institution has doubts about the veracity or adequacy of previously obtained customer identification data.

The principle that financial institutions should conduct CDD should be set out in law. Each country may determine how it imposes specific CDD obligations, either through law or enforceable means.

The CDD measures to be taken are as follows:

(a)   Identifying the customer and verifying that customer's identity using reliable, independent source documents, data or information.

(b)   Identifying the beneficial owner, and taking reasonable measures to verify the identity of the beneficial owner, such that the financial institution is satisfied that it knows who the beneficial owner is. For legal persons and arrangements this should include financial institutions understanding the ownership and control structure of the customer.

(c)   Understanding and, as appropriate, obtaining information on the purpose and intended nature of the business relationship.

(d)   Conducting ongoing due diligence on the business relationship and scrutiny of transactions undertaken throughout the course of that relationship to ensure that the transactions being conducted are consistent with the institution's knowledge of the customer, their business and risk profile, including, where necessary, the source of funds.

Financial institutions should be required to apply each of the CDD measures under (a) to (d) above, but should determine the extent of such measures using a risk-based approach (RBA) in accordance with the Interpretive Notes to this Recommendation and to Recommendation 1.

Financial institutions should be required to verify the identity of the customer and beneficial owner before or during the course of establishing a business relationship or conducting transactions for occasional customers. Countries may permit financial institutions to complete the verification as soon as reasonably practicable following the establishment of the relationship, where the money laundering and terrorist financing risks are effectively managed and where this is essential not to interrupt the normal conduct of business.

Where the financial institution is unable to comply with the applicable requirements under paragraphs (a) to (d) above (subject to appropriate modification of the extent of the measures on a risk-based approach), it should be required not to open the account, commence business relations or perform the transaction; or should be required to terminate the business relationship; and should consider making a suspicious transactions report in relation to the customer.

These requirements should apply to all new customers, although financial institutions should also apply this Recommendation to existing customers on the basis of materiality and risk, and should conduct due diligence on such existing relationships at appropriate times.

11. Record-keeping

Financial institutions should be required to maintain, for at least five years, all necessary records on transactions, both domestic and international, to enable them to comply swiftly with information requests from the competent authorities. Such records must be sufficient to permit reconstruction of individual transactions (including the amounts and types of currency involved, if any) so as to provide, if necessary, evidence for prosecution of criminal activity.

Financial institutions should be required to keep all records obtained through CDD measures (e.g. copies or records of official identification documents like passports, identity cards, driving licences or similar documents), account files and business correspondence, including the results of any analysis undertaken (e.g. inquiries to establish the background and purpose of complex, unusual large transactions), for at least five years after the business relationship is ended, or after the date of the occasional transaction.

Financial institutions should be required by law to maintain records on transactions and information obtained through the CDD measures.

The CDD information and the transaction records should be available to domestic competent authorities upon appropriate authority.

ADDITIONAL MEASURES FOR SPECIFIC CUSTOMERS AND ACTIVITIES

12. Politically exposed persons *

Financial institutions should be required, in relation to foreign politically exposed persons (PEPs) (whether as customer or beneficial owner), in addition to performing normal customer due diligence measures, to:

(a) have appropriate risk-management systems to determine whether the customer or the beneficial owner is a politically exposed person;

(b) obtain senior management approval for establishing (or continuing, for existing customers) such business relationships;

(c) take reasonable measures to establish the source of wealth and source of funds; and

(d) conduct enhanced ongoing monitoring of the business relationship.

Financial institutions should be required to take reasonable measures to determine whether a customer or beneficial owner is a domestic PEP or a person who is or has been entrusted with a prominent function by an international organisation. In cases of a higher risk business relationship with such persons, financial institutions should be required to apply the measures referred to in paragraphs (b), (c) and (d).

The requirements for all types of PEP should also apply to family members or close associates of such PEPs.

13. Correspondent banking *

Financial institutions should be required, in relation to cross-border correspondent banking and other similar relationships, in addition to performing normal customer due diligence measures, to:

(a)   gather sufficient information about a respondent institution to understand fully the nature of the respondent's business and to determine from publicly available information the reputation of the institution and the quality of supervision, including whether it has been subject to a money laundering or terrorist financing investigation or regulatory action;

(b)   assess the respondent institution's AML/CFT controls;

(c)   obtain approval from senior management before establishing new correspondent relationships;

(d)   clearly understand the respective responsibilities of each institution; and

(e)   with respect to "payable-through accounts", be satisfied that the respondent bank has conducted CDD on the customers having direct access to accounts of the correspondent bank, and that it is able to provide relevant CDD information upon request to the correspondent bank.

Financial institutions should be prohibited from entering into, or continuing, a correspondent banking relationship with shell banks. Financial institutions should be required to satisfy themselves that respondent institutions do not permit their accounts to be used by shell banks.

14.   Money or value transfer services *

Countries should take measures to ensure that natural or legal persons that provide money or value transfer services (MVTS) are licensed or registered, and subject to effective systems for monitoring and ensuring compliance with the relevant measures called for in the FATF Recommendations. Countries should take action to identify natural or legal persons that carry out MVTS without a license or registration, and to apply appropriate sanctions.

Any natural or legal person working as an agent should also be licensed or registered by a competent authority, or the MVTS provider should maintain a current list of its agents accessible by competent authorities in the countries in which the MVTS provider and its agents operate. Countries should take measures to ensure that MVTS providers that use agents include them in their AML/CFT programmes and monitor them for compliance with these programmes.

15.   New technologies

Countries and financial institutions should identify and assess the money laundering or terrorist financing risks that may arise in relation to (a) the development of new products and new business practices, including new delivery mechanisms, and (b) the use of new or developing technologies for both new and pre-existing products. In the case of financial institutions, such a risk assessment should take place prior to the launch of the new products, business practices or the use of new or developing technologies. They should take appropriate measures to manage and mitigate those risks.

16.   Wire transfers *

Countries should ensure that financial institutions include required and accurate originator information, and required beneficiary information, on wire transfers and related messages, and that the information remains with the wire transfer or related message throughout the payment chain.

Countries should ensure that financial institutions monitor wire transfers for the purpose of detecting those which lack required originator and/or beneficiary information, and take appropriate measures.

Countries should ensure that, in the context of processing wire transfers, financial institutions take freezing action and should prohibit conducting transactions with designated persons and entities, as per the obligations set out in the relevant United Nations Security Council resolutions, such as resolution

1267 (1999) and its successor resolutions, and resolution 1373(2001), relating to the prevention and suppression of terrorism and terrorist financing.

RELIANCE, CONTROLS AND FINANCIAL GROUPS

17. Reliance on third parties *

Countries may permit financial institutions to rely on third parties to perform elements (a)–(c) of the CDD measures set out in Recommendation 10 or to introduce business, provided that the criteria set out below are met. Where such reliance is permitted, the ultimate responsibility for CDD measures remains with the financial institution relying on the third party.

The criteria that should be met are as follows:

(a) A financial institution relying upon a third party should immediately obtain the necessary information concerning elements (a)-(c) of the CDD measures set out in Recommendation 10.

(b) Financial institutions should take adequate steps to satisfy themselves that copies of identification data and other relevant documentation relating to the CDD requirements will be made available from the third party upon request without delay.

(c) The financial institution should satisfy itself that the third party is regulated, supervised or monitored for, and has measures in place for compliance with, CDD and record-keeping requirements in line with Recommendations 10 and 11.

(d) When determining in which countries the third party that meets the conditions can be based, countries should have regard to information available on the level of country risk.

When a financial institution relies on a third party that is part of the same financial group, and (i) that group applies CDD and record-keeping requirements, in line with Recommendations 10, 11 and 12, and programmes against money laundering and terrorist financing, in accordance with Recommendation 18; and (ii) where the effective implementation of those CDD and record-keeping requirements and AML/CFT programmes is supervised at a group level by a competent authority, then relevant competent authorities may consider that the financial institution applies measures under (b) and (c) above through its group programme, and may decide that (d) is not a necessary precondition to reliance when higher country risk is adequately mitigated by the group AML/CFT policies.

18.   Internal controls and foreign branches and subsidiaries *

Financial institutions should be required to implement programmes against money laundering and terrorist financing. Financial groups should be required to implement group- wide programmes against money laundering and terrorist financing, including policies and procedures for sharing information within the group for AML/CFT purposes.

Financial institutions should be required to ensure that their foreign branches and majority-owned subsidiaries apply AML/CFT measures consistent with the home country requirements implementing the FATF Recommendations through the financial groups' programmes against money laundering and terrorist financing.

19.   Higher-risk countries *

Financial institutions should be required to apply enhanced due diligence measures to business relationships and transactions with natural and legal persons, and financial institutions, from countries for which this is called for by the FATF. The type of enhanced due diligence measures applied should be effective and proportionate to the risks.

Countries should be able to apply appropriate countermeasures when called upon to do so by the FATF. Countries should also be able to apply countermeasures independently of any call by the FATF to do so. Such countermeasures should be effective and proportionate to the risks.

REPORTING OF SUSPICIOUS TRANSACTIONS

20.   Reporting of suspicious transactions *

If a financial institution suspects or has reasonable grounds to suspect that funds are the proceeds of a criminal activity, or are related to terrorist financing, it should be required, by law, to report promptly its suspicions to the financial intelligence unit (FIU).

21.   Tipping-off and confidentiality

Financial institutions, their directors, officers and employees should be:

(a)   protected by law from criminal and civil liability for breach of any restriction on disclosure of information imposed by contract or by any legislative, regulatory or administrative provision, if they report their suspicions in good faith to the FIU, even if they did not know precisely what the underlying criminal activity was, and regardless of whether illegal activity actually occurred; and

(b)   prohibited by law from disclosing ("tipping-off") the fact that a suspicious transaction report (STR) or related information is being filed with the FIU.

DESIGNATED NON-FINANCIAL BUSINESSES AND PROFESSIONS

22.   DNFBPs: customer due diligence *

The customer due diligence and record-keeping requirements set out in Recommendations 10, 11, 12, 15, and 17, apply to designated non-financial businesses and professions (DNFBPs) in the following situations:

(a)   Casinos – when customers engage in financial transactions equal to or above the applicable designated threshold.

(b)   Real estate agents – when they are involved in transactions for their client concerning the buying and selling of real estate.

(c)   Dealers in precious metals and dealers in precious stones – when they engage in any cash transaction with a customer equal to or above the applicable designated threshold.

(d)   Lawyers, notaries, other independent legal professionals and accountants – when they prepare for or carry out transactions for their client concerning the following activities:

- buying and selling of real estate;

- managing of client money, securities or other assets;

- management of bank, savings or securities accounts;

- organisation of contributions for the creation, operation or management of companies;

- creation, operation or management of legal persons or arrangements, and buying and selling of business entities.

(e)   Trust and company service providers – when they prepare for or carry out transactions for a client concerning the following activities:

- acting as a formation agent of legal persons;

- acting as (or arranging for another person to act as) a director or secretary of a company, a partner of a partnership, or a similar position in relation to other legal persons;

- providing a registered office, business address or accommodation, correspondence or administrative address for a company, a partnership or any other legal person or arrangement;

- acting as (or arranging for another person to act as) a trustee of an express trust or performing the equivalent function for another form of legal arrangement;

- acting as (or arranging for another person to act as) a nominee shareholder for another person.

23. DNFBPs: Other measures *

The requirements set out in Recommendations 18 to 21 apply to all designated non-financial businesses and professions, subject to the following qualifications:

(a) Lawyers, notaries, other independent legal professionals and accountants should be required to report suspicious transactions when, on behalf of or for a client, they engage in a financial transaction in relation to the activities described in paragraph (d) of Recommendation 22. Countries are strongly encouraged to extend the reporting requirement to the rest of the professional activities of accountants, including auditing.

(b) Dealers in precious metals and dealers in precious stones should be required to report suspicious transactions when they engage in any cash transaction with a customer equal to or above the applicable designated threshold.

(c) Trust and company service providers should be required to report suspicious transactions for a client when, on behalf of or for a client, they engage in a transaction in relation to the activities referred to in paragraph (e) of Recommendation 22.

E. TRANSPARENCY AND BENEFICIAL OWNERSHIP OF LEGAL PERSONS AND ARRANGEMENTS

24. Transparency and beneficial ownership of legal persons *

Countries should take measures to prevent the misuse of legal persons for money laundering or terrorist financing. Countries should ensure that there is adequate, accurate and timely information on the beneficial ownership and control of legal persons that can be obtained or accessed in a timely fashion by competent authorities. In particular, countries that have legal persons that are able to issue bearer shares or bearer share warrants, or which allow nominee shareholders or nominee directors, should take effective measures to ensure that they are not misused for money laundering or terrorist financing. Countries should consider measures to facilitate access to beneficial ownership and control information by financial institutions and DNFBPs undertaking the requirements set out in Recommendations 10 and 22.

25. Transparency and beneficial ownership of legal arrangements *

Countries should take measures to prevent the misuse of legal arrangements for money laundering or terrorist financing. In particular, countries should ensure that there is adequate, accurate and timely information on express trusts, including information on the settlor, trustee and beneficiaries, that can be obtained or accessed in a timely fashion by competent authorities. Countries should consider measures to facilitate access to beneficial ownership and control information by financial institutions and DNFBPs undertaking the requirements set out in Recommendations 10 and 22.

F.   POWERS AND RESPONSIBILITIES OF COMPETENT AUTHORITIES, AND OTHER INSTITUTIONAL MEASURES

REGULATION AND SUPERVISION

26.   Regulation and supervision of financial institutions *

Countries should ensure that financial institutions are subject to adequate regulation and supervision and are effectively implementing the FATF Recommendations. Competent authorities or financial supervisors should take the necessary legal or regulatory measures to prevent criminals or their associates from holding, or being the beneficial owner of, a significant or controlling interest, or holding a management function in, a financial institution. Countries should not approve the establishment, or continued operation, of shell banks.

For financial institutions subject to the Core Principles, the regulatory and supervisory measures that apply for prudential purposes, and which are also relevant to money laundering and terrorist financing, should apply in a similar manner for AML/CFT purposes. This should include applying consolidated group supervision for AML/CFT purposes.

Other financial institutions should be licensed or registered and adequately regulated, and subject to supervision or monitoring for AML/CFT purposes, having regard to the risk of money laundering or terrorist financing in that sector. At a minimum, where financial institutions provide a service of money or value transfer, or of money or currency changing, they should be licensed or registered, and subject to effective systems for monitoring and ensuring compliance with national AML/CFT requirements.

27.   Powers of supervisors

Supervisors should have adequate powers to supervise or monitor, and ensure compliance by, financial institutions with requirements to combat money laundering and terrorist financing, including the authority to conduct inspections. They should be authorised to compel production of any information from financial institutions that is relevant to monitoring such compliance, and to impose sanctions, in line with Recommendation 35, for failure to comply with such requirements. Supervisors should have powers to impose a range of disciplinary and financial sanctions, including the power to withdraw, restrict or suspend the financial institution's license, where applicable.

28.   Regulation and supervision of DNFBPs *

Designated non-financial businesses and professions should be subject to regulatory and supervisory measures as set out below.

(a) Casinos should be subject to a comprehensive regulatory and supervisory regime that ensures that they have effectively implemented the necessary AML/CFT measures. At a minimum:

- casinos should be licensed;

- competent authorities should take the necessary legal or regulatory measures to prevent criminals or their associates from holding, or being the beneficial owner of, a significant or controlling interest, holding a management function in, or being an operator of, a casino; and

- competent authorities should ensure that casinos are effectively supervised for compliance with AML/CFT requirements.

(b) Countries should ensure that the other categories of DNFBPs are subject to effective systems for monitoring and ensuring compliance with AML/CFT requirements. This should be performed on a risk-sensitive basis. This may be performed by (a) a supervisor or (b) by an appropriate self-regulatory body (SRB), provided that such a body can ensure that its members comply with their obligations to combat money laundering and terrorist financing.

The supervisor or SRB should also (a) take the necessary measures to prevent criminals or their associates from being professionally accredited, or holding or being the beneficial owner of a significant or controlling interest or holding a management function, e.g. through evaluating persons on the basis of a "fit and proper" test; and (b) have effective, proportionate, and dissuasive sanctions in line with Recommendation 35 available to deal with failure to comply with AML/CFT requirements.

OPERATIONAL AND LAW ENFORCEMENT

29. Financial intelligence units *

Countries should establish a financial intelligence unit (FIU) that serves as a national centre for the receipt and analysis of: (a) suspicious transaction reports; and (b) other information relevant to money laundering, associated predicate offences and terrorist financing, and for the dissemination of the results of that analysis. The FIU should be able to obtain additional information from reporting entities, and should have access on a timely basis to the financial, administrative and law enforcement information that it requires to undertake its functions properly.

30. Responsibilities of law enforcement and investigative authorities *

Countries should ensure that designated law enforcement authorities have responsibility for money laundering and terrorist financing investigations within the framework of national AML/CFT policies. At least in all cases related to major proceeds-generating offences, these designated law enforcement authorities should develop a pro-active parallel financial investigation when pursuing money laundering, associated predicate offences and terrorist financing. This should include cases where the associated predicate offence occurs outside their jurisdictions. Countries should ensure that competent authorities have responsibility for expeditiously identifying, tracing and initiating actions to freeze and seize property that is, or may become, subject to confiscation, or is suspected of being proceeds of crime. Countries should also make use, when necessary, of permanent or temporary multi-disciplinary groups specialised in financial or asset investigations. Countries should ensure that, when necessary, cooperative investigations with appropriate competent authorities in other countries take place.

31. Powers of law enforcement and investigative authorities

When conducting investigations of money laundering, associated predicate offences and terrorist financing, competent authorities should be able to obtain access to all necessary documents and information for use in those investigations, and in prosecutions and related actions. This should include powers to use compulsory measures for the production of records held by financial institutions, DNFBPs and other natural or legal persons, for the search of persons and premises, for taking witness statements, and for the seizure and obtaining of evidence.

Countries should ensure that competent authorities conducting investigations are able to use a wide range of investigative techniques suitable for the investigation of money laundering, associated predicate offences and terrorist financing. These investigative techniques include: undercover operations, intercepting communications, accessing computer systems and controlled delivery. In addition, countries should have effective mechanisms in place to identify, in a timely manner, whether natural or legal persons hold or control accounts. They should also have mechanisms to ensure that competent authorities have a process to identify assets without prior notification to the owner. When conducting investigations of money laundering, associated predicate offences and terrorist financing, competent authorities should be able to ask for all relevant information held by the FIU.

32.   Cash couriers *

Countries should have measures in place to detect the physical cross-border transportation of currency and bearer negotiable instruments, including through a declaration system and/or disclosure system.

Countries should ensure that their competent authorities have the legal authority to stop or restrain currency or bearer negotiable instruments that are suspected to be related to terrorist financing, money laundering or predicate offences, or that are falsely declared or disclosed.

Countries should ensure that effective, proportionate and dissuasive sanctions are available to deal with persons who make false declaration(s) or disclosure(s). In cases where the currency or bearer negotiable instruments are related to terrorist financing, money laundering or predicate offences, countries should also adopt measures, including legislative ones consistent with Recommendation 4, which would enable the confiscation of such currency or instruments.

GENERAL REQUIREMENTS

33.   Statistics

Countries should maintain comprehensive statistics on matters relevant to the effectiveness and efficiency of their AML/CFT systems. This should include statistics on the STRs received and disseminated; on money laundering and terrorist financing investigations, prosecutions and convictions; on property frozen, seized and confiscated; and on mutual legal assistance or other international requests for cooperation.

34.   Guidance and feedback

The competent authorities, supervisors and SRBs should establish guidelines, and provide feedback, which will assist financial institutions and designated non-financial businesses and professions in applying national measures to combat money laundering and terrorist financing, and, in particular, in detecting and reporting suspicious transactions.

SANCTIONS

35.   Sanctions

Countries should ensure that there is a range of effective, proportionate and dissuasive sanctions, whether criminal, civil or administrative, available to deal with natural or legal persons covered by Recommendations 6, and 8 to 23, that fail to comply with AML/CFT requirements. Sanctions should be applicable not only to financial institutions and DNFBPs, but also to their directors and senior management.

G. INTERNATIONAL COOPERATION

36.   International instruments

Countries should take immediate steps to become party to and implement fully the Vienna Convention, 1988; the Palermo Convention, 2000; the United Nations Convention against Corruption, 2003; and the Terrorist Financing Convention,

1999. Where applicable, countries are also encouraged to ratify and implement other relevant international conventions, such as the Council of Europe Convention on Cybercrime, 2001; the Inter-American Convention against Terrorism, 2002; and the Council of Europe Convention on Laundering, Search, Seizure and Confiscation of the Proceeds from Crime and on the Financing of Terrorism, 2005.

37. Mutual legal assistance

Countries should rapidly, constructively and effectively provide the widest possible range of mutual legal assistance in relation to money laundering, associated predicate offences and terrorist financing investigations, prosecutions, and related proceedings. Countries should have an adequate legal basis for providing assistance and, where appropriate, should have in place treaties, arrangements or other mechanisms to enhance cooperation. In particular, countries should:

(a) Not prohibit, or place unreasonable or unduly restrictive conditions on, the provision of mutual legal assistance.

(b) Ensure that they have clear and efficient processes for the timely prioritisation and execution of mutual legal assistance requests. Countries should use a central authority, or another established official mechanism, for effective transmission and execution of requests. To monitor progress on requests, a case management system should be maintained.

(c) Not refuse to execute a request for mutual legal assistance on the sole ground that the offence is also considered to involve fiscal matters.

(d) Not refuse to execute a request for mutual legal assistance on the grounds that laws require financial institutions or DNFBPs to maintain secrecy or confidentiality (except where the relevant information that is sought is held in circumstances where legal professional privilege or legal professional secrecy applies).

(e) Maintain the confidentiality of mutual legal assistance requests they receive and the information contained in them, subject to fundamental principles of domestic law, in order to protect the integrity of the investigation or inquiry. If the requested country cannot comply with the requirement of confidentiality, it should promptly inform the requesting country.

Countries should render mutual legal assistance, notwithstanding the absence of dual criminality, if the assistance does not involve coercive actions. Countries should consider adopting such measures as may be necessary to enable them to provide a wide scope of assistance in the absence of dual criminality.

Where dual criminality is required for mutual legal assistance, that requirement should be deemed to be satisfied regardless of whether both countries place the offence within the same category of offence, or denominate the offence by the same terminology, provided that both countries criminalise the conduct underlying the offence.

Countries should ensure that, of the powers and investigative techniques required under Recommendation 31, and any other powers and investigative techniques available to their competent authorities:

(a) all those relating to the production, search and seizure of information, documents or evidence (including financial records) from financial institutions or other persons, and the taking of witness statements; and

(b) a broad range of other powers and investigative techniques;

are also available for use in response to requests for mutual legal assistance, and, if consistent with their domestic framework, in response to direct requests from foreign judicial or law enforcement authorities to domestic counterparts.

To avoid conflicts of jurisdiction, consideration should be given to devising and applying mechanisms for determining the best venue for prosecution of defendants in the interests of justice in cases that are subject to prosecution in more than one country.

Countries should, when making mutual legal assistance requests, make best efforts to provide complete factual and legal information that will allow for timely and efficient execution of requests, including any need for urgency, and should send requests using expeditious means. Countries should, before sending requests, make best efforts to ascertain the legal requirements and formalities to obtain assistance.

The authorities responsible for mutual legal assistance (e.g. a Central Authority) should be provided with adequate financial, human and technical resources. Countries should have in place processes to ensure that the staff of such authorities maintain high professional standards, including standards concerning confidentiality, and should be of high integrity and be appropriately skilled.

38.   Mutual legal assistance: freezing and confiscation*

Countries should ensure that they have the authority to take expeditious action in response to requests by foreign countries to identify, freeze, seize and confiscate property laundered; proceeds from money laundering, predicate offences and terrorist financing; instrumentalities used in, or intended for use in, the commission of these offences; or property of corresponding value. This authority should include being able to respond to requests made on the basis of non-conviction-based confiscation proceedings and related provisional measures, unless this is inconsistent with fundamental principles of their domestic law. Countries should also have effective mechanisms for managing such property, instrumentalities or property of corresponding value, and arrangements for coordinating seizure and confiscation proceedings, which should include the sharing of confiscated assets.

39.   Extradition

Countries should constructively and effectively execute extradition requests in relation to money laundering and terrorist financing, without undue delay. Countries should also take all possible measures to ensure that they do not provide safe havens for individuals charged with the financing of terrorism, terrorist acts or terrorist organisations. In particular, countries should:

(a)   ensure money laundering and terrorist financing are extraditable offences;

(b)   ensure that they have clear and efficient processes for the timely execution of extradition requests including prioritisation where appropriate. To monitor progress of requests a case management system should be maintained;

(c)   not place unreasonable or unduly restrictive conditions on the execution of requests; and

(d)   ensure they have an adequate legal framework for extradition.

Each country should either extradite its own nationals, or, where a country does not do so solely on the grounds of nationality, that country should, at the request of the country seeking extradition, submit the case, without undue delay, to its competent authorities for the purpose of prosecution of the offences set forth in the request. Those authorities should take their decision and conduct their proceedings in the same manner as in the case of any other offence of a serious nature under the domestic law of that country. The countries concerned should cooperate with each other, in particular on procedural and evidentiary aspects, to ensure the efficiency of such prosecutions.

Where dual criminality is required for extradition, that requirement should be deemed to be satisfied regardless of whether both countries place the offence within the same category of offence, or denominate the offence by the same terminology, provided that both countries criminalise the conduct underlying the offence.

Consistent with fundamental principles of domestic law, countries should have simplified extradition mechanisms, such as allowing direct transmission of requests for provisional arrests between appropriate authorities, extraditing persons based only on warrants of arrests or judgments, or introducing a simplified extradition of consenting persons who waive formal extradition proceedings. The authorities responsible for extradition should be provided with adequate financial, human and technical resources. Countries should have in place processes to ensure that the staff of such authorities maintain high professional standards, including standards concerning confidentiality, and should be of high integrity and be appropriately skilled.

40.   Other forms of international cooperation *

Countries should ensure that their competent authorities can rapidly, constructively and effectively provide the widest range of international cooperation in relation to money laundering, associated predicate offences and terrorist financing. Countries should do so both spontaneously and upon request, and there should be a lawful basis for providing cooperation. Countries should authorise their competent authorities to use the most efficient means to cooperate. Should a competent authority need bilateral or multilateral agreements or arrangements, such as a Memorandum of Understanding (MOU), these should be negotiated and signed in a timely way with the widest range of foreign counterparts.

Competent authorities should use clear channels or mechanisms for the effective transmission and execution of requests for information or other types of assistance. Competent authorities should have clear and efficient processes for the prioritisation and timely execution of requests, and for safeguarding the information received.

INTERPRETIVE NOTES TO THE FATF RECOMMENDATIONS

INTERPRETIVE NOTE TO RECOMMENDATION 1 (ASSESSING RISKS AND APPLYING A RISK-BASED APPROACH)

1.   The risk-based approach (RBA) is an effective way to combat money laundering and terrorist financing. In determining how the RBA should be implemented in a sector, countries should consider the capacity and anti-money laundering/countering the financing of terrorism (AML/CFT) experience of the relevant sector. Countries should understand that the discretion afforded, and responsibility imposed on, financial institutions and designated non-financial bodies and professions (DNFBPs) by the RBA is more appropriate in sectors with greater AML/CFT capacity and experience. This should not exempt financial institutions and DNFBPs from the requirement to apply enhanced measures when they identify higher risk scenarios. By adopting a risk-based approach, competent authorities, financial institutions and DNFBPs should be able to ensure that measures to prevent or mitigate money laundering and terrorist financing are commensurate with the risks identified, and would enable them to make decisions on how to allocate their own resources in the most effective way.

2.   In implementing a RBA, financial institutions and DNFBPs should have in place processes to identify, assess, monitor, manage and mitigate money laundering and terrorist financing risks. The general principle of a RBA is that, where there are higher risks, countries should require financial institutions and DNFBPs to take enhanced measures to manage and mitigate those risks; and that, correspondingly, where the risks are lower, simplified measures may be permitted. Simplified measures should not be permitted whenever there is a suspicion of money laundering or terrorist financing. Specific Recommendations set out more precisely how this general principle applies to particular requirements. Countries may also, in strictly limited circumstances and where there is a proven low risk of money laundering and terrorist financing, decide not to apply certain Recommendations to a particular type of financial institution or activity, or DNFBP (see below). Equally, if countries determine through their risk assessments that there are types of institutions, activities, businesses or professions that are at risk of abuse from money laundering and terrorist financing, and which do not fall under the definition of financial institution or DNFBP, they should consider applying AML/CFT requirements to such sectors.

A.   Obligations and decisions for countries

3.   **Assessing risk** – Countries[1] should take appropriate steps to identify and assess the money laundering and terrorist financing risks for the country, on an ongoing basis and in order to: (i) inform potential changes to the country's AML/CFT regime, including changes to laws, regulations and other measures; (ii) assist in the allocation and prioritisation of AML/CFT resources by competent authorities; and (iii) make information available for AML/CFT risk assessments conducted by financial institutions and DNFBPs. Countries should keep the assessments up-to-date, and should have

---

1   Where appropriate, AML/CFT risk assessments at a supra-national level should be taken into account when considering whether this obligation is satisfied.

mechanisms to provide appropriate information on the results to all relevant competent authorities and self-regulatory bodies (SRBs), financial institutions and DNFBPs.

4. **Higher risk** – Where countries identify higher risks, they should ensure that their AML/CFT regime addresses these higher risks, and, without prejudice to any other measures taken by countries to mitigate these higher risks, either prescribe that financial institutions and DNFBPs take enhanced measures to manage and mitigate the risks, or ensure that this information is incorporated into risk assessments carried out by financial institutions and DNFBPs, in order to manage and mitigate risks appropriately. Where the FATF Recommendations identify higher risk activities for which enhanced or specific measures are required, all such measures must be applied, although the extent of such measures may vary according to the specific level of risk.

5. **Lower risk** – Countries may decide to allow simplified measures for some of the FATF Recommendations requiring financial institutions or DNFBPs to take certain actions, provided that a lower risk has been identified, and this is consistent with the country's assessment of its money laundering and terrorist financing risks, as referred to in paragraph 3.

    Independent of any decision to specify certain lower risk categories in line with the previous paragraph, countries may also allow financial institutions and DNFBPs to apply simplified customer due diligence (CDD) measures, provided that the requirements set out in section B below ("Obligations and decisions for financial institutions and DNFBPs"), and in paragraph 7 below, are met.

6. **Exemptions** – Countries may decide not to apply some of the FATF Recommendations requiring financial institutions or DNFBPs to take certain actions, provided:

    (a) there is a proven low risk of money laundering and terrorist financing; this occurs in strictly limited and justified circumstances; and it relates to a particular type of financial institution or activity, or DNFBP; or

    (b) a financial activity (other than the transferring of money or value) is carried out by a natural or legal person on an occasional or very limited basis (having regard to quantitative and absolute criteria), such that there is low risk of money laundering and terrorist financing.

    While the information gathered may vary according to the level of risk, the requirements of Recommendation 11 to retain information should apply to whatever information is gathered.

7. **Supervision and monitoring of risk** – Supervisors (or SRBs for relevant DNFBPs sectors) should ensure that financial institutions and DNFBPs are effectively implementing the obligations set out below. When carrying out this function, supervisors and SRBs should, as and when required in accordance with the Interpretive Notes to Recommendations 26 and 28, review the money laundering and terrorist financing risk profiles and risk assessments prepared by financial institutions and DNFBPs, and take the result of this review into consideration.

B. Obligations and decisions for financial institutions and DNFBPs

8. **Assessing risk** – Financial institutions and DNFBPs should be required to take appropriate steps to identify and assess their money laundering and terrorist financing risks (for customers, countries or geographic areas; and products, services, transactions or delivery channels). They should document those assessments in order to be able to demonstrate their basis, keep these assessments up to date, and have appropriate mechanisms to provide risk

assessment information to competent authorities and SRBs. The nature and extent of any assessment of money laundering and terrorist financing risks should be appropriate to the nature and size of the business. Financial institutions and DNFBPs should always understand their money laundering and terrorist financing risks, but competent authorities or SRBs may determine that individual documented risk assessments are not required, if the specific risks inherent to the sector are clearly identified and understood.

9. **Risk management and mitigation** – Financial institutions and DNFBPs should be required to have policies, controls and procedures that enable them to manage and mitigate effectively the risks that have been identified (either by the country or by the financial institution or DNFBP). They should be required to monitor the implementation of those controls and to enhance them, if necessary. The policies, controls and procedures should be approved by senior management, and the measures taken to manage and mitigate the risks (whether higher or lower) should be consistent with national requirements and with guidance from competent authorities and SRBs.

10. **Higher risk** – Where higher risks are identified financial institutions and DNFBPs should be required to take enhanced measures to manage and mitigate the risks.

11. **Lower risk** – Where lower risks are identified, countries may allow financial institutions and DNFBPs to take simplified measures to manage and mitigate those risks.

12. When assessing risk, financial institutions and DNFBPs should consider all the relevant risk factors before determining what is the level of overall risk and the appropriate level of mitigation to be applied. Financial institutions and DNFBPs may differentiate the extent of measures, depending on the type and level of risk for the various risk factors (e.g. in a particular situation, they could apply normal CDD for customer acceptance measures, but enhanced CDD for ongoing monitoring, or vice versa).

INTERPRETIVE NOTE TO RECOMMENDATION 3 (MONEY LAUNDERING OFFENCE)

1. Countries should criminalise money laundering on the basis of the United Nations Convention against Illicit Traffic in Narcotic Drugs and Psychotropic Substances, 1988 (the Vienna Convention) and the United Nations Convention against Transnational Organized Crime, 2000 (the Palermo Convention).

2. Countries should apply the crime of money laundering to all serious offences, with a view to including the widest range of predicate offences. Predicate offences may be described by reference to all offences; or to a threshold linked either to a category of serious offences; or to the penalty of imprisonment applicable to the predicate offence (threshold approach); or to a list of predicate offences; or a combination of these approaches.

3. Where countries apply a threshold approach, predicate offences should, at a minimum, comprise all offences that fall within the category of serious offences under their national law, or should include offences that are punishable by a maximum penalty of more than one year's imprisonment, or, for those countries that have a minimum threshold for offences in their legal system, predicate offences should comprise all offences that are punished by a minimum penalty of more than six months imprisonment.

4. Whichever approach is adopted, each country should, at a minimum, include a range of offences within each of the designated categories of offences. The offence of money laundering should extend to any type of property, regardless of its value, that directly or indirectly represents the proceeds of crime. When

proving that property is the proceeds of crime, it should not be necessary that a person be convicted of a predicate offence.

5. Predicate offences for money laundering should extend to conduct that occurred in another country, which constitutes an offence in that country, and which would have constituted a predicate offence had it occurred domestically. Countries may provide that the only prerequisite is that the conduct would have constituted a predicate offence, had it occurred domestically.

6. Countries may provide that the offence of money laundering does not apply to persons who committed the predicate offence, where this is required by fundamental principles of their domestic law.

7. Countries should ensure that:

   (a) The intent and knowledge required to prove the offence of money laundering may be inferred from objective factual circumstances.

   (b) Effective, proportionate and dissuasive criminal sanctions should apply to natural persons convicted of money laundering.

   (c) Criminal liability and sanctions, and, where that is not possible (due to fundamental principles of domestic law), civil or administrative liability and sanctions, should apply to legal persons. This should not preclude parallel criminal, civil or administrative proceedings with respect to legal persons in countries in which more than one form of liability is available. Such measures should be without prejudice to the criminal liability of natural persons. All sanctions should be effective, proportionate and dissuasive.

   (d) There should be appropriate ancillary offences to the offence of money laundering, including participation in, association with or conspiracy to commit, attempt, aiding and abetting, facilitating, and counselling the commission, unless this is not permitted by fundamental principles of domestic law.

Appendix 2.4   FATF Standards 9 Special Recommendations (SR) on Terrorist Financing (TF)[1]

I.   Ratification and implementation of UN instruments

II.   Criminalising the financing of terrorism and associated money laundering

III.   Freezing and confiscating terrorist assets

IV.   Reporting suspicious transactions related to terrorism

V.   International co-operation

VI.   Alternative remittance

VII.   Wire transfers

VIII.   Non-profit organisations

IX.   Cash couriers

II.   CRIMINALISING THE FINANCING OF TERRORISM AND ASSOCIATED MONEY LAUNDERING

Each country should criminalise the financing of terrorism, terrorist acts and terrorist organisations. Countries should ensure that such offences are designated as money laundering predicate offences.

IV.   REPORTING SUSPICIOUS TRANSACTIONS RELATED TO TERRORISM

If financial institutions, or other businesses or entities subject to anti-money laundering obligations, suspect or have reasonable grounds to suspect that funds are linked or related to, or are to be used for terrorism, terrorist acts or by terrorist organisations, they should be required to report promptly their suspicions to the competent authorities.

VIII.   NON-PROFIT ORGANISATIONS

Countries should review the adequacy of laws and regulations that relate to entities that can be abused for the financing of terrorism. Non-profit organisations are particularly vulnerable, and countries should ensure that they cannot be misused:

(i)   by terrorist organisations posing as legitimate entities;

---

1 © FATF. Reproduced with the kind permission of FATF. For the full document please see http://www.fatf-gafi.org/topics/fatfrecommendations/documents/ixspecialrecommendations.html Exact acknowledgement wording still tbc

(ii) to exploit legitimate entities as conduits for terrorist financing, including for the purpose of escaping asset freezing measures; and

(iii) to conceal or obscure the clandestine diversion of funds intended for legitimate purposes to terrorist organisations.

Appendix 2.5   Wolfsberg Anti-Corruption Guidance (August 2011) (relates to Chapter 18)[1]

In August 2011 the Wolfsberg Group replaced its 2007 Wolfsberg Statement against Corruption with a revised, expanded and renamed version of the paper: Wolfsberg Anti-Corruption Guidance. This Guidance takes into account a number of recent developments and gives tailored advice to international financial institutions in support of their efforts to develop appropriate Anti-Corruption programmes, to combat and mitigate bribery risks associated with clients or transactions and also to prevent internal bribery.

The Wolfsberg Group periodically reviews documents it has issued to ensure they remain up to date and relevant to the financial industry. The impetus for this review includes the legal and regulatory developments and anti-bribery enforcement actions over recent years, particularly under the US Foreign Corrupt Practices Act. This, combined with increased regulatory scrutiny of financial institutions in the wake of the financial crisis, the increasing implementation across of world of the United Nations Convention Against corruption, as well as new law enacted to implement to OECD Convention Against Bribery in International Business Transactions and, finally, the coming into law of the UK Bribery Act, which introduce a wide reaching corporate offence of failing to prevent bribery as a result of not having implemented "adequate procedures" to address bribery and corruption risks, has resulted in a revised paper.

The Wolfsberg Anti-Corruption Guidance has an entirely new Appendix which set of the elements for an internal Anti-Corruption framework, suitable for an international financial institution. There are sections on roles and responsibilities, reporting policies and the programme framework. The latter includes risk assessments, due diligence in relation to third parties (including the use of intermediaries), political and charitable contributions, gifts and entertainment, whistleblowing, as well as controls (e.g. monitoring & surveillance) and communication, training & awareness. While the Guidance has greatly expanded the scope of the original paper, the risk focus for financial institutions remains as before: namely client risks continue to present the greatest risks for banks. The original guidance in this area has been updated but essentially remains as valid today as it did when the paper was original written.

Adherence to the Guidance paper is not à substitute for legal advice and financial institutions should therefore seek the assistance of their own internal and external counsel for advice on bribery and corruption risks, as may be relevant to their respective business.

---

1 Wolfsberg Principles reproduced with kind permission of the Wolfsberg Group. All rights reserved.

Appendix 3

Amnesty Programmes and Disclosure Facilities

Contents

433

Appendix 3.1　2014 Offshore Voluntary Disclosure Program (US)

The IRS began an open-ended offshore voluntary disclosure program (OVDP) in January 2012 on the heels of strong interest in the 2009 and 2011 programs. The IRS is offering people with undisclosed income from offshore accounts another opportunity to get current with their tax returns. The 2012 OVDP has a higher penalty rate than the previous program but offers clear benefits to encourage taxpayers to disclose foreign accounts now rather than risk detection by the IRS and possible criminal prosecution. This is a continuation of the program introduced in 2012 with modified terms, but for purposes of referring to this modified program, it may be referred to as the 2014 OVDP. The modifications are effective July 1, 2014. See below for links to both the original and modified program terms.

In addition to the OVDP, the IRS in 2013 offered a "Streamlined Amnesty" option, available for U.S. taxpayers with undisclosed foreign financial assets, where the situation is certified as not wilful.

For OVDP Documents and Forms please see – http://www.irs.gov/uac/2012-Offshore-Voluntary-Disclosure-Program"

OTHER TAX AMNESTIES:

Australia: tax amnesties launched in 2007 and 2009.[2] Also the project "DOIT" Amnesty (standing for "Disclose Offshore Income Today") was launched on 27 March 2014, with a final submission deadline of 19 December 2014.

Belgium: In 2004 the Belgian Parliament adopted a law allowing individuals subject to Belgian income tax to regularize the undeclared, or untaxed, assets they held before June 1, 2003.[3]

Canada: has had a general Tax Amnesty since the 1980s.

Germany: In 2004 Germany granted a tax amnesty in connection with tax evasion.[4]

Greece: On September 30, 2010, the Hellenic Parliament ratified a legislation pushed through by the Greek government in an effort to raise revenue, granting tax amnesty to millions of Greek citizens by paying just 55 percent of the outstanding debts.[5][6][7] In 2011, the European Commission requested Greece to modify its tax legislation as its tax amnesty was considered discriminatory and incompatible with European Union treaties.[8]

Italy: tax amnesty introduced in 2001 that came to be known as *Scudo Fiscale* (English: Tax Shield, which was extended in 2003.[9] In 2009 the Italian tax amnesty yielded €80 billion, while the Bank of Italy estimated that Italian citizens held around €500bn in undeclared funds outside the country.[10] A new initiative was launched in early 2014 originally by Law Decree 4/2014 of 24 January 2014, followed by Law Proposal 2247/2248 of 31.03.2014 and will be open until 30 September 2015.

Portugal: tax amnesties introduced in 2005 and 2010.[11]

Russia: In 2007, a Russian tax amnesty program collected $130 million in the first six months. The Russian program was not open to anyone previously convicted of tax crimes such as tax evasion.[12]

South Africa: In 2003 South Africa enacted the *Exchange Control Amnesty And Amendment of Taxation Laws Act*, a tax amnesty.[13]

Spain: In 2012 the Spanish Minister of Economy and Competitiveness announced a tax evasion amnesty for undeclared assets or those hidden in tax havens. Repatriation would be allowed by paying a 10 percent tax, with no criminal penalty.[14]

Appendix 3.2   France: The New Voluntary Disclosure Program[1]

On 21st June 2013, the French tax authorities issued their circular in respect of the new voluntary disclosure program for undeclared foreign assets. This is neither a tax amnesty nor a very generous program as compared to what has been put in place by some other European countries. The former tax regularisation unit ("regularisation cell") created in 2009 has not been reactivated, but the amended tax returns will be dealt with by one of the central services of the French tax authorities (DNVSF) and not with the taxpayer's local tax office

Appendix 3.3   Israel Voluntary Disclosure/ Tax Amnesty

Announced 23 September 2014

Appendix 3.4   The Swiss-UK Tax Cooperation Agreement

This required Swiss banks to identify those "in scope" and notify the affected individuals no later than 28 February 2013 ["in scope" referring to customers with significant UK connections, but excluding UK-Resident Non-Domiciliaries), and on 31 May 2013 to subject their Swiss bank accounts to a one-off levy of between 21% and 41% which resulted in payment of a total of £340 Million to the UK HMR&C. Annual deductions will thereafter be made and paid over, albeit on an anonymous basis. See **17.11**

---

1   Notes courtesy of Jean-Marc Tirard & Maryse Naudin of Tirard, Naudin.

Appendix 3.5   Memorandum of Understanding between the Government of the Isle of Man ("Government of the Isle of Man") and Her Majesty's Revenue and Customs ("HMRC") of the United Kingdom of Great Britain and Northern Ireland relating to Cooperation in Tax Matters

PREAMBLE

A.   On the terms of this Memorandum of Understanding, HMRC will, from 6 April 2013 until 30 September 2016 make available a disclosure facility (including a bespoke scheme) to persons eligible to participate in it as set out in Schedule 2 to assist those persons in complying with their obligations to HMRC.

B.   To support the objectives of the disclosure facility, the Government of the Isle of Man will require financial intermediaries to contact relevant persons to advise them of the disclosure facility and to ensure adherence to legislation for the prevention of money-laundering.

TERMS

1.   This Memorandum of Understanding must be interpreted in accordance with Schedule 1.

2.   HMRC will make the terms of the disclosure facility in Schedule 2 available from 6 April 2013 until 30 September 2016.

3.   The Government of the Isle of Man will–

   (a)   require financial intermediaries in the Isle of Man to contact their clients who are known to be relevant persons so that those clients are made aware of the disclosure facility before 31 December 2013 and to remind them about the disclosure facility during the six months period ending on 30 September 2016;

   (b)   continue to ensure that financial intermediaries in the Isle of Man properly apply Isle of Man legislation for the prevention of money-laundering.

4.   HMRC and the Government of the Isle of Man agree that they will provide (through a joint declaration, exchange of letters, issuance of "frequently asked questions" and answers, or otherwise) written guidance on Isle of Man investment and wealth management structures and their treatment as a general matter by HMRC, with a view to providing clarification to relevant persons investing in the Isle of Man.

5.   For the avoidance of doubt–

   (a)   this agreement and anything done in connection with it shall be without prejudice to–

(i)   any requirement for a person with any beneficial interest whatsoever in relevant property to account to HMRC for any UK tax payable in respect of such interest;

(ii)   the application of HMRC's published criminal investigation policy;

(b)   any tax withheld under the Agreement between the UK and the Isle of Man providing for measures equivalent to those laid down in the European Union Savings Directive (Council Directive 2003/48/EC) will be creditable and credited against any UK tax due under this disclosure facility;

(c)   the obligations of an eligible person to report any interest in relevant property to HMRC and to account for any UK tax in relation to it will be satisfied only if full and unprompted disclosure is made in respect of the relevant property and full UK tax (together with interest and applicable penalties) is paid thereon.

6.   HMRC may amend or withdraw the disclosure facility upon giving three months notice in writing to the Government of the Isle of Man.

7.   Signatures

SIGNED BY:

For, and on behalf of
Her Majesty's
Revenue and Customs of
The United Kingdom of Great Britain and
Northern Ireland
Edward Troup
(HMRC Tax Assurance Commissioner)

Date 19.Feb.2013

For, and on behalf of,
the Government of
of the Isle of Man

WE Teare MHK
Minister of the Treasury

Date 19.Feb.2013.

SCHEDULE 1

Defined words and phrases

1.   The following words and phrases have the following meanings–

"annuity contract" means a contract under which the issuer agrees to make payments for a period of time determined in whole or in part by reference to the life expectancy of one or more individuals, but does not include a non investment-linked, non-transferable immediate life annuity that is issued to an individual and monetises a pension or disability benefit provided under an account, product or arrangement identified as excluded from the definition of financial account;

"cash value insurance contract" means an insurance contract (other than an indemnity reinsurance contract between two insurance companies) that has a cash value (see paragraph 3);

"cut off day" means–

(a)   in the case of a natural person, 6 April 1999;

(b)   in the case of a legal person, 1 April 1999;

"financial account" means an account maintained by a financial institution;

"financial institution" means an Isle of Man Custodial Institution, a Depository Institution, an Investment Entity, or a Specified Insurance Company;

"financial intermediary" means a person who holds or is required to hold a licence under the Financial Services Act 2008 (an Act of Tynwald);

"HMRC" means Her Majesty's Revenue and Customs and, where the context requires, its predecessor organisations (the Inland Revenue and Her Majesty's Customs and Excise) as well as any successor organisations;

"insurance contract" means a contract (other than an annuity contract) under which the issuer agrees to pay an amount upon the occurrence of a specified contingency involving mortality, morbidity, accident, liability or property risk;

"investigation means"–

(a)   any criminal investigation conducted by HMRC relating to–

(i)   those functions for which the Commissioners for HMRC are responsible as set out in the Commissioners for Revenue and Customs Act 2005 (c. 11), and

(ii)   any money laundering offence within part 7 of the Proceeds of Crime Act 2002 (c. 29) which is associated with those functions;

(b)   any civil enquiry of any kind that is supported by statutory information powers and is carried out for the purposes of ascertaining whether the UK tax liabilities of a person are correct and up-to-date.

"person" means a natural or legal person or any other body of persons;

"published disclosure facility" means any facility (apart from this one) or campaign offered by HMRC under which it is or was possible to regularise a person's UK tax position;

"relevant person" means–

(a)   in respect of a natural person, a person who, in the period commencing on 6 April 1999 and ending on 31 December 2013–

(i)   has had a beneficial interest in relevant property; and

(ii)   has been resident in the UK for UK tax purposes,

for any part of the period.

     (b)   in respect of a legal person, a person that–

          (i)   in the period commencing on 1 April 1999 and ending on 31 December 2013 has had a beneficial interest in relevant property; and

          (ii)   is incorporated in the UK or has been resident in the UK for UK tax purposes in the period referred to in paragraph (i);

"relevant property" means–

     (a)   an account held with a bank or other financial institution in the Isle of Man;

     (b)   an annuity contract or cash value insurance contract issued or maintained by a financial institution in the Isle of Man; or

     (c)   a company (including a corporation and an institution structured as a corporation as well as a company without legal personality), partnership, foundation, establishment, trust, trust enterprise, or other fiduciary entity, estate, cash value insurance contract or annuity contract that is issued, formed, founded, settled, incorporated, administered, or managed in the Isle of Man;

"UK" means the United Kingdom of Great Britain and Northern Ireland;
  "UK Company" means a legal person that–

     (a)   has its place of incorporation in the UK, or

     (b)   has at any time on or after 1 April 1999 been resident in the UK for UK tax purposes;

"UK tax" means all taxes, duties and contributions under the care and management of or otherwise payable to HMRC;
  "UK tax year" means the period commencing on 6 April in any year and ending on 5 April of the following year.

2.   A relevant person has a beneficial interest in relevant property where–

     (a)   the person is a natural person who, on or at any time after 6 April 1999, has–

          (i)   held or controlled a share or voting rights in, or

          (ii)   received any of the profits of,

a legal person (other than those that are listed or which are collective investment vehicles) or a body of persons without legal personality.

     (b)   in the case of trusts or other fiduciary entities, the person is–

          (i)   the person or one of the person who established or funded it;

          (ii)   the person or one of the persons regarded as its principal beneficiary or principal beneficiaries;

          (iii)   a person entitled to any of its income or capital;

          (iv)   a person who has received a distribution or distributions, in a given UK tax year from the entity since 6 April 1999; or

          (v)   a person who has been provided with the benefit, in a given UK tax year, of an asset or any number of assets from such entity since 6 April 1999;

     (c)   in the case of an account with a bank or other financial institution that is relevant property–

    (i)   the person in whose name the account is held if the person is a UK Company or a natural person who is the beneficial owner of the account;

    (ii)   where the account is held in the name of a natural person who is not the beneficial owner or in the name of a legal person other than a UK company, the person identified as the "beneficial owner" in forms provided to the financial intermediary by that person pursuant to legislation for the prevention of money-laundering;

  (d)   in the case of a cash value insurance contract or an annuity contract–

    (i)   the person entitled to access the cash value or change the beneficiary of the contract;

    (ii)   if no person can access the cash value or change the beneficiary, the person named as the owner in the contract or has a vested entitlement to payment under the terms of the contract;

    (iii) the person entitled to receive a payment under a cash value annuity contract or annuity contract upon its maturity.

3.   In determining whether an insurance contract has a cash value, no account must be taken of–

  (a)   an amount payable in respect of a personal injury or sickness benefit or other benefit providing indemnification of an economic loss incurred upon the occurrence of the event insured against; or

  (b)   a refund to the policyholder of a previously paid premium under an insurance contract (other than under a life insurance contract) due to policy cancellation, decrease in risk exposure during the effective period of the insurance contract, or arising from a redetermination of the premium due to correction of posting or similar error.

4.   Except where the context otherwise requires–

  (a)   the singular includes the plural and vice versa;

  (b)   in Schedule 2, a reference to a person is a reference to a person eligible to participate in the disclosure facility.

SCHEDULE 2

The Disclosure Facility

Conditions for participation in the Disclosure Facility

1.   A person may participate in this disclosure facility if the person–

  (a)   is eligible to participate in the disclosure facility;

  (b)   applies to participate in the disclosure facility after 5 April 2013 and before 30 September 2016 in the manner required by HMRC;

  (c)   provides the level of disclosure required by HMRC for the purposes of the disclosure facility; and

  (d)   makes the financial commitment.

Persons eligible to participate in the disclosure facility

2.   A person is eligible to participate in the disclosure facility if the person is a relevant person who is not the subject of an investigation by HMRC on 6 April 2013 that has not been concluded by that day.

Level of disclosure required by HMRC

3.   A person provides the level of disclosure required by HMRC only if the person–

    (a)   makes full and unprompted disclosure in respect of all relevant property in which the person has had a beneficial interest after 5 April 1999;

    (b)   provides such information as HMRC reasonably deems necessary to ensure the person pays all UK tax (together with interest and penalties) required from that person taking account of the disclosure facility; and

    (c)   without prejudice to the generality of the foregoing, provides, at the time when application to participate in the disclosure facility is made–

        (i)   the person's name, address (or registered office), date of birth (or date of incorporation);

        (ii)   the persons' national insurance number or any other unique tax reference appropriate to the person;

        (iii)   in relation to a natural person, full details of all previously undisclosed UK tax liabilities in respect of every UK tax year commencing on or after 6 April 1999 and ending before the beginning of the UK tax year in which the disclosure is made;

        (iv)   in relation to a legal person, full details of all previously undisclosed UK tax liabilities in respect of every accounting period commencing on or after 1 April 1999 and ending before the beginning of a period of 12 months starting on 1 April in which the application for the disclosure facility is made;

        (v)   a computation of the overall UK tax liability of the person taking account of the disclosure facility;

        (vi)   a declaration that the disclosure made is correct and complete;

        (vii)   full contact details of any person who has provided professional advice in relation to making the application to participate in the disclosure facility.

Financial commitment

4.   A person makes the financial commitment where–

    (a)   at the time when the application to participate in the disclosure facility is made, the person–

        (i)   pays the overall UK tax liability computed in compliance with paragraph 3(c)(v); or

        (ii)   provides evidence of inability to make such payment together with a proposal for payment and an appropriate payment on account; and

    (b)   pays any further UK tax, interest and penalties notified as payable taking account of the disclosure facility within 30 days of such notification or such other period as HMRC agrees.

Persons who may participate in the facility conferred by paragraphs 6 to 8

5.   The facility conferred by paragraphs 6 to 8 is available only in relation to a person who–

   (a)   is eligible to participate in the disclosure facility;

   (b)   has not been the subject of an investigation by HMRC that concluded before 6 April 2013 or one that began after that day;

   (c)   has not engaged with, participated in or been contacted personally by HMRC in respect of any published disclosure facility before applying to HMRC to participate in the disclosure facility; and

   (d)   is not a "relevant person" for the purposes of the Agreement between the Swiss Confederation and the UK on cooperation in the area of taxation who could authorise disclosure of information to HMRC in relation to that person in accordance with that agreement.

Tax and Penalties

6.   In relation to a person to whom this paragraph applies (subject to paragraphs 8 and 9)–

   (a)   HMRC will not seek to recover from that person UK tax chargeable in respect of a UK tax year or an accounting period ending before the cut off day; and

   (b)   HMRC–

      (i)   will not impose a penalty on that person in respect of UK tax described paragraph (a); and

      (ii)   will not impose a penalty on that person exceeding the percentage determined in accordance with paragraph 7 ("specified percentage") in respect of other UK tax disclosed by virtue of the disclosure facility as being chargeable.

Specified percentage

7.   The specified percentage is–

   (a)   in relation to an inaccuracy falling for a penalty in accordance with Schedule 24 of the Finance Act 2007 (c. 11) ("Schedule 24") (other than a penalty described in (b) and (c)), 20% of the UK tax to which the penalty relates;

   (b)   in relation to an inaccuracy falling for a penalty in accordance with Schedule 24 under "category 2" by reason of paragraph 4A(2) of that Schedule, 30% of the UK tax to which the penalty relates;

   (c)   in relation to an inaccuracy falling for a penalty in accordance with Schedule 24 under "category 3" by reason of paragraph 4A(3) of that Schedule, 40% of the UK tax to which the penalty relates;

   (d)   in any other case, 10% of the UK tax to which the penalty relates.

Errors on tax returns

8.   Where–

   (a)   an error has been made in a tax return made to HMRC by virtue of the Taxes Management Act 1970 (c. 9) in respect of–

(i)   an accounting period ending more than four years before the beginning of a period of 12 months starting on 1 April in which the application for the disclosure facility is made, or

(ii)   a UK tax year ending more than four years before the beginning of the UK tax year in which the application for the disclosure facility is made,

(b)   the error led to a failure of a person to report to HMRC an interest in relevant property on which the person would have been subject to UK tax,

(c)   the error was made by that person and no one else, and

(d)   HMRC (after due consideration of any representations made by or on behalf of that person), considers the error was one that a reasonable person would have made,

any further UK tax that would have been disclosed as chargeable if the error had not occurred will be treated for the purposes of paragraph 6 as chargeable in respect of a UK tax year or an accounting period ending before the cut off day.

Property excluded from the facility in paragraph 6

9.   The facility in paragraph 6 does not apply in respect of UK tax or penalties relating to–

(a)   an account with a bank or other financial institution held outside the UK or Isle of Man which was opened through a UK branch or agency of a bank;

(b)   property constituting "criminal property" within the meaning in section 340 of the Proceeds of Crime Act 2002 (c. 29) by virtue of being a benefit from criminal conduct (other than conduct comprising only illegal tax evasion (not limited to UK tax)).

The Bespoke Service

10.   The bespoke service will be a personalised service available to a person and will have the following features–

(a)   the possibility of initial anonymous contact by a professional adviser (including a financial intermediary) to discuss with HMRC the circumstances of a person on a "no names" basis;

(b)   the possibility for a person or professional adviser acting on behalf of that person having a single point of contact within a discrete HMRC team to ensure consistency of treatment;

(c)   due consideration by HMRC of–

(i)   residence and domicile claims made by a person, subject to the provision of full supporting evidence;

(ii)   estimated offers to settle UK tax liability, subject to receipt of evidence justifying such estimate;

(iii)   offers to pay by instalments over a reasonable period of time (together with such interest as required by law on unpaid amounts), subject to the provision of evidence confirming hardship or the need for the sale of any property in order to make payment of UK tax, interest or penalties;

(d)   provided full and accurate disclosure is made by a person and where it is practical to do so, HMRC will fulfil its obligations in order to facilitate the determination of a person's liability to pay outstanding UK tax, interest and penalties within nine months of the making of the application to participate in the disclosure facility or such other period of time as HMRC agrees with the person.

(e)   where a penalty imposed on a person in relation to a liability to UK tax disclosed in consequence of the person's participation in the bespoke service is determined taking account the maximum reduction for disclosure from that penalty possible, HMRC will not, in relation to that penalty, publish information about that person in accordance with section 94 of the Finance Act 2009 (c. 10);

(f)   in respect of an accounting period ending before 1 April 2016 or UK tax year ending before 6 April 2016, assistance by HMRC to a person regarding compliance with UK tax law requirements without prejudice to HMRC's powers in relation to that person.

11.   For the purposes of making a disclosure of tax following an inaccuracy made in relation to a person's UK tax affairs, a person may request that the bespoke service applies in respect of all and any assets and income in respect of which UK tax may apply in respect of the period commencing on 6 April 2013 and ending on 5 April 2016.

Appendix 3.6   Memorandum of Understanding between the Government of Guernsey ("Government of Guernsey") and Her Majesty's Revenue and Customs ("HMRC") of the United Kingdom of Great Britain and Northern Ireland Relating to Cooperation in Tax Matters

PREAMBLE

A.   On the terms of this Memorandum of Understanding, HMRC will, from 6 April 2013 until 30 September 2016 make available a disclosure facility (including a bespoke scheme) to persons eligible to participate in it as set out in Schedule 2 to assist those persons in complying with their obligations to HMRC.

B.   To support the objectives of the disclosure facility, the Government of Guemsey will require financial intermediaries to contact relevant persons to advise them of the disclosure facility and to ensure adherence to legislation for the prevention of money-laundering.

TERMS

1.   This Memorandum of Understanding must be interpreted in accordance with Schedule 1.

2.   HMRC will make the terms of the disclosure facility in Schedule 2 available from 6 April 2013 until 30 September 2016.

3.   The Government of Guemsey will–

(a)   require financial intermediaries in Guemsey to contact their clients who are known to be relevant persons so that those clients are made aware of the disclosure facility before 31 December 2013 and to remind them about the disclosure facility during the six month period ending on 30 September 2016;

(b)   continue to ensure that financial intermediaries in Guemsey properly apply Guemsey legislation for the prevention of money-laundering.

4.   HMRC and the Government of Guemsey will provide (through a joint declaration, exchange of letters, issuance of "frequently asked questions" and answers, or otherwise) written guidance on Guemsey investment and wealth management structures and their treatment as a general matter by HMRC, with a view to providing clarification to relevant persons investing in Guemsey.

5.   For the avoidance of doubt–

(a)   this Memorandum of Understanding and anything done in connection with it shall be without prejudice to–

    (i)   any requirement for a person with any beneficial interest whatsoever in relevant property to account to HMRC for any UK tax payable in respect of such interest;

    (ii)   the application of HMRC's published criminal investigation policy;

(b)   any tax withheld under the Agreement between the UK and Guemsey providing for measures equivalent to those laid down in the European Union Savings Directive (Council Directive 2003/48/EC) will be creditable and credited against any UK tax due under this disclosure facility;

(c)   the obligations of an eligible person to report any interest in relevant property to HMRC and to account for any UK tax in relation to it will be satisfied only if full and unprompted disclosure is made in respect of the relevant property and full UK tax (together with interest and applicable penalties) is paid thereon.

6.   HMRC may amend or withdraw the disclosure facility upon giving three months notice in writing to the Government of Guemsey.

7.   Signatures

SIGNED BY:

For, and on behalf of,	For, and on behalf of,
Her Majesty's	the Government
Revenue and Customs of	of Guemsey
The United Kingdom of	
Great Britain and Northern	
Ireland	
Edward Troup	Nigel Garland
(HMRC Tax Assurance Commissioner)	Deputy Director (Compliance & International) of Income Tax
Date 11 March 2013	Date 11 March 2013

SCHEDULE 1

Defined words and phrases

1.   The following words and phrases have the following meanings–

"annuity contract" means a contract under which the issuer agrees to make payments for a period of time determined in whole or in part by reference to the life expectancy of one or more individuals, but does not include a non investment-linked, non-transferable immediate life annuity that is issued to an individual and monetises a pension or disability benefit provided under an account, product or arrangement identified as excluded from the definition of financial account;

"cash value insurance contract" means an insurance contract (other than an indemnity reinsurance contract between two insurance companies) that has a cash value (see paragraph 3);

"cut off day" means–

    (a)   in the case of a natural person, 6 April 1999;

    (b)   in the case of a legal person,1 April 1999;

"financial account" means an account maintained by a financial institution;

"financial institution" means a Guemsey Custodial Institution, a Depository Institution, an Investment Entity, or a Specified Insurance Company;

"financial intermediary" means a person who holds or is required to hold a licence under the Financial Services Commission (Bailiwick of Guemsey) Law (1987);

"HMRC" means Her Majesty's Revenue and Customs and, where the context requires, its predecessor organisations (the Inland Revenue and Her Majesty's Customs and Excise) as well as any successor organisations;

"insurance contract" means a contract (other than an annuity contract) under which the issuer agrees to pay an amount upon the occurrence of a specified contingency involving mortality, morbidity, accident, liability or property risk;

"investigation means"–

    (a)   any criminal investigation conducted by HMRC relating to–

        (i)   those functions for which the Commissioners for HMRC are responsible as set out in the Commissioners for Revenue and Customs Act 2005 (c. 11), and

        (ii)   any money laundering offence within part 7 of the Proceeds of Crime Act 2002 (c. 29) which is associated with those functions;

    (b)   any civil enquiry of any kind that is supported by statutory information powers and is carried out for the purposes of ascertaining whether the UK tax liabilities of a person are correct and up-to-date.

"person" means a natural or legal person or any other body of persons;

"published disclosure facility" means any facility (apart from this one) or campaign offered by HMRC under which it is or was possible to regularise a person's UK tax position;

"relevant person" means–

    (a)   in respect of a natural person, a person who, in the period commencing on 6 April 1999 and ending on 31 December 2013 –

        (i)   has had a beneficial interest in relevant property; and

        (ii)   has been resident in the UK for UK tax purposes,

for any part of the period.

    (b)   in respect of a legal person, a person that–

        (i)   in the period commencing on 1 April 1999 and ending on 31 December 2013 has had a beneficial interest in relevant property; and

        (ii)   is incorporated in the UK or has been resident in the UK for UK tax purposes in the period referred to in paragraph (i);

"relevant property" means–

    (a)   an account held with a bank or other financial institution in Guemsey;

(b) an annuity contract or cash value insurance contract issued or maintained by a financial institution in Guemsey; or

(c) a company (including a corporation and an institution structured as a corporation as well as a company without legal personality), partnership, foundation, establishment, trust, trust enterprise, or other fiduciary entity, estate, cash value insurance contract or annuity contract that is issued, formed, founded, settled, incorporated, administered, or managed in Guemsey;

"UK" means the United Kingdom of Great Britain and Northern Ireland;
   "UK Company" means a legal person that–

(a) has its place of incorporation in the UK, or

(b) has at any time on or after 1 April 1999 been resident in the UK for UK tax purposes;

"UK tax" means all taxes, duties and contributions under the care and management of or otherwise payable to HMRC;
   "UK tax year" means the period commencing on 6 April in any year and ending on 5 April of the following year.

2. A relevant person has a beneficial interest in relevant property where–

(a) the person is a natural person who, on or at any time after 6 April 1999, has–

     (i) held or controlled a share or voting rights in, or

     (ii) received any of the profits of,

a legal person (other than those that are listed or which are collective investment vehicles) or a body of persons without legal personality.

(b) in the case of trusts or other fiduciary entities, the person is–

     (i) the person or one of the persons who established or funded it;

     (ii) the person or one of the persons regarded as its principal beneficiary or principal beneficiaries;

     (iii) a person entitled to any of its income or capital;

     (iv) a person who has received a distribution or distributions, in a given UK tax year from the entity since 6 April 1999; or

     (v) a person who has been provided with the benefit, in a given UK tax year, of an asset or any number of assets from such entity since 6 April 1999;

(c) in the case of an account with a bank or other financial institution that is relevant property–

     (i) the person in whose name the account is held if the person is a UK Company or a natural person who is the beneficial owner of the account;

     (ii) where the account is held in the name of a natural person who is not the beneficial owner or in the name of a legal person other than a UK company, the person identified as the "beneficial owner" in forms provided to the financial intermediary by that person pursuant to legislation for the prevention of money-laundering;

(d) in the case of a cash value insurance contract or an annuity contract–

449

(i) the person entitled to access the cash value or change the beneficiary of the contract;

(ii) if no person can access the cash value or change the beneficiary, the person named as the owner in the contract or has a vested entitlement to payment under the terms of the contract;

(iii) the person entitled to receive a payment under a cash value annuity contract or annuity contract upon its maturity.

3. In determining whether an insurance contract has a cash value, no account must be taken of–

(a) an amount payable in respect of a personal injury or sickness benefit or other benefit providing indemnification of an economic loss incurred upon the occurrence of the event insured against; or

(b) a refund to the policyholder of a previously paid premium under an insurance contract (other than under a life insurance contract) due to policy cancellation, decrease in risk exposure during the effective period of the insurance contract, or arising from a redetermination of the premium due to correction of posting or similar error.

4. Except where the context otherwise requires–

(a) the singular includes the plural and vice versa;

(b) in Schedule 2, a reference to a person is a reference to a person eligible to participate in the disclosure facility.

SCHEDULE 2

The Disclosure Facility

Conditions for participation in the Disclosure Facility

1. A person may participate in this disclosure facility if the person–

(a) is eligible to participate in the disclosure facility;

(b) applies to participate in the disclosure facility after 5 April 2013 and before 30 September 2016 in the manner required by HMRC;

(c) provides the level of disclosure required by HMRC for the purposes of the disclosure facility; and

(d) makes the financial commitment.

Persons eligible to participate in the disclosure facility

2. A person is eligible to participate in the disclosure facility if the person is a relevant person who is not the subject of an investigation by HMRC on 6 April 2013 that has not been concluded by that day.

Level of disclosure required by HMRC

3. A person provides the level of disclosure required by HMRC only if the person–

(a) makes full and unprompted disclosure in respect of all relevant property in which the person has had a beneficial interest after 5 April 1999;

(b) provides such information as HMRC reasonably deems necessary to ensure the person pays all UK tax (together with interest and penalties) required from that person taking account of the disclosure facility; and

(c) without prejudice to the generality of the foregoing, provides, at the time when application to participate in the disclosure facility is made–

(i) the person's name, address (or registered office), date of birth (or date of incorporation);

(ii) the person's national insurance number or any other unique tax reference appropriate to the person;

(iii) in relation to a natural person, full details of all previously undisclosed UK tax liabilities in respect of every UK tax year commencing on or after 6 April 1999 and ending before the beginning of the UK tax year in which the disclosure is made;

(iv) in relation to a legal person, full details of all previously undisclosed UK tax liabilities in respect of every accounting period commencing on or after 1 April 1999 and ending before the beginning of a period of 12 months starting on 1 April in which the application for the disclosure facility is made;

(v) a computation of the overall UK tax liability of the person taking account of the disclosure facility;

(vi) a declaration that the disclosure made is correct and complete;

(vii) full contact details of any person who has provided professional advice in relation to making the application to participate in the disclosure facility.

Financial commitment

4. A person makes the financial commitment where–

(a) at the time when the application to participate in the disclosure facility is made, the person–

(i) pays the overall UK tax liability computed in compliance with paragraph 3(c)(v); or

(ii) provides evidence of inability to make such payment together with a proposal for payment and an appropriate payment on account; and

(b) pays any further UK tax, interest and penalties notified as payable taking account of the disclosure facility within 30 days of such notification or such other period as HMRC agrees.

Persons who may participate in the facility conferred by paragraphs 6 to 8

5. The facility conferred by paragraphs 6 to 8 is available only in relation to a person who–

(a) is eligible to participate in the disclosure facility;

(b) has not been the subject of an investigation by HMRC that concluded before 6 April 2013 or one that began after that day;

(c) has not engaged with, participated in or been contacted personally by HMRC in respect of any published disclosure facility before applying to HMRC to participate in the disclosure facility; and

(d)   is not a "relevant person" for the purposes of the Agreement between the Swiss Confederation and the UK on cooperation in the area of taxation who could authorise disclosure of information to HMRC in relation to that person in accordance with that agreement.

Tax and Penalties

6.   In relation to a person to whom this paragraph applies (subject to paragraphs 8 and 9)–

(a)   HMRC will not seek to recover from that person UK tax chargeable in respect of a UK tax year or an accounting period ending before the cut off day; and

(b)   HMRC–

    (i)   will not impose a penalty on that person in respect of UK tax described in paragraph (a); and

    (ii)   will not impose a penalty on that person exceeding the percentage determined in accordance with paragraph 7 ("specified percentage") in respect of other UK tax disclosed by virtue of the disclosure facility as being chargeable.

Specified percentage

7.   The specified percentage is–

(a)   in relation to anything falling for a penalty in accordance with Schedule 24 of the Finance Act 2007 (c. 11) ("Schedule 24"), Schedule 41 of the Finance Act 2008 (c. 9) ("Schedule 41") or Schedule 55 of the Finance Act 2009 (c. 10) ("Schedule 55") (other than anything falling for a penalty described in (b) and (c)), 20% of the UK tax to which the penalty relates;

(b)   in relation to anything the amount of penalty for which is determinable by reference to paragraph 4A(2) of Schedule 24, paragraph 6A(2) of Schedule 41 or paragraph 6A(2) of Schedule 55, 30% of the UK tax to which the penalty relates;

(c)   in relation to anything the amount of penalty for which is determinable by reference to paragraph 4A(3) of Schedule 24, paragraph 6A(3) of Schedule 41 or paragraph 6A(3) of Schedule 55, 40% of the UK tax to which the penalty relates;

(d)   in any other case, 10% of the UK tax to which the penalty relates.

Errors on tax returns

8.   Where–

(a)   an error has been made in a tax return made to HMRC by virtue of the Taxes Management Act 1970 (c. 9) in respect of–

    (i)   an accounting period ending more than four years before the beginning of a period of 12 months starting on 1 April in which the application for the disclosure facility is made, or

    (ii)   a UK tax year ending more than four years before the beginning of the UK tax year in which the application for the disclosure facility is made,

(b)   the error led to a failure of a person to report to HMRC an interest in relevant property on which the person would have been subject to UK tax,

(c)   the error was made by that person and no one else, and

(d)   HMRC (after due consideration of any representations made by or on behalf of that person), considers the error was one that a reasonable person would have made,

any further UK tax that would have been disclosed as chargeable if the error had not occurred will be treated for the purposes of paragraph 6 as chargeable in respect of a UK tax year or an accounting period ending before the cut off day.

Property excluded from the facility in paragraph 6

9.   The facility in paragraph 6 does not apply in respect of UK tax or penalties relating to–

(a)   an account with a bank or other financial institution held outside the UK or Guemsey which was opened through a UK branch or agency of a bank;

(b)   property constituting "criminal property" within the meaning in section 340 of the Proceeds of Crime Act 2002 (c. 29) by virtue of being a benefit from criminal conduct (other than conduct comprising only illegal tax evasion (not limited to UK tax)).

The Bespoke Service

10.   The bespoke service will be a personalised service available to a person and will have the following features–

(a)   the possibility of initial anonymous contact by a professional adviser (including a financial intermediary) to discuss with HMRC the circumstances of a person on a "no names" basis;

(b)   the possibility for a person or professional adviser acting on behalf of that person having a single point of contact within a discrete HMRC team to ensure consistency of treatment;

(c)   due consideration by HMRC of–

(i)   residence and domicile claims made by a person, subject to the provision of full supporting evidence;

(ii)   estimated offers to settle UK tax liability, subject to receipt of evidence justifying such estimate;

(iii)   offers to pay by instalments over a reasonable period of time (together with such interest as required by law on unpaid amounts), subject to the provision of evidence confirming hardship or the need for the sale of any property in order to make payment of UK tax, interest or penalties;

(d)   provided full and accurate disclosure is made by a person and where it is practical to do so, HMRC will fulfil its obligations in order to facilitate the determination of a person's liability to pay outstanding UK tax, interest and penalties within nine months of the making of the application to participate in the disclosure facility or such other period of time as HMRC agrees with the person;

(e)   where a penalty imposed on a person in relation to a liability to UK tax disclosed in consequence of the person's participation in the bespoke service is determined taking into account the maximum reduction for disclosure from that penalty possible, HMRC will not, in relation to that penalty, publish information about that person in accordance with section 94 of the Finance Act 2009 (c. 10);

(f)   in respect of an accounting period ending before 1 April 2016 or UK tax year ending before 6 April 2016, assistance by HMRC to a person regarding compliance with UK tax law requirements without prejudice to HMRC's powers in relation to that person.

11.   For the purposes of making a disclosure of tax, following an inaccuracy made in relation to a person's UK tax affairs, a person may request that the bespoke service applies in respect of all and any assets and income in respect of which UK tax may apply in respect of the period commencing on 6 April 2013 and ending on 5 April 2016.

Appendix 3.7 Memorandum of Understanding between the Government of Jersey ("Government of Jersey") and Her Majesty's Revenue And Customs ("HMRC") of the United Kingdom of Great Britain and Northern Ireland relating to Cooperation in Tax Matters

PREAMBLE

A.   On the terms of this Memorandum of Understanding, HMRC will, from 6 April 2013 until 30 September 2016 make available a disclosure facility (including a bespoke scheme) to persons eligible to participate in it as set out in Schedule 2 to assist those persons in complying with their obligations to HMRC.

B.   To support the objectives of the disclosure facility, the Government of Jersey will require financial intermediaries to contact relevant persons to advise them of the disclosure facility and to ensure adherence to legislation for the prevention of money-laundering.

TERMS

1.   This Memorandum of Understanding must be interpreted in accordance with Schedule 1.

2.   HMRC will make the terms of the disclosure facility in Schedule 2 available from 6 April 2013 until 30 September 2016.

3.   The Government of Jersey will–

    (a)   require financial intermediaries in Jersey to contact their clients who are known to be relevant persons so that those clients are made aware of the disclosure facility before 31 December 2013 and to remind them about the disclosure facility during the six month period ending on 30 September 2016;

    (b)   continue to ensure that financial intermediaries in Jersey properly apply Jersey legislation for the prevention of money-laundering.

4.   HMRC and the Government of Jersey will provide (through a joint declaration, exchange of letters, issuance of "frequently asked questions" and answers, or otherwise) written guidance on Jersey investment and wealth management structures and their treatment as a general matter by HMRC, with a view to providing clarification to relevant persons investing in Jersey.

5.   For the avoidance of doubt–

(a)   this Memorandum of Understanding and anything done in connection with it shall be without prejudice to–

    (i)   any requirement for a person with any beneficial interest whatsoever in relevant property to account to HMRC for any UK tax payable in respect of such interest;

    (ii)   the application of HMRC's published criminal investigation policy;

(b)   any tax withheld under the Agreement between the UK and Jersey providing for measures equivalent to those laid down in the European Union Savings Directive (Council Directive 2003/48/EC) will be creditable and credited against any UK tax due under this disclosure facility;

(c)   the obligations of an eligible person to report any interest in relevant property to HMRC and to account for any UK tax in relation to it will be satisfied only if full and unprompted disclosure is made in respect of the relevant property and full UK tax (together with interest and applicable penalties) is paid thereon.

6.   HMRC may amend or withdraw the disclosure facility upon giving three months notice in writing to the Government of Jersey.

7.   Signatures

SIGNED BY:

For, and on behalf of,	For, and on behalf of,
Her Majesty's	the Government
Revenue and Customs of	of Jersey
The United Kingdom of	
Great Britain and Northern	
Ireland	
Edward Troup	David Le Cuirot
(HMRC Tax Assurance Commissioner)	(Acting Comptroller of Taxes)
Date 13 March 2013	Date 13 March 2013

SCHEDULE 1

Defined words and phrases

1.   The following words and phrases have the following meanings–

"annuity contract" means a contract under which the issuer agrees to make payments for a period of time determined in whole or in part by reference to the life expectancy of one or more individuals, but does not include a non investment-linked, non-transferable immediate life annuity that is issued to an individual and monetises a pension or disability benefit provided under an account, product or arrangement identified as excluded from the definition of financial account;

"cash value insurance contract" means an insurance contract (other than an indemnity reinsurance contract between two insurance companies) that has a cash value (see paragraph 3);

"cut off day" means–

(a)   in the case of a natural person, 6 April 1999;

(b)   in the case of a legal person,1 April 1999; "financial account" means an account maintained by a financial institution;

"financial institution" means a Jersey Custodial Institution, a Depository Institution, an Investment Entity, or a Specified Insurance Company;

"financial intermediary" means a person who holds or is required to hold a licence under the Banking Business (Jersey) Law (1991), the Financial Services (Jersey) Law (1988), the Collective Investment Funds (Jersey) 1988, or the Insurance Business (Jersey) Law 1996;

"HMRC" means Her Majesty's Revenue and Customs and, where the context requires, its predecessor organisations (the Inland Revenue and Her Majesty's Customs and Excise) as well as any successor organisations;

"insurance contract" means a contract (other than an annuity contract) under which the issuer agrees to pay an amount upon the occurrence of a specified contingency involving mortality, morbidity, accident, liability or property risk;

"investigation means"–

(a)   any criminal investigation conducted by HMRC relating to–

(i)   those functions for which the Commissioners for HMRC are responsible as set out in the Commissioners for Revenue and Customs Act 2005 (c. 11), and

(ii)   any money laundering offence within part 7 of the Proceeds of Crime Act 2002 (c. 29) which is associated with those functions;

(b)   any civil enquiry of any kind that is supported by statutory information powers and is carried out for the purposes of ascertaining whether the UK tax liabilities of a person are correct and up-to-date.

"person" means a natural or legal person or any other body of persons;

"published disclosure facility" means any facility (apart from this one) or campaign offered by HMRC under which it is or was possible to regularise a person's UK tax position;

"relevant person" means–

(a)   in respect of a natural person, a person who, in the period commencing on 6 April 1999 and ending on 31 December 2013–

(i)   has had a beneficial interest in relevant property; and

(ii)   has been resident in the UK for UK tax purposes,

for any part of the period.

(b)   in respect of a legal person, a person that–

(i)   in the period commencing on 1 April 1999 and ending on 31 December 2013 has had a beneficial interest in relevant property; and

(ii)   is incorporated in the UK or has been resident in the UK for UK tax purposes in the period referred to in paragraph (i);

relevant property" means–

(a)   an account held with a bank or other financial institution in Jersey;

(b)   an annuity contract or cash value insurance contract issued or maintained by a financial institution in Jersey; or

(c)   a company (including a corporation and an institution structured as a corporation as well as a company without legal personality), partnership, foundation, establishment, trust, trust enterprise, or other fiduciary entity, estate, cash value insurance contract or annuity contract that is issued, formed, founded, settled, incorporated, administered, or managed in Jersey;

"UK" means the. United Kingdom of Great Britain and Northern Ireland;
  "UK Company" means a legal person that–

(a)   has its place of incorporation in the UK, or

(b)   has at any time on or after 1 April 1999 been resident in the UK for UK tax purposes;

"UK tax" means all taxes, duties and contributions under the care and management of or otherwise payable to HMRC;
  "UK tax year" means the period commencing on 6 April in any year and ending on 5 April of the following year.

2.   A relevant person has a beneficial interest in relevant property where–

(a)   the person is a natural person who, on or at any time after 6 April 1999, has–

(i)   held or controlled a share or voting rights in, or

(ii)   received any of the profits of,

a legal person (other than those that are listed or which are collective investment vehicles) or a body of persons without legal personality.

(b)   in the case of trusts or other fiduciary entities, the person is–

(i)   the person or one of the persons who established or funded it;

(ii)   the person or one of the persons regarded as its principal beneficiary or principal beneficiaries;

(iii)   a person entitled to any of its income or capital;

(iv)   a person who has received a distribution or distributions, in a given UK tax year from the entity since 6 April 1999; or

(v)   a person who has been provided with the benefit, in a given UK tax year, of an asset or any number of assets from such entity since 6 April 1999;

(c)   in the case of an account with a bank or other financial institution that is relevant property–

(i)   the person in whose name the account is held if the person is a UK Company or a natural person who is the beneficial owner of the account;

(ii)   where the account is held in the name of a natural person who is not the beneficial owner or in the name of a legal person other than a UK company, the person identified as the "beneficial owner" in forms provided to the financial intermediary by that person pursuant to legislation for the prevention of money-laundering;

(d)   in the case of a cash value insurance contract or an annuity contract–

(i)   the person entitled to access the cash value or change the beneficiary of the contract;

      (ii)   if no person can access the cash value or change the beneficiary, the person named as the owner in the contract or has a vested entitlement to payment under the terms of the contract;

      (iii)   the person entitled to receive a payment under a cash value annuity contract or annuity contract upon its maturity.

3.   In determining whether an insurance contract has a cash value, no account must be taken of–

    (a)   an amount payable in respect of a personal injury or sickness benefit or other benefit providing indemnification of an economic loss incurred upon the occurrence of the event insured against; or

    (b)   a refund to the policyholder of a previously paid premium under an insurance contract (other than under a life insurance contract) due to policy cancellation, decrease in risk exposure during the effective period of the insurance contract, or arising from a redetermination of the premium due to correction of posting or similar error.

4.   Except where the context otherwise requires–

    (a)   the singular includes the plural and vice versa;

    (b)   in Schedule 2, a reference to a person is a reference to a person eligible to participate in the disclosure facility.

SCHEDULE 2

The Disclosure Facility

Conditions for participation in the Disclosure Facility

1.   A person may participate in this disclosure facility if the person–

    (a)   is eligible to participate in the disclosure facility;

    (b)   applies to participate in the disclosure facility after 5 April 2013 and before 30 September 2016 in the manner required by HMRC;

    (c)   provides the level of disclosure required by HMRC for the purposes of the disclosure facility; and

    (d)   makes the financial commitment.

Persons eligible to participate in the disclosure facility

2.   A person is eligible to participate in the disclosure facility if the person is a relevant person who is not the subject of an investigation by HMRC on 6 April 2013 that has not been concluded by that day.

Level of disclosure required by HMRC

3.   A person provides the level of disclosure required by HMRC only if the person–

    (a)   makes full and unprompted disclosure in respect of all relevant property in which the person has had a beneficial interest after 5 April 1999;

(b)   provides such information as HMRC reasonably deems necessary to ensure the person pays all UK tax (together with interest and penalties) required from that person taking account of the disclosure facility; and

(c)   without prejudice to the generality of the foregoing, provides, at the time when application to participate in the disclosure facility is made–

     (i)   the person's name, address (or registered office), date of birth (or date of incorporation);

     (ii)   the person's national insurance number or any other unique tax reference appropriate to the person;

     (iv)   in relation to a natural person, full details of all previously undisclosed UK tax liabilities in respect of every UK tax year commencing on or after 6 April 1999 and ending before the beginning of the UK tax year in which the disclosure is made;

     (v)   in relation to a legal person, full details of all previously undisclosed UK tax liabilities in respect of every accounting period commencing on or after 1 April 1999 and ending before the beginning of a period of 12 months starting on 1 April in which the application for the disclosure facility is made;

     (vi)   a computation of the overall UK tax liability of the person taking account of the disclosure facility;

     (vii)   a declaration that the disclosure made is correct and complete;

full contact details of any person who has provided professional advice in relation to making the application to participate in the disclosure facility.

Financial commitment

4.   A person makes the financial commitment where–

(a)   at the time when the application to participate in the disclosure facility is made, the person–

     (i)   pays the overall UK tax liability computed in compliance with paragraph 3(c)(v); or

     (ii)   provides evidence of inability to make such payment together with a proposal for payment and an appropriate payment on account; and

(b)   pays any further UK tax, interest and penalties notified as payable taking account of the disclosure facility within 30 days of such notification or such other period as HMRC agrees.

Persons who may participate in the facility conferred by paragraphs 6 to 8

5.   The facility conferred by paragraphs 6 to 8 is available only in relation to a person who–

(a)   is eligible to participate in the disclosure facility;

(b)   has not been the subject of an investigation by HMRC that concluded before 6 April 2013 or one that began after that day;

(c)   has not engaged with, participated in or been contacted personally by HMRC in respect of any published disclosure facility before applying to HMRC to participate in the disclosure facility; and

(d)   is not a "relevant person" for the purposes of the Agreement between the Swiss Confederation and the UK on cooperation in the area of taxation who could authorise disclosure of information to HMRC in relation to that person in accordance with that agreement.

Tax and Penalties

6. In relation to a person to whom this paragraph applies (subject to paragraphs 8 and 9)–

    (a) HMRC will not seek to recover from that person UK tax chargeable in respect of a UK tax year or an accounting period ending before the cut off day; and

    (b) HMRC–

         (i)   will not impose a penalty on that person in respect of UK tax described in paragraph (a); and

         (ii) will not impose a penalty on that person exceeding the percentage determined in accordance with paragraph 7 ("specified percentage") in respect of other UK tax disclosed by virtue of the disclosure facility as being chargeable.

Specified percentage

7. The specified percentage is–

    (a) in relation to anything falling for a penalty in accordance with Schedule 24 of the Finance Act 2007 (c. 11) ("Schedule 24"), Schedule 41 of the Finance Act 2008 (c. 9) ("Schedule 41") or Schedule 55 of the Finance Act 2009 (c. 10) ("Schedule 55") (other than anything falling for a penalty described in (b) and (c)), 20% of the UK tax to which the penalty relates;

    (b) in relation to anything the amount of penalty for which is determinable by reference to paragraph 4A(2) of Schedule 24, paragraph 6A(2) of Schedule 41 or paragraph 6A(2) of Schedule 55, 30% of the UK tax to which the penalty relates;

    (c) in relation to anything the amount of penalty for which is determinable by reference to paragraph 4A(3) of Schedule 24, paragraph 6A(3) of Schedule 41 or paragraph 6A(3) of Schedule 55, 40% of the UK tax to which the penalty relates;

    (d) in any other case, 10% of the UK tax to which the penalty relates.

Errors on tax returns

8. Where–

    (a) an error has been made in a tax return made to HMRC by virtue of the Taxes Management Act 1970 (c. 9) in respect of–

         (i)   an accounting period ending more than four years before the beginning of a period of 12 months starting on 1 April in which the application for the disclosure facility is made, or

         (ii) a UK tax year ending more than four years before the beginning of the UK tax year in which the application for the disclosure facility is made,

    (b) the error led to a failure of a person to report to HMRC an interest in relevant property on which the person would have been subject to UK tax,

461

(c)   the error was made by that person and no one else, and

(d)   HMRC (after due consideration of any representations made by or on behalf of that person), considers the error was one that a reasonable person would have made,

any further UK tax that would have been disclosed as chargeable if the error had not occurred will be treated for the purposes of paragraph 6 as chargeable in respect of a UK tax year or an accounting period ending before the cut off day.

Property excluded from the facility in paragraph 6

9.   The facility in paragraph 6 does not apply in respect of UK tax or penalties relating to–

(a)   an account with a bank or other financial institution held outside the UK or Jersey which was opened through a UK branch or agency of a bank;

(b)   property constituting "criminal property" within the meaning in section 340 of the Proceeds of Crime Act 2002 (c. 29) by virtue of being a benefit from criminal conduct (other than conduct comprising only illegal tax evasion (not limited to UK tax)).

The Bespoke Service

10.   The bespoke service will be a personalised service available to a person and will have the following features–

(a)   the possibility of initial anonymous contact by a professional adviser (including a financial intermediary) to discuss with HMRC the circumstances of a person on a "no names" basis;

(b)   the possibility for a person or professional adviser acting on behalf of that person having a single point of contact within a discrete HMRC team to ensure consistency of treatment;

(c)   due consideration by HMRC of–

(i)   residence and domicile claims made by a person, subject to the provision of full supporting evidence;

(ii)   estimated offers to settle UK tax liability, subject to receipt of evidence justifying such estimate;

(iii)   offers to pay by instalments over a reasonable period of time (together with such interest as required by law on unpaid amounts), subject to the provision of evidence confirming hardship or the need for the sale of any property in order to make payment of UK tax, interest or penalties;

(d)   provided full and accurate disclosure is made by a person and where it is practical to do so, HMRC will fulfil its obligations in order to facilitate the determination of a person's liability to pay outstanding UK tax, interest and penalties within nine months of the making of the application to participate in the disclosure facility or such other period of time as HMRC agrees with the person;

(e)   where a penalty imposed on a person in relation to a liability to UK tax disclosed in consequence of the person's participation in the bespoke service is determined taking into account the maximum reduction for disclosure from that penalty possible, HMRC will not, in relation to that penalty, publish information about that person in accordance with section 94 of the Finance Act 2009 (c. 10);

    (f)   in respect of an accounting period ending before 1 April 2016 or UK tax year ending before 6 April 2016, assistance by HMRC to a person regarding compliance with UK tax law requirements without prejudice to HMRC's powers in relation to that person.

11.   For the purposes of making a disclosure of tax, following an inaccuracy made in relation to a person's UK tax affairs, a person may request that the bespoke service applies in respect of all and any assets and income in respect of which UK tax may apply in respect of the period commencing on 6 April 2013 and ending on 5 April 2016.

Appendix 3.8 Isle of Man Disclosure Facility – making a disclosure

The HM Revenue & Customs (HMRC) Isle of Man Disclosure Facility provides an opportunity for eligible customers with assets or investments held in the Isle of Man to bring their UK tax affairs up to date. You can use the facility to make a full disclosure of outstanding liabilities and pay any amount due.

The disclosure facility runs from 6 April 2013 until 30 September 2016.

If you are eligible you will be entitled to limit your disclosure to tax periods ending on or after 1 April 1999 and to pay penalties within prescribed limits.

The Isle of Man government will require all financial intermediaries in the Isle of Man to contact clients who may be eligible to use the disclosure facility. However it is your responsibility to make sure you submit your application to participate within the time limits above and you should not wait for your financial intermediary to contact you before you do this.

HMRC will provide a decision on your disclosure as soon as possible. Most disclosures will be finalised within nine months of your application.

This facility is governed by a Memorandum of Understanding (MOU) and associated schedules. Frequently Asked Questions are also available. Links to these can be found at the bottom of this page.

On this page:
- What you should do next
- Confirm that you are eligible
- Apply to make a disclosure
- Making your disclosure payment
- How to make your disclosure
- More useful links

What you should do next

To make a disclosure you need to:
- Confirm that you are eligible. You need to ensure that your circumstances meet the conditions for using this facility.
- Apply to HMRC to make a disclosure. You will receive a unique reference number and confirmation to tell you which disclosure pack you should use.
- Make a payment within 30 days of your application date that accurately reflects the total tax liability of your disclosure.
- Complete and return your disclosure pack to HMRC as soon as possible.

Confirm that you are eligible

You are not eligible to participate if you:

- are under criminal investigation on 6 April 2013

- are under non-criminal in depth investigation on 6 April 2013

- come under criminal investigation following your application to participate in the Isle of Man Disclosure Facility, but before HMRC has determined your liability to pay outstanding UK tax, interest and penalties.

There are also certain circumstances which might mean that you are not eligible for the full terms of the facility. These include circumstances where you:

- have previously been the subject of criminal or in depth investigation

- are already linked to any alternative HMRC disclosure facility

- were, on 19 February 2013, a 'relevant person' for the purposes of the Swiss/ UK Tax Cooperation Agreement

You can get further guidance from the Offshore Disclosure Facility Helpdesk.

Apply to make a disclosure

If you are eligible to participate you can apply and provide an outline of your disclosure to HMRC online by using the link below. You will then be issued a unique reference number and told which disclosure pack you should use. This reference number should be included when you make your disclosure and on any payments or correspondence you send to HMRC.

You can obtain a paper copy of the application form by ringing the Offshore Disclosure Facility Helpdesk.

Making your disclosure payment

You need to make a payment that accurately reflects the total tax liability of the disclosure. This must be made within 30 days of your disclosure application date. HMRC may withdraw the terms of the disclosure facility and associated benefits if this payment is significantly lower than your actual liability.

How to make your disclosure

You need to make your disclosure within six months of the application being made. If you think it will take longer then please ring the Offshore Disclosure Facility Helpdesk as soon as you have received your application reference number.

After your application HMRC will tell you which disclosure pack to complete.

You can get a paper copy of the disclosure packs by ringing the Offshore Disclosure Facility Helpdesk.

Appendix 3.9　Guernsey Disclosure Facility – making a disclosure

The HM Revenue & Customs (HMRC) Guernsey Disclosure Facility provides an opportunity for eligible customers with assets or investments held in Guernsey to bring their UK tax affairs up to date. You can use the facility to make a full disclosure of outstanding liabilities and pay any amount due.

The disclosure facility runs from 6 April 2013 until 30 September 2016.

If you are eligible you will be entitled to limit your disclosure to tax periods ending on or after 1 April 1999 and to pay penalties within prescribed limits.

The Guernsey government will require all financial intermediaries in Guernsey to contact clients who may be eligible to use the disclosure facility. However it is your responsibility to make sure you submit your application to participate within the time limits above and you should not wait for your financial intermediary to contact you before you do this.

HMRC will provide a decision on your disclosure as soon as possible. Most disclosures will be finalised within nine months of your application.

This facility is governed by a Memorandum of Understanding (MOU) and associated schedules. Frequently Asked Questions are also available. Links to these can be found at the bottom of this page.

On this page:

- What you should do next
- Confirm that you are eligible
- Apply to make a disclosure
- Making your disclosure payment
- How to make your disclosure
- More useful links

What you should do next

To make a disclosure you need to:

- Confirm that you are eligible. You need to ensure that your circumstances meet the conditions for using this facility.

- Apply to HMRC to make a disclosure. You will receive a unique reference number and confirmation to tell you which disclosure pack you should use.

- Make a payment within 30 days of your application date that accurately reflects the total tax liability of your disclosure.

- Complete and return your disclosure pack to HMRC as soon as possible.

Confirm that you are eligible

You are not eligible to participate if you:

- are under criminal investigation on 6 April 2013

- are under non-criminal in depth investigation on 6 April 2013

- come under criminal investigation following your application to participate in the Isle of Man Disclosure Facility, but before HMRC has determined your liability to pay outstanding UK tax, interest and penalties.

There are also certain circumstances which might mean that you are not eligible for the full terms of the facility. These include circumstances where you:

- have previously been the subject of criminal or in depth investigation

- are already linked to any alternative HMRC disclosure facility

- were, on 19 February 2013, a 'relevant person' for the purposes of the Swiss/UK Tax Cooperation Agreement

You can get further guidance from the Offshore Disclosure Facility Helpdesk.

Apply to make a disclosure

If you are eligible to participate you can apply and provide an outline of your disclosure to HMRC online by using the link below. You will then be issued a unique reference number and told which disclosure pack you should use. This reference number should be included when you make your disclosure and on any payments or correspondence you send to HMRC.

You can obtain a paper copy of the application form by ringing the Offshore Disclosure Facility Helpdesk.

Making your disclosure payment

You need to make a payment that accurately reflects the total tax liability of the disclosure. This must be made within 30 days of your disclosure application date. HMRC may withdraw the terms of the disclosure facility and associated benefits if this payment is significantly lower than your actual liability.

How to make your disclosure

You need to make your disclosure within six months of the application being made. If you think it will take longer then please ring the Offshore Disclosure Facility Helpdesk as soon as you have received your application reference number.

After your application HMRC will tell you which disclosure pack to complete.

You can get a paper copy of the disclosure packs by ringing the Offshore Disclosure Facility Helpdesk.

Appendix 3.10 Jersey Disclosure Facility – making a disclosure

The HM Revenue & Customs (HMRC) Jersey Disclosure Facility provides an opportunity for eligible customers with assets or investments held in Jersey to bring their UK tax affairs up to date. You can use the facility to make a full disclosure of outstanding liabilities and pay any amount due.

The disclosure facility runs from 6 April 2013 until 30 September 2016.

If you are eligible you will be entitled to limit your disclosure to tax periods ending on or after 1 April 1999 and to pay penalties within prescribed limits.

The Guernsey government will require all financial intermediaries in Guernsey to contact clients who may be eligible to use the disclosure facility. However it is your responsibility to make sure you submit your application to participate within the time limits above and you should not wait for your financial intermediary to contact you before you do this.

HMRC will provide a decision on your disclosure as soon as possible. Most disclosures will be finalised within nine months of your application.

This facility is governed by a Memorandum of Understanding (MOU) and associated schedules. Frequently Asked Questions are also available. Links to these can be found at the bottom of this page.

On this page:
- What you should do next
- Confirm that you are eligible
- Apply to make a disclosure
- Making your disclosure payment
- How to make your disclosure
- More useful links

What you should do next

To make a disclosure you need to:
- Confirm that you are eligible. You need to ensure that your circumstances meet the conditions for using this facility.

- Apply to HMRC to make a disclosure. You will receive a unique reference number and confirmation to tell you which disclosure pack you should use.

- Make a payment within 30 days of your application date that accurately reflects the total tax liability of your disclosure.

- Complete and return your disclosure pack to HMRC as soon as possible.

Confirm that you are eligible

You are not eligible to participate if you:

- are under criminal investigation on 6 April 2013
- are under non-criminal in depth investigation on 6 April 2013
- come under criminal investigation following your application to participate in the Isle of Man Disclosure Facility, but before HMRC has determined your liability to pay outstanding UK tax, interest and penalties.

There are also certain circumstances which might mean that you are not eligible for the full terms of the facility. These include circumstances where you:

- have previously been the subject of criminal or in depth investigation
- are already linked to any alternative HMRC disclosure facility
- were, on 19 February 2013, a 'relevant person' for the purposes of the Swiss/UK Tax Cooperation Agreement

You can get further guidance from the Offshore Disclosure Facility Helpdesk.

Apply to make a disclosure

If you are eligible to participate you can apply and provide an outline of your disclosure to HMRC online by using the link below. You will then be issued a unique reference number and told which disclosure pack you should use. This reference number should be included when you make your disclosure and on any payments or correspondence you send to HMRC.

You can obtain a paper copy of the application form by ringing the Offshore Disclosure Facility Helpdesk.

Making your disclosure payment

You need to make a payment that accurately reflects the total tax liability of the disclosure. This must be made within 30 days of your disclosure application date. HMRC may withdraw the terms of the disclosure facility and associated benefits if this payment is significantly lower than your actual liability.

How to make your disclosure

You need to make your disclosure within six months of the application being made. If you think it will take longer then please ring the Offshore Disclosure Facility Helpdesk as soon as you have received your application reference number.

After your application HMRC will tell you which disclosure pack to complete.

You can get a paper copy of the disclosure packs by ringing the Offshore Disclosure Facility Helpdesk.

Appendix 3.11 Liechtenstein Disclosure Facility (LDF)

Details of the terms of the Liechtenstein Disclosure Facility (LDF) are now available.

The LDF is a bespoke service to support the reviews to be carried out by the Financial Intermediaries in Liechtenstein to identify those who may have liability to UK tax. The LDF allows people with unpaid tax linked to investments or assets in Liechtenstein to settle their tax liability under this special arrangement.

The LDF will run from 1 September 2009 until 5 April 2016. To help you prepare in the run up to the registration date basic information will be posted on the HM Revenue & Customs (HMRC) website for anyone who thinks they may qualify to register, or if you are a tax agent or adviser with clients that may qualify to register.

You can read the Memorandum of Understanding and Joint Declaration by following the links below.

In this section

- Liechtenstein Disclosure Facility
- Liechtenstein Disclosure Pack
- Frequently asked questions
- Help & advice
- Joint Declaration
- Memorandum of Understanding
- Related information
- Tax Information Exchange Arrangement
- Samples of Confirmation of Relevance

Appendix 3.12   Berwin Leighton Paisner Disclosure Facility Comparison: Isle of Man, Jersey, Guernsey and Liechtenstein[1]

September 2014

You should consider using a disclosure facility if you are UK resident and have undisclosed UK tax liabilities. The facilities provide a straightforward way to settle all undisclosed UK tax liabilities. There are four available disclosure facilities: the Isle of Man Disclosure Facility (**IoMDF**), the Jersey Disclosure Facility (**JDF**), the Guernsey Disclosure Facility (**GDF**) (together the **IJGDF**) and the Liechtenstein Disclosure Facility (**LDF**).

This note explains whether you are able to take advantage of the key benefits of one of these facilities, and where you have a choice over which one to use, what factors may influence that choice.

---

1 '© Berwin Leighton Paisner. This flowchart and accompanying information was compiled by Anthony Bunker, Damian Bloom and Anya Martin of Berwin Leighton Paisner LLP. It is reproduced with the kind permission of Berwin Leighton Paisner LLP. For more information please visit www.blplaw.com.'

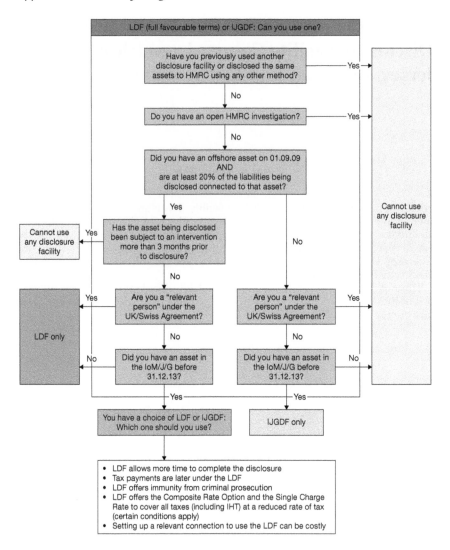

Key benefits of disclosure

Using a disclosure facility can provide significant advantages over an HMRC investigation process including:

- Lower fixed penalties: 10%-40% (instead of up to 200%)

- Immunity from investigation (IJGDF) or from criminal investigation/ prosecution (LDF) in relation to the disclosed assets

- Under the LDF, there is an option to cover all taxes including IHT for a fixed rate of 40%-50% tax on all income and gains being declared (restrictions apply)

- Reduced period of recovery assessments going back only to 1999 (instead of 20 years)

- Opportunity for an anonymous agreement on points such as domicile before registration

- Dedicated HMRC inspector, which significantly improves efficiency

- Anonymity from the "name and shame" list

Influencing factors between LDF and IJGDF

- The IJGDF and the LDF offer protection from HMRC investigation during the disclosure period, but the LDF also offers immunity from criminal prosecution unless the disclosed assets are the proceeds of crime (other than tax evasion). HMRC have implied that the IJGDF participants will not be criminally prosecuted but there is no certainty on this point.

- The LDF offers generous terms whereby IHT, VAT, SDLT, SDRT and SD are covered by a 40% composite rate (50% single charge rate (SCR) in later years) on income and gains. The SCR requires a relevant Liechtenstein connection on 30 Sept 2009.

Key definitions

Asset in IoM/J/G: for the IJGDF you will need to have had an asset in the relevant jurisdiction before 31.12.13. If you had assets in more than one of these jurisdictions you can chose between the facilities.

HMRC investigation: for the LDF this is an in-depth investigation for suspected serious fraud (or arrest for a criminal tax offence); for the IJGDF this is a criminal or non-criminal in depth investigation (open on 6 April 2013) or a criminal investigation following the application to participate in the IJGDF but before the liabilities have been determined by HMRC

IJGDF: Isle of Man/Jersey/Guernsey Disclosure Facility

Intervention: issues that are the subject of litigation, civil enquiries into tax liabilities supported by statutory information or investigation powers (i.e. tax return checks) or enquiries into multiple identified taxpayers stemming from third party information

LDF: Liechtenstein Disclosure Facility

LDF – full favourable terms: a 10% fixed penalty until 2009, limited assessment period to tax years from 1 April 1999, composite rate option/single charge rate

LDF – limited favourable terms: assurance about criminal prosecution and a single point of contact for disclosures

Offshore asset: any asset held outside the UK. This may include assets held in a trust or company, in any jurisdiction.

Relevant connection: a substantive link to Liechtenstein, which is required to access the LDF

Relevant person under the UK/Swiss Agreement: you are a relevant person if you have an asset in Switzerland, which again may include assets held in a trust or company

This guide is a summary of the disclosure facilities. It does not cover all circumstances and it is not a substitute for specific legal advice.

Appendix 4

OECD Exchange of Information, Early Adopters and Other Committed Parties (relates to Chapter 9)

Contents

Appendix 4.1   Extract from the OECD global forum on transparency and exchange of information for tax purposes – Tax Transparency 2013 Report on Progress[1]

TABLE 1: OVERALL RATINGS FOR JURISDICTIONS FOR WHOM PHASE 2 REVIEWS HAVE BEEN COMPLETED

Jurisdictions	Overall Ratings
Argentina	Largely Compliant
Australia	Compliant
Austria	Partially Compliant
The Bahamas	Largely Compliant
Bahrain	Largely Compliant
Belgium	Compliant
Bermuda	Largely Compliant
Brazil	Largely Compliant
Canada	Compliant
Cayman Islands	Largely Compliant
China	Compliant
Cyprus	Non-Compliant
Denmark	Compliant
Estonia	Largely Compliant
Finland	Compliant
France	Compliant
Germany	Largely Compliant
Greece	Largely Compliant
Guernsey	Largely Compliant
Hong Kong, China	Largely Compliant
Iceland	Compliant
India	Compliant
Ireland	Compliant
Isle of Man	Compliant
Italy	Largely Compliant
Jamaica	Largely Compliant
Japan	Compliant

1 © OECD. For further information please see http://www.oecd.org/tax/transparency/GFannualreport2013.pdf

Jurisdictions	Overall Ratings
Jersey	Largely Compliant
Korea	Compliant
Luxembourg	Non-Compliant
Macao, China	Largely Compliant
Malta	Largely Compliant
Mauritius	Largely Compliant
Monaco	Largely Compliant
Netherlands	Largely Compliant
New Zealand	Compliant
Norway	Compliant
Philippines	Largely Compliant
Qatar	Largely Compliant
San Marino	Largely Compliant
Seychelles	Non-Compliant
Singapore	Largely Compliant
South Africa	Compliant
Spain	Compliant
Sweden	Compliant
Turkey	Partially Compliant
Turks and Caicos Islands	Largely Compliant
United Kingdom	Largely Compliant
United States	Largely Compliant
Virgin Islands (British)	Non-Compliant

TABLE 2: JURISDICTIONS THAT CANNOT MOVE TO PHASE 2 REVIEW UNTIL THEY ACT ON THE RECOMMENDATIONS TO IMPROVE THEIR LEGAL AND REGULATORY FRAMEWORK

Botswana	Nauru
Brunei	Niue
Dominica	Panama
Guatemala	Switzerland*
Lebanon	Trinidad and Tobago
Liberia	United Arab Emirates
Marshall Islands	Vanuatu

* The Phase 2 of Switzerland is subject to conditions.

Appendix 4.2 Standard for Automatic Exchange of Financial Account Information – Common Reporting Standard[1]

PREFACE

This document was approved and de-classified by the Committee on Fiscal Affairs ("CFA") on 17 January and contains the global standard for automatic exchange of financial account information. It has been developed by the OECD, working with G20 countries, and in close co-operation with the EU. Part I contains the introduction[1] to the standard and Part II contains the text of the Model Competent Authority Agreement (CAA) and the Common Reporting and Due Diligence Standard (CRS).

1 Because of the OECD process on approval and de-restriction, the introduction may not fully reflect the latest developments. In particular it does not include all countries that recently committed to early adoption of the standard.

Under the standard, jurisdictions obtain financial information from their financial institutions and automatically exchange that information with other jurisdictions on an annual basis. The standard consists of two components: a) the CRS, which contains the reporting and due diligence rules and b) the Model CAA, which contains the detailed rules on the exchange of information. To prevent circumventing the CRS it is designed with a broad scope across three dimensions:

- The financial information to be reported with respect to reportable accounts includes all types of **investment income** (including interest, dividends, income from certain insurance contracts and other similar types of income) but also **account balances** and **sales proceeds** from financial assets.

- The financial institutions that are required to report under the CRS do not only include **banks** and **custodians** but also other financial institutions such as **brokers, certain collective investment vehicles and certain insurance companies**.

- Reportable accounts include accounts held by **individuals** and **entities (which includes trusts and foundations),** and the standard includes a requirement to look through passive entities to report on the individuals that ultimately control these entities.

The CRS also describes **the due diligence procedures that must be followed by financial institutions to identify reportable accounts.**

The CRS will need to be translated into domestic law, whereas the CAA can be executed within existing legal frameworks such as Article 6 of the Multilateral Convention on Mutual Administrative Assistance in Tax Matters or the equivalent of Article 26 in a bilateral tax treaty. Before entering into a reciprocal agreement

1 © OECD. For further information please see http://www.oecd.org/ctp/exchange-of-tax-information/automatic-exchange-financial-account-information-common-reporting-standard.pdf

478

to exchange information automatically with another country, it is essential that the receiving country has the legal framework and administrative capacity and processes in place to ensure the confidentiality of the information received and that such information is only used for the purposes specified in the instrument.

Consistent with previous OECD work in the area of automatic exchange, the common standard is intended to be used by those jurisdictions wishing to automatically exchange financial account information. Its aim is to avoid a proliferation of different standards which would increase costs for both governments and financial institutions.

This document does not yet contain: (1) a detailed commentary to help ensure the consistent application of the standard; or (2) information and guidance on the necessary technical solutions, including compatible transmission systems and a standard format for reporting and exchange. Work on these more technical modalities is ongoing. It is expected that both the commentary and the technical solutions will be completed by mid-2014. Subsequent changes to the standard or its commentary may of course become necessary as jurisdictions gain more experience with its implementation.

TABLE OF CONTENTS

STANDARD FOR AUTOMATIC EXCHANGE OF FINANCIAL ACCOUNT INFORMATION

Part I. Introduction and Overview

I. Background and Context

1.   As the world becomes increasingly globalised it is becoming easier for all taxpayers to make, hold and manage investments through financial institutions outside of their country of residence. Vast amounts of money are kept offshore and go untaxed to the extent that taxpayers fail to comply with tax obligations in their home jurisdiction. Offshore tax evasion is a serious problem for jurisdictions all over the world, OECD and non-OECD, small and large, developing and developed. Countries have a shared interest in maintaining the integrity of their tax systems. Cooperation between tax administrations is critical in the fight against tax evasion and in protecting the integrity of tax systems. A key aspect of that cooperation is exchange of information.

2.   The OECD has a long history of working on all forms of exchange of information – on request, spontaneous, and automatic – and the Multilateral Convention on Mutual Administrative Assistance in Tax Matters and Article 26 of the OECD Model Tax Convention provide a basis for all forms of information exchange. Over the past few years much progress has been made by the OECD, EU and the Global Forum on Transparency and Exchange of Information for Tax Purposes in improving transparency and exchange of information on request.

3.   More recently, political interest has also focused on the opportunities provided by automatic exchange of information. On 19 April 2013 the G20 Finance Ministers and Central Bank Governors endorsed automatic exchange as the expected new standard. The G20 decision followed earlier announcements by a number of European countries of their intention to develop and pilot multilateral tax information exchange based on the Model Intergovernmental Agreement to Improve International Tax Compliance and to Implement FATCA, developed between these countries and the United States (the "Model 1 IGA"). On 9 April 2013, the Ministers of Finance of France, Germany, Italy, Spain and the UK announced their intention to exchange FATCA-type information amongst themselves in addition to exchanging information with the United States. On 13 April, Belgium, the Czech Republic, the Netherlands, Poland, and Romania also expressed interest in this approach, which by May 14 had already been endorsed by 17 countries, with Mexico and Norway joining the initiative in early June and Australia in July. Further the United Kingdom agreed to automatically exchange information, on the basis of the intergovernmental approaches developed with the United States, with its Crown Dependencies and many of its Overseas Territories which also joined the pilot project.

4.   On 22 May 2013 the EU Council unanimously agreed to give priority to efforts to extend automatic exchange at the EU and global level and welcomed the on-going efforts made in the G8, G20 and OECD to develop a global standard. Shortly thereafter the OECD Ministerial called on "...all jurisdictions to move towards automatic exchange of information and to improve the availability, the quality and the accuracy of information on beneficial ownership, in order to effectively act against tax fraud and evasion." On 12 June the European Commission adopted a legislative proposal to extend the scope of automatic exchange of information in its directive on administrative co-operation to new items, including dividends, capital gains and account balances.

5.   Automatic exchange of information was also a key item on the G8 agenda. On 19 June the G8 leaders welcomed the OECD Secretary General report "A step change in tax transparency" which set out the concrete steps that need to be undertaken to put a global model of automatic exchange into practice.[2] G8 leaders agreed to work together with the OECD and in the G20 to implement its recommendations urgently.

2 http://www.oecd.org/ctp/exchange-of-tax-information/taxtransparency_G8report.pdf

6.   On 20 July the G20 Finance Ministers and Central Bank Governors endorsed the OECD proposals for a global model of automatic exchange in the multilateral context.[3] On 6 September the G20 leaders reinforced this message, and said: "Calling on all other jurisdictions to join us by the earliest possible date, we are committed to automatic exchange of information as the new global standard, which must ensure confidentiality and the proper use of information exchanged, and we fully support the OECD work with G20 countries aimed at presenting such a single global standard for automatic exchange by February 2014 and to finalizing technical modalities of effective automatic exchange by mid-2014."[4] They also asked the Global Forum to establish a mechanism to monitor and review the implementation of the new global standard on automatic exchange

of information and stressed the importance of developing countries being able to benefit from a more transparent international tax system.

3 "We commend the progress recently achieved in the area of tax transparency and we fully endorse the OECD proposal for a truly global model for multilateral and bilateral automatic exchange of information. We are committed to automatic exchange of information as the new, global standard and we fully support the OECD work with G20 countries aimed at setting such a new single global standard for automatic exchange of information. We ask the OECD to prepare a progress report by our next meeting, including a timeline for completing this work in 2014. We call on all jurisdictions to commit to implement this standard. We are committed to making automatic exchange of information attainable by all countries, including low-income countries, and will seek to provide capacity building support for them. We call on all countries to join the Multilateral Convention on Mutual Administrative Assistance in Tax Matters without further delay. We look forward to the practical and full implementation of the new standard on a global scale".

4 "We commend the progress recently achieved in the area of tax transparency and we fully endorse the OECD proposal for a truly global model for multilateral and bilateral automatic exchange of information. Calling on all other jurisdictions to join us by the earliest possible date, we are committed to automatic exchange of information as the new global standard, which must ensure confidentiality and the proper use of information exchanged, and we fully support the OECD work with G20 countries aimed at presenting such a new single global standard for automatic exchange of information by February 2014 and to finalizing technical modalities of effective automatic exchange by mid-2014. In parallel, we expect to begin to exchange information automatically on tax matters among G20 members by the end of 2015. We call on all countries to join the Multilateral Convention on Mutual Administrative Assistance in Tax Matters without further delay. We look forward to the practical and full implementation of the new standard on a global scale."

7.   The global model of automatic exchange is drafted with respect to financial account information. Many jurisdictions – OECD and non-OECD – already exchange information automatically with their exchange partners and also regionally (e.g. within the EU) on various categories of income and also transmit other types of information such as changes of residence, the purchase or disposition of immovable property, value added tax refunds, tax withheld at source, etc. The new global standard does not, nor is it intended to, restrict the other types or categories of automatic exchange of information. It sets out a minimum standard for the information to be exchanged. Jurisdictions may choose to exchange information beyond the minimum standard set out in this document.

8.   The Common Reporting Standard ("CRS"), with a view to maximizing efficiency and reducing cost for financial institutions, draws extensively on the intergovernmental approach to implementing FATCA. While the intergovernmental approach to FATCA reporting does deviate in certain aspects from the CRS, the differences are driven by the multilateral nature of the CRS system and other US specific aspects, in particular the concept of taxation on the basis of citizenship and the presence of a significant and comprehensive FATCA withholding tax. Given these features, that the intergovernmental approach to FATCA is a pre-existing system with close similarities to the CRS, and the anticipated progress towards widespread participation in the CRS, it is compatible and consistent with the CRS for the US to not require the look through treatment for investment entities in Non-Participating Jurisdictions.

II. Key features of a global model of automatic exchange of financial account information

9.   For a model of automatic exchange of financial account information to be effective it must be specifically designed with residence jurisdictions' tax compliance in mind rather than be a by-product of domestic reporting. Further,

it needs to be standardised so as to benefit the maximum number of residence jurisdictions and financial institutions while recognising that certain issues remain to be decided by local implementation. The advantage of standardisation is process simplification, higher effectiveness and lower costs for all stakeholders concerned. A proliferation of different and inconsistent models would potentially impose significant costs on both government and business to collect the necessary information and operate the different models. It could lead to a fragmentation of standards, which may introduce conflicting requirements, further increasing the costs of compliance and reducing effectiveness. Finally, because tax evasion is a global issue, the model needs to have a global reach so that it addresses the issue of offshore tax evasion and does not merely relocate the problem rather than solving it. Mechanisms to encourage compliance may be also required to achieve this aim.

10.   In 2012 the OECD delivered to the G20 the report "Automatic Exchange of Information: What it is, How it works, Benefits, What remains to be done",[5] which summarizes the key features of an effective model for automatic exchange. The main success factors for effective automatic exchange of financial information are: (1) a common standard on information reporting, due diligence and exchange of information, (2) a legal and operational basis for the exchange of information; and (3) common or compatible technical solutions.

5 http://www.oecd.org/ctp/exchange-of-tax-information/
   automaticexchangeofinformationreport.htm

1. Common standard on reporting, due diligence and exchange of information

11.   An effective model for automatic exchange of information requires a common standard on the information to be reported by financial institutions and exchanged with residence jurisdictions. This will ensure that the reporting by financial institutions is aligned with the interests of the residence country. It will also increase the quality and predictability of the information that is being exchanged. The result will be significant opportunities for the residence country to enhance compliance and make optimal use of the information (e.g. through automatic matching with domestic compliance information and data analysis).

12.   In order to limit the opportunities for taxpayers to circumvent the model by shifting assets to institutions or investing in products that are not covered by the model a reporting regime requires a broad scope across three dimensions:

- **The scope of financial information reported**: A comprehensive reporting regime covers different types of investment income including interest, dividends and similar types of income, and also address situations where a taxpayer seeks to hide capital that itself represents income or assets on which tax has been evaded (e.g. by requiring information on account balances).

- **The scope of accountholders subject to reporting**: A comprehensive reporting regime requires reporting not only with respect to individuals, but should also limit the opportunities for taxpayers to circumvent reporting by using interposed legal entities or arrangements. This means requiring financial institutions to look through shell companies, trusts or similar arrangements, including taxable entities to cover situations where a taxpayer seeks to hide the principal but is willing to pay tax on the income.

- **The scope of financial institutions required to report**: A comprehensive reporting regime covers not only banks but also other financial institutions such as brokers, certain collective investment vehicles and certain insurance companies.

13.   In addition to a common standard on the scope of the information to be collected and exchanged, an effective model of automatic exchange of financial

information also requires a common standard on a robust set of due diligence procedures to be followed by financial institutions to identify reportable accounts and obtain the accountholder identifying information that is required to be reported for such accounts. The due diligence procedures are critical as they help to ensure the quality of the information that is reported and exchanged. Finally feedback by the receiving jurisdiction to the sending jurisdiction regarding any errors in the information received can also be an important aspect of an effective automatic exchange model. Such feedback may take place in the form of spontaneous exchange of information, another important aspect of cooperation between tax authorities in itself.

2. Legal and operational basis for exchange of information

14.   Different legal basis for automatic exchange of information already exist. Whilst bilateral treaties such as those based on Article 26 of the OECD Model Tax Convention permit such exchanges, it may be more efficient to establish automatic exchange relationships on the basis of a multilateral exchange instrument. The Multilateral Convention on Mutual Administrative Assistance in Tax Matters (the "Convention"),[6] as amended in 2011, is such an instrument. It provides for all forms of administrative co- operation, contains strict rules on confidentiality and proper use of information, and permits automatic exchange of information. One of its main advantages is its global reach.[7] Automatic exchange under the Convention requires a separate agreement between the competent authorities of the parties, which can be entered into by two or more parties thus allowing for a single agreement with either two or more parties (with actual automatic exchange always taking place on a bilateral basis). Such a competent authority agreement then activates and "operationalizes" automatic exchange between the participants. Where jurisdictions rely on other information exchange instruments, such as bilateral treaties, a competent authority agreement can serve the same function.

6 The Multilateral Convention was developed jointly by the Council of Europe and the OECD and opened for signature by the member states of both organisations on 25 January 1988. The Convention was amended to respond to the call of the G20 at its April 2009 London Summit to align it to the international standard on exchange and to open it to all countries, in particular to ensure that developing countries could benefit from the new more transparent environment. It was opened for signature on 1st June 2011.

7 For information on jurisdictions covered by the Convention, signatories and ratifications see http://www.oecd.org/tax/exchange-of-tax-information/Status_of_convention.pdf

15.   All treaties and exchange of information instruments contain strict provisions that require information exchanged to be kept confidential and limit the persons to whom the information can be disclosed and the purposes for which the information may be used. The OECD released a Guide on Confidentiality, "Keeping it Safe"[8] which sets out best practices related to confidentiality and provides practical guidance on how to ensure an adequate level of protection. Before entering into an agreement to exchange information automatically with another jurisdiction, it is essential that the receiving jurisdiction has the legal framework and administrative capacity and processes in place to ensure the confidentiality of the information received and that such information is used only for the purposes specified in the instrument.

8 http://www.oecd.org/ctp/exchange-of-tax-information/keepingitsafe.htm

3. Common or compatible technical solutions

16.   Common or compatible technical solutions for reporting and exchanging information are a critical element in a standardised automatic exchange system – especially one that will be used by a large number of jurisdictions and financial institutions. Standardisation will reduce costs for all parties concerned.

17.   The technical reporting format must be standardised so that information can be captured, exchanged and processed quickly and efficiently in a cost effective

manner and secure and compatible methods of transmission and encryption of data must be in place.

III. Status and overview of work and next steps

18.   Part II of this report contains (1) a model competent authority agreement/ arrangement ("Model CAA") and (2) the common standard on reporting and due diligence for financial account information ("Common Reporting Standard"- "CRS"). Together they constitute the common standard on reporting, due diligence and exchange of information on financial account information. Under this standard jurisdictions obtain from reporting financial institutions and automatically exchange with exchange partners, as appropriate, on an annual basis financial information with respect to all reportable accounts, identified by financial institutions on the basis of common reporting and due diligence procedures. The term "financial information" means interest, dividends, account balance, income from certain insurance products, sales proceeds from financial assets and other income generated with respect to assets held in the account or payments made with respect to the account. The term "reportable account" means accounts held by individuals and entities (which includes trusts and foundations), and the standard includes a requirement to look through passive entities to report on the relevant controlling persons.

19.   Implementation of the standard will require translating the CRS into domestic law. Signing a competent authority agreement based on the model then allows putting in place the information exchange based on existing legal instruments, such as the Convention or bilateral income tax conventions. The exchange of information could also be implemented on the basis of a multilateral competent authority agreement/arrangement, or jurisdictions could enter into a multilateral intergovernmental agreement or multiple intergovernmental agreements that would be international treaties in their own right covering both the reporting obligations and due diligence procedures coupled with a more limited competent authority agreement. The legal basis could also be EU legislation that would cover the elements of the CRS.

20.   This report does not yet contain the more detailed commentary that is being developed to help in the consistent application of the standard. Given that implementation will be based on domestic law, it is important to ensure consistency in application across jurisdictions to avoid creating unnecessary costs and complexity for financial institutions in particular those with operations in more than one jurisdiction.

21.   Finally, this report does not yet contain information on the necessary technical solutions. It is expected that both the commentary and the technical solutions would be completed by mid-2014, noting of course that subsequent changes to the commentary may become necessary as jurisdictions gain more experience with the implementation of the standard.

1. Summary of the competent authority agreement

22.   The Model CAA links the CRS and the legal basis for the exchange (such as the Convention or a bilateral tax treaty) allowing the financial account information to be exchanged. The Model CAA consists of a number of whereas clauses and seven sections and provides for the modalities of the exchange to ensure the appropriate flows of information. The whereas clauses contain representations on domestic reporting and due diligence rules that underpin the exchange of information pursuant to the competent authority agreement. They also contain representations on confidentiality, safeguards and the existence of the necessary infrastructure for an effective exchange relationship. See also section 4 on collaboration on compliance and enforcement.

23.   The Model CAA contains a section dealing with definitions (Section 1), covers the type of information to be exchanged (Section 2), the time and manner of exchange (Section 3) and the confidentiality and data safeguards that must be respected (Section 5). Consultations between the competent authorities, amendments to the agreement and the term of the agreement, including suspension and termination, are dealt with in Sections 6 and 7.

24.   The Model CAA is drafted as a reciprocal agreement based on the principle that automatic exchange is reciprocal. There may also be instances where jurisdictions wish to enter into a non-reciprocal competent authority agreement (*e.g.* where one jurisdiction does not have an income tax). The Model CAA can easily be adapted for such non-reciprocal exchanges and further details on this will be included in the Commentary.

25.   The Model CAA contained in Part II refers to an "Annex" but once the CRS has been approved by the CFA the Model CAA would no longer require an Annex. References to the Annex could be replaced by a reference to the CRS developed by OECD and G20 countries (including a reference to the CRS as adopted on a fixed date) and available on the OECD website, and a corresponding definition would then be added to Section 1 of the Model CAA.

2. Summary of the Common Reporting Standard ("CRS")

26.   The CRS contains the reporting and due diligence standard that underpins the automatic exchange of financial account information. A jurisdiction implementing the CRS must have rules in place that require financial institutions to report information consistent with the scope of reporting set out in Section I and to follow due diligence procedures consistent with the procedures contained in Section II through VII. Capitalized terms used in the CRS are defined in Section VIII.

27.   The financial institutions (FI's) covered by the standard include custodial institutions, depository institutions, investment entities and specified insurance companies, unless they present a low risk of being used for evading tax and are excluded from reporting. The financial information to be reported with respect to reportable accounts includes interest, dividends, account balance, income from certain insurance products, sales proceeds from financial assets and other income generated with respect to assets held in the account or payments made with respect to the account. Reportable accounts include accounts held by individuals and entities (which includes trusts and foundations), and the standard includes a requirement to look through passive entities to report on the relevant controlling persons.

28.   The due diligence procedures to be performed by reporting financial institutions for the identification of reportable accounts are described in sections II through VII. They distinguish between individual accounts and entity accounts. They also make a distinction between pre-existing and new accounts, recognizing that it is more difficult and costly for financial institutions to obtain information from existing accountholders rather than requesting such information upon account opening.

●   For **Pre-existing Individual Accounts** FI's are required to review accounts without application of any de minimis threshold. The rules distinguish between Higher and Lower Value Accounts. For Lower Value Accounts they provide for a permanent residence address test based on documentary evidence or the FI would need to determine the residence on the basis of an indicia search. A self-certification (and/or documentary evidence) would be needed in case of conflicting indicia, in the absence of which reporting would be done to all reportable jurisdictions for which indicia have been

485

found. For Higher Value Accounts enhanced due diligence procedures apply, including a paper record search and an actual knowledge test by the relationship manager.

- For **New Individual Accounts** the CRS contemplates self-certification (and the confirmation of its reasonableness) without de minimis threshold.

- For **Pre-existing Entity Accounts**, FIs are required to determine: a) whether the entity itself is a Reportable Person, which can generally be done on the basis of available information (AML/KYC procedures) and if not, a self-certification would be needed; and b) whether the entity is a passive NFE and, if so, the residency of controlling persons. For a number of account holders the active/passive assessment is rather straight forward and can be made on the basis of available information, for others this may require self-certification. Pre-existing Entity Accounts below 250,000 USD (or local currency equivalent) are not subject to review.

- For **New Entity Accounts**, the same assessments need to be made as for Pre-existing Accounts. However, as it is easier to obtain self-certifications for new accounts, the 250,000 USD (or local currency equivalent) threshold does not apply.

29.   While the CRS contemplates due diligence procedures generally designed to identify reportable accounts, there are good reasons why jurisdictions may wish to go wider and, for instance, extend due diligence procedures for pre-existing accounts to cover all non-residents or cover residents of countries with which they have an exchange of information instrument in place. Such an approach could significantly reduce costs for financial institutions compared to an approach where due diligence has to be performed each time a new jurisdiction joins. Such wider rules or procedures are fully consistent with the narrower reporting and due diligence rules described in the CRS. The Commentary to the CRS will contain a version of the due diligence and reporting requirements that follows such a wider approach.

30.   Section IX of the CRS describes the rules and administrative procedures an implementing jurisdiction is expected to have in place to ensure effective implementation of, and compliance with, the CRS.

Part II: Text of model competent authority agreement and common reporting standard

Model agreement between the competent authorities of [jurisdiction a] and [jurisdiction b] on the automatic exchange of financial account information to improve international tax compliance

Whereas, the Government of [Jurisdiction A] and the Government of [Jurisdiction B] have a longstanding and close relationship with respect to mutual assistance in tax matters and desire to improve international tax compliance by further building on that relationship;

Whereas, the laws of their respective jurisdictions [are expected to require]/ [require]/[require or are expected to require] financial institutions to report information regarding certain accounts and follow related due diligence procedures, consistent with the scope of exchange contemplated by Section 2 of this Agreement and the reporting and due diligence procedures contained in the Annex;

Whereas, [Article [...] of the Income Tax Convention between [Jurisdiction A] and [Jurisdiction B]/[Article 6 of the Convention on Mutual Administrative Assistance in Tax Matters] (the "Convention")]/[other applicable legal instrument (the "Instrument")], authorises the exchange of information for tax purposes, including the exchange of information on an automatic basis, and allows the competent authorities of [Jurisdiction A] and [Jurisdiction B] (the "Competent Authorities") to agree the scope and modalities of such automatic exchanges;

Whereas, [Jurisdiction A] and [Jurisdiction B] have in place (i) appropriate safeguards to ensure that the information received pursuant to this Agreement remains confidential and is used solely for the purposes set out in the [Convention]/[Instrument], and (ii) the infrastructure for an effective exchange relationship (including established processes for ensuring timely, accurate, and confidential information exchanges, effective and reliable communications, and capabilities to promptly resolve questions and concerns about exchanges or requests for exchanges and to administer the provisions of Section 4 of this Agreement);

Whereas, the Competent Authorities desire to conclude an agreement to improve international tax compliance based on reciprocal automatic exchange pursuant to the [Convention]/[Instrument], and subject to the confidentiality and other protections provided for therein, including the provisions limiting the use of the information exchanged under the [Convention]/[Instrument];

Now, therefore, the Competent Authorities have agreed as follows:

SECTION 1

Definitions

1.   For the purposes of this agreement ("Agreement"), the following terms have the following meanings:

a)   The term **"[Jurisdiction A]"** means […].

b)   The term **"[Jurisdiction B]"** means […].

c)   The term **"Competent Authority"** means:

   (1)   in the case of [Jurisdiction A], […]; and

   (2)   in the case of [Jurisdiction B], […].

d)   The term **"[Jurisdiction A] Financial Institution"** means (i) any Financial Institution that is resident in [Jurisdiction A], but excludes any branch of that Financial Institution that is located outside [Jurisdiction A], and (ii) any branch of a Financial Institution that is not resident in [Jurisdiction A], if that branch is located in [Jurisdiction A].

e)   The term **"[Jurisdiction B] Financial Institution"** means (i) any Financial Institution that is resident in [Jurisdiction B], but excludes any branch of that Financial Institution that is located outside [Jurisdiction B], and (ii) any branch of a Financial Institution that is not resident in [Jurisdiction B], if that branch is located in [Jurisdiction B].

f)   The term **"Reporting Financial Institution"** means any [Jurisdiction A] Financial Institution or [Jurisdiction B] Financial Institution, as the context requires, that is not a Non-Reporting Financial Institution.

g)   The term **"Reportable Account"** means a [Jurisdiction A] Reportable Account or a [Jurisdiction B] Reportable Account, as the context requires, provided it has been identified as such pursuant to due diligence procedures, consistent with the Annex, in place in [Jurisdiction A] or [Jurisdiction B].

h)   The term **"[Jurisdiction A] Reportable Account"** means a Financial Account that is maintained by a [Jurisdiction B] Reporting Financial Institution and held by one or more [Jurisdiction A] persons that are Reportable Persons or by a Passive NFE with one or more Controlling Persons that is a [Jurisdiction A] Reportable Person.

i)   The term **"[Jurisdiction B] Reportable Account"** means a Financial Account that is maintained by a [Jurisdiction A] Reporting Financial Institution and held by one or more [Jurisdiction B] persons that are Reportable Persons or by a Passive NFE with one or more Controlling Persons that is a [Jurisdiction B] Reportable Person.

j)   The term **"[Jurisdiction A] Person"** means an individual or Entity that is identified by a [Jurisdiction B] Reporting Financial Institution as resident in [Jurisdiction A] pursuant to due diligence procedures consistent with the Annex, or an estate of a decedent that was a resident of [Jurisdiction A].

k)   The term **"[Jurisdiction B] Person"** means an individual or Entity that is identified by a [Jurisdiction A] Reporting Financial Institution as resident in [Jurisdiction B] pursuant to due diligence procedures consistent with the Annex, or an estate of a decedent that was a resident of [Jurisdiction B].

l)   The term **"TIN"** means a [Jurisdiction A] TIN or a [Jurisdiction B] TIN, as the context requires.

m)   The term **"[Jurisdiction A] TIN"** means a […].

n)   The term **"[Jurisdiction B] TIN"** means a […].

2.   Any capitalised term not otherwise defined in this Agreement will have the meaning that it has at that time under the law of the jurisdiction applying the Agreement, such meaning being consistent with the meaning set forth in the Annex. Any term not otherwise defined in this Agreement or in the Annex will, unless the context otherwise requires or the Competent Authorities agree to a common meaning (as permitted by domestic law), have the meaning that it has at that time under the law of the jurisdiction applying this Agreement, any meaning under the applicable tax laws of that jurisdiction prevailing over a meaning given to the term under other laws of that jurisdiction.

SECTION 2

Exchange of Information with Respect to Reportable Accounts

1.   Pursuant to the provisions of Article […] of the [Convention]/[Instrument] and subject to the applicable reporting and due diligence rules consistent with the Annex, each Competent Authority will annually exchange with the other Competent Authority on an automatic basis the information obtained pursuant to such rules and specified in paragraph 2.

2.   The information to be exchanged is, in the case of [Jurisdiction A] with respect to each [Jurisdiction B] Reportable Account, and in the case of [Jurisdiction B] with respect to each [Jurisdiction A] Reportable Account:

a)   the name, address, TIN and date and place of birth (in the case of an individual) of each Reportable Person that is an Account Holder of the account and, in the case of any Entity that is an Account Holder and that, after application of due diligence procedures consistent with the Annex, is identified as having one or more Controlling Persons that is a Reportable Person, the name, address, and TIN of the Entity and the name, address, TIN and date and place of birth of each Reportable Person;

b) the account number (or functional equivalent in the absence of an account number);

c) the name and identifying number (if any) of the Reporting Financial Institution;

d) the account balance or value (including, in the case of a Cash Value Insurance Contract or Annuity Contract, the Cash Value or surrender value) as of the end of the relevant calendar year or other appropriate reporting period or, if the account was closed during such year or period, the closure of the account;

e) in the case of any Custodial Account:

   (1) the total gross amount of interest, the total gross amount of dividends, and the total gross amount of other income generated with respect to the assets held in the account, in each case paid or credited to the account (or with respect to the account) during the calendar year or other appropriate reporting period; and

   (2) the total gross proceeds from the sale or redemption of property paid or credited to the account during the calendar year or other appropriate reporting period with respect to which the Reporting Financial Institution acted as a custodian, broker, nominee, or otherwise as an agent for the Account Holder;

f) in the case of any Depository Account, the total gross amount of interest paid or credited to the account during the calendar year or other appropriate reporting period; and

g) in the case of any account not described in subparagraph 2(e) or (f), the total gross amount paid or credited to the Account Holder with respect to the account during the calendar year or other appropriate reporting period with respect to which the Reporting Financial Institution is the obligor or debtor, including the aggregate amount of any redemption payments made to the Account Holder during the calendar year or other appropriate reporting period.

SECTION 3

Time and Manner of Exchange of Information

1. For the purposes of the exchange of information in Section 2, the amount and characterization of payments made with respect to a Reportable Account may be determined in accordance with the principles of the tax laws of the jurisdiction exchanging the information.

2. For the purposes of the exchange of information in Section 2, the information exchanged will identify the currency in which each relevant amount is denominated.

3. With respect to paragraph 2 of Section 2, information is to be exchanged with respect to [xxxx] and all subsequent years and will be exchanged within nine months after the end of the calendar year to which the information relates. Notwithstanding the foregoing sentence information is only required to be exchanged with respect to a calendar year if both jurisdictions have in effect legislation that requires reporting with respect to such calendar year that is consistent with the scope of exchange provided for in Section 2 and the reporting and due diligence procedures contained in the Annex.

4. Notwithstanding paragraph 3, the information to be exchanged with respect to [xxxx] is the information described in paragraph 2 of Section 2, except for gross proceeds described in subparagraph 2(e)(2) of Section 2.

5. The Competent Authorities will automatically exchange the information described in Section 2 in a common reporting standard schema in Extensible Markup Language.

6. The Competent Authorities will agree on one or more methods for data transmission including encryption standards.

SECTION 4

Collaboration on Compliance and Enforcement

A Competent Authority will notify the other Competent Authority when the first-mentioned Competent Authority has reason to believe that an error may have led to incorrect or incomplete information reporting or there is non-compliance by a Reporting Financial Institution with the applicable reporting requirements and due diligence procedures consistent with the Annex. The notified Competent Authority will take all appropriate measures available under its domestic law to address the errors or non-compliance described in the notice.

SECTION 5

Confidentiality and Data Safeguards

1. All information exchanged is subject to the confidentiality rules and other safeguards provided for in the [Convention]/[Instrument], including the provisions limiting the use of the information exchanged and, to the extent needed to ensure the necessary level of protection of personal data, in accordance with the safeguards which may be specified by the supplying Competent Authority as required under its domestic law.

2. Each Competent Authority will notify the other Competent Authority immediately regarding any breach of confidentiality or failure of safeguards and any sanctions and remedial actions consequently imposed.

SECTION 6

Consultations and Amendments

1. If any difficulties in the implementation or interpretation of this Agreement arise, either Competent Authority may request consultations to develop appropriate measures to ensure that this Agreement is fulfilled.

2. This Agreement may be amended by written agreement of the Competent Authorities. Unless otherwise agreed upon, such an amendment is effective on the first day of the month following the expiration of a period of one month after the date of the later of the signatures of such written agreement or the date of the later of the notifications exchanged for purposes of such written agreement.

SECTION 7

Term of Agreement

1. This Agreement will come into effect [...]/[on the date of the later of the notifications provided by each Competent Authority that its jurisdiction has the necessary laws in place to implement the Agreement].

2.   A Competent Authority may suspend the exchange of information under this Agreement by giving notice in writing to the other Competent Authority that it has determined that there is or has been significant non-compliance by the other Competent Authority with this Agreement. Such suspension will have immediate effect. For the purposes of this paragraph, significant non-compliance includes, but is not limited to, non-compliance with the confidentiality and data safeguard provisions of this Agreement and the [Convention]/[Instrument], a failure by the Competent Authority to provide timely or adequate information as required under this Agreement or defining the status of Entities or accounts as Non-Reporting Financial Institutions and Excluded Accounts in a manner that frustrates the purposes of the Common Reporting Standard.

3.   Either Competent Authority may terminate this Agreement by giving notice of termination in writing to the other Competent Authority. Such termination will become effective on the first day of the month following the expiration of a period of 12 months after the date of the notice of termination. In the event of termination, all information previously received under this Agreement will remain confidential and subject to the terms of the [Convention/Instrument].

Signed in duplicate in [...] on [...].

COMPETENT AUTHORITY FOR
[Jurisdiction A]:

COMPETENT AUTHORITY FOR
[Jurisdiction B]:

(ANNEX)

COMMON STANDARD ON REPORTING AND DUE DILIGENCE FOR FINANCIAL ACCOUNT INFORMATION ("COMMON REPORTING STANDARD")

Section I: General Reporting Requirements

A.   Subject to paragraphs C through F, each Reporting Financial Institution must report the following information with respect to each Reportable Account of such Reporting Financial Institution:

    1.   the name, address, jurisdiction(s) of residence, TIN and date and place of birth (in the case of an individual) of each Reportable Person that is an Account Holder of the account and, in the case of any Entity that is an Account Holder and that, after application of the due diligence procedures consistent with Sections V, VI and VII, is identified as having one or more Controlling Persons that is a Reportable Person, the name, address, jurisdiction(s) of residence and TIN of the Entity and the name, address, jurisdiction(s) of residence, TIN and date and place of birth of each Reportable Person;

    2.   the account number (or functional equivalent in the absence of an account number);

    3.   the name and identifying number (if any) of the Reporting Financial Institution;

4.   the account balance or value (including, in the case of a Cash Value Insurance Contract or Annuity Contract, the Cash Value or surrender value) as of the end of the relevant calendar year or other appropriate reporting period or, if the account was closed during such year or period, the closure of the account;

5.   in the case of any Custodial Account:

   a)   the total gross amount of interest, the total gross amount of dividends, and the total gross amount of other income generated with respect to the assets held in the account, in each case paid or credited to the account (or with respect to the account) during the calendar year or other appropriate reporting period; and

   b)   the total gross proceeds from the sale or redemption of property paid or credited to the account during the calendar year or other appropriate reporting period with respect to which the Reporting Financial Institution acted as a custodian, broker, nominee, or otherwise as an agent for the Account Holder;

6.   in the case of any Depository Account, the total gross amount of interest paid or credited to the account during the calendar year or other appropriate reporting period; and

7.   in the case of any account not described in subparagraph A(5) or (6), the total gross amount paid or credited to the Account Holder with respect to the account during the calendar year or other appropriate reporting period with respect to which the Reporting Financial Institution is the obligor or debtor, including the aggregate amount of any redemption payments made to the Account Holder during the calendar year or other appropriate reporting period.

B.   The information reported must identify the currency in which each amount is denominated.

C.   Notwithstanding subparagraph A(1), with respect to each Reportable Account that is a Preexisting Account, the TIN or date of birth is not required to be reported if such TIN or date of birth is not in the records of the Reporting Financial Institution and is not otherwise required to be collected by such Reporting Financial Institution under domestic law. However, a Reporting Financial Institution is required to use reasonable efforts to obtain the TIN and date of birth with respect to Preexisting Accounts by the end of the second calendar year following the year in which such Accounts were identified as Reportable Accounts.

D.   Notwithstanding subparagraph A(1), the TIN is not required to be reported if (i) a TIN is not issued by the relevant Reportable Jurisdiction or (ii) the domestic law of the relevant Reportable Jurisdiction does not require the collection of the TIN issued by such Reportable Jurisdiction.

E.   Notwithstanding subparagraph A(1), the place of birth is not required to be reported unless the Reporting Financial Institution is otherwise required to obtain and report it under domestic law and it is available in the electronically searchable data maintained by the Reporting Financial Institution.

F.   Notwithstanding paragraph A, the information to be reported with respect to [xxxx] is the information described in such paragraph, except for gross proceeds described in subparagraph A(5)(b).

Section II: General Due Diligence Requirements

A.   An account is treated as a Reportable Account beginning as of the date it is identified as such pursuant to the due diligence procedures in Sections

II through VII and, unless otherwise provided, information with respect to a Reportable Account must be reported annually in the calendar year following the year to which the information relates.

B.   The balance or value of an account is determined as of the last day of the calendar year or other appropriate reporting period.

C.   Where a balance or value threshold is to be determined as of the last day of a calendar year, the relevant balance or value must be determined as of the last day of the reporting period that ends with or within that calendar year.

D.   Each Jurisdiction may allow Reporting Financial Institutions to use service providers to fulfil the reporting and due diligence obligations imposed on such Reporting Financial Institutions, as contemplated in domestic law, but these obligations shall remain the responsibility of the Reporting Financial Institutions.

E.   Each Jurisdiction may allow Reporting Financial Institutions to apply the due diligence procedures for New Accounts to Preexisting Accounts, and the due diligence procedures for High Value Accounts to Lower Value Accounts. Where a Jurisdiction allows New Account due diligence procedures to be used for Preexisting Accounts, the rules otherwise applicable to Preexisting Accounts continue to apply.

Section III: Due Diligence for Preexisting Individual Accounts

The following procedures apply for purposes of identifying Reportable Accounts among Preexisting Individual Accounts.

A.   **Accounts Not Required to be Reviewed, Identified, or Reported.** A Preexisting Individual Account that is a Cash Value Insurance Contract or an Annuity Contract is not required to be reviewed, identified or reported, provided the Reporting Financial Institution is effectively prevented by law from selling such Contract to residents of a Reportable Jurisdiction.

B.   **Lower Value Accounts.** The following procedures apply with respect to Lower Value Accounts.

   1.   **Residence Address.** If the Reporting Financial Institution has in its records a current residence address for the individual Account Holder based on Documentary Evidence, the Reporting Financial Institution may treat the individual Account Holder as being a resident for tax purposes of the jurisdiction in which the address is located for purposes of determining whether such individual Account Holder is a Reportable Person.

   2.   **Electronic Record Search.** If the Reporting Financial Institution does not rely on a current residence address for the individual Account Holder based on Documentary Evidence as set forth in subparagraph B(1), the Reporting Financial Institution must review electronically searchable data maintained by the Reporting Financial Institution for any of the following indicia and apply subparagraphs B(3) through (6):

      a)   Identification of the Account Holder as a resident of a Reportable Jurisdiction;

      b)   Current mailing or residence address (including a post office box) in a Reportable Jurisdiction;

      c)   One or more telephone numbers in a Reportable Jurisdiction and no telephone number in the jurisdiction of the Reporting Financial Institution;

d)   Standing instructions (other than with respect to a Depository Account) to transfer funds to an account maintained in a Reportable Jurisdiction;

e)   Currently effective power of attorney or signatory authority granted to a person with an address in a Reportable Jurisdiction; or

f)   A "hold mail" instruction or "in-care-of" address in a Reportable Jurisdiction if the Reporting Financial Institution does not have any other address on file for the Account Holder.

3.   If none of the indicia listed in subparagraph B(2) are discovered in the electronic search, then no further action is required until there is a change in circumstances that results in one or more indicia being associated with the account, or the account becomes a High Value Account.

4.   If any of the indicia listed in subparagraph B(2)(a) through (e) are discovered in the electronic search, or if there is a change in circumstances that results in one or more indicia being associated with the account, then the Reporting Financial Institution must treat the Account Holder as a resident for tax purposes of each Reportable Jurisdiction for which an indicium is identified, unless it elects to apply subparagraph B(6) and one of the exceptions in such subparagraph applies with respect to that account.

5.   If a "hold mail" instruction or "in-care-of" address is discovered in the electronic search and no other address and none of the other indicia listed in subparagraph B(2)(a) through (e) are identified for the Account Holder, the Reporting Financial Institution must, in the order most appropriate to the circumstances, apply the paper record search described in subparagraph C(2), or seek to obtain from the Account Holder a self-certification or Documentary Evidence to establish the residence(s) for tax purposes of such Account Holder. If the paper search fails to establish an indicium and the attempt to obtain the self-certification or Documentary Evidence is not successful, the Reporting Financial Institution must report the account as an undocumented account.

6.   Notwithstanding a finding of indicia under subparagraph B(2), a Reporting Financial Institution is not required to treat an Account Holder as a resident of a Reportable Jurisdiction if:

a)   The Account Holder information contains a current mailing or residence address in the Reportable Jurisdiction, one or more telephone numbers in the Reportable Jurisdiction (and no telephone number in the jurisdiction of the Reporting Financial Institution) or standing instructions (with respect to Financial Accounts other than Depository Accounts) to transfer funds to an account maintained in a Reportable Jurisdiction, the Reporting Financial Institution obtains, or has previously reviewed and maintains a record of:

i.   A self-certification from the Account Holder of the jurisdiction(s) of residence of such Account Holder that does not include such Reportable Jurisdiction; and

ii.   Documentary Evidence establishing the Account Holder's non-reportable status.

b)   The Account Holder information contains a currently effective power of attorney or signatory authority granted to a person with an address in the Reportable Jurisdiction, the Reporting Financial Institution obtains, or has previously reviewed and maintains a record of:

  i. A self-certification from the Account Holder of the jurisdiction(s) of residence of such Account Holder that does not include such Reportable Jurisdiction; or

  ii. Documentary Evidence establishing the Account Holder's non-reportable status.

C. **Enhanced Review Procedures for High Value Accounts.** The following enhanced review procedures apply with respect to High Value Accounts.

  1. **Electronic Record Search.** With respect to High Value Accounts, the Reporting Financial Institution must review electronically searchable data maintained by the Reporting Financial Institution for any of the indicia described in subparagraph B(2).

  2. **Paper Record Search.** If the Reporting Financial Institution's electronically searchable databases include fields for, and capture all of the information described in, subparagraph C(3), then a further paper record search is not required. If the electronic databases do not capture all of this information, then with respect to a High Value Account, the Reporting Financial Institution must also review the current customer master file and, to the extent not contained in the current customer master file, the following documents associated with the account and obtained by the Reporting Financial Institution within the last five years for any of the indicia described in subparagraph B(2):

    a) The most recent Documentary Evidence collected with respect to the account;

    b) The most recent account opening contract or documentation;

    c) The most recent documentation obtained by the Reporting Financial Institution pursuant to AML/KYC Procedures or for other regulatory purposes;

    d) Any power of attorney or signature authority forms currently in effect; and

    e) Any standing instructions (other than with respect to a Depository Account) to transfer funds currently in effect.

  3. **Exception To The Extent Databases Contain Sufficient Information.** A Reporting Financial Institution is not required to perform the paper record search described in subparagraph C(2) to the extent the Reporting Financial Institution's electronically searchable information includes the following:

    a) The Account Holder's residence status;

    b) The Account Holder's residence address and mailing address currently on file with the Reporting Financial Institution;

    c) The Account Holder's telephone number(s) currently on file, if any, with the Reporting Financial Institution;

    d) In the case of Financial Accounts other than Depository Accounts, whether there are standing instructions to transfer funds in the account to another account (including an account at another branch of the Reporting Financial Institution or another Financial Institution);

e) Whether there is a current "in-care-of" address or "hold mail" instruction for the Account Holder; and

f) Whether there is any power of attorney or signatory authority for the account.

4. **Relationship Manager Inquiry for Actual Knowledge.** In addition to the electronic and paper record searches described above, the Reporting Financial Institution must treat as a Reportable Account any High Value Account assigned to a relationship manager (including any Financial Accounts aggregated with that High Value Account) if the relationship manager has actual knowledge that the Account Holder is a Reportable Person.

5. **Effect of Finding Indicia.**

a) If none of the indicia listed in subparagraph B(2) are discovered in the enhanced review of High Value Accounts described above, and the account is not identified as held by a Reportable Person in subparagraph C(4), then further action is not required until there is a change in circumstances that results in one or more indicia being associated with the account.

b) If any of the indicia listed in subparagraph B(2)(a) through (e) are discovered in the enhanced review of High Value Accounts described above, or if there is a subsequent change in circumstances that results in one or more indicia being associated with the account, then the Reporting Financial Institution must treat the account as a Reportable Account with respect to each Reportable Jurisdiction for which an indicium is identified unless it elects to apply subparagraph B(6) of this Section and one of the exceptions in such subparagraph applies with respect to that account.

c) If a "hold mail" instruction or "in-care-of" address is discovered in the electronic search and no other address and none of the other indicia listed in subparagraph B(2)(a) through (e) are identified for the Account Holder, the Reporting Financial Institution must obtain from such Account Holder a self-certification or Documentary Evidence to establish the residence(s) for tax purposes of the Account Holder. If the Reporting Financial Institution cannot obtain such self-certification or Documentary Evidence, it must report the account as an undocumented account.

6. If a Preexisting Individual Account is not a High Value Account as of 31 December [xxxx], but becomes a High Value Account as of the last day of a subsequent calendar year, the Reporting Financial Institution must complete the enhanced review procedures described in paragraph C with respect to such account within the calendar year following the year in which the account becomes a High Value Account. If based on this review such account is identified as a Reportable Account, the Reporting Financial Institution must report the required information about such account with respect to the year in which it is identified as a Reportable Account and subsequent years on an annual basis, unless the Account Holder ceases to be a Reportable Person.

7. Once a Reporting Financial Institution applies the enhanced review procedures described in paragraph C to a High Value Account, the Reporting Financial Institution is not required to re-apply such procedures, other than the relationship manager inquiry described in

subparagraph C(4), to the same High Value Account in any subsequent year unless the account is undocumented where the Reporting Financial Institution should re-apply them annually until such account ceases to be undocumented.

8.   If there is a change of circumstances with respect to a High Value Account that results in one or more indicia described in subparagraph B(2) being associated with the account, then the Reporting Financial Institution must treat the account as a Reportable Account with respect to each Reportable Jurisdiction for which an indicium is identified unless it elects to apply subparagraph B(6) and one of the exceptions in such subparagraph applies with respect to that account.

9.   A Reporting Financial Institution must implement procedures to ensure that a relationship manager identifies any change in circumstances of an account. For example, if a relationship manager is notified that the Account Holder has a new mailing address in a Reportable Jurisdiction, the Reporting Financial Institution is required to treat the new address as a change in circumstances and, if it elects to apply subparagraph B(6), is required to obtain the appropriate documentation from the Account Holder.

D.   Review of Preexisting Individual Accounts must be completed by [xx/xx/xxxx].

E.   Any Preexisting Individual Account that has been identified as a Reportable Account under this Section must be treated as a Reportable Account in all subsequent years, unless the Account Holder ceases to be a Reportable Person.

Section IV: Due Diligence for New Individual Accounts

The following procedures apply for purposes of identifying Reportable Accounts among New Individual Accounts.

A.   With respect to New Individual Accounts, upon account opening, the Reporting Financial Institution must obtain a self-certification, which may be part of the account opening documentation, that allows the Reporting Financial Institution to determine the Account Holder's residence(s) for tax purposes and confirm the reasonableness of such self-certification based on the information obtained by the Reporting Financial Institution in connection with the opening of the account, including any documentation collected pursuant to AML/KYC Procedures.

B.   If the self-certification establishes that the Account Holder is resident for tax purposes in a Reportable Jurisdiction, the Reporting Financial Institution must treat the account as a Reportable Account and the self-certification must also include the Account Holder's TIN with respect to such Reportable Jurisdiction (subject to paragraph D of Section I) and date of birth.

C.   If there is a change of circumstances with respect to a New Individual Account that causes the Reporting Financial Institution to know, or have reason to know, that the original self-certification is incorrect or unreliable, the Reporting Financial Institution cannot rely on the original self-certification and must obtain a valid self-certification that establishes the residence(s) for tax purposes of the Account Holder.

Section V: Due Diligence for Preexisting Entity Accounts

The following procedures apply for purposes of identifying Reportable Accounts among Preexisting Entity Accounts.

A.   **Entity Accounts Not Required to Be Reviewed, Identified or Reported.** Unless the Reporting Financial Institution elects otherwise, either with respect to all Preexisting Entity Accounts or, separately, with respect to any clearly identified group of such accounts, a Preexisting Entity Account with an account balance or value that does not exceed $250,000 as of 31 December [xxxx], is not required to be reviewed, identified, or reported as a Reportable Account until the account balance or value exceeds $250,000 as of the last day of any subsequent calendar year.

B.   **Entity Accounts Subject to Review.** A Preexisting Entity Account that has an account balance or value that exceeds $250,000 as of 31 December [xxxx], and a Preexisting Entity Account that does not exceed $250,000 as of 31 December [xxxx] but the account balance or value of which exceeds $250,000 as of the last day of any subsequent calendar year, must be reviewed in accordance with the procedures set forth in paragraph D.

C.   **Entity Accounts With Respect to Which Reporting Is Required.** With respect to Preexisting Entity Accounts described in paragraph B, only accounts that are held by one or more Entities that are Reportable Persons, or by Passive NFEs with one or more Controlling Persons who are Reportable Persons, shall be treated as Reportable Accounts.

D.   **Review Procedures for Identifying Entity Accounts With Respect to Which Reporting Is Required.** For Preexisting Entity Accounts described in paragraph B, a Reporting Financial Institution must apply the following review procedures to determine whether the account is held by one or more Reportable Persons, or by Passive NFEs with one or more Controlling Persons who are Reportable Persons:

1.   **Determine Whether the Entity Is a Reportable Person.**

a)   Review information maintained for regulatory or customer relationship purposes (including information collected pursuant to AML/KYC Procedures) to determine whether the information indicates that the Account Holder is resident in a Reportable Jurisdiction. For this purpose, information indicating that the Account Holder is resident in a Reportable Jurisdiction includes a place of incorporation or organisation, or an address in a Reportable Jurisdiction.

b)   If the information indicates that the Account Holder is resident in a Reportable Jurisdiction, the Reporting Financial Institution must treat the account as a Reportable Account unless it obtains a self-certification from the Account Holder, or reasonably determines based on information in its possession or that is publicly available, that the Account Holder is not a Reportable Person.

2.   **Determine Whether the Entity is a Passive NFE with One or More Controlling Persons Who Are Reportable Persons.** With respect to an Account Holder of a Preexisting Entity Account (including an Entity that is a Reportable Person), the Reporting Financial Institution must determine whether the Account Holder is a Passive NFE with one or more Controlling Persons who are Reportable Persons. If any of the Controlling Persons of a Passive NFE is a Reportable Person, then the account must be treated as a Reportable Account. In making these determinations the Reporting Financial Institution must follow the guidance in subparagraphs D(2)(a) through (c) in the order most appropriate under the circumstances.

a)   **Determining whether the Account Holder is a Passive NFE.** For purposes of determining whether the Account Holder is a Passive NFE, the Reporting Financial Institution must obtain a self-certification from the Account Holder to establish its status, unless it has information in its possession or that is publicly available, based on which it can reasonably determine that the Account Holder is an Active NFE or a Financial Institution other than an Investment Entity described in subparagraph A(6)(b) of Section VIII that is not a Participating Jurisdiction Financial Institution.

b) **Determining the Controlling Persons of an Account Holder.** For the purposes of determining the Controlling Persons of an Account Holder, a Reporting Financial Institution may rely on information collected and maintained pursuant to AML/KYC Procedures.

c) **Determining whether a Controlling Person of a Passive NFE is a Reportable Person.** For the purposes of determining whether a Controlling Person of a Passive NFE is a Reportable Person, a Reporting Financial Institution may rely on:

   i. Information collected and maintained pursuant to AML/ KYC Procedures in the case of a Preexisting Entity Account held by one or more NFEs with an account balance that does not exceed $1,000,000; or

   ii. A self-certification from the Account Holder or such Controlling Person of the jurisdiction(s) in which the Controlling Person is resident for tax purposes.

E. **Timing of Review and Additional Procedures Applicable to Preexisting Entity Accounts**.

   1. Review of Preexisting Entity Accounts with an account balance or value that exceeds $250,000 as of 31 December [xxxx] must be completed by 31 December [xxxx].

   2. Review of Preexisting Entity Accounts with an account balance or value that does not exceed $250,000 as of 31 December [xxxx], but exceeds $250,000 as of 31 December of a subsequent year, must be completed within the calendar year following the year in which the account balance or value exceeds $250,000.

   3. If there is a change of circumstances with respect to a Preexisting Entity Account that causes the Reporting Financial Institution to know, or have reason to know, that the self-certification or other documentation associated with an account is incorrect or unreliable, the Reporting Financial Institution must re-determine the status of the account in accordance with the procedures set forth in paragraph D.

Section VI: Due Diligence for New Entity Accounts

The following procedures apply for purposes of identifying Reportable Accounts among New Entity Accounts.

A. **Review Procedures for Identifying Entity Accounts With Respect to Which Reporting Is Required.** For New Entity Accounts, a Reporting Financial Institution must apply the following review procedures to determine whether the account is held by one or more Reportable Persons, or by Passive NFEs with one or more Controlling Persons who are Reportable Persons:

1. **Determine Whether the Entity Is a Reportable Person.**

   a) Obtain a self-certification, which may be part of the account opening documentation, that allows the Reporting Financial

Institution to determine the Account Holder's residence(s) for tax purposes and confirm the reasonableness of such self-certification based on the information obtained by the Reporting Financial Institution in connection with the opening of the account, including any documentation collected pursuant to AML/KYC Procedures. If the Entity certifies that it has no residence for tax purposes, the Reporting Financial Institution may rely on the address of the principal office of the Entity to determine the residence of the Account Holder.

b) If the self-certification indicates that the Account Holder is resident in a Reportable Jurisdiction, the Reporting Financial Institution must treat the account as a Reportable Account unless it reasonably determines based on information in its possession or that is publicly available, that the Account Holder is not a Reportable Person with respect to such Reportable Jurisdiction.

2. **Determine Whether the Entity is a Passive NFE with One or More Controlling Persons Who Are Reportable Persons.** With respect to an Account Holder of a New Entity Account (including an Entity that is a Reportable Person), the Reporting Financial Institution must determine whether the Account Holder is a Passive NFE with one or more Controlling Persons who are Reportable Persons. If any of the Controlling Persons of a Passive NFE is a Reportable Person, then the account must be treated as a Reportable Account. In making these determinations the Reporting Financial Institution must follow the guidance in subparagraphs A(2)(a) through (c) in the order most appropriate under the circumstances.

a) **Determining whether the Account Holder is a Passive NFE.** For purposes of determining whether the Account Holder is a Passive NFE, the Reporting Financial Institution must rely on a self-certification from the Account Holder to establish its status, unless it has information in its possession or that is publicly available, based on which it can reasonably determine that the Account Holder is an Active NFE or a Financial Institution other than an Investment Entity described in subparagraph A(6)(b) of Section VIII that is not a Participating Jurisdiction Financial Institution.

b) **Determining the Controlling Persons of an Account Holder.** For purposes of determining the Controlling Persons of an Account Holder, a Reporting Financial Institution may rely on information collected and maintained pursuant to AML/KYC Procedures.

c) **Determining whether a Controlling Person of a Passive NFE is a Reportable Person.** For purposes of determining whether a Controlling Person of a Passive NFE is a Reportable Person, a Reporting Financial Institution may rely on a self-certification from the Account Holder or such Controlling Person.

Section VII: Special Due Diligence Rules

The following additional rules apply in implementing the due diligence procedures described above:

A. **Reliance on Self-Certifications and Documentary Evidence.** A Reporting Financial Institution may not rely on a self-certification or Documentary

Evidence if the Reporting Financial Institution knows or has reason to know that the self-certification or Documentary Evidence is incorrect or unreliable.

B. **Alternative Procedures for Financial Accounts Held by Individual Beneficiaries of a Cash Value Insurance Contract or an Annuity Contract.** A Reporting Financial Institution may presume that an individual beneficiary (other than the owner) of a Cash Value Insurance Contract or an Annuity Contract receiving a death benefit is not a Reportable Person and may treat such Financial Account as other than a Reportable Account unless the Reporting Financial Institution has actual knowledge, or reason to know, that the beneficiary is a Reportable Person. A Reporting Financial Institution has reason to know that a beneficiary of a Cash Value Insurance Contract or an Annuity Contract is a Reportable Person if the information collected by the Reporting Financial Institution and associated with the beneficiary contains indicia as described in paragraph B of Section III. If a Reporting Financial Institution has actual knowledge, or reason to know, that the beneficiary is a Reportable Person, the Reporting Financial Institution must follow the procedures in paragraph B of Section III.

C. **Account Balance Aggregation and Currency Rules.**

1. **Aggregation of Individual Accounts.** For purposes of determining the aggregate balance or value of Financial Accounts held by an individual, a Reporting Financial Institution is required to aggregate all Financial Accounts maintained by the Reporting Financial Institution, or by a Related Entity, but only to the extent that the Reporting Financial Institution's computerized systems link the Financial Accounts by reference to a data element such as client number or TIN, and allow account balances or values to be aggregated. Each holder of a jointly held Financial Account shall be attributed the entire balance or value of the jointly held Financial Account for purposes of applying the aggregation requirements described in this subparagraph.

2. **Aggregation of Entity Accounts.** For purposes of determining the aggregate balance or value of Financial Accounts held by an Entity, a Reporting Financial Institution is required to take into account all Financial Accounts that are maintained by the Reporting Financial Institution, or by a Related Entity, but only to the extent that the Reporting Financial Institution's computerized systems link the Financial Accounts by reference to a data element such as client number or TIN, and allow account balances or values to be aggregated. Each holder of a jointly held Financial Account shall be attributed the entire balance or value of the jointly held Financial Account for purposes of applying the aggregation requirements described in this subparagraph.

3. **Special Aggregation Rule Applicable to Relationship Managers.** For purposes of determining the aggregate balance or value of Financial Accounts held by a person to determine whether a Financial Account is a High Value Account, a Reporting Financial Institution is also required, in the case of any Financial Accounts that a relationship manager knows, or has reason to know, are directly or indirectly owned, controlled, or established (other than in a fiduciary capacity) by the same person, to aggregate all such accounts.

4. **Amounts Read to Include Equivalent in Other Currencies.** All dollar amounts are in U.S. dollars and shall be read to include equivalent amounts in other currencies, as determined by domestic law.

Section VIII: Defined Terms

The following terms have the meanings set forth below:

A.   **Reporting Financial Institution**

1.   The term **"Reporting Financial Institution"** means any Participating Jurisdiction Financial Institution that is not a Non-Reporting Financial Institution.

2.   The term **"Participating Jurisdiction Financial Institution"** means (i) any Financial Institution that is resident in a Participating Jurisdiction, but excludes any branch of that Financial Institution that is located outside such Participating Jurisdiction, and (ii) any branch of a Financial Institution that is not resident in a Participating Jurisdiction, if that branch is located in such Participating Jurisdiction.

3.   The term **"Financial Institution"** means a Custodial Institution, a Depository Institution, an Investment Entity, or a Specified Insurance Company.

4.   The term **"Custodial Institution"** means any Entity that holds, as a substantial portion of its business, Financial Assets for the account of others. An Entity holds Financial Assets for the account of others as a substantial portion of its business if the Entity's gross income attributable to the holding of Financial Assets and related financial services equals or exceeds 20 per cent of the Entity's gross income during the shorter of: (i) the three-year period that ends on 31 December (or the final day of a non-calendar year accounting period) prior to th year in which the determination is being made; or (ii) the period during which the Entity has been in existence.

5.   The term **"Depository Institution"** means any Entity that accepts deposits in the ordinary course of a banking or similar business.

6.   The term **"Investment Entity"** means any Entity:

a)   that primarily conducts as a business one or more of the following activities or operations for or on behalf of a customer:

i.   trading in money market instruments (cheques, bills, certificates of deposit, derivatives, etc.); foreign exchange; exchange, interest rate and index instruments; transferable securities; or commodity futures trading;

ii.   individual and collective portfolio management; or

iii.   otherwise investing, administering, or managing Financial Assets or money on behalf of other persons; or

b)   the gross income of which is primarily attributable to investing, reinvesting, or trading in Financial Assets, if the Entity is managed by another Entity that is a Depository Institution, a Custodial Institution, a Specified Insurance Company, or an Investment Entity described in subparagraph A(6)(a).

An Entity is treated as primarily conducting as a business one or more of the activities described in subparagraph A(6)(a), or an Entity's gross income is primarily attributable to investing, reinvesting, or trading in Financial Assets for purposes of subparagraph A(6)(b), if the Entity's gross income attributable to the relevant activities equals or exceeds 50 per cent of the Entity's gross income during the shorter of: (i) the three-year period ending on 31 December of the year preceding the year in which the determination is made; or (ii) the period during which the Entity has been in existence. The term "Investment Entity" does not include an Entity that is an Active NFE because it meets any of the criteria in subparagraphs D(9)(d) through (g).

This paragraph shall be interpreted in a manner consistent with similar language set forth in the definition of "financial institution" in the Financial Action Task Force Recommendations.

7.   The term **"Financial Asset"** includes a security (for example, a share of stock in a corporation; partnership or beneficial ownership interest in a widely held or publicly traded partnership or trust; note, bond, debenture, or other evidence of indebtedness), partnership interest, commodity, swap (for example, interest rate swaps, currency swaps, basis swaps, interest rate caps, interest rate floors, commodity swaps, equity swaps, equity index swaps, and similar agreements), Insurance Contract or Annuity Contract, or any interest (including a futures or forward contract or option) in a security, partnership interest, commodity, swap, Insurance Contract, or Annuity Contract. The term "Financial Asset" does not include a non- debt, direct interest in real property.

8.   The term **"Specified Insurance Company"** means any Entity that is an insurance company (or the holding company of an insurance company) that issues, or is obligated to make payments with respect to, a Cash Value Insurance Contract or an Annuity Contract.

B.   **Non-Reporting Financial Institution**

1.   The term **"Non-Reporting Financial Institution"** means any Financial Institution that is:

a)   a Governmental Entity, International Organization or Central Bank, other than with respect to a payment that is derived from an obligation held in connection with a commercial financial activity of a type engaged in by a Specified Insurance Company, Custodial Institution, or Depository Institution;

b)   a Broad Participation Retirement Fund; a Narrow Participation Retirement Fund; a Pension Fund of a Governmental Entity, International Organization or Central Bank; or a Qualified Credit Card Issuer;

c)   any other Entity that presents a low risk of being used to evade tax, has substantially similar characteristics to any of the Entities described in subparagraphs B(1)(a) and (b), and is defined in domestic law as a Non-Reporting Financial Institution, provided that the status of such Entity as a Non-Reporting Financial Institution does not frustrate the purposes of the Common Reporting Standard;

d)   an Exempt Collective Investment Vehicle; or

e)   a trust established under the laws of a Reportable Jurisdiction to the extent that the trustee of the trust is a Reporting Financial Institution and reports all information required to be reported pursuant to Section I with respect to all Reportable Accounts of the trust.

2.   The term **"Governmental Entity"** means the government of a jurisdiction, any political subdivision of a jurisdiction (which, for the avoidance of doubt, includes a state, province, county, or municipality), or any wholly owned agency or instrumentality of a jurisdiction or of any one or more of the foregoing (each, a "Governmental Entity").

This category is comprised of the integral parts, controlled entities, and political subdivisions of a jurisdiction.

a)   An "integral part" of a jurisdiction means any person, organization, agency, bureau, fund, instrumentality, or other body, however designated, that constitutes a governing authority of a jurisdiction. The net earnings of the governing authority must be credited to its own account or to other accounts of the jurisdiction, with no portion inuring to the benefit of any private person. An integral part does not include any individual who is a sovereign, official, or administrator acting in a private or personal capacity.

b)   A controlled entity means an Entity that is separate in form from the jurisdiction or that otherwise constitutes a separate juridical entity, provided that:

   i.   The Entity is wholly owned and controlled by one or more Governmental Entities directly or through one or more controlled entities;

   ii.   The Entity's net earnings are credited to its own account or to the accounts of one or more Governmental Entities, with no portion of its income inuring to the benefit of any private person; and

   iii. The Entity's assets vest in one or more Governmental Entities upon dissolution.

c)   Income does not inure to the benefit of private persons if such persons are the intended beneficiaries of a governmental program, and the program activities are performed for the general public with respect to the common welfare or relate to the administration of some phase of government. Notwithstanding the foregoing, however, income is considered to inure to the benefit of private persons if the income is derived from the use of a governmental entity to conduct a commercial business, such as a commercial banking business, that provides financial services to private persons.

3.   The term **"International Organization"** means any international organization or wholly owned agency or instrumentality thereof. This category includes any intergovernmental organization (including a supranational organization) (1) that is comprised primarily of governments; (2) that has in effect a headquarters or substantially similar agreement with the jurisdiction; and (3) the income of which does not inure to the benefit of private persons.

4.   The term **"Central Bank"** means a bank that is by law or government sanction the principal authority, other than the government of the jurisdiction itself, issuing instruments intended to circulate as currency. Such a bank may include an instrumentality that is separate from the government of the jurisdiction, whether or not owned in whole or in part by the jurisdiction.

5.   The term **"Broad Participation Retirement Fund"** means a fund established to provide retirement, disability, or death benefits, or any combination thereof, to beneficiaries that are current or former employees (or persons designated by such employees) of one or more employers in consideration for services rendered, provided that the fund:

a)   Does not have a single beneficiary with a right to more than five per cent of the fund's assets;

b) Is subject to government regulation and provides information reporting to the tax authorities; and

c) Satisfies at least one of the following requirements:

    i. The fund is generally exempt from tax on investment income, or taxation of such income is deferred or taxed at a reduced rate, due to its status as a retirement or pension plan;

    ii. The fund receives at least 50 per cent of its total contributions (other than transfers of assets from other plans described in subparagraphs B(5) through (7) or from retirement and pension accounts described in subparagraph C(17)(a)) from the sponsoring employers;

    iii. Distributions or withdrawals from the fund are allowed only upon the occurrence of specified events related to retirement, disability, or death (except rollover distributions to other retirement funds described in subparagraphs B(5) through (7) or retirement and pension accounts described in subparagraph C(17)(a)), or penalties apply to distributions or withdrawals made before such specified events; or

    iv. Contributions (other than certain permitted make-up contributions) by employees to the fund are limited by reference to earned income of the employee or may not exceed $50,000 annually, applying the rules set forth in paragraph C of Section VII for account aggregation and currency translation.

6. The term **"Narrow Participation Retirement Fund"** means a fund established to provide retirement, disability, or death benefits to beneficiaries that are current or former employees (or persons designated by such employees) of one or more employers in consideration for services rendered, provided that:

a) The fund has fewer than 50 participants;

b) The fund is sponsored by one or more employers that are not Investment Entities or Passive NFEs;

c) The employee and employer contributions to the fund (other than transfers of assets from retirement and pension accounts described in subparagraph C(17)(a)) are limited by reference to earned income and compensation of the employee, respectively;

d) Participants that are not residents of the jurisdiction in which the fund is established are not entitled to more than 20 per cent of the fund's assets; and

e) The fund is subject to government regulation and provides information reporting to the tax authorities.

7. The term **"Pension Fund of a Governmental Entity, International Organization or Central Bank"** means a fund established by a Governmental Entity, International Organization or Central Bank to provide retirement, disability, or death benefits to beneficiaries or participants that are current or former employees (or persons designated by such employees), or that are not current or former employees, if the benefits provided to such beneficiaries or participants are in consideration of personal services performed for the Governmental Entity, International Organization or Central Bank.

8. The term **"Qualified Credit Card Issuer"** means a Financial Institution satisfying the following requirements:

    a) The Financial Institution is a Financial Institution solely because it is an issuer of credit cards that accepts deposits only when a customer makes a payment in excess of a balance due with respect to the card and the overpayment is not immediately returned to the customer; and

    b) Beginning on or before [xx/xx/xxxx], the Financial Institution implements policies and procedures either to prevent a customer from making an overpayment in excess of $50,000, or to ensure that any customer overpayment in excess of $50,000 is refunded to the customer within 60 days, in each case applying the rules set forth in paragraph C of Section VII for account aggregation and currency translation. For this purpose, a customer overpayment does not refer to credit balances to the extent of disputed charges but does include credit balances resulting from merchandise returns.

9. The term **"Exempt Collective Investment Vehicle"** means an Investment Entity that is regulated as a collective investment vehicle, provided that all of the interests in the collective investment vehicle are held by or through one or more Entities described in subparagraph B(1), or individuals or Entities that are not Reportable Persons.

    An Investment Entity that is regulated as a collective investment vehicle does not fail to qualify under subparagraph B(9) as an Exempt Collective Investment Vehicle, solely because the collective investment vehicle has issued physical shares in bearer form, provided that:

    a) The collective investment vehicle has not issued, and does not issue, any physical shares in bearer form after [xx/xx/xxxx];

    b) The collective investment vehicle retires all such shares upon surrender;

    c) The collective investment vehicle performs the due diligence procedures set forth in Sections II through VII and reports any information required to be reported with respect to any such shares when such shares are presented for redemption or other payment; and

    d) The collective investment vehicle has in place policies and procedures to ensure that such shares are redeemed or immobilized as soon as possible, and in any event prior to [xx/xx/xxxx].

C. **Financial Account**

1. The term **"Financial Account"** means an account maintained by a Financial Institution, and includes a Depository Account, a Custodial Account and:

    a) in the case of an Investment Entity other than an Investment Entity that is a Financial Institution solely because it manages an Investment Entity described in subparagraph A(6)(b), any equity or debt interest in the Financial Institution;

    b) in the case of a Financial Institution not described in subparagraph C(1)(a), any equity or debt interest in the Financial Institution, if the class of interests was established with a purpose of avoiding reporting in accordance with Section I; and

c)   any Cash Value Insurance Contract and any Annuity Contract issued or maintained by a Financial Institution, other than a noninvestment-linked, non-transferable immediate life annuity that is issued to an individual and monetizes a pension or disability benefit provided under an account that is an Excluded Account.

The term "Financial Account" does not include any account that is an Excluded Account.

2.   The term **"Depository Account"** includes any commercial, checking, savings, time, or thrift account, or an account that is evidenced by a certificate of deposit, thrift certificate, investment certificate, certificate of indebtedness, or other similar instrument maintained by a Financial Institution in the ordinary course of a banking or similar business. A Depository Account also includes an amount held by an insurance company pursuant to a guaranteed investment contract or similar agreement to pay or credit interest thereon.

3.   The term **"Custodial Account"** means an account (other than an Insurance Contract or Annuity Contract) for the benefit of another person that holds one or more Financial Assets.

4.   The term **"Equity Interest"** means, in the case of a partnership that is a Financial Institution, either a capital or profits interest in the partnership. In the case of a trust that is a Financial Institution, an Equity Interest is considered to be held by any person treated as a settlor or beneficiary of all or a portion of the trust, or any other natural person exercising ultimate effective control over the trust. A Reportable Person will be treated as being a beneficiary of a trust if such Reportable Person has the right to receive directly or indirectly (for example, through a nominee) a mandatory distribution or may receive, directly or indirectly, a discretionary distribution from the trust.

5.   The term **"Insurance Contract"** means a contract (other than an Annuity Contract) under which the issuer agrees to pay an amount upon the occurrence of a specified contingency involving mortality, morbidity, accident, liability, or property risk.

6.   The term **"Annuity Contract"** means a contract under which the issuer agrees to make payments for a period of time determined in whole or in part by reference to the life expectancy of one or more individuals. The term also includes a contract that is considered to be an Annuity Contract in accordance with the law, regulation, or practice of the jurisdiction in which the contract was issued, and under which the issuer agrees to make payments for a term of years.

7.   The term **"Cash Value Insurance Contract"** means an Insurance Contract (other than an indemnity reinsurance contract between two insurance companies) that has a Cash Value.

8.   The term **"Cash Value"** means the greater of (i) the amount that the policyholder is entitled to receive upon surrender or termination of the contract (determined without reduction for any surrender charge or policy loan), and (ii) the amount the policyholder can borrow under or with regard to the contract. Notwithstanding the foregoing, the term "Cash Value" does not include an amount payable under an Insurance Contract:

a)   Solely by reason of the death of an individual insured under a life insurance contract including a refund of a previously paid premium provided such refund is a Limited Risk Refund as the term is understood in the Commentary;

b)   As a personal injury or sickness benefit or other benefit providing indemnification of an economic loss incurred upon the occurrence of the event insured against;

c)   Subject to the application of subparagraph C(8)(a), as a refund of a previously paid premium (less cost of insurance charges whether or not actually imposed) under an Insurance Contract (other than a life insurance contract or an Annuity Contract) due to cancellation or termination of the contract, decrease in risk exposure during the effective period of the contract, or arising from the correction of a posting or similar error with regard to the premium for the contract;

d)   As a policyholder dividend (other than a termination dividend) provided that the dividend relates to an Insurance Contract under which the only benefits payable are described in subparagraph C(8)(b); or

e)   As a return of an advance premium or premium deposit for an Insurance Contract for which the premium is payable at least annually if the amount of the advance premium or premium deposit does not exceed the next annual premium that will be payable under the contract.

9.   The term **"Preexisting Account"** means a Financial Account maintained by a Reporting Financial Institution as of [xx/xx/xxxx].

10.   The term **"New Account"** means a Financial Account maintained by a Reporting Financial Institution opened on or after [xx/xx/xxxx].

11.   The term **"Preexisting Individual Account"** means a Preexisting Account held by one or more individuals.

12.   The term **"New Individual Account"** means a New Account held by one or more individuals.

13.   The term **"Preexisting Entity Account"** means a Preexisting Account held by one or more Entities.

14.   The term **"Lower Value Account"** means a Preexisting Individual Account with a balance or value as of 31 December [xxxx] that does not exceed $1,000,000.

15.   The term **"High Value Account"** means a Preexisting Individual Account with a balance or value that exceeds $1,000,000 as of 31 December [xxxx] or 31 December of any subsequent year.

16.   The term **"New Entity Account"** means a New Account held by one or more Entities.

17.   The term **"Excluded Account"** means any of the following accounts:

a)   A retirement or pension account that satisfies the following requirements:

    i.   The account is subject to regulation as a personal retirement account or is part of a registered or regulated retirement or pension plan for the provision of retirement or pension benefits (including disability or death benefits);

    ii.   The account is tax-favoured (i.e., contributions to the account that would otherwise be subject to tax are deductible or excluded from the gross income of the account holder or taxed at a reduced rate, or taxation of investment income from the account is deferred or taxed at a reduced rate);

iii. Information reporting is required to the tax authorities with respect to the account;

iv. Withdrawals are conditioned on reaching a specified retirement age, disability, or death, or penalties apply to withdrawals made before such specified events; and

v. Either (i) annual contributions are limited to $50,000 or less, or (ii) there is a maximum lifetime contribution limit to the account of $1,000,000 or less, in each case applying the rules set forth in paragraph C of Section VII for account aggregation and currency translation.

A Financial Account that otherwise satisfies the requirements of this subparagraph will not fail to satisfy such requirements solely because such Financial Account may receive assets or funds transferred from one or more Financial Accounts that meet the requirements of subparagraph C(17)(a) or (b) or from one or more retirement or pension funds that meet the requirements of any of subparagraphs B(5) through (7).

b) An account that satisfies the following requirements:

i. The account is subject to regulation as an investment vehicle for purposes other than for retirement and is regularly traded on an established securities market, or the account is subject to regulation as a savings vehicle for purposes other than for retirement;

ii. The account is tax-favoured (i.e., contributions to the account that would otherwise be subject to tax are deductible or excluded from the gross income of the account holder or taxed at a reduced rate, or taxation of investment income from the account is deferred or taxed at a reduced rate);

iii. Withdrawals are conditioned on meeting specific criteria related to the purpose of the investment or savings account (for example, the provision of educational or medical benefits), or penalties apply to withdrawals made before such criteria are met; and

iv. Annual contributions are limited to $50,000 or less, applying the rules set forth in paragraph C of Section VII for account aggregation and currency translation.

A Financial Account that otherwise satisfies the requirements of this subparagraph will not fail to satisfy such requirements solely because such Financial Account may receive assets or funds transferred from one or more Financial Accounts that meet the requirements of subparagraph C(17)(a) or (b) or from one or more retirement or pension funds that meet the requirements of any of subparagraphs B(5) through (7).

c) A life insurance contract with a coverage period that will end before the insured individual attains age 90, provided that the contract satisfies the following requirements:

    i.   Periodic premiums, which do not decrease over time, are payable at least annually during the period the contract is in existence or until the insured attains age 90, whichever is shorter;

    ii.   The contract has no contract value that any person can access (by withdrawal, loan, or otherwise) without terminating the contract;

    iii.   The amount (other than a death benefit) payable upon cancellation or termination of the contract cannot exceed the aggregate premiums paid for the contract, less the sum of mortality, morbidity, and expense charges (whether or not actually imposed) for the period or periods of the contract's existence and any amounts paid prior to the cancellation or termination of the contract; and

    iv.   The contract is not held by a transferee for value.

d)   An account that is held solely by an estate if the documentation for such account includes a copy of the deceased's will or death certificate.

e)   An account established in connection with any of the following:

    i.   A court order or judgment.

    ii.   A sale, exchange, or lease of real or personal property, provided that the account satisfies the following requirements:

        (i)   The account is funded solely with a down payment, earnest money, deposit in an amount appropriate to secure an obligation directly related to the transaction, or a similar payment, or is funded with a Financial Asset that is deposited in the account in connection with the sale, exchange, or lease of the property;

        (ii)   The account is established and used solely to secure the obligation of the purchaser to pay the purchase price for the property, the seller to pay any contingent liability, or the lessor or lessee to pay for any damages relating to the leased property as agreed under the lease;

        (iii)   The assets of the account, including the income earned thereon, will be paid or otherwise distributed for the benefit of the purchaser, seller, lessor, or lessee (including to satisfy such person's obligation) when the property is sold, exchanged, or surrendered, or the lease terminates;

        (iv)   The account is not a margin or similar account established in connection with a sale or exchange of a Financial Asset; and

        (v)   The account is not associated with an account described in subparagraph C(17)(f).

    iii.   An obligation of a Financial Institution servicing a loan secured by real property to set aside a portion of a payment solely to facilitate the payment of taxes or insurance related to the real property at a later time.

iv.   An obligation of a Financial Institution solely to facilitate the payment of taxes at a later time.

f)   A Depository Account that satisfies the following requirements:

i.   The account exists solely because a customer makes a payment in excess of a balance due with respect to a credit card or other revolving credit facility and the overpayment is not immediately returned to the customer; and

ii.   Beginning on or before [xx/xx/xxxx], the Financial Institution implements policies and procedures either to prevent a customer from making an overpayment in excess of $50,000, or to ensure that any customer overpayment in excess of $50,000 is refunded to the customer within 60 days, in each case applying the rules set forth in paragraph C of Section VII for currency translation. For this purpose, a customer overpayment does not refer to credit balances to the extent of disputed charges but does include credit balances resulting from merchandise returns.

g)   any other account that presents a low risk of being used to evade tax, has substantially similar characteristics to any of the accounts described in subparagraphs C(17)(a) through (f), and is defined in domestic law as an Excluded Account, provided that the status of such account as an Excluded Account does not frustrate the purposes of the Common Reporting Standard.

D.   **Reportable Account**

1.   The term **"Reportable Account"** means an account held by one or more Reportable Persons or by a Passive NFE with one or more Controlling Persons that is a Reportable Person, provided it has been identified as such pursuant to the due diligence procedures described in Sections II through VII.

2.   The term **"Reportable Person"** means a Reportable Jurisdiction Person other than: (i) a corporation the stock of which is regularly traded on one or more established securities markets; (ii) any corporation that is a Related Entity of a corporation described in clause (i); (iii) a Governmental Entity; (iv) an International Organization; (v) a Central Bank; or (vi) a Financial Institution.

3.   The term **"Reportable Jurisdiction Person"** means an individual or Entity that is resident in a Reportable Jurisdiction under the tax laws of such jurisdiction, or an estate of a decedent that was a resident of a Reportable Jurisdiction. For this purpose, an Entity such as a partnership, limited liability partnership or similar legal arrangement that has no residence for tax purposes shall be treated as resident in the jurisdiction in which its place of effective management is situated.

4.   The term **"Reportable Jurisdiction"** means a jurisdiction (i) with which an agreement is in place pursuant to which there is an obligation in place to provide the information specified in Section I, and (ii) which is identified in a published list.

5.   The term **"Participating Jurisdiction"** means a jurisdiction (i) with which an agreement is in place pursuant to which it will provide the information specified in Section I, and (ii) which is identified in a published list.

6.   The term **"Controlling Persons"** means the natural persons who exercise control over an Entity. In the case of a trust, such term means

the settlor, the trustees, the protector (if any), the beneficiaries or class of beneficiaries, and any other natural person exercising ultimate effective control over the trust, and in the case of a legal arrangement other than a trust, such term means persons in equivalent or similar positions. The term "Controlling Persons" must be interpreted in a manner consistent with the Financial Action Task Force Recommendations.

7. The term **"NFE"** means any Entity that is not a Financial Institution.

8. The term **"Passive NFE"** means any: (i) NFE that is not an Active NFE; or (ii) an Investment Entity described in subparagraph A(6)(b) that is not a Participating Jurisdiction Financial Institution.

9. The term **"Active NFE"** means any NFE that meets any of the following criteria:

a) Less than 50 per cent of the NFE's gross income for the preceding calendar year or other appropriate reporting period is passive income and less than 50 per cent of the assets held by the NFE during the preceding calendar year or other appropriate reporting period are assets that produce or are held for the production of passive income;

b) The stock of the NFE is regularly traded on an established securities market or the NFE is a Related Entity of an Entity the stock of which is regularly traded on an established securities market;

c) The NFE is a Governmental Entity, an International Organization, a Central Bank , or an Entity wholly owned by one or more of the foregoing;

d) Substantially all of the activities of the NFE consist of holding (in whole or in part) the outstanding stock of, or providing financing and services to, one or more subsidiaries that engage in trades or businesses other than the business of a Financial Institution, except that an NFE does not qualify for this status if the NFE functions (or holds itself out) as an investment fund, such as a private equity fund, venture capital fund, leveraged buyout fund, or any investment vehicle whose purpose is to acquire or fund companies and then hold interests in those companies as capital assets for investment purposes;

e) The NFE is not yet operating a business and has no prior operating history, but is investing capital into assets with the intent to operate a business other than that of a Financial Institution, provided that the NFE does not qualify for this exception after the date that is 24 months after the date of the initial organization of the NFE;

f) The NFE was not a Financial Institution in the past five years, and is in the process of liquidating its assets or is reorganizing with the intent to continue or recommence operations in a business other than that of a Financial Institution;

g) The NFE primarily engages in financing and hedging transactions with, or for, Related Entities that are not Financial Institutions, and does not provide financing or hedging services to any Entity that is not a Related Entity, provided that the group of any such Related Entities is primarily engaged in a business other than that of a Financial Institution; or

h) The NFE meets all of the following requirements:

    i. It is established and operated in its jurisdiction of residence exclusively for religious, charitable, scientific, artistic, cultural, athletic, or educational purposes; or it is established and operated in its jurisdiction of residence and it is a professional organization, business league, chamber of commerce, labour organization, agricultural or horticultural organization, civic league or an organization operated exclusively for the promotion of social welfare;

    ii. It is exempt from income tax in its jurisdiction of residence;

    iii. It has no shareholders or members who have a proprietary or beneficial interest in its income or assets;

    iv. The applicable laws of the NFE's jurisdiction of residence or the NFE's formation documents do not permit any income or assets of the NFE to be distributed to, or applied for the benefit of, a private person or non-charitable Entity other than pursuant to the conduct of the NFE's charitable activities, or as payment of reasonable compensation for services rendered, or as payment representing the fair market value of property which the NFE has purchased; and

    v. The applicable laws of the NFE's jurisdiction of residence or the NFE's formation documents require that, upon the NFE's liquidation or dissolution, all of its assets be distributed to a Governmental Entity or other non-profit organization, or escheat to the government of the NFE's jurisdiction of residence or any political subdivision thereof.

E. Miscellaneous

1. The term **"Account Holder"** means the person listed or identified as the holder of a Financial Account by the Financial Institution that maintains the account. A person, other than a Financial Institution, holding a Financial Account for the benefit or account of another person as agent, custodian, nominee, signatory, investment advisor, or intermediary, is not treated as holding the account for purposes of this Annex, and such other person is treated as holding the account. In the case of a Cash Value Insurance Contract or an Annuity Contract, the Account Holder is any person entitled to access the Cash Value or change the beneficiary of the contract. If no person can access the Cash Value or change the beneficiary, the Account Holder is any person named as the owner in the contract and any person with a vested entitlement to payment under the terms of the contract. Upon the maturity of a Cash Value Insurance Contract or an Annuity Contract, each person entitled to receive a payment under the contract is treated as an Account Holder.

2. The term **"AML/KYC Procedures"** means the customer due diligence procedures of a Reporting Financial Institution pursuant to the anti-money laundering or similar requirements to which such Reporting Financial Institution is subject.

3. The term **"Entity"** means a legal person or a legal arrangement, such as a corporation, partnership, trust, or foundation.

4. An Entity is a **"Related Entity"** of another Entity if either Entity controls the other Entity, or the two Entities are under common control. For this purpose control includes direct or indirect ownership of more than 50 per cent of the vote and value in an Entity.

5. The term **"TIN"** means Taxpayer Identification Number (or functional equivalent in the absence of a Taxpayer Identification Number).

6. The term **"Documentary Evidence"** includes any of the following:

    a) A certificate of residence issued by an authorized government body (for example, a government or agency thereof, or a municipality) of the jurisdiction in which the payee claims to be a resident.

    b) With respect to an individual, any valid identification issued by an authorized government body (for example, a government or agency thereof, or a municipality), that includes the individual's name and is typically used for identification purposes.

    c) With respect to an Entity, any official documentation issued by an authorized government body (for example, a government or agency thereof, or a municipality) that includes the name of the Entity and either the address of its principal office in the jurisdiction in which it claims to be a resident or the jurisdiction in which the Entity was incorporated or organized.

    d) Any audited financial statement, third-party credit report, bankruptcy filing, or securities regulator's report.

Section IX: Effective Implementation

A. A jurisdiction must have rules and administrative procedures in place to ensure effective implementation of, and compliance with, the reporting and due diligence procedures set out above including:

    1. rules to prevent any Financial Institutions, persons or intermediaries from adopting practices intended to circumvent the reporting and due diligence procedures;

    2. rules requiring Reporting Financial Institutions to keep records of the steps undertaken and any evidence relied upon for the performance of the above procedures and adequate measures to obtain those records;

    3. administrative procedures to verify Reporting Financial Institutions' compliance with the reporting and due diligence procedures; administrative procedures to follow up with a Reporting Financial Institution when undocumented accounts are reported;

    4. administrative procedures to ensure that the Entities and accounts defined in domestic law as Non-Reporting Financial Institutions and Excluded Accounts continue to have a low risk of being used to evade tax; and

    5. effective enforcement provisions to address non-compliance.

ORGANISATION FOR ECONOMIC CO-OPERATION AND DEVELOPMENT

The OECD is a unique forum where governments work together to address the economic, social and environmental challenges of globalisation. The OECD is also at the forefront of efforts to understand and to help governments respond to new developments and concerns, such as corporate governance, the information economy and the challenges of an ageing population. The Organisation provides a setting where governments can compare policy experiences, seek answers to common problems, identify good practice and work to co-ordinate domestic and international policies.

The OECD member countries are: Australia, Austria, Belgium, Canada, Chile, the Czech Republic, Denmark, Estonia, Finland, France, Germany, Greece, Hungary, Iceland, Ireland, Israel, Italy, Japan, Korea, Luxembourg, Mexico, the Netherlands, New Zealand, Norway, Poland, Portugal, the Slovak Republic, Slovenia, Spain, Sweden, Switzerland, Turkey, the United Kingdom and the United States. The European Union takes part in the work of the OECD.

OECD Publishing disseminates widely the results of the Organisation's statistics gathering and research on economic, social and environmental issues, as well as the conventions, guidelines and standards agreed by its members.

Appendix 4.3   Early Adopters and Other Committed Parties

Early adopters group

Argentina, Barbados, Belgium, Bulgaria, Chile, Colombia, Croatia, Curaçao, Cyprus, the Czech Republic, Denmark, Dominica, Estonia, the Faroe Islands, Finland, France, Germany, Greece, Greenland, Hungary, Iceland, India, Ireland, Italy, Korea, Latvia, Liechtenstein, Lithuania, Luxembourg, Malta, Mauritius, Mexico, the Netherlands, Niue, Norway, Poland, Portugal, Romania, San Marino, Seychelles, Slovak Republic, Slovenia, South Africa, Spain, Sweden, Trinidad and Tobago, the United Kingdom and Uruguay; the UK's Crown Dependencies of Isle of Man, Guernsey and Jersey; the UK's Overseas Territories of Anguilla, Bermuda, the British Virgin Islands, the Cayman Islands, Gibraltar, Montserrat, and the Turks & Caicos Islands.

Other committed parties (excluding the United States)

Albania, Andorra, Antigua and Barbuda, Aruba, Australia, Austria, The Bahamas, Belize, Brazil, Brunei Darussalam, Canada, China, Costa Rica, Grenada, Hong Kong (China), Indonesia, Israel, Japan, Marshall Islands, Macao (China), Malaysia, Monaco, New Zealand, Qatar, Russia, Saint Kitts and Nevis, Samoa, Saint Lucia, Saint Vincent and the Grenadines, Saudi Arabia, Singapore, Sint Maarten, Switzerland, Turkey, United Arab Emirates.

Appendix 4.4   EY Global Tax Alert

OECD ISSUES STANDARD FOR AUTOMATIC EXCHANGE OF INFORMATION IN TAX MATTERS

Executive summary[1]

By Stuart Chalcraft, James Guthrie, Julian Skingley, Peter Frost, Paul Radcliffe, David Wren

On 21 July 2014, the Organisation for Economic Co-operation and Development (OECD) published the *Standard for Automatic Exchange of Information in Tax Matters* (the Standard).

The Standard consists of the Model Competent Authority Agreement, intended as a template for intergovernmental agreements, and the Common Reporting Standard (CRS) that contains the reporting and due diligence standard that underpins the automatic exchange of information. There are also extensive commentaries and guidance on technical solutions for information exchange as well as a number of appendices.

The Standard has no direct legal force but it is expected that jurisdictions will follow it closely in adopting local rules and regulations, with many countries already agreeing to early adoption in 2016. There is, however, significant scope for variations to be incorporated as part of that implementation process.

The CRS represents an additional global compliance burden for financial institutions (FIs) and increases the risks and costs of servicing globally-mobile customers and non-individual customers in general.

One positive note for FIs is that the OECD has modelled the CRS on the intergovernmental approach to the Foreign Tax Account Compliance Act (FATCA), which means that in part it should be possible to leverage existing and planned FATCA processes and systems. It should be noted, however, that the data required under the CRS is different, and the volumes of customers and clients affected are likely to be significantly greater.

This Alert summarizes the background to the release of the Standard, the process for global implementation and key issues for effected FIs.

---

1 © 2014 EYGM Limited. All Rights Reserved. Reproduced by kind permission of EY. For additional information on this Alert please see: http://www.ey.com/Publication/vwLUAssets/OECD_issues_Standard_for_Automatic_Exchange_of_Information_in_Tax_Matters/$FILE/2014G_CM4656_OECD%20issues%20Standard%20for%20Automatic%20Exchange%20of%20Information%20in%20Tax%20Matters.pdf

Background

The Standard is intended by the OECD to be a "step change" in the way in which jurisdictions share tax information to combat tax evasion

The OECD acknowledges that many jurisdictions already exchange information automatically, often on certain common types of income, most notably within the EU. However the Standard is intended to be global in scope and to focus on a universal set of information relating to financial accounts, drawing heavily on the intergovernmental approach adopted under FATCA.

The Standard consists of a Model Competent Authority Agreement and the Common Reporting Standard on reporting and due diligence for financial account information. It contains detailed Commentary on both components and technical solutions for information exchange.

Model Competent Authority Agreement

The Model Competent Authority Agreement (Model CAA) links the CRS and the legal basis for information exchange (such as the OECD's Multilateral Convention on Mutual Assistance in Tax Matters or a bilateral tax treaty).

The Model CAA contains clauses setting out representations on the due diligence and domestic reporting undertaken as well as on data confidentiality and infrastructure in place for effective information exchange. There are also sections dealing the type of information to be exchanged, along with the time and manner of such exchanges. Other sections include provisions for collaboration between competent authorities on the issues of compliance and enforcement.

In order to encourage as much uniformity in such agreements as possible, the OECD has published a model bilateral agreement and a model multilateral agreement. There is also a model nonreciprocal agreement, to be used where one contracting state does not wish to receive information on its residents' banking activities in the partner country (for example, in a jurisdiction where no income tax regime exists

The Common Reporting Standard

The CRS contains the reporting and due diligence requirements that are the foundation of automatic information exchange.

Participating jurisdictions will have to enact rules in domestic laws that are consistent with the provisions of the CRS.

FIs covered by the scope of the CRS will be required to report financial account information on account holders that are tax resident in other participating jurisdictions.

The CRS draws heavily on the FATCA Model 1 Intergovernmental Agreement (IGA) albeit with some important differences to accommodate a global exchange of information, rather than one which is aimed at identifying and reporting financial accounts held by US persons only.

FIs in scope include custodial institutions, depository institutions, investment entities and specified insurance companies, unless they pose a low risk of being used for tax evasion and are therefore excluded from reporting. It is worth noting that the scope is broader than under FATCA in that a number of exemptions such as local Foreign Financial Institutions are not provided in the CRS.

The financial information to be reported includes interest, dividends, account balance or value, income from certain insurance products, sales proceeds from financial assets and other income generated with respect to assets held in the account or payments made into the account.

Reportable accounts include those held by individuals and entities (including trusts and foundations) and there is a requirement to look through passive entities to report on the relevant controlling persons.

As with FATCA, there are detailed due diligence requirements for new and pre-existing accounts held by individuals and entities. The diligence requirements are similar to those required under the Model 1 IGA, although significantly, the respective de minimis thresholds for individuals (US$50,000) and INSURANCE CONTRACTS (US$250,000) are not available under the CRS

Commentaries on the Model CAA and CRS

For each section of the Model CAA and CRS, there is an accompanying detailed Commentary, which is intended to further explain the provisions with a view to ensuring consistency in application across jurisdictions. The OECD notes that in some situations the Commentary does allow for alternative approaches to be adopted.

The Commentary deals with some key uncertainties and concerns expressed by industry, including the following:

- One particular concern expressed has been the treatment of new accounts for pre-existing customers. The Commentary deals with this issue and generally follows the position taken under FATCA, namely allowing new accounts for existing customers to be linked to the pre-existing account relationship. This will mean that due diligence requirements can be adapted from FATCA.

- The Commentary includes specific guidance on the definition and use of publicly available information to classify entity account holders, which will be welcome to all affected FIs. The definition in particular is widely drawn and should allow many FIs to leverage existing solutions built for FATCA purposes.

The Commentary also specifically indicates that participating jurisdictions will be expected to help taxpayers determine their tax residency and the OECD will support the distribution of information to help taxpayers determine their residency. This should help to alleviate FIs' concerns that customers may look to them to determine their tax residency.

The final release of the Commentary is a positive development for financial institutions and competent authorities as it provides detailed guidance on the requirements of the CRS.

The next step for both parties will be to understand the differences between approaches that have already been adopted for FATCA and those required for the CRS, in order to be able to assess the level of change necessary.

However, until participating jurisdictions implement the CRS into law, uncertainty will remain. So for financial institutions with operations in countries which have committed to early adoption of the rules from 2016, there will now be a focus on engaging with competent authorities to ensure the CRS can be implemented as efficiently – and as uniformly – as possible.

Technical solutions

The Standard contains guidance on relevant technical implementation recommendations. It includes a schema to be used to exchange information and provides a standard in relation to the information technology (IT) aspects of data safeguards of confidentiality and the transmission and encryption of information.

Implementation

The Standard is dependent on the relevant governmental bodies of participating jurisdictions entering into CAAs, either bilaterally or multilaterally, and appropriately incorporating the CRS into domestic law.

A key concern will be whether jurisdictions will take different positions in terms of implementation and interpretation. The industry hope is that any such differences are few and far between. An additional concern, given the number of adopting jurisdictions, will be how FIs will monitor such differences to ensure they remain compliant.

An *OECD Background Information Brief* released in February 2014 acknowledges this concern and states that the standard will be a "living system" and so may need to "evolve over time." Helpfully, the OECD also notes that "The OECD, working with G20 jurisdictions, will seek to ensure that the Standard remains a single Standard also over time and that as much as possible it continues to be interpreted and operated consistently across different jurisdictions."

Timeline

An Early Adopters Group (EU nations, along with the UK Crown Dependencies and Overseas Territories, as well as some others) indicated in March 2014 that they will implement the CRS with a view to the first exchange of information taking place in 2017. This would mean reporting FIs needing to implement new on-boarding requirements by 1 January 2016.

WHICH COUNTRIES ARE COMMITTED TO THE CRS?

Early adopters group

Argentina, Belgium, Bulgaria, Colombia, Croatia, Cyprus, the Czech Republic, Denmark, Estonia, the Faroe Islands, Finland, France, Germany, Greece, Hungary, Iceland, India, Ireland, Italy, Latvia, Liechtenstein, Lithuania, Malta, Mexico, the Netherlands, Norway, Poland, Portugal, Romania, Slovakia, Slovenia, South Africa, Spain, Sweden, and the United Kingdom; the UK's Crown Dependencies of Isle of Man, Guernsey and Jersey; the UK's Overseas Territories of Anguilla, Bermuda, the British Virgin Islands, the Cayman Islands, Gibraltar, Montserrat, and the Turks & Caicos Islands.

Other committed parties (excluding the United States)

Anguilla, Australia, Austria, Brazil, Canada, the People's Republic of China, Chile, Colombia, Costa Rica, Montserrat, Indonesia, Israel, Japan, Korea, Luxembourg,

Malaysia, New Zealand, Russian, Saudi Arabia, Singapore, Switzerland, and Turkey.

Implementation from 2016

A joint statement released by the Early Adopters Group envisages that the CRS will be implemented from 2016, with the probable timeline in those countries being:

- 1 January 2016: New account due diligence
- 31 December 2016: Complete review for high value individual accounts
- 31 December 2017: Complete review for low value individual accounts and entity accounts

First exchanges of information are due to take place in September 2017, which means that reporting by reporting FIs should take place between March and June 2017.

FIs may be skeptical of these deadlines, given the delays in the FATCA timelines. However, the evident determination of the OECD and the Early Adopters Group in particular means that FIs should not underestimate the likelihood that these timelines will become effective in some, if not all, of the 44 jurisdictions committed to early adoption.

Treaty relief and compliance enhancement

Throughout the process of developing the Standard, the OECD has indicated its intention to align the adoption of the CRS to the Treaty Relief and Compliance Enhancement (TRACE) project.

TRACE focuses on simplifying the process by which portfolio investors claim reduced rates of withholding tax pursuant to a double tax treaty or under relevant domestic law. Now that the Standard has been released it is anticipated that work on incorporating TRACE at an OECD level will begin.

These developments are positive for FIs with an interest in this area, such as asset-servicing organizations and portfolio investors. Such organizations should consider approaching their respective industry organizations to encourage engagement with both the OECD and relevant national governments to register support for this initiative.

DETAILED COMMENTS

Due diligence requirements

The overall process for obtaining customer classifications is broadly the same as the FATCA Model 1 IGA with one key difference being that the nature of the classifications is based on tax residency rather than citizenship or nationality. The OECD has recognized the significant investment in FATCA by the financial services industry and this will hopefully mean that FIs can leverage a significant amount of the work already performed for FATCA purposes when complying with this new standard.

The Commentary clarifies some of the due diligence requirements and provides much needed detail on the interpretation of requirements. The majority of requirements are as set out in the EY Global Tax Alert, *OECD releases Common*

Reporting Standard, dated 20 February 2014, while some key differences to the FATCA Model 1 IGA are highlighted here:

- Focus on tax residency of individuals and entities rather than citizenship as under FATCA. The rules for reporting specified entities resident in participating jurisdictions are maintained from FATCA and are likely to have significantly more impact under the CRS due to the cross-border nature of companies within Europe and Asia

- Removal of de minimis limits for existing and new individual accounts and also in relation to insurance contracts. However, the ability to rely on a residential address for pre-existing accounts should minimize the impact

- On benefit of the removal of de minimis limit is that aggregation challenges are eliminated for a number of accounts. Aggregation will be required to determine higher value accounts (higher than US$1m) for review and for entities, but it may be possible to apply more tactical solutions for these requirements based on business area or other criteria

- The CRS introduces the concept of an "undocumented account," which will be reported as such to the competent authority. These accounts will generally arise when an FI is unable to obtain information for a pre-existing account. It is not clear what needs to be reported in respect of undocumented accounts; however it is clear from the guidance that the number of accounts reported will drive the extent of any inquiry (see *Enforcement* section below)

Compared to the Model 1 IGA, more detailed guidance has been provided as to who must be deemed a Controlling Person, particularly in respect of a trust. Under the CRS, beneficiaries must always be treated as the Controlling Persons, regardless of whether or not any of them exercises control over the trust, and several other clarifications and definitions are included. This appears to set a more rigorous requirement than under FATCA.

For all accounts, FIs may not rely on certifications or documentary evidence if the FI (or, in the case of certain high-value accounts, a relationship manager) knows or has reason to know the certification or documentary evidence is incorrect or unreliable. This will require FIs to have processes to cross-validate information received against the information held for Know Your Customer/Anti-Money Laundering purposes.

As there is no globally standardized start and end date for the review of pre-existing accounts, it will be a challenge for multinational organizations to design and roll-out a program, and it is likely that identifying all non-domestic customers during any review will be the market standard.

LOCAL IMPLEMENTATION

Exchange of information

The expectation expressed in the Model CAA is that data will be exchanged through XML via a common schema, the specifications for which are provided in Annex 3 of the OECD publication.

Beyond this, the model CAA leaves discretion to participating jurisdictions to agree between themselves as to how data will be exchanged, while providing "appropriate minimum standards" of secure transmission and encryption. In particular, the use of memory sticks and other portable media is discouraged.

The CRS does not give an indication of how data will be exchanged between reporting FIs and competent authorities, leaving it to each jurisdiction to determine how best to collect the required information. A concern for multinational financial services groups will be the potential need to deploy a mixture of different technology solutions across the organization, depending on the protocols agreed upon in each country.

Enforcement

While FATCA relies on withholding and presumptions of US citizenship to manage non-responders, the CRS relies solely on the reporting of undocumented accounts (i.e., if the residency of the account owner cannot be documented, then the account is reportable). Therefore enforcement procedures adopted by local competent authorities will be critical to ensure global compliance.

The CRS sets out a number of rules and procedures that jurisdictions must employ in order to ensure effective implementation and compliance with the reporting and due diligence procedures.

In summary these include:

- Rules to prevent practices intended to circumvent the reporting requirements and due diligence procedures

- Administrative procedures to verify reporting FIs' compliance and follow-up steps when undocumented accounts are reported

- Effective enforcement provisions to address non-compliance

While recognizing that jurisdictions will already have a number of anti-avoidance rules in place, the CRS states that the effectiveness of the rule is more important than its form. The Commentary provides several situations for which it is expected that such anti-avoidance rules would apply as a minimum. These include the movement of accounts to non-participating jurisdictions, transfers of balances over year-end and the manipulation of data quality.

A notable inclusion in the CRS is the treatment of undocumented accounts, which will primarily apply to pre-existing accounts for which the financial institution cannot obtain documentation. The Commentary states there is always "cause for concern" if undocumented accounts arise, whether from inadequate processes being implemented by a reporting FI in obtaining the necessary information or as a result of the account holder being non-compliant.

A number of courses of action may be expected by a jurisdiction receiving information on undocumented accounts. This will range from a simple inquiry to the reporting FI in the case of a small number, up to a full audit where there is a larger than average number or a noticeable year on year increase.

Significantly, the Commentary adds that a jurisdiction may implement rules that provide for the imposition of fines or other penalties where a person does not provide information which could include a failure by an individual to provide self-certification.

It also suggests that jurisdictions may wish to make self-certification a condition of account opening, which could cause issues for a number of sectors, particularly where third parties are involved in any compliance process.

Local discretion on implementation

The CRS allows for a number of jurisdictional based variations and potential inconsistencies to be included on transposition into local legislation. Key areas include:

- Classification of Non-Reporting FIs may vary by jurisdiction depending on the application of local legislation and whether the entity presents a low risk of being used to evade tax. There may be some inconsistencies depending on the application of this definition

- Certain accounts may also be classified as Excluded Accounts by meeting a number of low risk requirements

The Commentary attempts to reduce any such inconsistencies, stating that they would typically expect excluded account definitions to be consistent with those excluded under FATCA IGAs.

Industry focus – Asset Management

A key difference between the CRS and FATCA is that under the CRS, the definition of financial account includes interests in funds that are regularly traded on a stock exchange. This means that exchange traded funds in jurisdictions that adopt the CRS will be within the scope for reporting under the CRS but not FATCA.

This will have a significant impact on the Exchange Traded Fund (ETF) industry and will be a challenging requirement to meet as listed funds do not perform due diligence on investors when they purchase shares. This issue is partly covered in the Commentary, where it is suggested that where due diligence is carried out by brokers, such brokers could be required to provide all information to the fund to enable the fund to comply with its obligations.

Another significant difference between the CRS and FATCA is the treatment of investment entities from jurisdictions that have not adopted the CRS. Under the CRS these will be classified as passive non-financial entities (NFEs). This will require FIs in jurisdictions that have adopted the CRS to classify the Controlling Persons of any investment entity outside a CRS jurisdiction that holds an account.

Industry focus – Insurance

There is no material difference between a specified insurance company as defined under FATCA for Model 1 IGA purposes and one as defined under the CRS. The focus remains squarely on identifying accounts described as Cash Value Insurance (CVI) contracts where there is a cash value payment on termination or surrender, or through collateralizing the account.

Under the CRS more individual accounts will be potentially reportable as in scope accounts are not limited to those valued at more than US$50,000 as under the FATCA Model 1 IGA. There are, however, a list of excluded accounts which include term life insurance, tax favored policies, and retirement and pension accounts. Reinsurance policies are also specifically excluded. There also appears to be an opportunity to exclude other "low risk" accounts which should help smaller product producers.

As with FATCA, most life insurance companies are likely to be FIs and in scope of CRS for account due diligence and reporting, while general insurance companies and insurance brokers will not. It should be noted, however, that the CRS does not contain a "FATCA like" concept of Fixed, Determinable, Annual, Periodical (FDAP) income payments.

Life insurance companies in scope of CRS and that operate within the EU may have additional due diligence work to perform on their insurance back book for CRS purposes than they have had to carry out under FATCA, where the back book is out of scope for a significant number of CVI products. The CRS retains the FATCA approach of exempting from review those pre-existing CVI accounts where the FI is effectively prevented by law from selling their products into the reportable jurisdiction. EU law, however, requires the free movement of services so that in theory a policy holder is able to effectively shop around the EU for their policy. Consequently, where an EU insurer is not prevented by law from selling their products into reportable jurisdictions within the EU the pre-existing exemption may not apply.

As many EU countries are expected to be early adopters of the Standard, due diligence of the back book will be an immediate and additional burden for life insurers as soon as CRS goes live.

Technology, Data and Reporting Implications

The Standard contains guidance on the use of technology solutions which will form a fundamental component of the reporting mechanism.

The OECD's approach is to set the expected level of standards around information exchange, data security, encryption, confidentiality and integrity, while allowing for variations in solutions that meet these standards. It does not mandate a single solution for data transmission or encryption, effectively allowing further use of systems and practices already in use, which vary by reporting financial institution and competent authority.

From a reporting FI's perspective, the main technology focus will be to firstly identify the reportable accounts, and then to compile the annual CRS reports for submission in the specified format to their local competent authority. This process will need to be replicated, addressing local variations from the common standard, for each jurisdiction the FI operates in. This presents a management control challenge and coordinating activities will require sharing of management information on reporting activities.

For competent authorities, the task of collecting data from domestic FIs, together with the production of the CRS reports and the receipt of reciprocal reports, will be a new task to resource and manage. A dedicated reporting solution, which includes the relevant data security and encryption standards may be required if the existing reporting mechanisms are not suitable for this new reporting activity.

In summary, while efforts at standardization have clearly been made, in practice there will be multiple variations from the standard which will require clarity of understanding of these variances in order to design the reporting technology support plus robust management of the technology solutions.

What next?

The approach adopted by FIs will be influenced by, among other things, the extent to which they consider that the anticipated timetable for implementation of the OECD proposals may change.

FIs will need to decide the best time to initiate a systems review and modification to ensure they can satisfy the requirements of the CRS, taking into account, in particular, the time required for implementing changes to customer classification processes.

Comparing the IRS FATCA and OECD schemas

A comparative analysis of the IRS FATCA Schema v1.1 and OECD Schema (Annex 3) illustrates that there are approximately 100 separate data elements across the two schemas. Of these 100, about one third have the same definition, one third have similar but different definitions, and the other third appear only in one, not both, of the schemas.

By way of example of the challenges of local implementation, the UK FATCA Submission schema also contains further differences. In many jurisdictions, it is likely that there will be more differences than similarities between the reports needed for FATCA and CRS reporting.

FIs should take therefore immediate steps to understand the key differences and similarities between the CRS and FATCA, and the corresponding impact on their approach to FATCA compliance. For example, there may be opportunities to reduce effort by combining FATCA planned activities with the CRS requirements, such as the review of high value accounts.

Local implementation of the rules will be critical to this process, and engagement with local tax authorities or other competent authorities may help ensure that businesses can comply with the CRS in a way that minimizes cost and disruption.

Using existing FATCA solutions

One of the most significant drivers determining the challenge, cost and complexity of CRS implementation will be the current capability of the FATCA compliance program and the ability to use existing programs to deliver CRS compliance.

FIs that have developed strategic solutions based on the Model 1 IGA may be able to amend those processes and system solutions to cater for CRS with relative ease, leveraging the investment made for FATCA.

Alternatively, organizations that have built "tactical" solutions for FATCA, organizations that have designed their solutions for compliance with FFI Agreements and US banks that have aligned Chapter 3 solutions with FATCA compliance may find that they have a more challenging task to adopt CRS in all countries.

Appendix 5

Customer Due Diligence

Contents

Appendix 5.1   House of Commons Library Report 25 September 2013 'Bank accounts: problems of identification'

Standard Note: SN/BT/3366

Last updated: 25 September 2013

Author: Timothy Edmonds

                   Business & Transport Section

This note gives practical guidance which Members may like to convey to constituents who find that their application for a bank account is refused. More detail on the general legislative background and policy comment should also see standard note *Money Laundering Regulations* SN/BT/2592 available on the intranet.

Contents

Standard Notes are compiled for the benefit of Members of Parliament and their personal staff. Authors are available to discuss the contents of these papers with Members and their staff but cannot advise others.

A. Introduction

Ever since legislation was introduced in this country to counter money laundering some individuals have encountered problems when they apply for a bank account. For some their lack of key identification documents has resulted in their applications being refused. The groups affected cover a broad spectrum of the public but mainly concentrate on the elderly, those from abroad, or the homeless and transient (for whatever reason).

B. Legal requirements.

The current regulations were made under the *Proceeds of Crime Act 2002*, which consolidated various money laundering offences. They have been amended at various stages due to European directives and the guiding legislation is now *The Money Laundering Regulations 2007* (SI 2007/2157).[1] These regulations were themselves amended by Regulations in 2012 – the *Money Laundering (Amendment) Regulations 2012* (SI 2012/2298).

Under the Regulations it is an offence to form a business relationship (in this case to open a bank[2] account) in the course of 'relevant financial business' unless

---

1 SI2007/2157 Explanatory Memorandum available at: http://www.opsi.gov.uk/si/em2007/uksiem_20072157_en.pdf

2 All references to 'bank' include building societies and other deposit taking institutions.

identification procedures have been carried out. Those procedures must ensure that new business applicants produce satisfactory evidence of their identity.

On the question of what evidence of identity is satisfactory, Regulation 5 states:

5.   "Customer due diligence measures" means—

   (a)   identifying the customer and verifying the customer's identity on the basis of documents,data or information obtained from a reliable and independent source;

   (b)   identifying, where there is a beneficial owner who is not the customer, the beneficial owner and taking adequate measures, on a risk-sensitive basis, to verify his identity so that the relevant person is satisfied that he knows who the beneficial owner is, including, in the case of a legal person, trust or similar legal arrangement, measures to understand the ownership and control structure of the person, trust or arrangement; and

   (c)   obtaining information on the purpose and intended nature of the business relationship.

The regulation does not stipulate specific documents. Each financial institution therefore, may decide what evidence it requires before it considers that satisfactory proof of identity has been given in order for it to discharge its legal obligation. Failure to meet these requirements can lead to a two year prison term or a fine or both. This may partly explain the inflexible attitude of bank staff which is common in these problem cases.

C. Evidential requirements

Normally, separate items of identity (i.e. that the individual is who he or she claims to be) and address are sought. Where there is no face to face contact, identity requirements are likely to be stricter, and more documentation may be asked for. In a document published jointly by the government, the Financial Servicers Authority (then the main financial regulator) and the Serious Organised Crime Agency the following examples of readily acceptable documents are described:

What proof of identity will you need?

The best documents are those that are issued by an official authority, cannot be easily forged, and include a photograph. Separate documents are needed to prove your identity and your home address. Some examples are shown below.

Documents you can use to confirm your identity:
- Current signed passport
- Current UK driving licence or a blue disabled driver's pass
- EU member state ID card
- Residence permit (issued by Home Office to EU nationals)
- Benefit book or original letter from benefits agency (e.g. Pensions Service, Jobcentre plus, Child Benefit Office, etc)

Documents you can use to confirm your home address:
- Bills – recent utility or council tax bills
- Official letters – UK solicitor confirming home purchase, benefits agency
- Statements – bank, building society, credit union, mortgage
- Others – council rent card, tenancy agreement[1]

---

1 Available online at: http://www.bba.org.uk/pdf/awareness2.pdf

As part of the Banking Code, banks are required to state clearly what documentation they accept. A survey, from a sample of banks' websites, of accepted forms of identification shows a wide variation between the banks:

Accepted identification

		Barclays	HSBC	Nat-West	Nation-wide
Identity					
Full passport		yes	yes	yes	yes
European Union National Identity Card		yes	yes		yes
UK photocard driving licence or UK full paper driving licence		yes	yes	yes	yes
UK Armed Forces ID card.		yes		yes	
Inland Revenue tax notification of benefits, coding or tax due			yes		yes
Police warrant card				yes	
Construction industry CIS4 & 6				yes	
Firearms or shotgun certificate				yes	
Current student identification card				yes	
Benefits agency book or notification of right to benefit OAP travel pass			yes	yes	yes
Disabled drivers pass				yes	
NHS medical card	(2)			yes	
Birth/adoption certificate	(2)			yes	yes
Provisional driving licence	(2)			yes	
Bank or building society statement with crdit or cheque guarantee card					yes
Address					
UK photocard driving licence or UK full paper driving licence.		yes		yes	
Gas bill (less than three months old) with evidence that the bill has been paid.	(1)	yes	yes	yes	yes
Water bill (less than 3 or 12 months old) with evidence that the bill has been paid.	(1)	yes	yes	yes	yes
Telephone bill for a fixed line, not a mobile (less than three months old).	(1)	yes	yes	yes	yes
Local authority (council) tax bill (less than three months old).		yes	yes	yes	yes
Bank statement (within recent past) from another bank. Bank credit card statement		yes	yes	yes	
Mortgage statement (less than 12 months old).		yes		yes	

Inland Revenue notice of tax coding (current tax year), or other notifications	yes	yes	yes	
European Union National Identity Card		yes		
Benefits agency book or notification of right to benefit			yes	
Current home or motor insurance			yes	

Note
1)   In case of Barclays the bill must have been paid too.
2)   for applicants 20 years old or under only.

Source: Company websites

It is important to stress that this list is simply a compilation of the items that the institutions advertise as being readily acceptable and should not deter individuals from persisting with an application. Some organisations appear more imaginative in what they accept than others but in practice, they all might accept the same items. It is usual for ID to be restricted to one category, i.e. a passport cannot confirm both identity and address.

D. What to do if you don't have the right documents

If there is an ID deficiency and the application is declined, it is important for the constituent not to simply 'give up'. The Government, through the FSA has as a policy goal the eradication as far as possible, of financial exclusion – where mainly poorer sections of society do not have access to things like bank accounts, loans or overdrafts. This conflict between policing of new accounts and encouragement of more accounts through various ways, including for example, government paying many social benefits through a bank, is at the core of the difficulties being experienced. To overcome this, a working group (the Joint Money Laundering Steering Group (JMLSG)) which liaises between government, the regulator and the industry, has produced guidance for the industry to follow.

The key section of its guidance, based upon the industry's rulebook is shown below (some sections are emphasised in bold):

Access to basic banking facilities and other financial services is a necessary requirement for most adults. It is important therefore that the socially/ financially disadvantaged should not be precluded from opening accounts or obtaining other financial services merely because they do not possess evidence of their identity in circumstances where they cannot reasonably be expected to do so. **Internal procedures must allow for such instances and must provide appropriate advice to staff on how identity can be confirmed under these exceptional circumstances and what local checks can be made.**

M3.1.5G states that the exceptions to guard against financial exclusion aim to help relevant firms ensure that where **people cannot reasonably be expected to produce detailed evidence of identity, they are not denied access to financial services.** Although a relevant firm must always take reasonable steps to check who its client is, relevant firms will sometimes be approached by clients who are at a disadvantage, or who otherwise cannot reasonably be expected to produce detailed evidence that helps to confirm identity. **Examples could be where a person does not have a passport or driving licence, or whose name does not appear on utility bills.**

531

ML 3.1.6G states that **where a relevant firm has reasonable grounds to conclude that an individual client is not able to produce the detailed evidence of his or her identity and cannot reasonably be expected to do so, the relevant firm may accept as identification evidence a letter or statement from a person in a position of responsibility who knows the client, that tends to show that the client is who s/he says s/he is, and to confirm his/her permanent address if s/he has one.**

4.110. ML 3.1.7G provides that examples of persons in a position of responsibility who know the client include solicitors, doctors, ministers of religion, teachers, hostel managers and social workers.

4.111. The list is not exhaustive and other examples might include, for example, district nurses or midwives who have visited the client in their homes, care home managers, prison governors, probation officers, police officers and civil servants, Members of Parliament, members of the Scottish Parliament or the Northern Ireland Assembly, a Justice of the Peace, a local or county councillor, or the staff in the registry of a higher education or further education institution.

It would be very helpful to an applicant when they are refused an account to ask the staff for a meeting with the branch '**money laundering reporting officer**'. It is their job to make decisions in non-standard cases and the guidance notes above quoted to this person could form the basis of a discussion.

In January 2006 the JMLSG produced *Guidance for the UK Financial Sector.* It included a table showing suitable alternatives to 'normal' id in difficult areas:[1]

Special Cases

Many customers in the categories below will be able to provide standard documents, and this will normally be a firm's preferred option. This annex is a non-exhaustive and non-mandatory list of documents (see Notes) which are capable of evidencing identity for special cases who either cannot meet the standard verification requirement, or have experienced difficulties in the past when seeking to open accounts, and which will generally be appropriate for opening a Basic Bank Account. These include:

Customer	Documents
Benefit claimants	Entitlement letter issued by DWP, HMRC or local authority, or
	Identity Confirmation Letter issued by DWP or local authority
Those in care homes/sheltered accommodation/ refuge	Letter from care home manager/warden of sheltered accommodation or refuge
	Homeless persons who cannot provide standard identification documentation are likely to be in a particular socially excluded category. A letter from the warden of a homeless shelter, or from an employer if the customer is in work, will normally be sufficient evidence.

1 JMLSG website http://www.jmlsg.org.uk/content/1/c4/68/87/Final_Part_II_030306. pdf

Those on probation	It may be possible to apply standard identification procedures. Otherwise, a letter from the customer's probation officer, or a hostel manager, would normally be sufficient.
Prisoners	It may be possible to apply standard identification procedures. Otherwise, a letter from the governor of the prison, or, if the applicant has been released, from a police or probation officer or hostel manager would normally be sufficient.
International students	Passport or EEA National Identity Card AND
	Letter of Acceptance or Letter of Introduction from Institution on the DfES list
	Guidance on identification for international students is available on the JMLSG website (see International Students: Basic Bank Account Opening Procedures 12 August 2005).
Economic migrants [here meaning those working temporarily in the UK, whose lack of banking or credit history precludes their being offered other than a basic bank account]	National Passport, or
	National Identity Card (nationals of EEA and Switzerland)
	Details of documents required by migrant workers are available at www.employingmigrants.org.uk and Home Office website www.homeoffice.gov.uk/. Firms are not required to establish whether an applicant is legally entitled to work in the UK but if, in the course of checking identity, it came to light that the applicant was not entitled to do so, the deposit of earnings from employment could constitute an arrangement under the Proceeds of Crime Act.
Refugees (those who are not on benefit)	Immigration Status Document, with Residence Permit, or
	IND travel document (ie Blue Convention Travel doc, or Red Stateless Persons doc, or Brown Certificate of Identity doc)
	Refugees are unlikely to have their national passports and will have been issued by the Home Office with documents confirming their status. A refugee is normally entitled to work, to receive benefits and to remain in the UK.
Asylum seekers	IND Application Registration Card (ARC)
	NB This document shows the status of the individual, and does not confirm their identity
	Asylum seekers are issued by the Home Office with documents confirming their status. Unlike refugees, however, information provided by an asylum seeker will not have been checked by the Home Office. The asylum seeker's Applicant Registration Card (ARC) will state whether the asylum seeker is entitled to take employment in the UK. Asylum seekers may apply to open an account if they are entitled to work, but also to deposit money brought from abroad, and in some cases to receive allowances paid by the Home Office. Firms are not required to establish whether an applicant is legally entitled to work in the UK but if, in the course of checking identity, it came to light that the applicant was not entitled to do so, the deposit of earnings from employment could constitute an arrangement under the Proceeds of Crime Act.

| Travellers | Travellers may be able to produce standard identification evidence; if not, they may be in a particular special case category. If verification of address is necessary, a check with the local authority, which has to register travellers' sites, may sometimes be helpful. |

Notes:

1. Passports, national identity cards and travel documents must be current, i.e. unexpired. Letters should be of recent date, or, in the case of students, the course dates stated in the Letter of Acceptance should reasonably correspond with the date of the account application to the bank. All documents must be originals. In case of need, consideration should be given to verifying the authenticity of the document with its issuer.

2. As with all retail customers, firms should take reasonable care to check that documents offered are genuine (not obviously forged), and where these incorporate photographs, that these correspond to the presenter.

The JMLSG is (mid 2013) in the process of releasing new guidance. However, from the point of view of the specified documents there is no real change to the main requirments. The preamble (5.3.72) states:

If documentary evidence of an individual's identity is to provide a high level of confidence, it will typically have been issued by a government department or agency, or by a court, because there is a greater likelihood that the authorities will have checked the existence and characteristics of the persons concerned. In cases where such documentary evidence of identity may not be available to an individual, other evidence of identity may give the firm reasonable confidence in the customer's identity, although the firm should weigh these against the risks involved.

| 5.3.73 | Non-government-issued documentary evidence complementing identity should normally only be accepted if it originates from a public sector body or another regulated financial services firm, or is supplemented by knowledge that the firm has of the person or entity, which it has documented. |
| 5.3.74 | If identity is to be verified from documents, this should be based on: |

Either a government-issued document which incorporates:

- the customer's full name and photograph, and
- **either** his residential address
- **or** his date of birth.

A section of the guidance dealing with 'customers who cannot provide the standard evidence' can be found in Part I, 5.3.98.

Some customers may not be able to produce identification information equivalent to the standard. Such cases may include, for example, some low-income customers in rented accommodation, customers with a legal, mental or physical inability to manage their affairs, individuals dependent on the care of others, dependant spouses/partners or minors, students, refugees and asylum seekers, migrant workers and prisoners. The firm will therefore need an approach that compensates for the difficulties that such customers may face in providing the standard evidence of identity.

The list of documents suggested as being acceptable for 'special cases' can be found in Annex 1-I (Part II, p13) of the new JMSL sectoral guidance for retail banks.

Appendix 5.2   Wolfsberg Anti-Money Laundering Principles for Private Banking (2012)[1]

Preamble

The following Principles are understood to be appropriate for private banking relationships. Principles for other market segments may differ.

The Principles were initially formulated in 2000 (and revised in 2002) to take into account certain perceived risks associated with private banking. Such risks continue to warrant appropriate levels of attention, no less today than ten years ago. Regulators continue to expect strong anti-money laundering ("AML") standards, robust controls, enhanced client due diligence and suitable AML policies and procedures. The Wolfsberg Group[2] takes this opportunity to provide a further revision of the Principles.

The objectives of suitable AML policies and procedures are to prevent the use of the bank's worldwide operations for criminal purposes and to protect the firm's reputation. Such policies and procedures are designed to mitigate the risk of money laundering and to cooperate with governments and their agencies in the detection of money laundering.

The bank will periodically assess the risk of its private banking business and the bank's Senior/Executive Management will be made aware of these risks. It is the responsibility of Senior/Executive Management of the bank to approve written policies and procedures to address these risks, reflecting a risk based approach and to oversee the implementation of these policies, procedures and relevant controls. Such policies and procedures will adhere to these Principles and will be periodically updated in light of relevant developments.

1   Client Acceptance: General Principles

1.1   General

The bank will endeavour to accept only those clients whose source of wealth and funds can be reasonably established to be legitimate. The primary responsibility for this lies with the private banker who sponsors the client for acceptance. Mere fulfilment of internal review procedures does not relieve the private banker of this basic responsibility. Bank policy will specify what such responsibility and sponsorship entail.

---

1 Wolfsberg Principles reproduced with kind permission of the Wolfsberg Group. All rights reserved.
2 The Wolfsberg Group consists of the following leading international financial institutions: Banco Santander, Bank of Tokyo-Mitsubishi-UFJ Ltd, Barclays, Citigroup, Credit Suisse, Deutsche Bank, Goldman Sachs, HSBC, JPMorgan Chase, Société Générale and UBS. These Principles were revised in conjunction with the Basel Institute on Governance.

1.2 Identification and Verification of Identity

1.2.1 Client Identity

The bank will establish the identity of its clients and beneficial owners prior to establishing business relationships with such persons. Identity is generally established by obtaining the name, date of birth (in the case of individuals), address and such further information that may be required by the laws of the relevant jurisdictions.

1.2.2 Verification of Identity

The bank will take reasonable measures to verify identity when establishing a business relationship as noted below, subject to applicable local requirements.

- Natural persons: identity will be verified to the bank's satisfaction on the basis of official identity papers or other reliable, independent source documents, data, or information as may be appropriate under the circumstances.
- Corporations, partnerships, foundations: identity will be verified on the basis of documentary evidence of due organisation and existence.
- Trusts: identity will be verified on the basis of appropriate evidence of formation and existence or similar documentation. The identity of the trustees will be established and verified.

Identification documents, if used for verification purposes, must be current at the time of opening and copies of such documents will be obtained.

1.2.3   Beneficial Owner

Beneficial ownership, for AML purposes, must be established for all accounts. Beneficial owners will ordinarily include the individuals (i) who generally have ultimate control through ownership or other means over the funds in the account and/or (ii) who are the ultimate source of funds for the account and whose source of wealth should be subject to due diligence. Mere signature authority does not necessarily constitute control for these purposes. The meaning of beneficial ownership for purposes of determining who should be subject to due diligence is dependent on the circumstances and due diligence must be done on all beneficial owners identified in applying the following principles:

- Natural persons: when the account is in the name of an individual, the private banker must establish whether the client is acting on his/her own behalf. If doubt exists, the bank will establish the capacity in which and on whose behalf the accountholder is acting.
- Legal entities: where the client is a private investment company, the private banker will understand the structure of the company sufficiently to determine the provider of funds, the beneficial owner(s) of the assets held by the company and those with the power to give direction to the directors of the company. This principle applies regardless of whether the share capital is in registered or bearer form.[1]
- Trusts: where the client is a trust, the private banker will understand the structure of the trust sufficiently to determine (i) the provider of funds (e.g. settlor), (ii) those who have control over the funds (e.g. trustees), (iii) any persons or entities who have the power to remove the trustees and (iv) the persons for whose benefit the trust is established.
- Partnerships: where the client is a partnership, the private banker will understand the structure of the partnership sufficiently to determine the provider of funds and the general partners.
- Foundations: where the client is a foundation, the private banker will understand the structure of the foundation sufficiently to determine the provider(s) of funds and how the foundation is managed.

---

1 Legal entities that are operating companies are not addressed in these Principles.

- Unincorporated associations: the above principles apply to unincorporated associations.

In each of the above cases, the private banker will make a reasonable judgment as to the need for further due diligence.

Local law may characterise beneficial owners by reference to specific minimum levels of ownership.

The identity of each beneficial owner will be established and, as appropriate, verified unless the identity is previously verified in accordance with the beneficial owner's role as a client. Identity will be verified to the bank's satisfaction on the basis of official identity papers or other reliable, independent source documents, data, or information as may be appropriate under the circumstances. In the event verification is based on identity papers, copies of such identity papers should be obtained.

"Beneficial ownership," as that term may be used for other purposes, may have different meanings.

1.2.4 Intermediaries

The nature of the relationship of the bank with an intermediary depends on the type of intermediary involved:

Introducing Intermediary: an introducing intermediary introduces clients to the bank, whereupon the introducing intermediary's clients become clients of the bank. The bank will generally obtain the same type of information with respect to an introduced client that would otherwise be obtained by the bank, absent the involvement of an introducing intermediary. The bank's policies will address the circumstances in, and the extent to, which, the bank may rely on the introducing intermediary in obtaining this information.

Managing Intermediary: a managing intermediary acts as a professional asset manager for another person and either (i) is authorised to act in connection with an account that such person has with the bank (in which case the considerations noted above with respect to introducing intermediaries would apply); or (ii) is itself the accountholder with the bank, to be treated as the client of the bank.

The private banker will perform due diligence on the introducing or managing intermediary and establish, as appropriate, that the intermediary has relevant due diligence procedures for its clients, or a regulatory obligation to conduct such due diligence, that is satisfactory to the bank.

1.2.5 Powers of Attorney/Authorised Signers

The relationship between the holder of a power of attorney or another authorised signer, the accountholder and if different, the beneficial owner of the account, must be understood.

The identity of a holder of general powers over an account (such as the power to act as a signatory for the account) will be established and, as appropriate, verified.

1.2.6 Practices for Walk-In Clients and Electronic Banking Relationships

A bank will determine whether walk-in clients or relationships initiated through electronic channels require a higher degree of due diligence prior to account opening. The bank will specifically address measures to satisfactorily establish and verify the identity of non-face-to-face customers.

1.3 Due Diligence

In addition to the information contemplated in 1.2, it is essential to collect and record information covering the client profile categories outlined in Appendix I.

Applying a risk based approach, the bank will corroborate the information set forth in Appendix I on the basis of documentary evidence or reliable sources. Unless other measures reasonably suffice to conduct the due diligence on a client (e.g. favourable and reliable references), a client will be met prior to account opening, at which time, if identity is verified on the basis of official identity documents, such documents will be reviewed.

1.4 Numbered or Alternate Name Accounts

Numbered or alternate name accounts will only be accepted if the bank has established the identity of the client and the beneficial owner. These accounts must be open to a level of scrutiny by the bank's appropriate control layers equal to the level of scrutiny applicable to other client accounts. Wire transfers from these accounts must reflect the true name of the accountholder.

1.5 Concentration Accounts

The bank will not permit the use of its internal non-client accounts (sometimes referred to as "concentration" accounts) to prevent association of the identity of a client with the movement of funds on the client's behalf, i.e., the bank will not permit the use of such internal accounts in a manner that would prevent the bank from appropriately monitoring the client's account activity.

1.6 Oversight Responsibility

There will be a requirement that new clients, subject to a risk based approach, be approved by at least one person other than the private banker.

2 Client Acceptance: Situations requiring Additional Diligence / Attention; Prohibited Customers

2.1 Prohibited Customers

The bank will specify categories of customers that it will not accept or maintain.

2.2 General

In its internal policies, the bank must define categories of persons whose circumstances warrant enhanced due diligence. This will typically be the case where the circumstances are likely to pose a higher than average risk to a bank.

2.3 Indicators

The circumstances of the following categories of persons are indicators for defining them as requiring Enhanced Due Diligence:

- Persons residing in and/or having funds sourced from countries identified by credible sources as having inadequate AML standards or representing high risk for crime and corruption.
- Persons engaged in types of economic or business activities or sectors known to be susceptible to money laundering.
- "Politically Exposed Persons," frequently abbreviated as "PEPs," referring to individuals holding or, as appropriate, having held, senior, prominent, or important public positions with substantial authority over policy, operations or the use or allocation of government-owned resources, such as senior government officials, senior executives of government corporations, senior politicians, important political party officials, etc., as well as their close family and close associates. PEPs from different jurisdictions may be subject to different levels of diligence.[1]

Clients who are not deemed to warrant enhanced due diligence may be subjected to greater scrutiny as a result of (i) monitoring of their activities, (ii) external inquiries, (iii) derogatory information (e.g. negative media reports) or (iv) other factors which may expose the bank to reputational risk.

---

1 For more information regarding Politically Exposed Persons, please see the Wolfsberg Group's "Wolfsberg Frequently Asked Questions ("FAQs") on Politically Exposed Persons ("PEPs")" available at http://www.wolfsberg-principles.com/pdf/PEP-FAQ-052008.pdf.

2.4 Senior Management Approval

The bank's internal policies should indicate whether, for any one or more among these categories, Senior Management must approve entering into new relationships.

Relationships with Politically Exposed Persons may only be entered into with the approval of Senior Management.

2.5 Cash Handling

The bank's policies and procedures will address client cash transactions, including specifically the receipt and withdrawal of large amounts of cash.

3 Updating Client Files

The private banker is responsible for updating the client file on a defined basis and/or when there are major changes. The private banker's supervisor or an independent control person will review relevant portions of client files on a regular basis to ensure consistency and completeness. The frequency of the reviews depends on the size, complexity and risk posed by the relationship.

With respect to clients classified under any category of persons mentioned in 2, the bank's internal policies will indicate whether Senior Management must be involved in these reviews and what management information must be provided to management and/or other control layers. The policies and/or procedures should also address the frequency of these information flows.

Reviews of PEPs must require Senior Management's involvement.

4 Practices when identifying Unusual or Suspicious Activities

4.1 Definition of Unusual or Suspicious Activities

The bank will have a written policy on the identification of, and follow-up on, unusual or suspicious activities. This policy and/or related procedures will include a definition of what is considered to be suspicious or unusual and give examples thereof.

Unusual or suspicious activities may include:

- Account transactions or other activities which are not consistent with the due diligence file
- Cash transactions over a certain amount
- Pass-through / in-and-out-transactions.

4.2 Identification of Unusual or Suspicious Activities

Unusual or suspicious activities can be identified through:

- Monitoring of transactions
- Client contacts (meetings, discussions, in-country visits etc.)
- Third party information (e.g. newspapers, other media sources, internet)
- Private banker's internal knowledge of the client's environment (e.g. political situation in his/her country).

4.3 Follow-up on Unusual or Suspicious Activities

The private banker, management and/or the control function will carry out an analysis of the background of any unusual or suspicious activity. If there is no plausible explanation a decision involving the control function will be made to:

- continue the business relationship with increased monitoring
- cancel the business relationship
- report the business relationship to the Authorities.

The report to the Authorities is made by the control function and Senior Management may need to be notified (e.g. Senior Compliance Officer, CEO, Chief Auditor, General Counsel). As required by local laws and regulations, the assets may be blocked and transactions may be subject to approval by the control function.

5 Monitoring and Screening

5.1 Monitoring Programme

The primary responsibility for reviewing account activities lies with the private banker. The private banker will be familiar with significant transactions and increased activity in the account and will be especially aware of unusual or suspicious activities (see 4.1). In addition, a sufficient monitoring programme must be in place. The bank will decide to what extent fulfilment of this responsibility will need to be supported through the use of automated systems or other means.

5.2 Ongoing Monitoring

With respect to clients classified under any category of persons mentioned in 2, the bank's internal policies will indicate how the account activities will be subject to monitoring.

5.3 Sanctions Screening

A sufficient Sanctions Programme must be in place. Prospective clients must be screened on the basis of applicable sanctions and existing clients must be screened as applicable sanctions are updated. Transactions must be screened on the basis of applicable sanctions.

6 No Inappropriate Assistance

Neither the private banker, nor any other bank employee, will provide clients with any assistance with the knowledge that such assistance will be used to deceive Authorities, including Tax Authorities.

7 Control Responsibilities

The bank's policies and procedures will include standard controls to be undertaken by the various "control layers" (private banker, line management, independent operations unit, Compliance, Internal Audit). These controls will cover issues of frequency, degree of control, areas to be controlled, responsibilities and follow-up, compliance testing, etc.

An independent audit function (which may be internal to the bank) will test the programmes contemplated by these controls.

8 Reporting

There will be regular management reporting established on money laundering issues (e.g. number of reports to authorities, monitoring tools, changes in applicable laws and regulations, the number and scope of training sessions provided to employees).

9 Education, Training and Information

The bank will establish a training programme on the identification and prevention of money laundering for employees who have client contact and for Compliance personnel. Regular training (e.g. annually) will also include how to identify and follow-up on unusual or suspicious activities. In addition, employees will be informed about any major changes in AML laws and regulations.

All new employees will be provided with guidelines on the AML procedures.

10 Record Retention Requirements

The bank will establish record retention requirements for all AML related documents. The documents must be kept for a minimum of five years, or longer, as may be required by local law and regulation.

11 Exceptions and Deviations

The bank will establish an exception and deviation procedure that requires risk assessment and approval by an independent unit.

12 AML Organisation

The bank will establish an adequately staffed and independent department responsible for the prevention of money laundering (e.g. Compliance, independent control unit, Legal).

Appendix I

Due Diligence of New Clients and Principal Beneficial Owners

Using a risk-based approach, the bank must ensure that it collects and records a sufficient amount of pertinent information when establishing a business relationship and must update the client profile with additional information as the relationship develops. The information should enable an independent reviewer (whether internal or external to the bank) to understand the client and the relationship on the basis of the information recorded. In the event the client is not the beneficial owner, not all of the information contemplated by this Appendix will be obtained with respect to the client; however, in these circumstances, the relevant information will be obtained with respect to the beneficial owner(s).

Source of Wealth

In order to evaluate the source of a client's (or beneficial owner's) wealth, the bank should gather information relevant to the manner in which the wealth was obtained. For example, the information collected by the bank will differ depending on whether the wealth was acquired through ownership of a business, employment or professional practice, inheritance, investments or otherwise.

Net Worth

Source of Initial Funding of Account

The financial institution and jurisdiction from which the assets funding the account will be transmitted (e.g. a transfer from the client's account at another financial institution). This is distinct from an explanation of the source of wealth.

Account Information
- Purpose for Account
- Expected Account Size
- Expected Account Activity

Occupation

Nature of Client's (or Beneficial Owner's) Business

Role/Relationship of Powers of Attorney or Authorised Third Parties

Other Pertinent Information (e.g. Source of Referral)

Appendix 5.3 The Wolfsberg AML Principles: FAQs with Regard to Beneficial Ownership in the Context of Private Banking (relates to Chapter 16)[1]

Questions sometimes arise with regard to the term "beneficial ownership" as used in the Anti-Money Laundering Principles (AML) for Private Banking (the "Principles"). Some of these questions, as well as answers, are noted below.

Q.1. What does "beneficial ownership" mean for AML purposes?

A. The term "beneficial ownership," when used to refer to beneficial ownership of an account in an AML context (such as the Principles), is conventionally understood as equating to ultimate control over funds in such account, whether through ownership or other means. "Control" in this sense is to be distinguished from mere signature authority or legal title.

The term reflects a recognition that a person in whose name an account is opened with a bank is not necessarily the person who ultimately controls such funds. This distinction is important because the focus of AML efforts – and this is fundamental to the Principles – needs to be on the person who has this ultimate level of control. Placing the emphasis on this person is typically a necessary step in determining the source of wealth.

Generally, the process of determining who should be viewed as the beneficial owner does not pose any particular challenges. For example, as noted in the answer to Question 3 below, it is readily apparent that an individual who establishes a personal investment company ("PIC"), transfers his own assets into the company, and is the sole shareholder, should be viewed as the beneficial owner. There may be situations, however, in which determining what "beneficial ownership" is for AML purposes may not be as straightforward as a conceptual matter. To accommodate these situations, beneficial owners should, for money laundering purposes, be broadly conceived of as including the individuals (i) who generally have ultimate control over such funds through ownership or other means and/ or (ii) who are the ultimate source of funds for the account and whose source of wealth should be subject to due diligence.[2] An example of the application of this framework to the different roles involved in the creation and management of trusts is discussed below in the answers to Questions 4 to 4C.

What "beneficial ownership" is intended to mean for purposes of the Principles should therefore be seen as dependent on the circumstances of the account involved. The Principles, consequently, do not seek to define the term "beneficial ownership" in the abstract; rather, the focus in the Principles is on identifying persons, in particular circumstances, who should be viewed as having the requisite "beneficial ownership."

---

1 Wolfsberg Principles reproduced with kind permission of the Wolfsberg Group. All rights reserved.
2 Such other means, as contemplated in clause (i) above, could include entitlement, although neither entitlement, nor ownership necessarily establishes beneficial ownership in the absence of control.

Accordingly, Paragraph 1.2.3 of the Principles begins with the general statement that beneficial ownership must be established for all accounts, sets forth general characteristics of beneficial owners (as per (i) and (ii) in the prior paragraph), but then qualifies these general principles by elaborating, in the particular contexts of (i) natural persons, (ii) legal entities, (iii) trusts and (iv) unincorporated associations, what the private banker should seek to understand so that he is in a position to determine the persons who warrant due diligence.

In the context of private banking relationships – which is what the Principles address – it should be noted that in circumstances in which the account holder is not a natural person, the general objective is to establish the identity of the natural person(s) who, ultimately, has the requisite beneficial ownership. In other contexts – e.g. lines of business of the bank in which the clients are operating corporate entities with many shareholders – this objective, of course, would not make sense.

Generally, for purposes of the Principles, it would be inappropriate to equate "beneficial owner" with "beneficiary" or "holder of any beneficial interest." To define the term "beneficial ownership" in this manner would yield a result that is too inclusive. See Questions 2-5 for a more concrete, practical approach.

These FAQs focus on beneficial ownership of accountholder assets in the typical private banking contexts (e.g. when the accountholder is a PIC or a trust). These situations are to be distinguished from those situations, not addressed in these FAQs, in which the accountholder is (i) a legal entity that is an operating company or (ii) an intermediary (e.g. an investment manager) acting on behalf of its clients. For a more detailed consideration of intermediaries in the context of private banking, see the Wolfsberg Frequently Asked Questions with Regard to Intermediaries and Holders of Powers of Attorney/Authorised Signers in the Context of Private Banking.

Q.2. What does the term "beneficial ownership" mean in the context of natural persons?

A. When a natural person seeks to open an account in his/her own name, the private banker should inquire whether such person is acting on his own behalf. If such person responds affirmatively, then, in the ordinary case, it is reasonable to presume that he/she is the beneficial owner.

There are circumstances, however, when this presumption may no longer be reasonable, that is, when "doubt exists" as to whether the apparent account holder is acting on his own behalf. In the client acceptance process, for example, such doubt could arise if there are inconsistencies in the information gathered in the due diligence process. For example, if a prospective client's explanation as to the sources of his/her wealth does not, on its face, make sense, further due diligence would be appropriate.

Moreover, after the account has been opened, subsequent activity in the account may become inconsistent with the originally anticipated account activity, in which event, it may be reasonable to revisit the initial presumption that the account holder was acting on his/her own behalf. For example, if it is anticipated that the client, after the account is opened, will have occasional transfers of US $100,000, and there are suddenly frequent transfers substantially in excess of that amount, further due diligence may be warranted, including further inquiry as to beneficial ownership.

Q.3. What does "beneficial ownership" mean in the context of a legal entity, such as a Personal Investment Company (PIC)?

A. There are situations in which the client (i.e. the accountholder) is a legal entity, but in which it is appropriate, for due diligence purposes, to understand the identity of the beneficial owners of the entity. In the event an individual wishes to hold assets through a PIC, the PIC is the client, and the individual is the beneficial owner of such company and appropriate due diligence would be done, including, for example, ascertaining the ownership and control structure, database checks and inquiring as to the beneficial owner's source of wealth. If appropriate, the banker should consider verifying the identity of the beneficial owner by reference to official identity papers or other reliable, independent source documents, data, or information.

The case of a PIC is to be distinguished from that of a corporate entity that is a typical operating company with many shareholders, with regard to which it would make no sense to do due diligence on the shareholders. Indeed, this type of entity would not ordinarily have a relationship with a private bank because such a client is institutional or commercial in nature and would presumably have relationships with other business units of the bank.

There may be situations where there is more than one beneficial owner. For instance, a successful entrepreneur may organise a private holding company in which he and his spouse are the shareholders, but in which he is the provider of funds. In this situation, due diligence as to the source of funds and wealth should be done on him, not his spouse. It may, however, be appropriate to engage in some due diligence with respect to the spouse's background and reputation.

It is appropriate for the private banker to develop an understanding of the company's structure. In the event, for example, there are shareholders owning a substantial amount of shares who are not related to the apparent provider of funds, the private banker should seek to understand why this is so. Similarly, if there are individuals who are in a position to exert control over the funds held by the company (e.g. directors or persons with power to give direction to the directors) and such individuals are not related to the apparent provider of funds, the private banker should consider why this might be so. In these types of situations, this further inquiry may disclose that the apparent provider of funds is not to be viewed as the beneficial owner with respect to such funds. If so, the focus of due diligence should be redirected to the beneficial owner, or indeed, the propriety of opening an account at all may be called into question.

Q.3A. What implications, if any, are there if corporate entities are not legally required to disclose, as a matter of public record or otherwise, who their ultimate beneficial owners are?

A. There may be situations in which applicable law does not require corporations to disclose publicly (e.g. in a registry) or otherwise who their beneficial owners are. If such a corporate entity were a potential client of the private bank, such law, however, would not preclude, as a matter of AML due diligence, an understanding of the beneficial ownership of the company. The private banker should conduct the appropriate due diligence with respect to the principal beneficial owners, regardless of the disclosure laws applicable to the company.

Q.3B. What implications, if any, are there, for due diligence purposes, if shares of a PIC are held in bearer form?

A. The fact that shares of a PIC are in bearer form does not preclude the usual due diligence standards with respect to the beneficial owner of assets held within the PIC. The initial inquiry should be to identify the beneficial owner of the assets held within the PIC (regardless of whether the shares are held in bearer form). In addition, given that in the case of bearer shares the ownership interest may be readily transferred, a bank should take measures to prevent the misuse of bearer shares by applying, for example, one or more of the following mechanisms: (i) certification as to beneficial ownership at the outset of the relationship and when there are changes in beneficial ownership structure; (ii) immobilisation of the shares by requiring them to be held by an appropriate party; (iii) conversion of such shares to registered shares; or (iv) prohibiting bearer shares.

Q.4. What does "beneficial ownership" mean in the context of trusts?

A. In the typical case, it would be clear which person has "beneficial ownership" for the purposes of the Principles. For instance, in the case of an industrialist who establishes a trust for the benefit of his wife or minor children, the "beneficial owner" would be the industrialist settlor, namely, the "provider of funds," as contemplated by Paragraph 1.2.3 of the Principles. The appropriate due diligence should be conducted with regard to the industrialist, including background checks and the requisite inquiry as to the source of wealth. If appropriate, the banker should consider identifying the beneficial owner by reference to official identity papers.

Even though the wife and children have a beneficial interest in the trust for trust law purposes (indeed for such purposes they might appropriately be referred to as "beneficial owners"), they should not be treated as "beneficial owners" for AML purposes. That is, it would not make sense to conduct due diligence with respect to the wife's or children's source of wealth, although it may be appropriate to do some due diligence with respect to their background and reputation.

This result, incidentally, highlights the consequences of a typical feature of trusts, the separation of legal title and beneficial interest. The person having legal title, i.e. the trustee, typically has control with respect to the assets; however, the parties to the arrangement who have beneficial interests, i.e. the beneficiaries, would typically not have control. As the prior example illustrates, it is yet a third party, the settlor, as the provider of funds (who may neither have control, nor a beneficial interest in the assets of the trust) who should, from an AML point of view, be the object of due diligence. Control in these circumstances is not the determinative criterion for AML purposes, nor is beneficial interest

The fact that the settlor is deceased does not preclude the need for due diligence with respect to his/her reputation and source of wealth. In this regard, it is presumptively reasonable to look to the trustee for information regarding the source of wealth, assuming the trustee is reputable.

Q.4A. Why is it appropriate for the private banker to understand who has control over the funds held in the trust structure or who has the power to remove the trustee, even if the person having such control or power is not the source of funds?

A. If there is a person who has this level of control or power, it is appropriate for the private banker to seek an explanation for this arrangement and to undertake further inquiry, if, on its face, the arrangements are not plausible.

Moreover, a person who has this level of control or power may present reputational risk to the bank, even if the ultimate explanation for the arrangement is plausible and due diligence as to such person's reputation is warranted, if such person is not already known by the bank to be reputable.

Q.4B. Why is it appropriate for the private banker to determine the persons for whose benefit the trust is established?

A. The private banker should consider for whose benefit the trust is established in order to determine whether more inquiry would be appropriate. As noted in the answer to Question 4, in the typical case, in which the beneficiaries are, for example, members of the settlor's family, applying the same level of inquiry to the beneficiaries that would be applied to the settlor would not be warranted. This would not ordinarily be a situation posing money laundering or terrorist financing risk. If, however, the private banker determines that a beneficiary exercises control over the arrangement, the beneficiary should be treated as a beneficial owner for AML purposes, i.e. as a person subject to due diligence. Furthermore, if the private banker, in his consideration of the circumstances, determines that the arrangement is unusual (e.g. the beneficiaries' relationship to the settlor is atypical), the private banker should conduct further inquiry.

Q.4C. What should the private banker review in seeking to understand the structure of the trust sufficiently for purposes of 1.2.3?

A. The private banker may rely on declarations or attestations given by the trustee as to the "provider of funds, those who have control over the funds (e.g. trustees) and any persons who have the power to remove the trustees" as well as persons for whose benefit the trust is established, if the trustee is an institution or individual who is well-known to the private banker. If the private banker is not familiar with the institution or individual, then the private banker should undertake due diligence with respect to such institution or individual with a view to establishing a basis for reasonably accepting such declaration or attestation. It is not necessary for the private banker to obtain a copy of the trust instrument. In atypical circumstances, the private banker may determine to engage in further inquiry.

Q.5. What does beneficial ownership mean in the context of partnerships, foundations and unincorporated associations?

A. Establishing beneficial ownership in these contexts generally entails the same principles as discussed above.

Partnerships: Partnerships are comprised of partners (sometimes referred to as general or equity partners) and sometimes include limited partners. Ordinarily, the principal general or equity partners would be considered to be the "beneficial owners" for purposes of Paragraph 1.2.3. In the event the partnership includes limited partners, there may be circumstances in which a limited partner could be considered to be a "beneficial owner."

Foundations: In some jurisdictions, "foundations" may be used by clients as investment or wealth planning vehicles, much as private holding companies are used for such purposes in other jurisdictions. Foundations, however, are not "owned" by particular individuals. The private bankers should understand who the founder (typically, the client) is. The private banker should do so even if the identity of the founder (i.e. the source of funds) is not discernible from the public record.

Unincorporated Associations: If such organisations are used by clients, the private banker should understand the structure of the association (which may not be "owned" by particular individuals) and identify who provides the association with its funds and subject such person to appropriate due diligence.

Appendix 5.4   Jonathan Goldsmith: 'Clients' Money in the News'[1]

A RAFT OF MEASURES TO PREVENT MONEY LAUNDERING HIGHLIGHTS THE DIFFICULTY LAWYERS FACE IN HOLDING CONFIDENTIAL FINANCIAL INFORMATION FOR CLIENTS IN A HIGH-TECH WORLD.

The treatment of clients' money has, surprisingly, become a hot topic. Who would have thought that so many developments would occur at once (three different strands). Is there a moral here?

The longest-running story emerges from the current draft money laundering directive, the discussions on which are about to be revived (now that the period of European elections and the appointment of commissioners is drawing to a close). You may recall that this is the 4th money laundering directive, and lawyers have been caught in the coils of the series since the 2nd directive, which was the one which introduced the notorious reporting duty around suspicious transactions. The current draft 4th directive was some way through its legislative process when it was noticed there was a difference in the treatment of what are called pooled accounts (which we know as client accounts) between this version and the 3rd directive.

According to the 3rd directive (Article 11.2.b), member states may allow customer due diligence not to be applied in respect of beneficial owners of pooled accounts run by independent legal professionals. This is good, because it eliminates a burden which would otherwise be considerable. The 4th directive aims to abolish this explicit exception. The authorities feel that the simplified due diligence provisions in the 3rd directive are overly permissive, because certain categories of client or transaction are given outright exemption. The revised directive proposes to tighten the rules. Under the new system, it would be left to the member states to determine which areas they believe present a lower risk, so resulting in simplified customer due diligence measures (article 13 of 4th directive).

My organisation, the Council of Bars and Law Societies of Europe (CCBE), believes that the current system of pooled accounts works smoothly, and meets the requirements of preventing money laundering. The Law Society agrees. If pooled accounts for lawyers are abolished, lawyers would have to open a separate account for each individual case, then make a separate transfer from that account and close the account afterwards, which would be extremely burdensome. The lobbying on this point continues.

Now along come two further measures, from different sources, both dealing with tax compliance. The first is the US Foreign Account Tax Compliance Act (FATCA). You might have read about it, as it is causing US citizens living abroad to give up their citizenship in increasing numbers. FATCA requires such citizens to report their financial accounts held outside the country, and – more to the point – requires foreign financial institutions to report to the US Internal Revenue Service about their US clients. (Unlike other developed countries, the US levies income tax on citizens regardless of residence, and requires citizens living abroad to pay US taxes on foreign income.) Although the act was passed in 2010, the reporting obligation has been introduced just this summer. Foreign banks are in any case suffering heavy fines at the moment from the long arm of US law, and so there are reports of foreign banks refusing to take on US citizens as customers, because of the risk of suffering penalties for not reporting back properly under FATCA. It does not take too much imagination to see that pooled accounts might not be a favourite of such banks, since in among the many deposits pooled in one lawyer's accounts might lurk a US citizen.

The third strand comes from the OECD in Paris. It has just published its 'Standard for Automatic Exchange of Financial Information in Tax Matters', which it describes as a new single global standard between key authorities worldwide. It might be described more accurately as 'Son of FATCA', but on a world-wide basis. Here the problem relates to the confidentiality of the information. Although section 5 of the Standard deals (briefly) with confidentiality, including provisions limiting the use of the information exchanged, the question is whether the level of the Standard's confidentiality is the equivalent of the strict requirements binding lawyers under ethical and legal rules. What are we to do if client financial information held by lawyers is transferred automatically out of the country?

There is a moral here (sorry). Technology and globalisation have made passage around the world easier. Everything is becoming quicker and easier all the time. But villains have taken advantage of it for their own ends. So now air travel is slowed up by queues to take off our shoes and hand over bottles of liquids. Similarly, opening and running a bank account for clients is made difficult to the point of impossible because others shift their money around to hide its provenance or to avoid paying taxes. The annoyance of travelling by donkey cart and communicating by smoke signals has been replaced by airport pat-downs and due diligence forms.

Appendix 5.5   Alan Binnington: 'Money Laundering and Tax Evasion – the Bankers' Dilemma' (relates to Chapter 8)[1]

BACKGROUND

Jersey has had anti-money laundering legislation since the 1980's but it was only on July 1st, 1999, with the implementation of the Proceeds of Crime (Jersey) Law 1999 ("the 1999 Law") that the money laundering offences which had been created by legislation such as the Drug Trafficking Offences (Jersey) Law 1988 were extended to cover other forms of serious criminal conduct. The 1999 Law was based largely on section 93 of the UK's Criminal Justice Act 1988 ("the 1988 Act") as amended by the Criminal Justice Act 1993 which, in turn, was intended to implement the EU Council Directive of June 10th, 1991 on the Prevention of the Use of the Financial System for the Purpose of Money Laundering[2]. The EU Directive required member states to legislate to prohibit money laundering in connection with the proceeds of criminal activity, such activity being defined by reference to the crimes specified in Article 3(1)(a) of the Vienna Convention of 1988 which was directed against illicit traffic in narcotic drugs and psychotropic substances, together with such other criminal activity designated as such for the purposes of the Directive by each member state. Interestingly, the Directive did not require Member States actually to criminalise money laundering nor did it specifically refer to criminal activity in the field of tax evasion.

When the 1988 Act was amended it is widely believed that the UK Treasury did not think that tax evasion was included in the Act's definition of criminal conduct. Indeed, the Parliamentary debate on the amendments to the 1988 Act[3] focused on the evils of drug trafficking and organised crime with no mention of the Act's possible use in the field of tax evasion. However within two years the UK Government was making clear that it regarded tax evasion as an issue which was just as serious as that of drug trafficking. In October 1995, at the Commonwealth Finance Ministers' Meeting held in Jamaica, the Chancellor of the Exchequer stated that:

> "we must recognise that money laundering is associated with all types of crime – from fraud to extortion, arms smuggling to kidnapping. It is quite artificial to draw a distinction between drug related crimes and other crimes. In Britain we have responded to the shifting threat by passing legislation to cover the proceeds of all indictable offences. There is no moral difference between drug trafficking and other serious offences, the risks from both are great, and this applies as much to fiscal offences as any other crime. All crimes should mean ALL crimes. Who is the victim is irrelevant. Tax crimes make the law abiding suffer. It is they who make up the shortfall caused by those who cheat".[4]

---

1 This article first appeared in the Jersey Law Review, March 2001. Reproduced by kind permission of the publisher.
2 EC Directive 91/308.
3 Hansard, April 4th, 1993.
4 HM Treasury Press Notice No 132/95 October 5th, 1995.

How then did a statute which, at the time it was debated, did not appear to apply to tax offences, come to be applied to such offences? The answer lies in the way in which "criminal conduct" is defined, not by reference to a list of particular offences but by reference to the mode of trial of offences.

The problem of definition

The money laundering offences created by the 1988 Act, as amended, create liability where the accused has in some way dealt with a person's "proceeds of criminal conduct" with a specified degree of knowledge of that person's criminal activity. "Criminal conduct" is defined as "conduct which constitutes an offence to which this Part of this Act applies or would constitute such an offence if it had occurred in England and Wales or (as the case may be) Scotland".[1] By virtue of Section 71 of the 1988 Act, as amended, Part 6 of the Act applies to offences which are listed in Schedule 4 to the Act or, if not so listed, which are indictable offences, other than drug trafficking offences or offences under Part 3 of the Prevention of Terrorism (Temporary Provisions) Act 1989. Broadly speaking, therefore, "proceeds of criminal conduct" refers to the proceeds of indictable offences. As far as fiscal offences are concerned, under English law tax evasion is dealt with not by means of trial on indictment but by means of proceedings for a penalty before the Commissioners of the Inland Revenue. On the face of it therefore the English legislation would not appear to apply to tax evasion. This may well be the reason why, when the Act was debated, no reference was made to its application to fiscal offences. However, tax evasion will usually, in addition, involve some other form of criminal activity which is triable on indictment such as forgery or false accounting. There is, of course, also the common law offence of cheating the public revenue which was expressly preserved by Section 32(2) of the Theft Act 1968. This offence comprises any form of fraudulent conduct which results in diverting money from the Revenue and thus requires no positive act of deception[2]. Failure to make a tax return could therefore constitute the offence of cheating.

Although it is now clear that offences committed within the context of tax evasion will fall within the definition of criminal conduct for the purposes of the 1988 Act there are nevertheless difficulties in applying the Act to such offences, these difficulties arising as a result of the definition of "proceeds", difficulties which also arise under the Jersey legislation discussed below.

The Jersey legislation

The 1999 Law follows a similar pattern to the 1988 Act. Thus it creates three principal money laundering offences, namely assisting another to retain the benefit of criminal conduct[3], acquiring possessing or using the proceeds of criminal conduct[4] and concealing or transferring the proceeds of criminal conduct[5]. For the purposes of the 1999 Law "criminal conduct" is defined, in Article 32(7), as "conduct which constitutes an offence to which this Law applies or would constitute such an offence if that conduct had occurred in the Island". By virtue of the First Schedule to the Law, offences to which the Law applies are "any offence for which a person is liable on conviction to imprisonment for a term of one or more years (whether or not he is also liable to any other penalty)".

1 Section 93A (7).
2 *R v Mavji* [1987] 2 All ER 759.
3 Article 32.
4 Article 33.
5 Article 34.

Under the Income Tax (Jersey) Law 1961 the penalty for fraudulently or negligently making incorrect statements in connection with a tax return is a fine rather than a sentence of imprisonment[1]. Accordingly, as in the UK, tax evasion *per se* does not constitute criminal conduct for the purpose of the 1999 Law. However, again as in the UK, tax evasion may involve other offences, such as forgery, false accounting or common law fraud, all of which are punishable by a sentence of one or more years' imprisonment and thus fall within the definition of criminal conduct.

Cheating the revenue authorities in Jersey

The position in relation to cheating may however be different. There does not appear to be a common law offence in Jersey of cheating the public revenue. This is perhaps not particularly surprising given that Jersey was described, in 1847, as an Island in which the taxes "are so light that the Island is generally looked upon as free from taxes"[2]. The position is not wholly free from doubt but it would seem strange if the Royal Court could suddenly discover an offence which does not appear to have been charged in this jurisdiction and which depends upon the distinction, under English law, between two forms of cheating. Under English common law cheating was only an offence if it involved physical interference with the property of another against the will of its owner. It was not an offence simply to trick someone into parting with his ownership of money or other property. In the words of Holt C.J.[3]: "Shall we indict one for making a fool of another?". Where the cheating was directed against the public as a whole the common law recognised the offence where any particular member of the public suffered by it. The acts complained of did however have to include the use of a misleading device in a permanent form rather than simply the making of a false statement. Thus in *R v Jones*[4] the court stated that the cheat was "not indictable unless he came with false tokens; playing with false dice is, for that is such a cheat as a person of ordinary capacity cannot discover". In *R v Hudson*[5] which concerned the submission of false statements to the Inland Revenue, Goddard L.C.J. delivering the judgment of the Court of Criminal Appeal, reviewed the earlier authorities, noting that if one subject merely cheats another by telling him lies, that is not indictable whereas if the false representation is used to defraud the Crown it is indictable as a fraud on the public. The court went on to hold that "all frauds affecting the Crown and public at large are indictable as cheats at common law". In the circumstances of *R v Hudson*[6] it was not necessary for the court to consider whether there was any difference between an act or an omission for these purposes, as the taxpayer in that case had made a false representation.

The distinction between an act and an omission fell to be considered some 30 years later by the English Court of Appeal in *R v Mavji*[7]. The case concerned the failure by a director of a company to file value added tax returns on behalf of the company in respect of gold which it had sold and on which it had charged the tax. The court noted that neither in *R v Hudson*[8] nor in the earlier authorities was the distinction between 'deceit' involving an act and 'non deceit' involving no more than an omission canvassed or regarded as vital or indeed relevant. The court stated that: "The distinction has always been and in our view remains between

---

1 See Article 137.
2 Evidence of Mr Peter Le Sueur, Advocate, at para 2018 of the 1847 *Report of the Commissioners appointed to inquire into the criminal law of the Channel Islands.*
3 In *R v Jones* (1703) 2 Ld.Raym.1013.
4 *Supra.*
5 [1956] 1 All ER 814.
6 *Supra.*
7 *Supra.*
8 *Supra.*

'frauds affecting the Crown and public at large', to repeat the words of Hawkins, and those which affect only individuals".

The Jersey position

The position under Jersey law would appear to be different. Cheating the revenue does not appear to have been charged as such in Jersey. It is more likely to be charged as fraud or false accounting. Furthermore, having conducted a comprehensive review of Jersey case law the Court of Appeal, in *Foster v Att. Gen*[1], concluded that whilst it is not easy to draw a general rule from local cases of criminal fraud the cases "justify the proposition that to establish criminal fraud it is necessary to show that the defendant deliberately made a false representation with intention of causing thereby – and with the result in fact of causing thereby – actual prejudice to someone and actual benefit to himself or somebody else". This would seem to suggest that a deliberate act is required rather than an omission. This would certainly be consistent with the Jersey authorities referred to in the Court of Appeal's judgement. The one exception referred to in that judgment would appear to be the case of *Attorney General v O'Brien*[2] which arose from the Out of Work Donations granted by the States after the First World War to demobilised soldiers until they found employment. The two defendants had both had a few days paid employment whilst receiving the allowance, but had not informed the Out of Work Donations Committee. They were convicted of having *"commis une fraude au préjudice des Etats"*. The judgment is silent as to whether there was any form of representation and as the defendants admitted the facts the matter was not argued. The difficulty with such cases is that, as the Court of Appeal itself stated in *Foster*, "it is not easy to draw a general rule from local cases with criminal fraud because it is very rare to find in the records any reasons for the court's decision".[3] Notwithstanding the O'Brien decision the position would seem to be in Jersey that a positive act is required rather than an omission. On this basis the failure to file a tax return would not constitute fraud whereas the filing of a false return would. This distinction may not be particularly problematical from the point of view of criminal law generally but, as will be seen, may pose difficulties in relation to the reporting requirements under the 1999 Law.

The problem of "Proceeds"

The difficulties of applying the 1999 Law to fiscal offences do not end with the definition of criminal conduct. Article 1(1) of the 1999 Law provides that "proceeds of criminal conduct" in relation to any person who has benefited from criminal conduct, means that benefit". Article 1(2) then provides that "where a person derives a pecuniary advantage as a result of or in connection with the commission of an offence or with criminal conduct, he is to be treated as if he had obtained as a result of or in connection with the commission of that offence, or that conduct, a sum of money equal to the value of the pecuniary advantage.

Where a person commits, for example, a robbery it is fairly easy to identify the proceeds of his criminal conduct. However in the case of tax evasion, which usually results in the taxpayer simply paying less tax than he should, it is likely to be difficult to identify the proceeds. Although Article 1(2) provides, in effect, that the tax evader is to be treated as if he had obtained a sum of money equal to the amount of the tax that he has saved, the 1999 Law provides no guidance as to where that sum is to be found. In the case of the robber it is relatively easy to identify the amount taken from say, a bank, and then to trace its progress through

---

1   1992 JLR 6.
2   (1919) 27 PC106.
3   1992 JLR 6 at 26.

the money laundering process. Although its character may be changed as a result of the laundering operation one is likely to be able to follow an audit trail and identify the ultimate destination of the funds. However in the case of the tax evader it is not possible to do this. Tax is not usually payable out of a specific fund. This difficulty in identifying "proceeds" in the case of fiscal offences is however a difficulty both for the prosecution and for the defence.

An illustration

One can illustrate the difficulties by reference to Article 32 of the 1999 Law which deals with the offence of assisting another to retain the benefit of criminal conduct. Article 32 provides:

"(1)   Subject to paragraph (3), if a person enters into or is otherwise concerned in an arrangement whereby -

    (a)   the retention or control by or on behalf of another (in this Article referred to as "A") of A's proceeds of criminal conduct is facilitated (whether by concealment, removal from the jurisdiction, transfer to nominees or otherwise); or

    (b)   A's proceeds of criminal conduct –

        (i)   are used to secure that funds are placed at A's disposal; or

        (ii)   are used for A's benefit to acquire property by way of investment, knowing or suspecting that A is a person who is or has been engaged in criminal conduct or has benefited from criminal conduct, he is guilty of an offence."

The prosecution therefore have to prove (1) the defendant's participation in an arrangement which assists in the retention or control of A's proceeds of criminal conduct; and (2) that the defendant knew or suspected that A is a person who is or has been engaged in criminal conduct or has benefited from criminal conduct. In a fiscal case the prosecution may be in some difficulty in proving that the particular funds being dealt with by the arrangement are the proceeds of criminal conduct for the reasons referred to above. However the defendant is not in a position to rely on that difficulty when it comes to proof of his knowledge of suspicion, as the knowledge or suspicion relates not to the question as to whether or not the funds are the proceeds of criminal conduct but as to whether or not A is a person 'who is or has been engaged in criminal conduct'. Accordingly the defendant may not suspect that the particular funds are the proceeds of a fiscal offence but if he suspected that A had previously engaged in any form of criminal conduct he could be found guilty if it turns out that the funds were the proceeds of entirely different criminal conduct, namely a fiscal offence. Article 32(4) does however provide a defence if the defendant can prove that "he did not know or suspect that the arrangement related to any person's proceeds of criminal conduct". However the burden of proof is then on the defendant and if the court is satisfied that the proceeds were in fact the proceeds of a fiscal offence academic arguments as to the difficulties of identifying proceeds in fiscal cases are unlikely to advance the matter much further.

The problem of suspicion

The difficulty of identifying "proceeds" in fiscal offences also presents a practical problem as a result of the indirect requirement imposed by the 1999 Law to report suspicious transactions.

Each of the principal money laundering offences provides, as a defence, that if the defendant carries out the act complained of with the consent of a police officer having disclosed his suspicion or belief that property is derived from or used in connection with criminal conduct then the offence is not committed. Thus although the 1999 Law does not impose a positive obligation to report it provides a substantial incentive, in the form of a potential defence, for doing so[1]. In the case of non fiscal offences, deciding whether or not there is knowledge or suspicion may well be relatively straight forward, albeit that there may be difficulties depending on whether the offence in question requires the application of an objective or a subjective test. However in the case of fiscal offences the problem is more acute. In the absence of decided cases on the point it would be unsafe to assume that merely because there are difficulties in identifying the proceeds of a fiscal offence one does not have to report a person who one suspects of evading tax. Some comfort may perhaps be drawn from the fact that if the offence of cheating the public revenue is unknown to Jersey law some positive act will be required over and above a mere failure to pay tax, which act is likely to arouse suspicion and thus trigger the desire to report. Until a case comes before the courts the debate will continue as to how much information about a taxpayer's affairs will lead to suspicion of fiscal criminal conduct.

Difficulties may also arise where there is a suspicion that the client is evading tax in his home country but for reasons which, whilst they involve illegality, are nevertheless understandable. The obvious example is where the client is resident in a country where corruption is endemic and where those responsible for tax collection routinely pass information to criminal groups who then kidnap a member of the taxpayer's family in the hope of extracting a large ransom. Whilst one may have every sympathy with the taxpayer in those circumstances, from a moral point of view, the strict legal position is that if an offence such as fraud is involved then one is dealing with criminal conduct and failing to disclose a suspicion renders one liable for an offence in the event that either the prosecutor or the court decides to take the strict, rather than the moral, view.

Conclusion

The history of the EU Council Directive and the 1988 Act, which are the sources of Jersey's 1999 Law suggest that in the drafting process little thought was given to the difficulties of applying this legislation to fiscal offences. For those who might one day find themselves charged with a money laundering offence relating to fiscal matters some comfort may be drawn from the fact that some of the difficulties may hinder the prosecutor in securing a conviction. However from the point of view of the operation of a financial services business, such as a bank, these difficulties of application will frequently pose significant problems given the indirect requirement to report suspicious transactions. Reporting one's customer to the police on the basis that one suspects him of having engaged in criminal conduct is a drastic step. On the other hand, failing to report a suspicious transaction and, as a result, being convicted of a money laundering offence, which carries with it a potential sentence of imprisonment of up to 14 years, is an extremely serious matter. For understandable reasons neither government nor prosecutors wish to give greater guidance as to the application of all crimes money laundering legislation to fiscal offences. This is an unsatisfactory state of affairs but it would seem that we shall have to wait for the first test case before the matter is clarified.

Alan Binnington is an advocate of the Royal Court and a Private Client Director at BBC Trust (International) Limited, La Motte Chambers, St Helier, Jersey, JE1 1PB.

---

1 This can be contrasted with Article 18A of the Drug Trafficking Offences (Jersey) Law 1988 where failure to disclose a suspicion relating to drug money laundering is a specific offence.

Appendix 6

Suspicious Transaction Reports ('STRS') and Reporting

NCA Suspicious Activity Reports ('SARs') Annual Report 2013

Statement by the Chair of the SARs Regime Committee

I am pleased to publish the Suspicious Activity Reports (SARs) Regime Committee Annual Report for 2013. This represents a milestone in the lifetime of the regime which started with Sir Stephen Lander's review of April 2006, with this report being the last under the Serious Organised Crime Agency (SOCA) before it transitioned into the newly created National Crime Agency (NCA).

It is opportune in that context to review progress made during the last seven years, which has seen a remarkable transformation under the oversight of the SARs Regime Committee. This has seen the development of a solid public and private sector partnership which, even in a period of economic austerity, has still managed to drive forward a strategy focused on improving performance and impactive outcomes.

This last year has seen significant operational challenges driven by: continuing increases in SARs submitted; an increased number of requests for consent; commitments arising from the Arab Spring; and an increased requirement to service the needs of our international partners and those in the financial counter terrorism community. Additionally, new initiatives, projects and proof of concept work for new ways of working under the NCA have provided new challenges and learning which will shape thinking in the new agency.

As in previous years, the regime's technology has required constant support and maintenance in order to provide added resilience and to maintain service until a replacement system can be implemented. We have continued to support users of the ARENA system with a view to ensuring the information is exploited to its fullest extent, whilst maintaining the necessary data protection measures and requirements.

Additionally, this year saw the implementation of a new model of engagement with stakeholders and whilst still relatively early days, the response has been overwhelmingly positive from all sectors, particularly reporters.

On the international front the UK Financial Intelligence Unit (UKFIU) has continued to engage with partners with a view to supporting and influencing arrangements going forward, particularly as they relate to the transition of FIU. Net into Europol, support to HM Treasury on the proposed Fourth European Union Money Laundering Directive, and the Financial Action Task Force (FATF). Internally we continue to explore enhancing our international relationships and upgrading our technology supporting the sharing of information internationally.

Over the year SOCA prioritised the UKFIU's technology and resourcing requirements in order to ensure the provision of an improved service to the regime's stakeholders. This has been successful to date although there remains more to be achieved.

As this report represents an important landmark in the history of the SARs Regime covering the last reporting year under SOCA, I wish to formally thank all regime participants, and members of the SARs Regime Committee, for their contribution over the past seven years in developing the regime to the strong position it now finds itself in today. I am confident that we have left SOCA with a lasting legacy and provided the NCA with a solid footing upon which to build further.

Trevor Pearce (Former Director General of SOCA)

Director, National Crime Agency
Chair of the SARs Regime Committee

Summary

This is the seventh Annual Report of the Suspicious Activity Reports (SARs) Regime Committee, and the final one recording progress of the UK Financial Intelligence Unit (UKFIU) under the governance of the Serious Organised Crime Agency (SOCA). On 7 October 2013, SOCA ceased to exist and the UKFIU became part of the Intelligence Hub of the newly formed National Crime Agency (NCA). Although this report is published by the NCA, it refers to the reporting period of October 2012 to September 2013 under the management of SOCA.

The format of recent Annual Reports followed the main aims of a three-year strategy set for the regime in 2009. These aims were:

1.   Appropriate SARs to be submitted by the full range of reporting sectors.

2.   Maximising the use of information provided by reporters while ensuring proportionality.

3.   Supporting and enhancing the technical capabilities and experience of all SARs Regime participants.

4.   Continuing improvement of the governance and transparency of the regime.

As this strategy concluded in 2012, and with the establishment of the NCA on the horizon, it was agreed by the Committee that setting a further strategy would not be appropriate until the NCA structures, roles and functions had been more clearly defined. It was agreed that an interim plan which focused on maintaining business as usual, with a view to ensuring a smooth transition into the NCA, would be appropriate. Business aims underscoring the UKFIU's activity would be:

1.   Continued engagement with end users and the reporting sectors.

2.   Continued focus on the resilience of ELMER[1] and work towards a subsequent replacement.

3.   Contribute to the development of the national and international operating and legislative environment influencing money laundering and terrorist financing, ensuring that the UKFIU is well placed upon creation of the NCA.

These areas will be the cornerstone of this year's report. As such the report will be structured as follows:

- Part One: Performance
- Part Two: Forward Look

Part One: Performance

Part One outlines the performance of the SARs Regime from October 2012 to September 2013, and is structured around the three overarching aims for the UKFIU as described in the last SARs Annual Report:

1.   Continued engagement with end users and the reporting sectors to improve the level of SAR submissions, activity taken from those SARs, and feedback to the reporting sectors.

---

1 The SARs database in SOCA/NCA.

2.   Increased focus on the resilience of ELMER and work towards a subsequent replacement.

3.   Comment on and develop the national and international operating and legislative environment influencing money laundering and terrorist financing, ensuring that the UKFIU is well placed upon creation of the NCA.

For new readers there is a brief overview of the SARs Regime included in Annex A, a list of SARs Regime Committee members in Annex B, and a Glossary of Terms in Annex G.

The SARs Regime Committee was set up in October 2006, and since then it has had active oversight of SOCA's/the NCA's discharge of its responsibilities within the regime and the effective involvement of stakeholders in the way in which the regime operates.[1]

The Annual Report contributes towards the UK's obligations under the Third European Union Money Laundering Directive to provide feedback to industry on SARs.

Key statistics

Since the publication of the first SARs Annual Report in 2007, the number of SARs has increased significantly year-on-year: in 2007 there were 220,484 SARs received. In this reporting period (2012–13) there were 316,527 – an increase of almost 38,000 from the previous year. The SARs Regime Committee members believe the upward trend to be the result of outreach work and awareness raising, rather than a greater risk of money laundering in the UK.

Although the volume presents challenges for the UKFIU and end users, it does mean that a larger pool of SARs information is available overall, which significantly improves opportunities to identify and develop intelligence on the criminal perpetrators and their activities.

Figures i and ii show the number of SARs received, the number of consent requests made to the UKFIU, and the methods of reporting in the past two reporting years.

Figure i: Key statistics for the SARs Regime

Key statistics	Oct 12 to Sept 13	Oct 11 to Sept 12
Total SARs	316,527	278,665
Consent SARs	14,103	12,915
Percentage submitted electronically	99.25%	98.87%
Percentage submitted manually	0.75%	1.13%
Breaches of confidentiality	2	0

Although Figure i records two formal allegations of a breach of confidentiality, one proved to be unfounded and the second, involving material sent to an overseas agency, was fully investigated and dealt with by the foreign financial intelligence unit.

---

1 For the reporting period of October 2006–October 2007.

Figure ii: Methods of reporting SARs

	SAR Online[1]	CSV file/ encrypted bulk data[2]	Word/ encrypted email	Paper	Total
Oct 2012	5,011	21,621	1	198	26,831
Nov 2012	5,316	21,231	3	227	26,777
Dec 2012	3,526	19,650	1	183	23,360
Jan 2013	4,812	20,435	4	182	25,433
Feb 2013	4,963	20,162	1	240	25,366
Mar 2013	4,599	19,127	0	199	23,925
Apr 2013	4,507	20,763	15	185	25,470
May 2013	4,694	23,766	0	215	28,675
Jun 2013	4,321	21,869	21	191	26,402
Jul 2013	5,443	23,562	21	205	29,231
Aug 2013	4,854	23,031	6	179	28,070
Sept 2013	4,372	22,430	8	177	26,987
Total SARs	56,418	257,647	81	2,381	316,527
Total Reporters	4,440	18	2	702	5,095

Electronic reporting

The ratio of reports submitted electronically and manually (i.e. on paper) remained consistent with last year's figures (see Figure i). This continues to assist the UKFIU in dealing with SARs more efficiently and effectively, and is a direct result of engagement between the UKFIU and reporters to encourage electronic reporting. This figure is in stark contrast to the 13.30% paper submissions during the period covered by the first SARs Annual Report (2006–2007) and represents a significant achievement. To strengthen this message, in 2013 the UKFIU created a communication product – 'Submitting a SAR Within The Regulated Sector' – providing further advice on using SAR Online, made available via the SOCA website.

The UKFIU has reviewed SAR Online and recognises there are issues with its usability; however, these should be redressed through the IT upgrade programme.

New reporters

There were 2,677 new SAR Online registrations (Figure iii) during this reporting year. This includes registrations from 1,946 unique institutions[3] (72.69% of all new

---

1 SAR Online is a secure web-based reporting mechanism that can be used by everyone with internet access.
2 The UKFIU provides 'Public Key Infrastructure' encryption certificates which allow high volume reporters to submit encrypted files directly onto the SARs database.
3 New registrants are classified as unique institutions if they are not an outlet of an existing SAR Online user.

registrations) that were completely new to SAR Online. The remaining registrations were from individuals working for institutions already using the system.

The number of new individual estate agent registrants increased by over 97.83% on 2011/12 (up from 46 to 91). This follows a large number of workshops the UKFIU has conducted with the Office of Fair Trading (OFT) to raise anti-money laundering (AML) awareness in this sector.

Figure iii: New individual registrants to SAR Online by sector[1]

	Oct 12 to Sept 13	Oct 11 to Sept 12
Accountants	23.80%	28.68%
Banks	3.21%	3.07%
Building Societies	0.75%	0.79%
Estate Agents	3.40%	1.81%
Financial Services	9.00%	9.64%
Gambling	0.90%	0.79%
Government	0.34%	0.55%
High Value Dealers	3.55%	2.60%
Legal	18.75%	20.97%
Money Service Businesses (MSBs)	9.64%	10.39%
Stocks & Shares	4.45%	4.52%
Other	22.23%	16.21%
Totals	2,677	2,542

Analysis of SARs reporting by sector

As in previous years, the largest reporter of SARs continued to be the banking sector. The sector made up 79.40% of all SARs. It is believed that this is possibly in response to regulatory actions within the global financial sector. As with last year, money service businesses (MSBs) were the second largest reporting sector (6.74% for 2012/13, compared to 8.40% last year). It is always difficult to attempt to establish what is a 'correct' level of reporting by the sectors – a more comprehensive breakdown can be found in Annex C at the back of this report.

---

1 Sector categories are chosen by reporters on registration.

Figure iv shows the proportion of total SARs submitted by sector.

Figure iv: SARs submitted by sector 2012/2013

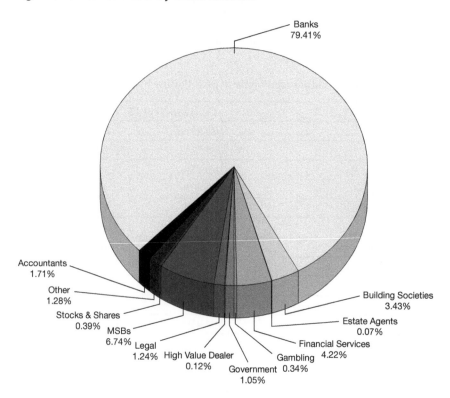

Figure v below breaks these numbers down by sector.

Figure v: SARs submitted by sector

Oct 12 to Sept 13	Volumes	% of Total
Accountants	5,428	1.71%
Banks	251,336	79.40%
Building Societies	10,844	3.43%
Estate Agents	215	0.07%
Financial Services	13,359	4.22%
Gambling	1,062	0.34%
Government	3,338	1.05%
High Value Dealer	383	0.12%
Legal	3,935	1.24%
Money Service Businesses (MSBs)	21,343	6.74%
Stocks & Shares	1,224	0.39%
Other	4,060	1.28%
Totals	316,527	100%

Figure vi: SARs submitted by the financial services sector

Oct 12 to Sept 13	Volumes	% of Total
Consumer Credit	148	1.11%
Credit Card	4,027	30.14%
Credit Union	330	2.47%
Electronic Payment	1,468	10.99%
Finance Company	4,517	33.81%
Friendly Society	8	0.06%
Independent Financial Advisor	7	0.05%
Insurance	2,254	16.87%
Mortgage Provider	155	1.16%
Pension Provider	217	1.62%
Retail Intermediary	228	1.71%
Totals	13,359	100%

Figure vii: SARs submitted by money service businesses

Oct 12 to Sept 13	Volumes	% of Total
Money Transmission	14,191	66.49%
Cheque Casher	5,063	23.72%
Bureau de Change	2,089	9.79%
Totals	21,343	100%

Engagement with regime participants

The UKFIU attended over 232 conferences, events, presentations and meetings during the year aimed at participants of the SARs Regime. This included 94 events for reporters, 102 for law enforcement agencies (LEAs), and 36 supervisor/ professional body/trade association visits. This does not however include the numerous telephone calls and emails conducted between the UKFIU and regime participants. These figures represent almost a doubling in the number of such visits reported in last year's report, which recorded a total of 128 events.

New model of engagement

In 2012, the SARs Regime Committee agreed that a 'new model of engagement' be developed with a view to delivering feedback and outreach more effectively, particularly taking into account available resources. This year saw the implementation of the model.

The key principles which support the new model of engagement are:

- To provide feedback on the SARs Regime for reporters.
- To provide greater analysis of SARs informing stakeholders of emerging thematic or geographical trends in a timely manner.
- To undertake analysis of SARs to inform engagement with the supervisors and professional bodies/ trade associations which represent stakeholders, in order to better understand, distil, design and communicate information to improve regime effectiveness.

Supervisors and professional bodies

Over the year, the focus has been on engagement with the reporting sectors, especially in relation to achieving the goal of providing effective feedback. This has included working with the Anti-Money Laundering Supervisors' Forum (AMLSF)[1] Affinity Groups regarding implementation, with overall feedback being positive. The UKFIU further liaised with regulators, supervisors and trade associations, who assisted in delivering key messages to their members through their pre-existing secure delivery mechanisms.

The UKFIU worked collaboratively with sector regulators such as the Gambling Commission and the Solicitors Regulation Authority to provide information related to the SARs supplied by, and also in respect of, their areas of business. This was done to assist the regulators in updating their own risk profiles. During the year two urgent UKFIU bulletins were sent to UK law societies around fraud typologies identified and developed by the Consent Team.

Financial services sector

The financial services sector continues to be the major contributor of SARs, in particular the retail banks. The UKFIU recognises the importance of its relationship with banks and building societies and chairs a quarterly meeting – the Proceeds of Crime Operational Group (POCG) – with the British Bankers' Association, Building Societies Association and their respective members. The POCG provides a mechanism for discussing and resolving operational matters concerning the effective operation of the regime and also offers an opportunity for feedback.

High volume reporters of SARs, including retail banks, continue to receive an annual feedback report on reporting quality and positive investigative outcomes, which is well received by the recipients.

To expand its reach under the new model, the UKFIU has initiated engagement with professional bodies representing banks encompassing the wholesale, investment and wealth sectors, particularly those which may have smaller operations within the UK. In this reporting year, the UKFIU has had positive engagement with the Association of Foreign Banks and the UK Chinese Bankers' Association, which has facilitated the improvement of communications and the provision of feedback.

Money service businesses

Through Project Quaver, SOCA worked closely with Her Majesty's Revenue & Customs (HMRC), the Financial Services Authority (FSA)[2] and other law enforcement agencies in the UK and overseas to reduce the risk of money laundering at MSBs. During the year, the UKFIU supported Project Quaver through engagement with MSBs by providing SAR related feedback and anti-money laundering guidance.

SOCA continued to tackle the threat from mass marketing fraud by focusing on key levers which enable organised criminals to conduct such fraud. MSBs are one such enabler. SOCA analysed information provided by a major MSB regarding all payments made over the six month period of June to November 2011 from a sample area in the UK. This resulted in the identification of a large number of victims and established that a high percentage of the payments were associated with fraud.

SOCA produced a victim profile which is now being used by the MSB to identify victims of fraud. SARs submitted by the MSB in question almost tripled as a result (from 1,389 in 2010 to 3,911 for the same quarter in 2012).

---

1 The AMLSF brings together those UK bodies with supervisory responsibilities under the Money Laundering Regulations 2007.
2 As of April 2013 the FSA became the Financial Conduct Authority (FCA).

Building societies

In 2010 and 2011 respectively, the number of SARs submitted by building societies averaged at 646 and 607 per month respectively. Following outreach work with building societies which began in January 2012 and continued into 2013, the number of SARs submitted has now increased to an average of 900 per month this year.

Estate agents

The programme of outreach continued with the property professionals sector, including UKFIU participation in Office of Fair Trading (OFT) workshops (one in Northern Ireland), and events by the National Association of Estate Agents (NAEA), National Association of Valuers and Auctioneers (NAVA) and Guild of Property Professionals. There were also meetings with individual estate agents and the professional bodies.

SARs Twice Yearly Reporter Booklet

One of the successes of the new model of engagement was the introduction of a new UKFIU communications product: the SARs Twice Yearly Reporter Booklet. The aim of the product – first issued in March, followed by a second in September – was:

- To share perspectives on the use of SARs with participants of the regime.
- To share and encourage best practice among reporters.
- To provide a feedback mechanism to the UKFIU about the operation of the regime.
- To highlight successful law enforcement outcomes in case studies.

Feedback from recipients has been very positive.

Guidance products

Other publications issued during this period included:

- Fraud typologies to UK law societies.
- 'Reporting Requirements on International Standards', done in conjunction with HM Treasury, the Financial Services Authority and the Home Office.
- 'Engagement with the UKFIU'.
- 'Submitting a SAR within the Regulated Sector'.
- 'Obtaining Consent Guidance from SOCA under Part 7 of the Proceeds of Crime Act (POCA) 2002 or under Part 3 of the Terrorism Act (TACT) 2000'.

End users

Based on the UKFIU's new model of engagement, officers undertook an extensive schedule of end user visits within their respective geographic regions of responsibility. Although the principal aim of these visits was to reinvigorate wider use of the ARENA[1] system and consequently further exploitation of SAR information, these visits also:

- Provided new and existing users with a better understanding of ARENA functionality and of best practice gathered from other end users through the ARENA user group.
- Sought to improve the knowledge of ARENA Subject Matter Experts (SMEs) and therefore their confidence in leading future ARENA training for their officers.

---

1 A search and analysis software tool for end users of SARs.

- Enabled UKFIU officers to establish closer working relationships with their respective end users.
- Provided an opportunity for UKFIU officers to discuss the current priorities and developments within the regime and ensure police forces are adhering to our policies on governance.

The aim of these visits has been to ultimately increase the analysis of SAR information through the use of ARENA. There is an ambition for the managed expansion of ARENA user access by police forces beyond their Economic Crime Units, and into different areas of end users such as Major Crime Units and Confidential Units. This will allow SAR information to be exploited beyond traditional Financial Investigation Units, while still maintaining SAR confidentiality.

SAR confidentiality

SOCA continued to work with investigators and prosecutors to ensure compliance with the guidance provided by 'Home Office Circular 53/2005: Money Laundering: The Confidentiality And Sensitivity of Suspicious Activity Reports And The Identity of Those Who Make Them'. In order to reinforce the Circular, SOCA maintained a dedicated hotline for reporters to raise concerns about the inappropriate use of SARs. This continues into the National Crime Agency.

In the reporting period, two formal allegations of a breach of confidentiality were made by reporters. One proved to be unfounded and the second, involving material disseminated to an overseas agency, was subject of a full investigation and report from the FIU which received the intelligence. As a consequence local procedures have been revised and the reporting institution informed.

A further breach of confidentiality was self-reported by a law enforcement agency (LEA). Although a formal risk assessment did not identify any risk to any reporter, SOCA suspended an individual's access to SARs pending a review by the LEA's professional standards department. As a result of the professional standards investigation, the individual responsible was given a written misconduct warning and removed from the LEA's Financial Investigation Unit. The matter has been discussed with the reporter and they were content with the action taken.

Over the year the UKFIU undertook a policy to up-skill its staff, as a result of which the vast majority of staff received specific training with the Proceeds of Crime Centre (POCC), formerly of the National Policing Improvement Agency (NPIA) and now with the NCA, to become accredited Financial Intelligence Officers. This training also emphasised the duty of care to reporters and how SARs material can be used.

Vulnerable persons

During the year there was an increase in partnership working across multiple agencies. One of the consequences has been the identification of members of the public who are vulnerable, or likely to become vulnerable to financial crime. The UKFIU (in its role of receiving, analysing and disseminating SARs), has a role in providing SAR information effectively and efficiently to support the activity of partners and protect the public.

While fulfilling their anti-money laundering and terrorist financing obligations, reporters sometimes identify those who are being exploited or who are potential victims of fraud. The UKFIU has implemented procedures to identify SARs containing information on various types of fraud that prey upon vulnerable members of society. Common types of fraud include romance fraud[1], boiler room

---

1 Dating or romance scam, when the 'perfect partner', usually online, gains the victim's trust and asks for money.

fraud[1], 419 fraud[2] and pension liberation fraud. Relevant SARs are identified and passed to police forces who will, in many cases, arrange visits by local officers to offer advice in order to prevent fraud or further losses. In the reporting period 552 such SARs were identified and disseminated to police partners.

Case study

SARs indicated that the subject had sent almost £70,000 from various financial institutions to a receiver in Ghana. Enquiries were made to establish any vulnerability issues and the subject was visited by officers. The subject agreed that they had been a victim of a romance scam and would refrain from sending any further cash.

Pension liberation – 'Project Bloom'

The UKFIU is a partner in Project Bloom, a multi-agency initiative, started in mid 2012 between industry, law enforcement and regulators, which aims to address the threat of pension liberation fraud. This is a form of fraud where members of the public are encouraged to access their pension before retirement, following false representations of anticipated levels of returns when investments are either non-existent, or incapable of providing such a return.

The full extent of the value of money being fraudulently liberated from existing pension schemes is estimated at £400 million annually.[3] In January the UKFIU introduced a new SAR Glossary Code specific to pension liberation fraud to assist reporters and end users in the reporting and identification of money laundering resulting from this type of fraud.

The statistics in Figure viii below illustrate the rise in SARs reporting on this type of fraud.

Figure viii: SARs relating to Pension Liberation Fraud

	Total SARs	Consent SARs	Consents as a percentage of total SARs
Oct 2012	34	32	94%
Nov 2012	57	38	67%
Dec 2012	19	18	95%
Jan 2012	32	26	81%
Feb 2013	107	86	80%
Mar 2013	128	98	77%
Apr 2013	167	112	67%
May 2013	261	149	57%
Jun 2013	188	66	35%
Jul 2013	123	36	29%
Aug 2013	105	14	13%
Sept 2013	124	22	18%

1 Involves bogus stockbrokers, usually based overseas, cold calling people to pressure them into buying shares that promise high returns. In reality, the shares are either worthless or non-existent.
2 Victims are targeted to make advance or upfront payments for goods/services/financial gains that do not materialise.
3 The Pensions Regulator Annual Report and Accounts, 2012–2013.

The UKFIU has supported the project through the identification of search parameters to enable the timely recognition of pension liberation frauds and also secured the agreement of the project's Delivery Group to allocate liberation cases to only two LEAs, thus maintaining a consistent approach to enforcement action.

In addition to this operational support, the team continues to assist a wide range of reporters in submitting consent requests when pension liberation is suspected. It also assists LEAs in identifying opportunities to intervene where a vulnerable person has been the victim of a pension fraud, or when a suspect may have been identified.

Themes and trends

The SARs Data Exploitation Team (SDET) was created in 2012 as an analytical unit within the UKFIU. The team's prime objective is to undertake analysis to identify those patterns and trends which could illustrate changes in criminal, reporter or end user behaviour in support of the new model of engagement with the ultimate objective being the improvement in the overall quality of SARs.

The team has begun partnership work with industry analysts from the reporting sector. The aim is to share information (where possible) across the sectors, cognisant that the reporting sectors sometimes identify new criminal trends first. This work will enable the identification of and subsequent sharing of good practice and intelligence across the SARs Regime.

Geography – jurisdictions of risk

Substantial criminal proceeds generated in the UK are laundered overseas and it is clear that some jurisdictions pose a greater risk in facilitating this criminality. SDET utilised a comprehensive matrix developed by the SOCA Criminal Finance and Profits Team. This matrix, recognised by the Home Office and HM Treasury, is being used by SDET as a prioritisation tool in their work.

500 euro note

The use of the 500 euro note has long been recognised as being attractive to money launderers owing to the ease of portability of large volumes of cash. Research undertaken during the year concluded that whilst the note is no longer issued in the UK, in a six month period in 2012, £2.2 million worth of this type of note was reported in SARs. This research is continuing to inform the strategic picture.

Glossary Codes

During the year the UKFIU, with the support of the SARs Regime Committee, embarked on a piece of work reviewing the SAR Glossary of Terms (also known as the SAR Glossary Codes), and their use by SARs Regime participants. The codes were introduced in 2007, following requests from reporters, to enhance the ability of end users to exploit reports and to reduce the effort expended by reporters in completing SARs. The codes are not mandatory but do assist in identifying reports which relate to certain activities.

The review, which took the form of questionnaires and interviews, entailed extensive consultation with the SARs Regime Committee, trade associations, supervisors, regulators, reporters and end users. Analysis of SARs was also conducted by the UKFIU.

The review concluded that the glossary codes served a worthwhile purpose for the major end users. Additionally, feedback from other end users suggested that greater use of the codes would be made if there was more consistency and reliability around their use.

The review and subsequent discussion with the SARs Committee took into account the planned replacement of the ELMER system, and it was acknowledged that any major changes would be unlikely to gain sufficient traction in the short term. Therefore it was agreed that some housekeeping of the codes would be undertaken, removing the emphasis on predicate offences and focusing on those codes which are necessary to identify the money laundering area rather than the predicate offence. This process has been supported by a re-issuing of the codes.

SOCA Alerts

SOCA shared assessed intelligence and information on specific or generic dangers or threats from serious organised criminality with the private sector, trade bodies and relevant regulators in the form of a SOCA Alert (now NCA Alerts). Each Alert is targeted to enable such organisations to take crime prevention action. SOCA also distributed one-to-one intelligence releases for more sensitive intelligence, such as potential corruption or specific attacks. SARs information can be used to inform the writing of Alerts.

Over this reporting period, 581 SARs were submitted by reporters as a result of SOCA Alerts. The vast majority of these SARs derived from two Alerts: one published in January 2011 called 'Protecting the Elderly and Vulnerable Through The Suspicious Activity Reports (SARs) Regime'; the other published in February 2013 entitled 'Update on the Remit of the Department for Work and Pensions (DWP) Fraud Investigation Service (FIS) and Single Fraud Investigation Service (SFIS)'.

The latter was issued on behalf of the DWP and enabled several banks to identify funds that might have been obtained through fraud. It outlined seven key areas of common fraud types and identified the intelligence most useful to investigations to counter each of these. This Alert led to at least £9,848 of fraudulent funds being recovered through the indemnity process.

Other Alerts published in this reporting period which were linked to SAR submissions included: 'Terrorist Funding Through UK-Based Fraud'; 'Maritime Piracy Ransom Payment Tracking'; 'Prepaid Debit Cards used for Criminal Activity'; 'Fraudulent Applications for DWP Crisis Loans'; 'Bank and Personal Data associated with Money Laundering'; 'Combating Sales of New Psychoactive Substances'; 'Department of Work and Pensions Update on the Launch of Universal Credit'; 'Compromised Accounts to Facilitate Fraud'; 'Eastern European Money Mules' and 'Title Implications of UK/Swiss Tax Agreements for Criminal Funds held in Switzerland'.

This last Alert was published to inform reporters of the potential implications of the UK/Swiss Tax Co-operation Agreement that was going to affect UK account holders. Due to the agreement, from 31 May 2013, individuals were to lose their anonymity and become subject to tax liabilities. The Alert sought to ensure that those individuals trying to conceal their assets by removing funds from the affected accounts were identified.

In addition, four other Alerts from previous reporting years led to further SARs being submitted: 'The Exploitation of UK Money Service Businesses (MSBs) by Organised Crime'; 'Criminal attacks on EU Emission Trading Scheme Registries'; 'Intelligence Release Pertaining to Romanian Nationals' and 'Abuse of UK Banking System by UK Money Service Businessmen to Facilitate Tax and Duty Evasion in Pakistan'.

Staffing and development

Throughout the year there were concerns around staffing within the UKFIU and its ability to meet SOCA's mandated regime responsibilities. These concerns were escalated to the SOCA Board, which prioritised the UKFIU business area and secured the allocation of additional resources.

The UKFIU establishment has been increased and currently has only a few vacant positions. The unique position of the UKFIU and its resourcing requirements was recognised in the transition from SOCA to the NCA and has been migrated as a complete entity.

Industry awareness

As part of the UKFIU's designated powers requirement, there is a need for the UKFIU staff's knowledge and understanding to remain current with regard to the law and to undergo continuous professional development.

In March, the UKFIU held two successful 'Industry Awareness' days for its staff, the first of their kind. The purpose of the events was to support UKFIU staff of all grades in developing their level of skill, knowledge, understanding and experience necessary to carry out their duties to the high standard expected of a national bureau, ensuring the FIU is recognised nationally and internationally as a centre of excellence.

Presentations were given by representatives from HM Treasury (HMT), the Home Office (HO), Gambling Commission, Law Society of England and Wales, Solicitors Regulation Authority (SRA), Financial Services Authority (FSA) and Barclays Bank. These addressed anti-money laundering/counter terrorist financing from the reporting context, looking at the difficulties and sensitivities, and rules and regulations with which regulators, supervisors, reporters and others wrestle.

Feedback from attendees and presenters was very positive, and similar awareness raising seminars are planned for the future.

FIO training

In preparation for the establishment of the NCA, some elements of the National Policing Improvement Agency (NPIA) transferred into SOCA; one of these was the Proceeds of Crime Centre (POCC). The POCC is responsible for the training, accreditation and monitoring of the performance of UK financial investigators. The UKFIU has benefited from co-location with POCC which has supported a close working relationship in areas of mutual interest. This has included the UKFIU undertaking POCC training to become accredited Financial Intelligence Officers (FIOs). This was part of a drive instigated by UKFIU senior management, and supported by POCC, to strengthen the knowledge and expertise of all staff across the various teams in the UKFIU.

Transparency and governance of the regime

Created in 2006, the purpose of the SARs Regime Committee has been to oversee, on behalf of the SOCA Board, SOCA's responsibilities in relation to the SARs Regime. The Committee's membership from the private sector, law enforcement and government bodies has sought to represent those sectors that participate in the regime. During the year, membership has widened to include representation from the counter terrorism community.

At the Committee's quarterly meeting in June, SOCA Director General Trevor Pearce addressed the Committee, and on behalf of SOCA Chairman Sir Ian Andrews and the SOCA Board, formally thanked members for their contribution over the past seven years. The Board recognised how much the regime had changed and that there had been significant challenges with regards to resourcing and IT, which had made the achievements to date even more impressive. The Board felt it was important, especially going into the NCA, that progress continued.

SARs Regime Tasked Group

The SARs Regime Tasked Group is an ad-hoc sub-group of the main SARs Committee, formed and tasked to undertake specific pieces of work. It is made up of individuals representing private and public sector bodies who are able to consider and advise on specific issues. During the year the Tasked Group was convened to identify how law enforcement and the regulated sector could work together to improve the collective understanding of the global environment and how this affected the SARs Regime. The work sought to identify sources of information, risks and threats, the use of technology to exploit international information, and to propose agreed ways of working that would derive benefit to stakeholders within the Regime. It was recognised from the outset that business models and issues were very different for the accountancy and legal sectors when compared with the banking sector, and therefore separate discussions were held.

The issues discussed included information sharing risks, the scope and scale of networks not being universal or as extensive in all areas, and resource constraints. Whilst the view of participants was positive around the exercise, divergence across the regime made it difficult to envisage how it could be taken to another level. It was concluded that the way forward was for actual risks and risk assessments that could be shared be fed into the ongoing work for the National Risk Assessment.

Retention and deletion of SARs

Following the Information Commissioner's Office (ICO) 2011 review on SOCA's operation and use of ELMER, the UKFIU has continued to comply with its recommendations. In January 2013, SOCA hosted a follow up visit from the ICO during which it demonstrated that the database no longer retained SARs beyond six years. SOCA also showed that procedure was in place to assess feedback indicating SARs were not linked to criminal funds and to delete such SARs where appropriate. The ICO confirmed that they were satisfied with the management of the overall process, and that there was no need for further review meetings pre-transition into the NCA.

HMRC increasing the use of SARs

Her Majesty's Revenue & Customs (HMRC) continued to seek opportunities to drive up its performance and maximise intervention opportunities afforded by the Proceeds of Crime Act 2002 (POCA) and the SARs Regime. HMRC utilise a system called CONNECT, a data matching tool that enables the organisation to cross match HMRC and third party data items to highlight patterns in HMRC's body of taxpayer data. CONNECT allows HMRC to identify anomalies between factors such as bank interest, property income, other lifestyle indicators, and a customer's stated tax liability.

In 2010 an 'in principle' agreement was reached between the UKFIU and HMRC to facilitate the sharing of SARs intelligence to reference against HMRC's CONNECT system. A trial proof of concept exercise concluded with the identification of nine cases for criminal investigation from a sample population of 100 cases. Development work has concluded and a full matching of data took place in October 2013. HMRC's ability to use SARs data matching against bespoke profiles will produce increased intervention opportunities across the full range of taxes, duties and entitlements administered by HMRC, generating yield and cases suitable for prosecution.

As HMRC becomes more effective in utilising this important intelligence facility, efficiency savings made will be recycled into case production and enhancement of the intelligence risk picture to inform future strategic direction.

The use of SARs is integral in supporting HMRC's Affluent Strategy (which targets those attempting to avoid or evade taxes). As part of intelligence-led research, SARs facilitate discovery of UK and non-UK based assets and financial transactions, leading to the identification of untaxed sources of income in the UK and the assets that generate that income.

HMRC continued to make improvements in the handling of consent SARs. In the financial year of April 2012 to March 2013 the HMRC Banking Liaison and Consent Team handled 2,921 requests for consent. The team repatriated £1,611,516 back to HMRC from 696 consents. HMRC prevented estimated revenue losses of £16,230,012 from 2,155 additional consent requests.

The HMRC Consent Team handled 70 requests for consent presented as a result of the Liechtenstein Disclosure Facility (LDF) which was created following a Memorandum of Understanding between the Government of Liechtenstein and

HMRC. This relates to cooperation in tax matters; by making a disclosure under the LDF, UK taxpayers with undeclared liabilities can get their tax affairs in order, whilst taking advantage of special terms. The 70 consents prevented revenue losses of £42,985,800.

Consent

The Proceeds of Crime Act 2002 (POCA), allows persons and businesses to avail themselves of a defence against money laundering charges by submitting an authorised disclosure[1] and seeking the consent of the NCA to undertake an activity (a "prohibited act" under s327, 328 or 329) about which they have concerns.

The UKFIU Consent Team grants or refuses such consent requests on behalf of the NCA. The team manages the receipt, assessment and resolution of all consent requests, and the team's work frequently leads to the development of new opportunities for intervention against criminal finances and profits. Legislation demands that consent decisions must be made within seven working days of receipt, and the UKFIU processed over 14,000 requests this year. As the work of the Consent Team has increased, the FIU has deployed more resources into this area both permanently and at times of peak demand.

Data on the value of seizures, restraints and the number of arrests made as a result of consent SARs is a useful indicator of the effectiveness of the consent regime in disrupting criminal finance. Figure ix shows seizure and restraint figures for interventions arising from requests that have been refused, and Figure x shows the same figures for requests that were granted.[2] However the effectiveness of the consent regime cannot be measured solely by intervention figures. The regime also has a preventative value, one example being the identification of fraud in action.

Figure ix: Outcomes of refused consent requests

Interventions arising from refused consent requests Oct 12 to Sept 13	
Restraint sums	£19,887,133
Cash seizure sums	£173,374
Funds indemnified by HMRC	£19,932,349
Funds repatriated to HMRC	£2,752,287
Total	£42,745,143
Cases with arrests recorded	32 (38 arrests)
Refusal rate for the period	9.8%

The restraint amount for refusals this reporting year is down on last year's figure of £104,747,007. This is because last year's figure was boosted by a single restraint for £70 million following identification of funds in the UK relating to a fraud investigation by a foreign jurisdiction. Overall there has been a drop in the refusal rate from 9.5% to 7.8% this year. However this is only just below the normal refusal rate which ranges from 8% to 12% per annum.

Cash seizure as a result of refused consent has increased from £119,143 last year to £173,374 this year, while arrests increased from 34 to 38.

---

1 Referred to as 'consent requests' throughout this Annual Report.
2 The data listed is based on information supplied by end users to the UKFIU, and as such is likely to represent a minimum, as 100% reporting was not achieved. This data was sought and supplied in the period immediately following receipt of the consent SAR, or when restraint has been obtained and further results may have been achieved at a later date that are not included here.

Figure x below details the outcomes of granted consent requests. There is no requirement for LEAs to inform the UKFIU of restraint, cash seizure or arrest figures as a result of granting consent (only refusal), and so these figures should only be considered as a guide to the impact of consent requests.

Figure x: Outcomes of granted consent requests

Interventions arising from granted consent requests Oct 12 to Sept 13	
Restraint sums	£217,081
Cash seizure sums	£148,374
Total	£365,455
Cases with arrests recorded	8 (8 arrests)

The figures for restraint sums and cash seizure sums are both down considerably on last year's figures (£5,557,900 and £609,047 respectively). The reasons for this will be reviewed by the UKFIU and considered if there is any underlying reason for this drop.

Figure xi: Consent requests refused

	Consent requests refused		Refused consent requests that are subsequently granted in the Moratorium Period	
	Number	Percentage of requests refused	Number	Percentage of overall refusals
Oct 2012	124	10.0%	22	17.7%
Nov 2012	111	9.5%	25	22.5%
Dec 2012	92	9.6%	12	13.0%
Jan 2013	109	10.7%	20	18.3%
Feb 2013	130	10.5%	26	20.0%
Mar 2013	85	7.0%	20	23.5%
Apr 2013	99	7.7%	29	29.3%
May 2013	159	12.0%	29	18.2%
Jun 2013	135	11.3%	27	20.0%
Jul 2013	120	9.5%	21	17.5%
Aug 2013	96	8.5%	19	19.8%
Sept 2013	127	11.7%	16	12.6%
Total	1,387	9.8%	266	19.2%

Turnaround of consent requests

Over this reporting period 12.8% of all consent requests were turned around on the day of receipt or the next working day; with just over a third of requests (35.8%) turned around on the day of receipt, day one or day two. The average turnaround time for all requests was 3.5 days. This is a slight increase on last year's reported turnaround of 3.1 days. This was mainly due to an increase in volume, the quality of the SARs and because more cases were allocated to LEAs for their advice than was granted in house. The views of LEAs were required more often, as the nature of the suspicion was more complex and there was greater potential for law enforcement interest.

Review of consent submissions by sector

During the year, the Consent Team identified an increase in the need to contact reporters with queries concerning the content of consent requests upon receipt, or during the notice period. This was compounded with difficulty contacting the relevant reporter. As both these issues affected the turnaround time for responding to requests, and tied up valuable resources in chasing contacts during the notice period, the team conducted a review of consent requests over a four month period from September 2012 to December 2012.

All 4,377 requests during this period were analysed individually to establish, by sector, areas for improvement including:

- Ensuring the five key elements[1] of a consent request were included in each request, and
- Which sectors were the most difficult to contact for follow up enquiries.

To identify specific issues and improve the efficiency of the consent regime, the report was shared with supervisors in accordance with the new model of engagement so they could engage with their sectors to improve the quality of the reports. Subsequently the main report has been split into individual sector reports so the detail can be used for training and educational purposes by the respective supervisors with their members.

Analysis of the Moratorium Period

During the reporting period, the Consent Team identified significant differences between LEAs in how refusals and the Moratorium Period[2] reviews were dealt with, and a disparity in outcome. As these issues affect the proportionality of the regime and reporters' relationship with their customers, the team reviewed and analysed Moratorium Period outcomes for the period October 2011 to September 2012.

All 1,238 refusals during this period were reviewed individually to establish, by LEA, areas for improvement including:

- Complying with the demands of the Moratorium Period reviews by SOCA.
- Barriers to obtaining restraint.
- Reducing the number of cases that go 'assumed' on day 32.
- Communication of outcome to SOCA.

To identify specific issues and improve the efficiency of the consent regime, the report was shared with the Association of Chief Police Officers (ACPO), the SOCA Proceeds of Crime Centre (formerly the National Policing Improvement Agency [NPIA] Proceeds of Crime Centre), and the regional and national Financial Investigators Working Groups (FIWGs), so they could engage with financial

---

1 Key elements are: 1) reporter's suspicion of money laundering; 2) the prohibited act they have been asked to do; 3) the value and whereabouts of the criminal property; 4) the identity of the subject; or 5) enough information to identify the subject or whereabouts of criminal property if not known.

2 The law specifies consent decisions must be made within seven working days (the 'notice period') from the day after receipt of the consent request. If consent is refused within the seven working days, law enforcement has a further 31 calendar days (the 'moratorium period') – from the day of refusal – to further the investigation into the reported matter and take further action.

investigation units and financial investigators to improve the outcomes of refusing consent.

In due course, it is hoped that this will have a positive influence on the NCA's ongoing assessments of the proportionality of continuing to refuse consent during the Moratorium Period, and a significant impact on LEAs' ability to recover assets where a consent refusal is involved. Both of these benefits should make a difference to reporters.

Consent legal sector bulletins

Two UKFIU bulletins were issued to the legal sector about specific fraud identified as being perpetrated against small and medium sized firms (these were identified via consent SARs).

Appendix 7

Lawyers, Law Reports and Cases

Contents

The 'all crimes' nature of the AML-CFT offences under PoCA 2002 (and in many of the offshore jurisdictions) should have simplified prosecution procedures. However, to date there have been few prosecutions or convictions for ML offences on a stand-alone basis. Law enforcement agencies prefer to prosecute the more substantive related crime (e.g. drug trafficking, etc.), and are understandably reluctant to get involved in the complexities of pure AML-CFT offences. This may be due to a combination of factors, including under-resourcing, and local political sensitivities in having the local Regional Crime Squad being seen to prioritise tackling higher profile street crimes.

Nevertheless, there are already a number of cautionary tales for practitioners.

Appendix 7.1   *Shah v HSBC*

WE CAN GO ON TOGETHER – WITH SUSPICIOUS MINDS: VICTORY FOR MLROs IN *SHAH v HSBC*

In *Shah & Anor v HSBC Private Bank (UK) Limited*[1], the High Court dismissed Mr Shah's $300m action against HSBC for losses he argued were caused by delays in executing his payment instructions. Those delays were due to HSBC raising internal suspicions over Mr Shah's source of funds and, pursuant to the relevant legislative regime, filing a Suspicious Activity Report ('**SAR**') and seeking the consent of the Serious and Organised Crime Agency ('**SOCA**') to proceed with the transaction. This decision of Mr Justice Supperstone has been widely welcomed by money laundering compliance professionals at financial firms. This articles summarises the history of this long running litigation, examines the key findings of Mr Supperstone, and sets out suggested practical steps firms can take in light of this decision.

FACTS

Mr Shah, a businessman with Zimbabwean interests, together with his wife brought a $300m action against his bank, HSBC, for damages caused by delays in executing four instructions to transfer funds from his account. The bank delayed processing the transfers because its nominated officer, Mr Wigley, suspected that the funds were proceeds of crime and, in the usual way and in accordance with the reporting regime in the Proceeds of Crime Act 2002 ('**POCA**'), delayed processing the transfers and filed a SAR. HSBC did not tell Mr Shah the precise reason for the delay and simply explained that it was *'complying with its UK statutory obligations'*. SOCA did provide its consent in respect of three of the transfers (Mr Shah cancelled one of the instructions) and they were executed shortly thereafter. Mr Shah claimed that the losses occurred when the intended transferee of one the payment instructions, an ex-employee of Mr Shah, tipped off Zimbabwean authorities that Mr Shah was being investigated for money laundering. Mr Shah submitted that this caused the Zimbabwean authorities to become suspicious and led to them freezing and then seizing his assets resulting in losses of over $300m.

PROCEDURAL HISTORY

This litigation has a chequered history.

In January 2009, Hamblen J disposed of the claim by way of summary judgment[2]. He rejected the four ways in which the claimants had pleaded their case and held that suspicion, for the purposes of POCA, was a purely subjective matter in which reasonableness was irrelevant unless the bank's good faith was in issue. Accordingly, the judge held that in light of the bank's evidence that it had held a genuine, subjective suspicion, the action would fail unless the claimants sought to argue that the bank acted in bad faith (which they had not pleaded).

---

1 [2012] EWHC 1283 (QB).
2 [2009] EWHC 79 (QB).

Mr Shah appealed against the summary disposal of his case. At the appeal, HSBC argued that a court would not expect bank employees to give evidence of their suspicion and neither would a court require the bank to disclose evidence of the basis of its suspicions. That argument was rejected by the Court of Appeal[1], who considered such an argument as tantamount *'to saying that the dispute is completely unjusticiable and that, therefore, the bank must win'*. Accordingly, the Court of Appeal held that the bank should be required to prove through disclosure and calling witness evidence in the ordinary way at a full trial that, as a matter of fact, it suspected Mr Shah of being involved in money laundering.

In July 2011, the bank applied for permission to redact from reports disclosed to Mr Shah in the course of the litigation the identities of the employees who had formed relevant suspicions and reported them to Mr Wigley. The bank argued that the identities were not relevant and did not need to be disclosed under the normal Civil Procedure Rules. Coulson J[2] considered that Mr Shah was put at a disadvantage by not knowing the identity of the individuals who raised the suspicions as it was relevant to the question of whether that suspicion was genuinely held. The judge therefore held that the bank was obliged by its obligation to provide standard disclosure to reveal the identity of those employees whose names had been redacted. However, the judge also held that the bank was nevertheless entitled to maintain their employee's anonymity as they enjoyed an exemption from the general rule on the ground of the public interest immunity, which applied in this case as it did for police informants. The judge considered that a balance ought to be struck and ordered the bank to produce an anonymous schedule of the relevant employees but one which identified the department in which they worked. For a more in depth discussion of Coulson J's judgment, please see Baker & McKenzie's previous article *'What's in a name? Would a SAR filed under any other name be as sweet?'* in *Money Laundering Bulletin* issue 186 of September 2011.

In October 2011, Mr Shah appealed against Coulson J's finding that the public interest immunity applied. The bank cross appealed against Coulson J's finding that the identities of its staff were disclosable at all. The Court of Appeal[3] refused Mr Shah's appeal and allowed the bank's cross appeal. The court found it was important to bear in mind that by this point, the ways in which Mr Shah had pleaded his case had already been rejected and all that was left was HSBC being put to proof that it held a genuine suspicion. The court's analysis was that the duty of standard disclosure did not extend to the names of employees who had reported suspicions of money laundering on the basis that their names did not assist Mr Shah's case (as he no longer put forward any positive case that the redacted names could support). Secondly, the redacted names could not be said to adversely affect HSBC's case, and therefore did not fall within the normal test of disclosable information. A more detailed discussion of the Court of Appeal's judgment can be found in Baker & McKenzie's previous article *'The case that dare not speak its name'* published in *Money Laundering Bulletin* in November 2011.

A further blow to Mr Shah's case came in November 2011 when the Court of Appeal[4] refused Mr Shah permission to amend his pleadings to make a further allegation that the bank acted in bad faith when it made the decision to file the SARs.

The full case finally came to be heard before Supperstone J, sitting in the Queen's Bench Division of the High Court, between November 2011 to March 2012.

---

1 [2010] EWCA Civ 31.
2 [2011] EWHC 1713 (QB).
3 [2011] EWCA Civ 1154.
4 [2011] EWCA Civ 1669.

Judgment was handed down on 16 May 2012, when all of Mr Shah's claims against the bank were dismissed.

THE DECISION

Mr Shah pleaded two principal submissions before Supperstone J:

- First, that HSBC was in breach of contract in failing to process the payment instructions; and

- Secondly, that HSBC was in breach of contract by not providing an explanation for failing to process the payment instructions.

BREACH OF CONTRACT 1 – FAILING TO PROCESS THE PAYMENT INSTRUCTIONS

Counsel for HSBC submitted that the effect of the POCA reporting regime was that the statute implied a term into the contract between a bank and its customer excusing the bank from processing instructions in the absence of consent from SOCA in circumstances where the bank suspected the transactions constituted money laundering. Counsel for Mr Shah resisted this argument and argued, inter alia, that it was *'ridiculously wide'*; that the court should not develop implied contractual terms to *'insulate a banker from the potentially harsh consequences of carrying on business as a banker'*; that such an implied term would not be obvious to a customer; and that a bank should not be absolved from liability where it cannot prove that its customer relationship team formed an actual suspicion.

Supperstone J rejected Mr Shah's arguments and found that such an implied term did exist. The judge said that the POCA regime:

> 'necessarily...makes inroads into the contractual duty of bankers to comply with a customer's payment instructions. It is plain that POCA has intervened in the contractual relationship between banker and customer in a way which may cause the customer prejudice. This has been recognised by the courts. However the courts also recognise that it is a price Parliament has deemed worth paying in the fight against money laundering'.

The judge considered that the balance of conflicting interests struck by Parliament in the POCA reporting regime requires the implication of such a term into the contract between a banker and his customer. In making this finding, Supperstone J referred to and followed the reasoning of the Court of Appeal in *K Limited v National Westminster Bank plc* [2007] 1 WLR 311. In that case, Longmore LJ noted:

> '...Parliament has struck a precise and workable balance of conflicting interests in the 2002 Act...to intervene between a banker and his customer in the performance of the contract mandate is a serious interference with the free flow of trade. But Parliament has considered that a limited interference is to be tolerated in preference to allowing the undoubted evil of money-laundering to run rife in the commercial community... Many people would think that a reasonable balance has been struck.'

WHOSE SUSPICION?

The existence of the implied term was not the end of the matter. The central issue in respect of the first breach of contract claim was whether HSBC in fact suspected money laundering – i.e. HSBC still had to show that it formed the relevant suspicion. In this context, the question arose: which natural person or persons constitute the bank for the purpose of establishing that HSBC did in fact suspect that the instructions constituted money laundering? In other words, whose suspicion should be imputed to HSBC?

Counsel for HSBC argued that Mr Wigley, in his capacity as the MLRO and the nominated officer pursuant to POCA, was the *'directing mind and will'* of HSBC for the purposes of forming the relevant suspicion. He further submitted that the structure of the POCA reporting regime is such that it is the bank's nominated officer that forms a suspicion and reports to SOCA if appropriate. Accordingly Mr Wigley's state of mind can be attributed to HSBC and was sufficient for the purpose of establishing that HSBC did in fact hold a suspicion.

HSBC faced several challenges on this point, including the fact that it could not put into evidence any document formally appointing Mr Wigley as the POCA nominated officer and the fact that Mr Wigley was employed by HSBC Bank plc, a different HSBC entity to the one that filed the SARs. Counsel for Mr Shah unsurprisingly sought to capitalise on these facts and pointed out that there was no evidence that the parent company had authority from the defendant entity to appoint its nominated officer. Indeed, Mr Wigley's own evidence was that he was not directly appointed as nominated officer but that he thought that the responsibility was delegated to him in respect of all UK HSBC entities by Mr Brownlee, the Senior Manager of Money Laundering Control. In cross examination, Mr Brownlee conceded that 'technically' Mr Wigley was not the nominated officer as he was not nominated by the organisation but by Mr Brownlee himself.

Despite the absence of a clear paper trail, the judge nevertheless was *'left in no doubt from the evidence that Mr Wigley was the Defendant's nominated officer'* within the meaning of ss 338(5) and 340(12) of POCA and that it was he who submitted each of the relevant SARs on behalf of the defendant HSBC entity. It was Mr Wigley who exercised management and control over these decisions, had autonomy to make these decisions, and exercised his judgment independently. Although the judge considered that the absence of formal appointment was not in his view fatal, Supperstone J did state that he *'would have expected HSBC Bank plc and the Defendant to have properly documented the appointment of Mr Wigley as the Defendant's nominated officer'*.

DEFINITION OF SUSPICION

The judge said that the meaning of suspicion was clear from the authorities. He cited the judgment of Longmore LJ in *R v Da Silva* [2007] 1 WLR 303, in which he held that 'suspicion' means:

> '...that the defendant must think that there is a possibility, which is more than fanciful, that the relevant facts exist. A vague feeling of unease would not suffice. But the statute does not require the suspicion to be 'clear' or 'firmly grounded'

The definition of suspicion in *R v Da Silva* was given in the context of a criminal charge of assisting another person to retain the benefit of criminal conduct knowing or *suspecting* that that other person was or had been engaged in criminal conduct, contrary to s 93A(1)(a) of the Criminal Justice Act 1988. However, in the later case of *K Limited*, Longmore LJ adopted that definition in facts similar to this case. He said:

> 'The existence of suspicion is a subjective fact. There is no legal requirement that there should be reasonable grounds for the suspicion. The relevant bank employee either suspects or he does not. If he does suspect he must (either himself or through the bank's nominated officer) inform the authorities'.

At the first appeal of this case, Longmore LJ expressly stated that the Court of Appeal was bound by the reasoning in *Da Silva* and *K Limited* that the relevant suspicion need not be based on reasonable grounds.

On the facts of the case, Supperstone J *'was left in no doubt that Mr Wigley honestly and genuinely suspected that the funds were criminal property when he submitted his report to SOCA...'*. Crucially, although Mr Wigley did not himself document why he was reporting the matter to SOCA (all that was before the court was a document produced by one of the clerks working under Mr Wigley), the judge found as matter of fact on the basis of Mr Wigley's evidence that Mr Wigley himself took the decision to make a report to SOCA and not, as alleged by counsel for Mr Shah, as a result of being influenced by suspicions generated by others lower down the chain without he himself knowing the reason for them.

BREACH OF CONTRACT 2 – FAILING TO PROVIDE AN EXPLANATION

Mr Shah argued that HSBC was in breach of contract by failing to provide information as to its communications with SOCA and failing to seek permission from SOCA to provide that information to him. It was submitted that this duty to provide information was to be implied into the banking contract as it was part and parcel of the bank's duty as the customer's agent to keep the customer informed of the reasons why the bank could not comply with his instructions. Mr Shah sought the following from HSBC:

- The name of the agency to whom the reports were made;

- SOCA reference numbers;

- Copies of the consent; and

- The primary facts that led HSBC to make the disclosure and documentary evidence of the same.

HSBC argued that the primary relationship between bank and customer is one of debtor and creditor, and does not give rise to a free standing duty on banks to provide to its customer the type of information sought by Mr Shah.

The judge held that there was no implied term in the banking contract requiring a bank to provide to its customer details of its communications with SOCA. Indeed, the judge found that HSBC was obliged to refuse to provide the information where it or its servants/agents, in providing that information, might commit offences under s 333 and/or 342 of POCA. An offence is committed under s 333 (which was the section that applied at the material time and has since been replaced by s 333A–333E) if a person knows or suspects that an authorised disclosure has been made and he makes a disclosure that is likely to prejudice any investigation which might be conducted following the original disclosure to the authorities. Furthermore, s 342 contains an offence of 'prejudicing an investigation' and is committed where a person knows or suspects that a money laundering investigation is being, or is about to be conducted and he makes a disclosure which is likely to prejudice that investigation.

The judge held that the principal argument against imposing such an implied term is that it is unlikely that banks will know whether their disclosure to SOCA has or will trigger an investigation; the likely scope of that investigation (for instance, whether it would extend to third parties and if so which third parties); and whether the customer seeking the information is wholly innocent. Therefore, banks will not be in a position to know whether providing the information to the customer might constitute offences of tipping off and/or prejudicing an investigation under s 333 and 342 POCA. Accordingly, any implied duty to provide information would *'cut across the statutory regime, operate as a disincentive to report suspicious activity and undermine the integrity of the reporting regime'*. The judge also observed that such an implied term would be unreasonable given the number of SARs that are made in the banking sector. Supperstone J went on to reject the submission that HSBC should have sought consent from SOCA to provide that information and, following extensive consideration of the facts of the Zimbabwe authorities' investigation into Mr Shah, rejected any causal link between HSBC's conduct and Mr Shah's losses.

COULD A CUSTOMER INVOKE PROVISIONS OF THE DATA PROTECTION ACT 1998 TO OBTAIN A COPY OF A SAR?

One interesting point in relation to the provision of SARs to a customer, but which does not appear to have been pleaded or discussed in this case, is whether a customer could obtain a copy of the SAR under the Data Protection Act 1998 (the '**DPA**').

The DPA applies to all individuals and businesses that process data in the UK. Data subjects have a right under the DPA to access personal data held about them. This creates a potential conflict between the tipping off provisions under POCA and the right of the data subject to obtain a copy of the SAR under the DPA.

However, the DPA provides certain exemptions to the rights of data subjects to access data processed about them. Section 29 of the DPA provides that in circumstances where the application of those rights would be likely to prejudice the prevention or detection of crime or the apprehension or the prosecution of offenders, data controllers are exempt from complying with them.

In July 2009, the Fraud Advisory Panel issued guidance on when this provision is likely to apply and there is also some guidance by HM Treasury and the Information Commissioner. The effect of the guidance is that where compliance with the data subject's rights under the DPA involves the disclosure of a SAR in circumstances which would in turn be likely to prejudice any investigation, disclosure would constitute a tipping off offence under POCA and the s 29 exemption would apply.

However, the exemption applies only 'to the extent to which' prejudice to an investigation is likely. Accordingly, where disclosure of a SAR to the data subject would not be likely to prejudice an investigation, no tipping off offence would be committed, and therefore the s 29 exemption would not be available to data controllers. The Fraud Advisory Panel guidance gives the example of where the existence and contents of a SAR have already been revealed in the course of criminal proceedings, it is unlikely that any prejudice would be caused by the subsequent disclosure of the SAR to the individual concerned.

In practice, there are likely to be parts of a SAR that fall within the exemption and parts that do not. In those cases, the bank would need to carefully mask those parts that fall within the exemption and disclose those parts that do not. If in doubt as to whether the disclosure is likely to prejudice an investigation, the reporting entity should seek prior consent from the investigating body (e.g. SOCA) before disclosing some or all of the contents of the SAR to its customer.

It should not be assumed that the s 29 exemption applies automatically to SARs. The data subject's rights and the s 29 exemption must be considered on a case-by-case basis. If challenged, either in front of the Information Commissioner or in court, then a data controller must be prepared to defend the decision made (i.e. whether to disclose the SAR or not). Any decision to rely on s 29 should therefore be taken at a senior level and the reasons for that decision should be documented.

As mentioned above, it does not appear that obtaining copies of the SARs under the DPA was an avenue explored by Mr Shah. If he had done, then HSBC may have been under an obligation to disclose at least parts of the SARs, possibly on a redacted basis.

COMMENT

This case highlighted and grappled with the difficult practical question of how to balance a bank's contractual duty to its clients and its statutory money-laundering obligations. The space in which these two considerations conflict is one frequently occupied by MLROs. Being unable to carry out customers' instructions invariably puts institutions at risk of damaging customer relationships and its reputation but equally banks and other institutions simply cannot afford to approach the statutory reporting regime in a cavalier fashion.

Although this long and drawn out litigation ultimately ended in vindication for banks and their compliance procedures, the overwhelming lesson to be learned is that steps could be taken to avoid this type of protracted case, for instance:

- ensuring that a proper 'audit trail' is kept showing formal appointment of nominated officers (and, where the nominated officer is employed by a different entity within the group, a record is kept formally giving the employing entity the power to nominate the individual on behalf of the entity for which he is nominated);

- that a record is kept of the scope of the role of the nominated officer;

- that standard terms of business expressly incorporate the terms that HSBC had to ask the court to imply.

It should also be borne in mind that the hearing before Supperstone J was necessary following the earlier decision of the Court of Appeal in this case that banks can be put to proof before the courts to explain the basis of their decision to file a SAR through disclosure and calling witness evidence in the ordinary way at a full trial. Accordingly, banks and other reporting institutions within the POCA reporting regime should put in place procedures to record in writing the existence and basis of a relevant suspicion, the identity of the individual who formed it, as well the decisions taken that lead to the making of a SAR.

In addition to the time and cost of having to engage in this type of litigation, such cases also invariably cause avoidable stress and business disruption. The personal cost to individuals should also not be underestimated. Although Supperstone J ultimately found Mr Wigley to have been a 'patently honest witness', it cannot have been an easy process – for instance his evidence before the court lasted six days and the HSBC compliance procedures; his personal role; and the contents of the SARs were forensically scrutinised by leading counsel in cross-examination. Ultimately the judge was persuaded by Mr Wigley's evidence but no doubt his time in the witness box would have been greatly improved if he had had the benefit of contemporaneous documentary evidence, for instance evidence of his formal appointment as POCA nominated officer.

A victory by Mr Shah would invariably have cast troubling doubts over the efficacy of commonly used money laundering reporting processes. This decision ought to provide comfort that the courts will stand behind MLROs acting in the proper discharge of their statutory duties.

Appendix 7.2   *Duff*

R. v Duff 2004 (2003) 10(2) JICTCP, an English solicitor, Jonathan Duff, was imprisoned for six months by the Manchester Crown Court for the AML-CFT offence of failing to report his suspicion in relation to money paid to his firm by a commercial client who was then convicted of drug trafficking. Duff did take independent advice in relation to reporting suspicion, but evidently decided that he had no such reportable suspicion. His misunderstanding may have been based on ambiguous wording in the statute, but despite accepting his was a genuine mistake of law, the Judge sent Duff to prison for his act of omission.

As noted in **10.5**, a JITCP article (Ryan Myint, 'Solicitors Beware: Money Laundering after R v Duff' [2003] 10(2)) analysed the Duff case. Two points in the case stand out as curious:

(i) the transactions which Duff failed to report involved some highly suspicious circumstances, but Duff seems to have missed all of the warning signals; and

(ii) Duff was prosecuted under s 52(1) of the Drug Trafficking Act 1994, which provided that a person who fails to disclose knowledge or suspicion of drug ML is guilty of an offence (PoCA introduces a similar offence, but on an 'all crimes' basis). Neither the trial Judge nor the Court of Appeal clarified why the s 52(2) exception did not apply to Duff. Section 52(2) provides an exception to s 52(1) where the information came to the professional legal advisor in privileged circumstances. Clearly, therefore, there must not have been any element of legal advice' being given.

Appendix 7.3   *Warren*

In the United States, former English solicitor Andrew R. Warren was extradited to the United States to stand trial (Law Society Gazette [2003] 25 April) for ML offences, securities, banking and tax violations, and using alleged 'bogus' corporations which he had set up in offshore jurisdictions.

Appendix 7.4   *Ferguson*

In 2004 also in the United States, a Miami lawyer was sentenced to over two years' imprisonment for AML-CFT offences for accepting a client's legal fees from a friend of the client who was involved in the Cali, Colombia, drug cartels. The Court showed that Donald Ferguson knew or should have known that the money came from illegal activity, even though his own client was not part of the cartels, and the money was paying for legitimate legal services. Ferguson was disbarred.

Appendix 7.5   *Double*

Peter Double (a former attorney from California, and before that a name Partner in a Hong Kong firm of Solicitors) established offshore structures for clients who were later accused of money laundering. The US Government accused Double of being part of a "conspiracy" to launder money. On Monday 3 May 2001, Peter Double was sentenced to five years imprisonment for his part in a "money laundering conspiracy" in which he claims to have been paid ordinary legal fees to set up offshore structures for a client who later testified against him in return for a reduced sentence. Mr Double drafted documents for loans and other financial transactions that later turned out to be false. Mr Double argued (unsuccessfully) that he would happily draft an employment contract for a corporate client without meeting the proposed employee; so why should he be required to establish the *bona fides* of a borrower under a financing agreement? At that time his conviction was of great concern to lawyers working in the field of offshore companies and finance, but its salutary warning has required them to be far more cautious about accepting new clients and to require extensive disclosure of a client's history and current financial affairs before assisting to move money through such structures.

Appendix 7.6   *Griffiths*

In 2006 a conveyancing solicitor Phillip Griffiths was jailed for 15 months (reduced to 6 months on appeal), for failing to make a disclosure to the authorities, knowing or suspecting ML offences were taking place, having been acquitted of being involved in the ML itself.

Appendix 7.7 *Dougan*

In 2006 Brian Dougan, a solicitor from Northern Ireland, was jailed in 2006 for three months at Liverpool Crown Court for converting or transferring the proceeds of criminal conduct. He was found to have allowed £66,000 to pass through his client account while carrying out conveyancing work for a convicted criminal.

Appendix 7.8 *Gauntlett and Beveridge*

In June 2006, in a case involving a small (two-Partner) firm of Solicitors, the High Court Judge criticised the partners as being grossly negligent, although both Matthew Gauntlett and Sarah Beveridge were acquitted of ML offences despite the fact that a legal executive in their firm had passed more than £200 million through their client account apparently without their knowledge. The legal executive received a six-year sentence. The Judge asked a copy of his remarks to be sent to the Law Society.

Reported on 7 August 2006 by Sue Mawdsley, solicitor and partner at Legal Risk.

Appendix 7.9   The Law Society Anti-money laundering Practice note October 2013[1]

CHAPTER 6 – LEGAL PROFESSIONAL PRIVILEGE

6.1 GENERAL COMMENTS

Solicitors are under a duty to keep the affairs of their clients confidential, and the circumstances in which they are able to disclose client communications are strictly limited.

However, sections 327–329, 330 and 332 of POCA contain provisions for disclosure of information to be made to the NCA.

Solicitors also have a duty of full disclosure to their clients. However, sections 333A and 342 of POCA prohibit disclosure of information in circumstances where a SAR has been made and/or where it would prejudice an existing or proposed investigation.

This chapter examines the tension between a solicitor's duties and these provisions of POCA. Similar tensions also arise with respect to the Terrorism Act and you should refer to the Law Society's practice note on anti-terrorism in those circumstances.

This chapter should be read in conjunction with Chapter 5 of this practice note and if you are still in doubt as to your position, you should seek independent legal advice.

The Law Society's AML directory may be of assistance in locating a solicitor who practises in this area of law.

6.2 APPLICATION

This chapter is relevant to any solicitor considering whether to make a disclosure under POCA.

6.3 DUTY OF CONFIDENTIALITY

A solicitor is professionally and legally obliged to keep the affairs of clients confidential and to ensure that his staff do likewise. The obligations extend to all matters revealed to a solicitor, from whatever source, by a client, or someone acting on the client's behalf. See Chapter 4 of the SRA Handbook.

In exceptional circumstances this general obligation of confidence may be overridden. See Chapter 4 of the SRA handbook. However, certain communications can never be disclosed unless statute permits this either expressly or by necessary implication. Such communications are those protected by legal professional privilege (LPP).

---

1 © Law Society. Reproduced by kind permission of the Law Society of England and Wales. For the full version of the Practice Note please see www.lawsociety.org.uk/advice/practice-notes/aml/.

6.4 LEGAL PROFESSIONAL PRIVILEGE

6.4.1 General overview

LPP is a privilege against disclosure, ensuring clients know that certain documents and information provided to lawyers cannot be disclosed at all. It recognises the client's fundamental human right to be candid with his legal adviser, without fear of later disclosure to his prejudice. It is an absolute right and cannot be overridden by any other interest.

LPP does not extend to everything lawyers have a duty to keep confidential. LPP protects only those confidential communications falling under either of the two heads of privilege – advice privilege or litigation privilege.

For the purposes of LPP, a lawyer only includes solicitors and their employees, barristers and in-house lawyers.

6.4.1 Advice privilege

Principle

Communications between a lawyer, acting in his capacity as a lawyer, and a client, are privileged if they are both:

- confidential
- for the purpose of seeking legal advice from a solicitor or providing it to a client

Scope

Communications are not privileged merely because a client is speaking or writing to you. The protection applies only to those communications which directly seek or provide advice or which are given in a legal context, that involve the lawyer using his legal skills and which are directly related to the performance of the lawyer's professional duties [Passmore on Privilege 2nd edition 2006].

Case law helps define what advice privilege covers.

Communications subject to advice privilege:

- a solicitor's bill of costs and statement of account [*Chant v Brown* (1852) 9 Hare 790] information imparted by prospective clients in advance of a retainer will attract

LPP if the communications were made for the purpose of indicating the advice required [*Minster v Priest* [1930] AC 558 per Lord Atkin at 584].

Communications not subject to advice privilege:
- notes of open court proceedings [*Parry v News Group Newspapers* (1990) 140 New Law Journal 1719] are not privileged, as the content of the communication is not confidential. conversations, correspondence or meetings with opposing lawyers [*Parry v News Group Newspapers* (1990) 140 New Law Journal 1719] are not privileged, as the content of the communication is not confidential.
- a client account ledger maintained in relation to the client's money [*Nationwide Building Society v Various Solicitors* [1999] P.N.L.R. 53.]
- an appointments diary or time record on an attendance note, time sheet or fee record relating to a client [*R v Manchester Crown Court, ex p. Rogers* [1999] 1 W.L.R. 832]

- conveyancing documents are not communication so not subject to advice privilege [*R v Inner London Crown Court ex p. Baines & Baines* [1988] QB 579]

Advice within a transaction

All communications between a lawyer and his client relating to a transaction in which the lawyer has been instructed for the purpose of obtaining legal advice are covered by advice privilege, not withstanding that they do not contain advice on matters of law and construction, provided that they are directly related to the performance by the solicitor of his professional duty as legal adviser of his client. [*Three Rivers District Council and others v the Bank of England* [2004] UKHL 48 at 111]

This will mean that where you are providing legal advice in a transactional matter (such as a conveyance) the advice privilege will cover all:

- communications with,
- instructions from, and
- advice given to

the client, including any working papers and drafts prepared, as long as they are directly related to your performance of your professional duties as a legal adviser.

6.4.3 Litigation privilege

Principle

This privilege, which is wider than advice privilege, protects confidential communications made after litigation has started, or is reasonably in prospect, between either:

- a lawyer and a client
- a lawyer and an agent, whether or not that agent is a lawyer
- a lawyer and a third party

These communications must be for the sole or dominant purpose of litigation, either:

- for seeking or giving advice in relation to it
- for obtaining evidence to be used in it
- for obtaining information leading to obtaining such evidence

6.4.4 Important points to consider

An original document not brought into existence for these privileged purposes and so not already privileged, does not become privileged merely by being given to a lawyer for advice or other privileged purpose.

Further, where you have a corporate client, communication between you and the employees of a corporate client may not be protected by LPP if the employee cannot be considered to be 'the client' for the purposes of the retainer. As such, some employees will be clients, while others will not. [*Three Rivers District Council v the Governor and Company of the Bank of England (no 5)* [2003] QB 1556]

It is not a breach of LPP to discuss a matter with your nominated officer for the purposes of receiving advice on whether to make a disclosure.

6.4.5 Crime/fraud exception

LPP protects advice you give to a client on avoiding committing a crime [*Bullivant v Att-Gen of Victoria* [1901] AC 196] or warning them that proposed actions could attract prosecution [*Butler v Board of Trade* [1971] Ch 680]. LPP does not extend to documents which themselves form part of a criminal or fraudulent act, or communications which take place in order to obtain advice with the intention of carrying out an offence [*R v Cox & Railton* (1884) 14 QBD 153]. It is irrelevant whether or not you are aware that you are being used for that purpose [*Banque Keyser Ullman v Skandia* [1986] 1 Lloyds Rep 336].

Intention of furthering a criminal purpose

It is not just your client's intention which is relevant for the purpose of ascertaining whether information was communicated for the furtherance of a criminal purpose. It is also sufficient that a third party intends the lawyer/client communication to be made with that purpose (eg where the innocent client is being used by a third party) [*R v Central Criminal Court ex p Francis & Francis* [1989] 1 AC 346].

Knowing a transaction constitutes an offence

If you know the transaction you're working on is a principal offence, you risk committing an offence yourself. In these circumstances, communications relating to such a transaction are not privileged and should be disclosed.

Suspecting a transaction constitutes an offence

If you merely suspect a transaction might constitute a money laundering offence, the position is more complex. If the suspicions are correct, communications with the client are not privileged. If the suspicions are unfounded, the communications should remain privileged and are therefore non-disclosable.

Prima facie evidence

If you suspect you are unwittingly being involved by your client in a fraud, the courts require prima facie evidence before LPP can be displaced [*O'Rourke v Darbishire* [1920] AC 581]. The sufficiency of that evidence depends on the circumstances: it is easier to infer a prima facie case where there is substantial material available to support an inference of fraud. While you may decide yourself if prima facie evidence exists, you may also ask the court for directions [*Finers v Miro* [1991] 1 W.L.R. 35].

The Crown Prosecution Service guidance for prosecutors indicates that if a solicitor forms a genuine, but mistaken, belief that the privileged circumstances exemption (see 6.5 below) applies (for example, the client misleads the solicitor and uses the advice received for a criminal purpose) the solicitor will be able to rely on the reasonable excuse defence. It is likely that a similar approach would be taken with respect to a genuine, but mistaken, belief that LPP applies.

We believe you should not make a disclosure unless you know of prima facie evidence that you are being used in the furtherance of a crime.

6.5 PRIVILEGED CIRCUMSTANCES

Quite separately from LPP, POCA recognises another type of communication, one which is received in 'privileged circumstances'. This is not the same as LPP, it is merely an exemption from certain provisions of POCA, although in many cases the communication will also be covered by LPP.

The privileged circumstances exemptions are found in the following places:

- POCA – section 330 (6)(b), (10) and (11)
- POCA – section 342 (4)
- Terrorism Act – section 19 (5) and (6)
- Terrorism Act – section 21A (8)

Although the wording is not exactly the same in all these sections, the essential elements of the exemption are:

- you are a professional legal adviser
- the information or material is communicated to you:
    - o by your client or their representative in connection with you giving legal advice
    - o by the client or their representative in connection with them seeking legal advice from you
    - o by any person for the purpose of/in connection with actual or contemplated legal proceedings
- the information or material cannot be communicated or given to you with a view to furthering a criminal purpose

The defence covers solicitors, their non-solicitor partners and their employees (see s 330 (7B) of POCA) [link to POCA], barristers and in-house lawyers.

Consider the crime/fraud exception [link to 6.4.5] when determining what constitutes the furthering of a criminal purpose.

Finally, section 330(9A) protects the privilege attaching to any disclosure made to a nominated officer for the purposes of obtaining advice about whether or not a disclosure should be made.

6.6 DIFFERENCES BETWEEN PRIVILEGED CIRCUMSTANCES AND LPP

6.6.1 Protection of advice

When advice is given or received in circumstances where litigation is neither contemplated nor reasonably in prospect, except in very limited circumstances communications between you and third parties will not be protected under the advice arm of LPP.

Privileged circumstances, however, exempt communications regarding information communicated by representatives of a client, where it is in connection with your giving legal advice to the client, or the client seeking legal advice from you. This may include communications with:

- a junior employee of a client (if it is reasonable in the circumstances to consider them to be a representative of the client)
- other professionals who are providing information to you on behalf of the client as part of the transaction

You should consider the facts of each case when deciding whether or not a person is a representative for the purposes of privileged circumstances.

6.6.2 Losing protection by dissemination

There may be circumstances in which a legal adviser has communicated to him information which is subject to legal professional privilege, but which does not fall within the definition of privileged circumstances.

For example, a lawyer representing client A may hold or have had communicated to him information which is privileged as between client B and his own lawyer, in circumstances where client A and client B are parties to a transaction, or have some other shared interest.

The sharing of this information may not result in client B's privilege being lost, if it is stipulated that privilege is not waived (*Gotha City v Sotheby's (no 1)* [1998] 1 WLR 114).

However, privileged circumstances will not apply because the information was not communicated to client A's lawyer by a client of his in connection with the giving by him of legal advice to that client. However if it was given to him by any person in connection with legal proceedings or contemplated legal proceedings, privileged circumstances would apply.

In such circumstances, the lawyer representing client A would not be able to rely on privileged circumstances, but the information might still be subject to LPP, unless the crime/fraud exemption applied.

6.6.3 Vulnerability to seizure

It is important to correctly identify whether communications are protected by LPP or if they are merely covered by the privileged circumstances exemption. This is because the privileged circumstances exemption exempts you from certain POCA provisions. It does not provide any of the other LPP protections to those communications. Therefore a communication which is only covered by privileged circumstances, not LPP, will still remain vulnerable to seizure or production under a court order or other such notice from law enforcement.

6.7 WHEN DO I DISCLOSE?

If the communication is covered by LPP and the crime/fraud exception does not apply, you cannot make a disclosure under POCA.

If the communication was received in privileged circumstances and the crime/fraud exception does not apply, you are exempt from the relevant provisions of POCA, which include making a disclosure to the NCA.

If neither of these situations applies, the communication will still be confidential. However, the material is disclosable under POCA and can be disclosed, whether as an authorised disclosure, or to avoid breaching section 330. Section 337 of POCA permits you to make such a disclosure and provides that you will not be in breach of your professional duty of confidentiality when you do so.

Appendix 7.10 House of Commons Library report, 14 November 2012 'The impact of AML legislation on professional services (accountants and solicitors)

MONEY LAUNDERING REGULATIONS

Standard Note: SN/BT/2592

Last updated: 14 November 2012

Author: Timothy Edmonds

Section   Business & Transport Section

This note sets out the main features of the UK's money laundering legislation and the proposals for change that arise because of the third money laundering Directive which came into effect in December 2007 and amendments to which came into force in October 2012.

This note concentrates especially on the impact of the legislation on the financial services industry and upon professional services, such as accountants and solicitors, who are most exposed to the law. Other aspects more closely connected to the criminal law and the recovery of assets and court procedures are dealt with by the Home Affairs Section, X4322.

Another Standard Note – SN/BT/3366 – deals with the practical problems of attempting to prove identity when trying to open a bank account.

Contents

1 Introduction

Money laundering describes the procedures used by criminals to make money which has been acquired from criminal activity appear to have been lawfully acquired. These procedures are typically highly complex and by design hard to trace. Funds, whether generated through organised crime, terrorism or drug trafficking, will be placed within the mainstream economy or financial sector and the source and origin of the funds will be progressively concealed with each transaction. These transactions must be carried out in such a way as to avoid attracting the attention of the authorities and with it the risk of detection, confiscation and criminal proceedings. Because of the laundering, the funds will appear to be lawful. The first EU money laundering Directive defined it thus:

> The conversion or transfer of property, knowing that such property is derived from serious crime, for the purpose of concealing or disguising the illicit origin of the property or of assisting any person who is involved in committing such an offence or offences to evade the legal consequences of his action, and the concealment or disguise of the true nature, source, location, disposition, movement, rights with respect to, or ownership of property, knowing that such property is derived from serious crime.[1]

2 Development of regulation

There have been several attempts to control money laundering, the focus having shifted over time, often in response to events, from general criminality to drug enforcement and, lately, terrorist activity. In England and Wales, the *Criminal Justice Act 1988* (as amended by the *Criminal Justice Act 1993*) made it an offence to assist in the retention or use of the proceeds of serious criminal conduct. Similar provisions also apply in Scotland and Northern Ireland and, for drug trafficking offences, under the *Drug Trafficking Act 1994*.[2] The legislation aimed to make it harder for criminals to enjoy the benefits of their crimes. Also, by encouraging the vigilance (backed up by criminal sanctions) of those whose work may bring them into contact with criminal funds, to increase the chance of detection.

It is difficult to entirely separate legislation dealing with money laundering with more general legislation aimed at, loosely defined, the assets of criminals. This section will try to outline the overall impact of legislation but will later concentrate upon money laundering and its impact on the financial services industry and associated professions.

Action on a European level began with the first *Money Laundering Directive*. This was implemented by Regulation in the UK[3] and came into force on 1 April 1994. Financial institutions are most vulnerable to being party (unwillingly or not) to money laundering and thus are in the 'front line' of restrictions. The main impact of the Directive was to require financial institutions to verify the identity of all customers opening business relations with them (and to keep records of their identification). Staff had to be trained in anti-money laundering practices and suspicions of money laundering must be reported through a designated officer (usually referred to as the money laundering reporting officer).

The *Terrorism Act 2000* (TA 2000) widened the definition of terrorist activity. Previously, powers set out in the *Prevention of Terrorism Act 1989* were available only in respect of acts of terrorism connected with the affairs of Northern Ireland, or international terrorism. They were not generally available in respect of acts of

---

1 First anti-money laundering Directive 91/308/EEC of 10 June 1991 on prevention of the use of the financial system for the purpose of money laundering, OJ L 344/76 of 28.12.2001.
2 The details of these offences are not discussed here; this note focuses on the obligations faced by financial institutions.
3 SI 1993 No 1993. These regulations, in the form in which they were first enacted, are available on the HMSO website, www.hmso.gov.uk.

"domestic" terrorism, that is, acts of terrorism connected solely with the affairs of the United Kingdom or any part of the United Kingdom other than Northern Ireland. The definition, which is set out in section 1 of the Act, was extended to cover a wider range of actions or threats of action, including those "made for the purpose of advancing a political, religious or ideological cause".[1] Other provisions in Part 3 of the TA 2000 imposed duties relating to the disclosure of information about terrorist finance.

Increasing both the volume and intensity of terrorist legislation was the *Anti-Terrorism, Crime and Security Act 2001 [ATCSA]*. This Act is a much longer and more wide-ranging than the TA 2000. It was passed in response to, and within a few months of, the attack on the World Trade Centre on 11 September 2001. ATCSA is in 14 parts; it contains numerous new powers and created many new offences. The first three parts of ATCSA deal with forfeiture of terrorist property and seizure of terrorist funds. They replace and add to measures in the 2000 Act. Part 3 also deals with the freezing of foreign property held by UK institutions.

The Home Office's Explanatory Memorandum to the 2001 Act includes the following summary of the provisions in Parts 1–2:

Terrorist property

5. Part 1 and Schedules 1 and 2 of the Act contain provisions to prevent terrorists from gaining access to their money. They complement provisions in the new Proceeds of Crime Bill and ensure that investigative and freezing powers are available wherever funds could be used to finance terrorism.

6. The introduction of account monitoring orders enable the police to require financial institutions to provide information on accounts for up to 90 days. The existing requirement to report knowledge or suspicion of terrorist financing has been strengthened, for the regulated sector, so that it is an offence not to report where there were "reasonable grounds" for suspicion.

7. The Act gives law enforcement agencies the power to seize terrorist cash anywhere in the UK, and the power to freeze assets at the start of an investigation, rather than when the person is about to be charged, reducing the risk that funds will be used or moved before they can be frozen.

Freezing orders

8. Part 2 creates a new power which enables the Treasury to freeze the assets of overseas governments or residents who have taken, or are likely to take, action to the detriment of the UK's economy or action constituting a threat to the life or property of a national or resident of the UK. The Treasury's previous power to freeze assets, contained in the 1964 Act, is repealed.[2]

The provisions allowing freezing orders (Section 4 of ATCS) were controversially used when the Treasury seized funds that could be used to compensate UK depositors with the failed Landsbanki Icelandic bank during the financial crisis of 2008.[3]

1 *Terrorism Act 2000*, s. 1(1)(c).
2 http://www.opsi.gov.uk/acts/en2001/2001en24.htm.
3 HM Treasury press notice, 103/08.

Although the Government had announced plans to reform the main money laundering offences before the 9/11 attack, the attack prompted a rethink of previous proposals.

On 15 October 2001, the then Chancellor, Gordon Brown, set out a range of new actions to be taken against terrorist finances, including the establishment of a regulatory regime for bureaux de change and a multi-agency terrorist finance unit within the National Criminal Intelligence Unit.[1] At the same time, the Home Secretary announced that in addition to the measures in the *Proceeds of Crime Bill*, special controls would be set out in an emergency Anti-Terrorism Bill that would allow the bank accounts of suspected terrorists to be monitored and frozen.

Provisions in the *Proceeds of Crime Act 2002* (POCA) enable the police and other law enforcement authorities to seize the proceeds of all crime, including terrorist crime. It brought together previous enactments and, together with the regulations made under it is the basis for most of the important, current, money laundering law. POCA was amended by the *Serious Organised Crime & Police Act 2005*.

2.1 The Money Laundering Offences (POCA) 2002

The main offences

The three principal money laundering offences are contained in sections 327, 328 and 329 of the Act. These offences are triable either in a Magistrates' Court or in the Crown Court and are punishable on conviction on indictment in the Crown Court by a maximum of 14 years imprisonment and/or a fine.

Section 327 – An offence is committed if a person conceals, disguises, converts, transfers or removes from the jurisdiction property which is, or represents, the proceeds of crime which the person knows or suspects represents the proceeds of crime.

Section 328 – An offence is committed when a person enters into or becomes concerned in an arrangement which he knows or suspects will facilitate another person to acquire, retain, use or control criminal property and the person knows or suspects that the property is criminal property.

Section 329 – An offence is committed when a person acquires, uses or has possession of property which he knows or suspects represents the proceeds of crime.

The 2005 Act made several minor, though welcomed by the professions, amendments. For example, Section 102 allows that if the source of the funds is criminal in this country but not in the country of origin then the funds are clean. For example, proceeds of bullfighting remitted to the UK are clean despite the fact that bullfighting is a criminal act in the UK. Section 104 eliminates the need to make what are called 'limited value reports' where there is very little to report other than the fact that suspicious activity has taken place. For example if neither the identity whereabouts nor address of the suspect is known, making a report is no longer necessary.

All three of the principal money laundering offences contain certain defences. For example, in the case of each of these offences, it is a defence to have made an authorised disclosure to, and obtain appropriate consent from, the authorities before doing the act which would constitute the offence (see sections 335 and 338 of the Act).

Obtaining consent

Appropriate consent is the consent of a constable, customs officer or an officer from the Serious Organised Crime Agency (SOCA) to proceed with a prohibited act (s 335). A key element of consent is the specification of time limits within which

---

1 'UK action plan on terrorist financing', HM Treasury, 15 October 2001. See also HC Deb 15 October 2001 cc 923–53.

the authorities must respond to an authorised disclosure in circumstances where a consent decision is required. The law specifies that consent decisions must be made within seven working days. If nothing is heard within that time, then the discloser can go ahead with an otherwise prohibited act without an offence being committed. If consent is withheld within the seven working days, then the authorities have a further 31 calendar days in which to take further action such as seeking a court order to restrain the assets in question. If nothing is heard after the end of the 31 day period, then the discloser can proceed with the transaction without committing an offence.

2.2 The second money laundering Directive

The second money laundering Directive was given effect by the *Money Laundering Regulations 2003/3075*, made under the *POCA 2002*. This revised the *Money Laundering Regulations 1993*[1] *and 2001*.[2] It is still the basis of many of the procedural aspects of the current money laundering specific legislation.

The main changes brought about by the regulation was in the way it affects financial and credit institutions, money services businesses, firms providing legal or accountancy services, casinos, estate agents, and some dealers in high value goods. They were laid as statutory instruments 2003/3074–3076 on 1st December 2003 and came into force on 1 March 2004.

The regulations prescribe arrangements that must be in place within firms carrying on relevant business, to forestall and prevent their being used for money laundering. They apply[3], inter alia, to:

- The regulated activities of all financial sector firms i.e. banks, building societies and other credit institutions; individuals and firms engaging in regulated investment activities under FSMA; issuers of electronic money; insurance companies undertaking long term life business, including the life business of Lloyd's of London;
- Bureaux de change, cheque encashment centres and money transmission services (money service businesses);
- The National Savings Bank; Corporate service providers, company formation agents, trust companies and trust service providers or managers;
- Casinos;
- Dealers in high value goods (including auctioneers) who accept payment in cash of Euro 15,000 or more (either single or linked transactions);
- Lawyers and accountants, when undertaking relevant business.

Persons carrying on relevant business under the regulations are required to establish and maintain appropriate systems and controls to forestall and prevent the firm being used in connection with money laundering covering:

- internal controls and communication;
- identification procedures;
- recognition of suspicious transactions and reporting procedures;
- awareness raising and training of employees; and
- record keeping.

Detailed advice as to the application and implementation of the regulations can be found in a document produced by the Joint Money Laundering Steering Group (JMLSG) in November 2007 and which has been subsequently amended. The main document, which is in two parts, can be found on the JMLSG website here:[4]

1 SI 1993/1933.
2 SI 2001/3641.
3 Regulation 2.
4 JMLSG website at http://www.jmlsg.org.uk/bba/jsp/polopoly.jps?d=758 retrieved 14 July 2009.

The Issues

The Treasury was aware that the regulations introduced many new requirements affecting potentially thousands of practitioners, hundreds of thousands of individuals and millions of individual transactions. There were many issues to be considered.

It consulted on the draft regulations in November 2002[1] and published a short analysis of responses in April 2003.[2] By April, the Government had recognised that it would not be able to keep the implementation deadline of June 2003. It said that the delay was necessary to take into account issues raised during the consultation period.

The consultation document[3] explained that in implementing the Directive the Government was trying to make the UK regime both a 'proportionate response to the risk of money laundering' but also to minimise 'competitive distortion' between different professions. The latter aim in particular means that in some cases the proposed scope of the regulatory regime may be wider than strictly necessary in order to avoid some unattractive consequences. The consultation document discussed a range of policy options and why extending its scope may be desirable.

The arguments and concerns over aspects of the regulations are set out in the consultation document. They are shown below.

Client confidentiality

Some correspondents mentioned the problem of client confidentiality. It is difficult to see, however, what action a government could take on client confidentiality without rendering the whole Directive impotent. The whole point of the Directive is for advisers and financial agents to alert the authorities to suspected activity. The point was raised some time ago in an article in the Financial Times it said:

> The parliamentary members of the special conciliation committee accepted virtually all of a text governing the professional secrecy of lawyers and their clients as proposed by the Belgian presidency of the EU. Tackling the big outstanding problem, the Maps agreed legal advice could be exempted from professional secrecy where a lawyer was taking part in money-laundering activities or knew that his client was seeking advice for money-laundering purposes. But the committee voted down a presidency proposal that lawyers should report their clients to the authorities when there was "reason to believe" the client was seeking advice to launder funds.

> Yesterday's discussions in the parliament have thus left resolution of an increasingly bitter dispute between the parliament and member states over money-laundering rules hanging on a phrase. If parliament and member states cannot resolve their differences by mid-November, the legislation will collapse. "The ball is now in the member states' court," declared James Provan, the UK Conservative MEP who leads the parliamentary side in the conciliation committee. Klaus-Heiner Lehne, the German Christian Democrat MEP who has steered the money-laundering legislation through parliament, strongly defended the MEPs' decision to amend the Belgian text. He said 28 Directive on the prevention of the use of the financial system for the purpose of money laundering

1 http://www.hm-treasury.gov.uk./media/F5B/68/monlaund_proprev_93and01_condoc. pdf. Retrieved 27 April 2007.

2 Treasury press notice, 29 April 2003, summarising responses available at http://www. hm-treasury.gov.uk./consultations_and_legislation/consult_monlaunreg/consult_ monlaunreg93_summary.cfm. Retrieved 27 April 2007.

3 http://www.hm-treasury.gov.uk/media//3F064/monlaund_propev_93and01_condoc. pdf.

the phrase "reason to believe" was unsuitable for criminal law. Belief, he said, "was a matter for theologians, not for prosecutors.[1]

De minimus reporting value

Another concern expressed has been the lack of a de minimus reporting value.

The Treasury analysis of responses to the consultation document included a section on the definition of high value dealers:

> Dealers in High Value Goods: The majority of respondents expressed the preference for businesses to be able to choose whether to accept cash transactions for Euro 15,000 or above. The other options of designating certain luxury goods or banning the use of cash over the limit were seen as impractical for the reasons stated in the consultation document. There were several objections to a registration fee being charged.

In this case, there is a de minimus limit, namely £10,000 (approx). This point was picked up in another Financial Times article:

> Retailers such as jewellers, antique shops and car dealers who accept payments of more than about £10,000 could unwittingly fall foul of new anti-money laundering regulations, lawyers have warned.

> Shops that are paid in cash for big-ticket items will face hefty fines if they cannot formally identify their customers once the laws come into effect in June. The moves, which implement a European Union Directive, are aimed at cracking down on money launderers who invest "dirty" money in luxury goods which are easy to transport and sell.

> But few shops are even aware of the rules, which will be slipped into UK law as a statutory instrument under the Financial Services and Markets Act. Fewer still have plans in place to make sure they can comply with the rules, according to retail sector specialists Simon White, retail lawyer at Browne Jacobson, said: "At present there is a complete lack of information being provided for retailers to prepare them for this legislation. "Retailers who accept large sums of money in cash, even innocently, could find themselves under investigation."

> Under the rules, any retailer who wishes to accept more than €15,000 will have to implement compliance procedures that include: registering with Customs & Excise, appointing a compliance officer, and training staff in the legislation.

> Customers looking to pay in cash will have to show proof of identity, such as a passport or new-style driving licence, and evidence of a current address.

> Even if a requested ID has been provided, sellers will have a legal duty to report suspicious transactions to the National Criminal Intelligence Service.

> The laws could mean many businesses stop accepting large cash payments in a bid to avoid the cost and effort of complying. Mr White said his firm was advising clients to stop taking such payments unless they really had to. He added: "While the penalties for non-compliance have yet to be confirmed, they will certainly be punitive as this is always the case with anti-money laundering regulations. They will certainly involve the potential for very large fines, even for accidental non-compliance.

---

1 'EU fails to find accord on anti-terrorist financing rules', *Financial Times*, 3 October 2001.

The laws are also likely to affect more businesses in Britain than many other EU countries because the government has chosen to interpret the term "high-value dealers" in the widest possible sense. It will include builders and other tradesmen and even less formal cash businesses such as horse auctions.[1]

The professions

The comments with respect to client confidentiality are obviously important here too. The professions though were exercised about the cost of the regulations. In the consultation document, the compliance costs for accountancy and legal services were considered together:

6(ii) Compliance costs for a typical business.

Accountancy and legal services

Approximately 65,000 firms operate in the UK in proving auditing, book-keeping, tax consultancy and other accountancy services. Approximately 2,000 of these are members of the CCAB bodies. Over 100,000 qualified solicitors are members of the Law Societies of England and Wales, Scotland and Northern Ireland. Many law and accountancy firms, including most of the major players, are registered to carry on investment business, and are thus already subject to the Money Laundering Regulations. Many other businesses already have extensive systems in place pursuant to a code of conduct, and could therefore comply with the regulations with minimal additional cost.

Estimates from the Law Society indicate that a medium sized firm (10 partners and 20 associates) whose system was not yet substantially in compliance with the Regulations would incur the following costs:-

Training: 1 day per year for the Money Laundering Reporting Officer (£1,000) and 2 hours training session for each fee earner every 3 years (£300 per person) Reporting system: ongoing monthly costs of £1,000

Storage costs: minimal. Solicitors typically keep client files for a minimum of 6 years and other affected sectors keep client records for tax or business reasons.

Total annual costs: £16,000

Total sector costs (excluding firms that are already compliant)

Option 1: Assuming that an additional 5,000–10,000 legal professionals and 10,000–20,000 accountants (equivalent to 500–1,000 medium-sized firms) would become subject to the Regulations, total sector costs would be in the range of £8 million to £16 million.

Options 2 and 3: In addition to the firms covered by option 1, approximately 43,000 firms of unqualified practitioners would be covered by the Regulations.

However, many of these would be much smaller than the average firm outlined above, and the sector includes a large number of sole practitioners. Assuming an average firm size of 4 practitioners, and using the Law Society estimates above, we estimate average costs to be just under £3,000 per firm. This would imply total sector costs in the range of £130 million to £150 million.

---

1 *Retailers face fines under new law to track big cash payments*, Financial Times 5 May 2203.

Identification

In terms of its impact upon the public, there is probably no bigger issue than the identification rule, the 'know your customer' rule. The extreme difficulty with which many people and groups of people, (returning ex-pats, students, migrants, the elderly etc) faced in trying to open a bank account has to many been the public face of money laundering.[1] This specific issue is dealt with in a practical way in another Library standard note – Bank Accounts problems of identification (SN/BT/3366) which is available on the intranet.

A detailed statement of identification needs mentioned in the last line can be found in part two (sectoral guidance) of the JMSLG Report mentioned above at: http://www.jmlsg.org.uk/content/1/c6/01/14/57/Part_II_HMT_approved.pdf

2.3 Serious Organised Crime Agency[2]

Although complex, the existing money laundering rules have at their heart a simple requirement, namely that, after careful procedures have been followed, if a worker or institution in the financial services or related sectors, has suspicions about a transaction it should be reported to the National Criminal Intelligence Service (NCIS). Subsequently NCIS was subsumed within the Serious Organised Crime Agency (SOCA) formed on 3 April 2006. Suspicious Activity Reports (SARS) have to be made in a prescribed manner on a special form. Given the nature of what accountants, lawyers, bankers, estate agents etc were being asked to report upon, i.e. 'suspicions', and the severity of the penalties if they did not report, there have been worries that regulated persons report anything on the 'better safe than sorry' principle. Taken to extremes this would swamp the resources of the receiving agency and render the entire system unworkable. There was also concern that for the effort put in to SARS very little emerged from it, and, there were concerns about the use of SAR related findings, especially the confidentiality of reported data.

These concerns lead to a review that reported in March 2006 *REVIEW OF THE SUSPICIOUS ACTIVITY REPORTS REGIME (The SARs Review)* written by the Head of SOCA Sir Stephen Lander.[3] With respect to the money laundering aspects the Review noted these criticisms:

> There is a perception in the regulated sectors that the SARs regime is broken: that institutions are spending some millions of pounds complying with burdensome legal obligations, yet Government is not similarly committed and there are virtually no results in terms of crimes prosecuted and the seizure of terrorist or criminal funds as a consequence of their efforts. This perception is principally focussed on the AML arrangements, but similar concerns, while muted by a reluctance to criticise post the events of 7 July 2005, were expressed during the review about the parallel CTF arrangements. While it is understandable that these perceptions may have arisen, they are, however, inaccurate. Not only is Government itself also spending sizeable sums on the regime, but there have continued to be significant SAR-related law enforcement successes and intelligence gains from its operation, albeit usually out of sight of those who provided the original lead information. However, as the KPMG, Jill Dando Institute and HMIC reports referred to already

1 This specific issue is dealt with in a practical way in another Library standard note – Bank Accounts problems of identification (SN/BT/3366) which is available on the intranet.
2 http://www.soca.gov.uk/index.html.
3 *The Sars Review: http://www.soca.gov.uk/downloads/SOCAtheSARsReview_FINAL_Web.pdf*, retrieved 28 April 2007.

have all indicated, and as NCIS as the current FIU itself accepts, there is significant room for improvement in the way the regime functions.[1]

The Report noted that there had been slightly less than 195,000 SARs in 2005, up from 20,000 in 2000. SOCA commented on the level of reporting:

> The main argument against seeking to suppress the numbers of SARs against some conception of a right size of reporting is however, a more fundamental one. In passing TA and POCA, Parliament determined to set wide definitions of terrorist and criminal property and significant penalties for money laundering, and to retain a low threshold for disclosures, involving "suspicion", not "knowledge" or "belief". The consequence appears to have been the significant growth in reporting already noted. Two conclusions follow. First, it would be improper for SOCA as the FIU to seek, against some concern about reporting volumes, to insert its judgement about the threshold for suspicion in place of the duty to make that judgement laid on the reporters by Parliament. In any event, it is self evident that SOCA would never be better qualified to determine what is suspicious in the context of the reporters' business than the reporters themselves.
>
> Second, it could be argued that in inviting Parliament to establish the regime set out in TA Part 3 and POCA Part 7, Government was accepting the responsibility for ensuring that the resulting volumes of information were handled effectively. Finally, it is worth remembering that UK volumes of SARs are not out of range of the volumes being reported in some other comparable jurisdictions.
>
> 54. Accordingly **I recommend (Recommendation 10)** that, while it would clearly be appropriate for SOCA to assist the reporting sectors to fulfil their statutory obligations, it would be inappropriate, given current legislation, for SOCA as the FIU, or Government more generally, to seek to suppress the overall number of SARs. In short, the correct Government position on numbers of SARs should be volume neutral.
>
> In practice, as already noted in Part III of this report, the current suspicion based approach has been delivering operational benefits to law enforcement, and there are thus grounds for believing that the arrangements are not fundamentally flawed. This does not, of course, mean that reporters should be released from the obligation to distinguish effectively between the unusual and the truly suspicious, nor that the regime would be well served by the removal of the due diligence arrangements put in place by many to make that distinction.
>
> 55. I have already set out earlier in this report the responsibility that I recommend should fall to SOCA to assist reporters. In particular, I identified a need for better guidance and training support (paragraph 47), reform of the arrangements for electronic reporting of SARs (paragraph 43), and the provision of agreed performance measurement information for the regime as a whole.
>
> 56. The uneven volumes and mixed quality of reporting both between and within sectors was noted in Part III of this report. Although these are at heart issues for the reporting institutions themselves and their regulators, **I recommend (Recommendation 11)** that SOCA should commit effort to identifying such problems and helping reporters address them. Changes already envisaged, such as a standard reporting form, and

---

1 Ibid para 25.

others now proposed, such as a glossary of terms to be used in describing the grounds for suspicion, should help the weaker performers; but identifying and remedying gaps in reporting would require collaboration with regulators and, given the size of the reporting community, a risk-based approach. **I recommend (Recommendation 12)** that this should be the subject of further discussion with regulators with the aim of devising joint programmes of work going forward.

Information about the workings of the regime can be had from the annual SOCA Report – one of the recommendations of the Lander Review – and a SARs-specific Annual Report, which includes activity numbers.

Successive Reports reveal the continuing balance sought between volume of SARS reports and their quality.

Between October 2007 and September 2008 there were 210,524 SAR notifications, of which 956 were passed to the National Terrorist Finance Unit.[1] The table below gives recent figures:

Key statistics

	Oct 09 to Sept 10	Oct 10 to Sept 11
	240,582	247,601
Total SARs Consent SARs	14,334	13,662

Source: SARS Activity Annual Report 2011, p10

The SARS work is now undertaken by the UK Financial Intelligence Unit which sits within SOCA and was a requirement of the third money laundering Directive (see below).

2.4 The third money laundering Directive (3MLD)

Following on from work by international bodies – the Financial Action Taskforce – a new set of regulations were drawn up. These came down to the UK as the third money laundering Directive (3MLD) of 15 December 2007.[2]

3MLD reproduces much of the second Directive but is more detailed and contains some new provisions.

In particular, it explicitly deals with terrorist financing; provides new definitions for Politically exposed Persons (PEPs); introduces the requirement for Money Service Businesses, Trust, and Company Service Providers to be licensed or registered under a fit and proper test; enhances the customer due diligence regime, encourages a risk based approach and prohibits anonymous accounts. It requires there to be monitoring and supervision of all the institutions covered by the Directive, and the collection of statistics on the effectiveness of the regime and on feedback. It also carries forward from earlier Directives a system in which institutions should refrain from suspicious transactions until they have informed the FIU (Article 24), and a requirement for something like a tipping off offence (Article 28).

1 SARs Annual Report 2007–8.
2 Directive 2005/60/EC, available at (retrieved 28 April 2007): http://europa.eu.int/eur-lex/lex/LexUriServ/site/en/oj/2005/l_309/l_30920051125en00150036.pdf.

The Treasury published its consultation document in July 2006[1] and the draft regulations consultation on the 22 January 2007.[2] Issues that required comment or were much debated included such things as:

- Definition of accountant and tax advisor
- Some organisations would escape the Directive if their dealings were small and of an occasional basis. 'Small' remains to be defined, currently the Treasury suggest £61,000 or €91,500.
- Should the Directive apply to a wider group of businesses? Currently not, however, the Government has clearly considered the possible inclusion of letting agents.
- The level at which casino's should exercise due diligence with customers – the current Government suggestion is that the threshold above which casinos should act should be set at €2,000 chips exchanged or gambled. There is a substantial section on casinos in the document.
- What customers or products should qualify under the new, risk-based simplified due diligence procedures.[3]
- Enforcement – what powers of entry, search and interrogation should the various supervisory bodies have and which bodies should they be?
- The definition of what activities are included in the operations of a trust or company service provider;
- The 'fit and proper' test – the government wants a limited definition of what makes a company fit and proper, largely based on a list of negative criterion – thou shalt nots – consultation is required on whether a broader 'holistic' approach should be adopted, if so is the new 'catch all' provision adequate for this purpose?

The new regulations were published in July 2007 as *The Money Laundering Regulations 2007* (SI 2007/2157).[4] Resolving some of the issues raised by consultation:

- 'Small' is defined as total turnover of less than £64,000, no transaction more than €1,000, the financial activity is less than 5% of the total annual turnover. (Schedule 2);
- Estate agents are included;
- Casinos are required to either verify the identity of all their customers before they gamble, either in house or remotely, or they are required to do so if the €2,000 threshold is breached. (Regulation 10);
- The 'fit and proper test' is essentially a list of specific thou shalt not have done this or that, capped by a catch-all: *(h) is otherwise not a fit and proper person with regard to the risk of money laundering or terrorist financing.*(Regulation 28);

An article outlining the working of the Directive was published by a partner in Simmons and Simmons solicitors. It said:

> The provisions of the Third Money Laundering Directive will be implemented in the UK in December 2007 when the Money Laundering Regulations 2007 ("the Regulations") are brought into force. The Third Directive and the Regulations raise a number of practical concerns for solicitors.

1 HM Treasury July 2006. http://www.hm-treasury.gov.uk/media/B60/AC/moneylaundering310706.pdf.

2 HM Treasury January 2007 http://www.hm-treasury.gov.uk/media/4EC/49/consult_thirdmoney_2007.pdf.

3 It is a source of surprise to this author to see how things have changed. MPs and hence the Library received many complaints about banks and other institutions refusing to open accounts for (amongst others) newly arrived individuals because of the ML rules. Now, the banks, in particular, are in great competition for the accounts of, especially, Polish migrants who years ago would have had no chance of getting one.

4 SI 2007/2157 Explanatory Memorandum available at: http://www.opsi.gov.uk/si/em2007/uksiem_20072157_en.pdf.

The Third Directive broadens the scope of applicability of the Second Directive, which was introduced in 2001. In 2001 the anti-money laundering regime was applied for the first time to "gatekeepers". It has now been extended to cover all traders in goods for transactions in cash of €15,000 or more. It also applies to more entrants to the regulated sector, including trust and company service providers and insurance intermediaries. This is one area of the Third Directive that may cause practical issues. Trust and company service providers are often consulted for privacy reasons and they may have the new customer due diligence and supervision requirements. They are currently grappling with the issues presented by this.

The Third Directive is more prescriptive than the Second Directive in that it has mandatory provisions for customer due diligence ("CDD") requirements. Most solicitors practising in England and Wales are well versed in the process of verifying their clients' identities but in a more flexible regime. However, the Third Directive does encourage a risk-based approach.

Article 8 of the Third Directive adds the requirement to identify, where applicable, the ultimate beneficial owner, including, for legal persons, trusts and similar legal arrangements, taking risk-based and adequate measures to understand the ownership and control structure of the customer. Those covered by the Third Directive will also now be required to obtain information on the intended nature and purpose of the business relationship and to monitor that relationship.

Obligations to identify the beneficial owner and understand the ownership and control structure of legal entities are new and difficulties are expected. Legal entities often have companies as shareholders or directors, making it hard to identify the beneficial owner. The issue is also a problem with customers/ clients domiciled in countries with no trade registry.

The Third Directive does on the one hand introduce a detailed regime for CDD but it also introduces a risk-based approach, which the regulated sector in the UK has applied for many years. This allows organisations to tailor their efforts more efficiently to their own business needs. Reduced CDD measures can be applied when the client is a credit or financial institution situated in a non-EU member state, which imposes requirements similar to the Directive. The reduced system can also be used in certain designated cases. Conversely, enhanced CDD measures must be taken in cases where there is a higher risk of money laundering or terrorist financing. This includes those cases where a customer is not physically present for identification purposes and special measures for PEPs (politically exposed persons). In these circumstances there is a requirement to take specific and adequate measures to compensate for the higher risk by requesting more documents or information.

It is likely that lawyers, in order to save time, rely on others to comply with the CDD requirements. The Third Directive now specifically states that a person may rely on a third party for CDD, but the ultimate responsibility for compliance remains with the institution covered by the Directive. This is part of a risk-based approach and should be carefully documented.

The Regulations will also introduce a new scheme of supervisors for each of the sectors not currently supervised or monitored for money laundering purposes. Solicitors will continue to be regulated by the Solicitors Regulation Authority.[1]

3MLD was itself amended by Regulations in 2012 – *the Money Laundering (Amendment) Regulations 2012* (SI2012/2298). The explanatory note on the effect of the amendments can be found here.
  The main changes are that it has:

- increased the powers of professional supervisory bodies to share information with each other. This means, for example that HMRC, which is responsible for supervising unqualified accountants, will now have wider scope to take matters into consideration to decide whether a person is "fit and proper".
- Relaxed the rules regarding reliance on other bodies 'due diligence' searches, so that fewer checks by different bodies on the same person need be made.
- Estate agents in the UK, but who dealt only with overseas sales are now included

Proposals that would have abolished some criminal penalties for breaches of 3MLR to be replaced by civil penalties imposed by the supervisory bodies were not taken forward.

3 Conclusion

Money laundering legislation has had a major impact upon business and individuals in the UK in terms of cost and time to set up systems and in the inconvenience faced by people struggling to find adequate identification to prove to their banks or solicitors who they are, often when they have been customers for years.
  The benefits of all this remain at best, literally, incalculable. Arrests and successful prosecutions, by number, appear very small. SOCA defines success in its Action Plan as:

> The broad performance framework identified for SOCA by the Home Secretary is designed to reflect the reality of what it has been tasked to achieve. The SOCA Board has determined that, in response to that framework set by the Home Secretary, SOCA will be governed by a performance regime that bears as closely as possible to the reality of outcomes that matter to the people of this country. Its main measures will be:
>
> - the quality of knowledge and understanding of serious organised crime;
> - criminal asset performance, where SOCA will contribute to Government wide asset recovery targets. These targets, and SOCA's contribution to them, are currently under review elsewhere within Government;
> - dislocation of criminal markets, assessed through evaluation of the impact of SOCA's activity, with an aim of generating evidence of that impact in the form of upward pressure on the price of criminal goods or services, a reduction in UK availability or quality, or evidence that criminals are finding the UK a less attractive market; and

---

1 Louise Delahunty, Simmons & Simmons, published Law Society's *Brussels Agenda*, 7 December 2007.

- the quality of SOCA's relationships with others, which will be measured through regular structured surveys.[1]

Evidence suggest that, for example, the price of most Class A drugs has fallen fairly consistently since 2001,[2] but, SOCA point out in their latest annual report, the purity of drugs has also declined. So hard evidence for success is still difficult for outside observers to obtain.

A detailed survey of the impact of the combined effects of the legislation was published by an academic at Newcastle Business School.[3] The author's conclusions were that there was very little hard evidence of the benefits of the legislation. Evidence is mainly 'second hand' in the sense that the indicators used are those derived from the system itself, i.e. number of SARS reported. Also, whereas the costs of the regime are born almost entirely by the industry, the 'rewards' are enjoyed by the law enforcement agencies by virtue of increased confiscations etc. The supposed benefit to industry of a 'clean reputation' was thought by some in the industry to be hard to calculate and more thought that publishing how much they spent on enforcement would have a negative impact on their shareholders.

More positively, however, industry, in particular the financial services industry, does appear to be more at ease with the legislation than it was. Responses from a limited sample of industry representatives suggests that the new risk-based approach works and has made life simpler. The sector is getting better at knowing when to report and when not to, and, crucially in retail sectors appears to be providing better training for its 'front line' staff. There is, perhaps inevitably, a feeling that public sector prosecutions do not match private industry's considerable efforts sufficiently. Another concern is that where companies have operations in a multiple jurisdictions, efforts made in the UK are undone by lower requirements overseas.[4]

The response to the third Directive too is generally positive. The Finance & Leasing Association state:

> We believe that, on the whole, these draft regulations are a positive response to most of our feedback and more generally to industry input. The Treasury has accepted most of the minor amendments we requested and generally reacted positively to most of our key concerns.
>
> We also welcome the Treasury's continuing consultation and dialogue with experts within the Joint Money Laundering Steering Group (JMLSG) and with sector and industry experts within trade bodies such as the BBA, IMA, ABI and the FLA. It is essential the Treasury maintains this dialogue in order to be able to iron out definitional, scope and supervisory concerns.[5]

The Electronic Money Association think that "overall the AML regime is workable" although

> "There is some frustration over the investment put into combating financial crime by the public sector however, when the private sector's compliance requirements are increasing. Law enforcement resources and ability to address industry concerns could be improved significantly.[6]

---

1 SOCA *Annual Plan 2006/07*, p 12.
2 Dept of Health *Drug Situation 2005*, p 110.
3 *Just How Effective is Money Laundering Legislation?* Jackie Harvey, Security Journal 2008.
4 Unofficial briefing Association of Foreign Banks.
5 Unofficial briefing.
6 Unofficial briefing.

Appendix 7.11 Torn? How do banks juggle duty to their customers with money-laundering obligations, asks Simon Goldstone[1]

IN BRIEF

The banker's dilemma: how to escape prosecution for money-laundering offences while complying with your customer's lawful instructions?

A bank is contractually obliged to honour its customers' transaction requests, provided that sufficient funds are in the customer's account; a bank is obliged by statute not to deal in the fruits of money-laundering, and faces prosecution under the Proceeds of Crime Act 2002 (POCA 2002) if it does so.

Shah v HSBC Private Bank Ltd [2012] EWHC 1283 (QB), [2012] All ER (D) 155 (May) gave a stark illustration of the potential for conflict between these duties: the defendant bank refused to execute certain transactions, on the basis that it suspected the account contained laundered money; those refusals led to the customer sustaining losses; the customer sought to recover those losses – around $300m – in an action for breach of contract.

The recent judgment of Mr Justice Supperstone shows how the courts will assess the bank's attempts to navigate a safe path between those conflicting duties. In this article I consider the case of Shah and its practical and legal implications.

THE TRANSACTION REQUESTS

Mr Shah was a Zimbabwean national of great wealth. He had held accounts at the bank since 2002. From time to time he would move large sums into and out of his account. This was consistent with his business as a dealer in the world's commodity and currency markets. On occasion his larger transfers raised the eyebrows of those in the bank's anti money-laundering function. In November 2003 Shah had requested that $19m be transferred to and from a Zimbabwean account on a short-term basis. The compliance team had queried, internally, whether it was necessary to inform the Serious Organised Crime Agency (SOCA). They decided that the transaction was not suspicious – despite the sum and destination of the funds – and SOCA was never informed. In December 2004, the bank's compliance officer had sent a communiqué to SOCA, following receipt into one of Shah's accounts of a modest (£3,500) transfer which the bank suspected to be the proceeds of crime.

The events which triggered the claim took place in 2006. First, Shah transferred into HSBC $28m from an account he held with Credit Agricole in Geneva. His reason for moving this sum was that a fraudulent attempt had been made to access the Swiss account; Shah wanted the money safe while security was tightened in Geneva. Following the transfer, the money was held in a rolling account, which earned interest on a monthly basis. Some weeks later, Shah asked for the funds to

1 © LexisNexis. All rights reserved. This article has been reproduced by kind permission of Simon Goldstone of 4 Pump Court and the New Law Journal.

be returned to Switzerland. However, he was persuaded by the defendant to retain the money in London for a further month. When that month passed, he renewed his request for the money to be wired to Geneva. The request was declined; the bank was unable to comply on account of its "statutory obligations".

This delphic response signified that the bank had sent a suspicious activity report (SAR) to SOCA, and would not be able to execute his request until SOCA had consented. Furthermore, the bank considered itself unable to inform their customer of the reason for this delay.

While it may be thought extraordinary that a bank could refuse to do what its customer asked of it, and then to offer no explanation for such refusal, the bank's position was that this response was necessary and consistent with the reporting regime under POCA 2002. The interplay of the various relevant sections of POCA 2002 is as follows:

(i)   The bank faces prosecution if it deals in money that is the proceeds of crime (s 327).

(ii)   Where it suspects that the account from which it has been asked to effect a transfer is tainted by laundered money, the bank must inform SOCA of that suspicion (s 330).

(iii)   As and when SOCA consent to the transaction, the bank may comply with its customer's transfer request (s 338).

(iv)   The bank is committing a criminal offence if it "tips off" the customer about a report to SOCA in circumstances where a police investigation might be prejudiced by the customer's awareness of the report (s 333).

In due course, SOCA gave its consent and the money was returned to Geneva.

Shortly after this episode, Shah made a second request which the bank again refused to action. This was a distinctly modest request, for a transfer of $7,200 to a Mr Kabra, Shah's previous bookkeeper. The transfer would settle a debt arising from the termination of his employment. Again, the bank offered no explanation other than that it was "complying with statutory obligations". The effect of this refusal was, on Shah's case, cataclysmic. Shah told Mr Kabra about the bank's explanation; Kabra put two and two together, and concluded that Shah was suspected of moneylaundering.The Harare grapevine did the rest: within a matter of days the Zimbabwean authorities had carried out a dawn raid at Shah's home and frozen his accounts with the Reserve Bank of Zimbabwe (RBZ). Shah begged HSBC to explain their actions – this would give RBZ the comfort they needed to release his assets; however the bank, mindful of the "tipping-off" provisions of POCA 2002, declined to provide Shah with the information he required. His Zimbabwean assets remained locked until RBZ softened their position, permitting him to re-invest in government bonds. However, those gilts gave a miserly return compared to what was available in the markets in which Shah had been operating. The difference came to approximately $300m, and this is what Shah claimed against the bank.

THE DEFENCE

The bank's reaction to the claim was simple: at the time of the SARs they suspected that the money in the accounts was criminal property, and therefore were unable to effect the transactions without SOCA's consent; second, if they had given Shah the explanation he sought, they would have faced the risk of prosecution for tipping-off.

SUSPICION

Back in 2009, Mr Justice Hamblen gave summary judgment for the bank on the basis that Shah would never be able to gainsay the bank's averment that it suspected that the accounts contained criminal property (*Shah v HSBC Private Bank (UK) Ltd* [2009] EWHC 79 (QB), [2009] All ER (D) 204 (Jan)). This ruling was overturned on appeal (*Shah v HSBC Private Bank (UK) Ltd* [2010] EWCA Civ 31, [2010] 3 All ER 477): since the bank was, on the face of it, in breach of contract by refusing to honour its customer's request, it was for the bank to prove that it held the suspicion that it alleged.

Supperstone J found that there was an implied term permitting the bank to refuse to execute a payment instruction in the absence of SOCA's consent if, as a matter of fact, it suspected the transaction constituted money-laundering.

The factual evidence as to suspicion was given by a Mr Wigley, the officer who made the ultimate decision as to whether to report transactions to SOCA. He was cross-examined for some six days. Part of the reason for such a long stint in the witness box was that there was limited documentary evidence as to the state of mind of the bank at the time of the SARs; furthermore, what documentary evidence there was did not demonstrate with any great clarity the basis of any suspicion. That said, the SARs themselves were deployed, and Wigley was able to persuade the court that he would not have sent the SARs if he had not been suspicious: after all, he had no particular axe to grind with Shah, and bad faith was not alleged.

The judge accepted that:

(i) the sheer size of the $28m transaction probably caused suspicion (even though this was not made explicit in the SAR itself, and the 2003 transaction had not been reported even though for a comparably vast sum);

(ii) the fact that personnel working closer to the coal-face had recorded suspicions probably influenced Mr Wigley's own suspicion (notwithstanding that his evidence was that he had formed his own independent suspicion); and

(iii) Wigley found suspicious the explanation that Shah had given for wanting to move his funds from Switzerland and back again (even though, by the time of the trial, a transcript of a telephone conversation had been disclosed which indicated that Shah's account manager had checked this explanation with Credit Agricole who backed it up);

Importantly, the judge found that although certain aspects of the bank's account management seemed inconsistent with suspicion, it did not follow that Wigley himself was not suspicious. For example, in persuading Shah to retain the $28m for a further month the bank, if suspicious, would (if the money had in fact been laundered) have committed a s 327 offence. Rather, the emphasis of the judicial enquiry was squarely on whether there was, as a matter of fact, a suspicion at the time of the SARs, not on whether every detail of the bank's conduct throughout its dealings with Shah was consistent with suspicion.

Interestingly, there was a possibility that the $7,200 which was the subject of the second SAR did not originate from the $28m funds that the bank suspected to be criminal property. This was a question of accounting which the court was unable to resolve; Wigley's understanding was that the funds came from the same account, and that was sufficient for the court: even if it transpired that the smaller sum came from a different pot the bank's suspicion made it impossible for them not to report the second smaller transaction to SOCA.

WITHHOLDING INFORMATION

The second limb of Shah's case was that it was "part and parcel of the bank's duty that it would keep the customer informed of the reasons why its instructions could not be complied with"; and that bank's refusal to provide RBZ with the information which would have led to them releasing his Zimabawean assets was in breach of that duty. Supperstone J held that the bank was under no such duty: often the bank would not know whether a SAR had triggered an investigation, or might lead to an investigation in the future and therefore whether the provision of the information might constitute a tipping-off offence. The term would be "unworkable".

CONCLUSION

Four and a half years after proceedings were issued, and following two visits to the Court of Appeal, Shah's claim has finally been laid to rest. It is clear from the judgment that even where a bank's accounting and record-keeping leave much to be desired, a claim will be dismissed if a bank can provide plausible evidence of suspicion. Further, the mere fact that SOCA has consented to a transaction does not oblige the bank to give chapter and verse as to why the transaction was delayed: the potential liability for tipping-off survives the consent, and can last for as long as the bank thinks that an investigation is a realistic possibility.

The judgment reads like a shoulder massage for compliance officers at banks who might have nervously feared a torrent of similar claims. In reality, unless a claimant in Mr Shah's position can prove that a bank acted in bad faith, he will have a mountain to climb in proving that a SAR was unaccompanied by the suspicion necessary to suspend the bank's usual duties to honour its customer's mandate.

Appendix 7.12 *May*

This is the first of a trilogy of appeals relating to the confiscation of criminal assets. On 24 September 2001 in the Central Criminal Court before Judge Samuels QC, the appellant pleaded guilty to a count of conspiracy to cheat contrary to section 1(1) of the Criminal Law Act 1977. On 3 October 2001 he was sentenced to five years' imprisonment. On 2 August 2002 a confiscation order was made against him in the sum of £3,264,277 with six years' imprisonment in default of payment under the Criminal Justice Act 1988 as amended.

The conspiracy involved the wrongful withholding and reclaiming of VAT from HM Customs & Excise, resulting in a loss to public funds of around £11m. There were a number of other conspirators, some before the court, some not. Limited companies had been incorporated solely for the purpose of dishonestly retaining and reclaiming the VAT on sales of high value computer processing units ("CPUs"). Between February 1999 and September 2000 four such companies in turn imported CPUs from the European Union, no VAT being payable on importation. The goods were then sold on to a trader in the UK, thereby attracting a liability to VAT at the standard rate of 17.5%. The UK trader (also party to the fraud and commonly known as the "buffer company") ostensibly paid the purchase price plus VAT for the goods. The dishonest import company (commonly known as the "missing trader"), however, instead of accounting for the VAT received, retained it and then disappeared as a trading entity before enforcement action could be taken. The UK trader would then export the same goods (another zero-rated supply) back to the dishonest foreign supplier and itself reclaim the VAT which it had ostensibly paid to the importing company. This practice, with each importing company disappearing after a short trading life, is known as a "missing trader" or "carousel" fraud. It is a prevalent form of fraud, causing (the committee was told) very large losses to public funds. There were four phases of this conspiracy, referable to each of the four successive missing trader companies.

The appellant himself joined the conspiracy about halfway through and was involved only with the last two phases. With regard to these phases, however, he was found to be a joint principal, indeed the driving force, behind the fraud. The VAT unaccounted for during phases 3 and 4 totalled £4,439,533. The essential structure of the [old] regime requires the court, before making a confiscation order, to address and answer three questions:

- The first question is: has the defendant (D) benefited from the relevant criminal conduct? If the answer to that question is negative, the inquiry ends.

- If the answer is positive, the second question is: what is the value of the benefit D has so obtained?

- The third question is: what sum is recoverable from D?

The questions are distinct and the answer given to one does not determine the answer to be given to another. The questions and answers should not be elided.

Although "confiscation" is the name ordinarily given to this process, it is not confiscation in the sense in which schoolchildren and others understand it. A criminal caught in possession of criminally-acquired assets will, it is true, suffer their seizure by the state. Where, however, a criminal has benefited financially from crime but no longer possesses the specific fruits of his crime, he will be deprived of assets of equivalent value, if he has them. The object is to deprive him, directly or indirectly, of what he has gained. "Confiscation" is, as Lord Hobhouse of Woodborough observed in *In re Norris* [2001] UKHL 34, [2001] 1 WLR 1388, para 12, a misnomer.

The first question: benefit: The court first [has] to determine whether D had benefited from [the crime]. In *R v Moran* [2001] EWCA Crim 1770, [2002] 1 WLR 253, a case under the unamended 1988 Act. The defendant, a market trader, had cheated the Inland Revenue by failing to disclose profits. A confiscation order had been made in the amount of tax underpaid plus interest. This was rightly held to be the pecuniary advantage, within the meaning of section 71(5), which the defendant had obtained. In *R v Olubitan* [2003] EWCA Crim 2940, [2004] 2 Cr App R (S) 70, a case under the amended 1988 Act, the defendant was convicted of conspiracy to defraud. At the confiscation hearing he was found to have benefited to the extent of £123,000 and an order was made in the smaller sum of £88,000. The evidence, however, showed that he had joined the conspiracy on the day that police action brought it to an end by interception of a dummy consignment arranged to trap the conspirators. On these facts the Court of Appeal rightly held that the defendant had obtained nothing from his participation in this conspiracy, observing (p 78) that section 71 (1A) and (5) are

> *"not to be construed so that a person may be held to have obtained property or derived a pecuniary advantage when a proper view of the evidence demonstrates that he has not in fact done so".*

The second question: the value of the benefit: The defendant's benefit [is] the value of the property he had obtained as a result of or in connection with the commission of the relevant criminal offence, and the value of a pecuniary advantage …was the money value of that advantage. The [2002 Act] simply provides that if a person benefits from conduct his benefit is the value of the property obtained. This simplicity is, however, to some extent deceptive, since sections 79–80 contain detailed rules, which need not for present purposes be summarised, for assessing the value of property obtained. It is unsurprising, given the severity of the potential consequences, that the answering of this second question has given rise to many problems, some of detail which do not call for mention here, and some of principle which do.

The defendant in the recent case of *R v Sharma* [2006] EWCA Crim 16, [2006] 2 Cr App R (S) 416 was convicted of conspiracy to defraud. The fraud in which he was engaged obtained about £179,000, paid into a company account of which the defendant was the sole signatory. A confiscation order was made against him in the sum of £179,000. It was argued on appeal (paras 2(1) and 14) that this figure should have been reduced to take account of sums paid out by the defendant to his fellow conspirators. This argument was rejected. It was rightly held (para 19), applying general principles of law, that a person who receives money into his bank account obtains it from the source from which it is derived and, where he is the sole signatory on the account, he obtains the money and has possession of it for his own benefit. Where (ibid) the defendants have not jointly obtained the benefit, but there has been a disposal by one member of a criminal enterprise to another who knowingly receives it, each is treated as the recipient of a benefit to the extent of the value of the money which has come into the possession of each of them. The amount of the benefit a defendant obtains (para 25) is not affected by the amount which might be obtained by others to whom he transfers any part of the benefit.

The third question: the recoverable amount: From the 1986 Act onwards, the courts have been required to reinforce confiscation orders by the imposition of a term of imprisonment to be served in default of payment. But it has been recognised that a defendant may lack the means to pay a sum equal to the aggregate of the payments or rewards he has received, or the value of the property or pecuniary advantages he has obtained. It has also been recognised that it would be unjust to imprison a defendant for failure to pay a sum which he cannot pay. Thus provision has been made for assessing the means available to a defendant and, if that yields a figure smaller than that of his aggregate benefit, making a confiscation order in the former, not the latter, sum. The answering of this third question is a very important stage in the procedure for making confiscation orders since, however great the payments a defendant may have received or the property he may have obtained, he cannot be ordered to pay a sum which is beyond his means to pay.

Conclusion: The sum which the appellant, jointly with others, was found to have fraudulently obtained from HM Customs and Excise was, in law, as much his as if he had acted alone. That conclusion leads ineluctably to the further conclusions that he benefited from his offending, and benefited to an extent substantially greater than the confiscation order made against him (because of the deduction erroneously made by the judge as recorded in para 6 above). The order made was less than his realisable assets. It is entirely consistent with the legitimate objects of the legislation, and it requires, that he be ordered to pay such sum, which involves no injustice or lack of proportionality. The legislation is, as Lord Steyn described it in *R v Rezvi* [2003] 1 AC 1099, para 17, "a precise, fair and proportionate response to the important need to protect the public". *R v Porter* [1990] 1 WLR 1260 is not authority that the court has power to apportion liability between parties jointly liable, a procedure which would be contrary to principle and unauthorised by statute. No error was shown in the reasoning of Keene LJ, with which the committee generally agrees, while stressing that in any given case the statutory questions must be answered by applying the statutory language, shorn of judicial glosses and paraphrases, to the facts of that case. The appeal must be dismissed.

COMMENT

Although in the period April 2007–February 2008 [immediately before this judgement] the courts in England and Wales made 4,504 such orders in sums totalling £225.87 million, the 17 December 2013 Report of the National Audit Office notes that in 2012–13, 673,000 offenders were convicted of a crime (many of which had a financial element), yet only 6,392 confiscation orders were set [this an increase of less than 50% some 5 years later]

Figure 4

Confiscation orders imposed since 1987, by order size

Order size	Orders	Benefit assessed (£m)	Current order amount (£m)	Amount confiscated (£m)	Accrued interest (£m)	Collection rate (including interest) (%)
£0 or less	611	473.7	– 3.1	– 3.1	0.7	N/A
£0.01–£1,000	23,400	1,721.2	6.5	6.3	0.5	89
£1,000.01–£25,000	19,202	1,991.9	135.8	118.7	6.4	84
£25,000.01–£100,000	5,631	2,303.3	285.8	219.5	20.1	72
£100,000.01–£500,000	2,566	4,138.3	544.7	35 6.1	59.8	59
£500,000.01–£1,000,000	358	1,026.6	252.4	124.1	47. 0	41
£1,000,000.01–£50,000,000	261	4,151.0	911.6	2 07.3	215.9	18
Total	**52,029**	**15,806.1**	**2,133.6**	**1,029.0**	**350.3**	**41**

Notes

1 158 orders have negative amounts to correct accrued interest reporting. 453 orders are for £0.

2 Figure includes more recent orders where there has been less time to collect monies.

Source: National Audit Office analysis. Data taken from Joint Asset Recovery Database in September 2013.

Appendix 8

Trustees and Money Laundering

Contents

Appendix 8.1   Trustees and Money Laundering Case studies (updated)

Case study 1

Consider the following facts and identify the criminal offences and by whom committed, if any.

Nice Profit Company Limited ('NPC') is a Hong Kong incorporated company, doing business in import export. Its entire issued share capital, HK$2, is legally and beneficially owned by its two directors, Mr P and Mr Q, who are HK residents.

It commenced business in June 2012, having been incorporated by the owners' solicitors in April 2012. The service company of these solicitors acts as company secretary to NPC. The registered office is the principal place of business, an office owned by a BVI company ('PropCo') owned as to 50% each by the trustee of the P and Q family trusts; the trustee is the HK service company of the accountants of Mr P and Mr Q who are the auditors of NPC, which also acts as director of PropCo.

The rental paid for the office is at a rate more than three times the market rate, but PropCo has a lot of HK tax losses and the solicitors and accountants, who both advised in respect of the structuring of NPC, thought that this was a good way to minimise the profits of NPC.

The profits of NPC are also minimised by the payment of a 3% commission on all sales introduced to NPC by, ComCo, a sister company of PropCo with the same director. The commission arrangement was recommended by the two advisors and the agreement was drafted by the solicitors. ComCo, also a BVI company, has no staff or activity; the commission payments are paid to the client account of the accountants, as there has been some difficulty in opening a bank account for ComCo.

NPC gets nearly all the products it sells and exports manufactured in China by various third parties; it assists the directors of some of those third parties by paying the invoices less 'agreed charges of 5%' and then paying that amount to the BVI company owned by the directors whom it is assisting, companies set up by the same solicitors, the payment being to the solicitors' client account and against invoicing done by the solicitors' firms staff 'for services rendered'.

NPC sells nearly all of the products it buys from China around the region, mostly to companies in Indonesia, Korea or The Philippines. It generally assists the directors of the buyer companies to minimise their companies' taxes by over-invoicing and then paying out the surplus over the real price to the accounts of banks in Hong Kong or Singapore nominated by the buyers' directors; in the records of NPC these payments appear as 'finance charges on trade facilities arranged for and due by overseas customers'.

NPC elected to have a short first financial period, to 30 November; this was done in the expectation that there would be losses and that NPC would then get the usual four year exemption from filing profits tax returns. The audit of the accounts of NPC has just been signed by the directors and accountants with a clean audit report.

Some of the items which NPC is able to source and sell are subject to quota restrictions in either the US, or the EU; in anticipation of finding buyers for these goods, at meetings in Hong Kong Mr Q made an arrangement with his brother in Dubai, and Mr P with his brother in Mauritius, for the issue of Certificates of Origin from those countries whenever needed, 'costing a little more if the goods weren't shipped via there'; both relatives are Government officials in their respective countries of residence.

Case study 2

Consider the following facts and identify and comment upon any reporting obligations which you may determine the facts suggest could require, upon whom they fall, and with whom liability for failure to report rests.

ABC Ltd is a Hong Kong company wholly owned by the partners of ABC & Associates, a firm of Accountants practicing in Hong Kong. The directors are some of partners of the firm, as well as some of the employees.

The firm is affiliated to XY International and as such has access to the 'world-wide XY partnership'. The firm holds itself out as possessing 'multinational, multi-disciplinary staff and expertise'. The firm routinely gives tax advice other than in respect of Hong Kong, sometimes having checked the same with overseas affiliated offices – if the client so requested and was paying for the same. One such affiliate is in the PRC.

ABC Ltd often receives referrals of work from the overseas affiliates of the firm, as well as receiving instructions on corporate structures, and the like, from the partners of the firm in Hong Kong. The standing instructions are to accept such referrals and instructions without needing to check further.

For the most part ABC conducts a corporate secretarial practice for clients – that is to say it sets up local and foreign companies, acts as the Company Secretary, either directly or through a wholly-owned 'nominee company', provides a registered office or a correspondence address to foreign companies, and provides administrative support.

The services do not include directors or employees of ABC acting as director of client companies. Where clients require directors of record, this work is given to retired partners of the firm who have no direct dealing with the clients and merely collect a fee and sign whatever is prepared and sent round to them for signature by ABC.

These former partners are all indemnified by the current partners in respect of all liabilities arising from their acting as directors of client companies.

One of the wholly-owned 'nominee companies' is ABC Nominees Ltd, a Hong Kong incorporated company, the directors of which are the same as those of ABC Ltd, plus some extra members of the firm's staff; it acts as nominee shareholder and trustee of trusts declared for the benefit of clients, generally to 'put a bit of distance' between the client and the underlying company managed by ABC Ltd.

Two of the directors of 'Nominees' are HK admitted solicitors who are employed by ABC.

In June 2011 one of the partners of the firm, who is also a director of both ABC and ABC Nominees was approached by the partner of the affiliated firm in the PRC to set up a structure for the managing director of a formerly state-owned company there, now privatised and listed in Shanghai, which gentleman, Mr X, will be running the soon to be set-up in Hong Kong subsidiary of the listed company.

The partner from the PRC affiliate informed the HK partner that the Hong Kong company will be used to reinvoice goods of the parent to overseas buyers, 'trapping the profits in Hong Kong' and making it easier to 'manage the parent's cash flow and exchange control problems'. Whilst the structure to be set up for Mr X, was to be used to enable him, who will continue to reside in the PRC but just come to HK for board meetings, to benefit from a 'split contract type arrangement'.

Due to the 'market sensitive nature' of the transactions, the Hong Kong partner was asked to keep the identity of Mr X, the client, to himself. He did so, but later advised the firm's management committee of the fact of the structure having been set up.

That structure which was set up upon his instructions, consists of a 'blind trust' owning a BVI company. 'Nominees' is the trustee of said trust and 'Corporate Services' manages the BVI company, with one of the former partners acting as its sole director. Corporate Services also provides secretarial accounting and administration (consisting of the reinvoicing activity) to the subsidiary of the PRC company and the firm audit its accounts.

There is a contract between the said subsidiary and the said BVI company, written by one of the solicitor directors of ABC Nominees, under which the services of Mr X are provided to the subsidiary for USD20,000 per quarter, plus an annual profit share. There is no contract between Mr X and the BVI company.

The activity of the HK subsidiary gradually built up, and all of the profits from the reinvoicing, net of the quarterly fee to the BVI company and various professional charges for the company and the trust/BVI company structure, were retained in the subsidiary.

On 31 December 2013 Mr X declared that the profit share due to the BVI company for the period from commencement to date would be USD1,500,000 – approximately 80% of the profits from the reinvoicing activity; the director of the BVI company duly signed the invoice for this amount when it was presented to him by 'Corporate Services' on 2 January 2014 and at the same time he signed documentation for the same amount to be paid by the BVI company, as dividend, in favour of ABC Nominees, its shareholder; against the instructions of the partner in charge, ABC Nominees immediately made a 'distribution' to the three adult children of Mr X who are now studying in the US as soon as the money was received by ABC Nominees – having been transferred directly there from the HK company 'to save time and bank charges.

On 10 January 2014 it was reported that Mr X had sadly died in a car accident.

Case study 3

Consider the following facts and identify and comment upon any issues of possible criminal or civil liability, other than in respect of any breach of trust, which you may determine the facts suggest.

ABC Ltd is the sole trustee of a trust subject to BVI Law, T Family Trust. ABC Ltd is incorporated in Hong Kong and is managed and controlled by a board of directors all of whom are HK resident individuals. ABC Ltd carries on its business from offices in HK. The funds of T Family Trust are for the most part held in an account with LM Bank in Hong Kong, an account which is operated by various operated by staff of ABC Ltd; a small sum, being the initial settlement sum of HKD100 is held in the file of T Family Trust maintained by ABC Ltd at its HK offices.

The settlor of T Family Trust, who provided the HKD100 out of her own money, was at the time a member of staff of ABC Ltd, who is not a member of the T Family; she was later dismissed for stealing money from various clients' funds, but no report was made to the police and no money was recovered.

The named beneficiaries of T Family Trust are The International Red Cross HK Branch and The Community Chest of HK.

The balance of the trust funds were received by a series of transfers to ABC Ltd from a HK bank account of a BVIIBC of which Mr T is the sole director and bank account signatory; ABC Ltd provide a correspondence address and a corporate 'authorised signatory' to that company; the bearer share certificate was delivered by ABC Ltd to Mr T, a HK resident at the time, but now a resident of Australia, as he has been since November 2012. One of the directors of ABC Ltd knows that the BVI company was funded by transfers from Mr T's personal bank account in Hong Kong and that the bearer share certificate is kept in the safety deposit box which Mr T still has with that bank.

On several occasions since March 2013, at the request of Mr T, various invoices for 'services rendered' have been issued by the BVI IBC, signed by various persons allowed to represent the corporate authorised signatory, and addressed to a company in Australia and to the attention of Mr T. Mr T advised ABC Ltd that the payments were to reduce his tax exposure in Australia, by reducing the amount of his salary from the Australian company.

All of these invoices have been paid and the funds then immediately transferred to ABC Ltd, for the A/c of T Family Trust Over the same period, again at the request of Mr T, various payments have been made out of the trust funds held at LM Bank to persons in the US, Australia and the UK. All of these payments were recorded in the records of T Family Trust as loans to Mr T and then, one week later, forgiven.

Some of the interest earned on the bank deposits of T Family Trust has been given to The Community Chest.

Case study 4

Consider the following facts and identify and comment upon any issues of possible criminal or civil liability, or reporting obligations, which you may determine the facts suggest.

R, S & T, HK Representative Office, is the HK Representative Office of one of Switzerland's oldest private banks, which, in turn, is wholly owned by a large English bank, D Bank.

X, Y & Co are D Bank's Hong Kong solicitors.

The staff of the Rep Office routinely instruct X, Y & Co to set up structures to hold the money of the banks new clients, whilst the solicitors routinely suggest to their clients that they should consider appointing the Swiss bank to manage their money and arrange appointments at the Rep Office.

Most of the structures advised upon by the solicitors end up being managed by D Bank Trustees Ltd, a BVI licensed trustee company with offices in various parts of the world, including with a Part XI registration in Hong Kong. A partner of X, Y & Co is a director of D Bank Trustees Ltd.

Mr K is a US citizen, resident in both Thailand and Hong Kong; he runs a large and successful company in Hong Kong dealing in Asian antiques and artifacts,

LK Ltd. That company is BVI incorporated, but has a Part XI registration in HK. It is owned as to 50% by D Bank Trustees Ltd, operating via their HK branch, as nominee for the wife of Mr K, who is a Philippine citizen resident in Hong Kong – where she works for an airline as a flight attendant; and as to the other 50% by D Bank Trustees Ltd, operating via their Jersey branch, as trustee for Mr L and his issue, he being a Swiss citizen and resident with a business there, 'Asia-Europe Exchange' importing Asian antiques and artifacts from LK Ltd. Administration to that business is provided by D Bank Trustees Ltd, Zug branch.

Asia-Europe Exchange makes merely nominal profits from its business, enough to cover Mr L's costs.

Mrs. K approaches one of the staff of the Rep Office, Zinkie, and tells her that she is concerned that Mr K might be about to leave her and so she wants to get a structure set up that will protect her and the K children if that happens – she wants to take the remainder of the 50% of the profits paid out over the years as dividends from LK Ltd to D Bank Trustees Ltd, HK branch, that were not paid directly to Mr K, which remainders have always been and are presently held on one month call deposits in D Bank's Singapore branch, and place them into a trust and then have the Swiss bank manage the money.

Zinkie sends Mrs. K along to X, Y & Co for confirmation of the 'trust structuring' advice she has given Mrs K, via the brochure of D Bank Trustees Ltd.

Co-incidentally, the HK wife of Mr L has just instructed the same firm to act for her in her intended divorce of Mr L She has told the solicitor handling the matter that once the divorce is out of the way and she has got her share she intends to report Mr L to the Swiss authorities, because she is sure he has never told them about his 'hidden ownership' of LK Ltd and she thinks that he also imports entertainers and domestic helpers from Thailand into Europe under the Asia-Europe Exchange business, ladies who are officially employed by LK Ltd to do market research amongst customers – contracts of employment actually prepared by the firm upon instructions from Mr K.

Appendix 8.2   Extracts from 'Practical Implications of Money Laundering Regulations – Tax Evasion'

by John Nugent

Director PKF (Isle of Man) Limited
for the STEP Winter Conference 2003

Introduction

This paper deals with the potential implications of advance money laundering legislation for organisations that have, perhaps unconsciously, assisted in the evasion of taxes. Whilst this is only one aspect of money laundering legislation it is by no means a narrow issue and if the following analysis is correct its short and long-term effects could be substantial.

The implications of money laundering legislation for tax evasion are dealt with from the perspective of the offshore financial centres, but this is a reasonable perspective given that they have probably been the natural home for the bulk of pure tax evasion. However, the potential implications do not only attach to those latter day tax havens and their businesses, but may involve onshore clients and professional advisors who have had no involvement in any culpable activity. The problems highlighted therefore need to be taken seriously by a wide range of individuals and organisations in offshore and onshore locations.

Tax evasion

The UK tax authorities may consider tax evasion and tax avoidance to be equally unacceptable activities but the real difference between them can be highlighted by the way in which they are identified, and by the remedies that are then available to attack and counteract them. In the case of tax evasion, the tax authorities have the full force of their investigative armoury, supplemented by flows of information from voluntary tip-offs, exchanges of information with other departments, exchanges of information with other jurisdictions, money laundering disclosures and more recently the extraction of information from organisations which are suspected of harbouring certain species of tax evasion arrangements. The action they can then take to discourage tax evasion includes well publicised criminal prosecutions resulting in jail sentences. On the other hand, tax avoidance is identified by the careful scrutiny of tax returns and other tax records and by the systematic investigation of suspected wide-ranging avoidance techniques. Avoidance arrangements are then dealt with by means of technical challenges which the tax authorities hope will prove that the arrangements do not work and which will then lead to a financial settlement. Future tax avoidance is tackled by means of detailed anti-avoidance legislation.

Although both are economically unacceptable it is therefore clear that tax evasion is considered at some level to be more serious than tax avoidance. It is quite simply a criminal activity.

Tax evasion involves some blameworthy act or omission and is in reality equivalent to fraud. It is typified by a deliberate failure to report something to the tax authorities which the law requires should be reported; or by a distortion or falsification of information or documents knowing that such falsehoods may reduce a liability which would otherwise be due. In essence tax evasion therefore involves the concealment of the true facts of an arrangement.

In contrast tax avoidance can be considered as an attempt to reduce a tax liability in a manner which is contrary to the intentions of the authority who set out the law which enforces the system of taxation. Importantly though, it does not involve any element of concealment or alteration of the true facts of an arrangement. It does not involve fraud. Tax avoidance seeks to reduce a potential tax liability by the exploitation of opportunities which exist because of the structure of the taxing legislation, but to do so in a way that can be fully and properly disclosed to the taxing authorities. Indeed the only safe approach for an organisation which does not want to be involved with tax evasion is to focus on full and proper disclosure.

The Inland Revenue have traditionally only prosecuted in a small number of the investigations they carry out each year, but (during 2003) they have been told that they must boost their rate of prosecutions, at a time when they are increasing their focus on offshore tax evasion. Publicising such prosecutions is obviously part of their strategy and the selection of cases for prosecution will no doubt sometimes be influenced by the impact they will have on the public and professionals. From the Inland Revenue's point of view, a prosecution which results in an accountant in Jersey going to jail is an extremely worthwhile exercise in the fight against offshore tax evasion. Publicity of this nature has two major implications for the Inland Revenue:

–   It hopefully leads to improving standards and some reduction in the willingness of professionals and offshore service providers to be involved in tax evasion or shoddy tax avoidance.

–   At least up until the abandonment of the Hansard procedure it fed the system by ensuring co-operation during investigations and by driving out new voluntary disclosures.

It can therefore be envisaged that further offshore related prosecutions will follow, and that these may be as a result of one or more of the following key issues:

(a)   The Inland Revenue will continue to come across cases which are so unacceptable as to warrant prosecution on their own merits. Unfortunately, the offshore world may have a plentiful supply of such cases.

(b)   The *Charlton* and *Dimsey and Allen* cases were largely focused on the Channel Islands, and may well have had a greater impact there than in other offshore locations. It could therefore be that the Inland Revenue will want to specifically identify professionals and offshore service providers who are exposed to possible prosecution in relation to arrangements in other specifically targeted jurisdictions.

(c)   The prosecutions mentioned above were also in connection with relatively small scale offshore operations, and it may be convenient for the Inland Revenue to send a suitable message to larger organisations by a carefully selected prosecution. This would however have to be balanced against the risk of disturbing the growing willingness for these organisations to face up to and sort out any problems they have offshore.

(d)   Mass marketed offshore tax schemes are held in particularly low esteem and it may be that the Inland Revenue seek to undermine this approach to tax planning by finding examples that are so objectionable that they can categorise them as tax evasion and so institute criminal proceedings. There are already hints that a new approach to marketed tax schemes is emerging.

(e)   From a strategic point of view, the SCO may want to quickly demonstrate its new sources of information from NCIS or even the offshore jurisdictions themselves. They may therefore seek to identify potential prosecutions which have come through these new routes to be able to say: *look we have just put an offshore service provider in jail as a result of information we received from a money laundering report.*

(f)   Taking the points made above, they may seek to identify potential prosecution cases relating to offshore service providers involved in regular tax evasion or marketed schemes which they can classify as tax evasion, which have come to their attention through money laundering reports.

Ignoring tax evasion

Cynics have argued the case that tax evasion has not been reported because: certain professionals have not fully appreciated either the scope of the relevant legislation or the extent of their responsibilities under it; or the subjective test imposed by the legislation meant that even those who were fully aware of their obligations could effectively ignore situations where they could claim they did not have a suspicion.

Both of these perceived restrictions on the flow of information may be stripped away by PoCA because the new regime is forcing a new level of awareness on the regulated sector and because it makes it much harder to ignore certain situations.

Money laundering legislation does of course exist in offshore locations, but there is no indication that these regimes have provided much assistance in the identification of any widespread tax evasion. This may be because tax evasion is not covered by the local reporting requirements, it is not thought to be covered, any information regarding possible tax offences is not routinely passed to the UK, or the tests for when tax evasion must be reported are set so high that they can effectively be ignored.

There is no indication that on its own the offshore based 'triumvirate' of Regulation, KYC, and EoI is fundamentally undermining offshore tax evasion. That does however appear to be on the verge of changing, and the UK provides a perfect example of the way in which onshore legislation may work to greater effect than anything that can be imposed on the offshore world. Despite the intense pressure that offshore locations have been under to co-operate with the fight against tax evasion, the most dramatic change is likely to come from the type of legislation found in the PoCA. The reporting requirements introduced in this legislation cut through the apparent loopholes mentioned above by imposing an objective test on the UK 'regulated sector'. Importantly, it raises the stakes from a minimum of suspicion to 'reasonable grounds' for suspicion. This immediately puts those who worry that their poor vision may mean that they are missing something under pressure to get an eye test. It will now be necessary for those caught by PoCA to go beyond the point at which they do not have a suspicion of tax evasion to ensure that there are no circumstances surrounding the matter which are known or should be investigated which would give reasonable grounds for a suspicion.

The business proposition

So does this all mean that the evasion of UK taxes has been dealt a death blow and that such activities will be impossible in the future? It seems unlikely. Any student of human nature will sensibly answer that as long as there are taxes there will be some who will seek to evade those taxes, and onshore and offshore there will be those who are foolish or greedy enough to want to help them.

What does seem to be fatally wounded by objectively biased anti-money laundering legislation is 'institutionalised tax evasion'. This is in effect mass tax evasion facilitated by organisations who honestly do not know [or] turn a blind eye to [or] do not care about [or] actively encourage the fact that their clients and customers are evading taxes. These organisations are normally based in offshore centres, although they may be owned by or have related entities in the onshore jurisdictions. Indeed those most immediately affected by the problems explored in this paper will be medium to large size organisations who have wide-ranging business interests beyond the entity containing the tax evasion arrangements.

It is interesting to consider why on earth such an industry could have grown up, especially when some of those involved in it seem otherwise to be reputable financial institutions. Its genesis would seem to rest on a relatively simple business proposition, which may be adopted consciously or unconsciously, but which runs broadly as follows.

The original business proposition

1   Large-scale offshore services are profitable;

2   There are potentially substantial amounts of undeclared funds that can be held in offshore arrangements;

3   The obtaining and servicing of such business requires a lower level of skill, care and attention (and hence investment) than legitimate tax avoidance;

4   The customer or client has an interest in being discrete;

5   Such arrangements do not seem to break local laws and in any case it may be someone else who is breaking a law; and

6   There is no obligation to report or otherwise be concerned about someone else breaking someone else's law.

This may have allowed that ever useful 'blind eye' to be turned on tax evasion.

However, in some cases the basic business proposition was then subject to the following amendments.

The first amendments

7   There may be an obligation to report the breaking of someone else's laws but only if there is knowledge or suspicion; and

8   Even if a money laundering report has to be made it may not go beyond the local jurisdiction.

The view seems to have been taken that this First Amendment did not necessarily reduce the attractions of the Business Proposition, but it then suffered a further potential set back:

The second amendment

9   The local jurisdiction may supply information, but only at some point in the future, and only on request, or in relation to clearly defined situations which can probably be avoided.

This may have made some people stop and think seriously about the type of business in their organisation and perhaps to even consider cleaning up certain aspects of that work, but the indications are that it has not yet led to an unravelling of the offshore tax evasion industry.

There now appear to be two key issues which will or should cause offshore organisations who have followed the business proposition to seriously rethink their positions:

- Firstly, there is the apparent refocusing of attention by tax investigators on the facilitators of offshore tax evasion; and

- Secondly, and timed almost perfectly to build on the first point is the potentially substantial amount of new intelligence that will flow to the tax authorities as a result of legislation like PoCA.

Offshore organisations

Organisations which provide offshore arrangements need urgently to review the services they provide, to ensure that they are not running the risk of attracting new tax evasion arrangements and to analyse their existing clients and customers to identify any existing tax evasion arrangements.

Offshore service providers who do not want the nature of their work to be misunderstood need to be careful about the way they present themselves. Their adverts, marketing literature and websites must not give any hint that they are prepared to deal with anything other than legitimate tax avoidance arrangements. Just as importantly, their staff must be properly briefed on the nature of the work that the organisation is prepared to deal with. To protect themselves, their staff, and their customers and clients, they must adopt a culture that is set firmly against any involvement in tax evasion.

A thorough review of existing clients and customers is needed to identify cases which may represent tax evasion so that decisions can be made on the action needed to clean up those cases. It is vital that this review is undertaken by competent and suitably qualified in-house or external tax specialists. The aim here is to identify those situations which do or could involve tax evasion, or which are at risk of being classified as tax evasion by the tax authorities. At this stage the organisations must not rely on vague assurances given to them by their clients or customers, or by their clients' or customers' advisers, unless perhaps those advisers are themselves reputable taxation specialists.

The first difficulty that such organisations face is the identification of cases which involve evasion or which have aspects to them which could be classified as evasion. This involves trying to identify:

(a) Actual evasion where the situation is known or suspected by the offshore organisation.

(b) Hidden evasion where there is no current knowledge or suspicion but where there may be reasonable grounds for suspecting that evasion has taken place.

(c) Default evasion where cases were originally intended as legitimate tax avoidance exercises, but which have, because of subsequent events, turned into evasion.

(d) Assumed evasion involving arrangements which do work to legitimately avoid tax but which have some element to them (such as dummy settlors or bearer shares) which is indicative of tax evasion and which could lead to an attack by the tax authorities.

(e) Deemed evasion in which legitimate avoidance schemes may be found not to work and which because of the way they have been handled may be classed as evasion by the tax authorities.

Having identified the various categories of evasion or potential evasion, the organisation involved then needs to decide what action should be taken. This will again require specialist advice and will vary depending on the nature of the cases involved, but it is likely to have to meet the following key requirements:

(a)   Any approach which needs to be made to the tax authorities and any money laundering reports which are required will have to be dealt with as quickly as possible.

(b)   Any approach to the tax authorities must be handled extremely carefully, to ensure that the organisation itself is protected as far as possible and that any future negotiations with the Inland Revenue by any other party are not prejudiced.

(c)   Similarly any approach that is needed to any other party involved in the arrangements needs to be dealt with as quickly as possible, but again in a way which as far as possible protects the offshore organisation and does not prejudice future negotiations.

Those organisations who do find themselves burdened with some element of tax evasion or potential tax evasion have various options available to them depending on whether:

–   a large proportion of their business is represented by tax evasion;

–   they find a substantial number of cases which could be tax evasion, but they also deal with a wide-range of legitimate commercial or tax avoidance arrangements; or

–   they have limited exposure to tax evasion risks.

Depending on the extent of their infection with tax evasion these organisations could be considered as critically ill, seriously ill or poorly.

Critically ill: Those organisations that find that a very substantial proportion of their business could be classed as tax evasion face serious and urgent problems. They have to realise that for the reasons outlined above, that business could in future come to the attention of the tax authorities, and unless they face up to that fact and take the appropriate action, they face uncontrolled assaults on their finances, reputation and wider business interests. Perhaps more worrying for individuals involved is the fact that the spectre of prosecution could well become a reality if it is felt that tax evasion monies have been actively sought or that the organisations welcomed such business when it arrived.

Although incomprehensible to most onshore professionals, the fact is that such organisations do exist. What may be even harder to comprehend is the fact that, whilst some of these organisations are well known local and grubby, some are parts of well known reputable international businesses. These offshore anomalies cannot be explained away only by the Business Proposition put forward above. It does not seem feasible that the serious minded onshore owners of such organisations would have allowed such a situation to develop. There must therefore be other factors involved in addition to the basic Business Proposition, and it seems likely that these may have included a lack of control of the offshore entities, a lack of parental understanding of the business, and the need for the offshore management to strive for easy profits. Add to these explanations the fact that certain offshore organisations seem to have bought themselves into trouble by acquiring offshore services providers to access the funds within the client base, and the growth and spread of these organisations starts to make some sense. *The fact is though that some onshore parents may not be fully aware of the deep seated problem that their seemingly successful offshore children have stored up.*

Organisations in this situation clearly need to handle matters extremely carefully, and will no doubt need a range of specialist help to try to protect themselves and their employees from the wrath of the authorities, their customers and clients, and the market place. It may well be that the problems are so extensive that, when faced with the task of trying to remodel and rebuild, the client base has to be pared so much, or that the risk and reward analysis of the owner swings so far in favour of the former, that it is not worth continuing with the business. Unfortunately, a sale of the business is unlikely to be viable. There may not be much worth selling, and in any case some understanding of the problems identified here are already starting to dawn on the consciousness of the offshore world, to the extent that the market for certain sorts of businesses may have already evaporated. There may therefore be no choice but to break up the business, but this itself has to be managed very carefully. It may be necessary to work closely with regulators to ensure that the wider interests of the organisation are not tainted by the infected business unit. Clients and customers will obviously have to be handled with kid gloves to get rid of problem cases and find new homes for good cases, without jeopardising their position further and again to seek to ensure that the process does not damage the reputation of the organisation.

Seriously ill: For the sake of the offshore centres themselves it must be hoped that there are not too many organisations that are as infected with tax evasion as those described above, but there are likely to be some in most jurisdictions. More common will be organisations who it may be unfair to claim have engaged in institutionalised tax evasion, but who do have a reasonable weight of cases which are at risk of being classed as tax evasion. Once again these organisations need to take urgent and careful action. This is not only to identify and sort out old problems, but also to ensure no new tax evasion business is accepted and to protect the good quality businesses, because unlike the basket cases mentioned above, it will be possible to save these businesses. The business unit will to some extent contract, but with care it may be possible for it to be saved and rebuilt. The biggest problem faced by this category of organisation may well be managing the way they are perceived by the regulatory and tax authorities, by their introducers of business and by their good quality clients and customers.

Poorly: The final category of organisation that needs to be taking some action consists of businesses which identify a relatively small proportion of evasion or possible evasion. These will be able to sort themselves out and still have viable ongoing businesses, but it is vital that their lack of exposure does not lead to complacency. They must be vigorous in their determination to create a business which is based solely on good quality, legitimate arrangements which are not tainted by any risk of tax evasion. If they handle matters properly they will, together with those healthy organisations who are free from tax evasion, be thriving offshore service providers in future years.

Appendix 8.3   Client Alert

THE *CAVERSHAM* CASE

Jersey's Royal Court imposes fines totalling £100,000 for failure to comply with anti-money laundering requirements

On 25 November 2005, the Royal Court passed sentence on Caversham Fiduciary Services Limited ('Caverhsam'), Caversham Trustees Limited ('Caversham Trustees') and director Nicholas Bell for offences dating back to 2002, when the identity of a person known only as 'Mr Lee' was not verified. Caversham was fined £40,000, Caversham Trustees £25,000 and Mr Bell £35,000; and the defendants were ordered to pay the prosecution costs.

Facts

In 2002, Mr Bell was contacted by an English solicitor explaining that:

> 'Mr Stevens, as attorney for Mr Lee, received monies from the proceeds of the sale of a sauna in London and they now wish to re-invest those monies. Mr Lee is non-resident who wishes the monies to be kept offshore in the first instance.'

A discretionary trust was requested; and the initial settled assets into the trust were described as the 'sale proceeds for M. Lee'. The identity of Mr Lee as the disclosed principal was never verified. Within days, £850,000 was received into Caversham's client account, and Caversham paid the monies to the client account of Caversham Trustees. Immediately following receipt, Mr Bell received instructions to pay away £825,000 to four, unknown third parties. The trust was established the following day by Caversham Trustees, with Mr Stevens as sole beneficiary. The following working day, Caversham Trustees effected the payments away. The Court heard that Jersey Financial Services Commission ('JFSC') identified the above facts during an inspection visit, and notified the Attorney General.

Law

Article 2 of the Money Laundering Jersey Order 1999 ('the Order'), pursuant to Article 37 of the Proceeds of Crime (Jersey) Law ('the Law'), requires financial institutions to maintain procedures for the purposes of forestalling and preventing money laundering. These include identification and internal control and communication procedures. Where an applicant for business appears to be acting on behalf of another (ie Mr Lee), under the Order that other person's identity must be verified.

The Anti-Money Laundering Guidance Notes to the Finance Industry, issued by the JFSC, are admissible in legal proceedings as evidence of best practice. The Notes clearly state that, if verification of identity has not been completed prior to entering into a business relationship, assets should not be paid away, under any circumstances, until verification of identity has taken place.

Issues

During trial, at the close of the prosecution case, the Royal Court ruled that the maintenance of anti-money laundering procedures is an absolute duty on financial institutions. The defendants would have been able to present evidence and seek to rely on the statutory defence of having taken reasonable steps to avoid the commission of an offence. However, further to the Court's ruling that an absolute duty is imposed, the defendants did not call any evidence as to their procedures or otherwise, and entered guilty pleas. Mr Bell pleaded guilty on the basis that the companies' commission of the offences was attributable to his negligence.

The Court was referred by the Crown to certain facts considered to aggravate the offences:

(a) the arrangement facilitated the layering of substantial funds;

(b) the very short period of time (four working days) over which the funds were received by Caversham, paid to Caversham Trustees and then paid away, without knowing who Mr Lee was or if he exists;

(c) the provision of effectively total anonymity to Mr Lee (if he exists) through the discretionary trust structure; and

(d) the payment away of monies to unknown entities, without commercial purpose or apparent justification under the trust, with no internal control or communication to ensure the identity of Mr Lee was known.

As is customary, the Crown made submissions to the Court on the sentences to impose and observed that this is the first case of its kind in Jersey and elsewhere, and the level of fines reflects this. Should there be further prosecutions for such offences within the finance industry, the Attorney General stated that he will move for substantially higher penalties.

When Sentencing, the Court observed these to be very serious breaches of the Law, as there was a serious breakdown in internal controls. Mr Lee's identity was never verified and Mr Bell's level of autonomy was responsible. Also, the failures were not realised by either company. The defence explained that Mr Bell would face financial difficulty if the Crown's conclusions were followed (ie a fine at the same level as the companies).

The Court, when imposing the fines detailed above, went on to state that Jersey's reputation as a premier offshore finance centre is capable of being destroyed in an instant. If actual money laundering had taken place here, the sentence of the Court may well have been higher.

Observations

The Court issued a stark warning: robust anti-money laundering procedures and internal controls and systems must be in place and applied, including appropriate levels of supervision and audit, to ensure full compliance with the Law.

All staff must understand that client verification is to be carried out properly and in a timely manner. A single failure, depending on the facts, may result in a substantial fine. Where money laundering has taken place, any individual whose conduct causes the breach in any way may face imprisonment. Procedures should ensure that, under no circumstances, should transfers internally or away be made (potential layering) without first having obtained satisfactory evidence of identity.

Jersey Court of Appeal guidance on obligations to 'maintain' procedures to forestall money laundering

The appeal against conviction was heard by the Jersey Court of Appeal in January 2006. The decision of the Court of Appeal sets out some useful guidance on the standards that Jersey financial institutions are expected to meet and interpretation of the requirements under the Money Laundering (Jersey) Order 1999 ('the Order').

Failure to comply with the requirements in the Order is an offence and can, as it had in the Caversham case itself, lead to prosecution under the Proceeds of Crime (Jersey) Law 1999 ('the Law').

The appeal to the Jersey Court of Appeal was on the ground that the Royal Court had erred in Law. The appellants' primary argument was that, contrary to the Royal Court's earlier findings, the duties under Article 2(1) of the Order to 'maintain' procedures (as set out in that Order) would require a "systemic failure" and that one single breach was insufficient for a prosecution for breach of the Law.

The Court of Appeal upheld the decision of the Royal Court and held that the obligations on a financial institution were not merely to establish the procedures set out in the Order to prevent and forestall money laundering but also to keep them in proper working order, so that they would be effective in relation to every relevant relationship or transaction. These duties could therefore be shown to have been breached by a single failure.

In reaching its conclusions, the Court of Appeal focused on the interpretation of the word 'maintain' and, in so doing, gave consideration to the intention behind the legislation in place. The Court of Appeal's view was that the States of Jersey had chosen to combat money laundering in Jersey, not simply by listing a series of offences but, by requiring financial institutions to avoid the facilitation of money laundering and laying down the means by which they should do so. The objective, therefore, was not to 'lock the stable door after the horse (in the form of the money) has bolted' but rather that 'dirty money' should not enter Jersey or its financial system in the first place.

As such, the thrust of the appellant's contention, namely that in a particular case the procedures could fail to bite but still be said to have been 'maintained' was, in the Court of Appeal's view, 'untenable'.

The Court of Appeal Judgment, therefore, further highlights the need for businesses to not only have procedures in place, but also to keep them in proper working order.

It is not sufficient for those procedures to be 'in routine use', rather they must be in use and effective in each relationship formed and transaction carried out.

Mourant du Feu & Jeune

Cayman | Guernsey | Jersey | London | New York

www.mourant.com

© Mourant | August 2007

AML in selected non-UK jurisdictions

Contents

The following extracts are taken from Chapters that published in International Guide to Money Laundering Law and Practice (4th Edition) published by Bloomsbury Professional in October 2013. The paragraph numbers used in the extracts correspond to the paragraph numbers used in the original chapters. For more information on *International Guide to Money Laundering Law and Practice* (4th Edition) please see: www.bloomsburyprofessional.com/uk/international-guide-to-money-laundering-law-and-practice-9781847669797/.

Appendix 9.1   The Bahamas

Dr Peter D Maynard

Counsel and Attorney at Law, Peter D Maynard Counsel & Attorneys, Nassau

[Bold material in square brackets has been contributed by Tim Bennett and does not appear in the chapter as written by Barbara Padega and published in *International Guide to Money Laundering Law and Practice,* **4th edition]**

INTRODUCTION

10.3   The Bahamas' tax neutrality is not new. Throughout its history, The Bahamas has had no taxes on sales, income, companies, capital gains, inheritance and other fields common in the metropolitan countries, which may be a legitimate disincentive for investment from abroad. Custom duties are the most important source of government revenues. Thus The Bahamas has served, and continues to serve, as a tax-neutral platform for international business.

BACKGROUND

10.7   … The Bahamas was removed from the FATF blacklist in June 2001. Even before the blacklist, the Caribbean FATF promoted a process of mutual evaluation among the countries in the region. Even before being placed on the blacklist, The Bahamas had undergone a favourable Caribbean FATF mutual evaluation in 1997. There was considerable dissatisfaction about the variance between the FATF and the Caribbean FATF findings.

MONEY LAUNDERING

10.16   The Bahamas adopts an 'all crimes' approach to money laundering offences. The offences governed by PCA 2000 and set out in PCA 2000, Sch include:

'(a) an offence under the Prevention of Bribery Act, Chapter 88;

(b) an offence under section 40, 41, or 42 (money laundering);

(c) An offence under the Anti Terrorism Act, Chapter 107;

(d) an offence which may be tried on information in The Bahamas other than a drug trafficking offence;

(e) an offence committed anywhere that, if it had occurred in The Bahamas, would constitute an offence in The Bahamas as set out in this Schedule.'

10.17   What crimes are predicate offences for money laundering purposes? In PCA 2000, Sch, as indicated above, money laundering offences are referred to in para (b). However, a comprehensive range of predicate offences is covered in paras (a), (c), (d) and (e). The limitation is that the offence is to be mutual or reciprocal, as suggested by the language of (d).

10.18   Is foreign corruption a predicate offence? The Bahamas is a party to the relevant international and regional conventions and resolutions. But there is no specific offence of foreign (or local) corruption. However, applying PCA 2000, Sch, para (d),[1] it is likely that such an offence would be caught under bribery, stealing, fraud or related offences. Therefore, such an offence would qualify as a predicate offence.

---

1   See para 10.16 above.

10.19   Is foreign tax evasion a predicate offence? Under international law, The Bahamas is not required to enforce the tax and revenue laws of other countries. The Bahamas has not entered into treaties with other countries, except the Tax Information Exchange Agreement with the US, concluded on 25 January 2002, which creates an obligation to assist the US in obtaining tax information which may be the foundation of a charge in the US of tax evasion. In any event, tax evasion is frequently accompanied by a charge of fraud or a related offence which is reciprocal, and which would fall into PCA 2000, Sch, para (d).

10.21   Does the predicate offence have to be proved to a criminal or civil standard of proof? The criminal standard of proof would apply to the predicate offences, as it would apply to all offences in The Bahamas.

10.22   It may be asked whether The Bahamas has a suspicion-based reporting system or a transaction based reporting system (or hybrid of the two). The reporting system is suspicion-based. Transaction-based systems are regarded as even more costly and ineffective than suspicion-based systems.

10.23   What is the definition of suspicious? Is the definition of suspicion objective or subjective, and what is a suspicious transaction for these purposes? There is no definition of 'suspicious' in the legislation. It is intended to have its ordinary meaning, and is subjective. However, due diligence and Know Your Customer rules have been in place for a considerable time. In addition, voluminous manuals of suspicious transaction and anti-money guidelines have been issued by the FIU which contain examples of suspicious transactions. A transaction, as defined in the Financial Transactions Reporting Act (Ch 368), s 2:

'(a)   means any deposit, withdrawal, exchange or transfer of funds (in whatever currency denominated), whether

    (i)   in cash,

    (ii)   by cheque payment order or other instrument, or

    (iii)   by electronic or other non-physical means; and

(b)   without limiting the generality of its foregoing, includes any payment made in satisfaction, in whole or in part, or any contractual or other legal obligation;

but does not include any of the following—

(c)   the placing of any bet;

(d)   participation in any game of chance defined in the Lotteries and Gaming Act;

(e)   any transaction that is exempted from the provisions of this Act by or under regulations made under section 42 [sic]?.'

It is the Financial Transactions Reporting Act 2000 (Ch 368), s 51 that empowers the minister to make regulations.

10.24   Separate suspicious transaction and anti-money laundering guidelines, tailored for particular sectors, have been issued to each of the following groups: banks and trust companies; financial service providers; co-operative societies; the insurance sector; the securities industry; and licensed casino operators. They contain copious examples of suspicious transactions and are designed to be used as a reference and a training tool.

FINANCIAL TRANSACTIONS REPORTING ACT 2000

10.47   FTRA 2000, Pt III deals with the obligation to report suspicious transactions. Where a financial institution has reasonable grounds to suspect that a transaction is relevant to the enforcement of PCA 2000, the financial institution is required to report the transaction to the FIU.[1]

DISCLOSURE AND TIPPING OFF

10.55   How is a disclosure report made? To what agency? As for the procedures, as set out, for example, in the guidelines for financial and corporate service providers, employees are required to report suspicious transactions to the Money Laundering Reporting Officer (MLRO), an internal officer to be appointed by each financial institution. If the employee has reported their suspicion to the MLRO, they have satisfied this obligation. The financial institution must ensure that prospective suspicions are passed without delay to the MLRO, who facilitates the expeditious reporting to the FIU, which is the national reception point for the disclosure of STRs. The MLRO, who may be a senior member of the compliance, internal audit or fraud department or, indeed, the chief executive in smaller institutions, determines whether the information rises to the level of knowledge or suspicion of money laundering.

10.56   Do they apply to operations abroad? No – they apply only to financial institutions within the jurisdiction.

10.57   Could disclosure result in a breach of customer confidentiality? Yes. However, the legislation requires that no civil liability will arise as a result of a disclosure.

10.58   Does the agency consent to transactions? No. The system is not based on transaction reporting. However, on the basis of an STR, the FIU may object to a transaction and take other steps, such as issuing a monitoring, restraining or freezing order.

10.59   How much feedback is given? The FIU must give feedback to the reporting institution. A form has been developed by the FIU for this purpose. What use is made of the intelligence obtained? The information may be the foundation of a charge for a criminal offence. For the purpose of laying a charge, the FIU works in co-ordination with the Attorney-General's Office. The information may also be used for interim measures by the FIU, such as the orders referred to at para 10.58 above.

OTHER LEGISLATIVE PROVISIONS
International Tax Cooperation Act 2010

10.175   The International Tax Cooperation Act 2010 (No 18 of 2010) (ITCA 2010) came into effect 1 July 2010 and its primary purpose is to implement international agreements between The Bahamas and foreign states that provide for cooperation in tax matters including the exchange of information for related purposes. ITCA 2010 is comprised of 15 sections and two schedules. ITCA 2010, addresses the procedure for requesting tax information,[2] the power to require production of information,[3] the power to enter premises to obtain information,[4] the conducting of tax interviews and examinations[5] and specific offences under the act. The Act makes it an offence to wilfully tamper with or alter information, to destroy, damage or conceal any information requested by the Minister. Under s 4 of ITCA 2010, any person who commits any offence in the act and is liable to summary conviction and a fine not exceeding $25,000 or imprisonment for a term not to exceed 12 months or both.

---

1   FTRA 2000, s 14.
2   ITCA 2000, s 4.
3   ITCA 2000, s 5.
4   ITCA 2000, s 6.
5   ITCA 2000, s 9.

INFORMATION AND PROSECUTIONS

10.179   In 2008 against a backdrop of heightened political attention, several significant developments occurred. Interestingly, almost 30 tax information exchange agreements have been signed or announced since November 2008.[1] Further, the OECD confirmed that several countries have announced measures to combat tax evasion and implement its standards.

10.180   The Bahamas continues to make progress in partnering with other countries to allow for exchange of tax information. In March 2010, The Bahamas entered into agreements with the seven Nordic economies (Denmark, the Faroe Islands, Finland, Greenland, Iceland, Norway and Sweden) to allow bilateral exchange of tax information. Prior to this, The Bahamas has also maintained agreements with important regional and economic partners in Mexico, the United States and the United Kingdom. The Bahamas is a member of the Global Forum on Transparency and Exchange of Information for Tax Purposes and an active member of the Global Forum's Peer Review Group, and it is participating in a peer review of its laws and practices in this area.

For the purposes of the progress report on the implementation of the standards, jurisdictions having signed at least 12 agreements that meet the internationally agreed tax standard, are considered to have substantially implemented that standard. Accordingly, The Bahamas moved into the substantially implemented category, becoming the 22nd jurisdiction to do so since the progress report was first issued in April 2009.[2]

10.181   The Mutual Evaluation/Detail Assessment Report stated that thus so far 14 money laundering prosecutions have taken place, yielding 6.6 million of forfeited proceeds that were placed in the confiscated assets fund.[3] The Report confirmed the commencement of a comprehensive program of on-site and off-site supervision of licensees and regular anti-terrorist financing warnings to licensees and public warnings on unauthorised banks allegedly operating out of The Bahamas.[4]

CONCLUSION

10.182   Quite an extensive array of new legislation has been enacted by The Bahamas as a result of the pressure of the OECD and related organisations upon the financial centres. It is not an exaggeration to suggest that The Bahamas has become one of the most highly regulated anti-money laundering jurisdictions. A new financial architecture is in effect. It is quite possible that there have been negative effects on its competitive position as a financial centre, particularly as the continuing demands by the OECD for tax information exchange may erode its niche market as a domicile for trusts. The limited case law suggests also that those external demands have been excessive. But, with the passage of time, the environment has settled. The financial sector seems to have weathered the storm by making the necessary legislative, procedural and law enforcement adjustments to meet or exceed international standards.

10.183   Thus, the country's determination to combat money laundering cannot reasonably be doubted. The Bahamas has polished its image as an international financial centre which is firmly against money laundering.
[The OECD's phase-two review process in 2013 accorded The Bahamas a largely compliant rating.]

1   November 2011, Global Forum on Transparency and Exchange Information for Tax Purposes, www.oecd.org/dataoecd/52/35/48981620.pdf
2   OECD (2010, March. 'OECD announces the Bahamas removal from 'grey list' – The Bahamas expands its network for international exchange of tax information', thebahamasweekly.com
3   December 2007, 'Mutual Evaluation/Detailed Assessment Report: Anti-Money Laundering and Combating the Financing of Terrorism'.
4   Ibid.

Appendix 9.2   Bermuda

Anthony Whaley

Barrister and Attorney, Conyers Dill & Pearman, Bermuda

[Bold material in square brackets has been contributed by Tim Bennett and does not appear in the chapter as written by Barbara Padega and published in *International Guide to Money Laundering Law and Practice,* **4th edition]**

INTRODUCTION

Bermuda

12.4   Bermuda has a reputation for stricter oversight than offshore financial centres in the Caribbean. Over the years, Bermuda has strived through legislation and codification of practices to meet the highest international standards in order to ensure that its name would be synonymous with ethics and quality. By being diligent in 'knowing its customers', it has often declined lucrative business when provenance was in doubt.

THE REGULATORS

12.8   Responsibility for the detection, investigation and prosecution of money laundering and similar crimes in Bermuda lies with the Minister responsible for justice (the 'Minister of Justice'), typically in cooperation with the BMA, the Bermuda Police Service and the Financial Intelligence Agency ('FIA'). Bermuda also established the National Anti-Money Laundering Committee ('NAMLC') for the purpose of advising the Minister of Justice in relation to the detection and prevention of money laundering in Bermuda, and on the development of a national plan of action to include recommendations concerning the development and implementation of policies and activities to combat money laundering and advising the Minister of Justice as to the participation of Bermuda in the international effort against money laundering. NAMLC is chaired by an independent Chairman and is made up of senior officers from the Ministry of Finance, the Ministry of National Security, the Attorney General's Chambers, the Department of Public Prosecutions, the Ministry of Justice, the Bermuda Monetary Authority, the Bermuda Police Service, HM Customs and the FIA.

BERMUDA'S AML REGIME

Ongoing commitment

12.9   The government of Bermuda has always been committed to ensuring that Bermuda has a strong, robust and effective regime for the combating of money laundering and terrorist financing. NAMLAC engages in an ongoing process of consultation and review to ensure that Bermuda's legislative and regulatory framework continues to operate effectively and to the highest of international standards. A visit from the IMF review team in mid 2007 was met by government and industry alike with enthusiasm for the underlying goals of the international community with respect to money laundering. Bermuda has been careful and deliberate in its response, adopting a phased approach to tackling its Action Plan to implement international requirements and importantly, there has been real action on the part of Bermuda's legislators. Working closely and cooperatively with the IMF review team, the government of Bermuda formulated a series of significant legislative reforms. Among other things, these reforms expand the obligations on financial institutions affected by the legislation and increased the scope of the regulated sector. New regulations dealing with wire transfers have also been implemented. In that regard, the government of Bermuda has reiterated to the international community its full commitment to completing, in a timely fashion, its ongoing programme of work designed to bring Bermuda's already strict controls into alignment with the FATF 40 Recommendations and FATF 9 Special Recommendations.

12.10   In earlier phases of the Action Plan, the focus was on implementing the statutory and operational international requirements that are specific to the financial sector. During the current phase, the focus is on implementing the requirements set out in the FATF Recommendations 12, 16 and 24, which deal with designated non-financial businesses and professions ('DNFBP'). DNFBP includes lawyers and accountants when they act for their clients in transactions related to specified activities, as well as casinos, trust and corporate service providers, real estate dealers and dealers in precious metals and stones. Having received a non-compliant rating in relation to the FATF Recommendations 12, 16 and 24, Bermuda sought the advice of the IMF to become compliant with these Recommendations, particularly those relating to lawyers and accountants and the establishment of an appropriate supervisory structure for all DNFBPs, and therefore amended key legislation to achieve this objective. This is all part of Bermuda's ongoing commitment to ensure full compliance with the FATF 40 Recommendations and FATF 9 Special Recommendations.

12.11   In the meantime, on 15 February 2012, the FATF adopted revised FATF Recommendations, which are now considered to be the international standards to combat money laundering, terrorist financing and the financing of proliferation of nuclear and other such weaponry. The Bermuda Government supports these new Recommendations and acknowledges that Bermuda's AML/ATF regime will need to be updated, as appropriate in the Bermuda context, to meet these enhanced global standards.[1] The revised FATF Recommendations deal with: (i) AML/ATF policies and co-ordination (risk-based approach and national co-operation and co-ordination); (ii) transparency; (iii) international co-operation; (iv) operational standards; (v) new threats and new priorities; and (vi) terrorist financing. In relation to AML/ATF policies and co-ordination, the FATF now requires jurisdictions to conduct a national risk assessment and then to determine an appropriate AML/ATF framework to address these risks and jurisdictions will also have to have regularly reviewed risk-based AML/ATF policies, with the relevant domestic authorities co-operating/co-ordinating the development, implementation and update of these AML/ATF policies. In relation to transparency, the FATF has strengthened the transparency requirements for the ownership and control of legal persons and legal arrangements, and the parties to electronic fund transfers. The FATF has enhanced the scope of international co-operation between Government agencies, and between financial groups and has expanded the requirements in relation to law enforcement and Financial Intelligence Units ('FIUs'). The FATF has also identified and addressed the following new and aggregated threats, namely financing of proliferation of weapons of mass destruction, corruption and politically exposed persons ('PEPs') and has expanded the list of designated offences for money laundering to include tax crimes, as well as other categories of offences, such as participation in an organised criminal group and racketeering. Finally, in relation to terrorist financing, the FATF has incorporated the requirements of the 9 Special Recommendations on terrorist financing within the 40 Recommendations. NAMLC has indicated that it will continue to take the required steps to ensure that Bermuda's framework has a high level of compliance with these new international requirements.

---

1   'FATF adopts the revised FATF Recommendations on 15 February 2012', NAMLC, March 2012.

CURRENT LEGISLATION

12.21 The Minister of Justice may by order designate a professional body as a supervisory authority in relation to the relevant persons regulated by it. Under the legislation in Bermuda regulating the legal and accounting professions respectively, a new Barristers and Accountants AML/ATF Board (the 'Board') has been established jointly by both bodies. This Board, which was designated as a supervisory authority in relation to regulated professional firms, will supervise such 'regulated professional firms' for compliance with the Regulations and laws. The Board has appointed a Supervisor for the purposes of assisting the Board in carrying out the day-to-day supervisory function. The Board is vested with the functions, powers and responsibilities set out in the SE Act. Under new provisions in the SE Act, all designated professional bodies are given the same range of powers as are available to other supervisory authorities although these powers will be tailored to take account of the fact that these are self-regulatory bodies. Guidance Notes for the prevention and detection of money laundering and the financing of terrorism have been issued by the Board.

12.22 The purpose of the Guidance Notes is to provide an outline of the regulatory framework for AML and ATF requirements and systems for Bermuda's Institutions as well as to interpret the requirements of the relevant AML/ATF law and regulations, indicating good industry practice procedures through a proportionate, risk-based approach. The Guidance Notes also assist institutions with the process of designing and implementing the systems and controls necessary to mitigate the risks of institutions being used in connection with money laundering and the financing of terrorism.

12.23 The Guidance is of direct relevance to the senior management of 'AML/ ATF regulated financial institutions' and to their respective Money Laundering Reporting Officers and other staff. It is not intended that the guidance be applied unthinkingly, as a checklist of steps to take but rather that financial institutions encourage their staff to 'think risk' as they carry out their duties within the AML/ATF regime. The BMA expects financial institutions under its supervision to address their management of risk in a thoughtful and considered way, and to establish and maintain systems and procedures which are appropriate and proportionate to the risks identified.

MONEY LAUNDERING OFFENCES

Application of money laundering offences to non-regulated persons

12.48 Even those persons in Bermuda not presently falling within the definition of relevant persons must be keenly aware of their obligations under the Act. Particular care will be required by persons involved in international business when considering the scope of their liability under the Act for 'knowing assistance of another in the retention of proceeds of crime'.

12.49 The concept of 'knowing assistance' traditionally arises in the context of the civil law cases on constructive trusts and duty of care, in which parties to a relationship, such as trustees, can be liable for a breach of duty to third parties. In civil cases, liability for 'knowingly assisting' a breach of duty can arise where a person recklessly disregards circumstances or facts known to him which would give rise to actual knowledge or suspicion of a dishonest breach of trust. The cases suggest that such recklessness is practically 'dishonest' *vis à vis* the relevant duty. Accordingly, the concern is whether a similar approach would be applied by the courts when considering whether a person 'knows or suspects' that a person he is assisting has been involved in or benefited from criminal conduct.

12.50   It could be difficult for a lawyer to argue he did not know or suspect misconduct if, on an objective basis, the court could find that an honest and reasonable advisor in a similar position with similar experience would be put on notice or would have had a suspicion. In such circumstances, the lawyer involved could be found guilty of 'assisting' a money launderer. In short, as in the civil context, 'turning a blind eye' or not making appropriate enquiries will probably undermine a successful defence.

Client confidentiality

12.51   The Act specifically provides that no liability will be incurred for breach of client confidentiality when reporting suspicions of money laundering. It is generally a defence to the offences, where it can be shown that a person becoming aware of money laundering activity made or intended to make disclosure to the authorities.

SUSPICIOUS TRANSACTIONS

12.81   Relevant persons are *required* to be alert to unexpected and unexplained changes in the pattern of transactions relating to a customer and to consider whether or not such changes may give rise to a suspicion of money laundering or terrorist financing activity. All employees of relevant persons (and relevant employees) are thus required to know enough about a customer's business to recognise that a transaction or series of transactions are unusual. Suspicious transactions are not exhaustively defined but typically fall within one or more of the following categories:

(i)   unusual activity of the customer (ie activities which are inconsistent with the customer's known legitimate business activities);

(ii)   unusual transaction in the course of some usual financial activity;

(iii)   unusually linked transactions;

(iv)   unusual employment of an intermediary in the course of some usual transaction;

(v)   unusual method of settlement;

(vi)   unusual or disadvantageous early redemption of an investment product;

(vii)   the formation of trusts or companies without any apparent commercial or other purpose;

(viii) the receipt of unexplained funds into a trust fund or underlying companies;

(ix)   the regular receipt of large cash payments (in excess of $10,000) which are immediately or nearly immediately transferred out of the structure;

(x)   long delays over the production of company accounts;

(xi)   formation of subsidiaries in circumstances where there appears to be no commercial or other proper purpose;

(xii)   appointment of solicitors as directors with little or no commercial involvement;

(xiii) large payments for unspecified services to consultants, related parties, employees etc;

(xiv)   unauthorised transactions or improperly recorded transactions (particularly where company has poor/inadequate accounting systems);

(iv)   purchase of property using a corporate vehicle where there is no good commercial or other reason.

PENDING CHANGES

Legislative developments

12.110   Following Bermuda's last AML/AFT evaluation conducted by the IMF in May 2007, Bermuda has taken great strides to ensure it becomes compliant with the relevant FATF recommendations in respect of which it received a non-compliant rating. New legislation was introduced which intended to primarily address some of the recommendations made by the IMF, specifically those relating to lawyers and accountants and the establishment of an appropriate supervisory structure for all DNFBPs. Amendments were made to four pieces of legislation, namely: (i) The Proceeds of Crime Regulations (Supervision and Enforcement) Act 2008; (ii) The Bermuda Bar Act 1974; (iii) The Institute of Charted Accountants of Bermuda Act 1973; and (iv) The Financial Intelligence Agency Act 2007. The result of all of these changes was to bring lawyers and accountants within the scope of the comprehensive AML/ATF regime described herein. The Corporate Service Provider Business Act 2012 was passed in the House of Assembly and the Senate during the Summer 2012 Parliamentary Session, and come into force on 1 January 2013. Corporate service providers were brought within scope as a result.

12.111   The updating of Bermuda's AML/ATF framework will continue to take place, but in various stages. The final phase will involve bringing into scope other stakeholders as required by the FATF recommendations. These will probably include other designated professionals, real estate agents, jewellers and high value dealers.

12.112   On 1 July 2011, The Bribery Act 2010 (the 'Bribery Act') came into force in the UK. The Bribery Act provides a comprehensive range of bribery offences, including offences of offering or receiving bribes, bribery of foreign public officials, and of failure to prevent a bribe being paid on an organisation's behalf. Further, the Bribery Act criminalises both bribery of public officials and bribery in the public sector. A number of the offences created by the Bribery Act have extensive extra-territorial reach, with activities which may take place outside of the UK being criminalised – the Bribery Act therefore has potentially significant implications for businesses operating in Bermuda. Bermuda persons and entities, particularly those businesses with international operations, will therefore need to check if any of their operations fall within the scope of the Bribery Act.

12.113   In the past decade, there has been increasing global attention on, and efforts made to combat, issues of corruption, or the 'use of public office for private gain.' Whilst the problems of corruption and bribery are ever increasing, there has also been continued progress made with a global anti-corruption ('AC') agenda. It is acknowledged that the fight against corruption is inextricably intertwined with that against money laundering, and that the stolen assets of a corrupt public official are useless unless they are placed, layered, and integrated into the global financial network. It is acknowledged that the prevention and detection of the proceeds of corruption are addressed by a broad range of the FATF Recommendations; it must therefore be highlighted that when financial institutions fail to follow AML procedures, particularly customer due diligence, it can give corrupt PEPs easy access to the global financial system. There is clearly a pressing need for the AML standards to be properly implemented by financial institutions, as well as stringent enforcement of the AML laws and regulations by the regulatory authorities or supervisors in Bermuda. The Ministry of Finance as well as its key stakeholders are therefore committed to ensuring that Bermuda adopts and enforces each and every such recommendation and will continue to ensure that legislative reform in Bermuda keeps step with the continuing and evolving global AML/ATF standards set by the FATF and other global standard-setting bodies.

12.114   Bermuda is cognisant of the fact that the revised FATF Recommendations which were adopted on 15 February 2012 are particularly relevant in light of the anticipated review of Bermuda's AML/ATF regime expected in 2014, as this review will assess the extent to which the revised FATF Standards have been effectively embedded into Bermuda's regime. Considerable legislative and other action must therefore be taken to ensure that there continues to be a strong and robust AML/ATF framework in Bermuda and that Bermuda continues to play a key role in the global fight against money laundering and terrorist financing and proliferation financing. Bermuda will continue to take the required steps to ensure that its framework has the highest level of compliance with international recommendation, standards and requirements.

BMA GENERAL GUIDANCE NOTES

12.115   The BMA has issued general guidance notes to assist AML/ATF regulated financial institutions in the implementation of the new Regulations and other relevant AML/ATF obligations. It is intended that sectoral guidance will also be prepared in conjunction with the relevant sectors of the financial services industry. Guidance Notes have already been prepared by the Barristers and Accountants AML/ATF Board to provide regulated professional firms for whom the Board has supervisory authority (ie lawyers and accountants) with guidance as to how they should carry out their obligations as required under Bermuda's AML/ATF regime. Other sector specific guidance is likely to follow.

[On 31 December 2013, the International Cooperation (Tax Information Exchange Agreements) Amendment Act 2013 came into force, amending the procedures pertaining to requests for information.]

Appendix 9.3   Canada[1]

Lisa M Douglas

Baker & McKenzie LLP, Toronto

INTRODUCTION

15.1   With its sophisticated financial system, long borders, multicultural population, and one of the world's highest rates of electronic banking and commerce, Canada may be considered an attractive place for money laundering. The Financial Action Task Force ('FATF') has identified drug trafficking as a significant source of illicit funds in Canada along with prostitution rings, illegal arms sales, migrant smuggling, and white-collar crime such as securities offences and payment system, real estate and telemarketing fraud.[2]

BACKGROUND

15.2   Canada adopted its first anti-money laundering statute in 1991 with a focus on record-keeping rather than reporting.[3] ... in 2000 the legislation was extended to cover a greater range of financial intermediaries and to require the reporting of prescribed financial transactions involving amounts of C$10,000 or more as well as suspicious transactions in any amount based upon reasonable grounds to suspect that the transaction is related to a money laundering offence.[4] At the same time, in July 2000, the Financial Transactions and Reports Analysis Centre of Canada ('FINTRAC') was established as Canada's independent financial intelligence agency with a mandate to collect, analyse and disclose financial information to police and intelligence agencies.[5] Suspicious transactions have been reportable since November 2001 while the reporting of large cash transactions and the cross-border importation and exportation of currency and monetary instruments of C$10,000 or more have been reportable since January 2003. With the enactment of Canada's Anti-terrorism Act in December 2001,[6] the existing anti-money laundering statute was renamed the Proceeds of Crime (Money Laundering) and Terrorist Financing Act ('PCMLTFA'), and its scope extended to include the reporting of transactions where there are reasonable grounds to suspect a transaction is related to a 'terrorist financing offence'.

15.6   Around the same time, as further indication of Canada's renewed focus on AML/ATF initiatives, the federal government provided financial support for the selection of Toronto as the home of the Egmont Group of Financial Intelligence Units, establishing the group's permanent secretariat in Canada's major financial centre.

---

1   Up to date to 1 February 2013.
2   Financial Action Task Force, Third Mutual Evaluation on Anti-Money Laundering and Combating the Financing of Terrorism: Canada, 29 February 2008.
3   Proceeds of Crime (Money Laundering Act), SC 1991, c 26.
4   Proceeds of Crime (Money Laundering Act), SC 2000, c 17.
5   http://www.fintrac.gc.ca/. Since that time FINTRAC has been integrated even more closely with the security intelligence community and shares financial intelligence with a greater range of domestic and international partners in government, policing and security intelligence.
6   Anti-terrorism Act, SC 2001, c 41.

The PCMLTFA was amended most recently in 2010, although many of these amendments are not yet in force.[1] However, 2010 amendments to regulations relating to the Criminal Code made both tax evasion and copyright infringement designated offences, meaning that laundering the proceeds of these crimes is now a money laundering offence and suspicions of this type of money laundering must be reported to FINTRAC by reporting entities.

In December 2011, the federal government released a consultation paper[2] regarding proposed amendments to Canada's AML/ATF legislative framework in support of the five-year parliamentary review mandated by the PCMLTFA which was conducted in 2012.[3] The proposed changes are significant and generally aimed at strengthening compliance and enforcement and closing gaps identified by various stakeholders.

CANADIAN MONEY LAUNDERING AND TERRORIST FINANCING LAWS

Proceeds of Crime (Money Laundering) and Terrorist Financing Act

15.26 The objective of the PCMLTFA is to combat the laundering of proceeds of crime and the financing of terrorist activities. The Act implements client identification, record keeping and reporting requirements for financial institutions and other financial intermediaries and professionals that are susceptible to being used for money laundering and terrorist financing. Financial institutions and intermediaries subject to the PCMLTFA must appoint a compliance officer, identify risk, establish policies and procedures to control risk and ensure compliance with their AML/ATF obligations, prepare a compliance manual describing those policies and procedures, train personnel in AML/ATF compliance, develop a review process to monitor compliance and changes to the law, and implement a self-assessment program to determine the effectiveness of measures taken to identify and control risk.

15.27 Financial entities and intermediaries subject to the PCMLTFA are required to keep records and report on the following transactions: (i) 'suspicious transactions' in any amount; (ii) international electronic funds transfers of C$10,000 or more; and (iii) large cash transactions of C$10,000 or more. The Proceeds of Crime (Money Laundering) and Terrorist Financing Regulations and the Proceeds of Crime (Money Laundering) and Terrorist Financing Suspicious Transaction Reporting Regulations implement Part 1 of the PCMLTFA by requiring financial institutions and intermediaries to comply with client identification requirements, maintain certain records, report on suspicious transactions and on large cash transactions and international electronic funds transfers of C$10,000 or more, and implement a compliance regime.[4]

FINTRAC

15.32 ...the Financial Transactions and Reports Analysis Centre of Canada ('FINTRAC') is Canada's financial intelligence unit, an independent federal government agency that operates at arm's length from law enforcement agencies.

---

1   Jobs and Economic Growth Act, SC 2010, c 12, Part 14; ss 1862 to 1866, ss 1874 and 1875 in force 14 February 2011 (SI/2011–13); remainder to come into force by order of the Governor in Council.
2   Canada, Department of Finance, *Strengthening Canada's Anti-Money Laundering and Anti-Terrorist Financing Regime* (Ottawa, 2011).
3   PCMLTFA, s 72(1).
4   SOR/2002–184 and SOR/2001–317.

15.33   FINTRAC's mandate is to analyse the information it collects to identify patterns of suspicious financial activity and to uncover associations among people and businesses linked to the patterns of suspected money laundering. Based on its analysis, if FINTRAC determines that there are reasonable grounds to suspect that the information would be relevant to the investigation or prosecution of a money laundering and/or terrorist activity financing offence and/or other threat to the security of Canada, FINTRAC must disclose designated information to the appropriate Canadian and international law enforcement authorities.

15.34   In addition to the information that it collects through the statutory reporting requirements, FINTRAC may collect other information that it considers relevant to money laundering activities and that is publicly available, including on commercial databases, and certain information that is maintained by the federal or provincial governments for law enforcement purposes.

15.35   FINTRAC's role also includes public education, awareness and prevention of money laundering and terrorist financing activity.

Canada Revenue Agency and tax implications

15.38   Once FINTRAC has determined that it has reasonable grounds to suspect that designated information would be relevant to investigating or prosecuting a money laundering or terrorist activity financing offence, it must disclose the information to the Canada Revenue Agency ('CRA'), if it also determines that the information is relevant to an offence of obtaining or attempting to obtain a rebate, refund or credit to which a person or entity is not entitled, or of evading or attempting to evade paying taxes or duties imposed under a federal statute administered by the Minister of National Revenue.[1]

Tax evasion became a 'designated offence' on 12 July 2010, allowing FINTRAC to build a case for disclosure to the Canada Revenue Agency when the criminal activity giving rise to the proceeds was tax evasion. Furthermore, in early 2011 the threshold for disclosing information to the Canada Revenue Agency was lowered from 'determining' to 'reasonable grounds to suspect' that the information being disclosed is relevant to tax evasion.

15.39   As a result, the number of cases being disclosed by FINTRAC to the Canada Revenue Agency has increased significantly, and this trend can be expected to continue.[2]

15.40   FINTRAC can disclose information to the CRA where it also has reasonable grounds to suspect that the information is relevant to determining whether a registered charity has ceased to comply with the requirements of the Income Tax Act for its registration as such, or whether an entity that FINTRAC has reasonable grounds to suspect has applied to be a registered charity is eligible to be registered as such.[3]

---

1   PCMLTFA, s 55(3)(b).
2   In a keynote address delivered on 17 October 2011 to the Money Laundering in Canada Conference 2011, the Director of FINTRAC indicated that in 2005–2006 only three case disclosures were made to the CRA whereas FINTRAC disclosed 136 cases to the CRA in 2010–2011 which 'helped the CRA to identify cases of significant tax non-compliance, and resulted in the reassessment of more than $27 million in federal taxes.'
3   PCMLTFA, s 55(3)(c).

PRIVACY

15.45   There is clearly a significant loss of personal privacy in the disclosure mandated by Canada's AML/ATF regime. However, the privacy of personal information disclosed to FINTRAC is protected to some extent through application of the federal Privacy Act to FINTRAC, criminal penalties for the unauthorised use or disclosure of personal information under the control of FINTRAC, and the need for law enforcement agencies to obtain a court order in order to obtain access to additional information from FINTRAC.

The Office of the Privacy Commissioner of Canada ('OPC') has a statutory mandate to conduct a biennial review of measures taken by FINTRAC to protect the information that it receives or collects under the PCMLTFA. The results of these reviews are reported to Parliament. The OPC continues to express certain privacy-related concerns including the amount of personal information required to be collected by reporting entities beyond what is needed for business purposes and the subjective and speculative assessments made by reporting entities based on the transactions of their clients. The OPC is also concerned about the staggering amount of information about individuals that FINTRAC collects which can be used to compile a comprehensive profile of an individual's life and behaviour, as well as cases identified by the OPC of suspicious transaction reports failing to meet the reporting threshold.[1]

In January 2010, the OPC released a guidance document providing a series of questions and answers recognising the obligation of reporting entities under the PCMLTFA to comply with Canada's privacy legislation in the course of collecting personal information and reporting to FINTRAC.

SUSPICIOUS TRANSACTION

15.52   The PCMLTFA also requires that completed or attempted 'suspicious transactions' be reported to FINTRAC by Reporting Entities.

15.53   Although the PCMLTFA and its regulations do not provide a specific definition of what constitutes a 'suspicious transaction', the reporting obligation is triggered when there are reasonable grounds to suspect that a transaction or a series of transactions is related to the commission or attempted commission of a money laundering offence or a terrorist activity financing offence. FINTRAC has developed guidelines regarding the type of transactions that it will monitor, which should be used by Reporting Entities for compliance purposes.

15.54   The concept of what constitutes a 'suspicious' financial transaction is largely dependent on the particular circumstances of a particular transaction or series of transactions within the context of the overall client relationship. Although FINTRAC has identified possible indicia of a 'suspicious' transaction, there are no specific criteria that apply to any particular situation. What is considered to be 'suspicious' will vary depending on the type of business that is monitoring transactions, and within the same business what is 'suspicious' will vary from client to client. Any assessment of suspicion should therefore be based on a reasonable evaluation of relevant factors, including knowledge of the client's business, financial history, background and usual behaviour. Transactions may be suspicious regardless of the sum of money involved. There is no monetary threshold for reporting suspicious transactions.

---

1   Office of the Privacy Commissioner of Canada, *Submission to the Department of Finance's Public Consultation* (Ottawa, March 2012).

15.55   Accordingly, when considering whether a financial transaction is 'suspicious', reporting entities, their management and staff should consider all available information about transactions including the nature of money laundering and terrorist activity financing offences, whether a suspicion is reasonably based (in reference to the context of the transaction and what is known about the client); and the common indicators and industry-specific indicators applicable to the particular financial entity as suggested by FINTRAC and augmented or customised through business experience. As a general guide, a transaction may be connected to money laundering or terrorist activity financing if it (or a group of transactions) raises questions or concerns about legitimacy or motive, or gives rise to discomfort, apprehension or mistrust about the nature of or reasons for the transaction.

15.58   No Reporting Entity or its employees may disclose to anyone, including the client in question, the contents of a suspicious transaction report or even that such a report has been made to FINTRAC.

REAL ESTATE DEVELOPERS, DEALERS IN PRECIOUS METALS AND STONES, AND LAWYERS

15.89   Until 2008, Canada's AML/ATF regime applied to financial entities (such as banks and trust companies); life insurers, agents and brokers; securities dealers including portfolio managers and investment counsellors; accountants (when carrying out certain activities on behalf of clients); real estate agents and brokers (when carrying out certain activities on behalf of clients); money services businesses including foreign exchange dealers; and certain types of casinos. Three additional sectors were identified as posing a significant risk as potential conduits for money laundering and terrorist financing: real estate developers, lawyers, British Columbia notaries, and dealers in precious metals and stones. The PCMLTFA was amended to require certain client identification and record-keeping measures in each of these sectors, while dealers in precious metals and stones are also required to comply with certain reporting requirements.[1]

LAWYERS

15.91   When the PCMLTFA was initially enacted many professionals including accountants, stockbrokers and lawyers were concerned about the impact on their professional and ethical duties to their clients. As a result of pressure from Canadian law societies concerned about the erosion of solicitor-client privilege, and faced with a constitutional challenge in the courts, the government repealed parts of the relevant regulations, effectively suspending application of the record-keeping and reporting requirements to lawyers and law firms in Canada with respect to suspicious and large cash transactions. The hearing of the constitutional challenge on the merits was adjourned generally while the government continued consultations with the legal profession in order to establish a regulatory compliance regime that would balance the government's AML/ATF imperative with the stringent ethical rules binding Canadian lawyers in their dealings with clients.

15.92   Amendments to the PCMLTFA came into force in February 2007 which clarified that legal counsel are not subject to the transaction reporting requirements. However, regulations effective from 30 December 2008 include provisions that purport to apply to legal counsel and law firms and require the formal identification

---

1   Dealers in precious metals and stones and British Columbia notaries have been required to report to FINTRAC since 30 December 2008, and real estate developers since 20 February 2009.

of their clients as well as detailed record-keeping and compliance obligations for financial transactions involving C\$3,000 or more in cash or negotiable instruments (excluding professional fees, disbursements, expenses and bail). However, the court order adjourning the constitutional challenge mentioned above provides that the consent of the Federation of Law Societies of Canada and other parties to the litigation is required for any new PCMLTFA regulations to apply to lawyers.

15.93   Meanwhile, the Federation of Law Societies of Canada and law societies across Canada have developed their own client identification measures in acknowledgement that lawyers are targets for money laundering by virtue of their trust accounts. The Federation's Model Rule on Client Identification and Verification codifies the steps that a prudent lawyer should take to verify a client's identity and is being adopted by the law societies. For example, in April 2008, the Law Society of Upper Canada, the self-governing body for lawyers in the Province of Ontario, approved bye-law amendments in relation to operational obligations and responsibilities that establish client identification and verification obligations for lawyers and paralegals in that province, which became effective on 1 January 2009. The Law Society's rules go beyond the federal requirements which apply only when C\$3,000 or more is involved, and apply when the lawyer is retained to provide professional services.

15.94   It appears to be the intention of the Canadian law societies to demonstrate responsible self-regulation in order to avoid application of the PCMLTFA, which the legal profession continues to oppose in order to protect solicitor-client privilege.

British Colombia Notaries

15.95   British Columbia notaries public and notary corporations are subject to certain obligations under the PCMLTFA when, on behalf of any individual or entity, they receive or pay funds (other than for professional fees, disbursements, expenses or bail); purchase or sell securities, real property or business assets or entities; or transfer funds or securities.

FINANCIAL ACTION TASK FORCE EVALUATION

15.118   The most recent evaluation of Canada by the FATF was released on 29 February 2008 based upon AML/ATF measures the country had in place as of mid-2007 prior to the implementation of legislative changes contemplated in Bill C-25 that the Canadian government made to strengthen its AML/ATF regime.[1] Nevertheless, Canada received a reasonably positive review, much improved over its previous FATF evaluation, although still non-compliant in certain respects. Among its less favourable findings the FATF identified issues with respect to the effectiveness of enforcement and the degree of regulatory supervision in certain sectors, and found that Canada's preventative system did not apply comprehensively to the range of financial and non-financial businesses and professions identified by the FATF standards. However, the February 2008 report acknowledged that many of the FATF requirements already had been addressed by the new regulations implemented after the evaluation was conducted.

A number of deficiencies were, however, identified by the FATF in relation to customer identification and due diligence, and Canada was found to be non-compliant with the FATF's standards in this area.[2] As a result of increasing

---

1   Implemented in stages, 2007–2009.
2   FATF's '40 Recommendations'.

pressure from the FATF, in October 2012 the Department of Finance proposed amendments to the regulations under the PCMLTFA to address these deficiencies.[1] The proposed new customer identification and due diligence requirements would come into force one year after being finalised.

---

1   Regulations Amending the Proceeds of Crime (Money Laundering) and Terrorist Financing Regulations, Canada Gazette, Part 1, Vol 146, No 41 (13 October 2012).

Appendix 9.4   Cayman Islands

Barbara Padega

Appleby, Cayman Islands

[Bold material in square brackets has been contributed by Tim Bennett and does not appear in the chapter as written by Barbara Padega and published in *International Guide to Money Laundering Law and Practice*, 4th edition]

INTRODUCTION

The Cayman Islands

16.1   Cayman remains a British Overseas Territory, but is responsible for its own internal self-government and law courts. Cayman has an independent legal and judicial system, with a right of final appeal to the Privy Council in London.

The regulators

16.3   The Cayman Islands Monetary Authority ('CIMA') is the competent authority responsible for supervising, regulating and inspecting financial institutions operating in or from the Cayman Islands. It is also the principal body responsible for the regulation of investment funds, banks and insurance companies.

16.4   The reporting authority in the Cayman Islands is the Financial Reporting Authority (the 'Reporting Authority') which consists of representatives of various professions appointed by the Governor following consultation with a steering group and the cabinet. The Reporting Authority is responsible for receiving, requesting, analysing and disseminating disclosures of financial information concerning proceeds of criminal conduct or suspected proceeds of criminal conduct. The Financial Reporting Unit ('FRU') of the Reporting Authority was admitted to the Egmont Group of Financial Intelligence Units in June of 2001. The FRU has cooperated on an 'all crimes' basis, exchanging information with other jurisdictions in the fight against financial crime.

CAYMAN ISLANDS' ANTI-MONEY LAUNDERING REGIME

Current legislation

16.5   ...The PCL [**Proceeds of Crime Law 2008**] is substantially based on the UK Proceeds of Crime Act.

PROCEEDS OF CRIME OFFENCES

The specific money laundering offences

16.11   Part V of the PCL sets out the money laundering offences, including those aimed at actively discouraging bankers and other professionals from remaining oblivious to the source of the wealth of their clients. These offences are discussed below.

Concealing, Disguising, Converting, Transferring or Removing Criminal Property

16.12   PCL, s 133 provides that a person commits an offence if he conceals, disguises, converts, transfers or removes from Cayman criminal property. 'Criminal Property' is defined as property that constitutes a person's benefit from criminal conduct or property that represents such a benefit (in whole or in part, and whether directly or indirectly) and the alleged offender knows or suspects that it constitutes or represents such a benefit. Criminal property includes terrorist property.[1] Concealing or disguising criminal property includes concealing or disguising its nature, source, location, disposition, movement, ownership or any rights with respect to it.

16.13   Certain statutory defences are provided. A person does not commit the offence if he makes[2] a disclosure to the Reporting Authority (but this does not apply to the person who committed or was a party to the act from which the property derives). An offence is not committed if the person knows, or believes on reasonable grounds, that the relevant criminal conduct occurred outside of Cayman and that the relevant conduct was not, at the time it occurred, unlawful under the criminal laws then applying in that country. A professional legal advisor does not commit the offence if he comes to have the information in privileged circumstances (unless the information is communicated or given with the intention of furthering a criminal purpose).

16.14   The central element of this offence is 'knowing or suspecting' that the property represents the benefit of 'criminal conduct'. The meaning of knowledge is discussed in *Baden v Societe Generale pour Faroviser le Developpement du Commerce et de Industrie en France SA*.[3] Although this case is concerned with the requisite knowledge of a constructive trust, the concepts are relevant. Five different mental states were described:

(i)   actual knowledge;

(ii)   wilfully shutting one's eyes to the obvious;

(iii)   wilfully and recklessly failing to make such inquiries as an honest and reasonable man would make;

(iv)   knowledge of circumstances which would indicate the facts to an honest and reasonable man; and

(v)   knowledge of circumstances which would put an honest and reasonable man on inquiry.

Gibson J. held: 'the court will treat a person as having constructive knowledge of the facts if he wilfully shuts his eyes to the relevant facts which would be obvious if he opened his eyes.'[4] The court accepted (i) above as knowledge and (ii) and (iii) above as constructive knowledge. The tests in (ii) and (iii) require wilfulness and recklessness in varying degrees. These terms indicate conscious acts of neglect, the supposition being that sufficient awareness of the surrounding circumstances led the person not to investigate any further. The tests in (iv) and (v) are cases of carelessness where the honest and reasonable man would have reacted differently,[5]

---

1   PCL, s 144(3).
2   Or intended to make such disclosure, but has a reasonable excuse for not doing so.
3   [1992] 4 All ER 161.
4   [1992] 4 All ER 161 at 235.
5   C Howard, 'The Mens Rea Tests for Money Laundering' [1998] NJL 1818. Howard makes the distinction as being between 'wilfully' and 'wilfully and recklessly' and gross carelessness tested by what a reasonable man would have done or realised.

the distinction being between wilful ignorance of the true facts and ignorance caused by carelessness.

16.15   In *R v Stewart, Cuhna, Burges and Doegan*[1] (one of a series of rulings dealing with what is commonly referred to as the Euro Bank matter), the Grand Court considered the issue of proving *mens rea* in the context of a preliminary evidentiary hearing in a prosecution under the previous legislation (which was also concerned with the meaning of knowledge and suspicion). The defendants in the case were employees of Euro Bank, which was separately charged with money laundering offences under the Proceeds of Criminal Conduct Law. In the instant matter, the Crown alleged that the defendants had entered into or been concerned in arrangements whereby the retention by others of the proceeds of their criminal conduct was facilitated, knowing or suspecting that those others had been engaged in criminal conduct or benefited from it.[2] Euro Bank was alleged to have had a long history of lax banking practices which made it particularly vulnerable to money launderers. The charges related to events which occurred after the enactment of the PCCL, but evidence of the lax practices extended back many years. The Crown wished to adduce evidence of the lax practices, and their lengthy duration, as proof of *mens rea*: knowledge or suspicion on the part of the bank's employees could be made out when one considered the institutionalised nature of the conspiracy to launder money.

16.16   In ruling on what evidence might be presented in the trial, Smellie CJ noted that 'there must be some evidential basis upon which the jury can properly conclude that the defendants must have known or suspected that the underlying original activity was criminal'. Further along in the judgment, in considering the role that suspicious circumstances might play in such a prosecution, Smellie CJ stated:

> 'Here, the prosecution will have to be able to demonstrate that the jury would first "be bound to conclude" that the original activity was such indictable criminal activity. Only then will the prosecution be allowed to invite the jury to conclude that the necessary knowledge or suspicion – as a matter of inference, must have resided in the defendant's mind.'

This language suggests a subjective, rather than a purely objective, test of knowledge or suspicion.

16.17   Central to the offence as well is the notion of 'criminal conduct'. Criminal conduct is defined in the PCL as conduct which constitutes an offence in Cayman or would constitute an offence in Cayman if it occurred there. The notion of criminal conduct was examined under the previous legislation in another decision in the Euro Bank saga.[3] In that case, the Crown sought to adduce evidence that the defendant bank employees assisted a person in laundering the proceeds of criminal conduct though a bank account held in Cayman. The account contained lawful earnings from a Florida resident which had been moved into a Cayman bank account, allegedly in an attempt to thwart a potential (but not yet existing) claim from his ex-wife. Smellie CJ held that the Crown was not permitted to adduce evidence of the bank account, as it had failed to show that the money in it constituted the proceeds of criminal conduct. Even if it were assumed that the lawful earnings in the account could become the proceeds of criminal conduct – for example, if the account holder intended to defraud his ex-wife and to pervert the course of justice – the defendants nevertheless could not be convicted of a

---

1   [2002] CILR 420.
2   Separate conspiracy charges were also raised.
3   *R v Stewart, Cunha, Burges and Donegan* [2003] CILR 443.

money laundering offence. It is not enough that the money might become 'dirty': it has to be the proceeds of criminal conduct.

KNOW YOUR CLIENT

The Money Laundering Regulations

16.39   The Money Laundering Regulations (2009 Revision) (the 'Regulations') have been brought into place to ensure compliance with worldwide 'Know Your Client' and general compliance standards. The Regulations have introduced offences to which relevant financial businesses may be subjected even if they do not have any clients that are dealing with the proceeds of criminal conduct. These offences will apply simply because the procedures as set out in the Regulations are not followed.

16.40   The Regulations were designed to supplement the offences that were originally created under the PCCL and continue to apply under the new PCL. They are specifically designed to cover areas including the following:

Internal reporting procedures

16.44   Procedures must be in place to ensure that a relevant financial business' employees are aware of the process for internal reporting of suspicious transactions and the line of internal reporting. These internal reporting procedures and such other procedures of internal control and communication must be appropriate for the purposes of identifying and preventing money laundering.

16.45   While guidance is given as to what is required in relation to the above areas, the Regulations have been purposely drafted in a very wide and broad manner and have further introduced or made it an offence if they are contravened. Where an offence is committed by the relevant financial business with the consent, connivance of, or is attributable to any neglect on the part of an officer of the financial service provider, that person as well as the financial service provider will be guilty of the offence and proceeded against and punished accordingly. On conviction on indictment for breach of the Regulations, a person may be liable to imprisonment not exceeding a term of two years or a fine or both, or on summary conviction to a fine not exceeding CI$5,000.

The Guidance Notes

16.46   CIMA first issued Guidance Notes on the Prevention and Detection of Money Laundering in the Cayman Islands (the 'Guidance Notes') on 1 June 2001. The most recent edition of the Guidance Notes was issued in March of 2010. CIMA states in the introduction to the Guidance Notes that in some respects they go beyond the requirements of the Regulations. Therefore, whilst the financial service provider may not be liable for prosecution for a breach of the Guidance Notes, CIMA has indicated that it expects all institutions conducting relevant financial business to pay due regard to them. If it appears to CIMA that the financial service provider is not paying due regard to the Guidance Notes, it will seek an explanation and may conclude that the financial service provider is carrying on business in a manner that may give rise to sanctions under the applicable legislation. Further, the Guidance Notes, whilst not having statutory force, may be taken into account by the Courts in determining whether a party has complied with the Regulations.

16.47   The overriding aim of the Guidance Notes is to ensure that appropriate identification information is obtained in relation to the customers of financial service providers and the payments made between them. This is to assist in the detection of suspicious transactions and to create an effective audit trail in the event of an investigation. The Guidance Notes provide nuts and bolts particulars of identification procedures, the documentation required as evidence of identity, the different procedures to follow with respect to politically exposed persons and interactions with those in high risk countries. The recommended methods for on-going monitoring, reporting of suspicious transactions, record keeping, audits and compliance management are also set out in the Guidance Notes.

CONCLUSION

16.51   Former US Treasury Secretary Paul O'Neill commended the Cayman Islands during the signing of a tax information treaty with the United States, saying:

'The Cayman Islands is undeniably the most important financial centre in the Caribbean and ranks among the largest and most important financial centres in the world…We commend the Cayman Islands for emphatically demonstrating that those who seek to engage in tax evasion or other financial crimes are not welcome within its jurisdiction.'[1]

Financial service providers in the Cayman Islands are noted for their culture of compliance and dedication to the prevention and detection of money laundering. Preliminary independent research by Professor Jason Sharman of Griffith University of Australia[2] reveals that the Cayman Islands is one of only two surveyed *jurisdictions* that obtained the full suite of due diligence required under international money laundering regulations.

16.52   The Cayman Islands has recently been given a positive review by the Caribbean Financial Action Task Force assessment committee, but as with any jurisdiction the responsibility to remain vigilant against money laundering in ongoing. This responsibility is heightened and subjected to increased international scrutiny for no other reason than the Cayman Islands is involved in a great many offshore transactions. The legislation in place, the standard of regulatory intervention and the compliance culture present in the private sector is such to ensure that the Cayman Islands maintains its commitment to fighting international crime.

[On 27 March 2014, CIMA issued a public statement about delegation of AML–CFT obligations, so as to clarify certain provisions in the Guidance Notes.]

---

1   Speech given November 2001.
2   J C Sharman, The Money Laundry: Regulating Criminal Finance in the Global Economy (Ithaca: Cornell University Press, 2011).

Appendix 9.5   Guernsey

Mark Dunster

Guernsey Advocate, Partner, Carey Olsen, Guernsey
MLRO of Carey Olsen
Chairman of the Guernsey Association of Compliance Officers

Stephen Hellman

Judge of the Supreme Court of Bermuda

[Bold material in square brackets has been contributed by Tim Bennett and does not appear in the chapter as written by Mark Dunster and Stephen Hellman published in *International Guide to Money Laundering Law and Practice*, 4th edition]

BACKGROUND

Introduction

22.1   Over the past few decades, the Bailiwick of Guernsey has become one of the world's foremost offshore centres. As such, it is an attractive target for money launderers. To counteract this threat, the Bailiwick has introduced strict anti-money laundering and anti-terrorist financing legislation. The offshore finance industry is of great importance to the Bailiwick as its main export earner and largest industry. This makes it essential for the industry to retain its good name internationally. Today, the Bailiwick deservedly has the reputation of being a modern, well-regulated jurisdiction. It is recognised as such by international bodies such as Financial Action Task Force ('FATF'), the IMF and others...

THE CONSTITUTIONAL POSITION

22.2   The Bailiwick consists of the islands of Guernsey, Alderney and Sark, and some smaller islands. Of these, Guernsey is the largest and most populous, and the site of most of the offshore business in the Bailiwick. Save where otherwise indicated, 'Guernsey' will be used as synonymous with 'the Bailiwick' in this chapter. Like Jersey and the Isle of Man, the islands in the Bailiwick are dependencies of the British Crown. Thus the Bailiwick is neither a sovereign state, nor a British Overseas Territory like Cayman or Bermuda. The Crown has ultimate responsibility for the good government of the Bailiwick. However, Guernsey, Alderney and Sark all have their own legislatures. The island of Guernsey is responsible for the enactment of criminal legislation throughout the Bailiwick.

22.3   It is a matter for debate whether the Bailiwick is subject to the supremacy of the UK Parliament. In practice, however, the UK government is responsible for the Bailiwick's international relations and for its defence, but does not seek to bind the constituent islands of the Bailiwick to international treaties without their prior consent.

INTERNATIONAL EVALUATIONS

22.8   Guernsey was most recently evaluated by the International Monetary Fund ('IMF') in 2010. This visit by the IMF was as a result of an invitation to them by Guernsey's government. The IMF's report broadly held that Guernsey had a 'high level of compliance' for each of the international standards against which the Bailiwick was judged. Certain recommendations were made which led to either new legislation, amendments to existing legislation or changed regulations or Guidance Notes. There was a suggestion by the IMF (which was not accepted by the Guernsey authorities) that although the legislation was in place it may not be being used vigorously enough in practice. The convictions and imprisonments of two money launderers in recent years should have put that issue to bed.[1]

ANTI-MONEY LAUNDERING LEGISLATION IN THE NEW MILLENNIUM

22.9   The new millennium has seen the introduction of all crimes and revised drug trafficking and anti-terrorist legislation and a revised set of Guidance Notes for the financial services industry. The law relating to the obtaining of evidence in Guernsey for use in investigations and prosecutions overseas has been overhauled.

22.10   Increasingly legislation has been aimed at improving international cooperation and transfer of evidence. This coupled with an ever increasing amount of bilateral tax information exchange agreements and the implementation of the European Withholding Tax Directive has kept Guernsey at the forefront of cooperative and compliant offshore finance centres. Guernsey now has agreements for exchange of tax information with some 35 countries.

MONEY LAUNDERING LEGISLATION

Tertiary provisions

Codes of Practice for Corporate Service Providers, Trust Service Providers and Company Directors

22.40   These Codes of Practice were issued by the Commission under the Regulation of Fiduciaries, Administration Businesses and Company Directors, etc (Bailiwick of Guernsey) Law 2000 (the Fiduciary Law). They were made on 20 March 2001 and came into effect on 1 April 2001.

Handbook for Financial Services Businesses on Countering Financial Crime and Terrorist Financing ('The Handbook'.)

22.41   This was issued by the Commission on 15 December 2007 and last updated in **[March/April 2013]**. It replaces the Guidance Notes on the Prevention of Money Laundering and Countering the Financing of Terrorism ('The Guidance Notes 2002'), which were issued by the Commission on 22 August 2002. They were known colloquially as 'the Rainbow Guide' on account of the brightly coloured, loose-leaf binder in which they were issued. The Guidance Notes 2002 in turn replaced the Guidance Notes on the Prevention of Money Laundering issued by the Commission on 1 January 2000, which were amended on 31 May 2000 and 4 October 2001. These were a revision of the Guidance Notes on the Prevention of Money Laundering issued by the Guernsey Joint Money Laundering Steering Group in March 1997. They were in turn based on similar Guidance Notes issued by the equivalent Steering Group in the UK and replaced the Money Laundering Avoidance Guidance Notes issued by the Commission in July 1991. Further amendment to the Guidance Notes is under consultation at the time of updating this chapter (1 July 2012).

---

1   *Law Officers of the Crown v Taylor* (Royal Court of Guernsey 2011) (two and half years' imprisonment) and *Law Officers of the Crown v Ludden* (Royal Court of Guernsey 2012) (five years' imprisonment). Both of these cases related to activity that had taken place (broadly) during the 2000s so are somewhat historic. It is also worth noting that there has also been one successful appeal against a drug trafficking conviction (and hence the confiscation order attaching thereto) confirming the independence of the Guernsey judiciary – *Hutchinson v Law Officers of the Crown* (Guernsey Court of Appeal 2012).

22.42   As with the regulations for Guernsey lawyers, accountants and estate agents the Commission has issued (on 7 November 2008) a Handbook for those groups of professionals. It is in substantially the same form as for other parts of the finance industry.

22.43   In addition to primary and secondary legislation and regulations etc the [GFSC] also issued 'Instructions' to the regulated industry. The exact status of these is unclear[1] but topics included:

(1)   corporate governance and controls;

(2)   taking business from sensitive sources, eg Iran;

(3)   screening of employees; and

(4)   dealing with wire transfers.

OFFENCES IN RELATION TO MONEY LAUNDERING AND TERRORIST FUNDS

22.46   The mental element necessary to commit an offence in relation to money laundering or terrorist funds under any of the above laws is typically either 'having reasonable grounds to suspect' or 'knowing or suspecting'. 'Having reasonable grounds to suspect' is an objective test. A person will be guilty of an offence having this element if they ought to have suspected but did not. 'Knowing or suspecting' is a subjective test. To be guilty of an offence having this element, a person must actually have known or suspected. They will not be guilty of an offence if they ought to have known or suspected but did not. 'Suspicion' and its cognates are not defined in any of the statutes. But, applying English case law, it need not be 'clear', 'firmly grounded and targeted on specific facts', or based on 'reasonable grounds'.[2]

The Criminal Justice (Proceeds of Crime) Bailiwick of Guernsey Law 1999

22.50   Criminal conduct' means any conduct, other than drug trafficking (which is covered by DT(BG)L 2000), which constitutes a criminal offence under the laws of the Bailiwick and is triable on indictment or which would constitute such an offence if it were to take place in the Bailiwick. It is therefore irrelevant whether the conduct is criminal in the jurisdiction in which it was committed.

22.51   Certain categories of criminal conduct call for brief comment.

22.52   *Fiscal offences.* It is a common law offence to cheat the Revenue. The States of Guernsey, which is the legislature for the island, levies income, property and other taxes and import duties for Guernsey and Alderney. In the case of the proceeds of the evasion of tax due in another jurisdiction, it is submitted that the correct approach would be to ask whether tax evasion is also an offence in the Bailiwick rather than to ask whether it is an offence in the Bailiwick to evade taxes due in that jurisdiction.[3] But the point is not free from doubt. In any case, tax evasion in other jurisdictions will tend to involve conduct, such as false accounting, which is indictable in the Bailiwick.

22.53   *Exchange control offences.* There are no general exchange control regulations in the Bailiwick. However, the Control of Borrowing (Bailiwick of Guernsey) Ordinance 1959, as amended, in effect imposes exchange controls with

---

1   We understand that compliance with these instructions is a matter which the Commission will take into account when considering if a person or entity is a 'fit and proper person' to be licensed to undertake a specific activity.

2   *Da Silva* [2006] EWCA Crim 1654, [2007] 1 WLR 303.

3   In England and Wales the Court of Appeal took this approach in analogous circumstances in *Quattrocchi* [2004] EWCA Civ 40; *The Times* 28 January 2004.

respect to borrowing by companies.[1] Moreover, as with tax evasion, exchange control offences in other jurisdictions will tend to involve conduct, such as false accounting, which is indictable in the Bailiwick.

22.54 *Bribery*. Bribery and other corrupt practices are offences under the Prevention of Corruption (Bailiwick of Guernsey) Law 2003. It is irrelevant whether the corrupt practice takes place outside the jurisdiction. It is also of note that the provisions of the UK Bribery Act 2010 often extend to Guernsey in practice because many companies here are subsidiaries of those in the UK or because Guernsey residents are also British citizens.

22.55 If a person is charged with an offence in connection with the proceeds of criminal conduct, then applying English case law the prosecution must prove to the criminal standard that the alleged proceeds are in fact the proceeds of criminal conduct other than drug trafficking, but need not prove the precise type of criminal conduct.[2]

The Handbook

22.72 The Handbook has been issued to assist financial services businesses to comply with the requirements of the relevant laws. Although technically the Handbook is for guidance only, its provisions are expressed to be a statement of the standard expected by the Commission of all financial services businesses in Guernsey. In practical terms, therefore, they are mandatory, and are universally regarded as such. The courts may take account of the Handbook in any proceedings brought under the relevant laws or in determining whether a person has complied with the requirements of the CJ(PC)BG Regulations.

RECOGNITION OF SUSPICIOUS CUSTOMERS/TRANSACTIONS

22.78 A suspicious transaction will often be one which is inconsistent with a customer's known legitimate business or activities, or with the normal business for that type of financial services product. It is, therefore, important that the financial services business knows enough about the customer's business to recognise that a transaction or a series of transactions is unusual. Further, that the financial services business knows enough about the type of transactions or structures commonly used in the particular area to recognise when a customer's particular requirements are unusual.

DISCLOSURE/TIPPING OFF

Disclosure reports[3]

22.144 Where, as a result of an internal report, a MLRO knows or suspects, or has reasonable grounds for knowing or suspecting, that a person is engaged in money laundering, they must make a disclosure to the Guernsey Financial Intelligence Service (FIS)...

22.145 Disclosures must be made using a standard form. Previously the system relied on the manual filing and submission of a form. The system has now gone electronic. An advanced and secure system ('Themis') links each regulated business to the FIS. The MLRO and his deputy are given passwords to access the secure website to both make reports electronically and to be notified of any changes in investigations or other matters by the FIS.

---

1   Although even these are under consideration for repeal.
2   *Montila* [2004] UKHL 50, [2004] 1 WLR 3141. This principle was also affirmed as the one that will be followed by the Guernsey courts in the Ludden case (supra) in which the Guernsey author was counsel for the defence.
3   The contents of this section draw heavily on the Handbook.

22.146   The financial services business should provide as much information and documentation as possible to show the basis of the suspicion and to enable the FIS to understand the intended nature of the business relationship.

22.147   The FIS will acknowledge receipt of a disclosure promptly in writing – now via the status update on the electronic system. If consent is sought to carry out a particular transaction, the FIS will consider this. Any consent will be in writing. In urgent cases, consent may be given orally, but will be followed by written confirmation. If consent is not given, the FIS will discuss the way forward with the financial services business. The FIS may follow up a disclosure with a request for further information.

22.148   The FIS will, as far as possible, supply on request information about the current status of investigations resulting from a disclosure, as well as more general information about trends and indicators.

22.149   Access to disclosures will be restricted to what the FIS describes in the Handbook as 'appropriate authorities'. Information from disclosures will normally be in a sanitised format and will not identify the source. If there is a prosecution, the FIS will protect the source of the information as far as the law allows. In practice this can be limited.[1]

22.150   In addition to reporting to the FIS, and at the same time, financial services businesses should make disclosures to the Commission where: the financial services business' systems failed to detect the transaction and the matter has been brought to its attention in another way, for example, by the FIS; the transaction may present a significant reputational risk to Guernsey and/or the financial services business; it is suspected that an employee of the financial services business was involved; or a member of the financial services business' staff has been dismissed for a serious breach of its internal policies, procedures and controls.

22.151   The disclosures for the past five years break down as follows:[2]

Year	2008	2009	2010	2011	2012*
Total no of STRs	519	627	680	1136	313
STRs made under T&CL 2002	6	4	5	0	N/A
Other STRs with terrorist finance link	3	1	0	3	N/A

* Up to 30 June 2012.

22.152   ...there have now been two money laundering offence convictions in Guernsey. In addition there have been numerous drug trafficking convictions and confiscation orders of varying degrees of seriousness. In addition the FIS has been of assistance in overseas money laundering inquiries which have led to a number of successful prosecutions in other jurisdictions.

THE FUTURE

22.196   An assessment team from the IMF last visited Guernsey between 17 May 2010 and 1 June 2010. The team produced a *Detailed Assessment Report on Anti-Money Laundering and Combating the Financing of Terrorism* in Guernsey which was published in January 2011.

---

1   In one criminal case in Guernsey the author spent some time cross examining the MLRO over his report and notes as submitted to the FIS. In England a similar situation occurred in the *Shah v HSBC* case during 2011/12.
2   Statistics supplied by FIS. The authors gratefully acknowledge the assistance of the FIS and, in particular, Investigation Officer Paul Yabsley of the Cross Border Crime Division.

22.197   The Report found that Guernsey's comprehensive anti-money laundering/combating terrorist financing legal framework provides a sound basis for an effective anti-money laundering/combating terrorist financing regime. Various shortcomings were identified during the assessment, but these were mainly technical in nature. Some of the deficiencies were addressed by the authorities immediately after the onsite visit. Money laundering and the financing of terrorism are criminalised fully in line with the FATF standard and the legal framework provides an ability to freeze and confiscate assets in appropriate circumstances...

22.198   However the Report stated that the Financial Intelligence Service and other law enforcement agencies should endeavour to enhance their performance in terms of cases for investigation for money laundering activity, particularly as a stand-alone offence. It expressed the view that, given the size of the Bailiwick's financial sector and its status as an international financial centre, the modest number of cases involving third party money laundering by financial sector participants and the disconnect between the number of money laundering cases investigated versus the number of cases prosecuted and eventually resulting in a conviction calls into question the effective application of the local money laundering provisions.

22.199   The Report further noted with respect to confiscation and provisional measures that, although the Bailiwick's provisions are robust, and they are used routinely in all prosecutions where they can be applied, they had not yet been used in a fully effective manner because of the few cases instituted in proceeds-generating matters other than drug trafficking.

22.200   The *Authorities' Response to the Assessment* is at Annex 1 to the Report. The Bailiwick Authorities affirmed that they were fully committed to meeting the standards set by the FATF Forty Recommendations on Money Laundering and Nine Special Recommendations. They noted that, as stated in the Report, most of the recommendations made by the assessors are technical in nature, with some relating to the improvement of implementation of legislation.

22.201   The Response noted that the first prosecution for autonomous money laundering has come to trial and the defendant has been convicted on nine different counts. There has also been a further successful money laundering prosecution involving two counts of money laundering. This trend is expected to continue, with further successful money laundering prosecutions for both self-laundering and autonomous money laundering anticipated in the future.

22.204   A Tax Information Exchange Agreement ('TIEA'), between Guernsey and the UK was signed at the end of January 2009. This new tax information exchange agreement is seen as a significant step in the UK's efforts to counter tax evasion. The number of TIEAs signed between Guernsey and other jurisdictions has now risen to 35. It is hoped that tax evaders will find it clear that money launderers are not able to use Guernsey as a safe haven. The G20 Summit in April 2009 declared that Guernsey was on the 'White List' of fully co-operating jurisdictions.

22.205   This agreement may also be of significance to UK residents who hold bank accounts in Guernsey. This agreement could assist HMRC in its quest to identify holders of such accounts.

22.206   The agreement provides that the parties, through their competent authorities, shall provide assistance through exchange of information that is foreseeably relevant to the administration or enforcement of the domestic laws of the parties concerning taxes covered by the agreement, including information that is foreseeably relevant to the determination, assessment, enforcement or collection of tax with respect to persons subject to such taxes or to the investigation of tax matters or the prosecution of criminal tax matters in relation to such persons.

22.207   The law in this chapter is stated as at 1 July 2012.

Appendix 9.6   Hong Kong

Kareena Teh,

Dechert LLP, Hong Kong

Lee Travis Benjamin

Registered Foreign Lawyer, Deacons, Hong Kong

[Bold material in square brackets has been contributed by Tim Bennett and does not appear in the chapter as written by Barbara Padega and published in *International Guide to Money Laundering Law and Practice,* **4th edition]**

INTRODUCTION

One country, two systems

23.1   On 1 July 1997, Hong Kong became a Special Administrative Region of the People's Republic of China. Despite that landmark constitutional event, Hong Kong continues to enjoy, under the Basic Law of Hong Kong,[1] a high degree of executive, legislative and judicial autonomy.[2] This includes matters relating to the legislation, investigation, prosecution, trial, and sentencing of money laundering and terrorist financing offences, which remain within the jurisdiction of Hong Kong as prescribed by the Basic Law.

Money laundering and terrorist financing

23.4   The three main pieces of legislation in Hong Kong that are concerned with money laundering are the Drug Trafficking (Recovery of Proceeds) Ordinance (Chapter 405 of the Laws of Hong Kong) (DTROP), the Organized and Serious Crimes Ordinance (Chapter 455 of the Laws of Hong Kong) (OSCO) and the Anti-Money Laundering and Counter-Terrorist Financing (Financial Institutions) Ordinance (Chapter 615 of the Laws of Hong Kong) (AMLO), whilst the United Nations (Anti-Terrorism Measures) Ordinance (Chapter 575 of the Laws of Hong Kong) (UNATMO) deals with combating terrorism and terrorist financing. From a technical perspective, there is no offence under the UNATMO that is not caught under the OSCO.

23.5   The AMLO empowers certain authorities to supervise compliance with the requirements under AMLO, as well as to publish guidelines regarding the application of its customer due diligence and record-keeping provisions. These authorities are the Hong Kong Monetary Authority (HKMA), the Securities and Futures Commission (SFC), the Office of the Commissioner of Insurance (OCI) and the Hong Kong Customs & Excise Department (CED). An analysis of these very proscriptive guidelines is beyond the scope of this chapter.

23.6   Both the Hong Kong Police Force and the CED have been empowered to investigate money laundering and terrorism and terrorist financing activities in Hong Kong and a Joint Financial Intelligence Unit (JFIU), run jointly by the two

---

1   The Basic Law is the constitutional document of Hong Kong. It was passed by the National People's Congress of China in order to implement China's basic policies regarding Hong Kong and the way in which Hong Kong would be administered for the next 50 years.

2   Basic Law, arts 2 and 12.

departments, was set up in 1989 to receive reports concerning suspicious financial activity. Since the enactment of the UNATMO, the JFIU also receives suspicious transaction reports related to terrorist property.

23.7   The role of the JFIU is not to investigate suspicious transactions, but simply to receive, analyse and store reports of suspicious transactions and refer them to the appropriate investigative unit. A suspicious transaction report will usually be referred to either the Narcotics Bureau, the Organized Crime & Triad Bureau of the Hong Kong Police Force or the Customs Drug Investigation Bureau of the CED.

23.8   The JFIU also advises on money laundering issues generally, both domestically and internationally, and offers practical guidance and assistance to the financial sector on the subject of money laundering.

PRIMARY LEGISLATION

Money laundering

The money laundering offence

23.10   Under the DTRPO and OSCO, it is an offence to deal with any property knowing or having reasonable grounds to believe that such property in whole or in part, directly or indirectly represents the proceeds of drug trafficking or of an indictable offence.[1]

23.11   In Hong Kong, crimes are defined by statute as being triable either summarily or on indictment. Generally, indictable offences are more serious offences, and include tax evasion, murder, kidnapping, drug trafficking, assault, theft, robbery, obtaining property by deception, false accounting, firearms offences, manslaughter, bribery, illegal gambling and smuggling.

23.12   It is irrelevant where the drug trafficking or indictable offence took place. Drug trafficking is defined to include drug trafficking anywhere in the world.[2] An indictable offence includes conduct which would constitute an indictable offence if it had occurred in Hong Kong,[3] regardless of whether the conduct is illegal in the jurisdiction where it is committed. Accordingly, money laundering can be of proceeds of drug trafficking or of an indictable offence committed either in Hong Kong or elsewhere. The purpose is to deter people from using Hong Kong to launder proceeds of crime. Moreover, from a technical perspective, dealing in Hong Kong with the proceeds from conduct which is legal (or at least not illegal) in another jurisdiction but which is illegal in Hong Kong is caught under the OSCO (eg, the proceeds of non-Hong Kong legal gambling). Similarly, dealing with the proceeds from conduct which is illegal outside Hong Kong but which is not illegal in Hong Kong is not caught by the OSCO (eg, the proceeds of non-Hong Kong exchange control violation).

Actus reus

23.13   The actus reus of a money laundering offence is 'dealing in property'. Dealing is defined broadly to include:

(i)   receiving, acquiring, concealing, disguising, disposing of or converting the property;

(ii)   bringing the property into or removing it from Hong Kong; and

(iii)   using the property to borrow money, or as security.[4]

---

1   DTRPO, s 25 and OSCO, s 25.
2   DTRPO, s 2(1).
3   OSCO, s 25(4).
4   DTRPO, s 2(1) and OSCO, s 2(1).

A person can be convicted of the money laundering offence under the DTRPO or OSCO for 'dealing' with property representing the proceeds of his or her own crime or someone else's crime.[1]

23.14   There is no requirement to prove the actual drug trafficking or indictable offence,[2] nor that the property actually represented the proceeds of the crime. In the case of *HKSAR v Wong Ping Shui Adam*,[3] it was held that the actus reus of the offence was 'dealing in property' and there were no words qualifying or restricting such property. It was not open to the interpretation that the property must be confined to property which must have been or could only have been the proceeds of an indictable offence. The wrongdoing intended was the conspiracy to put into effect a criminal enterprise, and the argument that the proceeds had to be those of an indictable offence was not sustainable in law. Accordingly, a person commits a money laundering offence under the DTRPO or OSCO once he or she 'deals with property' with the requisite mens rea.

Mens rea

23.15   The mens rea of a money laundering offence consists of two parts. A person must either 'know' or 'have reasonable grounds to believe' that the property he or she is dealing with represents proceeds of drug trafficking or of an indictable offence.

23.16   The term 'know' includes evidence of the person's involvement with the commission of the crime, or by admission that they knew that the property was proceeds of a crime.[4] In *Atwal v Massey*,[5] knowledge was found to be a subjective test unrelated to the objective determination of what a reasonable man would have known in the situation. Notwithstanding this, 'knowledge' for the purposes of s 25(1) of the DTRPO and the OSCO is broader than 'actual knowledge', and encompasses constructive knowledge. For example, in the English case of *James & Son Ltd v Smee*, Parker J held that: 'knowledge ... includes the state of mind of a man who shuts his eyes to the obvious or allows his servant to do something in the circumstances where a contravention is likely not caring whether a contravention takes place or not.'[6]

23.17   The term 'reasonable grounds to believe' involves both objective and subjective elements. The objective element requires proof that a common-sensed, right-thinking member of the public would consider that there were grounds sufficient to lead a person to believe that the property in whole or in part represented any person's proceeds of a crime. The subjective element requires proof that those grounds were known to the defendant.[7] In the case of *Seng Yuet Fong v HKSAR*,[8] on an application for leave to appeal against conviction, the applicant was the accountant of a third party who allegedly received an income of HK $6,000 per month as a salesman. Without explanation, large sums of money belonging to the third party were repeatedly deposited into accounts of the applicant, which were subsequently withdrawn by her and passed on to the third party. The third party was eventually convicted of drug trafficking and the applicant, having reasonable grounds for believing that the third party was a drug trafficker, was convicted of money laundering. The application for leave to appeal against conviction was dismissed by the Hong Kong Court of Final Appeal.

---

1   *Lok Kar-win v HKSAR* [1999] 4 HKC 796, CFA.
2   *HKSAR v Li Ching* [1997] 14 HKC 108, HKCA.
3   [2001] 1 HKLRD 346, CFA.
4   *Seng Yuet-fong v HKSAR* [1999] 2 HKC 833 (a case under the former DTRPO, s 25).
5   [1971] 3 All ER 881.
6   [1954] 3 All ER 273.
7   *HKSAR v Shing Siu-ming* [1999] 2 HKC 818; and *Seng Yuet-fong v HKSAR* [1999] 2 HKC 833 (both cases under the former DTRPO, s 25).
8   [1999] 2 HKC 833.

Reporting of suspicious money laundering transactions

Statutory obligation to report

23.23   Both the DTRPO and OSCO were amended in 1995[1] to tighten money laundering provisions by imposing a statutory duty on all persons to report suspicious transactions relating to money laundering. The disclosure obligation applies to all persons and overrides contractual confidentiality and personal data protection obligations. It does not, however, override legal professional privilege. The DTRPO and OSCO do not contain any geographical restriction on the disclosure obligation but, presumably, only persons subject to Hong Kong jurisdiction will be subject to Hong Kong law.

23.24   According to the DTRPO and OSCO,[2] any person who knows or suspects that any property, in whole or in part, directly or, indirectly, represents the proceeds of drug trafficking, or of an indictable offence, or was or is intended to be used in that connection, must report such knowledge or suspicion to an authorised officer as soon as it is reasonable for them to do so.

23.25   The suspicion test is a subjective test. As a result, a person who does not suspect that property represents the proceeds of crime will not be guilty of an offence under s 25A(1). Notwithstanding this, a defendant may encounter difficulty in convincing a court that his lack of suspicion was honestly held where an ordinary man would have been suspicious about the property in question. It is possible that the personal knowledge and experience of the defendant will be a significant consideration in determining his state of mind. Finally, knowledge may include constructive knowledge, and therefore wilful blindness may not be a defence.

23.26   The case law implies that s 25A(1) has a lower mens rea benchmark than the test of having 'reasonable grounds to believe' in s 25(1). In the case of *Hussien v Chong Fook Kam*,[3] the Privy Council considered the test of 'reasonable suspicion' contained in the Malaysian Criminal Procedure Code, which authorised a police officer to arrest a person whom he reasonably suspected of being guilty of an offence. Lord Devlin said: 'Suspicion in its ordinary meaning is a state of conjecture or surmise where proof is lacking: "I suspect but I cannot prove. Suspicion arises at or near the starting-point of an investigation of which the obtaining of prima facie proof is the end".' The view in *Hussien v Chong Fook Kam* is supported by the case of *Pang Yiu Hung Robert v Commissioner of Police*.[4] In this case, Justice Hartman cited Lord Devlin and Scott LJ with approval, stating that: 'suspicion is not to be equated with prima facie proof'.

23.27   An authorised officer includes any police officer, any member of the CED and the JFIU. A suspicious transaction report may be made to the JFIU by mail, fax or telephone in accordance with the instructions contained on its website.[5] Following receipt of a suspicious transaction report, the JFIU will conduct preliminary research to determine whether the report merits further investigation and, where appropriate, allocate the matter to trained financial investigation officers in the police and the CED for further investigation. This may involve seeking supplementary information from the person making disclosure and from other sources. Discreet inquiries are also made to confirm the basis for suspicion.

---

1   The Drug Trafficking (Recovery of Proceeds) (Amendment) Ordinance 1995 and the Organised and Serious Crimes (Amendment) Ordinance 1995.
2   DTRPO, s 25A and OSCO, s 25A.
3   [1970] AC 942.
4   [2002] 4 HKC 579.
5   www.jfiu.gov.hk/.

23.28   The JFIU will send the person making the suspicious transaction report a letter acknowledging receipt of the report. In the case of suspicious transactions involving a bank account, if there is no immediate need for action against the relevant account, consent will usually be given by the JFIU within a few days of receipt of the report allowing the person filing the report to continue to operate the account in accordance with normal banking practices. Until such consent is obtained, further transactions in respect of the account could constitute the offence of dealing, and should therefore be avoided.

23.29   On request, the JFIU, the police or the CED to whom the suspicious transaction report has been made may, but are not obliged to, provide to the person making the report a status report on the relevant investigation.

23.30   For an employee, he or she may report any knowledge or suspicion of a money laundering transaction to the person designated by his or her employer[1] and he or she would not be prosecuted for the offence under the DTRPO or the OSCO, notwithstanding that his or her employer or the person designated by his or her employer fails to, or determines not to, report the transaction to the relevant authorities.

23.31   Failure to report any such knowledge or suspicion is an offence, carrying a maximum penalty of three months' imprisonment and a fine, currently HK $50,000.[2]

Statutory protection for disclosure

23.32   Under Hong Kong law, banks are under a duty of confidentiality to customers.[3] It is an implied term of the contract between a bank and its customer that the bank will not divulge to any third party either the state of the customer's account or any of his or her transactions with the bank, or any information relating to the customer acquired through the keeping of his or her account unless:

(i)   disclosure is required under Hong Kong law;

(ii)   disclosure is made with the express or implied consent of the customer;

(iii)   there is a duty to the public to disclose; or

(iv)   the interests of the bank require disclosure.

23.33   Further, personal data in Hong Kong is protected by the Personal Data (Privacy) Ordinance (Chapter 486 of the Laws of Hong Kong) (PDPO), which prohibits the use of personal information (including the transfer or disclosure of such information) for any purpose other than the purpose for which it was collected, unless with the consent of the person in question. Personal information includes any information about a living individual from which it is reasonably practicable to ascertain the identity of the person in question.

23.34   In order to encourage the reporting of suspicious financial activity and to ensure a person is not penalised for making such a report, statutory protection is afforded to any person who has disclosed information pursuant to a report of known or suspected money laundering transactions. Such disclosure shall not be treated as a breach of any contract or of any enactment or rule of conduct restricting disclosure of information (including the banker's duty of confidentiality to customers and the prohibition contained in the PDPO against disclosure) and shall not render the person making the disclosure liable in damages for any loss arising out of the disclosure.[4]

---

1   DTRPO, s 25A(4) and OSCO, s 25A(4).
2   DTRPO, s 25A(7) and OSCO, s 25A(7).
3   *Tournier v National Provincial and Union Bank of England* [1924] 1 KB 461, CA.
4   DTRPO, s 25A(3) and OSCO, s 25A(3).

CIVIL REMEDIES

23.79   In addition to criminal liability, a money launderer may be liable to account for the money being laundered. Depending on the manner in which the money launderer obtained the proceeds and the form of those proceeds, a number of claims may be brought against the money launderer in Hong Kong. If the illegal proceeds are beneficially owned by the person whose money is being laundered (for example, in cases of theft) and the money is still identifiable in the hands of the money launderer, it is possible to bring a proprietary claim, either at law or in equity, to follow the money into the hands of the money launderer. Additionally, the owner may be able to bring a personal action at law for money had and received against the money launderer or a personal action in equity against whoever was responsible for initiating the misapplication of his or her property.

23.80   If the conduct which gave rise to the illicit proceeds involved a disposition of property in breach of trust, and the money launderer had dishonestly been an accessory to or assisted in the disposition of that property, or the money launderer had knowingly received that property or its proceeds disposed of in breach of trust, a constructive trust may be imposed on the money launderer in respect of that property or its proceeds.[1] The trust need not be a formal trust and may arise should there be a fiduciary relationship between the 'trustee' and the property of another person[2] or if a constructive trust is imposed due to fraudulent or unconscionable conduct[3] or criminal behaviour.[4]

23.81   This area of the law is extremely complex, principally due to the existence of what has been described[5] as 'arbitrary and anomalous distinctions' between the claims at law and the claims in equity.

[The Hong Kong prosecuting authorities have adopted a more aggressive prosecution strategy and the Judiciary are now imposing tough sentences. The last two years have seen some high profile convictions, including:

- **Lue Juncheng convicted in January 2013 for laundering HKD13.1 billion, and imprisoned for 10½ years**

- **Yet Lam Mei-ling convicted in March 2013 for laundering HKD6.7 billion, and imprisoned for 10 years**

- **Carson Yeung (former president of English football club Birmingham City F.C.) was convicted in March 2014 on five counts of money laundering a total of HK$720 million and sentenced to 6 years' imprisonment, with the trial judge commenting that Yeung was "not a witness of truth", and that his sentence included a necessary element of deterrence**

And in March 2014 two Hong Kong tycoons (Joseph Lau and Stephen Lo) were convicted in absentia in the Macau Courts (a separate SAR of China) for bribery and money laundering: their extradition from Hong Kong is being sought. The bribe recipient (a former Macau public works minister) received a 29-year prison sentence.]

---

1   *Royal Brunei Airlines Sdn Bhd v Tan* [1995] 2 AC 378, PC.
2   *Baden v Société Générale pur Favoriser le Developpement du Commerce et de l'Industrie en France SA* [1993] 1 WLR 509n.
3   Eg, the obtaining of property as a result of undue influence (*Barclays Bank plc v O'Brien* [1994] 1 AC 180) or an attempt to renege on an undertaking or agreement (*Bannister v Bannister* [1948] WN 261).
4   Eg, the obtaining of property or inheritance as a result of unlawful killing (*Re Crippen's Estate* [1911] P 108). In very few cases will a constructive trust be imposed in cases of theft as a thief acquires no title to the property he or she steals.
5   By Millett J in *El Ajou v Dollar* Land Holdings plc [1993] BCLC 735 at 757B–C.

Appendix 9.7   The Isle of Man

Peter Clucas

Cains, Douglas

[Bold material in square brackets has been contributed by Tim Bennett and does not appear in the chapter as written by Peter Clucas and published in *International Guide to Money Laundering Law and Practice*, 4th edition]

INTRODUCTION

25.1   The Isle of Man is a British Crown Dependency, having The Queen as Head of State. However, the Island is constitutionally and politically independent of the United Kingdom ('UK'), having its own legislature (Tynwald), established in the tenth century, which legislates on all internal matters, including taxation. The British Government is responsible only for the Island's defence and foreign representation, although the trend is for the Island to take greater responsibility for negotiating its own foreign agreements in relation to matters over which it already exercises a domestic jurisdiction, for example, the tax information exchange agreements which the Isle of Man has agreed with 27 countries (and an additional eight Double Taxation Agreements) to date were negotiated and settled by the Island's Treasury department. UK law does not normally extend to the Isle of Man, although by Order in Council British statutes can be extended to the Island with the express consent of Tynwald.

25.2   The Isle of Man is not a member of the European Union ('EU'), but enjoys a special relationship with the EU by virtue of Protocol 3 to the UK's Act of Accession annexed to the 1972 Treaty of Accession by which the UK became a member of the EU. Apart from the application of Value Added Tax ('VAT'), the Island is outside the EU in the field of financial services and products and is not bound by EU directives in this area. Nor is it subject to EU regulations on harmonisation of tax, corporate and other laws, except in respect of the common customs tariff and certain agricultural levies.

25.4   The Isle of Man actively participates in and cooperates with a number of international organisations, including the Financial Action Task Force ('FATF'), the Organisation for Economic Co-operation and Development ('OECD'), the Financial Stability Forum (an IMF body), the Basle Committee on Banking Supervision, the International Organisation of Securities Commissions ('IOSCO'), the International Association of Insurance Supervisors ('IAIS'), the Offshore Group of Banking Supervisors ('OGBS') and the Egmont Group. In particular, the Isle of Man participates in those specific international legislative initiatives aimed at combating the prevalence of drug trafficking, terrorism and associated money laundering activities. The Island's primary legislation in respect of money laundering is broadly in line with EU legislation and regulations and the international initiatives being undertaken by those countries who are members of FATF.

25.5   ...The Island's desire to cooperate with international law enforcement agencies was affirmed more recently by the IMF in its 2009 evaluation of the Island's AML/CFT measures.

25.6   ...Updated anti-money laundering regulations were introduced in September 2010 and a large scale revision of the Island's primary legislation dealing with the proceeds of crime came into force from 1 August 2009.

LEGISLATION AND REGULATION OVERVIEW – MONEY LAUNDERING IN THE ISLE OF MAN

25.8   The Isle of Man's primary anti-money laundering offences largely mirror their equivalent in the UK. This is perhaps not surprising. The two jurisdictions not only maintain a close relationship, both politically and geographically, but each have a shared, if independent, common law system of jurisprudence. Whilst the Isle of Man's independent legal status should always be emphasised, it is a feature of Manx law which was affirmed by the Privy Council in *Frankland v R*,[1] that decisions of the English courts, especially those from England's appellate courts, whilst not binding are of high persuasive value in the Isle of Man. Notwithstanding, the Isle of Man Court of Appeal has stated in *Gilberson SL and other & Dominator Ltd*,[2] that the Isle of Man's legal system is becoming increasingly independent of English statutes and procedures, and frequently chooses to be informed by or to adopt the common law and practices found in jurisdictions other than England. Although this demonstrates a preparedness on the part of the Manx courts to seek guidance from other jurisdictions, in the context of its primary anti-money laundering laws, the Isle Man will undoubtedly still be highly influenced by decisions of the English courts given that the Island's legislation in this field is either materially equivalent to or has been adapted from corresponding legislation in the UK. In 2002, the UK passed the Proceeds of Crime Act 2002 ('UK POCA'). The Island's primary offences relating to anti-money laundering now mirror the equivalent provisions of UK POCA (with minor modifications or exceptions) in the form of the Isle of Man's Proceeds of Crime Act 2008 ('IOM POCA') which received Royal Assent on 22 October 2008. The primary anti-money laundering offences within IOM POCA came into force on 1 August 2009 and introduced UK POCA style anti-money laundering criminal offences in the Isle of Man.

25.12   The secondary legislation, in the form of the Proceeds of Crime (Anti-Money Laundering) Code 2010 as amended (the 'Code'), the Prevention of Terrorist Financing Code 2011 (the 'PTF Code')...(or as they are more often referred to together as 'the AML/CFT Codes'), aims to impose requirements on business activities that are perceived to be exposed to the risk of money laundering and terrorist financing and obliges them to establish and maintain AML/CFT procedures, principally customer due diligence ('CDD') measures, similar but not identical to the requirements imposed in the UK under the Money Laundering Regulations 2007...

FUTURE MEASURES

25.13   The fight against international money laundering is an ever-constant one. Even in the relatively short period since the introduction in the Isle of Man of legislation in this area (1987), the Island's anti-money laundering measures have developed apace and, importantly, in a direction that has generally brought with it accolades from the international community. However the reality of the Island's position and status as an international financial centre is that it is under constant international pressure to be seen to lead the way in introducing ever more stringent anti-money laundering laws. The IMF's report containing its evaluation of the Island's measures in this area was published in September 2009, and stated

---

1   Manx Law Reports (MLR) 1987–80 65.
2   Unreported, 1 May 2009.

that: '*With the significant upgrading of requirements, particularly between August and mid-December 2008, the IOM has brought its AML/CFT preventive measures largely into compliance with the FATF Recommendations*'.

25.15   In line with the approach under UK POCA, IOM POCA refers to money laundering by reference to the concept of criminal property. Under s 158 of IOM POCA, criminal property is defined as:

> 'property constituting a person's benefit from criminal conduct or representing such a benefit in whole or in part and whether directly of indirectly where the alleged offender knows or suspects that it constitutes or represents such a benefit'.

> ...

THE ISLE OF MAN'S CURRENT PRIMARY LEGISLATION

IOM POCA, s 140 – arrangements

25.22   Property is 'criminal property' for the purposes of IOM POCA if it: (a) constitutes a person's benefit from criminal conduct or it represents such a benefit (in whole or part and whether directly or indirectly); and (b) the alleged offender knows or suspects that it constitutes or represents such a benefit. For this purpose 'criminal conduct' is conduct which: (a) constitutes an offence in the Isle of Man; or (b) would constitute an offence in the Isle of Man if it occurred there.

25.23   It follows that all criminal offences in the Isle of Man are capable of being [**predicate**] offences for money laundering under IOM POCA. The extension of the definition of criminal conduct to also include conduct which would constitute an offence in the Isle of Man if it had occurred in the Isle of Man gives the anti-money laundering measures within IOM POCA an extra territorial dimension. Clearly such a measure is intended to cover situations where the factual constituents of the criminal conduct in question occur outside the Isle of Man. Crucially this part of the definition of criminal conduct contained within IOM POCA does not require dual criminality. Therefore, if it is conduct outside the Isle of Man which is in issue, technically it does not matter whether or not such conduct constitutes a criminal offence under the laws of the jurisdiction in which it took place provided that it would constitute an offence if it had occurred in the Isle of Man. However, ss 139, 140 and 141 each provide that a person does not commit an offence if that person knows, or believes on reasonable grounds, that the relevant criminal conduct occurred in a particular country or territory outside the Island and the criminal conduct was not at the time it occurred unlawful under the criminal law then applying in that country and is not of a description prescribed by the Department of Home Affairs. No conduct has been so prescribed to date.

25.24   The precise meanings of 'knowledge' and 'suspicion' within the context of these provisions have not as yet received judicial comment in the Isle of Man. It is reasonable to assume though that the Manx courts will look to and apply the meanings that have been ascribed to such terms in comparable circumstances by the Commonwealth courts. In particular Isle of Man law will construe the meanings of 'knowledge' and 'suspicion' within the definition of 'criminal property' by applying the meanings ascribed to such expressions under English law under UK POCA.

Fiscal offences

25.25   A degree of uncertainty was initially expressed as to whether the legislation pre-dating the introduction of IOM POCA was intended to capture fiscal offences. There were no provisions within the CJA 1990 that carved out an exception for fiscal crimes. Whilst this remains the position under IOM POCA, it is generally agreed that any conduct wherever transacted in relation to a fiscal or revenue offence that is sufficiently serious to be capable of constituting a criminal offence in the Isle of Man is caught by IOM POCA. As far as particular fiscal offences are concerned, the Isle of Man has made provision for offences under its VAT legislation and Income Tax Acts. In the UK there are common law offences of defrauding and/or cheating the public revenue. It is by no means clear whether these offences have Manx equivalents (there as yet being no decision of the Manx Courts directly on point), but if there is such a common law offence in the Isle of Man it would undoubtedly be capable of supporting a money laundering offence under IOM POCA. In addition, there are offences under the Isle of Man Theft Act 1981, such as false accounting, which may be relevant in the context of tax evasion schemes and also fall within its scope.

IOM POCA, ss 142–143 – failure to disclose

25.46   ...special provision is made for a defence of reasonable non-disclosure and for legal professional privilege in the context of mandatory disclosures. Legal professional privilege is considered under s 142(8)(b), (15) and (16) which provide that:

'(8) But a person does not commit an offence under this section if–

(a)   ...

(b)   that person is a professional legal adviser or relevant professional adviser and–

(i)   if the person knows either of the things mentioned in subsection (6)(a) and (b), the person knows the thing because of information or other matter that came to the person in privileged circumstances, or

(ii)   the information or other matter mentioned in subsection (3) came to the person in privileged circumstances ...'

'(15) Information or other matter comes to a professional legal adviser or relevant professional adviser in privileged circumstances if it is communicated or given to the adviser–

(a)   by (or by a representative of) a client of the adviser in connection with the giving by the adviser of legal advice to the client;

(b)   by (or by a representative of) a person seeking legal advice from the adviser; or

(c)   by a person in connection with legal proceedings or contemplated legal proceedings.'

'(16) But subsection (15) does not apply to information or other matter which is communicated or given with the intention of furthering a criminal purpose.'

25.47   Having regard to the provision which allows for the making of defensive disclosures within ss 139–141 (which refer to authorised disclosures – an authorised disclosure being a disclosure prescribed by s 154 made to a constable or nominated officer) and the requirement for mandatory disclosures under s 142 (again to a constable or nominated officer), separate offences are established under ss 143 and 144 in respect of nominated officers who receive a disclosure from an employee, but fail to disclose in the appropriate circumstance. Under s 143, nominated officers of businesses within the regulated sector who receive a disclosure report under s 142 commit an offence if, knowing or suspecting, or having reasonable grounds for so knowing or suspecting, that another person is engaged in money laundering, commit an offence if they fail to make the required disclosure to the FCU. A similar offence exists under s 144 in respect nominated officers employed outside the regulated sector who receive disclosures from employees in the course of business. The major difference for nominated officers working outside the regulated sector is that they are only required to make a disclosure to the FCU if they know or suspect (as opposed to having reasonable grounds to suspect) that another person is engaged in money laundering. There are no legal privilege defences to the offences created under ss 143 and 144.

HOW EFFECTIVE IS THE CURRENT PRIMARY LEGISLATION?

25.55   The Isle of Man has, to date, used the provisions of the anti-money laundering acts that are identified above to bring prosecutions sparingly. In the decision of *Re Miller*[1], the court examined its discretionary power to appoint a receiver under the DTA 1996 to enforce a confiscation order made following a conviction for drug trafficking – the case related to confiscating the proceeds of crime rather than the active laundering of such proceeds. In October 2009, the Manx High Court entered convictions in *R v Baines*, its highest profile and most complex criminal action for offences which included charges of money laundering under the CJA 1990, s 17A. Whilst the action against Mr Baines attracted considerable attention within the Island, the Court did not deliver a written judgment and consequently the case has not provided any commentary upon the wider AML legal issues involved. Accordingly, in the absence of other case commentaries, it remains difficult to judge the practical effectiveness of the IOM POCA type offences in some respects. The Baines prosecution and conviction aside, the absence of any significant number of money laundering convictions to date may reflect the fact that these primary offences are complex and undoubtedly create a significant burden for any prosecution. However, the picture from the UK was that after a similarly slow start, increasing use was made of the UK's equivalent legislation to bring criminal prosecutions for alleged money laundering offences in that jurisdiction. There is little doubt that international pressure continues to mount for the Island to use its criminal sanctions to the full (this point was made by the IMF when its 2009 evaluation of the Isle of Man was published).

25.56   The most practical issues to arise out of the legislation have been the introduction of the disclosure regime and the problems faced by financial institutions by the creation of the tipping off offences,

DISCLOSURES

25.60   The disclosure regime provides a highly effective source of intelligence which should not be measured against the fact that few money laundering prosecutions have taken place in the Isle of Man to date. Invaluable information disclosed in the Isle of Man has led to onward disclosures to SOCA, and by SOCA to overseas authorities which in turn has led to numerous formal applications from foreign territories for evidence to be obtained in the Isle of Man for use in criminal proceedings or criminal investigations.

TIPPING OFF

25.61   The rise in the number of disclosures has led to practical difficulties in the context of tipping off. As discussed earlier, the legislation provides that once

1   [2005–06] MLR N.22.

a disclosure has been made, any person with knowledge or suspicion of that fact is guilty of an offence if he discloses information which is likely to prejudice any investigation which might be conducted following the disclosure. This has created some concerns for banks and other financial institutions, especially where the ground for suspicion leading to the disclosure is serious fraud carrying with it a concomitant risk of constructive trusteeship. Banks faced with such a situation have expressed concern that they may not be able to investigate the provenance of a customer's funds in such circumstances without running the risk of tipping off the customer that a suspicious transaction disclosure may have been made to the FCU. A not dissimilar issue arose for consideration by the Manx High Court in *Re Petition of Alliance & Leicester International Limited*[1] in which the Manx High Court considered the English Court of Appeal authority in *Bank of Scotland v A Limited*[2] and held that 'it is open to a bank to seek directions from the Court if it has a reasonable apprehension that it might be held as a constructive trustee'. Whilst the Manx High Court would appear from this case to be reasonably receptive to genuine cases where financial institutions face a dilemma due to fears of tipping off, the court still expects a party to consult with the FCU in the first place and only where a reasonable and workable solution cannot be reached with the FCU should an application be made to the court. With the Island's enactment of UK POCA style offences, the decisions of the English courts relating to the extent to and circumstances under which the courts may assist organisations that are faced with real dilemma due to tipping off concerns continue to guide and persuade the Isle of Man courts.

INCHOATE OFFENCES

25.62   It is a general principle of Manx criminal law that a person need not be wholly involved in the commission of a complete offence to incur criminal liability. A person may be guilty of an offence if he has:

(i)   attempted to commit it;

(ii)   conspired with another person(s) to commit it; or

(iii)   incited another person(s) to commit it.

25.63   In addition, a person may be guilty as a secondary party to a criminal offence if he aids, abets, counsels or otherwise procures a commission of the principal offence.

25.64   IOM POCA defines money laundering by reference to an act which constitutes an offence under ss 139 to 141 and includes an act constituting an attempt, conspiracy or incitement to commit, or an act constituting aiding, abetting, counselling or procuring the commission of, money laundering offences.

IOM POCA – FURTHER PROVISIONS

Changes to Anti-Money Laundering legislation

25.73   Under the Island's previous anti-money laundering legislation, money laundering and the seizure of cash where these related to drug offences and other crimes was treated separately. IOM POCA brings the offences and procedures for drugs crime and other crime (excluding that related to terrorism) together within one statute – repealing and replacing those previously found in Part 1 of the CJA and the DTA.

1   Unreported, 4 May 2001.
2   [2001] All ER 58.

25.74 IOM POCA has introduced an objective standard in relation to suspicion of money laundering in the context of disclosures where the information or other matter upon which the person's knowledge or suspicion (or reasonable ground for suspicion) is based came to that person in the course of a regulated business. Regulated businesses are defined in Sch 4 to IOM POCA and include those businesses or activities that are also defined as relevant businesses under the Code.

The secondary legislation

The Criminal Justice (Anti-Money Laundering) Code 2010 ('the Code')

25.81 The Code was introduced on 1 September 2010. The explanatory note to the Code states that:

> '... the Code contains anti-money laundering provisions in line with Financial Action Task Force's recommendations on money laundering and terrorist financing and accompanying methodology.'

25.82 The Code is not of general application and only imposes obligations upon those businesses listed in schedule 1 to the Code. The businesses mentioned in schedule 1 to the Code are each defined as a 'relevant business'. The list of relevant businesses encompasses a very wide range of activities, each susceptible to being targeted by money launderers. The list of relevant businesses is based upon the list of activities defined as falling within the regulated sector for the purposes of IOM POCA. The list of relevant businesses is as follows:

...

'6.

(1) Any activity specified in paragraph (2) that is undertaken by:

  (a) an Advocate;

  (b) a registered legal practitioner within the meaning of the Legal Practitioners Registration Act 1986;

  (c) a Notary;

  (d) an accountant or a person who, in the course of business, provides accountancy services.

(2) The activities referred to in paragraph (1) are:

  (a) holding or managing any assets belonging to a client;

  (b) the provision of legal services which involves participation in a financial or real property transaction (whether by assisting in the planning or execution of any such transaction or otherwise) by acting for, or on behalf of, a client in respect of:

   (i) the sale or purchase of land;

   (ii) managing bank, savings or security accounts;

   (iii) organising contributions for the promotion, formation, operation or management of bodies corporate;

   (iv) the sale or purchase of a business.

...

12. Investment business within the meaning of Section 3 of the Financial Services Act 2008 and Class 2 of Schedule 1 to the Regulated Activities Order 2008 as if the exclusions contained within the Order or the Financial Services (Exemptions) Regulations 2008 had not been made.

...

16. Corporate services or trust services within the meaning of Section 3 of the Financial Services Act 2008 and Class 4 and 5 of Schedule 1 to the Regulated Activities Order 2008 ignoring any exclusions for that class contained in the Order or the Financial Services (Exemptions) Regulations 2008.

...

29. Administering or managing money on behalf of other persons.

GUIDANCE ISSUED BY ISLE OF MAN AUTHORITIES

25.110   ...with the introduction of anti-money laundering codes, regulators and some professional bodies in the Isle of Man have issued bespoke guidance notes addressing the specific requirements of the Code. All deposit taking, investment (including mutual funds) and corporate and trust administration activities carried on by way of business in and from the Isle of Man require a licence issued by the FSC. In relation to its licence holders, the FSC has issued the Anti-Money Laundering and Countering the Financing of Terrorism Handbook. The Handbook contains the FSC's Guidance Notes for deposit takers, investment businesses, corporate and trust service providers. The Handbook may be accessed via the FSC's own website at www.fsc.gov.im ... Industry guidance notes for accountants follow the practice notes issued by the Institute (which invariably means that the guidance is issued with primary regard to the UK's Money Laundering Regulations 2007 rather than the Code). Manx qualified lawyers (Advocates) are regulated by the Isle of Man Law Society which has incorporated compliance with the Code into its Practice Rules and since 1 August 2008 has issued its own Guidance Notes...

CIVIL LAW ASPECTS

25.146   Whilst the measures considered within this chapter have concentrated on the Isle of Man's criminal law provisions enacted to combat the threat of money laundering, it should not be overlooked that the Isle of Man has well developed and sophisticated system of civil laws that may be of assistance in retaining and recovering the proceeds of criminal conduct. As highlighted earlier, the Isle of Man's legal system is grounded in the common law which, in the absence of local statutory or customary laws to the contrary, follows established common law principles in the UK. Accordingly, the Isle of Man has developed its own jurisdictions in relation to freezing assets (*Mareva*-type orders) and in relation to tracing the proceeds of crime along broadly similar lines to English law. This includes the enactment of a statutory basis[1] for granting interim relief in the absence of substantive Manx proceedings. Prior to this the Manx High Court had found at first instance in the case of *SIB v Braff*[2] that under its inherent jurisdiction a claim for a *Mareva*-type injunction may stand alone as a form of relief granted in support of proceedings in another jurisdiction. Section 56B of the High Court Act 1991 is important in not only confirming the jurisdiction of the court to grant free-standing relief, it also confirms that such interim relief is not restricted to orders for freezing but may also encompass disclosure orders for tracing assets. For instance, the Manx High Court will allow an aggrieved party to trace assets on the principles identified in *Bankers Trust v Shapiro*[3] or to seek disclosure against third parties under *Norwich Pharmacal* principles.[4]

---

1   High Court Act 1991, s 56B as introduced by Civil Jurisdiction Act 2001, s 1.
2   [1997/98] 1 OFLR 553.
3   [1980] 3 All ER 353.
4   See *Norwich Pharmacal Co v Customs and Excise Comrs* [1973] 2 All ER 943.

25.147   Furthermore, the Isle of Man also recognises the concept of trusts and the use of constructive trusts, including the imposition of liability on third parties in relation to knowing receipt or dishonest assistance, is well established.[1] The leading English authorities in relation to knowing assistance such as *Agip (Africa) Limited v Jackson & Others*[2] and *Royal Brunei Airlines v Tan*[3] are fully recognised, the former case involving a claim against a firm of Manx chartered accountants which succeeded in establishing liability as if a constructive trustee for funds paid away in what was at that time knowing assistance. The Manx High Court at first instance has also approved the use of remedial constructive trusts in order to provide a just remedy in appropriate circumstances.[4]

1   *Barlow Clowes Int Ltd & Others and Eurotrust Int Ltd & Others* [2005–06] MLR 112, Privy Council.
2   [1992] 4 All ER 451.
3   [1995] 2 AC 378.
4   *Cusack v Scroop Limited* [1996–98] MLR N-20 and *In Re Petition of Scottish Life*, (unreported, 19 July 2000).

Appendix 9.8 Jersey

David Cadin

Bedell Cristin, St Helier

[Bold material in square brackets has been contributed by Tim Bennett and does not appear in the chapter as written by David Cadin and published in *International Guide to Money Laundering Law and Practice*, 4th edition]

INTRODUCTION

28.1   Jersey, the largest of the Channel Islands, is established as a leading international finance centre, with an enviable reputation for stability, integrity, quality of service, professionalism and high standards of regulation. Jersey is, however, exposed to the same risks faced by all financial centres: its reputation may be undermined and its financial services subverted by the activities of money launderers and organised

CONSTITUTIONAL POSITION

28.5   Jersey is a British Crown Dependency. The UK is responsible for the Jersey's defence and representation in relation to foreign affairs, but otherwise the Island is an independent jurisdiction, governed by its own 'Parliament', the States of Jersey, which legislates for all internal matters, including taxation. Generally, UK statutes do not apply to Jersey. Jersey has its own court system, although the final Court of Appeal is the Privy Council of England and Wales.

28.6   Jersey is not a member of the EU, but has a special relationship with the EU pursuant to the Act of Accession, Protocol 3[1] of the UK to the EU. Whilst being inside the EU's common external tariff wall, Jersey is not required to adopt EU fiscal policies, nor is it required to implement EU directives on such matters as movement of capital, company law or rules regarding insurance, investment and banking business.

JERSEY'S FINANCE INDUSTRY

28.7   Jersey is one of the most solidly established international financial centres, having been offering offshore banking and finance services for over 40 years. Jersey is well known for its banking services, fund management services, trust and company administration services and for securitisations and structured finance generally. In the Global Financial Centres Index ('GFCI') published in March 2012, Jersey featured in the world's top ten for private banking and wealth management. According to the GFCI, Jersey is the highest-rated offshore financial centre. The Financial Stability Board and Financial Action Task Force both also refer to Jersey as a top tier jurisdiction. Notwithstanding the challenges posed by the recent global financial crisis, the size of Jersey's industry has continued to grow with the value of funds administered in Jersey reaching its highest level in December 2011 since June 2009 (£197.6 billion). The funds sector too has experienced a 10.5%

---

1   Act of Accession (1972): TS 17 (1979); Cmnd 7463.

year-on-year growth, bank deposits have increased and the number of companies registered in Jersey grew to its highest level in December 2011.

EVALUATIONS

28.16   In November 2008, the IMF conducted a Financial System Stability Assessment Update ('FSAP') in Jersey concluding that financial sector regulation and supervision in Jersey are of a high standard.

The FSAP noted that Jersey has a 'high level of compliance' with the FATF Recommendations, being compliant or largely compliant with 44 of the 49 general FATF recommendations.

28.17   Whilst there is presently no FATF Mutual Evaluation Report on Jersey, the FSAP showed that Jersey is well positioned to achieve full compliance with international standards.

LEGISLATIVE AND REGULATORY STRUCTURE

Guidance

28.29   The final part of Jersey's anti-money laundering regime consists of guidance issued by the JFSC in the form of sector-specific 'Handbooks for the Prevention and Detection of Money Laundering and the Financing of Terrorism'. The JFSC initially provided guidance in the form of a 'Handbook' for the prudentially regulated sector (ie the banking sector) and has subsequently proceeded to adapt this guidance for the different sectors, albeit whilst attempting to maintain a common approach and ethos. As at the date of writing, the JFSC has issued handbooks for the prudentially regulated sector, the accountancy sector, the legal sector, and estate agents and high value dealers. Sector specific handbooks for trust companies, banks and funds are currently being written. These 'Handbooks' together with any future 'Handbooks', herein after referred to collectively as the 'Handbooks' will be updated continually and are available publicly on the JFSC website.

28.30   The Handbooks are intended to provide a self-contained, practical interpretation of all of Jersey's anti-money laundering legislation aimed at specific business sectors. They are intended to set out what currently represents 'best practice' and to assist businesses in complying with their obligations. The Handbooks do not have the force of law, but may be taken into account where a court has to determine whether a relevant business or profession has complied with the ML(J)O 2008. In addition, the JFSC has made it clear that it is prepared to use its regulatory powers to address failures to follow the Handbooks. Accordingly, for practical purposes, one may consider the Handbooks to be mandatory.

PRIMARY LEGISLATION

Assisting another to retain the proceeds of crime

The offence

28.34   PC(J)L 1999, art 32 provides that:

'(1) Subject to paragraph (3), if a person enters into or is otherwise concerned in an arrangement whereby—

    (a)   the retention or control by or on behalf of another (in this Article referred to as "A") of A's proceeds of criminal conduct is facilitated (whether by concealment, removal from the jurisdiction, transfer to nominees or otherwise); or

    (b)   A's proceeds of criminal conduct—

        (i)   are used to secure that funds are placed at A's disposal; or

        (ii)   are used for A's benefit to acquire property by way of investment,

knowing or suspecting that A is a person who is or has been engaged in criminal conduct or has benefited from criminal conduct, he is guilty of an offence.'

28.35   'Criminal conduct' for the purposes of PC(J)L 1999 is defined as:[1]

(a)   conduct which constitutes an offence in Jersey for which a person is liable on conviction to imprisonment for a term of one or more years; or

(b)   conduct which if it occurs or has occurred outside Jersey (whether or not the person is also liable to any other penalty) would have constituted an offence under (a) if occurring in Jersey.

28.36   Criminal conduct, as defined, does not include offences involving drug trafficking or terrorism, as such offences are dealt with under DTO(J)L 1988 and T(J)L 2002 respectively.

28.38   In relation to conduct which takes place outside Jersey, whether such conduct constitutes an offence under the laws of the jurisdiction in which it took place is not relevant, there is no requirement for 'dual criminality', rather, it is simply necessary to show that such conduct, if it had been committed in Jersey, could have resulted in a term of imprisonment of one year or more.

28.39   The question of whether conduct which takes place outside Jersey constitutes an offence under the laws of Jersey was considered most recently in the case of *Bhojwani v AG*.[2] In determining whether such conduct constitutes an offence under the laws of Jersey, the Jersey Court is concerned with the essence of the conduct. If the conduct in question would have constituted an offence in Jersey if committed at the same time as the conduct under consideration, it will be sufficient for establishing that an offence has been committed under the laws of Jersey.

28.40   The question of whether fiscal offences constitute 'criminal conduct' for the purposes of PC(J)L 1999 has received particular attention in the past. There is no exception or 'special category' for tax-related offences, the question is simply whether a fiscal offence constitutes an offence in Jersey for which a person is liable, on conviction, to imprisonment for a term of one or more years. The penalty under the Income Tax (Jersey) Law 1961 ('IT(J)L 1961') for fraudulently or negligently making incorrect statements in connection with a tax return is a fine, rather than imprisonment.[3] However, a recent decision of the Court of Appeal[4] has clarified the position. Although tax evasion is normally prosecuted under the IT(J)L 1961 which provides for financial penalties only, more serious conduct can also be prosecuted as customary law fraud[5] (notwithstanding the views expressed by the House of Lords in *Rimmington*[6] that because of the existence of a specific statutory

---

1   PC(J)L 1999, art 1(1) and PC(J)L 1999, Sch 1.
2   2010 JLR 78.
3   Income Tax (Jersey) Law 1961, art 137.
4   *Michel and Gallichan v Attorney General* [2006] JLR 287.
5   As to which, see Foster v A–G 1992 JLR 6.
6   *R v Rimmington* [2005] UKHL 63.

offence, a common law offence could not be charged). As a customary law offence of fraud would have a minimum sentence of one year's imprisonment, tax evasion whether in Jersey or elsewhere can constitute criminal conduct for the purposes of PC(J)L 1999.

28.41   Moreover, a tax-related offence may (and often will) involve other offences, such as forgery or false accounting, which can also lead to imprisonment for a term of one or more years. Accordingly, the commission of tax-related offences can constitute criminal conduct for the purposes of PC(J)L 1999, and the proceeds of a tax-related offence may be the subject of money laundering offences under that law.

28.42   In PC(J)L 1999, art 32, references to any person's 'proceeds of criminal conduct' include any property that in whole or in part, directly or indirectly, represent in his hands the proceeds of criminal conduct, that is property obtained by such person as a result of or in connection with criminal conduct. Where the criminal conduct comprises non-declaration of assets for taxation purposes, the actual proceeds of the criminal conduct will be the tax charge on the non-declared funds. However given the wide definition of 'proceeds of criminal conduct' (to include property obtained 'in connection with criminal conduct'), all the undeclared funds held in a Jersey bank account will constitute the proceeds of crime.

Knowledge or suspicion?

28.43   PC(J)L 1999, art 32, requires a mens rea of knowledge or suspicion. Neither is defined in PC(J)L 1999 and, to date, the Jersey courts have not been required to comment on the precise meaning of such terms in this context, save to note that it is a question of fact for the tribunal in each case. Whilst actual knowledge may be relatively easy to identify, suspicion can create rather more difficulties. However, given the similarity of PC(J)L 1999 to the UK Criminal Justice Act 1988, the Jersey courts are likely to be influenced by the decisions of the English courts as to interpretation on this point. In the case of 'suspicion', the definition given in *R v Da Silva*[1] and approved in *K Limited*,[2] would be applied.

Defences

28.51   A final point to note relates to the provision of PC(J)L 1999, art 32(3) (a), which ensures that any disclosure made will not be treated as a breach of any duty of confidentiality, and the person making it will not be liable for such breach. These provisions should not be regarded as providing a general immunity from criminal or civil actions in relation to any conduct of the person making the disclosure following the making of it, but rather should properly be regarded as providing specific protection from liability arising directly from the making of such disclosure. Further, in order to benefit from this protection from liability, the making of the report may well need to be reasonably justifiable.

28.52   Article 32 of the PC(J)L 1999 is widely drawn and there is no provision exempting lawyers, or information subject to legal privilege, from its ambit. This is not necessarily surprising. The Article is specifically concerned with arrangements which assist another to retain the benefit of criminal conduct. If a lawyer has been party to such an arrangement, none of the advice given can be subject to privilege on the basis of the crime/fraud exception. Notwithstanding that, arts 40 and 41 of the PC(J)L 1999 and equivalent provisions in the DTO(J)L 1988 do not permit the

1   [2006] EWCA Crim 1654.
2   *K Ltd v National Westminster Bank Plc and others* 2005/ 2189 A3.

police access to privileged information. Difficulties may arise in practice where the lawyer's involvement falls short of being a party to the arrangement. Further guidance has recently been given by the JFSC in its Handbook for the Legal Sector.[1]

Acquisition, possession or use of the proceeds of crime

The offence

28.56   PC(J)L 1999, art 33 provides that:

'(1) A person is guilty of an offence if, knowing that any property is or in whole or in part directly or indirectly represents another person's proceeds of criminal conduct, he acquires or uses that property or has possession of it.'

Knowledge or suspicion?

28.57   This offence requires knowledge, rather than knowledge or suspicion.

Failure to disclose knowledge or suspicion of money laundering

The offence

28.65   The offence of failing to disclose knowledge or suspicion of money laundering (under PC(J)L 1999, arts 34A–34D) was brought in by an amendment to the PC(J)L 1999 in 2008 and provides as follows:

'(1) A person shall be guilty of an offence if:

(a)   the person knows or suspects that another person is engaged in money laundering;

(b)   the information, or other matter, on which that knowledge or suspicion is based comes to the person's attention in the course of his or her trade, profession, business or employment; and

(c)   the person does not disclose the information or other matter to a police officer as soon as is reasonably practicable after it comes to his or her attention.

(2)   It is not an offence under this Article for a professional legal adviser to fail to disclose any information or other matter that comes to him or her in circumstances of legal privilege.

(3)   Where a person discloses to a police officer:

(a)   the person's suspicion or belief that another person is engaged in money laundering ; or

(b)   any information or other matter on which that suspicion or belief is based,

the disclosure shall not be treated as a breach of any restriction imposed by statute, contract or otherwise.'

28.66   This offence does not apply to professional legal advisers acting in circumstances of legal privilege or employers and/or employees who receive

---

1   Available on the JFSC website.

information in the course of carrying on a financial services business.[1] In addition, the States of Jersey, has the power to make regulations excusing other categories of individuals from the ambit of the provision for regulatory, supervisory, investigative and registration purposes.

28.67 The offence is only committed if the information or other matter comes to the attention of the accused in the course of their trade, profession, business or employment and, beyond this, PC(J)L 1999, art 34A does not impose obligations upon the public at large.

28.69 As elsewhere, provisions of PC(J)L 1999, art 34A provide that any disclosure shall not be treated as a breach of any restriction imposed by statute, contract or otherwise, but the additional provision that such disclosure will not involve the person making it in liability of any kind (PC(J)L 1999, art 32(3) and elsewhere) is missing.

28.70 In the case of financial services businesses, the obligation is wider and applies to anyone who has 'reasonable grounds for knowing or suspecting'. Article 34D of the PC(J)L 1999 provides:

'(i) A person commits an offence if each of the following 3 conditions is satisfied:

(ii) The first condition is that the person:

    (a)   knows or suspects; or

    (b)   has reasonable grounds for knowing or suspecting,

that another person is engaged in money laundering.

(iii) The second condition is that the information or other matter:

    (a)   on which the person's knowledge or suspicion is based; or

    (b)   that gives reasonable grounds for such knowledge or suspicion,

comes to him or her in the course of the carrying on of a financial services business.

(iv) The third condition is that the person does not disclose the information or other matter to a police officer or to a nominated officer as soon as is practicable after it comes to him or her.'

28.71 For the purposes of art 34D, a nominated officer is a person (such as the MLRO or his deputies) who has been nominated by the employer of the person making the disclosure to receive disclosures. The disclosure to the nominated officer must be in the course of the discloser's employment and in accordance with procedures maintained by the employer.

28.72 The offence cannot be committed by professional legal advisers acting in circumstances where legal privilege applies.

28.73 Whereas disclosure under PC(J)L 1999 has historically given rise to a defence from prosecution, arts 34A–34D of PC(J)L 1999 create a mandatory

---

1   Financial services businesses are defined in art 36 of PC(J)L 1999 as those businesses described in Sch 2 to PC(J)L 1999 namely businesses regulated by the JFSC, lawyers, accountants, estate agents, dealers in high value goods, and providers of certain other defined services. See para 28.112 for further details.

requirement to disclose to the police any suspicion of money laundering arising within a commercial setting.

28.74 Knowledge or suspicion? The offence under art 34A of PC(J)L 1999 is a generally applicable offence that requires actual knowledge or suspicion and the test will be a subjective one. In relation to suspicion, the court is likely to apply the definition given in *R v Da Silva*[1] and approved in *K Limited*.[2] **[contrast the position in relation to Terrorism offences where 28.87 notes that 'here, the duty to disclose arises if a person knows or suspects or has reasonable grounds for knowing or suspecting a person has committed an offence ... [and] the duty differs ...in that actual knowledge or suspicion is not essential ... [and] It is enough that the person ought to have known of or suspected the offence having regard to the information in their possession: an objective rather than a subjective test'].**

28.75 The offence under art 34D of PC(J)L 1999 applies only to those employed in financial services businesses and requires only reasonable grounds for knowledge or suspicion, importing an objective test into the elements of the offence.

Tipping off

The offence

28.88 PC(J)L 1999, art 35 provides that, broadly, a person will commit an offence if they disclose to any other person information or any other matter which is likely to prejudice any actual or proposed investigation into money laundering when they know or suspect that:

(a) a disclosure has been made to the police;

(b) an investigation into money laundering is being or is proposed to be conducted; or

(c) a disclosure has been made to the money laundering reporting officer at their place of employment.

28.90 PC(J)L 1999, art 35 can pose particular problems for financial services businesses. This is especially so in the context of civil proceedings, where a disclosure to the JFCU under art 32 or 33 of PC(J)L 1999 may have resulted in an informal freeze.[3] Not only will the financial services businesses be facing particular difficulties caused by the tension between their duties to their customer and their obligations under the substantive provisions of the PC(J)L, but they may also face difficulties in explaining why they are unable to act given the provisions of art 35.

28.91 One way of resolving the apparent tension is provided by art 35(4) and (5) which state as follows:

'(4) Nothing in paragraph (1), (2) or (3) makes it an offence for a professional legal adviser to disclose any information or other matter:

(a) to or to a representative of a client of the legal adviser in connection with the giving by the adviser of legal advice to the client; or

---

1   [2006] EWCA Crim 1654.
2   *K Ltd v National Westminster Bank Plc and others* 2005/ 2189 A3.
3   See para 28.168 below.

    (b)   to any person:

        (i)   in contemplation of or in connection with legal proceedings, and

        (ii)   for the purpose of those proceedings.

    (5) Paragraph (4) does not apply in relation to any information or other matter that is disclosed with a view to furthering a criminal purpose.'

28.92   As was noted by Longmore LJ in *K Ltd*,[1] these provisions enable the financial services business with an appropriate method of informing the customer of its disclosure, namely by procuring its professional legal adviser to pass the information on (ie the fact that a report has been made) to a person in connection with legal proceedings (ie proceedings by the customer against the financial services business for breach of mandate).

Concealing or transferring proceeds to avoid prosecution or a confiscation order

The offences

28.100   PC(J)L 1999, art 34 provides for two separate, but related, offences, as follows:

    '(1) A person is guilty of an offence if the person:

        (a)   conceals or disguises any property that is or in whole or in part represents the person's proceeds of criminal conduct; or

        (b)   converts or transfers that property or removes it from the jurisdiction,

    for the purpose of avoiding prosecution for an offence specified in the First Schedule or the making or enforcement in his case of a confiscation order.

    (2) A person is guilty of an offence if, knowing or having reasonable grounds to suspect that any property is or in whole or in part directly or indirectly represents another's proceeds of criminal conduct, the person:

        (a)   conceals or disguises that property; or

        (b)   converts or transfers that property or removes it from the jurisdiction,

    for the purpose of assisting any person to avoid prosecution for an offence specified in Schedule 1 or the making or enforcement in the person's case of a confiscation order.

    (3) In paragraphs (1) and (2), the references to concealing or disguising any property include references to concealing or disguising its nature, source, location, disposition, movement or ownership or any rights with respect to it.'

Knowledge or suspicion?

28.102   It is a requirement under PC(J)L 1999, art 34(2), that the person knows or has 'reasonable grounds' to suspect that the property represents the proceeds of

---

1   2005/ 2189 A3.

another's criminal conduct. This sets a more objective standard of suspicion than that within PC(J)L 1999, art 32 (which requires actual suspicion).[1]

SECONDARY LEGISLATION

The ML(J)O 2008: Application

28.111   Although relevant to all types of money laundering, the ML(J)O 2008... only applies to a person carrying on financial services business in or from within Jersey or either a Jersey body corporate, or a Jersey limited liability partnership carrying on a financial services business in any part of the world (called a 'relevant person').

Duty to comply with procedures

28.122   PC(J)L 1999, art 37 provides that if any person carrying on a financial services business contravenes or fails to comply with a requirement in the ML(J)O 2008 which applies to that business, it shall be an offence, punishable by up to two years' imprisonment or an unlimited fine, or both, irrespective of whether money laundering has taken place. However, this strict position is mitigated somewhat by the provisions of art 37(10), which provides that it is a defence for a person to prove that they took all reasonable steps and exercised due diligence to avoid committing the offence of breaching a requirement of the order.

28.124   In deciding whether a person has complied with the requirement to maintain these procedures, the court may take into account any relevant guidelines issued or endorsed by the JFSC and, in practice, the Anti-Money Laundering Handbooks issued by the JFSC.

28.125   The case of *Bell and Caversham v AG*[2] in 2006 highlighted the importance of complying with both the legislation and the guidance, and provided the first example of how the court in Jersey, and possibly elsewhere, might deal with such matters. Caversham was a financial services provider subject to the requirements of the 1999 Order, Mr Bell was a director of Caversham and they were both charged with failing to comply with the 1999 Order on the grounds that they failed to identify a client. The obligation under the 1999 Order was to 'maintain' certain listed procedures, including identification measures 'for the purposes of forestalling and preventing money laundering'.

28.126   A UK sole practitioner introduced a potential intermediary client to Caversham with a request that a trust be established for him. Information was sought on the client and the beneficiaries and five days later, before those enquiries had been completed, Caversham received the sum of £850,000. Some two days later Caversham was asked to transfer £825,000 out to four accounts in UK banks, which was done by Mr Bell. Caversham was paid £2,600 for its work. It had no identification information on the recipients who were in any event, wholly different to those originally proposed as beneficiaries under the trust. Caversham's defence to the charges was that it had procedures to combat money laundering and to identify recipients of funds but that those procedures failed in this case. The court rejected this submission both at first instance and on appeal. There was no need for there to be any systemic failure for an offence to be committed, the obligation was to maintain procedures and as the judge at first instance held, 'maintenance is an absolute duty and one breach, if it is more than mere oversight, is in my view sufficient for the purposes of a criminal

---

1   See para 28.43 above.
2   [2006] JCA 14.

trial'. The Court of Appeal went further and held that maintenance required the procedures to be kept in proper working order and 'met in respect of every relevant transaction, subject only to the defendants being excused where there are circumstances which are beyond their control'. In the particular case, the court said that there were two options: either Caversham had no procedures or alternatively, it had them, but given that they failed to work, had not been kept them in proper working order. Caversham was fined £65,000 and Mr Bell, £35,000, along with the costs of the prosecution.

28.127   Given the increased, international vigilance against money laundering and terrorist financing, courts may well deal with money laundering offences more seriously in the future. The key message to be learnt in the aftermath of the *Caversham* case is that a single failure can be a criminal offence.

GUIDANCE FROM THE JFSC

General

28.134   The guidance issued by the JFSC takes the form of sector-specific Handbooks. As at the date of writing, the JFSC has produced a Handbook for the regulated sector[1], for the accountancy sector, the legal sector and for estate agents and high value dealers[2] ('Handbooks'). The JFSC is working towards providing separate Handbooks for trust companies, banks and funds.

28.135   The Handbooks outline the requirements of Jersey's money laundering legislation, provide a practical interpretation of the ML(J)O 2008 and give examples of current 'best practice'. As noted above, although the Handbooks do not have the force of law, they may be taken into account where a court has to determine whether a financial services business has complied with the ML(J)O 2008. The JFSC draws a distinction in the Handbooks between statutory requirements (failure to follow these is a criminal offence and may also attract regulatory sanction) and regulatory requirements (failure to follow these may attract regulatory sanction).

28.136   The JFSC is likely to regard failures to follow the Handbooks seriously and, as such, compliance with the Handbooks is effectively mandatory.

28.137   The Handbooks themselves are significant documents (running to in excess of 100 pages). The content of the Handbooks is summarised below under the following headings:

- Corporate governance

- Customer due diligence requirements

- Identification and verification of identity

- Monitoring activity and transactions

- Reporting money laundering and financing terrorism activity and transactions

---

1   See www.jerseyfsc.org/anti-money_laundering/regulated_financial_services_busines sesaml_cft_handbook.asp **[updated 11 December 2013]**
2   See www.jerseyfsc.org/anti-money_laundering/other_businesses_and_organisations /aml_cft_handbook.asp

LEGAL PROFESSIONAL PRIVILEGE

Corporate governance

28.139   The language used in the Handbooks leaves no room for doubt as to the intentions of the JFSC, or the seriousness with which the JFSC views the issue of money laundering. At the heart of the new requirements is the business risk assessment. The requires the board to analyse and document the risks presented by its own organisation and the different areas thereof, its customers, geographic factors, the particular business or businesses conducted, and how it delivers its service. The risk assessment must be revisited from time to time as may be appropriate. Informed by that risk assessment, the board is obliged to implement and maintain appropriate systems and controls to prevent and detect money laundering and the financing of terrorism.

28.140   For the first time, a new role is mandated for relevant persons, namely that of MLCO.[1] The MLCO will be tasked with monitoring compliance with applicable legislation relating to money laundering and the financing of terrorism. This is a senior appointment, which must be notified to the JFSC, who should report directly to the board and have sufficient 'seniority and authority within the business so that the board reacts to and acts upon any recommendations made'.[2] In order to discharge his functions, the MLCO must have unfettered access to all business lines, support departments and information necessary to appropriately perform the function.

28.141   The role of MLCO is different to that of MLRO although in some cases, the same person will fulfil both roles. The MLRO is tasked with dealing with both internal disclosures of money laundering or suspicions of the same, along with external reports to the police. In addition, the MLRO must manage relationships effectively to avoid tipping off any third parties following a disclosure. The MLRO will also act as the liaison point with the JFSC and the JFCU and in any other third party enquiries in relation to money laundering or financing of terrorism. **[The MLRO is tasked with evaluating the reports, determining whether to make any external report to the JFCU and if one be made, assisting in managing the customer relationship thereafter to avoid any tipping off issues. Once a report has been filed with the JFCU, the relevant person may find itself subject to an informal freeze.[3]]**

...

28.162   The Handbook for the Legal Sector provides detailed guidance and examines the tension between a lawyer's duty of confidentiality to his/her client and the disclosure obligations imposed by the PC(J)L 1999, DTO(J)L 1988 and T(J) L 2002 and the circumstances in which the direct disclosure obligations otherwise imposed by the primary legislation do and do not apply.

THE INFORMAL FREEZE

28.168   Whilst the offences under the PC(J)L 1999 and other statutes, along with the mechanism for raising suspicions with the JFCU may be familiar to those in the UK and other jurisdictions, a crucial distinction between the Jersey legislation and that in other jurisdictions, is the absence of any time limits on the JFCU for responding to disclosures or indeed taking proceedings or any other steps. If a

---

1   Article 7 of the ML(J)O 2008.
2   Per Handbook.
3   [See para 28.168 below.]

disclosure has been made to the JFCU, the relevant person making the report would clearly have the requisite knowledge or suspicion to found an offence under art 32 were it to continue without the consent of the JFCU. However, were the JFCU to refuse to consent, the relevant person could find itself in a difficulty.

28.169   For example, in the case of a bank which has made a disclosure on its customer, were that customer to request payments out of his account, the bank could not action the request in the absence of consent from the JFCU, nor could it simply ignore the customer's request, lest it be subject to proceedings for breach of mandate. However, the tipping off provisions might also prevent the bank from telling its customer about the difficulties it faces and the fact that it has made a disclosure.

28.170   Having initially followed the guidance in *Amalgamated Metal Trading*,[1] which involved the bank allowing, if not encouraging the customer, to bring proceedings against it, the Royal Court has now definitively determined the issue in the decision of *Gichuru v Walbrook Trustees (Jersey) Limited and others*.[2] If an institution has concerns, it should explore those concerns with its customer. If it is unable to allay its concerns it should then make a disclosure. If the JFCU refuses to provide the necessary consent, the institution is unlikely to act on the customer's instructions and the customer then has the choice of either judicially reviewing the decision of the police (on the usual judicial review grounds) or of bringing a private action against the institution for breach of mandate. In such proceedings, the burden will be on the customer to establish, on a balance of probabilities, the legitimacy of the funds or assets. It is always possible that the court may, on the basis of the information before it, determine that the assets are legitimate, only for it to be discovered subsequently, that they are definitely not. If the institution wishes to rely upon the earlier judgment to protect itself from subsequent criminal proceedings, it will need to show that it took 'such steps as are reasonable in all the circumstances to resist proceedings'.[3]

28.171   A recent example of a customer bringing a claim for breach of mandate is the English case of *Shah and another v HSBC Private Bank (UK) Ltd ('Shah')*.[4] The bank in that case delayed in executing payment instructions because it suspected the funds were criminal property. The bank filed a suspicious activity report and awaited the consent of SOCA (the English equivalent of the JFCU) before making the payments requested. The bank declined to provide its customer with any information concerning its failure to make the payments. The customer brought a claim against the bank for breach of mandate claiming damages for the bank's failure to process the payment instructions and provide the customer with information as to the facts which had caused the bank not to process the payment instructions. The English High Court ruled that there must be an implied term in the contract that permitted the bank to refuse to execute payment instructions in the absence of appropriate consent where it suspected a transaction constituted money laundering. The court also ruled that the bank was under no duty to provide its customer with information and that there had to be an implied term that allowed a bank to refuse to provide the information where to otherwise do so might result in 'tipping off' for example.

28.172   Under art 32 of the PC(J)L 1999 dealing with the funds in question with the consent of the JFCU is a defence. Where consent is not given by the JFCU

---

1   [2003] 1 WLR 2711, as applied in Ani v Barclays Private Bank and Trust Limited and Attorney General [2004] JLR 165.
2   [2008] JRC 068.
3   As per Tomlinson J in *Amalgamated Metal Trading* at para 32.
4   [2012] EWHC 1283.

whether to a bank or a trustee for example who has filed a suspicious activity report ('SAR') funds or assets are generally treated as informally frozen for fear of prosecution otherwise for money laundering. That informal freeze is not however inviolable.

28.173   In *Re Bird*[1] a trustee filed a SAR after the protector of the trusts in question was charged (but not yet convicted) with illegal gambling, racketeering and tax evasion. The trustee refused to make payments out of the trusts without the consent of the JFCU or to communicate with the protector. After the trustee made the SAR, the protector purported to appoint a successor protector who in turn appointed additional trustees who sought to change the law of the trusts from Jersey to Lichtenstein to circumvent the restrictions imposed by the trustee who was refusing to make payments from the trusts without the consent of the JFCU. The trustee applied for directions as to the validity of the appointments and said that the appointments amounted to a fraud on a power as the protector, the trustee said, had tried to extract assets from Jersey which were otherwise subject to the PC(J)L 1999 restrictions. The Jersey Court found that the protector's intention in appointing a successor was to ensure the smooth running of the trusts in the event he was remanded in custody and held that the appointment had been made in good faith in the best interests of the beneficiaries. The appointments to circumvent the restrictions imposed by Jersey law and to make payments which the law prohibited were found not to be improper as they were made in good faith in the interests of the beneficiaries. The intention was found to be consistent with the purpose for which the powers of appointment had been conferred. The intention to remove control of the trust from the trustee in Jersey was also found not be unlawful either because the appointments were not seeking to achieve something that was prohibited by Jersey law. In *Re Bird* the trustee had refused to make payments without the consent of the JFCU but the court said it was not prevented under art 32 from making payments without such consent. Unless and until the trust assets were proved to be the proceeds of crime, the Jersey Court held that it was not unlawful to make a payment. The intention to remove control from the Jersey trustee was to circumvent a restriction which the trustee itself had imposed rather than Jersey law. The change in identity of the protector and trustees did not result in assets being moved. If the appointments had been made following the conviction of the protector on the other hand, then the court is unlikely to have recognised the appointments which would have been seen in those circumstances as intending to commit a crime.

ENFORCEMENT

Enforcement agencies

28.174   The enforcement of Jersey's anti-money laundering regime involves the JFSC, the JFCU, and the Department of the Law Officers of the Crown.

JFSC

28.175   The JFSC is the regulator of Jersey's finance industry and is responsible for monitoring Jersey financial services business compliance with all legislation and guidance related to money laundering. The JFSC's compliance division undertakes a structured programme of compliance visits on all regulated financial institutions, which includes a detailed assessment of the institutions' anti-money laundering and counter-terrorism procedures.

---

1   [2008] JLR 1.

JFCU

28.176   The JFCU is responsible for receiving, disseminating and investigating reports of suspicions of money laundering made under the anti-money laundering legislation. The JFCU comprises both police and customs officers.

The Law Officer's Department

28.177   The Law Officers' Department, headed by Her Majesty's Attorney General ('HMAG') is responsible for the public prosecution of all criminal matters in Jersey. The Law Officers' Department also acts as the gateway between Jersey's and overseas authorities in relation to the investigation and prosecution of offences under the anti-money laundering legislation.

Domestic enforcement

Prosecutions

28.178   In March 2006, following the *Caversham* case, the JFSC issued a Policy on Referrals to the Attorney General under the PC(J)L 1999 and the Money Laundering (Jersey) Order 1999. The policy was in the following terms:

> 'The present policy of the Commission is that if it should come across an apparent breach of the Order in the course of its supervision, including as a result of an onsite examination, the Commission will refer it to the Attorney General if the breach is considered to be sufficiently serious. It should be stressed, however, that a decision on whether to prosecute a breach of the Order will be a matter solely for the Attorney General.

> The Commission will generally regard a breach of the Order as sufficiently serious to the extent that it poses a threat to clients or potential clients or to the reputation of the Island and/or where it casts doubt on the integrity, competence or financial standing of the person concerned. It will also be relevant if the breach was deliberate or premeditated rather than accidental, or if the person (individual or body corporate) has failed to report a material breach to the Commission.

> Failure, inability or refusal to cooperate with the Commission to rectify a breach, and a history of past breaches or poor regulatory compliance (which may give grounds to believe that the breach is likely to be repeated and/or is part of a systemic failure), will also be taken into account.'

Civil law aspects

28.200   In addition to the criminal law provisions designed to combat money laundering that have been considered above, Jersey's civil law is of assistance in tracing and recovering the proceeds of crime.

28.201   Whilst Jersey law has its roots in Norman customary law, in practice, English judicial decisions are regarded as persuasive in many areas, and Jersey's civil law tends to follow the same principles as are found in English law. Accordingly, freezing orders, disclosure orders (including orders against a third party on the basis of the *Norwich Pharmacal* principles[1]) and the tracing of assets on the principles of the *Bankers Trust* case[2] are all available in Jersey (even when there may be no substantive cause of action within the island and the only link is

---

1   *Norwich Pharmacal Co v Customs and Excise Comrs* [1973] 2 All ER 943.
2   *Bankers Trust Co v Shapira* [1980] 3 All ER 353, CA.

the presence of money in an account). Claims may also be asserted based on unjust enrichment and/or liability as an accessory to a breach of trust.

28.202   There is insufficient space here to consider civil law aspects in any detail, other than to note that dealing with the matrix of obligations to the client, obligations arising under anti-money laundering legislation and obligations arising out of civil proceedings can present difficult issues for financial services businesses.

Appendix 9.9   Singapore

Alvin Yeo SC

WongPartnership LLP, Singapore

Joy Tan

WongPartnership LLP, Singapore

[**Bold material in square brackets has been contributed by Tim Bennett and does not appear in the chapter as written by Alvin Yeo and Joy Tan and published in** *International Guide to Money Laundering Law and Practice*, **4th edition**]

INTRODUCTION

35.3   The Singapore Government 'places a high premium on safeguarding [**its**] integrity as a world class financial and commercial centre,' and has been proactive in establishing a sound and comprehensive legal, institutional, policy and supervisory framework designed to be anti-money laundering ('AML') and to counter the financing of terrorism ('CFT').

35.4   The Government's robust approach has resulted in a total of 76 persons being charged in court for money laundering offences under the CDSA between 2007 and the first half of 2010.[1] In these money laundering cases, the sums involved in each transaction ranged from about SGD1,000 to SGD500,000, while the sentences varied from two months' imprisonment to 54 months' imprisonment.[2] Between 2010 and 2011, a total of 44 persons were convicted of money laundering offences, with nearly SGD130 million worth of criminal proceeds being seized or frozen as they were linked to money-laundering investigations.[3]

35.7   In 2007, the FATF conducted its 3rd Mutual Assessment of Singapore. FATF assessed that Singapore operates a strict and rigorous AML/CFT regime, centred on a comprehensive and sound legal, institutional, policy, and supervisory framework.[4] Following efforts by Singapore to address the feedback from FATF to make the AML/CFT regime more stringent,[5] FATF in its Second Follow-up Report of February 2011 determined that Singapore has improved its level of compliance to the standard of 'Largely Compliant' at a minimum. As such, Singapore has been

---

1   17 in 2007, 23 in 2008, 26 in 2009 and 10 in the first half of 2010.
2   *Hansard, Parliamentary* Debates, Vol 87, Col 159, 26 April 2010.
3   Asiaone News website, see: http://news.asiaone.com/News/AsiaOne%2BNews/ Crime/Story/A1Story20121110-382709.html (accessed 15 February 2013); see also The New York Times website: http://www.nytimes.com/2012/10/16/business/global/ singapore-fights-image-as-tax-haven.html?pagewanted=all&_r=0> (accessed 15 February 2013).
4   Singapore was found to be compliant with 11; largely compliant with 32; partially complaint with 4; and non-compliant with 2 of the 40 + 9 Recommendations.
5   Notably through amendments to ss 46 and 47 of the CDSA to remove both the technical difficulties identified in FATF's 2nd Mutual Evaluation Report of Singapore.

upgraded from being subject to regular follow-ups to being required to provide only biennial updates.[1]

LEGISLATIVE FRAMEWORK

Money laundering as an offence

35.9   'Money laundering' in Singapore is a derivative offence involving the handling and processing of proceeds obtained from criminal conduct, with the final effect of disguising its origins such that they appear to have stemmed from a legitimate source.[2]

35.11   In the face of escalating international terrorist threats beginning with the 11 September 2001 attacks on the USA and abortive Al Qaida-affiliated Jemaah Islamiyah plots within Singapore's national borders, the CDSA [**The Corruption, Drug Trafficking and Other Serious Crimes (Confiscation of Benefits) Act (Cap 65A)**] was supplemented by the Terrorism (Suppressing of Financing) Act (the TSOFA) in January 2003, which focuses in particular on benefits owned by terrorist entities, or intended for their use.[3] The CDSA and the TSOFA comprise the primary legislation governing the AML/CFT framework in Singapore today.

Particulars

35.12   The CDSA criminalises the laundering of benefits derived from corruption, drug trafficking and other serious crimes[4] and prohibits the handling of benefits from drug trafficking and serious criminal conduct by direct[5] as well indirect[6] means, but without express mention of the words 'money laundering'. Instead, language specific to particular acts and the 'benefits'[7] originating therefrom is used.

Mens rea

35.18   An offence can be committed not only where the would-be launderer knows of the taint to the money but also where he 'has reason to believe' that it exists – a standard which has been determined to involve 'a lesser degree of conviction than certainty and a higher one than speculation'. In applying this standard, 'the court must assume the position of the actual individual involved (ie including his knowledge and experience), but must reason (ie infer from the facts known to such individual) from that position like an objective reasonable man'[8] who 'would have thought it probable that the property he retains is [**property obtained from criminal conduct**]'.[9]

---

1   *Anti Money-Laundering and Combating the Financing of Terrorism*, FATF Mutual Evaluation Second Follow-Up Report -- Singapore, 25 February 2011 at para 15.
2   Guidelines to MAS Notice 626 on Prevention of Money Laundering and Countering the Financing of Terrorism ('Guidelines to MAS Notice 626'), para 10.
3   Other relevant primary and subsidiary legislation in Singapore includes the United Nations Act 2001 (Cap 339) and United Nations (Anti-Terrorism Measures) Regulations 2001, as well as the Monetary Authority of Singapore (Anti-Terrorism Measures) Regulations 2002.
4   *Luyono Lam v PP* [2010] 4 SLR 37, at [13].
5   Sections 46 and 47 of the CDSA.
6   Sections 43 and 44 of the CDSA.
7   Part VI of the CDSA.
8   *Koh Hak Boon v Public Prosecutor* [1993] 3 SLR 427 at [13].
9   *Ow Yew Beng v Public Prosecutor* [2003] 1 SLR 536 at [10], following Koh Hak Boon v Public Prosecutor [1993] 3 SLR 427.

35.19   The CDSA provisions were amended in 2010[1] to remove the need to show motive for an offender's actions. There is no longer a requirement to show that the accused committed the act for the purpose of assisting the launderer to avoid prosecution for a drug trafficking or serious offence or the making or enforcement of a confiscation order. This was done so as to 'make it clear that an offence is committed so long as the accused does the act knowing or having reasonable grounds to believe that the property represents another person's proceeds of crime'.[2]

Presumption

35.21   There is additionally an express presumption that persons who hold or have held interests in property disproportionate to their known sources of income have (unless they provide the court with a satisfactory alternative explanation), obtained the same as the benefit of criminal conduct,[3] thereby reversing the burden of proof in demonstrating that the property in question was not in fact the benefit of criminal conduct.

35.22   This presumption was used to impose restraint orders on the property of Thor Beng Huat (Thor), the brother-in-law of wanted fugitive Ng Teck Lee, former CEO of Citiraya Industrial Limited, who fled Singapore pending corruption and criminal breach of trust charges after his scheme between 2003 and 2004 of selling computer chips meant for destruction was uncovered in January 2005. Thor had seen his annual income increase from $36,536 in 1998 to $600,017.92 in 2004, and additionally had, in the 12 months from February 2004, purchased three luxury cars that were well beyond his stated income.[4]

Cross-border currency controls

The predicate offences

35.24   As previously indicated, money laundering under the CDSA is an offence predicated on the relevant property being tainted by certain listed existing or impending[5] criminal conduct. Such criminal conduct is set out in the First Schedule of the CDSA (drug trafficking offences), and in the Second Schedule of the CDSA. In 2010 and 2011, ten offences were added to the list of serious offences in the Second Schedule of the CDSA.

35.25   The 'serious offences' category includes kidnapping, sexual exploitation (including women and children), the illicit trafficking of drugs, arms and human beings, copyright infringement, criminal conspiracy and the abetment of organised criminal groups in the commission of transnational crimes, the failure to provide disclosure relating to the financing of terrorism, hostage-taking, casino offences and immigration offences.[6]

35.26   In October 2011, the Monetary Authority of Singapore ('MAS') announced its intention to criminalise the laundering of proceeds from tax offences.[7] The FATF Recommendations released in February 2012 have confirmed

---

1   Sections 46(2) and 47(2) of the CDSA.
2   *Hansard, Parliamentary* Debates, Vol 86, Col 2045, 12 January 2010.
3   Sections 4(4) and 5(6) of the CDSA.
4   Re *Thor Beng Huat*, [2006] 4 SLR 581.
5   In relation to TSOFA offences classified as 'serious offences' under ss 326–329, Second Schedule of the CDSA.
6   Second Schedule of the CDSA.
7   *'A Competent, Trusted, and Clean Financial Centre'*, Ravi Menon, Keynote Speech at the WMI Connection, 27 October 2011.

that tax crimes are within the 'designated categories of offences.[1] In line with the FATF Recommendations,[2] MAS released a consultation paper in October 2012 designating certain tax crimes as money laundering predicate offences (the 'MAS Consultation Paper 2012'). These offences include direct and indirect tax offences under the Income Tax Act[3] and the Goods and Services Tax Act[4] respectively. The Second Schedule to the CDSA is scheduled to be updated by June 2013 to reflect the proposed changes, and the criminalisation of the laundering of proceeds from these tax offences will come into effect on 1 July 2013.[5]

35.27   From a public policy perspective, courts have held that financial crimes involving public funds committed against public institutions have to be dealt with sternly as they 'amount(ed) to an assault on the common weal and undermine good administration'.[6] This approach was taken in the *SLA* case where the two SLA employees were charged with cheating, conspiracy to cheat and money laundering for concealment or conversion of properties representing benefits from their criminal conduct.[7] It was observed that such financial crimes often have repercussions extending beyond the facts of the case, including the heightened costs and manpower involved in putting in place more stringent checks, as well as the potentially leading to costly litigation.[8]

35.28   Acts and omissions amounting to serious offences in Singapore that take place in foreign countries also qualify as 'criminal conduct' for the purpose of constituting a money laundering offence under the CDSA provided such acts are prohibited by the laws of the foreign country in question.[9]

35.29   The courts in Singapore have attempted to facilitate the AML/CFT regime here by stating that the predicate offences need not be proved at the standard of 'beyond reasonable doubt' because to do so is 'awkward and costly' and would '[**rob the CDSA**] of its intended efficacy'.[10] Instead, the Prosecution needs to 'adduce some evidence in question with particular criminal conduct'.[11]

NON-LEGISLATIVE MEASURES

Regulating high-risk industries (financial institutions)

The Monetary Authority of Singapore ('MAS')

35.81   The government has recognised that the business and financial sectors are key partners in combating money laundering and terrorist financing'[12] Integrated supervisory and regulatory oversight of the financial sector falls to the Monetary Authority of Singapore ('MAS'), which in turn has, pursuant to ss 27A and 27B

---

1   International Standards on Combating Money Laundering and the Financing of Terrorism and Proliferation, The FATF Recommendations, Feb 2012, printed March 2012 at p 111.
2   Consultation Paper on Designation of Tax Crimes as Money Laundering Predicate Offences in Singapore, MAS, 9 October 2012 at p 1.
3   Sections 96 and 96A of the Income Tax Act.
4   Sections 62 and 63 of the Goods and Services Tax Act.
5   Consultation Paper on Designation of Tax Crimes as Money Laundering Predicate Offences in Singapore, MAS, 9 October 2012 at p 3.
6   *Public Prosecutor v Koh Seah Wee and another* [2012] 1 SLR 292 at [57].
7   *Ibid*, at [57] and [59].
8   *Ibid*, at [60].
9   Section 2(1) of the CDSA.
10   *Ang Jeanette v Public Prosecutor* [2011] 4 SLR 1 at [58].
11   Above n 30 at [58].
12   Above n 106, at para [5].

of the MAS Act, prescribed rigorous directions and regulations for the 'financial institutions'[1] within its purview.

Suspicious transaction reporting

35.99   Apart from requiring the financial institutions within its control to adhere to the above reporting requirements, examples of suspicious transactions to be red-flagged are set out in the MAS Guidelines. Such examples include[2]:

(a)   transactions which do not make economic sense, such as:

    (i)   bank customers with large numbers of accounts among which frequent transfers occur, or with exaggeratedly high liquidity;

    (ii)   transactions that cannot be reconciled with the usual activities of the customer, including requests for investment management service;

    (iii)   buying and selling of securities with no discernible purpose, especially where inappropriate for the customer's apparent standing;

(b)   transactions involving large amounts of cash, such as:

    (i)   exchanging unusually large amounts of currency notes in small denominations without plausible reason;

    (ii)   frequent withdrawal of large cash amounts by means of cash cheques, including travellers' cheques;

    (iii)   company transactions denominated by unusually large amounts of cash, rather than by way of cheques, letters of credit, etc;

(c)   transactions involving transfers abroad (with no plausible reason) such as:

    (i)   large regular payments or similar dealings that cannot be clearly identified as bona fide transactions, from and to countries associated with (i) the production, processing or marketing of narcotics of other illegal drugs; (ii) other criminal conduct; (iii) terrorist activities or (iv) with persons designated as terrorists;

    (ii)   substantial increase in cash deposits or securities purchases without reason, especially if such funds or securities are subsequently transferred out within a short period to accounts in unusual destinations or overseas;

(d)   transactions involving unidentified parties, such as:

    (i)   transfers of money to other banks with no indication of beneficiaries;

    (ii)   use of pseudonyms or numbered accounts for effecting commercial transactions by enterprises active in trade and industry;

    (iii)   holding in trust shares of unlisted companies whose activities cannot be ascertained.

...

---

1   Defined at ss 27A(6) and 27B(3) to include licensed banks, licensed finance companies, approved financial institutions, money changers, registered insurers and insurance intermediaries or those regulated under the Insurance Act, licensed financial advisers, entities licensed under the Securities and Futures Act, trustees for authorised collective investment schemes, trustee-managers of registered business trusts, licensed trust companies, holder of stored value facilities and other persons licenced or regulated by the MAS.
2   Based on Guidelines to MAS Notice 626 (to banks).

35.100 It is to be noted that financial institutions in Singapore are advised that cash transactions of SGD20,000 are sufficient to raise suspicions, especially in the case of new customers. However, Singapore has expressly vetoed implementation of routine threshold reporting[1] after consideration of the practical efficiency and effectiveness of such requirements.

Regulating high-risk industries (others)

Legal profession

35.102 The legal profession is regulated by the Legal Profession Act and in particular, professional conduct rules in the form of the LP(PC)R. Such rules amount to subsidiary legislation, and are enforced by the Law Society of Singapore (the Law Society). A breach of these rules has been viewed by the courts to be a 'serious matter'[2] and a breach thereof will lead to disciplinary proceedings,[3] following which sanctions may range from being disbarred and suspended, to being fined or reprimanded.[4]

35.103 Recently, a lawyer was found guilty of serious misconduct[5] for repeatedly evading the Law Society's attempts to conduct inspections of the financial records of his practice in furtherance of its AML obligations under Rule 11I of the LP(PC)R.[6] The Disciplinary Tribunal highlighted the importance of Rules 11D to 11H of the LP(PC)R, which form part of the legal framework to combat money laundering in Singapore. It stated that '(t)hese provisions were introduced in order to meet Singapore's international obligations as a member of the intergovernmental body, the Financial Action Task Force, set up to develop and promote policies to combat money laundering and funding of terrorist activities'.[7] Accordingly, disciplinary action[8] was taken against the lawyer in question. He was also subsequently charged with eight counts of misappropriating a total of SGD1.2 million.[9]

35.104 Although s 39(4) of the CDSA does protect lawyers, in part, from the duty to disclose information under the reporting requirements by way of exemption in relation to information subject to legal privilege, lawyers are now subject to CDD and suspicious transaction reporting requirements on a similar basis to the obligations of financial institutions pursuant to the LP(PC)R and the Law Society Practice Directions[10] issued in guidance of its application.

35.105 In particular, the focus of the LP(PC)R relates to proper identification and verification of the basis for matters and transactions which may cause clients to deposit significant sums in lawyers' client accounts. For example, matters dealing with transfers of real estate, changes in company ownership, unusually complex matters or those involving an unusually large quantum. Detailed recommendations have since been provided by the Law Society in the form of two

---

1   Where reporting is mandatory whenever the value of the transaction exceeds a threshold level, regardless of the whether there is a real question as to whether the transaction stemmed from legitimate or suspicious sources.
2   *Law Society of Singapore v Mustaffa bin Abu Bakar* [2011] SGDT 1, at [24].
3   Sections 82A and 82B of the Legal Profession Act.
4   Sections 88 and 94 of the Legal Profession Act.
5   *Supra* n 142, at [25]; see also section 83(2)(b) of the Legal Profession Act.
6   IBA Anti-Money Laundering Forum – Singapore, http://www.anti-moneylaundering.org/asiapacific/Singapore.aspx, accessed on 15 May 2012.
7   Above n 142 at [20]–[21].
8   Section 93(1)(c) of the Legal Profession Act.
9   'Lawyer charged with $1.2 million fraud', The Straits Times, 20 Feb 2012.
10 Enforceable in that breach thereof would open the way for an allegation of improper conduct under s 83(2)(d) of the Legal Profession Act.

Council's Practice Directions[1] clarifying and detailing lawyers' obligations under the new rules, including detailed compliance, accounting, and reporting measures. Thus the purposes of the new provisions, being to reduce the possibility of large unmonitored transactions being carried through lawyers' client accounts, and laundered by way of having tainted monies retrieved from said accounts through withdrawals on the part of innocent firms, are undoubtedly being effected.

35.106   The Conveyancing and Law of Property (Conveyancing) Rules 2011 were enacted to cover the holding of conveyancing money by solicitors, appointed banks or by the Singapore Academy of Law. The objective of these rules is to safeguard conveyancing money without unduly compromising the efficiency of conveyancing practice. These Rules we enacted in order to address cases about lawyers absconding with their clients' money. It prescribes that money held by lawyers for the purposes of purchasing property for a client must be held in a Conveyancing Account. In order to withdraw money from this account, there must be authorisation from two parties.[2]

35.107   This new set of Rules assists in terms of preventing of money laundering offences. The acts which it is intended to prevent commonly form the stepping stones to the commission of certain predicate offences, such as criminal breach of trust. It is envisioned that this framework will assist to prevent the commission of money laundering by solicitors absconding with their clients' money.

EDUCATION AND TRAINING

MAS efforts

35.117   MAS has prescribed detailed procedures for institutions within its purview, and has additionally conducted and participated in seminars and conferences with a view to general improvement and public education. In addition, MAS conducts scheduled on-site inspections and supervision of each financial institution, with recommendations and procedures specifically targeted at the relevant institution in question.

The private banking industry

35.121   The Private Banking Advisory Group recently released a Private Banking Code of Conduct. Part 3 of the Code deals with continuing professional development and clause 3.1.2 states that all people to which the Code applies must achieve a minimum of 15 hours of continuing professional development every year. This was lauded as an example of MAS-industry collaboration, and the industry has been working closely with MAS to promote compliance with AML/ CFT measures by organising seminars to raise awareness, conducting training programmes, and issuing industry guidelines.

---

1   Practice Direction 3 of 2007 and Practice Direction 1 of 2008.
2   *Hansard*, Parliamentary Debates, Vol 87, Col 4794, 11 April 2011.

Appendix 9.10   United States of America

Jerome P Tomas

Baker & McKenzie, Chicago, Illinois USA

William V Roppolo

Baker & McKenzie, Miami, Florida, USA

INTRODUCTION

41.1   While the war on tax evasion and drug kingpins of the 1970s, 1980s and 1990s brought money laundering to attention of law enforcement authorities and practitioners, the events of 11 September 2001 and the resulting amendments to the US criminal money laundering laws and the US Bank Secrecy Act pursuant to the USA PATRIOT Act culminated in the sudden expansion of the reach and scope of the US money laundering laws. The last decade has seen an explosion in the complexity and stakes of financial crime. The growth of international terrorism, international financial and organised criminal activity all of which require funding for their operations are clear evidence of the challenges posed to the US and international financial institutions. As the financial world continues to develop and become more complex, so too does criminal conduct. If past is prologue, the US money laundering regime and enforcement priorities will also change to reflect the changing financial and criminal environment. The US has chosen to combat that threat by compelling financial institutions to initiate robust know-your-customer programs, or strengthen existing compliance regimes, to effectively identify and report money laundering efforts touching upon its financial system. In the last two years, regulators have significantly expanded their enforcement of anti-money laundering laws. The typical pattern has been for financial institutions against which enforcement actions have been initiated to enter into deferred prosecution agreements in exchange for revamping their internal compliance capabilities and, with increasing frequency, paying large fines.

41.2   Following the terrorist attacks of 11 September 2001, the regulatory and prosecutorial focus of US anti-money laundering policy shifted from drug trafficking to international terrorism, and in particular the role that correspondent banking and private banking relationships of US financial institutions with foreign financial firms (ie offshore banks, securities brokerage firms and insurance companies) may play in international money laundering. Recently, in light of the financial downturn and the credit and mortgage crisis, it is clear that the regulators are focusing their attention on money laundering-related conduct and its role in these recent events. Another trend following 11 September 2001 was the expansion of the potential scope of the US money laundering regime to professionals, financial intermediaries and other third parties. Regulations were proposed subjecting many of these types of entities to regulation under the Bank Secrecy Act. While some of these proposed regulations were finalised, many of them fell by the wayside, including those requiring investment advisers and private investment funds (eg hedge funds) to implement policies and procedures under the BSA. Nevertheless, intermediaries still face exposure to serious civil and criminal penalties if they do not take adequate steps to ensure that they are not providing support to those who traffic in the proceeds of criminal activities.

2007 United States National Money Laundering Strategy[1]

41.4   On 5 May 2007, the US government released its 2007 National Money Laundering Strategy (the 'Money Laundering Strategy') as a direct response to the US inter-agency Money Laundering Threat Assessment completed in December 2005 (the 'Threat Assessment'). The Money Laundering Strategy focuses exclusively on preventing money laundering separately from efforts to combat the financing of terror, but at the same time attempts to level the playing field internationally by working to ensure that US financial institutions are not disadvantaged by efforts to combat money laundering and terrorist financing. The Money Laundering Strategy addresses issues identified by the Threat Assessment by expounding nine specific goals, described as follows.

1   *Continue to safeguard the banking system*

41.5...

2   *Enhance financial transparency in money services business*

41.6...

3   *Stem the flow of illicit bulk cash out of the United States*

41.7...

4   *Attack trade-based money laundering at home and abroad*

41.8...

5 *Promote transparency in the ownership of legal entities*

41.9   States make it relatively easy for individuals to register certain business entities, such as corporations, limited liability companies, and trusts. This simplicity makes it difficult for financial institutions to identify suspicious transactions and hinders law enforcement investigations and prosecutions. FinCEN will raise awareness of the misuse of these legal entities for money laundering and will work with state administrators to explore options to increase transparency in the beneficial ownership of legal entities. The government will also issue guidance on the risks of providing financial services to shell companies.

6   *Examine anti-money laundering regulatory oversight and enforcement at casinos*

41.10...

7   *Implement and enforce anti-money laundering regulations for the insurance industry*

41.11...

8   *Support global anti-money laundering capacity building and enforcement efforts*

41.12...

9   *Improve how we measure our progress*

---

1   As of the date of publication, the 2007 US Money Laundering Strategy is the most recent published strategy.

41.13…

CRIMINAL ANTI-MONEY LAUNDERING LAWS

General concepts under US AML laws

Jurisdictional scope of AML laws

41.36   The US AML laws apply to both US and non-US persons, as well as to domestic and extraterritorial conduct. Section 1956 applies to extraterritorial conduct if the conduct is by a United States citizen and the transaction or series of transactions involves funds or monetary instruments valued in excess of $10,000. Under s 1956 for non-US persons, the AML laws will apply extraterritorially if the conduct occurs in part in the United States and the transaction or series of transactions involves funds or monetary instruments valued in excess of $10,000.

41.37   Under s 1956(b)(2), US Federal courts have jurisdiction over foreign persons, which specifically includes any financial institution charted under the laws of a foreign country, for purposes of a money laundering prosecution if two conditions are met. First, service of process upon the foreign person must be made pursuant to the Federal Rules of Civil Procedure or the laws of the country in which the foreign person is found. Secondly:

(i)   the foreign person has committed a money laundering offence involving a financial transaction that occurred in whole or in part in the United States;

(ii)   the foreign person has converted, for their personal use, property in which the US has an ownership interest arising out of an order of forfeiture issued by a US court; or

(iii) the foreign person is a financial institution that maintains a bank account at a financial institution in the US.

41.38   Section 1957 applies to US persons regardless of the location of the offence.[1] Section 1957 applies to non-US persons only if the offence takes place within the United States or a maritime or territorial jurisdiction of the United States.[2]

41.39   The 2006 money laundering indictment of Martin Tremblay, a Canadian national and president and managing director of the Bahamas-based investment firm Dominion Investments, Ltd, demonstrates how the US criminal money laundering laws apply to foreign persons. The indictment alleged that Tremblay, through Dominion Investments, laundered approximately $1 billion in criminally tainted property derived from international narcotics trafficking, securities fraud scams, income tax evasion, mail and wire fraud schemes, and bank fraud, among other crimes. After receiving these proceeds, Tremblay allegedly laundered the illicit funds by transferring them into US bank accounts and offshore bank accounts. The indictment alleged that in order to further the money laundering scheme, Tremblay used shell companies and fictitious entities, using the same false nominees, addresses, and telephone numbers, to launder these illegal proceeds. In assessing the application of the US criminal AML laws, a key factor in this case was that Tremblay effected transactions through US bank accounts.

---

1   18 USC § 1957(d)(2).
2   18 USC § 1957(d)(1).

State of mind – intent and knowledge

41.40   The AML laws, as a general matter, require 'knowledge' that the property or funds involved in a transaction represents the proceeds of unlawful activity.[1] The criminal money laundering laws predicate liability upon, among other things, a defendant acting while 'knowing that the property involved in a financial transaction represents the proceeds of some form of unlawful activity'. The knowledge requirement under the AML laws does not require that a defendant know that the proceeds at issue in the transaction are the proceeds of SUA. Rather, the criminal AML laws merely require evidence sufficient to prove that a defendant knew that the property involved in the transaction represented proceeds from some form of activity that constitutes a felony under State, Federal, or foreign law. The unlawful activity that represents the source of the funds, of which the defendant must have knowledge, does not necessarily need to be SUA. This is important because SUA is a defined term comprised of a finite number of offences. Therefore, a prosecutor, when left to establish this 'knowledge' may seek to establish knowledge based on an almost limitless number of federal, state, or foreign laws. Under US federal criminal law, the requirement of knowledge can also be satisfied by constructive knowledge through what is known as the doctrine of 'conscious avoidance' (also known as 'wilful blindness' or 'deliberate ignorance').[2] The doctrine seeks to prevent a person from wilfully and intentionally remaining ignorant of a fact that is material to his or her conduct in order to avoid criminal liability. For example, a defendant's constructive knowledge of a fact required to prove guilt may arise from proof that they intentionally avoided learning of the fact whilst aware of a high probability of its existence. US courts frequently apply this doctrine in money laundering cases where a party has deliberately avoided learning facts about the conduct of another party to the transaction, even though the circumstances of the case made it highly likely that the defendant party was aware that the other party was seeking to launder the proceeds of criminal activity. In practice, wilful blindness requires a showing of more than that the defendant 'should have known' that the relevant facts constituting the violation.[3] With respect to a corporation's state of mind, the knowledge of a corporation or other collective entity may be established through the collective knowledge of the employees gained during the course of their employment.[4]

---

1   18 USC § 1956(a)(1), (2). In addition to this 'knowledge', under many of the provisions of the AML laws, there are additional 'specific intent' requirements which must be proved in a prosecution for violations of these laws.
2   *United States v Antzoulatos*, 962 F2d 720, 725 (7th Cir 1992) (upholding sentence for s 1956 violation, stating that '[i]t is well settled that wilful blindness or conscious avoidance is the legal equivalent of knowledge' and that 'courts of appeals have consistently upheld the use of so-called ostrich instructions based on conscious avoidance when supported by the evidence.'). Whether particular conduct constitutes wilful blindness requires a fact intensive analysis.
3   *Antzoulatos*, 962 F2d at 725.
4   *United States v Bank of New England, NA*, 821 F.2d 844, 855 (1st Cir. 1987), cert. denied, 484 US 943, 108 s Ct 328, 98 L. Ed. 2d 356 (upholding collective knowledge jury instruction in an appeal from a criminal conviction of a bank for failing to file Currency Transaction Reports, and stating: '… you have to look at the bank as an institution. As such, its knowledge is the sum of the knowledge of all of the employees. That is, the bank's knowledge is the totality of what all of the employees know within the scope of their employment. So, if Employee A knows one facet of the currency reporting requirement, B knows another facet of it, and C a third facet of it, the bank knows them all. So if you find that an employee within the scope of his employment knew that CTRs had to be filed, even if multiple checks are used, the bank is deemed to know it. The bank is also deemed to know it if each of several employees knew a part of that requirement and the sum of what the separate employees knew amounted to knowledge that such a requirement existed.').

41.41   A section 1956 offence in many cases requires proof of knowledge with respect to the criminally derived nature of the proceeds and, for example, proof that a defendant entered into the financial transaction with the intent to promote the carrying on of SUA. The specific intent requirements of s 1956 are not present in s 1957. Section 1957 prohibits defendants from knowingly engaging in a monetary transaction with criminally derived property valued at more than US$10,000. Here, like under s 1956, the prosecution does not need to show that that the defendant knew that the property was derived from a specified unlawful activity. Rather, the prosecution must simply prove that a defendant knew that the proceeds at issue in the transaction were criminally derived. However, the prosecution must still prove, along with the other elements of a s 1957 violation, that the proceeds were in fact derived from SUA.

Conspiracy,[1] aiding and abetting,[2] and extraterritorial jurisdiction for money laundering violations

41.42   US courts have interpreted the federal aiding and abetting statute as creating equal criminal liability for any person who aids or abets another person in committing any federal crime. Similarly, the federal conspiracy statute creates an offence of conspiring to commit any federal offence, including the substantive offences found in ss 1956 and 1957. The conspiracy statute contains two distinct clauses that create two different conspiracy offences; it states in the relevant part:

> 'If two or more persons conspire either to commit any offense against the United States, or to defraud the United States, or any agency thereof in any manner or for any purpose, and one or more of such persons do any act to effect the object of the conspiracy, each shall be fined under this title or imprisoned not more than five years, or both.'

41.43   If the conspiracy involves a non-US party who conspires in a foreign territory to violate a US federal offence, the US courts may assume extraterritorial jurisdiction over the foreign conspirator.[3] Moreover, a non-US national who has agreed and participated in a scheme outside the US that violates the extraterritorial provisions of US criminal law will also be subject to the extraterritorial reach of the US conspiracy statute if the agreement and conduct entered into by the foreign party is 'intended to take effect' or has a direct effect in the US.[4] For example, a foreign institution with no business presence in the US could incur liability under the substantive money laundering offences based on the US federal statutes criminalising conspiracies to commit crimes and aiding and abetting crimes against the US.[5] The Second Circuit Court of Appeals ruled in *Melia v United States*[6] that the US could exercise jurisdiction over a party outside the US who conspired with persons within the US.

41.44   Regarding aiding and abetting, a US District Court ruled in *United States v Noriega*[7] that the federal aiding and abetting and conspiracy statutes could be applied extraterritorially to overseas conduct that was defined as criminal by

---

1   Codified at 18 USC, s 371 (2000).
2   Codified at 18 USC s 2 (2000).
3   62 Stat 701, c 645 (25 June 1948) (original language of conspiracy statute); *Chua Han Mow v United States* 730 F 2d 1308 at 1311 (9th Cir, 1984), cert den 470 US 1031 (1985); see also *United States v Cotten* 471 F 2d 744 at 750 (9th Cir, 1972), cert den 411 US 936 (1973). The federal conspiracy statute has been codified at 18 USC, s 371 (1998).
4   Department of Justice Manual, para 33.32 n 2 above, s 9–2128.2 (1994–1 Supp), citing 18 USC, s 1871.
5   See 18 USC, s 2 (1998); see also 18 USC, s 371 (1998).
6   667 F 2d 300 (2nd Cir, 1981).
7   764 F Supp 1506 at 1516 (SD Fla., 1990).

the underlying substantive offence. The court in the Noriega case adopted the reasoning of the Eleventh Circuit Court of Appeals in *United States v Inco Bank & Trust Corp*,[1] where it was recognised as a well-settled principle of US criminal law that the US government has the power to prosecute every member of a conspiracy regardless of their territorial location if any act or agreement of the conspiracy occurred in the US.

41.45   As a defence, a non-US person or institution could argue that they should not be subject to liability because they did not have the necessary *mens rea* to commit the offence under US law. A foreign defendant could assert that the US government had failed to provide adequate notice that the transaction (involving a money laundering offence under the extraterritorial provisions of US law) for which the foreign defendant was providing assistance, or was involved in a conspiracy, was an offence under US law. Indeed, because of this lack of notice, foreign defendants could argue that they did not possess the culpable intent or required knowledge necessary to be liable, either criminally or civilly, under US anti-money laundering law, and thus the extraterritorial application and enforcement would violate due process under the US Constitution. The imputation of criminal liability, however, will likely be justified if the foreign defendant has availed itself of the privileges of conducting any type of business in US territory and, therefore, would be presumed to be aware of the laws of the US. The more difficult issue, however, concerns the non-US person who has no business activity in US markets, but who may still be subject to extraterritorial third-party liability because it knowingly advised a transaction, lawful under the laws of its own country, but which violated the extraterritorial provisions of US anti-money laundering law or other financial sanction laws

BANK SECRECY ACT

Institution specific requirements

Suspicious activity reports

41.63   Section 5318 of the BSA provides that the US Secretary of Treasury may, by regulation require any financial institution to report any suspicious transaction relevant to a possible violation of a law regulation. Like the AML compliance program requirement, when Congress amended the BSA in 1992 it provided the Treasury Department with the authority to require financial institutions to make and file reports of suspicious activities. Although this power was granted in 1992, before the passage of the USA PATRIOT Act, other than the banking industry, Treasury had only exercised this authority to require certain categories of money services businesses to make and file suspicious activity reports. The passage of the USA PATRIOT Act, which resulted in an expansion of the BSA definition of 'financial institution', exposed a great deal of other types of business, or 'financial institutions' to the suspicious activity report requirement. To date, the Secretary of Treasury has implemented regulations requiring banks, casinos, money services businesses, mutual funds, loan or finance companies, insurance companies, securities broker-dealers, introducing brokers in commodities and futures commission merchants to implement and maintain procedures for reporting suspicious transactions. As a general matter, the SAR procedures for

---

1   845 F 2d 919 at 923–24 (11th Cir, 1988). In this case, US conspirators had begun the conspiracy in the US and it continued to function in the US until the US conspirators took it to the Cayman Islands, where Inco Bank agreed to launder money on behalf of the US conspirators. The court held that although Inco Bank joined the conspiracy in the Cayman Islands and undertook no acts in US territory, it had knowingly become part of a conspiracy that would continue to operate in the US, and thus was liable as a co-conspirator.

these categories of financial institutions must be tailored to cover transactions conducted through the financial institution in an amount of $5,000 or more (or one or more related transactions totalling $5,000 or more), where the financial institution knows, suspects or has reason to suspect that:

(i)   the transaction involves illegally derived funds or is intended to hide or disguise funds or assets derived from illegal activity (including the ownership, source, location, nature, or control of these proceeds) as part of a scheme to violate or evade US law or regulation, including transaction reporting requirements;

(ii)   the transaction is designed to evade BSA requirements;

(iii)   the transaction has no business or apparent lawful purpose, or is not the sort of transaction in which the customer would normally be expected to engage; or

(iv)   involves the use of the financial institution/entity to facilitate criminal conduct and, after examining the transaction and the attendant facts, the bank knows of no such reasonable explanation.[1] Financial institutions satisfy this requirement by reporting these transactions to FinCEN on a designated Form, as well as identifying, collecting and maintaining supporting documentation for a period of five years.[2] Banks are also subject to similar, but somewhat different, reporting requirements under regulations passed by the banking regulators.[3]

41.64   The BSA prohibits a financial institution, as well as its officers, directors, and employees from disclosing to any person involved in the suspicious transaction, that a SAR has been filed with respect to the transaction. The SAR rule provides that if any person is subpoenaed requesting a SAR or information contained within the SAR, that person shall refuse to produce the SAR, or any information that would disclose that a SAR has been prepared or filed, unless the US government requests the disclosure.[4] Financial institutions, and their officers, directors, employees and agents who make and file a SAR (either compulsory or voluntary) are shielded from liability arising out of any disclosure made in the report.[5] Notwithstanding the general blanket prohibition on disclosure or sharing of the SAR or the information contained within the SAR, FinCEN has issued guidance permitting a US branch or agency of a foreign bank to share a SAR with its head office outside of the US.[6]

41.65   *Banking Intra Agency Guidance on Sharing Suspicious Activity Reports with Head Offices and Controlling Companies,* published on 20 January 2006, provides that a US bank or savings association can share a SAR with its controlling company or companies, and that a US branch or agency of a foreign bank may share a SAR with its head office outside the US. FinCEN has now concluded that a depository institution that has filed a SAR may share the SAR, or any information that would reveal the existence of the SAR, with an affiliate, as defined herein, provided the affiliate is subject to a SAR regulation. There is a limitation on the use and disclosure of this information by the head office, along with potential liability for

---

1   31 CFR § 1020.320, 1021.320, 1022.320, 1023.320, 1024.320, 1025.320, 1026.320.
2   Id.
3   12 CFR § 21.11; 12 CFR. § 208.62; 12 CFR § 353.3.
4   31 CFR § 103.18(e).
5   31 CFR § 103.18(e).
6   *Interagency Guidance on Sharing Suspicious Activity Reports with Head Offices and Controlling Companies,* issued by Financial Crimes Enforcement Network, Board of Governors of the Federal Reserve System, Federal Deposit Insurance Corporation, Office of the Comptroller of the Currency, and Office of Thrift Supervision, 20 January 2006.

disclosure of the SAR. Similar guidance was published by FinCEN with respect to securities broker dealers, future commission merchants, mutual funds and introducing brokers in commodities. Guidance issued in 2010 clarified that while SARs may be shared with affiliates, it is not appropriate for the affiliate to share the SAR with an affiliate of its own, even if that affiliate is subject to a SAR filing requirement.

41.66   A financial institution must generally file a SAR within 30 calendar days after it has detected facts that may constitute a basis for the filing of a SAR.[1] Where the suspicious activity/potential violations require immediate attention, for example, ongoing money laundering schemes, in addition to the actual filing of a SAR, a financial institution is required to immediately notify the appropriate law enforcement authority by telephone.

USA PATRIOT Act amendments to the BSA – significant developments

Correspondent accounts and private banking account requirements – section 312 of the USA PATRIOT Act

Private banking accounts

41.78   Another modification to the BSA by the USA PATRIOT Act was the requirement for certain categories of financial institutions to conduct due diligence on its private banking accounts.

41.79   Where a covered financial institution maintains a private bank account for a non-US person, it must implement procedures designed to: (1) identity all nominal and beneficial owners of the private banking account; (2) determine whether this person(s) is a senior foreign political figure; (3) determine the source(s) of funds deposited into the account, as well as the purpose and expected use of the account; and (4) monitor and review the account activity to ensure that it is consistent with the information obtained by the covered financial institution concerning the client's source of funds, and the stated purpose and expected use of the account, as well as to report any known or suspected money laundering or suspicious activity conducted to, from, or through the private banking account.[2] Where the account is directly or indirectly held by a senior foreign political figure, the covered financial institution must conduct enhanced due diligence that is 'reasonably designed' to detect and report transactions that may involve proceeds of foreign corruption.[3] Private banking accounts that do not fall within this definition are still subject to the covered financial institution's risk-based AML program. The covered financial institution must also have procedures for when this due diligence cannot be conducted, including, but not limited to, determining whether to not open the account and filing a SAR.[4]

41.80   In order for a private banking account to be subject to this regulation the private bank account must:

(i)   require a minimum aggregate deposit of funds/other assets of $1 million or more;

(ii)   be established for, on behalf of, or for the benefit of, one or more non-US persons who are direct or beneficial owners of the account; and

---

1   103 CFR § 103.18(b)(2). Under certain circumstances, an additional 30-day period is provided.
2   31 CFR § 1010.610(a); (b).
3   See, eg, 31 CFR § 1010.610(c).
4   See, eg, 31 CFR § 1010.620(d).

(iii)   be assigned to, or be administered or managed by an employee or representative of the covered financial institution which acts as a liaison between the covered financial institution and the direct or beneficial owner of the account.[1]

CORPORATE AND BUSINESS ENTITY LIABILITY AND COMPLIANCE PROGRAMS

41.115   US courts apply the common law theory of *respondeat superior* to impose criminal liability on business entities for the acts or omissions of their officers and employees while acting within the course and scope of their responsibility. US courts have also developed the doctrine of collective intent, so that the intent or acts of individual employees can be attributed to the corporation or entity which employed them. Corporations may be deemed to have the collective knowledge or intent of all of their employees. Collective intent has been attributed to financial institutions for the cumulative acts and knowledge of their employees with respect to violations of BSA 1970.

41.116   Because of these principles of corporate and entity liability under US law, Congress considered it necessary to enact statutory requirements that corporations and business entities covered by the money laundering laws maintain anti-money laundering compliance programs. The Treasury Department administers and monitors compliance with these programs. The programs focus on internal risk management practices, procedures and controls that include, among other things, designation of compliance officers, maintenance of an ongoing employee training program and implementing an independent audit function to test the adequacy of the compliance programs.

---

1   31 CFR § 1010.610(m)(3).

AML-CFT Prosecutions & Fines

1990s	Bank of Credit and Commerce International: Unknown amount, estimated in billions, of criminal proceeds, including drug trafficking money, laundered during the mid-1980s. "BCCI's Criminality". Globalsecurity.org.
1991	Ferdinand Marcos: Unknown amount, estimated at US$10 billion of government assets laundered through banks and financial institutions in the United States, Liechtenstein, Austria, Panama, Netherlands Antilles, Cayman Islands, Vanuatu, Hong Kong, Singapore, Monaco, the Bahamas, the Vatican and Switzerland Dunlap, David W. (January 13, 1991). "Commercial Property: The Bernstein Brothers; A Tangled Tale of Americas Towers and the Crown". *The New York Times*
late 1990s	Nauru: US$70 billion of Russian capital flight laundered through unregulated Nauru offshore shell banks Hitt, Jack (10 December 2000). "The Billion Dollar Shack". *The New York Times.*
late 1990s	Bank of New York: US$7 billion of Russian capital flight laundered through accounts controlled by bank executives, O'Brien, Timothy L. (9 November 2005). "Bank of New York Settles Money Laundering Case". *New York Times*
2002	Sani Abacha (died in 1998): US$2–5 billion of government assets laundered through banks in the UK, Luxembourg, Jersey (Channel Islands), and Switzerland, by the president of Nigeria "Sani Abacha". Asset Recovery Knowledge Center. Also in March 2014 the United States froze the current accounts containing USD458 million belonging to the late President.
January 2004	£2.3 million fine on Abbey National for breaches of UK AML-CFT Regulations which (along with Royal Bank of Scotland's £750,000 fine in December 2002) was noteworthy, as, in imposing the fines, the Regulator specifically admitted that <u>no actual ML had been detected</u>, but that the fines were nevertheless being imposed as the two banks did not have adequate CDD information concerning their customers' and their activities.
May 2004	US $25 million fine on Riggs Bank for violations of AML-CFT laws
November 2005	US $38 million fine on Bank of New York, including for failure to file SARs$
December 2005	US $25 million civil penalty on Israel Discount Bank, including for failure to file SARs
December 2005	US $80 million fine paid by ABN AMRO Bank NV for poor monitoring of its correspondent and international clearing business

2008	Lloyds: £218 Million
2008	Credit Suisse: £333 Million
2009	UBS: USD789 Million for AML-CFT/ Tax Evasion
2009	Institute for the Works of Religion: Italian authorities investigated suspected money laundering transactions amounting to US$218 million made by the IOR to several Italian banks Josephine McKenna (7 December 2009). "Vatican Bank reported to be facing money-laundering investigation". *The Times*
2010	ABN-AMRO: £311 Million for AML-CFT
December 2012	HSBC: USD1.9 Billion for failing to enforce AML-CFT rules throughout the 2000s (exposing it to drug traffickers, terrorists and sanctioned governments such as Iran).
	"HSBC to Pay Record Fine to Settle Money-Laundering Charges". *New York Times*. 11 December 2012
2012	Standard Chartered: paid $330 million in fines for money-laundering hundreds of billions of dollars for Iran in the 2000s and occurred for "nearly a decade to hide 60,000 transactions worth $250 billion"
	"Standard Chartered to Pay $330 Million to Settle Iran Money Transfer Claims". *New York Times*. 6 December 2012.
2012	ING: £385 Million for AML-CFT

March 2012–April 2013:

- Coutts: £8.75 MIO
- Habib Bank £525,000
- Turkish bank: £294,000
- EFG Bank: £4.2MIO

May 2013	Liberty Reserve was seized by United States federal authorities for laundering $6 billion
May 2014	Credit Suisse: USD2.8 Billion for Aiding Tax Evasion
August 2014	Standard Chartered a further fine of USD300 Million for failing to identify suspicious transactions (despite and in addition to the fine in 2012)
October 2014	UBS: French Government considering a fine of €5 Billion

Appendix 11

Data Leaks, Penetrations and Thefts; Whistleblowing; the Financial Secrecy Index

Contents

Appendix 11.1   Examples of Data Leaks, Penetration and Thefts

See Chapter 9.3

The Castle Bank Bahamas "caper" in the 1970s:

Guardian Bank (John Mathewson), Cayman Islands 1996

LGT, Liechtenstein, 2002 (where Heinrick Kieber stole information on 1,400 bank customers and sold the DVD to the German Tax Authorities for €5Million (paid to him net of German withholdong tax!).

UBS Zürich, 2008 (where a disgruntled ex-employee who was unhappy with His severance package, provided information to the US SEC) in October 2014. Renzo Gadola (who worked at UBS form 1995 to 2009) was found guilty and of breaching the Swiss law of economic espionage.

HSBC in Geneva: According to the Financial Times, "a list of 15,000 clients from around the world was allegedly stolen in 2006 and 2007 by Herve Falciani, a former IT employee who worked at HSBC's offices in Geneva. The data fell into the hands of the French authorities in 2009 when they searched his home in the South of France at the request of Swiss prosecutors after he absconded from Switzerland. France since passed it onto other governments, including Spain and the UK, following requests made under the terms of their double tax treaties. It is reported that Mr Falciani denies breaking any laws."

HSBC in Jersey: in November 2012 the UK Inland Revenue obtained details of every British client of HSBC in Jersey after a whistleblower secretly provided a detailed list of names, addresses and account balances earlier this week.

In early 2013, two BVI CSPs had data leaks/penetrations, and the information on approximately 120,000 BVI companies was passed to the *International Consortium of Investigative Journalists*. This information was painstakingly processed by ICIJ, and most of it was placed on the Internet (on the ICIJ website) where in many cases the name of the company and the name of the UBO client and his/her offshore companies are revealed.

May 2014 *Standard Chartered* Singapore advised their Private Bank Clients that in December 2013 *"an unfortunate incident occurred involving the theft of bank statements belonging to some of our Private Bank Clients via our third party service provider...."* The outsource company who apparently handled the printing and mailing of their bank statements seems to have perpetrated a data theft.

Appendix 11.2   Whistleblowers (and see 8.16)

Bradley Birkenfeld (formerly of UBS) was awarded USD104 Million under the US Whistleblower programme for shopping UBS to the US authorities, despite having been sentenced to 40 months in a Federal Prison (thus earning USD4,600 per hour for each hour he spends behind bars). In April 2012 Birkenfeld's boss (Martin Liechti, Head of UBS North America) was taken off a plane while in transit through the US on the way to the Bahamas. And then in due course, his boss (Raoul Weill, former head of UBS private clients) was arrested on 21 October 2013 in Bologna and extradited to the US. On 4 November 2014 Raoul Weill was acquitted by a South Florida jury.

Appendix 11.3   Financial Secrecy Index 2013

Eighty-two countries and territories were included in the 2013 Financial Secrecy Index.[1]

Rank	Country or territory	FSI Value	Secrecy Score	Global Scale Weight
1	Switzerland	1,765.2	78	4.916
2	Luxembourg	1,454.4	67	12.049
3	Hong Kong	1,283.4	72	4.206
4	Cayman Islands	1,233.5	70	4.694
5	Singapore	1,216.8	70	4.280
6	USA	1,212.9	58	22.586
7	Lebanon	747.8	79	0.354
8	Germany	738.3	59	4.326
9	Jersey	591.7	75	0.263
10	Japan	513.1	61	1.185
11	Panama	489.6	73	0.190
12	Malaysia (Labuan)	471.6	80	0.082
13	Bahrain	461.1	72	0.182
14	Bermuda	432.3	80	0.061
15	Guernsey	419.3	67	0.257
16	United Arab Emirates (Dubai)	419.0	79	0.061

1   "Financial Secrecy Index – 2013 Results". Tax Justice Network. November 7, 2013. http://www.financialsecrecyindex.com/PDF/FSI-Rankings-2013.pdf

Rank	Country or territory	FSI Value	Secrecy Score	Global Scale Weight
17	Canada	418.5	54	2.008
18	Austria	400.8	64	0.371
19	Mauritius	397.8	80	0.047
20	British Virgin Islands	385.4	66	0.241
21	United Kingdom	361.3	40	18.530
22	Macao	360.4	71	0.108
23	Marshall Islands	329.6	82	0.022
24	Korea	328.7	54	0.978
25	Russia	325.2	60	0.318
26	Barbados	317.4	81	0.021
27	Liberia	300.8	83	0.014
28	Seychelles	293.4	85	0.011
29	Brazil	283.9	52	0.768
30	Uruguay	277.4	72	0.040
31	Saudi Arabia	274.2	75	0.028
32	India	254.5	46	1.800
33	Liechtenstein	240.9	79	0.011
34	Isle of Man	237.2	67	0.049
35	Bahamas	226.8	80	0.009
36	South Africa	209.7	53	0.260
37	Philippines	206.6	67	0.033
38	Israel	205.9	57	0.132
39	Netherlands	204.9	50	0.430
40	Belgium	199.2	45	1.031
41	Cyprus	198.9	52	0.264
42	Dominican Republic	193.7	73	0.012
43	France	190.9	41	2.141
44	Australia	168.1	47	0.394
45	Vanuatu	164.9	87	0.002
46	Costa Rica	157.6	71	0.008
47	Ireland	155.5	37	2.646
48	New Zealand	151.4	52	0.126
49	Gibraltar	147.8	79	0.003
50	Norway	142.7	42	0.667
51	Guatemala	142.4	77	0.003
52	Belize	129.8	80	0.002
53	Latvia	128.1	51	0.090
54	Italy	118.9	39	0.748
55	Aruba	113.3	71	0.003
56	Spain	111.3	36	1.504
57	Ghana	109.9	66	0.005
58	Curacao	106.4	77	0.001
59	U.S. Virgin Islands	102.8	69	0.003
60	Botswana	98.9	73	0.002
61	Anguilla	96.7	76	0.001
62	Saint Vincent and the Grenadines	85.1	78	0.001
63	Turks and Caicos Islands	81.8	78	0.000
64	Malta	78.0	44	0.079
65	Saint Lucia	66.8	84	0.000

Appendix 11   Data Leaks, Penetrations and Thefts; Whistleblowing etc.

Rank	Country or territory	FSI Value	Secrecy Score	Global Scale Weight
66	Denmark	63.1	33	0.605
67	Antigua & Barbuda	60.4	80	0.000
68	San Marino	59.5	80	0.000
69	Portugal (Madeira)	57.9	39	0.092
70	Grenada	55.7	78	0.000
71	Sweden	55.7	32	0.440
72	Hungary	54.6	40	0.056

Index